Lecture Notes in Computer Science 4085

Commenced Publication in 1973
Founding and Former Series Editors:
Gerhard Goos, Juris Hartmanis, and Jan van Leeuwen

Editorial Board

David Hutchison
Lancaster University, UK

Takeo Kanade
Carnegie Mellon University, Pittsburgh, PA, USA

Josef Kittler
University of Surrey, Guildford, UK

Jon M. Kleinberg
Cornell University, Ithaca, NY, USA

Friedemann Mattern
ETH Zurich, Switzerland

John C. Mitchell
Stanford University, CA, USA

Moni Naor
Weizmann Institute of Science, Rehovot, Israel

Oscar Nierstrasz
University of Bern, Switzerland

C. Pandu Rangan
Indian Institute of Technology, Madras, India

Bernhard Steffen
University of Dortmund, Germany

Madhu Sudan
Massachusetts Institute of Technology, MA, USA

Demetri Terzopoulos
University of California, Los Angeles, CA, USA

Doug Tygar
University of California, Berkeley, CA, USA

Moshe Y. Vardi
Rice University, Houston, TX, USA

Gerhard Weikum
Max-Planck Institute of Computer Science, Saarbruecken, Germany

Jayadev Misra   Tobias Nipkow
Emil Sekerinski (Eds.)

FM 2006:
Formal Methods

14th International Symposium on Formal Methods
Hamilton, Canada, August 21-27, 2006
Proceedings

 Springer

Volume Editors

Jayadev Misra
University of Texas at Austin
Department of Computer Sciences, Taylor Hall
1 University Station, C0500, Austin, Texas 78712-1188, USA
E-mail: misra@cs.utexas.edu

Tobias Nipkow
Technische Universität München
Institut für Informatik
Boltzmannstr. 3, 85748 Garching, Germany
E-mail: nipkow@in.tum.de

Emil Sekerinski
McMaster University
Department of Computing and Software
1280 Main Street West, Hamilton, Ontario, L8S 4K1 Canada
E-mail: emil@mcmaster.ca

Library of Congress Control Number: 2006930417

CR Subject Classification (1998): D.2, F.3, D.3, D.1, J.1, K.6, F.4

LNCS Sublibrary: SL 2 – Programming and Software Engineering

ISSN   0302-9743
ISBN-10   3-540-37215-6 Springer Berlin Heidelberg New York
ISBN-13   978-3-540-37215-8 Springer Berlin Heidelberg New York

This work is subject to copyright. All rights are reserved, whether the whole or part of the material is concerned, specifically the rights of translation, reprinting, re-use of illustrations, recitation, broadcasting, reproduction on microfilms or in any other way, and storage in data banks. Duplication of this publication or parts thereof is permitted only under the provisions of the German Copyright Law of September 9, 1965, in its current version, and permission for use must always be obtained from Springer. Violations are liable to prosecution under the German Copyright Law.

Springer is a part of Springer Science+Business Media

springer.com

© Springer-Verlag Berlin Heidelberg 2006

Typesetting: Camera-ready by author, data conversion by Scientific Publishing Services, Chennai, India
Printed on acid-free paper   SPIN: 11813040   06/3142   5 4 3 2 1 0

Preface

This volume contains the proceedings of Formal Methods 2006, the 14th International Symposium on Formal Methods, held at McMaster University, Hamilton, Canada, during August 21-27, 2006. Formal Methods Europe (FME, www.fmeurope.org) is an independent association which aims to stimulate the use of, and research on, formal methods for system development. The first symposium in this series was VDM Europe in 1987. The scope of the symposium has grown since then, encompassing all aspects of software and hardware which are amenable to formal analysis. As in the previous years, this symposium brings together researchers, tool developers, vendors and users.

We received 145 submissions from 31 countries, making it a truly international event. Each submission was carefully refereed by at least three reviewers. The Program Committee selected 36 papers for presentation at the symposium, after an intensive, in-depth discussion. We would like to thank all the Program Committee members and the referees for their excellent and efficient work.

Apart from the regular contributions, there were five invited talks for the general symposium (Ernie Cohen, Nicholas Griffin, Thomas A. Henzinger, Peter Lindsay and George Necula); the contribution of Henzinger (with Sifakis as a co-author) and an abstract from Cohen are included in this volume.

Nicholas Griffin gave a general and informal talk about Russell's work in logic and the foundations of mathematics in the early years of the twentieth century. It focussed on the philosophical views that underlay Russell's attempts to solve the Russell paradox (and several others) which culminated in the ramified theory of types.

The FM 2006 symposium was planned to include four workshops and ten tutorials. Additionally, there was a Doctoral Symposium which included presentations by doctoral students, and a Poster and Tool Exhibition.

An Industry Day was organized by the Formal Techniques Industrial Association (ForTIA) alongside the main symposium. This was directly related to the main theme of the symposium: the use of well-founded formal methods in the industrial practice of software design, development and maintenance. The theme of the Industry Day in this symposium was "Formal Methods for Security and Trust in Industrial Applications." There were eight invited talks for Industry Day (Randolph Johnson, Jan Jürjens, Scott A. Lintelman, Dusko Pavlovic, Werner Stephan, Michael Waidner, Jim Woodcock and David von Oheimb); abbreviated versions of some of the talks are included in this volume.

The electronic submission, refereeing and Program Committee discussions would not have been possible without support of the EasyChair system, developed by Andrei Voronkov at the University of Manchester, UK. In addition to developing a system of great flexibility, Andrei was available for help and advice throughout; our heart-felt thanks to him. Our thanks to Springer, and, particularly, Ursula Barth, Anna Kramer and Frank Holzwarth, for help with preparation of this volume.

August 2006

Jayadev Misra
Tobias Nipkow
Emil Sekerinski

Symposium Organization

We are grateful to the Computing and Software Center at McMaster University, Hamilton, Canada and Formal Methods Europe for organizing FM 2006. Our special thanks to the faculty, students and staff of McMaster University who volunteered their time in the Organizing Committee.

Symposium Chairs

General Chair	Emil Sekerinski, McMaster University, Canada
Program Chairs	Jayadev Misra, University of Texas, Austin, USA
	Tobias Nipkow, Universität München, Germany
Industry Day Chairs	Volkmar Lotz, SAP Research Labs, France
	Asuman Suenbuel, SAP Research Labs, USA
Tools and Poster Chair	Marsha Chechik, University of Toronto, Canada
Workshops Chair	Tom Maibaum, McMaster University, Canada
Tutorials Chair	Jin Song Dong, National University, Singapore
Doctoral Symposium Chair	Ana Cavalcanti, University of York, UK
	Augusto Sampaio, UFPE, Brazil
	Jim Woodcock, University of York, UK
Sponsorship Chair	Jürgen Dingel, Queen's University, Canada

Organizing Committee at McMaster University

Publicity	Wolfram Kahl, Alan Wassyng, Jeff Zucker
Book Exhibition	Spencer Smith
Tools and Posters	Spencer Smith
Social Events	Ridha Khedri
Facilities Co-ordination	William Farmer, Mark Lawford
Events Co-ordination	Ryszard Janicki
Finances	Ryszard Janicki
Website Services	Doris Burns, Jan Maibaum

Program Committee

Jean-Raymond Abrial, ETH, Zurich, Switzerland
Alex Aiken, Stanford University, Stanford, USA
Keijiro Araki, Kyushu University, Fukuoka, Japan
Ralph-Johan Back, Abo Akademi, Turku, Finland

Gilles Barthe, INRIA at Sophia-Antipolis, France
David Basin, ETH, Zurich, Switzerland
Frank de Boer, CWI, Amsterdam, The Netherlands
Ed Brinksma, Embedded Systems Institute, Eindhoven, The Netherlands
Michael Butler, University of Southampton, Southampton, UK
Rance Cleaveland, University of Maryland, College Park, USA
Jorge Cuellar, Siemens Research, Munich, Germany
Werner Damm, OFFIS, Oldenburg, Germany
Javier Esparza, University of Stuttgart, Stuttgart, Germany
José Fiadeiro, University of Leicester, UK
Susanne Graf, Verimag, Grenoble, France
Ian Hayes, University of Queensland, Queensland, Australia
Gerard Holzmann, NASA/JPL Labs, Pasadena, USA
Cliff Jones, University of Newcastle upon Tyne, UK
Axel van Lamsweerde, Université Catholique de Louvain, Belgium
Gary T. Leavens, Iowa State University, Ames, USA
Rustan Leino, Microsoft Research, Redmond, USA
Xavier Leroy, INRIA, Rocquencourt, France
Dominique Méry, LORIA and Université Henri Poincaré, Nancy, France
Carroll Morgan, University of New South Wales, NSW, Australia
David Naumann, Stevens Institute of Technology, Hoboken, USA
Ernst-Rüdiger Olderog, University of Oldenburg, Oldenburg, Germany
Paritosh Pandya, TIFR, Mumbai, India
Sriram Rajamani, Microsoft Research, Bangalore, India
John Rushby, SRI International, Menlo Park, USA
Steve Schneider, University of Surrey, Guildford, UK
Vitaly Shmatikov, University of Texas, Austin, USA
Bernhard Steffen, University of Dortmund, Dortmund, Germany
P.S. Thiagarajan, National University of Singapore, Singapore
Martin Wirsing, Universität München, Germany
Pierre Wolper, Université de Liège, Liège, Belgium

External Reviewers

J. Abendroth	Andrew Appel	Krzysztof Apt
Yuji Arichika	Eugene Asarin	Anindya Banerjee
Mike Barnett	Don Batory	Maurice ter Beek
Yves Bertot	Sylvie Boldo	Marcello Bonsangue
Laura Brandan Briones	Achim Brucker	Dominique Cansell
David Carrington	Paul Caspi	Antonio Cau
Patrice Chalin	Tom Chothia	Dave Clarke
Joey Coleman	Robert Colvin	Olivier Constant
Phil Cook	William Cook	Karl Crary
Maximiliano Cristia	Adrian Curic	Roberto Delicata

Henning Dierks
Guillaume Dufay
E. Allen Emerson
Bernd Fischer
Marcelo Frias
Madhu Gopinathan
Stefan Hallerstede
Tobias Heindel
Wim Hesselink
Hardi Hungar
Johan Jeuring
Aditya Kanade
Joseph Kiniry
Piotr Kordy
Tomas Krilavicius
Ruurd Kuiper
Linas Laibinis
David Lesens
Michael Luttenberger
Erik Arne Mathiesen
Farhad Mehta
Ali Mili
Anders Moller
Prasad Naldurg
Dirk Nowotka
Anne Pacalet
Mariela Pavlova
David Pichardie
Mike Poppleton
Alexander Pretschner
Hridesh Rajan
Abdolbaghi Rezazadeh
Abhik Roychoudhury
David Rydeheard
Norbert Schirmer
Paul Sevinc
Colin Snook
Marielle Stoelinga
Douglas Stuart
Helen Treharne
Laurent Voisin
Thai Son Wang
Bernd Westphal
Jim Woodcock
Letu Yang

Juegen Doser
Andy Edmunds
Neil Evans
John Fitzgerald
Paul Gibson
Bhargav Gulavani
Klaus Havelund
Rolf Hennicker
Matthias Hölzl
Daniel Jackson
Warren A. Hunt Jr.
Stephanie Kemper
Alexander Knapp
Piotr Kosiuczenko
Ingolf Krueger
Marcel Kyas
Rom Langerak
Kamal Lodaya
Monika Maidl
Tim McComb
Roland Meyer
Antoine Mine
Michael Möller
Rocco De Nicola
Peter O'Hearn
Joachim Parrow
Thomas Peikenkamp
Ken Pierce
Sanjiva Prasad
Cyril Proch
H. Rajasekaran
M. Birna van Riemsdijk
Oliver Ruething
Mannu Satpathy
Gerardo Schneider
Murali Sitaraman
Martin Steffen
Ketil Stølen
Martyn Thomas
Stavros Tripakis
Marina de Vos
Andrzej Wasowski
Luke Wildman
Fei Xie
Pamela Zave

Paul Hankes Drielsma
Martin Ellis
Dirk Fahland
Martin Fränzle
Simon Goldsmith
Christian Haack
James Heather
Martin Henson
Marieke Huisman
Suresh Jagannathan
Sven Jörges
Stefan Kiefer
Barbara König
Pavel Krcal
Wouter Kuijper
Ralf Laemmel
Kim Larsen
Antònia Lopes
Joao Marques-Silva
Alistair McEwan
Ronald Middelkoop
Bill Mitchell
Peter Müller
Aditya Nori
David von Oheimb
Dirk Pattinson
Simon Peyton-Jones
Jaco van de Pol
Viorel Preoteasa
Harald Raffelt
Axel Rauschmayer
Robby
Theo Ruys
Andreas Schäfer
Stefan Schwoon
Graeme Smith
Mark-Oliver Stehr
Harald Störrle
Christian Topnik
Emilio Tuosto
Thomas Wahl
Heike Wehrheim
Martin Wildmoser
Alex Yakovlev
Gefei Zhang

Sponsors

We are thankful for the organizational support from FME and Formal Techniques Industrial Association (ForTIA). We gratefully acknowledge sponsorships from the following organizations: Microsoft Research, Tourism Hamilton, SAP Labs France, Software Quality Research Laboratory of McMaster University, and Faculty of Engineering of McMaster University.

Table of Contents

Invited Talk

The Embedded Systems Design Challenge 1
  Thomas A. Henzinger, Joseph Sifakis

Interactive Verification

The Mondex Challenge: Machine Checked Proofs
for an Electronic Purse 16
  *Gerhard Schellhorn, Holger Grandy, Dominik Haneberg,
  Wolfgang Reif*

Interactive Verification of Medical Guidelines 32
  *Jonathan Schmitt, Alwin Hoffmann, Michael Balser,
  Wolfgang Reif, Mar Marcos*

Certifying Airport Security Regulations Using the Focal Environment 48
  *David Delahaye, Jean-Frédéric Étienne,
  Véronique Viguié Donzeau-Gouge*

Proving Safety Properties of an Aircraft Landing Protocol Using I/O
Automata and the PVS Theorem Prover: A Case Study 64
  Shinya Umeno, Nancy Lynch

Invited Talk

Validating the Microsoft Hypervisor 81
  Ernie Cohen

Formal Modelling of Systems

Interface Input/Output Automata 82
  Kim G. Larsen, Ulrik Nyman, Andrzej Wąsowski

Properties of Behavioural Model Merging 98
  Greg Brunet, Marsha Chechik, Sebastian Uchitel

Automatic Translation from Circus to Java 115
  Angela Freitas, Ana Lucia Caneca Cavalcanti

Quantitative Refinement and Model Checking for the Analysis
of Probabilistic Systems 131
  Annabelle K. McIver

Real Time

Modeling and Validating Distributed Embedded Real-Time Systems
with VDM++ 147
  Marcel Verhoef, Peter Gorm Larsen, Jozef Hooman

Towards Modularized Verification of Distributed Time-Triggered
Systems 163
  *Jewgenij Botaschanjan, Alexander Gruler, Alexander Harhurin,
  Leonid Kof, Maria Spichkova, David Trachtenherz*

Industrial Experience

A Story About Formal Methods Adoption by a Railway Signaling
Manufacturer 179
  *Stefano Bacherini, Alessandro Fantechi, Matteo Tempestini,
  Niccolò Zingoni*

Partially Introducing Formal Methods into Object-Oriented
Development: Case Studies Using a Metrics-Driven Approach 190
  Yujun Zheng, Jinquan Wang, Kan Wang, Jinyun Xue

Specification and Refinement

Compositional Class Refinement in Object-Z 205
  Tim McComb, Graeme Smith

A Proposal for Records in Event-B 221
  Neil Evans, Michael Butler

Pointfree Factorization of Operation Refinement 236
  José Nuno Oliveira, César Jesus Rodrigues

A Formal Template Language Enabling Metaproof 252
  Nuno Amálio, Susan Stepney, Fiona Polack

Programming Languages

Dynamic Frames: Support for Framing, Dependencies and Sharing
Without Restrictions (**Best Paper**) 268
  Ioannis T. Kassios

Type-Safe Two-Level Data Transformation 284
  Alcino Cunha, José Nuno Oliveira, Joost Visser

Algebra

Feature Algebra 300
    Peter Höfner, Ridha Khedri, Bernhard Möller

Education

Using Domain-Independent Problems for Introducing Formal
Methods 316
    Raymond Boute

Formal Modelling of Systems

Compositional Binding in Network Domains 332
    Pamela Zave

Formal Modeling of Communication Protocols by Graph
Transformation 348
    Zarrin Langari, Richard Trefler

Feature Specification and Static Analysis for Interaction Resolution 364
    Marc Aiguier, Karim Berkani, Pascale Le Gall

A Fully General Operational Semantics for UML 2.0 Sequence
Diagrams with Potential and Mandatory Choice 380
    Mass Soldal Lund, Ketil Stølen

Formal Aspects of Java

Towards Automatic Exception Safety Verification 396
    Xin Li, H. James Hoover, Piotr Rudnicki

Enforcer – Efficient Failure Injection 412
    Cyrille Valentin Artho, Armin Biere, Shinichi Honiden

Automated Boundary Test Generation from JML Specifications 428
    Fabrice Bouquet, Frédéric Dadeau, Bruno Legeard

Formal Reasoning About Non-atomic JAVA CARD Methods
in Dynamic Logic 444
    Wojciech Mostowski

Programming Languages

Formal Verification of a C Compiler Front-End 460
    Sandrine Blazy, Zaynah Dargaye, Xavier Leroy

A Memory Model Sensitive Checker for C# 476
  Thuan Quang Huynh, Abhik Roychoudhury

Changing Programs Correctly: Refactoring with Specifications 492
  Fabian Bannwart, Peter Müller

Mechanical Verification of Recursive Procedures Manipulating Pointers
Using Separation Logic 508
  Viorel Preoteasa

Model Checking

Model-Based Variable and Transition Orderings for Efficient Symbolic
Model Checking 524
  Wendy Johnston, Kirsten Winter, Lionel van den Berg,
  Paul Strooper, Peter Robinson

Exact and Approximate Strategies for Symmetry Reduction in Model
Checking... 541
  Alastair F. Donaldson, Alice Miller

Monitoring Distributed Controllers: When an Efficient LTL Algorithm
on Sequences Is Needed to Model-Check Traces 557
  Alexandre Genon, Thierry Massart, Cédric Meuter

PSL Model Checking and Run-Time Verification Via Testers 573
  Amir Pnueli, Aleksandr Zaks

Industry Day: Abstracts of Invited Talks

Formal Methods for Security: Lightweight Plug-In or New Engineering
Discipline 587
  Werner Stephan

Formal Methods in the Security Business: Exotic Flowers Thriving
in an Expanding Niche 592
  David von Oheimb

Connector-Based Software Development: Deriving Secure Protocols...... 598
  Dusko Pavlovic

Model-Based Security Engineering for Real 600
  Jan Jürjens

Cost Effective Software Engineering for Security 607
  D. Randolph Johnson

Formal Methods and Cryptography 612
  Michael Backes, Birgit Pfitzmann, Michael Waidner

Verified Software Grand Challenge 617
    Jim Woodcock

Author Index 619

The Embedded Systems Design Challenge*

Thomas A. Henzinger[1] and Joseph Sifakis[2]

[1] EPFL, Lausanne
[2] VERIMAG, Grenoble

Abstract. We summarize some current trends in embedded systems design and point out some of their characteristics, such as the chasm between analytical and computational models, and the gap between safety-critical and best-effort engineering practices. We call for a coherent scientific foundation for embedded systems design, and we discuss a few key demands on such a foundation: the need for encompassing several manifestations of heterogeneity, and the need for constructivity in design. We believe that the development of a satisfactory Embedded Systems Design Science provides a timely challenge and opportunity for reinvigorating computer science.

1 Motivation

Computer Science is going through a maturing period. There is a perception that many of the original, defining problems of Computer Science either have been solved, or require an unforeseeable breakthrough (such as the P versus NP question). It is a reflection of this view that many of the currently advocated challenges for Computer Science research push existing technology to the limits (e.g., the semantic web [4]; the verifying compiler [15]; sensor networks [6]), to new application areas (such as biology [12]), or to a combination of both (e.g., nanotechnologies; quantum computing). Not surprisingly, many of the brightest students no longer aim to become computer scientists, but choose to enter directly into the life sciences or nanoengineering [8].

Our view is different. Following [18,22], we believe that there lies a large uncharted territory within the science of computing. This is the area of embedded systems design. As we shall explain, the current paradigms of Computer Science do not apply to embedded systems design: they need to be enriched in order to encompass models and methods traditionally found in Electrical Engineering. Embedded systems design, however, should not and cannot be left to the electrical engineers, because computation and software are integral parts of embedded systems. Indeed, the shortcomings of current design, validation, and maintenance processes make software, paradoxically, the most costly and least

---

* Supported in part by the ARTIST2 European Network of Excellence on Embedded Systems Design, by the NSF ITR Center on Hybrid and Embedded Software Systems (CHESS), and by the SNSF NCCR on Mobile Information and Communication Systems (MICS).

J. Misra, T. Nipkow, and E. Sekerinski (Eds.): FM 2006, LNCS 4085, pp. 1–15, 2006.
© Springer-Verlag Berlin Heidelberg 2006

reliable part of systems in automotive, aerospace, medical, and other critical applications. Given the increasing ubiquity of embedded systems in our daily lives, this constitutes a unique opportunity for reinvigorating Computer Science.

In the following we will lay out what we see as the Embedded Systems Design Challenge. In our opinion, the Embedded Systems Design Challenge raises not only technology questions, but more importantly, it requires the building of a new scientific foundation — a foundation that systematically and even-handedly integrates, from the bottom up, computation and physicality [14].

2   Current Scientific Foundations for Systems Design, and Their Limitations

2.1   The Embedded Systems Design Problem

What Is an Embedded System? An *embedded system* is an engineering artifact involving computation that is subject to physical constraints. The physical constraints arise through two kinds of interactions of computational processes with the physical world: (1) reaction to a physical environment, and (2) execution on a physical platform. Accordingly, the two types of physical constraints are *reaction constraints* and *execution constraints*. Common reaction constraints specify deadlines, throughput, and jitter; they originate from the behavioral requirements of the system. Common execution constraints put bounds on available processor speeds, power, and hardware failure rates; they originate from the implementation requirements of the system. Reaction constraints are studied in control theory; execution constraints, in computer engineering. Gaining control of the interplay of computation with both kinds of constraints, so as to meet a given set of requirements, is the key to embedded systems design.

Systems Design in General. *Systems design* is the process of deriving, from requirements, a model from which a system can be generated more or less automatically. A *model* is an abstract representation of a system. For example, software design is the process of deriving a program that can be compiled; hardware design, the process of deriving a hardware description from which a circuit can be synthesized. In both domains, the design process usually mixes bottom-up and top-down activities: the reuse and adaptation of existing component models; and the successive refinement of architectural models in order to meet the given requirements.

Embedded Systems Design. Embedded systems consist of hardware, software, and an environment. This they have in common with most computing systems. However, there is an essential difference between embedded and other computing systems: since embedded systems involve computation that is subject to physical constraints, the powerful separation of computation (software) from physicality (platform and environment), which has been one of the central ideas enabling the science of computing, does not work for embedded systems. Instead, the design of embedded systems requires a holistic approach that integrates essential paradigms from hardware design, software design, and control theory in a consistent manner.

We postulate that such a holistic approach cannot be simply an extension of hardware design, nor of software design, but must be based on a new foundation that subsumes techniques from both worlds. This is because current design theories and practices for hardware, and for software, are tailored towards the individual properties of these two domains; indeed, they often use abstractions that are diametrically opposed. To see this, we now have a look at the abstractions that are commonly used in hardware design, and those that are used in software design.

2.2 Analytical Versus Computational Modeling

Hardware Versus Software Design. *Hardware systems* are designed as the composition of interconnected, inherently parallel components. The individual components are represented by analytical models (equations), which specify their transfer functions. These models are deterministic (or probabilistic), and their composition is defined by specifying how data flows across multiple components. *Software systems*, by contrast, are designed from sequential components, such as objects and threads, whose structure often changes dynamically (components are created, deleted, and may migrate). The components are represented by computational models (programs), whose semantics is defined operationally by an abstract execution engine (also called a virtual machine, or an automaton). Abstract machines may be nondeterministic, and their composition is defined by specifying how control flows across multiple components; for instance, the atomic actions of independent processes may be interleaved, possibly constrained by a fixed set of synchronization primitives.

Thus, the basic operation for constructing hardware models is the composition of transfer functions; the basic operation for constructing software models is the product of automata. These are two starkly different views for constructing dynamical systems from basic components: one *analytical* (i.e., equation-based), the other *computational* (i.e., machine-based). The analytical view is prevalent in Electrical Engineering; the computational view, in Computer Science: the netlist representation of a circuit is an example for an analytical model; any program written in an imperative language is an example for a computational model. Since both types of models have very different strengths and weaknesses, the implications on the design process are dramatic.

Analytical and Computational Models Offer Orthogonal Abstractions. Analytical models deal naturally with concurrency and with quantitative constraints, but they have difficulties with partial and incremental specifications (nondeterminism) and with computational complexity. Indicatively, equation-based models and associated analytical methods are used not only in hardware design and control theory, but also in scheduling and in performance evaluation (e.g., in networking).

Computational models, on the other hand, naturally support nondeterministic abstraction hierarchies and a rich theory of computational complexity, but they have difficulties taming concurrency and incorporating physical constraints. Many major paradigms of Computer Science (e.g., the Turing machine; the thread model of concurrency; the structured operational semantics of programming languages) have succeeded precisely because they abstract away from all physical notions of concurrency and from all physical constraints on computation. Indeed, whole subfields of Computer Science are built on and flourish because of such abstractions: in operating systems and distributed computing, both time-sharing and parallelism are famously abstracted to the same concept, namely, nondeterministic sequential computation; in algorithms and complexity theory, real time is abstracted to big-O time, and physical memory to big-O space. These powerful abstractions, however, are largely inadequate for embedded systems design.

Analytical and Computational Models Aim at Different System Requirements. The differences between equation-based and machine-based design are reflected in the type of requirements they support well. System designers deal with two kinds of requirements. *Functional requirements* specify the expected services, functionality, and features, independent of the implementation. *Extra-functional requirements* specify mainly performance, which characterizes the efficient use of real time and of implementation resources; and robustness, which characterizes the ability to deliver some minimal functionality under circumstances that deviate from the nominal ones. For the same functional requirements, extra-functional properties can vary depending on a large number of factors and choices, including the overall system architecture and the characteristics of the underlying platform.

Functional requirements are naturally expressed in discrete, logic-based formalisms. However, for expessing many extra-functional requirements, real-valued quantities are needed to represent physical constraints and probabilities. For software, the dominant driver is correct functionality, and even performance and robustness are often specified discretely (e.g., number of messages exchanged; number of failures tolerated). For hardware, continuous performance and robustness measures are more prominent and refer to physical resource levels such as clock frequency, energy consumption, latency, mean-time to failure, and cost. For embedded systems integrated in mass-market products, the ability to quantify trade-offs between performance and robustness, under given technical and economic constraints, is of strategic importance.

Analytical and Computational Models Support Different Design Processes. The differences between models based on data flow and models based on control flow have far-reaching implications on design methods. Equation-based modeling yields rich analytical tools, especially in the presence of stochastic behavior. Moreover, if the number of different basic building blocks is small, as it is in circuit design, then automatic synthesis techniques have proved extraordinarily successful in the design of very large systems, to the point of creating an entire industry (Electronic Design Automation). Machine-based models, on the other hand, while sacrificing powerful analytical and synthesis techniques, can be executed directly. They give the designer more fine-grained control and provide a greater space for design variety and optimization. Indeed, robust software architectures and efficient algorithms are still individually designed, not automatically generated, and this will likely remain the case for some time to come. The emphasis, therefore, shifts away from design synthesis to design verification (proof of correctness).

Embedded systems design must even-handedly deal with both: with computation and physical constraints; with software and hardware; with abstract machines and transfer functions; with nondeterminism and probabilities; with functional and performance requirements; with qualitative and quantitative analysis; with booleans and reals. This cannot be achieved by simple juxtaposition of analytical and computational techniques, but requires their tight integration within a new mathematical foundation that spans both perspectives.

3   Current Engineering Practices for Embedded Systems Design, and Their Limitations

3.1   Model-Based Design

Language-Based and Synthesis-Based Origins. Historically, many methodologies for embedded systems design trace their origins to one of two sources: there are language-based methods that lie in the software tradition, and synthesis-based methods that come out of the hardware tradition. A *language-based* approach is centered on a particular programming language with a particular target run-time system. Examples include Ada and, more recently, RT-Java [5]. For these languages, there are compilation technologies that lead to event-driven implementations on standardized platforms (fixed-priority scheduling with preemption). The *synthesis-based* approaches, on the other hand, have evolved from hardware design methodologies. They start from a system description in a tractable (often structural) fragment of a hardware description language such as VHDL and Verilog and, ideally automatically, derive an implementation that obeys a given set of constraints.

Implementation Independence. Recent trends have focused on combining both language-based and synthesis-based approaches (hardware/software codesign) and on gaining, during the early design process, maximal independence from a specific implementation platform. We refer to these newer aproaches collectively as *model-based*, because they emphasize the separation of the design level from the implementation level, and they are centered around the semantics of abstract system descriptions (rather than on the implementation semantics). Consequently, much effort in model-based approaches goes into developing efficient code generators. We provide here only a short and incomplete selection of some representative methodologies.

Model-Based Methodologies. The synchronous languages, such as Lustre and Esterel [11], embody an abstract hardware semantics (synchronicity) within different kinds of software structures (functional; imperative). Implementation technologies are available for several platforms, including bare machines and time-triggered architectures. Originating from the design automation community, SystemC [19] also chooses a synchronous hardware semantics, but allows for the introduction of asynchronous execution and interaction mechanisms from software (C++). Implementations require a separation between the components to be implemented in hardware, and those to be implemented in software; different design-space exploration techniques provide guidance in making such partitioning decisions. A third kind of model-based approaches are built around a class of popular languages exemplified by MATLAB Simulink, whose semantics is defined operationally through its simulation engine.

More recent modeling languages, such as UML [20] and AADL [10], attempt to be more generic in their choice of semantics and thus bring extensions in two directions: independence from a particular programming language; and emphasis on system architecture as a means to organize computation, communication, and constraints. We believe, however, that these attempts will ultimately fall short, unless they can draw on new foundational results to overcome the current weaknesses of model-based design: the lack of analytical tools for computational models to deal with physical constraints; and the difficulty to automatically transform noncomputational models into efficient computational ones. This leads us to the key need for a better understanding of relationships and transformations between heterogeneous models.

Model Transformations. Central to all model-based design is an effective theory of model transformations. Design often involves the use of multiple models that represent different views of a system at different levels of granularity. Usually design proceeds neither strictly top-down, from the requirements to the implementation, nor strictly bottom-up, by integrating library components, but in a less directed fashion, by iterating model construction, model analysis, and model transformation. Some transformations between models can be automated; at other times, the designer must guide the model construction. The ultimate success story in model transformation is the theory of compilation: today, it is difficult to manually improve on the code produced by a good optimizing compiler from programs (i.e., computational models) written in a high-level language. On the other hand, code generators often produce inefficient code from equation-based models: fixpoints of equation sets can be computed (or approximated) iteratively, but more efficient algorithmic insights and data structures must be supplied by the designer.

For extra-functional requirements, such as timing, the separation of human-guided design decisions from automatic model transformations is even less well understood. Indeed, engineering practice often relies on a 'trial-and-error' loop of code generation, followed by test, followed by redesign (e.g., priority tweaking when deadlines are missed). An alternative is to develop high-level programming languages that can express reaction constraints, together with compilers that guarantee the preservation of the reaction constraints on a given execution platform [13]. Such a compiler must mediate between the reaction constraints specified by the program, such as timeouts, and the execution constraints of the platform, typically provided in the form of worst-case execution times. We believe that an extension of this approach to other extra-functional dimensions, such as power consumption and fault tolerance, is a promising direction of investigation.

3.2   Critical Versus Best-Effort Engineering

Guaranteeing Safety Versus Optimizing Performance. Today's systems engineering methodologies can be classified also along another axis: critical systems engineering, and best-effort systems engineering. The former tries to guarantee system safety at all costs, even when the system operates under extreme conditions; the latter tries to optimize system performance (and cost) when the system operates under expected conditions. Critical engineering views design as a constraint-satisfaction problem; best-effort engineering, as an optimization problem.

Critical systems engineering is based on worst-case analysis (i.e., conservative approximations of the system dynamics) and on static resource reservation. For tractable conservative approximations to exist, execution platforms often need to be simplified (e.g., bare machines without operating systems; processor architectures that allow time predictability for code execution). Typical examples of such approaches are those used for safety-critical systems in avionics. Real-time constraint satisfaction is guaranteed on the basis of worst-case execution time analysis and static scheduling. The maximal necessary computing power is made available at all times. Dependability is achieved mainly by using massive redundancy, and by statically deploying all equipment for failure detection and recovery.

Best-effort systems engineering, by contrast, is based on average-case (rather than worst-case) analysis and on dynamic resource allocation. It seeks the efficient use of resources (e.g., optimization of throughput, jitter, or power) and is used for applications where some degradation or even temporary denial of service is tolerable, as in telecommunications. The 'hard' worst-case requirements of critical systems are replaced by 'soft' QoS (quality-of-service) requirements. For example, a hard deadline is either met or missed; for a soft deadline, there is a continuum of different degrees of satisfaction. QoS requirements can be enforced by adaptive (feedback-based) scheduling mechanisms, which adjust some system parameters at run-time in order to optimize performance and to recover from deviations from nominal behavior. Service may be denied temporarily by admission policies, in order to guarantee that QoS levels stay above minimum thresholds.

A Widening Gap. The two approaches —critical and best-effort engineering— are largely disjoint. This is reflected by the separation between 'hard' and 'soft' real time. They correspond to different research communities and different practices. Hard approaches rely on static (design-time) analysis; soft approaches, on dynamic (run-time) adaptation. Consequently, they adopt different models of computation and use different execution platforms, middleware, and networks. For instance, time-triggered technologies are considered to be indispensable for drive-by-wire automotive systems [17]. Most safety-critical systems adopt very simple static scheduling principles, either fixed-priority scheduling with preemption, or round-robin scheduling for synchronous execution. It is often said that such a separation is inevitable for systems with uncertain environments. Meeting hard constraints and making the best possible use of the available resources seem to be two conflicting requirements. The hard real-time approach leads to low utilization of system resources. On the other hand, soft approaches take the risk of temporary unavailability.

We believe that, left unchecked, the gap between the two approaches will continue to widen. This is because the uncertainties in embedded systems design keep increasing for two reasons. First, as embedded systems are deployed in a greater variety of situations, their environments are less perfectly known, with greater distances between worst-case and expected behaviors. Second, because of the rapid progress in VLSI design, embedded systems are implemented on sophisticated, hardware/software layered multicore architectures with caches, pipelines, and speculative execution. The ensuing difficulty of accurate worst-case analysis makes conservative, safety-critical solutions ever more expensive, in both resource and design cost, in comparison to best-effort solutions. The divide between critical and best-effort engineering already leads often to a physical separation between the critical and noncritical parts of a system, each running on dedicated hardware or during dedicated time slots. As the gap between worst-case and average-case solutions increases, such separated architectures are likely to become more prevalent.

Bridging the Gap. We think that technological trends oblige us to revise the dual vision and separation between critical and best-effort practices. The increasing computing power of system-on-chip and network-on-chip technologies allows the integration of critical and noncritical applications on a single chip. This reduces communication costs and increases hardware reliability. It also allows a more rational and cost-effective management of resources. To achieve this, we need methods for guaranteeing a sufficiently strong, but not absolute, separation between critical and noncritical components that share common resources. In particular, design techniques for adaptive systems should make flexible use of the available resources by taking advantage of any complementarities between hard and soft constraints. One possibility may be to treat the satisfaction of critical requirements as minimal guaranteed QoS level. Such an approach would require, once again, the integration of boolean-valued and quantitative methods.

4   Two Demands on a Solution

Heterogeneity and Constructivity. Our vision is to develop an Embedded Systems Design Science that even-handedly integrates analytical and computational views of a system, and that methodically quantifies trade-offs between critical and best-effort engineering decisions. Two opposing forces need to be addressed for setting up such an Embedded Systems Design Science. These correspond to the needs for encompassing heterogeneity and achieving constructivity during the design process. *Heterogeneity* is the property of embedded systems to be built from components with different characteristics. Heterogeneity has several sources and manifestations (as will be discussed below), and the existing body of knowledge is largely fragmented into unrelated models and corresponding results. *Constructivity* is the possibility to build complex systems that meet given requirements, from building blocks and glue components with known properties. Constructivity can be achieved by algorithms (compilation and synthesis), but also by architectures and design disciplines.

The two demands of heterogeneity and constructivity pull in different directions. Encompassing heterogeneity looks outward, towards the integration of theories to provide a unifying view for bridging the gaps between analytical and computational models, and between critical and best-effort techniques. Achieving constructivity looks inward, towards developing a tractable theory for system construction. Since constructivity is most easily achieved in restricted settings, an Embedded Systems Design Science must provide the means for intelligently balancing and trading off both ambitions.

4.1 Encompassing Heterogeneity

System designers deal with a large variety of components, each having different characteristics, from a large variety of viewpoints, each highlighting different dimensions of a system. Two central problems are the meaningful composition of heterogeneous components to ensure their correct interoperation, and the meaningful refinement and integration of heterogeneous viewpoints during the design process. Superficial classifications may distinguish between hardware and software components, or between continuous-time (analog) and discrete-time (digital) components, but heterogeneity has two more fundamental sources: the composition of subsystems with different execution and interaction semantics; and the abstract view of a system from different perspectives.

Heterogeneity of Execution and Interaction Semantics. At one extreme of the semantic spectrum are fully synchronized components, which proceed in lock-step with a global clock and interact in atomic transactions. Such a tight coupling of components is the standard model for most synthesizable hardware and for hard real-time software. At the other extreme are completely asynchronous components, which proceed at independent speeds and interact nonatomically. Such a loose coupling of components is the standard model for most multithreaded software. Between the two extremes, a variety of intermediate and hybrid models exist (e.g., globally-asynchronous locally-synchronous models). To better understand their commonalities and differences, it is useful to decouple execution from interaction semantics [21].

Execution Semantics. Synchronous execution is typically used in hardware, in synchronous programming languages, and in time-triggered systems. It considers a system's execution as a sequence of global steps. It assumes synchrony, meaning that the environment does not change during a step, or equivalently, that the system is infinitely faster than its environment. In each execution step, all system components contribute by executing some quantum of computation. The synchronous execution paradigm, therefore, has a built-in strong assumption of fairness: in each step all components can move forward. Asynchronous execution, by contrast, does not use any notion of global computation step. It is adopted in most distributed systems description languages such as SDL [16] and UML, and in multithreaded programming languages such as Ada and Java. The lack of built-in mechanisms for sharing computation between components can be compensated through constraints on scheduling (e.g., priorities; fairness) and through mechanisms for interaction (e.g., shared variables).

Interaction Semantics. Interactions are combinations of actions performed by system components in order to achieve a desired global behavior. Interactions can be atomic or nonatomic. For atomic interactions, the state change induced in the participating components cannot be altered through interference with other interactions. As a rule, synchronous programming languages and hardware description languages use atomic interactions. By contrast, languages with buffered communication (e.g., SDL) and multithreaded languages (e.g., Java) generally use nonatomic interactions. Both types of interactions may involve strong or weak synchronization. Strongly synchronizing interactions can occur only if all participating components agree (e.g., CSP rendezvous). Weakly synchronizing interactions are asymmetric; they require only the participation of an initiating action, which may or may not synchronize with other actions (e.g., outputs in synchronous languages).

Heterogeneity of Abstractions. System design involves the use of models that represent a system at varying degrees of detail and are related to each other in an abstraction (or equivalently, refinement) hierarchy. Heterogeneous abstractions, which relate different styles of models, are often the most powerful ones: a notable example is the boolean-valued gate-level abstraction of real-valued transistor-level models for circuits.

In embedded systems, a key abstraction is the one relating application software to its implementation on a given platform. Application software is largely untimed, in the sense that it abstracts away from physical time. References to physical time may occur in the parameters of real-time statements, such as time-outs, which are treated as external events. The application code running on a given platform, however, is a dynamical system that can be modeled as a timed or hybrid automaton [1]. The run-time state includes not only the variables of the application software, but also all variables that are needed to characterize its dynamic behavior, including clock variables. Modeling implementations may require additional quantitative constraints, such as probabilities to describe failures, and arrival laws for external events. We need to find tractable theories to relate the application and implementation layers. In particular, such theories must provide the means for preserving, in the implementation, all essential properties of the application software.

Another cause of heterogeneity in abstractions is the use of different abstractions for modeling different extra-functional dimensions (or 'aspects') of a system. Some dimensions, such as timing and power consumption in certain settings, may be tightly correlated; others, such as timing and fault tolerance, may be achievable through independent, composable solutions. In general we lack practical theories for effectively separating orthogonal dimensions, and for quantifying the trade-offs between interfering dimensions.

Metamodeling. We are not the first to emphasize the need for encompassing heterogeneity in systems design. Much recent attention has focused on so-called 'metamodels,' which are semantic frameworks for expressing different models and their interoperation [2,9,3]. We submit that we need a metamodel which is not just a disjoint union of submodels within a common (meta)language, but one which preserves properties during model composition and supports meaningful analyses and transformations across heterogeneous model boundaries. This leads to the issue of constructivity in design.

4.2 Achieving Constructivity

The system construction problem can be formulated as follows: "build a system meeting a given set of requirements from a given set of components." This is a key problem in any engineering discipline; it lies at the basis of various systems design activities, including modeling, architecting, programming, synthesis, upgrading, and reuse. The general problem is by its nature intractable. Given a formal framework for describing and composing components, the system to be constructed can be characterized as a fixpoint of a monotonic function which is computable only when a reduction to finite-state models is possible. Even in this case, however, the complexity of the algorithms is prohibitive for real-world systems.

What are the possible avenues for circumventing this obstacle? We need results in two complementary directions. First, we need construction methods for specific, restricted application contexts characterized by particular types of requirements and constraints, and by particular types of components and composition mechanisms. Clearly, hardware synthesis techniques, software compilation techniques, algorithms (e.g., for scheduling, mutual exclusion, clock synchronization), architectures (such as time-triggered; publish-subscribe), as well as protocols (e.g., for multimedia synchronization) contribute solutions for specific contexts. It is important to stress that many of the practically interesting results require little computation and guarantee correctness more or less by construction.

Second, we need theories that allow the incremental combination of the above results in a systematic process for system construction. Such theories would be particularly useful for the integration of heterogeneous models, because the objectives for individual subsystems are most efficiently accomplished within those models which most naturally capture each of these subsystems. A resulting framework for incremental system construction is likely to employ two kinds of rules. *Compositionality* rules infer global system properties from the local properties of subsystems (e.g., inferring global deadlock-freedom from the deadlock-freedom of the individual components). *Noninterference* rules guarantee that during the system construction process, all essential properties of subsystems are preserved (e.g., establishing noninterference for two scheduling algorithms used to manage two system resources). This suggests the following action lines for research.

Constructivity for Performance and Robustness. The focus must shift from compositional methods and architectures for ensuring only functional properties, to extra-functional requirements such as performance and robustness.

Performance. The key issue is the construction of components (schedulers) that manage system resources so as to meet or optimize given performance requirements. These cover a large range of resource-related constraints involving upper and lower bounds, averages, jitter, and probabilities. Often the requirements for different resources are antagonistic, for instance, timeliness and power efficiency, or respecting deadlines and maximizing utilization. Thus we need construction methods that allow the joint consideration of performance requirements and the analysis of trade-offs.

Another inherent difficulty in the construction of schedulers comes from uncertainty and unpredictability in a system's execution and external environments. In this context, poor precision for time constants used in static scheduling techniques implies poor performance [23]. One approach is to build adaptive schedulers, which control execution by dynamically adjusting their scheduling policies according to their knowledge about the system's environment. However, currently there is no satisfactory theory for combining adaptive techniques for different kinds of resources. Such an approach must address the concerns of critical systems engineering, which currently relies almost exclusively on static techniques. The development of a system construction framework that allows the joint consideration of both critical and noncritical performance requirements for different classes of resources is a major challenge for the envisioned Embedded Systems Design Science.

Robustness. The key issue is the construction of components performing as desired under circumstances that deviate from the normal, expected operating environment. Such deviations may include extreme input values, platform failures, and malicious attacks. Accordingly, robustness requirements include a broad spectrum of properties, such as safety (resistance to failures), security (resistance to attacks), and availability (accessibility of resources). Robustness is a transversal issue in system construction, cutting across all design activities and influencing all design decisions. For instance, system security must take into account properties of the software and hardware architectures, information treatment (encryption, access, and transmission), as well as programming disciplines. The current state of the art in building robust systems is still embryonic. A long-term and continuous research effort is necessary to develop a framework for the rigorous construction of robust systems. Our purpose here is only to point out the inadequacy of some existing approaches.

In dynamical systems, robustness can be formalized as continuity, namely, that small perturbations of input values cause small perturbations of output values. No such formalization is available for discrete systems, where the change of a single input or state bit can lead to a completely different output behavior. Worse, many of our models for embedded systems are nonrobust even in the continuous domain. For example, in timed automata, an arbitrarily small change in the arrival time of an input may change the entire behavior of the automaton.

In computer science, redundancy is often the only solution to build reliable systems from unreliable components. We need theories, methods, and tools that support the construction of robust embedded systems without resorting to such massive, expensive overengineering. One hope is that continuity can be achieved in fully quantitative models, where quantitative information expresses not only probabilities, time, and other resource consumption levels, but also functional characteristics. For example, if we are no longer interested in the absolute (boolean-valued) possibility or nonpossibility of failure, but in the (real-valued) mean-time to failure, we may be able to construct continuous models where small changes in certain parameters induce only small changes in the failure rate.

Incremental Construction. A practical methodology for embedded systems design needs to scale, and overcome the limitations of current algorithmic verification and synthesis techniques. One route for achieving scalability is to rely on compositionality and noninterference rules which require only lightweight analyses of the overall system architecture. Such correct-by-construction techniques exist for very specific properties and architectures. For example, time-triggered architectures ensure timely and fault-tolerant communication for distributed real-time systems; a token-ring protocol guarantees mutual exclusion for strongly synchronized processes that are connected in a ring. It is essential to extend the correct-by-construction paradigm by studying more generally the interplay between architectures and properties.

A related class of correct-by-construction techniques is focused on the use of component interfaces [7]. A well-designed interface exposes exactly the information about a component which is necessary to check for composability with other components. In a sense, an interface formalism is a 'type theory' for component composition. Recent trends have been towards rich interfaces, which expose functional as well as extra-functional information about a component, for example, resource consumption levels. Interface theories are especially promising for incremental design under such quantitative constraints, because the composition of two or more interfaces can be defined as to calculate the combined amount of resources that are consumed by putting together the underlying components.

5   Summary

We believe that the challenge of designing embedded systems offers a unique opportunity for reinvigorating Computer Science. The challenge, and thus the opportunity, spans the spectrum from theoretical foundations to engineering practice. To begin with, we need a mathematical basis for systems modeling and analysis which integrates both abstract-machine models and transfer-function models in order to deal with computation and physical constraints in a consistent, operative manner. Based on such a theory, it should be possible to combine practices for critical systems engineering to guarantee functional requirements, with best-effort systems engineering to optimize performance and robustness. The theory, the methodologies, and the tools need to encompass heterogeneous execution and interaction mechanisms for the components of a system, and they need to provide abstractions that isolate the subproblems in design that require human creativity from those that can be automated. This effort is a true grand challenge: it demands paradigmatic departures from the prevailing views on both hardware and software design, and it offers substantial rewards in terms of cost and quality of our future embedded infrastructure.

Acknowledgments. We thank Paul Caspi and Oded Maler for valuable comments on a preliminary draft of this manuscript.

References

1. R. Alur, C. Courcoubetis, N. Halbwachs, T.A. Henzinger, P.-H. Ho, X. Nicollin, A. Olivero, J. Sifakis, and S. Yovine. The algorithmic analysis of hybrid systems. *Theoretical Computer Science*, 138(1):3–34, 1995.
2. F. Balarin, Y. Watanabe, H. Hsieh, L. Lavagno, C. Passerone, and A.L. Sangiovanni-Vincentelli. Metropolis: An integrated electronic system design environment. *IEEE Computer*, 36(4):45–52, 2003.
3. K. Balasubramanian, A.S. Gokhale, G. Karsai, J. Sztipanovits, and S. Neema. Developing applications using model-driven design environments. *IEEE Computer*, 39(2):33–40, 2006.
4. T. Berners-Lee, J. Hendler, and O. Lassila. The Semantic Web. *Scientific American*, 284(5):34–43, 2001.
5. A. Burns and A. Wellings. *Real-Time Systems and Programming Languages*. Addison-Wesley, third edition, 2001.
6. D.E. Culler and W. Hong. Wireless sensor networks. *Commununications of the ACM*, 47(6):30–33, 2004.
7. L. de Alfaro and T.A. Henzinger. Interface-based design. In M. Broy, J. Grünbauer, D. Harel, and C.A.R. Hoare, editors, *Engineering Theories of Software-intensive Systems*, NATO Science Series: Mathematics, Physics, and Chemistry 195, pages 83–104. Springer, 2005.
8. P.J. Denning and A. McGettrick. Recentering Computer Science. *Commununications of the ACM*, 48(11):15–19, 2005.
9. J. Eker, J.W. Janneck, E.A. Lee, J. Liu, X. Liu, J. Ludvig, S. Neuendorffer, S. Sachs, and Y. Xiong. Taming heterogeneity: The Ptolemy approach. *Proceedings of the IEEE*, 91(1):127–144, 2003.
10. P.H. Feiler, B. Lewis, and S. Vestal. The SAE Architecture Analysis and Design Language (AADL) Standard: A basis for model-based architecture-driven embedded systems engineering. In *Proceedings of the RTAS Workshop on Model-driven Embedded Systems*, pages 1–10, 2003.
11. N. Halbwachs. *Synchronous Programming of Reactive Systems*. Kluwer Academic Publishers, 1993.
12. D. Harel. A grand challenge for computing: Full reactive modeling of a multicellular animal. *Bulletin of the EATCS*, 81:226–235, 2003.

13. T.A. Henzinger, C.M. Kirsch, M.A.A. Sanvido, and W. Pree. From control models to real-time code using Giotto. *IEEE Control Systems Magazine*, 23(1):50–64, 2003.

14. T.A. Henzinger, E.A. Lee, A.L. Sangiovanni-Vincentelli, S.S. Sastry, and J. Sztipanovits. *Mission Statement: Center for Hybrid and Embedded Software Systems*, University of California, Berkeley, http://chess.eecs.berkeley.edu, 2002.

15. C.A.R. Hoare. The Verifying Compiler: A grand challenge for computing research. *Journal of the ACM*, 50(1):63–69, 2003.

16. ITU-T. *Recommendation Z-100 Annex F1(11/00): Specification and Description Language (SDL) Formal Definition*, International Telecommunication Union, Geneva, 2000.

17. H. Kopetz. *Real-Time Systems: Design Principles for Distributed Embedded Applications*. Kluwer Academic Publishers, 1997.

18. E.A. Lee. Absolutely positively on time: What would it take? *IEEE Computer*, 38(7):85–87, 2005.

19. P.R. Panda. SystemC: A modeling platform supporting multiple design abstractions. In *Proceedings of the International Symposium on Systems Synthesis (ISSS)*, pages 75–80. ACM, 2001.

20. J. Rumbaugh, I. Jacobson, and G. Booch. *The Unified Modeling Language Reference Manual*. Addison-Wesley, second edition, 2004.

21. J. Sifakis. A framework for component-based construction. In *Proceedings of the Third International Conference on Software Engineering and Formal Methods (SEFM)*, pages 293–300. IEEE Computer Society, 2005.

22. J.A. Stankovic, I. Lee, A. Mok, and R. Rajkumar. Opportunities and obligations for physical computing systems. *IEEE Computer*, 38(11):23–31, 2005.

23. L. Thiele and R. Wilhelm. Design for timing predictability. *Real-Time Systems*, 28(2-3):157–177, 2003.

The Mondex Challenge: Machine Checked Proofs for an Electronic Purse

Gerhard Schellhorn, Holger Grandy, Dominik Haneberg, and Wolfgang Reif

Lehrstuhl für Softwaretechnik und Programmiersprachen,
Universität Augsburg, D-86135 Augsburg, Germany
{schellhorn, grandy, haneberg, reif}@informatik.uni-augsburg.de

Abstract. The Mondex case study about the specification and refinement of an electronic purse as defined in [SCJ00] has recently been proposed as a challenge for formal system-supported verification. This paper
reports on the successful verification of the major part of the case study
using the KIV specification and verification system. We demonstrate that
even though the hand-made proofs were elaborated to an enormous level
of detail, we still could find small errors in the underlying data refinement
theory as well as the formal proofs of the case study.

We also provide an alternative formalisation of the communication
protocol using abstract state machines.

Finally the Mondex case study verifies functional correctness assuming
a suitable security protocol. Therefore we propose to extend the case
study to include the verification of a suitable security protocol.

1 Introduction

Mondex smart cards implement an electronic purse [MCI]. They have become
famous for having been the target of the first ITSEC evaluation of the highest
level E6 [CB99], which requires formal specification and verification.

The formal specification and proofs were done in [SCJ00] using the Z specification language [Spi92]. Two models of electronic purses were defined: an abstract one which models the transfer of money between purses as elementary
transactions, and a concrete level that implements money transfer using a communication protocol that can cope with lost messages using a suitable logging of
failed transfers. A suitable data refinement theory was developed in [CSW02].

Although the refinement proofs based on this theory were done manually
(with an auxiliary type checker) they were elaborated to the detail of almost
calculus level. The Mondex case study has been recently proposed as a challenge
for theorem provers [Woo06].

In this paper we show that verifying the refinement mechanically, using the
KIV theorem prover, can be done within a few weeks of work. We verify the
full Mondex case study except for the operations that archive failure logs from a
smart card to a central archive. These are independent of the protocol for money
transfer.

J. Misra, T. Nipkow, and E. Sekerinski (Eds.): FM 2006, LNCS 4085, pp. 16–31, 2006.
© Springer-Verlag Berlin Heidelberg 2006

The Mondex case study is too big to be presented completely within a paper of 16 pages ([SCJ00] has 240 pages, [CSW02] additional 54 pages). Therefore we unfortunately will have to refer to these papers quite often. To view the details of the KIV proofs we have prepared a technical report [SGHR06] and a Web presentation of the full KIV specifications and of all proofs, which can be found at [KIV]. The interested reader can find all details there.

Nevertheless we have tried to extract the core of the refinement problem and to give a concise definition of the case study in section 2. To this purpose we introduce the case study using abstract state machines (ASM, [Gur95], [BS03]). Since the relational approach of Z is quite different from the operational description of ASMs, this paper can also be used to compare the two specification styles. To check the adequacy of the ASM formalization we have also verified the central proof obligations of [SCJ00]: backward simulation and an invariant for the concrete level. We discuss these proofs in section 3. Doing them was sufficient to uncover small problems in the invariant of the concrete level.

While the proofs could be elaborated to a full ASM refinement proof which would be our traditional verification approach ([BR95], [Sch01], [Bör03]), we decided to mimic the data refinement proofs faithfully to succeed in verifying the challenge. Therefore we formalised the underlying data refinement theory. We report on a correction for this theory and an extension using invariants in section 4.

Finally we instantiated the data refinement theory with the operations of the Mondex case study. Our proofs improve the ones of [SCJ00] by using one refinement instead of two. Section 5 also reports on the additional complexity caused by using operations similar to Z instead of a simple ASM, and gives some statistics of the effort required.

When we discovered the Mondex case study, we were astonished to find that it has been given the highest security level ITSEC E6, when in fact the case study *assumes* a suitable security protocol rather than proving it. Since the real security protocol of Mondex smart cards has never been published, we discuss a probable security protocol in section 6 and propose a refinement of the concrete Mondex level to a specification that includes such a security protocol as an extension of the case study.

2   Two Simple ASMs for the Mondex Case Study

The Mondex case study is based on smart cards that are being used as electronic purses. Each card has a balance and may be used to transfer money to other cards. Unfortunately it is very hard to get a clear picture of their use in real life. The original web site [MCI] says that the smart cards are used to transfer money over the internet using a card reader on each end. [RE03] says one card reader is used, the 'from' purse (where money is taken from) is first put in the card reader, then the 'to' purse (which receives the money). This seems not really compatible with the protocol given later on. Finally, the Mondex paper [SCJ00] and the ITSEC evaluation [CB99] suggest an interface device, which seems to be a card reader with two slots, where both cards can be inserted simultaneously.

It is also not clear how cryptography is used, [CCW96] suggest that this was never disclosed, and that the Mondex card therefore is a classical example of "security by obscurity". Maybe this is the reason why a security protocol is not considered in the Mondex case study.

The smart cards of the formal specification are specified on two levels: An abstract level which defines transfer of money between purses as an atomic transaction, and a concrete level which defines a protocol to transfer money.

In this section we now give an alternative version of the Mondex refinement problem using abstract state machines (ASMs, [Gur95], [BS03]) and algebraic specifications as used in KIV [RSSB98].

The abstract state machines can also be found on the Web [KIV] in the *Mondex* project as *simple-AASM* and *simple-BASM*. We have tried to stay as close as possible to the notation of the original Mondex case study, but we have removed all details that we thought were not essential to understand the problem described by the Mondex refinement.

2.1   The Abstract Level

The abstract specification of a purse consists of a function balance from purse names to their current balance. Since the transfer of money from one to another purse may fail (due to the card being pulled abruptly from the card reader, or for internal reasons like lack of memory) the state of an abstract purse also must log the amount of money that has been lost in such failed transfers.

In the formalism of ASMs this means that the abstract state consists of two dynamic functions

balance : name $\rightarrow$ $\mathbb{N}$
lost : name $\rightarrow$ $\mathbb{N}$

Purses may be faked, so we have a finite number of names which satisfy a predicate authentic[1]. How authenticity is checked (using secret keys, pins etc.) is left open on both levels of the specification, so the predicate is simply left unspecified. We will come back to this point in section 6.

Transfer of money between authentic purses is done with the following simple ASM rule[2]

ABTRANSFER#
choose from, to, value, fail?
with authentic(from) $\wedge$ authentic(to) $\wedge$ from $\neq$ to $\wedge$ value $\leq$ balance(from)
in if $\neg$ fail? **then** balance(from) := balance(from) $-$ value
                      balance(to) := balance(to) $+$ value
             else balance(from) := balance(from) $-$ value
                      lost(from) := lost(from) $+$ value

---

[1] In the original Z specification, authentic is defined to be the domain of partial AbAuthPurse and ConAuthPurse functions. For simplicity, we use total functions instead, and use authentic to restrict their domain.

[2] By convention our rule names end with a # sign to distinguish them from predicates.

The rule nondeterministically chooses two different, authentic purses with names from and to, and an amount value for which the from purse has enough money and transfers it. The transfer may fail for internal reasons as indicated by the randomly chosen boolean variable fail?. In this case the from purse logs the lost money in its lost component.

This already completes the specification of the abstract level. Compared to the Z specification in [SCJ00] we have left out the operation ABIGNORE# which skips (i.e. does nothing): In data refinement such a skip operation is needed, since every operation must be refined by a 1:1 diagram. ASM refinement directly allows to use 0:1 diagrams, therefore such a skip operation is not needed.

2.2 The Concrete Level

On the concrete level transferring money is done using a protocol with 5 steps. To execute the protocol, each purse needs a status that indicates how far it has progressed executing the protocol. The possible states a purse may be in are given by the enumeration status = idle | epr | epv | epa. Compared to [SCJ00] we have merged the two states eaFrom and eaTo into one idle state. The behavior of a purse in eaTo state is exactly the same as that of a purse in eaFrom state, so we saw no necessity to distinguish them.

Purses not participating in any transfer are in the idle state. To avoid replay attacks each purse stores a sequence number nextSeqNo that can be used in the next transaction. This number is incremented during any run of the protocol. During the run of the protocol each purse stores the current payment details in a variable pdAuth of type PayDetails. These are tuples consisting of the names of the from and to purse, the transaction numbers these use for this transaction and the amount of money that is transferred. In KIV we define a free data type PayDetails =
    mkpd(. .from : name; . .fromno : nat; . .to : name; . .tono : nat; . .value : nat)
with postfix selectors (so pd.from is the name of the from purse stored in payment details pd). The state of a purse finally contains a log exLog of failed transfers represented by their payment details. The protocol is executed sending messages between the purses. The ether collects all messages that are currently available. A purse receives a message by selecting a message from the ether. Since the environment of the card is assumed to be hostile the message received may be any message that already been sent, not just one that is directed to the card (this simple model of available messages is also used in many abstract specifications of security protocols, e.g. the traces of [Pau98]). The state of the concrete ASM therefore is:

    balance : name → IN
    state : name → status
    pdAuth : name → PayDetails
    exLog : name → set(PayDetails)
    ether : set(message)

The protocol is started by two messages startFrom(msgna, value, msgno) and startTo(msgna, value, msgno) which are sent to the from and to purse respectively by the interface device. These two messages are assumed to be always available, so the initial ether already contains every such message. The arguments msgna and msgno of startFrom(msgna, value, msgno) are assumed to be the name and nextSeqNo of the to purse, value is the amount of value transfered. Similarly, for startTo(msgna, value, msgno) msgna and msgno are the corresponding data of the from purse.

On receiving a startFrom message msg from ether (selecting a message from ether is defined in the full ASM rule BOP# at the end of this section) in the idle state a purse named receiver[3] executes the following step:

```
STARTFROM#
let msgna = msg.name, value = msg.value, msgno = msg.nextSeqNo
in if    authentic(msgna) ∧ receiver ≠ msgna
      ∧ value ≤ balance(receiver) ∧ ¬ fail?
   then choose n with nextSeqNo(receiver) < n in
          pdAuth(receiver) := mkpd(receiver, nextSeqNo(receiver),
                                        msgna, msgno, value)
          state(receiver) := epr
          nextSeqNo(receiver) := n
          outmsg := ⊥
      else outmsg := ⊥
```

If the purse msgna which shall receive money is not authentic, the receiver purse has not enough money or the transition fails due to internal reasons (a flag fail? is used for this purpose just as on the abstract level), then the purse simply produces an empty output message ⊥ and does nothing else. Otherwise the purse stores the requested transfer in its pdAuth component, using its current nextSeqNo number as one component and proceeds to the epr state ("expecting request"). Thereby it becomes the from purse of the current transaction. nextSeqNo is incremented to make it unavailable in further transactions. An empty output message ⊥ is generated in the success case too that will be added to the ether (see the full ASM rule below).

The action for a purse receiving a startTo message in idle state is similar except that it goes into the epv state ("expecting value") and becomes the to purse of the transaction. Additionally it sends a request message to the from purse:

```
STARTTO#
let msgna = msg.name, value = msg.value, msgno = msg.nextSeqNo
in if authentic(msgna) ∧ receiver ≠ msgna ∧ ¬ fail?
   then choose n with nextSeqNo(receiver) < n in
          pdAuth(receiver) := mkpd(msgna, msgno, receiver,
                                        nextSeqNo(receiver), value)
          state(receiver) := epv seq
          outmsg := req(pdAuth(receiver))
          nextSeqNo(receiver) := n
      else outmsg := ⊥
```

---

[3] Receiver is always a purse receiving a message. This can be a from purse sending money as well as a to purse receiving money and should not be confused with the latter.

The request message req(pdAuth(receiver)) contains the payment details of the current transaction. Although this is not modeled, the message is assumed to be securely encrypted. Since an attacker can therefore never guess this message before it is sent, it is assumed that the initial ether does not contain any request message. When the from purse receives the request in state epr, it executes

```
REQ#
if msg = req(pdAuth(receiver)) ∧ ¬ fail?
then balance(receiver) := balance(receiver) − pdAuth(receiver).value
     state(receiver) := epa
     outmsg := val(pdAuth(receiver))
else outmsg := ⊥
```

The message is checked to be consistent with the current transaction stored in pdAuth and if this is the case the money is sent with an encrypted value message val(pdAuth(receiver)). The state changes to epa ("expecting acknowledge"). On receiving the value the to purse does

```
VAL#
if msg = val(pdAuth(receiver)) ∧ ¬ fail?
then balance(receiver) := balance(receiver) + pdAuth(receiver).value
     state(receiver) := idle
     outmsg := ack(pdAuth(receiver))
else outmsg := ⊥
```

It adds the money to its balance, sends an encrypted acknowledge message back and finishes the transaction by going back to state idle. When this acknowledge message is received, the from purse finishes similarly:

```
ACK#
if msg = ack(pdAuth(receiver)) ∧ ¬ fail?
then state(receiver) := idle
     outmsg := ⊥
else outmsg := ⊥
```

To put the steps together it finally remains to define the full ASM rule BOP#[4] which executes all the steps above:

```
BOP#
choose msg, receiver, fail? with msg ∈ ether ∧ authentic(receiver) in
  if isStartTo(msg) ∧ state(receiver) = idle then STARTTO#
  else if isStartFrom(msg) ∧ state(receiver) = idle then STARTFROM#
  else if isreq(msg) ∧ state(receiver) = epr then REQ#
  else if isval(msg) ∧ state(receiver) = epv then VAL#
  else if isack(msg) ∧ state(receiver) = epa then ACK#
  else ABORT#
  seq ether := ether ++ outmsg
```

The ASM rule chooses an authentic receiver for some message msg from ether. Like in the abstract ASM the fail? flag indicates failure due to internal reasons. At

---

[4] BOP# is called BSTEP# in the web presentation.

the end of the rule the produced message outmsg is added to the set ether of available messages. Therefore our ASM corresponds to the "between" level as defined in [SCJ00]. For the concrete level the ether is assumed to lose messages randomly (due to an attacker or technical reasons like power failure). Therefore the ASM rule COP# that models the concrete level replaces ether := ether ++ outmsg in BOP# with LOSEMSG# where:

> LOSEMSG#
> **choose** ether′ **with** ether′ ⊆ ether ++ outmsg **in** ether := ether′

If a purse is sent an illegal message ⊥ or a message for which it is not in the correct state, the current transaction is aborted by

> ABORT#
> **choose** n **with** nextSeqNo(receiver) ≤ n **in**
>   LOGIFNEEDED#
>   state(receiver) := idle
>   nextSeqNo(receiver) := n
>   outmsg := ⊥
>
> LOGIFNEEDED#
> **if** state(receiver) = epa ∨ state(receiver) = epv
> **then** exLog(receiver) := exLog(receiver) ++ pdAuth(receiver)

This action logs if money is lost due to aborting a transaction. The idea is that the lost money of the abstract level can be recovered by comparing the two logs of the from and to purses involved. Logging takes place if either the purse is a to purse in the critical state epv or a from purse in critical state epa.

This completes the description of the concrete level. Although the ASM is much simpler than the full Z specification (no promotion was used, none of the Z schemas in [SCJ00] that describe which variables are *not* allowed to change in operations are necessary, STARTFROM# is not prefixed with ABORT#, since the ASM can do this step separately by choosing ⊥ from ether, etc.) it still captures the essence of the refinement as we will see in Section 5.

3   Verification of Backward Simulation and Invariance for the ASMs

The ASMs of the previous section were not intended to be a 1:1 representation of the original Z operations. Rather they were intended as a concise description of the essential refinement problem contained in the case study. To check this we tried to prove the main theorems of the Mondex case study for these ASMs, namely

- The concrete ASM preserves the invariant BINV, that is used to restrict the "concrete" state to the "between" state ([SCJ00], sections 28-29).
- The concrete ASM satisfies the correctness condition of backward refinement using a backward simulation ABINV ([SCJ00], sections 14-20).

This section reports on the results. The first thing we had to do is to extract the properties of the invariants from the Z specification. We found that they are distributed in 3 places in [SCJ00]: The property of payment details that requires pd.from $\neq$ pd.to for every relevant pd used (section 4.3.2), the properties of purses P-1 to P-4 (section 4.6) and the properties B-1 to B-16 of the intermediate state that define an invariant for the concrete state (section 5.3).

Collecting these properties and the required definitions of AuxWorld (section 5.2) gives a suitable definition of BINV: full details can be found in the technical report [SGHR06] and in specification *BINV* in project *Mondex* [KIV].

There is one interesting modification: we had to strengthen properties P-3 and P-4. We found that although the proofs of [SCJ00] are very detailed they *still* contain minor flaws. The problems were detected when the proof for invariance theorem *BINV* failed. This theorem is written using Dynamic Logic [HKT00] and proved in KIV using sequent calculus:

$$\mathsf{BINV(\underline{cs})} \vdash \langle\!| \mathsf{BOP}\#(;\ \underline{cs})|\!\rangle\ \mathsf{BINV(\underline{cs})}$$

$\vdash$ is the sequent arrow (semantics: the conjunction of antecedent formulas before the sequent arrow implies the disjunction of succedent formulas after the sequent arrow). $\underline{cs}$ is the vector of variables that denote the concrete state, i.e. $\underline{cs}$ = balance, state, nextSeqNo, pdAuth, ether. $\langle\!|\mathsf{BOP}\#(;\ \underline{cs})|\!\rangle$ BINV($\underline{cs}$) states that all runs of BOP# terminate in a state where BINV holds again.

The first proof for the invariance theorem used the original properties P-3 and P-4. Specification *BINV-orig* on [KIV] contains a failed proof attempt. Its first open premise is one of the subgoals for proving invariance for the VAL# rule. The case can be traced back to the original Mondex paper. The problem is in section 29.4 in the proof of B-10 where it must be proved that toInEpv $\vee$ toLogged $\Rightarrow$ req $\wedge \neg$ ack for every payment details pd. Now the problem is as follows: the implication *can* be proved for pdAuth(receiver), where receiver is the (to) purse receiving the val message (to which it responds with an ack message). But this is not sufficient: if it would be possible that receiver is *different* from some na := pdAuth(receiver).to but has state(na) = epv and pdAuth(na) = pdAuth(receiver), then for *this* na the implication would be violated. The solution to this problem is obvious: add pdAuth(receiver).to = receiver when state(receiver) = epv to P-3.

A similar problem also exists for state(receiver) = epa (property P-4) where pdAuth(receiver).from = receiver has to be known (second open goal in the proof). Finally, we had to add the fact that every val(pd) message in the ether has authentic(pd.from). Like property authentic(pd.to) (B-1) is needed to make the application of partial function ConAuthPurse to pd.to defined in B-2, this property is needed in order to have a determined value for ConAuthPurse pd.from in B-3 (the proof of *BINV* in *BINV-orig* already has this property added).

We also added the requirement that pdAuth(receiver).to resp. .from must be authentic to P-3 and P-4. In early proof attempts this seemed necessary since these lacked the authentic clauses in the definition of the predicates toInEpr, toInEpv and toInEpa. After adding such clauses this addition to P-3 and P-4 may be redundant.

With these additions the invariant proof was successful. The standard heuristics and automation features of KIV (simplifier rules and problem specific patterns to guide the proof search as described in [RSSB98]) were sufficient for the proof. None of the complex lemma structure of [SCJ00] was necessary, although in some situations where it was not clear why our proof got stuck, it was helpful to cross-check details with the original proofs.

After this proof we verified the backward simulation condition:

$$\mathsf{ABINV}(\underline{as}', \underline{cs}'), \mathsf{BINV}(\underline{cs}), \langle \mathsf{BOP}\#(\underline{cs}) \rangle \ \underline{cs} = \underline{cs}'$$
$$\vdash \exists \ \underline{as}.\mathsf{ABINV}(\underline{as}, \underline{cs}) \wedge (\langle \mathsf{AOP}\#(\underline{as}) \rangle \ \underline{as} = \underline{as}' \vee \underline{as} = \underline{as}')$$

$\mathsf{ABINV}(\underline{as}, \underline{cs})$ is the backward simulation. The definition is basically identical to the simulation relation defined in [SCJ00].

The meaning of $\langle \mathsf{BOP}\#(\underline{cs}) \rangle \ \underline{cs} = \underline{cs}'$ is that $\mathsf{BOP}\#$ called with $\underline{cs}$ terminates and yields $\underline{cs}'$. This is equivalent to $\mathsf{BOP}(\underline{cs}, \underline{cs}')$. The proof obligation for ASM refinement allows a 1:1 diagram, where the concrete rule $\mathsf{BOP}\#$ refines an abstract operation $\mathsf{AOP}\#$ as well as a 0:1 diagram, where the concrete operation refines skip (second disjunct).

The proof for the simulation condition has 655 proof steps and 197 interactions. Compared to the invariance proof, which has 447 proof steps with 71 interactions, it is somewhat harder to achieve a high degree of automation due to the more complex quantifier structure of ABINV compared to BINV.

The proofs can be found in project *Mondex* in the web presentation [KIV]. Specification *BINV* contains the proof for invariance (theorem *BINV*), specification *Mondex-ASM-refine* contains the proof for the simulation condition (theorem *correctness*).

4   Specifying the Data Refinement Theory

The data refinement theory underlying the Mondex case study is defined in [CSW02] in 3 steps: first, the general data refinement theory of [HHS86] is given. Second the contract embedding [WD96] of partial relations is defined and corresponding proof rules for forward and backward simulation are derived. Third the embedding of input and output into the state is discussed.

We have formalised the first two parts of the theory already for [Sch05]. The corresponding algebraic specifications in KIV are available in the project named *DataRef* on the Web [KIV]. The third part is formalised in theory *Z-refinement*.

The central specification construct used in these projects (apart from standard constructs like enrichment, union, actualisation and renaming as present in all algebraic specification languages with lose semantics, e.g. CASL [CoF04]) is specification *instantiation*. Instantiating a subspecification PSPEC (the parameter) of a generic specification GSPEC with an actual specification ASPEC using a mapping σ (a morphism, that allows to instantiate sorts resp. operations with tuples of types resp. arbitrary expressions) requires to prove the axioms of $\sigma(\mathsf{PSPEC})$ over ASPEC. The resulting specification is $\sigma(\mathsf{GSPEC})$, with all theorems of ASPEC available as lemmas. Instantiating specifications is used to prove that forward and backward simulation imply refinement correctness and to prove that the contract approach instantiates the original approach [HHS86] for total relations (sections 3 and 4 in [CSW02]).

While the specifications and proofs in project *DataRef* mimic the ones of chapter 2 and 3 of [CSW02], those in *Z-refinement* differ from the ones in chapter 4. We found, that the embedding used is not correct: input and output sequences are embedded into the initialisation and finalisation relation using an *empty[X, Y]* relation (e.g. empty[GO, CO] in section 4.4.1 to embed output in initialisation). This relation is defined in Appendix A.4 as the relation that comprises only a pair of empty sequences. This is not a total relation, and leads to a partial initialisation relation. The correct definition should relate every sequence to the empty sequence (e.g. for empty[GO, CO] the global output GO of the initial global state is discarded, so that the initial concrete state has empty output CO) just as it has been done in the closely related approach of [DB01].

The correction results in an additional proof obligation (from the finalisation proof) for refinement correctness: every concrete input must be related to some abstract input via relation ι_b: Our web presentation calls this relation IT using the notation of theorem 10.5.2 in [DB01], which also requires totality. Adding the proof obligation it can be proved that backward simulation implies refinement correctness.

In the Mondex case study the proof obligations are applied restricting the state space of the concrete level to those states for which an invariant holds: this implies that all refinement proof obligations can assume the invariant for every concrete state. While this is adequate for the total operations of Mondex, it seems there is a problem when using invariants to restrict the state space for the general case of partial operations. More details on this can be found in the technical report [SGHR06].

Nevertheless it is possible to use invariants without restricting the state space, but a backward simulation theorem using invariants cannot be derived as an instance of the contract approach. Therefore we proved the following theorem directly by instantiating the original approach of [HHS86]. The theorem is given here for the approach without IO in a slightly simplified form with total initialisation and finalisation relations. The theorem with IO can be derived from this theorem with a similar proof as in [CSW02] (but with the corrected *empty* relation). It is given in the technical report [SGHR06]. The proof obligations can also be found as axioms without and with IO in the theories *conbackward-INV* in project *DataRef* and *IOconbackward-INV* in project *Z-refinement*.

Theorem 1. (Backward Simulation using Invariants)
Given an abstract data type ADT = (AINIT, AIN, AOP, AFIN, AOUT) *with total* AINIT $\subseteq$ GS $\times$ AS, AOP$_i$ $\subseteq$ AS $\times$ AS, *total* AFIN $\subseteq$ AS $\times$ GS, *a similar data type* CDT = (CINIT, CIN, COP, CFIN, COUT) *which uses states from* CS *instead of* AS, *a backward simulation* T $\subseteq$ CS $\times$ AS *and two invariants* AINV $\subseteq$ AS *and* CINV $\subseteq$ CS, *then the refinement is correct using the contract approach provided the following proof obligations hold:*

- CINIT $\subseteq$ CINV, AINIT $\subseteq$ AINV *(initially invariants)*
- ran(AINV $\lhd$ AOP) $\subseteq$ AINV, ran(CINV $\lhd$ COP) $\subseteq$ CINV *(invariance)*

- (CINIT $\triangleright$ CINV) $\mathbin{{}^\circ_\circ}$ T $\subseteq$ AINIT *(initialisation)*
- (CINV $\lhd$ CFIN) $\subseteq$ T $\mathbin{{}^\circ_\circ}$ (AINV $\lhd$ AFIN) *(finalisation)*
- dom(COP$_i$) $\vartriangleleft$ CINV $\subseteq$ dom((T $\lhd$ AINV) $\vartriangleleft$ dom(AOP$_i$)) *(applicability)*
- dom(T $\vartriangleleft$ dom(AOP$_i$)) $\vartriangleleft$ (COP$_i$ $\mathbin{{}^\circ_\circ}$ T) $\subseteq$ T $\mathbin{{}^\circ_\circ}$ (AINV $\lhd$ AOP$_i$) *(correctness)*

Instead of the usual embedding of the contract approach $\overset{\circ}{\mathsf{T}}=\mathsf{T} \cup \{\bot\} \times \mathsf{AS}_\bot$ the proof uses $\overset{\circ}{\mathsf{T}}=(\mathsf{T} \triangleright \mathsf{AINV}) \cup \{\mathsf{CS}_\bot \setminus \mathsf{CINV}\} \times \mathsf{AS}_\bot$. The idea is that those concrete states that do not satisfy the invariant behave like the undefined $\bot$ state and therefore get mapped to every abstract state. The proof proceeds as usual by eliminating $\bot$ from the resulting proof obligations.

5   Verification of the Data Refinement

Our specification faithfully replicates the data types and operations of the original Mondex refinement. The operations are defined in the specifications *Mondex-AOP* and *Mondex-COP*. The only difference to the original Mondex refinement is that we used ASM rules as an auxiliary means to specify operations:

$$\mathsf{OP}(\mathsf{cs}, \mathsf{cs}') \leftrightarrow \langle \mathsf{OP}\#(\mathsf{cs}) \rangle \; \mathsf{cs} = \mathsf{cs}'$$

This equivalence defines the relation $\mathsf{OP}(\mathsf{cs}, \mathsf{cs}')$ to hold if and only if ASM rule OP# started with cs can compute cs' as one possible result. Because of the relational semantics of programs, ASM rules adequately represent operation schemas: schema composition becomes sequential composition of programs. For example the composition ABORT $\mathbin{{}^\circ_\circ}$ STARTFROM $\vee$ IGNORE is represented as $\langle$ABORT#; STARTFROM# **or** IGNORE#$\rangle$ where **or** is the nondeterministic choice between two programs. Compared to using operations on relations directly, using auxiliary ASM rules allows to execute programs symbolically (see [RSSB98]), which improves proof automation.

Apart from the auxiliary use of operational definitions instead of pure relations the specification mimics the structure of the Z specifications faithfully: STARTFROM# is now prefixed with ABORT#, input is read from a list of inputs, disjunctions with IGNORE# operations that skip have been added etc.

The use of auxiliary operational definitions has the effect that the main proof obligations for data refinement, "Correctness" and "Concrete invariant preserved", have proofs which are nearly identical to the ones we did for ASM refinement (see the proofs of theorems *correctness* and *cinv-ok* in specification *Mondex-refine* in project *Mondex* on the web [KIV]). The only important differences are that instead of one proof for the full ASM rule we now have several proof obligations for the individual operations corresponding to cases in the ASM proof (lemmas *ABORT-ACINV*, *REQ-ACINV* etc. for correctness, *ABORT-CINV*, *REQ-CINV* etc. for invariance) and that the lemmas for ABORT# and IGNORE# are used several times, since several operations now refer to it.

We have decided to merge the two refinements of the Mondex case study into one, so each operation calls LOSEMSG# at the end, just as described for the ASM at the end of section 2.

This means that our concrete invariant cannot be BINV since the properties of the ether which have been specified with a predicate etherok(ether,...), that is part of the definition of BINV, do not hold for an ether where messages have been dropped. Instead we replace the old definition of etherok with

$$\text{newetherok(ether,...)} \leftrightarrow \exists \text{ fullether. ether} \subseteq \text{fullether} \wedge \text{etherok(fullether,...)}$$

The new predicate[5] claims the existence of fullether, where no messages have been dropped, such that fullether has the properties specified in the old etherok predicate. fullether does not change during LOSEMSG#, otherwise it is modified just like ether. The new definition of etherok is used in the definition of the new invariant CINV for the concrete level. The backward simulation ABINV is left unchanged. It is just renamed to ACINV.

Summarizing, there is a little extra work required to cope with the redundancy of operations and the lossy ether, but essentially proofs are done by "copy-paste" from the ASM proofs.

Summarizing, the effort to do the full case study was as follows:

- 1 week was needed to get familiar with the case study and to set up the initial ASMs (Section 2).
- 1 week was needed to prove the essential proof obligations "correctness" and "invariance" for the ASM refinement as shown in (Section 3).
- 1 week was needed to specify the Mondex refinement theory of [CSW02] and to generalise the proof obligations to cope with invariants (Section 4).
- Finally, 1 week was necessary to prove the data refinement and to polish the theories for the web presentation (this section).

Of course the four weeks needed for verification are not comparable to effort for the original case study, which had to develop the formal specifications, refinement notions and proofs from scratch: in private mail, Jim Woodcock sent us an estimation of 1.5 pages of specification/proof per day, which results in at least 10 person months of effort.

The task we solved here is the mechanisation of an already existing proof. This time was of course significantly reduced by having a (nearly) correct simulation, since usually most of the time is needed to find invariants and simulation relations incrementally. On the other hand, sticking to ASM refinement would have shortened the verification time. The main data refinement proofs for the Mondex refinement consist of 1839 proof steps with 372 interactions.

The effort required can be compared to the effort required for refinement proofs from another application domain which we did at around the same time as the original Mondex case study: verification of a compiler that compiles Prolog to code of the Warren abstract machine ([SA97], [SA98], [Sch99], [Sch01]). This case study required 9 refinements, and the statistical data ([Sch99], Chapter 19) show that proving each refinement needed on average about the same number of proof steps in KIV as the Mondex case study.

---

[5] The web presentation [KIV] uses the modified etherok definition given in specification *Mondex-CINV*, not a new predicate.

The ratio of interactions to proof steps is somewhat better in the Prolog case study, since automation of refinement proofs increases over time: investing time to improve automation by adding rewrite rules becomes more important when similar steps are necessary in several refinements and when developing simulation relations iteratively. Summarizing our proof effort shows that the Mondex case study is a medium-sized case study and a good benchmark for interactive theorem provers.

6   A Security Model for Mondex Purses

Although the Mondex case study was the basis of an ITSEC E6 certification ([CB99]), the formal model abstracts away an important part of the security of the application. As the cryptographic protocols used to realize the value transfer were and are still, to our knowledge, undisclosed ([CCW96]) the formal model assumes the existence of unforgeable messages for requesting, transferring and acknowledging the transfer of a value. To complete the analysis of the application a model based on a theory of messages with abstract representations of the used cryptographic mechanisms should be specified and used to proof that the 'dangerous' messages actually cannot be forged.

The Mondex application is prepared to use different cryptographic algorithms in the value transfer protocol. It is generally assumed that DES and RSA were used to authenticate the value transfer ([CB99]). It is not too difficult to come up with a cryptographic protocol that ensures that its messages have the properties that are required for the abstract messages req, val and ack. Using DES as cryptographic algorithm a shared secret key is used for authentication of messages ([BGJY98]). A possible protocol written in a commonly used standard notation for cryptographic protocols is:

1. to → from : $\{$REQ,pdAuth(to)$\}_{K_S}$
2. from → to : $\{$VAL,pdAuth(from)$\}_{K_S}$
3. to → from : $\{$ACK,pdAuth(to)$\}_{K_S}$

In this protocol K_S : key denotes a secret key shared between all valid Mondex cards. REQ, VAL and ACK are pairwise distinct constants used to distinguish the three message types.

Using RSA makes things somewhat more complicated since individual key pairs and digital certificates should then be used. To ensure security for the next years keys with at least 1024 Bit length must be used. Given this key size the public key and the associated certificate of a Mondex card and the payload of the protocol messages cannot be transferred to the smart card in one step, due to restrictions of the communication interface of smart cards. Therefore some of the steps that are atomic on the concrete level of Mondex would have to be split up into several steps on the implementation level. This further complicates the refinement.

Assuming the DES-based protocol, the challenge to be solved is to verify the security of the Mondex application with this real cryptographic protocol instead of the special messages postulated as unforgeable in the Mondex case study in Z. Possible approaches generally used in the verification of cryptographic protocols are model-checking ([Low96], [BMV03]) or interactive verification ([Pau98]). Paulson's inductive approach has proven to be especially powerful by tackling complex industrial protocols ([Pau01]). We plan to use our ASM-based model for cryptographic protocols ([HGRS05]) for verification. Particularly interesting is the question whether the protocol with cryptographic operations can be proven to be a refinement of the concrete protocol of the original Mondex case study. We think such a refinement is possible, and the Mondex case study shows an elegant way to separate functional correctness and security into two refinements.

7   Conclusion and Further Work

We have specified and formally verified the full communication protocol of the Mondex case study with the KIV system. We have slightly improved the protocol to use one idle instead of two eaFrom and eaTo states. We have improved the theory of backward simulation in the contract approach to include invariants for the data types. Using the improved theory, the correctness proof for Mondex could be done as one refinement instead of two. We think that the additional effort to do this was rather small compared to the effort needed to write down the proofs in [SCJ00] at nearly calculus level. Despite this great detail we were still able to find two small flaws: one in the underlying data refinement theory, where a proof obligation was missing and one in the invariant, where we had to add a totality property. Therefore we feel justified to recommend doing machine proofs as a means to increase confidence in the results.

As a second contribution we gave an alternative, concise specification of the refinement problem using ASMs. The fact that the main proofs are nearly identical to those for the original refinement indicates, that the ASMs are a good starting point to further improve the invariant and the verification technique.

One idea for further work is therefore to take the ideas of [HGRS05] to do a proper ASM refinement proof (that probably would use generalised forward simulation [Sch01] instead of backward simulation).

Another idea contained in the Mondex case study that we will try to address is that functional correctness and a security protocol as proposed Section 6 may be verified independently as two separate refinements.

Acknowledgement. We like to thank Prof. Börger for pointing out the Mondex challenge to us.

References

[BGJY98]   M. Bellare, J. Garay, C. Jutla, and M. Yung. VarietyCash: a Multi-purpose Electronic Payment System. In *Proceedings of the 3rd USENIX Workshop on Electronic Commerce.* USENIX, September 1998. URL: http://citeseer.ist.psu.edu/bellare98varietycash.html.

[BMV03]   David Basin, Sebastian Mödersheim, and Luca Viganò. An On-The-Fly Model-Checker for Security Protocol Analysis. In *Proceedings of Esorics'03*, LNCS 2808, pages 253–270. Springer-Verlag, Heidelberg, 2003.

[Bör03]   E. Börger. The ASM Refinement Method. *Formal Aspects of Computing*, 15 (1–2):237–257, November 2003.

[BR95]   E. Börger and D. Rosenzweig. The WAM—definition and compiler correctness. In Christoph Beierle and Lutz Plümer, editors, *Logic Programming: Formal Methods and Practical Applications*, volume 11 of *Studies in Computer Science and Artificial Intelligence*, pages 20–90. North-Holland, Amsterdam, 1995.

[BS03]   E. Börger and R. F. Stärk. *Abstract State Machines—A Method for High-Level System Design and Analysis*. Springer-Verlag, 2003.

[CB99]   UK ITSEC Certification Body. UK ITSEC SCHEME CERTIFICATION REPORT No. P129 MONDEX Purse. Technical report, UK IT Security Evaluation and Certification Scheme, 1999. URL: http://www.cesg.gov.uk/site/iacs/itsec/media/certreps/CRP129.pdf.

[CCW96]   E. K. Clemons, D. C. Croson, and B. W. Weber. Reengineering Money: The Mondex Stored Value Card and Beyond. In *Proceedings of the 29th Annual Hawaii International Conference on Systems Sciences 1996*. IEEE, 1996. URL: http://doi.ieeecomputersociety.org/10.1109/HICSS.1996.495345.

[CoF04]   CoFI (The Common Framework Initiative). CASL *Reference Manual*. LNCS 2960 (IFIP Series). Springer, 2004.

[CSW02]   D. Cooper, S. Stepney, and J. Woodcock. Derivation of Z Refinement Proof Rules: forwards and backwards rules incorporating input/output refinement. Technical Report YCS-2002-347, University of York, 2002. URL: http://www-users.cs.york.ac.uk/$\sim$susan/bib/ss/z/zrules.htm.

[DB01]   J. Derrick and E. Boiten. *Refinement in Z and in Object-Z : Foundations and Advanced Applications*. FACIT. Springer, 2001.

[Gur95]   Yuri Gurevich. Evolving algebras 1993: Lipari guide. In E. Börger, editor, *Specification and Validation Methods*, pages 9 – 36. Oxford Univ. Press, 1995.

[HGRS05]   D. Haneberg, H. Grandy, W. Reif, and G. Schellhorn. Verifying Security Protocols: An ASM Approach. In D. Beauquier, E. Börger, and A. Slissenko, editors, *12th Int. Workshop on Abstract State Machines, ASM 05*. University Paris 12 – Val de Marne, Créteil, France, March 2005.

[HHS86]   He Jifeng, C. A. R. Hoare, and J. W. Sanders. Data refinement refined. In B. Robinet and R. Wilhelm, editors, *Proc. ESOP 86*, volume 213 of *Lecture Notes in Computer Science*, pages 187–196. Springer-Verlag, 1986.

[HKT00]   D. Harel, D. Kozen, and J. Tiuryn. *Dynamic Logic*. MIT Press, 2000.

[KIV]   Web presentation of the mondex case study in KIV. URL: http://www.informatik.uni-augsburg.de/swt/projects/mondex.html.

[Low96]   Gavin Lowe. Breaking and fixing the Needham-Schroeder public-key protocol using FDR. In *Tools and Algorithms for the Construction and Analysis of Systems (TACAS)*, volume 1055, pages 147–166. Springer-Verlag, 1996.

[MCI]   MasterCard International Inc. *Mondex*. URL: http://www.mondex.com.

[Pau98]   L. C. Paulson. The Inductive Approach to Verifying Cryptographic Protocols. *J. Computer Security*, 6:85–128, 1998.

[Pau01]   Lawrence C. Paulson. Verifying the SET Protocol. In R. Gore, A. Leitsch, and T. Nipkow, editors, *IJCAR 2001: International Joint Conference on Automated Reasoning*, Siena, Italy, 2001. Springer LNCS 2083.

[RE03]   W. Rankl and W. Effing. *Smart Card Handbook*. John Wiley & Sons, 3rd edition, 2003.

[RSSB98]   Wolfgang Reif, Gerhard Schellhorn, Kurt Stenzel, and Michael Balser. Structured specifications and interactive proofs with KIV. In W. Bibel and P. Schmitt, editors, *Automated Deduction—A Basis for Applications*, volume II: Systems and Implementation Techniques, chapter 1: Interactive Theorem Proving, pages 13 – 39. Kluwer Academic Publishers, Dordrecht, 1998.

[SA97]   Gerhard Schellhorn and Wolfgang Ahrendt. Reasoning about Abstract State Machines: The WAM Case Study. *Journal of Universal Computer Science (J.UCS)*, 3(4):377–413, 1997. URL: http://hyperg.iicm.tu-graz.ac.at/jucs/.

[SA98]   Gerhard Schellhorn and Wolfgang Ahrendt. The WAM Case Study: Verifying Compiler Correctness for Prolog with KIV. In W. Bibel and P. Schmitt, editors, *Automated Deduction—A Basis for Applications*, pages 165 – 194. Kluwer Academic Publishers, Dordrecht, 1998.

[Sch99]   Gerhard Schellhorn. *Verification of Abstract State Machines*. PhD thesis, Universität Ulm, Fakultät für Informatik, 1999. URL: http://www.informatik.uni-augsburg.de/lehrstuehle/swt/se/publications/.

[Sch01]   G. Schellhorn. Verification of ASM Refinements Using Generalized Forward Simulation. *Journal of Universal Computer Science (J.UCS)*, 7(11):952–979, 2001. URL: http://hyperg.iicm.tu-graz.ac.at/jucs/.

[Sch05]   G. Schellhorn. ASM Refinement and Generalizations of Forward Simulation in Data Refinement: A Comparison. *Journal of Theoretical Computer Science*, vol. 336, no. 2-3:403–435, May 2005.

[SCJ00]   S. Stepney, D. Cooper, and Woodcock J. AN ELECTRONIC PURSE Specification, Refinement, and Proof. Technical monograph PRG-126, Oxford University Computing Laboratory, July 2000. URL: http://www-users.cs.york.ac.uk/~susan/bib/ss/z/monog.htm.

[SGHR06]   Gerhard Schellhorn, Holger Grandy, Dominik Haneberg, and Wolfgang Reif. The Mondex Challenge: Machine Checked Proofs for an Electronic Purse. Technical Report 2006-2, Universität Augsburg, 2006.

[Spi92]   J. M. Spivey. *The Z Notation: A Reference Manual*. Prentice Hall International Series in Computer Science, 2nd edition, 1992.

[WD96]   J. C. P. Woodcock and J. Davies. *Using Z: Specification, Proof and Refinement*. Prentice Hall International Series in Computer Science, 1996.

[Woo06]   J. Woodcock. Mondex case study, 2006. URL: http://qpq.csl.sri.com/vsr/shared/MondexCaseStudy/.

Interactive Verification of Medical Guidelines

Jonathan Schmitt[1], Alwin Hoffmann[1], Michael Balser[1],
Wolfgang Reif[1], and Mar Marcos[2]

[1] Lehrstuhl für Softwaretechnik und Programmiersprachen
Universität Augsburg, D-86135 Augsburg, Germany
{schmitt, balser, reif}@informatik.uni-augsburg.de
[2] Dept. of Computer Engineering and Science, Universitat Jaume I
Campus de Riu Sec, E-12071 Castellón, Spain
Mar.Marcos@icc.uji.es

Abstract. In the medical domain, there is a tendency to standardize
health care by providing medical guidelines as summary of the best
evidence concerning a particular topic. Based on the assumption that
guidelines are similar to software, we try to carry over techniques from
software engineering to guideline development. In this paper, we show
how to apply formal methods, namely interactive verification to improve
the quality of guidelines. As an example, we have worked on a guideline from the American Academy of Pediatrics for the management of
jaundice in newborns. Contributions of this paper are as follows: (I) a
formalized model of a nontrivial example guideline, (II) an approach to
verify properties of medical guidelines interactively, and (III) verification
of a first example property.[1]

1 Introduction

There is a tendency in the medical domain to standardize health care. This
is because the amount of medical studies conducted per year has long passed a
point, where every doctor can keep track of all results and also judge their quality.
To ease the workload, the instrument of guidelines has been devised. Guidelines
represent a summary of the best evidence concerning the interventions to manage
a particular clinical condition. Guideline developers take over the cumbersome
work of literature search and the evaluation of the quality of the relevant studies.
All this data is then compiled into a document, usually of 50 to 150 pages, where
medical staff can access the relevant recommendations in a fast, efficient way.
This makes guidelines very important documents, as hundreds to thousands of
physicians may act upon them, treating several thousands of patients according
to these guidelines. An error within such a guideline may cause great harm and
therefore, the quality of the guideline itself must be assured.

A first step to improve the quality of guidelines has been to introduce the
AGREE instrument[2], which is an informal review, mainly concerned with the

---

[1] This work has been partially funded by the European Commission's IST program,
under contract number IST-FP6-508794 Protocure II.
[2] http://www.agreecollaboration.org

J. Misra, T. Nipkow, and E. Sekerinski (Eds.): FM 2006, LNCS 4085, pp. 32–47, 2006.
© Springer-Verlag Berlin Heidelberg 2006

guideline development process. However, the quality of the content is less in the focus. Guidelines are written as natural language text and may therefore contain ambiguities in the formulation, ambiguities in the description of the treatment process or even wrong information, wrongly transferred into the document. The quality of the content of guidelines is the scope of a European research project called Protocure[3].

Fig. 1. Formalization and verification of medical guidelines

The Protocure project aims to assist the guideline development process by providing tools and techniques to evaluate not the process but the contents of a guideline during its complex development process. Based on the assumption that guidelines are similar to software, we try to carry over techniques from software engineering to guideline development. Our approach is to formalize guidelines and to verify properties (see Fig. 1). Guidelines are modeled in Asbru [1,2], which is a planning language especially designed for the medical domain. The modeling process already improves the quality of the guideline [3]. With formal verification, more errors can be revealed. For this, we have defined a formal semantics of Asbru in [4] and have translated Asbru to the SMV model checker [5]. In this paper, we take a different approach and focus on interactive verification of Asbru. As an example, we have worked on a guideline from the American Academy of Pediatrics for the management of jaundice in newborns.

Contributions of this paper are as follows: (I) a formal Asbru model of a nontrivial example guideline, (II) an approach to verify properties of medical guidelines interactively, and (III) verification of a first example property. In Sect. 2, we give an overview of the Asbru language, Sect. 3 introduces the medical guideline. Support for Asbru in the interactive theorem prover KIV [6] is described in Sect. 4, and the example property is verified in Sect. 5. Section 6 gives related work and Sect. 7 concludes.

2   Introduction to Asbru

Asbru is a hierarchical planning language. Basis of the Asbru semantics is the concept of plans with a defined plan state model visualized in Figure 2. All transitions within this state-chart are guarded, where the guards SC, RA and E represent external signals, which are sent to the plan by its respective super-plan. Evaluation of the other guards are dependent on the so called Asbru conditions. These are mappings from medical relevant data to boolean values. Details of the mappings are dependent on the individual Asbru plan.

---

[3] http://www.protocure.org

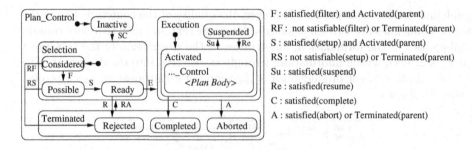

F : satisfied(filter) and Activated(parent)
RF : not satisfiable(filter) or Terminated(parent)
S : satisfied(setup) and Activated(parent)
RS : not satisfiable(setup) or Terminated(parent)
Su : satisfied(suspend)
Re : satisfied(resume)
C : satisfied(complete)
A : satisfied(abort) or Terminated(parent)

Fig. 2. Asbru semantics

Behavior of Asbru plans during their execution phase is dependent on their plan type. A plan can be of type `sequential`, meaning that the plan will start all of its sub-plans sequentially in the given order. If the plan type is `anyorder`, plans are still executed sequentially but the order of the execution of the sub-plans is arbitrary. It is also possible to start multiple sub-plans at a time. For this, Asbru provides the `parallel` and `unordered` plan types, where parallel-arranged sub-plans are synchronized, the unordered-controlled sub-plans are not. Furthermore, special plan types are defined for the request of medical data, calculations or deterministic choices.

2.1 State

For a graphical representation of an abstracted view of the data flow, see Figure 3. An Asbru system, consisting of Asbru plans and an environment, can be seen as a plan based implementation of a medical decision support system. The system bases its decisions upon data being provided by medical staff. This data is provided in a data structure called Patient Data *PD* for the system. In the Asbru implementation, the provider of medical data – the medical staff – is called the `monitoring unit`. Data may be abstracted from numerical values to symbolic values. As all data types in Asbru are discrete, data can be transformed to the smallest occuring unit in the case study, thus eliminating the need to annotate physical units.

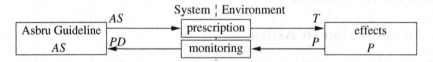

Fig. 3. Abstracted data flow within Asbru

The monitored data is processed according to the guideline represented as Asbru plans, and the output of this processing is provided to the medical staff as an abstracted description of the states of several Asbru plans, which are combined into the variable Asbru state *AS*. Medical staff, receiving this data, interprets it to come up with a set of treatments *T* to be administered to the patient *P*.

The condition of the patient changes in the environment. This transformation is described by `effects`. Treatments applied to the patient may restrict the otherwise indeterministic patient behavior. Effects are applied to the patients condition and the result of this application is then handed over to the monitoring unit. The monitoring unit compiles this data according to the decision of the medical staff. Therefore, there may be a discrepancy between the real condition of the patient and the known subset of it.

2.2   Plan State Model

The plan state model is depicted in Figure 2. A detailed description of a Structured Operational Semantics is given in [4]. For example, a plan, currently `considered` has the options of either advancing its state to `possible` or to change its state to `rejected`. This choice is dependent on the guards F and RF, where the F guard is satisfied, if and only if the filter condition of the plan is satisfied and the super-plan is still active. The RF guard is satisfied, if the super-plan is terminated or the filter condition is no longer satisfiable.

Six conditions define the transitions of an Asbru plan through the plan state model: `filter`, `setup`, `suspend`, `reactivate`, `abort` and `complete` conditions. Termination and suspension behavior is also affected by the states of sub- and super-plans.

2.3   Time-Annotated Conditions

Conditions are first order formulas φ mapping a state to a truth value. Conditions can be time-annotated. A time-annotated condition is written as follows

$$\varphi \; [ess, \; lss][efs, \; lfs][minDu, \; maxDu] \; ref$$

where ess is the earliest starting shift, lss the latest starting shift, efs the earliest finishing shift, lfs the latest finishing shift, and $[minDu, maxDu]$ the duration interval. The starting interval is defined as $[ess + ref, lss + ref]$. The finishing interval is defined accordingly. Any value but the reference point may be omitted and is then written as '_'. As a reference point, an absolute time point can be given as well as enter($planState$, $name$) and leave($planState$, $name$) to refer to the time when plan $name$ enters or leaves state $planState$. Also, with *now*, we refer to the time of evaluation.

Time annotations represent sets of intervals ranging over time. An interval is member of a time annotation if and only if its starting point is member of the starting interval, its finishing point is member of the finishing interval and its duration is member of the duration interval. A time-annotated condition evaluates to true, if and only if there is an interval I which is element of the time annotation and for which the condition is true at all times. Furthermore, if an earliest starting shift or a maximum duration is given, the condition must be initially false, more precise, in the time point prior to the starting point of I the condition must evaluate to false. Similarly, if a latest starting shift or a maximum duration is given, the condition must finally evaluate to false.

2.4   Intention

Asbru intentions model the aims of a plan. They are formulated in terms of temporal patterns making reference to plans and/or state variables that should be maintained, achieved or avoided, during or after the execution of a particular plan. In this sense, they can be regarded as proof obligations for Asbru. Intentions are written down similar to conditions. Intentions can also be time-annotated.

3   Example Medical Guideline

3.1   Jaundice Guideline

Jaundice (or hyperbilirubinemia) is a common disease in newborn babies. Under certain circumstances, elevated bilirubin levels may have detrimental neurological effects. In many cases jaundice disappears without treatment but sometimes needs phototherapy to reduce the levels of total serum bilirubin (TSB), which indicates the presence and severity of jaundice. In a few cases, however, jaundice is a sign of a severe disease.

The jaundice guideline of the American Association of Pediatrics (AAP) [7] is intended for the management of the disease in healthy term newborn babies. The main reason for choosing this guideline was that it is considered a high-quality one: as a matter of fact, the AAP jaundice guideline has been included in the repository of the National Guideline Clearinghouse[4] until it was replaced by a more recent update.

This particular guideline is a 10 pages document. It consists of an evaluation (or diagnosis) part and a treatment part, to be performed in sequence. During the application of the guideline, as soon as the possibility of a more serious disease is uncovered, the recommendation is to exit without any further action. The rationale behind this is that the guideline is exclusively intended for the management of jaundice in otherwise healthy newborns.

3.2   Jaundice Guideline in Asbru

Like the AAP guideline, the Asbru version has as main components a diagnostics part and a treatment part. It is made up of about 40 plans and has a length of 16 pages in an intermediate Asbru notation. Figure 4 shows part of the Asbru model for the jaundice guideline with an emphasis on treatment. The links represent the decomposition of plans into steps or sub-plans, and the plan type is represented by different kinds of arrows. Besides, the waiting strategy is indicated either with bold font keywords (e.g. **one** or **all**) or with bold font plan names (e.g. the "Observation" plan is a compulsory part of the plan group marked "*" in Figure 4).

The "Check-for-..." plans model monitoring of TSB level and check-ups at specific time intervals. The most important entry point of the guideline is the plan "Diagnostics-and-treatment-hyperbilirubinemia". It is divided into a diagnostics sub-plan and a treatment one, to be executed sequentially. Next we will focus on the latter.

---

[4] http://www.guideline.gov/

The treatment phase consists of two parallel parts, namely the actual treatments and a cyclical plan asking for the input of TSB values and updating the infants age every 12 to 24 hours. Regarding the treatments (label (**) in Fig. 4), either the regular ones ("Regular-treatments") or a transfusion ("Exchange-transfusion") can take place depending on the bilirubin level.

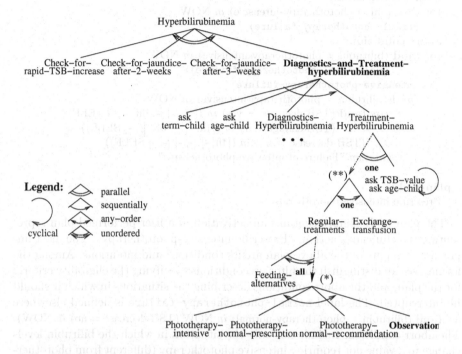

Fig. 4. Overview of the jaundice model in Asbru, with details of the treatment part

The "Regular-treatments" plan contains the proper treatment procedures. It consists of two parts to be performed in parallel (unordered): the study of feeding alternatives and the different therapies (see label (*)). The plans in group (*) can be tried in any order, one at a time. The intentions of "Regular-treatments" plan are both avoiding toxic bilirubin levels and attaining normal (or observation) ones at the end. The plan completes when the feeding alternatives and the therapies complete (waiting strategy all). The latter in turn depends on the completion of observation (compulsory plan in bold).

3.3 Plan "Phototherapy-Intensive"

As an illustration, we describe the plan "Phototherapy-intensive" together with its conditions and intentions. The intermediate Asbru notation for the plan is shown below:

plan Photherapy-intensive
  intentions
    maintain intermediate-state:
    (**and** (TSB-decrease = yes) *in* ([4h, -] [-, 6h] [-, -] SELF)
        (TSB-change ≥ 1) *in* ([4h, -] [-, 6h] [-, -] SELF))
  conditions
    filter-precondition:
    (**or** (bilirubin = phototherapy-intensive) *in* NOW
        normal-phototherapy-failure)
    abort-condition:
    (**or** (**and** (bilirubin ≠ phototherapy-intensive) *in* NOW
            (**not** normal-phototherapy-failure))
        intensive-phototherapy-failure:
        (**and** (bilirubin = phototherapy-intensive) *in* NOW
            (**or** (**and** (TSB-decrease = yes) *in* ([4h, -] [-, 6h] [-, -] SELF)
                    (TSB-change < 1) *in* ([4h, -] [-, 6h] [-, -] SELF))
                (TSB-decrease = no) *in* ([4h, -] [-, -] [-, -] SELF))
) *explanation* "Failure of intensive phototherapy."
)
  plan-body
    Prescribe-intensive-phototherapy

The plan body simply contains an activation of a user-performed plan representing the clinician's action, "Prescribe-intensive-phototherapy". The most important elements of the above plan are its conditions and intentions. Among the former we can distinguish the filter preconditions specifying the eligibility criteria for the plan, and the abort conditions describing the situations in which it should be interrupted. The label normal-phototherapy-failure is defined elsewhere as (**and** (bilirubin = phototherapy-normal) *in* NOW (TSB-decrease = no) *in* NOW). The abort conditions include not only the situation in which the bilirubin levels change to a value not requiring intensive phototherapy (different from phototherapy-intensive), but also the case of therapy failure – according to the guideline, *"Intensive phototherapy should produce a decline in the TSB level of 1 to 2 mg/dl within 4 to 6 hours ..."* and *"...failure of intensive phototherapy to lower the TSB level strongly suggests the presence of hemolytic disease or some other pathologic process and warrants further investigation"*.

An intention was specified by the modelers for the plan "Phototherapy-intensive". Since the guideline states that intensive phototherapy should produce a decline in the bilirubin levels of 1 to 2 mg/dl in 4 to 6 hours, it has been considered that this therapy aims at lowering the TSB levels in such a degree within this time range. This intention is intimately related to part of the abort conditions of the plan. It is specified to abort if there is an insufficient or no decrease in the TSB levels in the specified time range. In our verification case-study we have analyzed this intention.

4   Integration of Asbru in KIV

KIV is an integrated development environment to develop systems using formal methods. Systems are specified with algebraic specifications. System properties are verified by constructing proofs in an interactive theorem prover which is based on higher order logic with special support for temporal logic. KIV has been very useful for the development of sequential programs. Support for the development of concurrent systems and especially Asbru has recently been added.

4.1 Temporal Logic in KIV

KIV offers support for future-time linear temporal logic. Reactive systems can be described in KIV by means of state-charts or parallel programs; here we use parallel programs. A state of a system is encoded in first-order logic. Static variables v, which have the same values at each time point, are distinguished from dynamic variables V. A specialty of KIV is the use of primed and double-primed variables [8]: a primed variable V' represents the value of this variable after a system transition, the double-primed variable V'' is interpreted as the value after an environment transition. System and environment transitions alternate, with V'' being equal to V in the successive state. Here, an Asbru guidelines defines the system transition and the patient is interpreted as the environment. The supported future-time temporal operators include $\Box \, \varphi$ ("always φ"), $\Diamond \, \varphi$ ("eventually φ) and others.

4.2 Specification of Asbru

We have modeled the Asbru language in the interactive theorem prover KIV as follows. The data types are defined with algebraic specifications, the dynamic behavior, i.e. the plan state model of Asbru, is encoded in a parallel program. An overview of the algebraic specifications is given in Figure 5.

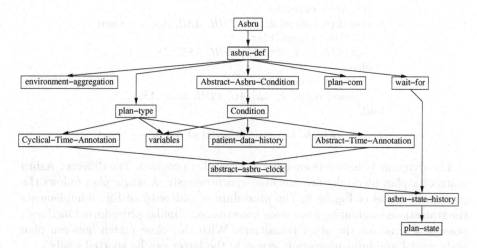

Fig. 5. Algebraic specifications defining the Asbru language

Asbru is based on a discrete micro/macro step semantics. Micro steps are internal plan transitions. If the plan state is stable a macro step is executed and the systems interacts with the environment. A discrete Asbru clock AC with micro and macro step counter is defined in *abstract-asbru-clock*. The definition of time annotations in *Abstract-Time-Annotation* is based on Asbru clocks. The specification defines a tuple containing the starting and finishing shifts, the duration and the reference point. The tuple represents a set of intervals. Conditions are modeled as higher order predicates which are evaluated for a given state. Non-trivial predicates satisfied and satisfiable in specification *Condition* define the semantics of time annotated conditions. *Abstract-Asbru-Condition* extends normal conditions by additional signals, necessary for advanced Asbru features which are omitted here.

The patient data PD stores knowledge about the state of the patient. A generic container is defined in *patient-data-history* and can be instantiated for the concrete case study. The patient data history PDH maps time to patient data. This history is important to evaluate time annotated conditions. An enumeration type *plan-state* defines the different plan states `inactive`, `considered`, etc. An Asbru state AS maps plan names to plan states. A history of Asbru states ASH is defined in *asbru-state-history*. The different plan types such as `sequential`, `anyorder`, `unordered`, and `parallel` are defined in *plan-type*. Description of further features such as the wait-for construct defining optional and mandatory sub plans (specification *wait-for*), and cyclical plan types (specification *Cyclical-Time-Annotation*) are omitted here. Specifications *environment-aggregation* and *plan-com* accumulate the environment signals.

considered#(sk, $sk0$; **var** AC, PDH, ASH, AS, ...)
begin
    if plan-not-filter(sk, AC, PDH, ASH, AS, ...) **then**
        $AS[sk]$:= `rejected`
        else if plan-filter(sk, AC, PDH, ASH, AS, ...) **then**
            $AS[sk]$:= `possible`;
            possible#(sk, $sk0$; AC, PDH, ASH, AS, ...)
        else
            $AS[sk]$:= `considered`;
            considered#(sk, $sk0$; AC, PDH, ASH, AS, ...)
    end

Fig. 6. Dynamic behavior of Asbru

The dynamic behavior is encoded as a parallel program. The different Asbru plans of a plan hierarchy are executed synchronously. A single plan follows the plan state model of Figure 2. The procedure considered# of Fig. 6 implements the transitions originating from state `considered`. Similar procedures inactive#, possible# exist for the other transitions. With this close match between plan state model and implementation, errors in the latter can be spotted easily.

4.3   Translation of Intentions

Intentions are translated to a temporal formula with two boolean variables SET (Start Event Trigger) and EET (End Event Trigger). Initially, the variables are set to false. Once the interval is entered, during which the intention must be satisfied, *SET* is set to true. *EET* signals the end of the interval. An intermediate-state maintain intention can be translated as follows [9]:

$$\Box \ (SET \land \neg\ EET \rightarrow \quad PDH\,[AC\,][\texttt{'TSB-decrease'}].\mathrm{val}$$
$$\land\ PDH\,[AC\,][\texttt{'TSB-change'}].\mathrm{val} > 1)$$

In our verification example, we need to reference the time point, where plan "Phototherapy-intensive" (abb. '**pti**') gets activated, which can be assessed with the predicate time-enter-state(...). Adding four or six hours to that time point gives us the times, where *SET* and *EET* have to be set. This setting is done by a TL formula, describing the environment transition of *SET* and *EET*. The desired behavior during the now defined timing period is a constant high decrease of bilirubin in the blood. For increased readability the predicates SET-pred and EET-pred can be used, where

$$\text{SET-pred}(ASH, AC, SET)$$
$$\leftrightarrow \textbf{if } \text{time-enter-state}(ASH, \texttt{'pti'}, \texttt{activated}, AC) + 4 = AC$$
$$\textbf{then } SET'' \textbf{ else } SET'' \leftrightarrow SET'$$

and EET-pred is defined analogously.

5   Interactive Verification of Asbru

Formal verification of the indicator for the jaundice guideline is rather complex, because of the nontrivial semantics of time annotations. In Section 5.1, we define the proof obligation which is to be verified and in the following sections give an overview of our proof and the errors which were discovered.

5.1   Proof Obligation

The proof obligation falls into four different parts. The current system configuration, the system description, the environment assumption, and the property to verify. Plan Phototherapy-intensive (which is abbreviated with '**pti**') is initially **inactive**, and the consider signal has been sent. Procedure inactive# defines the dynamic behavior of the Asbru plan in state **inactive** (see Sect. 4.2).

In the *environment assumption*, we ensure that the environment leaves the local system variable $AS\,[\texttt{'pti'}]$ unchanged. Furthermore, either a micro step is executed and the patient data history *PDH* does not change, or a macro step is executed and the patient state changes arbitrarily. A macro step is only possible, if the system is stable, i.e. variable *Tick'* is true. The property is already described in Section 4.3.

5.2   Proof Structure

In principle, verification of concurrent systems in KIV is based on symbolic execution with induction [8,10]. The Asbru guideline is executed step by step.

/* current system configuration */
$AS\,[\text{'pti'}] = \texttt{inactive}, PC\,[\text{'pti'}].\text{consider}, \neg\, SET, \neg\, EET,$
$\text{time-enter-state}(ASH, \text{'pti'}, \texttt{activated}, AC\,) + \text{num}(4) < AC, \ldots$
/* system description */
$[\text{inactive}\#(\text{'pti'}, \text{'rt'}; AC, PDH, ASH, AS, \ldots)],$
/* environment assumption */
$\square\,(\quad AS\,''[\text{'pti'}] = AS\,'[\text{'pti'}] \wedge \ldots$
$\qquad \wedge\, (\quad \text{micro}(AC\,'', AC\,') \wedge PDH\,''[AC\,''] = PDH\,[AC\,]$
$\qquad\qquad \vee\; Tick\,' \wedge \text{macro}(AC\,'', AC\,')))$
/* definition of flags SET and EET */
$\square\,(\text{SET-pred}(ASH, AC, SET) \wedge \text{EET-pred}(ASH, AC, EET)),$
$\vdash$ /* property */
$\square\,(SET \wedge \neg\, EET \rightarrow \quad PDH\,[AC\,][\text{'TSB-decrease'}].\text{val}$
$\qquad\qquad\qquad\quad \wedge\, PDH\,[AC\,][\text{'TSB-change'}].\text{val} > 1)$

Fig. 7. Sequent to verify

With the verification of an always property, after performing a TL step, it is
necessary to verify a FOL proof obligation and afterwards continue TL execution.
Symbolic execution may not terminate, because the guideline may contain loops.
For executing loops, induction is necessary.

In order to verify the intention, a proof for the correctness of the sequent of
Fig. 7 must be constructed. The execution, in principle, follows the abstracted
proof tree of Figure 8. The proof tree presented is drawn bottom up. The lowest
node in the proof tree is the initial node, marked "1" in Figure 8.

In the initial state, the plan "Phototherapy-intensive" (abb. 'pti') is in
inactive state, as is the sub-plan "Prescribe-intensive-phototherapy" (abb.

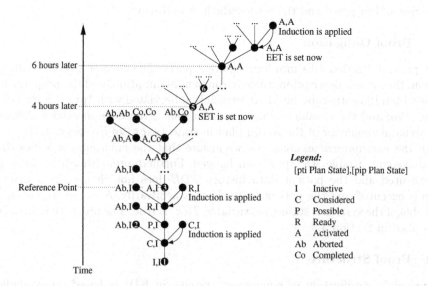

Fig. 8. Abstracted proof tree

'pip'). This is annotated in Fig. 8 as I, I. After advancing one TL step, the plan is considered. After each TL step, the possibility has to be considered, that the super-plan of 'pti' is terminated. This will result in the 'pti' plan to terminate as well. An example can be seen with node 2 in Figure 8. Status of the plans there is abbreviated to Ab, I.

We continue to progress until plan 'pti' reaches the activated state (see node 3 in Fig. 8). The transition of 'pti' from ready to activated marks a reference time. The function time-enter-state(ASH, 'pti', activated, AC) is used to determine that time. This is necessary, as this reference time is used as a reference point for time annotations in the abort condition as well as the intention. Also, a procedure representing 'pip' is started.

Further progression along the time line leads to an activation of the 'pip' plan, to be seen in node 4 in Figure 8. After 'pip' is activated, there is the possibility of a successful termination of 'pip'. It is not possible for 'pip' to abort because of its abort condition.

Advancing further along the time line, a point is reached, where 4 hours have passed since the activation of 'pti' (see node 5 in Fig. 8). From this point on for the next 2 hours, it has to be verified, that a large enough decrease of bilirubin in the blood of the newborn is measured or that the 'pti' plan aborts. This additional proof obligation is represented by node 6 in Figure 8.

Assuming this proof obligation is possible to verify, it is necessary to advance 2 hours further along the time line in the last open premise and close the remaining proof obligations with induction.

5.3 First Error

Proof proceeds as explained in Sect. 5.2 to node 6. There it has to be verified, that the intention is satisfied or the 'pti' plan aborts. However, neither is happening.

abort-condition of pti:

      (or (and (bilirubin $\neq$ photofherapy-intensive) in NOW
           (not (and (bilirubin $=$ photofherapy-normal) in NOW
                (TSB-decrease $=$ no) in NOW))
        (and (bilirubin $=$ photofherapy-intensive) in NOW
          (or (and (TSB-decrease $=$ yes) in ([4h, -] [-, 6h] [-, -] SELF)
              (TSB-change < 1) in ([4h, -] [-, 6h] [-, -] SELF))
           (TSB-decrease $=$ no) in ([4h, -] [-, -] [-, -] SELF))))

If the bilirubin level is not photofherapy-intensive, only the first half of the abort condition can become true. Therefore, with the TSB on a level different than photofherapy-intensive, the plan may only abort, if the bilirubin is not on level photofherapy-normal or **some** decrease in TSB is measured.

The automatically generated proof obligation is now to verify, that TSB level is unequal to photofherapy-normal or that there is some decrease of bilirubin measured now. If either did hold, the abort condition would have triggered, resulting in an abortion of the 'pti' plan which would in consequence satisfy the intention. Verification of this obligation is not feasible, as no side formulas imply either the decrease or the bilirubin blood level. The culprit here is the negation of

(and (bilirubin = phototherapy-normal) *in* NOW
        (TSB-decrease = no) *in* NOW **)**

Without this negation, the plan would react according to the intuition, aborting, once the bilirubin is on level `phototherapy-normal` and **no** decrease is measured. However, simply discarding the negation would lead to the next problem. If a minor decrease is measured, the plan still would not abort, but also the intention would not be satisfied.

corrected abort-condition of pti:
    (or (and (bilirubin ≠ phototherapy-intensive) *in* NOW
            (and (bilirubin = phototherapy-normal) *in* NOW
                (or (TSB-decrease = no) *in* NOW
                    (TSB-change < 1) *in* NOW **)))**
        (and (bilirubin = phototherapy-intensive) *in* NOW
            (or (and (TSB-decrease = yes) *in* ([4h, -] [-, 6h] [-, -] SELF)
                (TSB-change < 1) *in* ([4h, -] [-, 6h] [-, -] SELF))
            (TSB-decrease = no) *in* ([4h, -] [-, -] [-, -] SELF))))**

5.4   Second Error

After modifying the abort condition, the proof has to be reconstructed. Fortunately, most of the original proof can be replayed and the degree of automation is about 95%. The second proof attempt fails at node 6, where again it is necessary to verify that either plan `'pti'` is aborted or the intention is satisfied.

The failed proof attempt can be analyzed to discover a principle problem with time annotations. The original time annotation in the abort condition reads

$$[4h,\_][\_,6h][\_,\_] \text{ enter(activated, 'pti')}$$

As the latest finishing shift is given, the time-annotated condition must be finally false (see Sect. 2.3). In order to determine whether the abort condition holds, we have to wait until the condition is falsified. If, after four hours there is a decrease, but the change is not large enough, the abort condition does not necessarily trigger. This violates the intention.

In our example, we must neither give an earliest starting shift nor a latest finishing shift. The corrected time annotation reads:

$$[\_,6h][4h,\_][\_,\_] \text{ enter(activated, 'pti')}$$

5.5   Final Verification

With this new time annotation and the changed abort condition, the proof is replayed once more. Again, an automation grade between 95 and 99% is achieved.

It can now be shown in the proof obligation in node 5 in Fig. 8, that a violation of the intention may not occur without the plan being aborted. Using temporal logic induction the proof can be closed.

All in all, the proof had to be replayed twice and both times the abort condition had to be corrected. Thereafter the proof obligation can be verified. The complete proof consists of more than 600 proof steps. The symbolic execution is done almost automatically apart from the generalizations. Most of the manual work has to be done in the first order proof parts.

It would now be necessary to take the verification results and communicate them back to the guideline developers and Asbru modelers to assess the impact of the flaws found as well as the proposed solution.

6   Related Work

In addition to Asbru, a number of languages have been devised for the representation of medical guidelines (see [11] for a comparison of the most outstanding ones). Many of these languages are not formal enough, e.g. they often incorporate many free-text elements without a clear semantics. Exceptions to this are PROforma [12] and Asbru. The formal semantics defined for Asbru makes formal verification of Asbru guidelines possible. This is, to our knowledge, a rather novel approach in the area of guideline representation languages.

Besides KIV, there are a number of powerful theorem provers, e.g. Isabelle [13], STeP [14], and others, which can also be considered for the verification of medical guidelines. We have focused on KIV, because this theorem prover offers the intuitive strategy of symbolic execution with induction to verify temporal properties of concurrent systems.

While interactive verification is convenient for validating the semantics of Asbru and for reasoning about complex details such as time annotations, it is promising to provide automatic methods to effectively apply formal methods in practice. For this, a number of tools can be considered. In [5], we have used the SMV model checker [15] to verify properties of medical guidelines. Alternatives are SPIN [16], Kronos [17], etc. Especially the latter is an alternative to SMV for verifying time annotations. Dealing with time annotations usually implies the necessity for histories ranging over infinite data. As we expect the effort to find abstractions to be somewhat equal to the effort for interactive verification, we concentrate on the latter.

7   Conclusion

Our overall experiences with the jaundice case study suggest that the quality of medical guidelines could be improved by carrying over standard techniques from software engineering. As a matter of fact, we have identified a small number of errors in the formulation of a single plan of a particular Asbru hierarchy. This is a significant finding, given the degree of complexity of guideline languages. Not less important, we have shown how to apply formal methods to a non-standard application field. The procedure consists of modelling the guideline in Asbru and then verifying properties with an interactive theorem prover. In [5], we also considered model checking of guidelines.

The verification example has shown that symbolic execution is an intuitive strategy to verify guidelines interactively and offers a high degree of automation. Support for the reuse of proofs is essential, because in practice errors are found, the model is changed and proofs have to be reconstructed frequently.

For model checking Asbru guidelines it has been necessary to abstract from time annotations. Therefore, only part of the errors described in Sect. 5 have been found in [5]. Errors concerning the use of time annotations still requires interactive verification. Furthermore, we have found interactive verification very useful to validate the semantics of Asbru.

We have only considered a small sub part of the overall guideline. The selected part has been nontrivial because of time-annotated conditions and the complex semantics involved. The challenge remains to tackle the complete guideline with interactive verification. For this, we are currently working on a modular strategy based on the well known assumption guarantee approach. It would be interesting to also apply other approaches to the verification of medical guidelines. For this, the jaundice guideline could serve as an interesting case study. Other languages besides Asbru should also be considered.

References

1. Seyfang, A., Kosara, R., Miksch, S.: Asbru 7.3 reference manual. Technical report, Vienna University of Technology (2002)
2. Seyfang, A., Miksch, S., Marcos, M.: Combining diagnosis and treatment using Asbru. International Journal of Medical Informatics **68**((1-3)) (2002) 49–57
3. Marcos, M., Roomans, H., ten Teije, A., van Harmelen, F.: Improving medical protocols through formalisation: a case study. In: Proc. of the Session on Formal Methods in Healthcare, 6th International Conference on Integrated Design and Process Technology (IDPT-02). (2002)
4. Balser, M., Duelli, C., Reif, W.: Formal semantics of Asbru – An Overview. In: Proceedings of IDPT 2002, Society for Design and Process Science (2002)
5. Bäumler, S., Balser, M., Dunets, A., Reif, W., Schmitt, J.: Verification of medical guidelines by model checking – a case study. In: SPIN conference proceedings. (2006) to appear.
6. Balser, M., Reif, W., Schellhorn, G., Stenzel, K., Thums, A.: Formal system development with KIV. In Maibaum, T., ed.: Fundamental Approaches to Software Engineering. Number 1783 in LNCS, Springer-Verlag (2000)
7. AAP: American Academy of Pediatrics, Provisional Committee for Quality Improvement and Subcommittee on Hyperbilirubinemia. Practice parameter: management of hyperbilirubinemia in the healthy term newborn. Pediatrics **94** (1994) 558–565
8. Balser, M.: Verifying Concurrent System with Symbolic Execution – Temporal Reasoning is Symbolic Execution with a Little Induction. PhD thesis, University of Augsburg, Augsburg, Germany (2005)

9. Stegers, R.: From natural language to formal proof goal: Structured goal formalisation applied to medical guidelines. Master's thesis, Vrije Universiteit, Amsterdam (2006)
10. Balser, M., Duelli, C., Reif, W., Schellhorn, G.: Verifying concurrent systems with symbolic execution. Journal of Logic and Computation **12**(4) (2002) 549–560
11. Peleg, M., Tu, S., Bury, J., Ciccarese, P., Fox, J., Greenes, R., Hall, R., Johnson, P., Jones, N., Kumar, A., Miksch, S., Quaglini, S., Seyfang, A., Shortliffe, E., Stefanelli, M.: Comparing Computer-interpretable Guideline Models: A Case-study Approach. Journal of the American Medical Informatics Association **10**(1) (2003) 52–68
12. Fox, J., Johns, N., Lyons, C., Rahmanzadeh, A., Thomson, R., Wilson, P.: PROforma: a general technology for clinical decision support systems. Computer Methods and Programs in Biomedicine **54** (1997) 59–67
13. Paulson, L.C.: Isabelle: A Generic Theorem Prover. LNCS 828. Springer (1994)
14. Manna, Z., the STeP group: Step: The stanford temporal prover. Technical report, Computer Science Department, Stanford University (1994)
15. McMillan, K.L.: Symbolic Model Checking. Kluwer Academic Publishers (1990)
16. Holzmann, G.J.: The SPIN Model Checker. Addison-Wesley (2003)
17. Bozga, M., Daws, C., Maler, O., Olivero, A., Tripakis, S., Yovine, S.: Kronos: A model-checking tool for real-time systems. In Hu, A.J., Vardi, M.Y., eds.: Proc. 10th International Conference on Computer Aided Verification, Vancouver, Canada. Volume 1427., Springer-Verlag (1998) 546–550

Certifying Airport Security Regulations Using the Focal Environment

David Delahaye, Jean-Frédéric Étienne, and Véronique Viguié Donzeau-Gouge

CEDRIC/CNAM, Paris, France
David.Delahaye@cnam.fr, etien_je@auditeur.cnam.fr,
donzeau@cnam.fr

Abstract. We present the formalization of regulations intended to ensure airport security in the framework of civil aviation. In particular, we describe the formal models of two standards, one at the international level and the other at the European level. These models are expressed using the Focal environment, which is also briefly presented. Focal is an object-oriented specification and proof system, where we can write programs together with properties which can be proved semi-automatically. We show how Focal is appropriate for building a clean hierarchical specification for our case study using, in particular, the object-oriented features to refine the international level into the European level and parameterization to modularize the development.

1 Introduction

The security of civil aviation is governed by a series of international standards and recommended practices that detail the responsibilities of the various stake-holders (states, operators, agents, etc). These documents are intended to give the specifications of procedures and artifacts which implement security in airports, aircraft and air traffic control. A key element to enforce security is the conformance of these procedures and artifacts to the specifications. However, it is also essential to ensure the consistency and completeness of the specifications. Standards and recommended practices are natural language documents (generally written in English) and their size may range from a few dozen to several hundred pages. Natural language has the advantage of being easily understood by a large number of stake-holders, but practice has also shown that it can be interpreted in several inconsistent ways by various readers. Moreover, it is very difficult to process natural language documents automatically in the search for inconsistencies. When a document has several hundred pages, it is very difficult to ensure that the content of a particular paragraph is not contradicted by some others which may be several dozen pages from the first one.

This paper aims to present the formal models of two standards related to airport security in order to study their consistency: the first one is the international standard Annex 17 [7] (to the Doc 7300/8) produced by the International Civil Aviation Organization (ICAO), an agency of the United Nations; the second one

J. Misra, T. Nipkow, and E. Sekerinski (Eds.): FM 2006, LNCS 4085, pp. 48–63, 2006.
© Springer-Verlag Berlin Heidelberg 2006

is the European standard Doc 2320 [2] (a public version of the Doc 30, which has a restricted access status) produced by the European Civil Aviation Conference (ECAC) and which is supposed to refine the first one at the European level. More precisely, from these models, we can expect:

1. to detect anomalies such as inconsistencies, incompleteness and redundancies or to provide evidence of their absence;
2. to clarify ambiguities and misunderstandings resulting from the use of informal definitions expressed in natural language;
3. to identify hidden assumptions, which may lead to shortcomings when additional explanations are required (e.g. in airport security programmes);
4. to make possible the rigorous assessment of satisfaction for a concrete regulation implementation and w.r.t. the requirements.

This formalization was completed in the framework of the EDEMOI[1] [8] project, which aims to integrate and apply several requirements engineering and formal methods techniques to analyze regulation standards in the domain of airport security. The methodology of this project may be considered as original in the sense that it tries to apply techniques, usually reserved to critical software, to the domain of regulations (in which no implementation is expected). The project used a two-step approach. In the first step, standards described in natural language were analyzed in order to extract security properties and to elaborate a conceptual model of the underlying system [5]. The second step, which this work is part of, consists in building a formal model and to analyze/verify the model by different kinds of formal tools. In this paper, we describe two formal models of the two standards considered above, which have been carried out using the Focal [12] environment, as well as some results that have been analyzed from these models.

Another motivation of this paper is to present the Focal [12] (previously Foc) environment, developed by the Focal team, and to show how this tool is appropriate to model this kind of application. The idea is to assess and validate the design features as well as the reasoning support mechanism offered by the Focal specification and proof system. In our case study, amongst others, we essentially use the features of inheritance and parameterization. Inheritance allows us to get a neat notion of refinement making incremental specifications possible; in particular, the refinement of the international level by the European level can be expressed naturally. Parameterization provides us with a form of polymorphism so that we can factorize parts of our development and obtain a very modular specification. Finally, regarding the reasoning support, the first-order automated theorem-prover of Focal, called Zenon, bring us an effective help by automatically discharging most of the proofs required by the specification.

The paper is organized as follows: first, we give a brief description of the Focal language with its main structures and features; next, we present our case study,

[1] The EDEMOI project is supported by the French National "Action Concertée Incitative Sécurité Informatique".

i.e. the several standards regulating security in airports and in particular, those we chose to model; finally, we describe the global formalization made in Focal, as well as the properties that could be analyzed and verified.

2   The Focal Environment

2.1   What Is Focal?

Focal [12], initiated by T. Hardin with R. Rioboo and S. Boulmé, is a language in which it is possible to build applications step by step, going from abstract specifications, called species, to concrete implementations, called collections. These different structures are combined using inheritance and parameterization, inspired by object-oriented programming; moreover, each of these structures is equipped with a carrier set, providing a typical algebraic specification flavor. Moreover, in this language, there is a neat separation between the activities of programming and proving. A compiler was developed by V. Prevosto for this language, able to produce Ocaml [11] code for execution, Coq [10] code[2] for certification, but also code for documentation (generated by means of structured comments). More recently, D. Doligez provided a first-order automated theorem prover, called Zenon, which helps the user to complete his/her proofs in Focal through a declarative-like proof language. This automated theorem prover can produce pure Coq proofs, which are reinserted in the Coq specifications generated by the Focal compiler and fully verified by Coq.

2.2   Specification: Species

The first major notion of the Focal language is the structure of *species*, which corresponds to the highest level of abstraction in a specification. A species can be roughly seen as a list of attributes and there are three kinds of attributes:

- the carrier type, called *representation*, which is the type of the entities that are manipulated by the functions of the species; representations can be either abstract or concrete;
- the functions, which denote the operations allowed on the entities; the functions can be either *definitions* (when a body is provided) or *declarations* (when only a type is given);
- the properties, which must be verified by any further implementation of the species; the properties can be either simply properties (when only the proposition is given) or theorems (when a proof is also provided).

---

[2] Here, Coq is only used as a proof checker, and not to extract, from provided proofs and using its Curry-Howard isomorphism capability, Ocaml programs, which are directly generated from Focal specifications.

More concretely, the general syntax of a species is the following:

species <name> =

  rep [= <type>];   *(* abstract/concrete*
                                         representation *)

  sig <name> **in** <type>;   *(* declaration *)*
  let <name> = <body>;   *(* definition *)*

  property <name> : <prop>; *(* property *)*
  theorem <name> : <prop>   *(* theorem *)*
  proof : <proof>;

  end

where <name> is simply a given name, <type> a type expression (mainly typing of core-ML without polymorphism but with inductive types), <body> a function body (mainly core-ML with conditional, pattern-matching and recursion), <prop> a (first-order) proposition and <proof> a proof (expressed in a declarative style and given to Zenon). In the type language, the specific expression **self** refers to the type of the representation and may be used everywhere except when defining a concrete representation.

As said previously, species can be combined using (multiple) inheritance, which works as expected. It is possible to define functions that were previously only declared or to prove properties which had no provided proof. It is also possible to redefine functions previously defined or to reprove properties already proved. However, the representation cannot be redefined and functions as well as properties must keep their respective types and propositions all along the inheritance path. Another way of combining species is to use parameterization. Species can be parameterized either by other species or by entities from species. If the parameter is a species, the parameterized species only has access to the interface of this species, i.e. only its abstract representation, its declarations and its properties. These two features complete the previous syntax definition as follows:

species <name> (<name> **is** <name>, <name> **in** <name>, ...)
         inherits <name>, <name> (<pars>), ... = ...
  end

where <pars> is a list of <name> and denotes the names which are used as parameters. When the parameter is a species, the keyword is **is**, when it is an entity of a species, the keyword is **in**.

To better understand this notion of species, let us give a small example:

Example 1 (Finite stacks). To formalize finite stacks, an abstract way is to specify stacks (possibly infinite) first, and to refine them as finite stacks afterwards.

The specification of stacks might be the following: c

species stack (typ **is** setoid) **inherits** setoid =

    sig empty **in self**;
    sig push **in** typ −> **self** −> **self**;
    sig pop **in self** −> **self**;
    sig last **in self** −> typ;
    let is_empty (s) = !equal (s, !empty);

    property ie_empty : !is_empty (!empty);
    property ie_push : **all** e **in** typ, **all** s **in self**,
                          not (!is_empty (!push (e, s))); ...

    end

where setoid is a predefined species representing a non-empty set with an equality
(in the first line, the parameter and the inheritance from setoid show respectively
that we want to be able to compare two items of a stack, but also two stacks),
the "!" notation is equivalent to the common dot notation of message sending
in object-oriented programming (**self** is the default species when there is no
receiver species indicated; e.g. !empty is for **self**!empty).

    Next, before specifying finite stacks, we can be more modular and formalize
the notion of finiteness separately as follows:

species is_finite (max **in** int) **inherits** basic_object =

    sig size **in self** −> int;
    property size_max : **all** s **in self**, #int_leq (!size (s), max);

    end

where basic_object is a predefined species supposed to be the root of every Focal
hierarchy, int the predefined type of integers and "#int_" the prefix of operations
over the type int. Here, we can remark that the species is parameterized by an
entity of a species and not by a species.

    Finally, we can formalize finite stacks using a multiple inheritance from the
species stack and is_finite:

species finite_stack (typ **is** setoid, max **in** int)
        inherits stack (typ), is_finite (max) =

    let is_full (s) = #int_eq (!size (s), max);

    property size_empty : #int_eq (!size (!empty), 0);
    property size_push : **all** e **in** typ, **all** s **in self**, **not** (!is_full (s)) −>
        #int_eq (!size (!push (e, s)), #int_plus (!size (s), 1)); ...

    end

2.3   Implementation: Collection

The other main notion of the Focal language is the structure of *collection*, which corresponds to the implementation of a specification. A collection implements a species in such a way that every attribute becomes concrete: the representation must be concrete, functions must be defined and properties must be proved. If the implemented species is parameterized, the collection must also provide implementations for these parameters: either a collection if the parameter is a species or a given entity if the parameter denotes an entity of a species. Moreover, a collection is seen (by the other species and collections) through its corresponding interface; in particular, the representation is an abstract data type and only the definitions of the collection are able to manipulate the entities of this type. Finally, a collection is a terminal item and cannot be extended or refined by inheritance. The syntax of a collection is the following:

   collection <name> implements <name> (<pars>) = ... end

We will not detail examples of collections here since our formalization (see Section 4) does not make use of them. Actually, the airport security regulations considered in this paper are rather abstract and do not expect any implementation. Regarding our previous example of finite stacks, a corresponding collection will have to provide a concrete representation (using lists for example), definitions for only declared functions (empty, push, pop, last) and proofs for properties (ie_empty, ie_push, etc). For complete examples of collections, the reader can refer to the standard library of Focal (see Section 2.5).

2.4   Certification: Proving with Zenon

The certification of a Focal specification is ensured by the possibility of proving properties. To do so, a first-order automated theorem prover, called Zenon and based on the tableau method, helps us to complete the proofs. Basically, there are two ways of providing proofs to Zenon: the first one is to give all the properties (proved or not) and definitions needed by Zenon to build a proof with its procedure; the second one is to give additional auxiliary lemmas to help Zenon to find a proof. In the first option, Zenon must be strong enough to find a proof with only the provided properties and definitions; the second option must be considered when Zenon needs to be helped a little more or when the user likes to present his/her proof in a more readable form. In the first option, proofs are described as follows:

   theorem <name> : <prop>
   proof : by <props> def <defs>;

where <props> is a list of properties and <defs> a list of definitions.

   The proof language of the second option is inspired by a proposition by L. Lamport [6], which is based on a practical and hierarchical structuring of proofs using number labels for proof depth. We do not describe this language here but some examples of use can be found in the formalization of our case study (see Section 4.4 to get the development).

Let us describe a small proof in our example of finite stacks:

Example 2 (Finite stacks). In the species stack, we can notice that with the definition of is_empty, Property ie_empty can already be proved in the following way:

> **theorem** ie_empty : !is_empty (!empty)
> **proof** : **by** !equal_reflexive **def** !is_empty;

where equal_reflexive is the property of reflexivity for equality, which is inherited from the species setoid.

This proof uses the definition of is_empty, which means that any redefinition of is_empty in any further inheritance invalidates this proof (which has to be completed again using the new definition). Thus, w.r.t. usual object-oriented programming, redefinitions may have some additional effects since they directly influence the proofs in which they are involved.

2.5   Further Information

For additional information regarding Focal, the reader can refer to [3], as well as to the Focal Web site: `http://focal.inria.fr/`, which contains the Focal distribution (compiler, Zenon and other tools), the reference manual, a tutorial, some FAQs and also some other references regarding, in particular, Focal's formal semantics (e.g. see S. Boulmé and S. Fechter's PhD theses).

3   Case Study: Airport Security Regulations

The primary goal of the international standards and recommended practices regulating airport security is to safeguard civil aviation against acts of unlawful interference. These normative documents detail the roles and responsibilities of the various stake-holders and pinpoint a set of security measures (as well as the ways and means to implement them) that each airport serving civil aviation has to comply with. In addition, the entire regulatory system is organized in a hierarchical way, where each level has its own set of regulatory documents that are drafted and maintained by different bodies. At the international level, Annex 17 [7] of the International Civil Aviation Organization (ICAO) lays down the general principles and recommended practices to be adopted by each member state. It is refined at the European level by the Doc 2320 [2] of the European Civil Aviation Conference (ECAC), where the standard is made more detailed and more precise. At the national level, each member state has to establish and implement a national civil aviation security programme in compliance with international standards and national laws. Finally, at the airport level, the national and international standards are implemented by an airport security programme.

All these documents are written in natural language and due to their voluminous size, it is difficult to manually assess the consistency of the entire regulatory system. Moreover, informal definitions tend to be inaccurate and may be interpreted in various inconsistent ways by different readers. Consequently, it may happen that two inspectors visiting the same airport at the same time reach contradictory conclusions about its conformity. However, these documents have the merit of being rigorously structured. Ensuring their consistency and completeness while eliminating any ambiguity or misunderstanding is a significant step towards the reinforcement of airport security.

3.1   Scope Delimitation

After a deep study of the above-mentioned documents and several consultations with the ICAO and ECAC, we decided to take as a starting point the preventive security measures described in Chapter 4 of Annex 17. Chapter 4 begins by stating the primary goal to be fulfilled by each member state, which is:

> *4.1 Each Contracting State shall establish measures to prevent weapons, explosives or any other dangerous devices, articles or substances, which may be used to commit an act of unlawful interference, the carriage or bearing of which is not authorized, from being introduced, by any means whatsoever, on board an aircraft engaged in international civil aviation.*

Basically, this means that acts of unlawful interference can be avoided by preventing unauthorized dangerous objects from being introduced on board aircraft[3]. To be able to achieve this goal, the member states have to implement a set of preventive security measures, which are classified in Chapter 4 according to six specific situations that may potentially lead to the introduction of dangerous objects on board. These are namely:

- persons accessing restricted security areas and airside areas (A17, 4.2);
- taxiing and parked aircraft (A17, 4.3);
- ordinary passengers and their cabin baggage (A17, 4.4);
- hold baggage checked-in or taken in custody of airline operators (A17, 4.5);
- cargo, mail, etc, intended for carriage on commercial flights (A17, 4.6);
- special categories of passengers like armed personnel or potentially disruptive passengers that have to travel on commercial flights (A17, 4.7).

At the lower levels of the regulatory hierarchy, the security measures are refined and detailed in such a way as to preserve the decomposition presented above. This structure allowed us to easily identify the relation between the different levels of refinement. Due to the restricted access nature of some of the regulatory documents, the formalization presented in Section 4 only considers Chapter 4 of Annex 17 and some of the refinements proposed by the European Doc 2320. Moreover, for simplification reasons, we do not cover the security measures 4.3 and 4.6.

---

[3] Note that the interpretation given to the quoted paragraph may appear wrong to some readers. In fact, Paragraph 4.1 is ambiguous as it can be interpreted in two different ways (see Section 4.4 for more details).

3.2 Modeling Challenges

Modeling the regulations governing airport security is a real world problem and is therefore a good exercise to identify the limits of the inherent features of the Focal environment. Moreover, the ultimate objective of such an application is not to produce certified code but rather to provide an automated support for the analysis of the regulatory documents. For this case study, the formalization needs to address the following modeling challenges:

1. the model has to impose a structure that facilitates the traceability and maintainability of the normative documents. Moreover, through this structure, it should be possible to easily identify the impact of a particular security measure on the entire regulatory system;
2. the model must make the distinction between the security measures and the ways and means of implementing them. Most of the security measures are fairly general and correspond to reachable objectives. However, their implementation may differ from one airport to another due to national laws and local specificities;
3. for each level of the regulatory hierarchy, the model must determine (through the use of automated reasoning support tools) whether or not the fundamental security properties can be derived from the set of prescribed security measures. This will help to identity hidden assumptions made during the drafting process. In addition, the model has to provide evidence that the security measures defined at refined levels are not less restrictive than those at higher levels.

4 Formalization

4.1 Model Domain

In order to formalize the meaning of the preventive security measures properly, we first need to identity the subjects they regulate, together with their respective properties/attributes and the relationships between them. It is also essential to determine the hierarchical organization of the identified subjects in order to effectively factorize functions and properties during the formalization process. This is done by determining the dependencies between the security measures, w.r.t. the definitions of terms used in the corresponding normative document. For example, let us consider the following security measure described in Chapter 4 of Annex 17:

> *4.4.1 Each Contracting State shall establish measures to ensure that originating passengers of commercial air transport operations and their cabin baggage are screened prior to boarding an aircraft departing from a security restricted area.*

To be able to formalize this security measure, it is obvious that we will have to define the subjects *originating passenger*, *cabin baggage*, *aircraft* and *security restricted area*, together with the relations between them. Moreover, we will need to define appropriate attributes for the *originating passenger* subject to characterize the state of being *screened* and of being *on board*. Finally, to complete the formalization, we will have to specify the integrity constraints induced by the regulation (e.g. screened passengers are either in security restricted areas or on board aircraft). The hierarchies of subjects obtained after analyzing all the

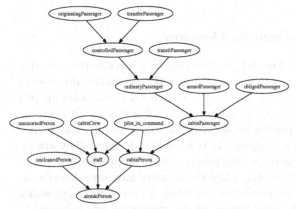

preventive security measures of Annex 17 are represented by a Focal model, where each subject is a species. For instance, the Focal model for airside persons is given in Figure 1 (where nodes are species and arrows inheritance relations s.t. $A \leftarrow B$ means species B inherits from A).

For possible extensions during the refinement process, the *representation* of the species is left undefined

Fig. 1. Hierarchy for airside persons in Annex 17

(abstract) and their functions are only declared. Moreover, since we are not concerned with code generation, our formalization does not make use of collections. For example, the following species corresponds to the specification of the *cabin person* subject:

> **species** cabinPerson (obj **is** object, obj_set **is** basic_set (obj),
>   do **is** dangerousObject, do_set **is** basic_set (do),
>   wp **is** weapon, wp_set **is** basic_set (wp), id **is** identity,
>   c_luggage **is** cabinLuggage (obj, obj_set, do, do_set, wp, wp_set),
>   cl_set **is** basic_lset (obj, obj_set, do, do_set, wp, wp_set, c_luggage))
>   **inherits** airsidePerson (obj, obj_set, do, do_set, wp, wp_set, id) =
>
>   **sig** embarked **in self** −> bool;
>   **sig** get_cabinLuggage **in self** −> cl_set;
>
>   **property** invariant_weapons : **all** w **in** wp, **all** s **in self**,
>   wp_set!member (w, !get_weapons (s)) −> **not** (wp!inaccessible (w));
>
>   **end**

The species cabinPerson specifies the common functions and properties for the different types of persons who are eligible to travel on board an aircraft. In order to specify the relations between cabin persons and the different items they can have access to during flight time, the species cabinPerson is parameterized with the species object, dangerousObject, weapon and cabinLuggage. The parameters obj_set, do_set, wp_set and cl_set describe the sets of the previously identified items; they are introduced to express the fact that a cabin person can own more than one item at a time. Since most of these relations are already specified in the species airsidePerson, they are inherited automatically. The function get_cabinLuggage is only introduced to make accessible the set of cabin luggage associated to a given instance of cabinPerson. Property invariant_weapons is a typical example of integrity constraints imposed by the regulation. It states that when weapons are carried by cabin persons, they are *by default* considered to be accessible during flight time.

4.2   Annex 17: Preventive Security Measures

As said in Section 3.2, the formal model needs to impose a certain structure that will facilitate the traceability and maintainability of the normative documents. To achieve this purpose, our model follows the structural decomposition proposed in Chapter 4 of Annex 17 (using inheritance), while taking into account the dependencies between the preventive security measures. In our model, since most of the security measures correspond to reachable objectives, they are defined as invariants and each airport security programme must provide procedures which satisfy these invariants. However, when the security measures describe actions to be taken when safety properties are violated, a procedural approach is adopted. The consistency and completeness of the regulation are achieved by establishing that the fundamental security property, defined in Paragraph 4.1 of Annex 17, is satisfied by all the security measures, while ensuring their homogeneity. The general structure of the Annex 17 model is represented in Figure 2.

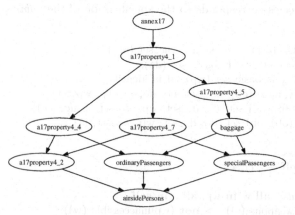

Fig. 2. Structure of Annex 17

The species airsidePersons, ordinaryPassengers, specialPassengers and baggage introduce the set domain of the subjects presented in Section 4.1 as well as their relational constraints (e.g. two passengers cannot have the same luggage). The preventive security measures are formalized in species a17property4_2, a17property4_4, a17property4_5, a17property4_7 and their dependencies are defined according to the hierarchical organization of the subjects they regulate. The fundamental security property is defined in species a17property4_1. It is at this level that the set of on board objects is defined. Finally, the theorems establishing the consistency and completeness of the regulation are defined in the species annex17.

Security Measures Related to Ordinary Passengers. As an example, we can focus on Property 4.4 of Annex 17 related to security measures for ordinary passengers. This property is divided into four sub-properties and, for example, we can describe how Property 4.4.1 (cited in Section 4.1) was formalized:

Example 3 (Property 4.4.1). Security measure 4.4.1 states that originating passengers and their cabin baggage should be screened prior to boarding an aircraft. In species a17property4_4, this statement is formalized as follows:

> **property** property_4_4_1 : **all** p **in** op, **all** s **in** self,
> op_set!member (p, !originatingPassengers (s)) ->
> op!embarked (p) -> op!screened (p);

where p represents an originating passenger and s the current state of species a17property4_4. It should be noted that the scope of the boolean function screened extends to cabin baggage as well, since cabin baggage remains with its owners throughout the boarding process. The fact of being a screened ordinary passenger is defined in the species controlledPassengers (see Figure 1) as follows:

> **property** invariant_screened : **all** s **in** self,
> !screened (s) -> wp_set!is_empty (!get_weapons (s)) **and**
> wp_set!is_empty (cl_set!get_weapons (!get_cabinLuggage (s))) **and**
> **all** o **in** do, do_set!member (o, !get_dangerousObjects (s)) **or**
> do_set!member (o, cl_set!get_dangerousObjects
> (!get_cabinLuggage (s))) -> do!is_authorized (o);

where s represents a controlledPassenger. Property invariant_screened states that if a passenger is screened, he/she does not have any weapons and if the passenger does have a dangerous object (other than weapons), it is authorized. A similar property also exists for Property 4.4.2 (which concerns transfer passengers) and could be factorized via the parameterization mechanism of Focal.

From this property and the three others (4.4.2, 4.4.3 and 4.4.4), we can prove the global property 4.4 that ordinary passengers admitted on board an aircraft do not have any unauthorized dangerous objects. This intermediate lemma is used afterwards when proving the consistency of the fundamental security property (4.1) w.r.t. the preventive security measures.

Consistency of Annex 17. Once we completed the formalization for each of the different categories of preventive security measures and derived the appropriate intermediate lemmas, we can consider Paragraph 4.1 (see Section 3.1) of Annex 17. It is formalized as follows in species a17property4_1:

> **property** property_4_1 : **all** a **in** ac, **all** s **in** self,
> ac_set!member (a, !departureAircraft (s)) ->
> (**all** o **in** do, do_set!member (o, !onboardDangerousObjects (a, s)) ->
> do!is_authorized (o)) **and**
> (**all** o **in** wp, wp_set!member (o, !onboardWeapons (a, s)) ->
> wp!is_authorized (o));

where a represents an aircraft. This states that dangerous objects are admitted on board a departing aircraft only if they are authorized. In addition, the set of on board objects for each departing aircraft is defined according to the different types of cabin persons (together with their cabin luggage) and according to the different types of hold baggage loaded into the aircraft. This correlation is necessary since it will allow us to establish the following consistency theorem:

> **theorem** consistency : !property_4_2 –> !property_4_4 –>
> !property_4_5 –> !property_4_7 –> !property_4_1
> **proof** : **by** do_set!union1, wp_set!union1 **def** !property_4_2, !property_4_4,
> !property_4_5, !property_4_7, !property_4_1;

where property_4_2, property_4_4, property_4_5 and property_4_7 corres-pond to the intermediate lemmas defined for each category of preventive security measures. The purpose of Theorem consistency is to verify whether the fundamental security property can be derived from the set of preventive security measures. This allowed us to identify some hidden assumptions done during the drafting process (see Section 4.4). However, this theorem does not guarantee the absence of contradictions in the regulation. A way to tackle this problem is to try to derive False from the set of security properties and to let Zenon work on it for a while. If the proof succeeds then we have a contradiction, otherwise we can only have a certain level of confidence.

4.3 Doc 2320: Some Refinements

The document structure of Doc 2320 follows the decomposition presented in Chapter 4 of Annex 17. Refinement in Doc 2320 appears at two levels. At the subject level, the refinement consists in enriching the characteristics of the existing subjects or in adding new subjects. At the security property level, the security measures become more precise and sometimes more restrictive. The verification of the consistency and completeness of Doc 2320 is performed in the same way as for Annex 17 (see the modeling described in Section 4.2). However, since Doc 2320 refines Annex 17, an additional verification is required to show that the security measures that it describes do not invalidate the ones defined in Annex 17. Thus, in addition to consistency proofs, another kind of proofs appears, that are refinement proofs. The model structure obtained for Doc 2320 is described in Figure 3 (where the existing species coming from

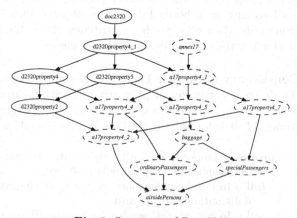

Fig. 3. Structure of Doc 2320

Annex 17 are distinguished with dashed nodes). As can be seen, the refinement is performed in such a way as to preserve the dependencies between the security measures. Moreover, it can be observed that unlike species a17property4_2, a17property4_4 and a17property4_5, species a17property4_7 does not have a Doc 2320 counterpart. This is because, in Doc 2320, no mention to special categories of passengers is made. We assume that in this case, the international standard still prevails.

A Refinement Example. In Doc 2320, Property 4.4.1 of Annex 17 is refined by Property 4.1.1, which states that originating passengers are either searched by hand or screened prior to boarding an aircraft. In species d2320property4, this statement is formulated as follows:

> **property** d2320property_4_1_1 : **all** p **in** op, **all** s **in self**,
> op_set!member (p, !originatingPassengers (s)) −>
> op!embarked (p) −> op!screened (p) **or** op!handSearched (p);

To prove that Property d2320property_4_1_1 does not invalidate Property property_4_4_1, the following theorem is used:

> **theorem** refinement : !d2320property_4_1_1 −> !property_4_4_1
> **proof** : **by** op!invariant_handSearched, op!invariant_screened
> **def** !d2320property_4_1_1, !property_4_4_1;

The above theorem is provable since in species controlledPassenger2320, which is a refined version of species controlledPassenger, the boolean function handSearched is characterized by the same properties than the boolean function screened (e.g. Property invariant_screened).

4.4   Analyses and Results

An Example of Ambiguity. As seen in Section 3, Paragraph 4.1 of Annex 17 is very important as it states the primary goal of the preventive security measures to be implemented by each member state. However, it appears to be ambiguous since it can be interpreted in two different ways: either dangerous objects are *never* authorized on board or they are admitted on board *only if* they are authorized. According to the ICAO, the second interpretation is the correct one as Paragraph 4.1 needs to be considered in the general context of the regulation to clarify this ambiguity.

Hidden Assumptions. In trying to demonstrate that Paragraph 4.1 of Annex 17 is consistent w.r.t. the set of preventive security measures, we discovered, for instance, the following hidden assumptions:

1. since disruptive passengers who are obliged to travel are generally escorted by law enforcement officers, they are considered not to have any dangerous objects in their possession;

2. unlike other passengers, transit passengers are not subjected to any specific security control but should be protected from unauthorized interference at transit spots. This implies that they are considered to be secure and hence do not have any unauthorized dangerous objects.

Development. The entire formalization takes about 10000 lines of Focal code, with in particular, 150 species and 200 proofs. It took about 2 years to be completed. The development is freely available (sending a mail to the authors) and can be compiled with the latest version of Focal (0.3.1).

5   Conclusion

Summary. A way to improve security is to produce high quality standards. The formal models of Annex 17 and Doc 2320 regulations, partially described in this paper, tend to bring an effective solution in the specific framework of airport security. From these formalizations, some properties could be analyzed and in particular, the notion of consistency. This paper also aims to emphasize the use of the Focal language, which provides a strongly typed and object-oriented formal development environment. The notions of inheritance and parameterization allowed us to build the specifications in an incremental and modular way. Moreover, the Zenon automated theorem prover (provided in Focal) discharged most of the proof obligations automatically and appeared to be very appropriate when dealing with abstract specifications (i.e. with no concrete representation).

Related Work. Currently, models of the same regulations, by D. Bert and his team, are under development using B [1] in the framework of the EDE-MOI project. In the near future, it could be interesting to compare the two formal models (in Focal and B) rigorously in order to understand if and how the specification language influences the model itself. It should be noted that the same results (see Section 4.4) were obtained from this alternative formalization, since some of these results were already analyzed before the formalization itself (during the conception step). Very close to the EDEMOI project is the SAFEE project [9], funded by the 6th Framework Programme of the European Union (FP6) and which aims to use similar techniques for security but on board the aircraft. Regarding similar specifications in Focal, we must keep in mind that the compiler is rather recent (4/5 years at most) and efforts have been essentially provided, by R. Rioboo, to build a Computer Algebra library, which is currently the standard library of Focal. However, some more applicative formalizations are under development like certified implementations of security policies [4] by M. Jaume and C. Morisset.

Future Work. We plan to integrate a test suite into this formalization using an automatic generation procedure (working from a Focal specification) and using stubs for abstract functions (i.e. only declared). Amongst other things, this will allow us to imagine and build attack scenarios which, at least in this context, appear to be quite interesting for official certification authorities. Such an automatic procedure is currently work in progress, by C. Dubois and M. Carlier, but is still limited (to universally quantified propositions) and needs to be extended to be applied to our development. We also plan to produce UML documents automatically generated from the Focal specifications and which is an effective solution to interact with competent organizations (ICAO, ECAC). Such a tool has been developed by J. F. Étienne but has to be completed to deal with all the features of Focal. Regarding the Focal language itself, some future evolutions might be appropriate, in particular, the notion of subtyping (there is a notion of subspecies but it does not correspond to a relation of subtyping), but which still needs to be specified in the case of properties. Also, it might be necessary to integrate temporal features in order to model behavioral properties, since in fact, our formalization, described in this paper, just shows a static view of the specified regulations.

References

1. J. R. Abrial. *The B Book, Assigning Programs to Meanings*. Cambridge University Press, Cambridge (UK), 1996. ISBN 0521496195.
2. The European Civil Aviation Conference. *Regulation (EC) N° 2320/2002 of the European Parliament and of the Council of 16 December 2002 establishing Common Rules in the Field of Civil Aviation Security*, December 2002.
3. C. Dubois, T. Hardin, and V. Viguié Donzeau-Gouge. Building Certified Components within Focal. In *Symposium on Trends in Functional Programming (TFP)*, volume 5, pages 33–48, Munich (Germany), November 2004. Intellect (Bristol, UK).
4. M. Jaume and C. Morisset. Formalisation and Implementation of Access Control Models. In *Information Assurance and Security (IAS), International Conference on Information Technology (ITCC)*, pages 703–708, Las Vegas (USA), April 2005. IEEE CS Press.
5. R. Laleau, S. Vignes, Y. Ledru, M. Lemoine, D. Bert, V. Viguié Donzeau-Gouge, and F. Peureux. Application of Requirements Engineering Techniques to the Analysis of Civil Aviation Security Standards. In *International Workshop on Situational Requirements Engineering Processes (SREP), in conjunction with the 13th IEEE International Requirements Engineering Conference*, Paris (France), August 2005.
6. L. Lamport. How to Write a Proof. *American Mathematical Monthly*, 102(7):600–608, August 1995.
7. The International Civil Aviation Organization. *Annex 17 to the Convention on International Civil Aviation, Security - Safeguarding International Civil Aviation against Acts of Unlawful Interference, Amendement 11*, November 2005.
8. The EDEMOI project, 2003. http://www-lsr.imag.fr/EDEMOI/.
9. The SAFEE project, 2004. http://www.safee.reading.ac.uk/.
10. The Coq Development Team. Coq, *version 8.0*. INRIA, January 2006. Available at: http://coq.inria.fr/.
11. The Cristal Team. Objective Caml, *version 3.09.1*. INRIA, January 2006. Available at: http://caml.inria.fr/.
12. The Focal Development Team. Focal, *version 0.3.1*. CNAM/INRIA/LIP6, May 2005. Available at: http://focal.inria.fr/.

Proving Safety Properties of an Aircraft Landing Protocol Using I/O Automata and the PVS Theorem Prover: A Case Study*

Shinya Umeno and Nancy Lynch

Massachusetts Institute of Technology,
Computer Science and Artificial Intelligence Laboratory,
32 Vassar Street, Cambridge MA 02139, USA
{umeno, lynch}@csail.mit.edu

Abstract. This paper presents an assertional-style verification of the aircraft landing protocol of NASA's SATS (*Small Aircraft Transportation System*) concept [1] using the I/O automata framework and the PVS theorem prover. We reconstructed the mathematical model of the landing protocol presented in [2] as an I/O automaton. In addition, we translated the I/O automaton into a corresponding PVS specification, and conducted a verification of the safety properties of the protocol using the assertional proof technique and the PVS theorem prover.

1 Introduction

Safety critical systems have been the subject of intensive study of applications of formal verification techniques. As a case study, we conduct an assertional-style verification of one such safety critical system in this paper: the aircraft landing protocol that is part of NASA's SATS (*Small Aircraft Transportation System*) concept of operation [1].

The SATS program aims to increase access to small and medium sized airports. The situation is significantly different in these airports from large airports, where separation assurance services are provided by the Air Traffic Control (ATC). Due to the limited facilities and inferior infrastructure in such airports, in the SATS concept of operations, a centralized air traffic management system is automated as the Airport Management Module (AMM), and does a minimal job to achieve the safe landing of the aircraft. It is the pilots' responsibility to determine the moment when their aircraft initiate the final approach initiation to the ground. Pilots follow the procedures defined in the SATS concept of operation to control their aircraft in a designated area in the air space of the airport, called the Self Controlled Area.

It is crucial to guarantee a safe separation of the aircraft in the Self Controlled Area when each pilot follows the procedures of the SATS concept. For this reason, a mathematical model of the landing and departure protocol of

---

* The project is supported by Air Force Contract FA9550-04-C-0084.

J. Misra, T. Nipkow, and E. Sekerinski (Eds.): FM 2006, LNCS 4085, pp. 64–80, 2006.
© Springer-Verlag Berlin Heidelberg 2006

SATS is presented in [2]. The model is a finite-state transition system obtained from a mathematical abstraction of the real system. In addition, in the paper, some properties of the model that represent the safe separation of the aircraft have been exhaustively checked using a model-checking technique. These include properties such as a bound on the number of aircraft on a particular portion of the airport (for example, no more than four aircraft are in the entire Self Controlled Area; or there is at most one aircraft at a certain part of the airspace in the airport).

Our objective in this paper is to carry out a proof of properties of the model proposed in [2] using inductive proof techniques that have been used in computer science literature, as opposed to an exhaustive state exploration used in [2]. We used I/O automata framework [3] to reconstruct the model, and have rigorously checked all proofs in this paper using the PVS mechanical theorem prover [4].[1] I/O automata have been successfully used to model nondeterministic distributed systems and to prove properties of them. Their treatment of nondeterminism is suitable for the model in this paper in which the next possible step that the model can take is nondeterministically defined.

There are three main contributions in this study. First, we present a reconstructed mathematical model of the SATS landing protocol using the I/O automata framework. This model gives us a more standardized and comprehensive description of the protocol than the model in [2]. Second, our inductive proof brings more insight into the protocol. Though a proof of our style may cost more than a state exploration method in terms of time and manpower, it often brings us a clearer view of how the system works, and what kinds of properties are crucial for guaranteeing the required behavior of the system. In this paper, we define a notion of *blocking of aircraft* in Section 4.2, which captures an auxiliary information of why the protocol works correctly. Third, this case study demonstrates the feasibility of using a mechanical theorem prover to prove properties of a moderately large and complex system in the context of the I/O automata framework.

The paper is constructed as follows. In Section 2, we present a reconstructed mathematical model of the SATS landing protocol, both the formal definition of the actual I/O automaton and the informal explanation of how the system works. In Section 3, we introduce the seven main properties that we will prove in this paper. Section 4 is devoted to the proof of the main properties, some of which have to be strengthened to make an inductive proof work. Finally, in Section 5, we summarize the results in the paper and discuss future work.

2   Abstract Model

In this section, we present an I/O automaton model for SATS, based on the model presented in [2]. In the model, the space of the airport is discretized, and

---

[1] Complete I/O automata and PVS specification codes, and PVS proof scripts are available at http://theory.csail.mit.edu/~umeno/. The full version of this paper [5] includes more detailed discussions on the model, the main properties, the auxiliary lemmas, and their proof.

is divided into several zones. These zones are represented as part of the state components of the automata, and the model can be used to check if the desirable upper bound on the number of aircraft in a specific zone is satisfied.

We will present a formal definition of the model as an I/O automaton in Section 2.5.

2.1   Logical Zones

The space of the airport used for landings is logically divided into 13 zones (see Figure 1). Each zone is modeled as a first-in first-out queue of aircraft. Only the first aircraft of a zone can move to another zone, and when an aircraft moves from one zone to another, it is removed from the head of the queue that it leaves, and is added to the end of the queue that it joins. Some zones have a symmetric structure with respect to the left side and the right side, for instance, holding3(right) and holding3(left).[2]

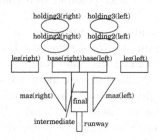
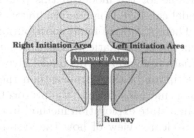

Fig. 1. 13 logical zones in SATS   **Fig. 2.** Logical zones divided into four areas

For the sake of an easier understanding of the big picture of how each zone is used, we group these 13 zones into the following four areas, depending on how they are used in the system (see Figure 2). The *left initiation area* consists of holding3(left) and holding2(left), which represent the zones to hold the aircraft at 3000 feet and 2000 feet, respectively, and which are used for the vertical approach initiation from the left side of the airport; lez(left) (*lateral entry zone*), which is used for the lateral approach initiation from the left side; and maz(left) (*missed approach zone*), which is used as the path that an aircraft that has missed the approach goes through to initiate the approach operation again. The *right initiation area* is a symmetric counterpart of the left initiation area, and is analogously defined. The *approach area* consists of base(right), base(left), intermediate, and final, which make a T-shaped area for the aircraft to land. The *runway* consists of zone runway. We say that an aircraft is *on the approach* if it is in the approach area. In addition, we often refer to the combined area of the two initiation areas and the approach area (thus, it consists of all logical zones except for runway) as the *operation area*. Actually, this area is the abstraction of

---

[2] Note that this right and left are determined with respect to a pilot's view; thus it is the opposite to what we actually see in the picture (for instance, holding3(right) is on the *left* side in the picture.).

the Self Controlled Area that we mentioned in Section 1. In this paper, we focus on the safety conditions in the operation area.

2.2   Aircraft

An aircraft is defined as a tuple that has two attributes: the mahf assignment, which will be explained shortly, mahf of type Side (an enumeration of left and right); and a unique ID, id, which is encoded as a natural number in the abstract model.

```
Aircraft tuple [
        mahf: Side, % Missed approach holding fix assignment.
        id  : ID  ] % ID of the aircraft
```

2.3   Landing Sequence

When an aircraft enters the system, the system (AMM) assigns its *leader* aircraft, or the aircraft it has to follow. This relation of a leader constructs a chain: the first aircraft that enters the system does not have a leader, the second aircraft that enters the system is assigned the first aircraft as the leader, the third one is assigned the second one as the leader, and so on. A leader is an important notion of the system since it is used as a part of the conditions to decide if an aircraft can initiate the final approach to the ground. As we will examine closely later, an aircraft cannot go to the approach area until its leader has gone there. We will see formally defined conditions in Section 2.5.

In our abstract model, we encode this notion of the leader aircraft as an explicit queue of aircraft, called the *"landing sequence."* When an aircraft enters the operation area, it is also added to the end of the landing sequence. We define the leader of aircraft a in the landing sequence as the aircraft just in front of a in the sequence. By this definition of the leader, this abstract sequence represents the chain of the *leader* relation in reality discussed above. When an aircraft lands or exits from the operation area, it is removed from the landing sequence.

The assignment of the leader for an aircraft does not change once it is assigned if that aircraft lands successfully in the first try. However, an aircraft does not always succeed in landing at the first attempt, that is, it may miss the approach. In such a case, its leader is *reassigned* and it has to redo the landing process. We will later look at the case when an aircraft misses the approach.

2.4   Paths of Aircraft

Here we present a high level picture of how an aircraft enters and moves in the logical zones, initiates the approach to the ground, and lands on the runway. All movements are represented as the transitions of the model. We refer to the corresponding transitions' names in parentheses when explaining the movements of aircraft in the following. In Section 2.5, we will examine the details of the important transitions.

An aircraft can enter the logical zones by entering either holding3 (VerticalEntry) or lez (LateralEntry) of either side. An aircraft that has entered holding3 descends to holding2 of the same side (HoldingPatternDiscend), and initiates the approach to the ground from there (VerticalApproachInitiation). An aircraft that has entered lez can go directly to the approach area if specific conditions are met; otherwise, it first goes to holding2 (LateralApproachInitiation). Every aircraft that initiates the approach first goes to the base zone of the same side where it initiates the approach. Once aircraft enter base, they merge into intermediate (Merging), then proceed to final (FinalSegment) and land on runway (Landing). This progression of the movement of aircraft is depicted in Figure 3.

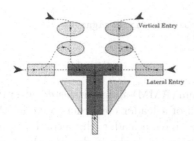
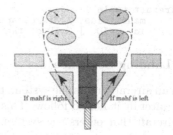

Fig. 3. Paths of aircraft   **Fig. 4.** Paths of aircraft that have missed the approach

An aircraft may miss the approach to the ground at the final zone. In such a case, it once again goes back to a zone where it can initiate the approach again, and make the next try to land.

An aircraft has to determine the side of an initiation area to which it has to go in case it misses the approach. For this purpose, the assignment of the side, called the *"mahf (missed approach holding fix)"* is given by the AMM to an aircraft when it enters the system, based on a system variable nextmahf. The variable nextmahf is of type Side, and is used by the AMM to keep track of the last assignment of mahf to aircraft that have entered the system. The system flips the value of nextmahf, either from left to right or vice versa, every time it assigns the mahf to an aircraft. This produces an *alternate assignment* of the left side and the right side to the aircraft in the landing sequence.

In the logical zones, a missed aircraft, with the reassignment as stated above, first goes to maz of the side assigned as its mahf (MissedApproach), and from there it goes back to either holding2 or holding3 of the side of maz where it leaves (LowestAvailableAltitude). Whether it goes to holding2 or holding3 is determined by the situation at the moment it leaves maz. These paths for aircraft that have missed the approach are shown in Figure 4.

2.5   Transitions

Twelve transitions are defined in the model based on the original procedures in SATS. Each one represents either a movement of an aircraft from one logical zone to another, an entry of an aircraft into the logical zones, or a removal of an aircraft from the logical zones.

Some transitions have an attribute of Side because they can be performed either from the right side or the left side of the airport. For example, VerticalApproachInitiation(right) represents the approach initiation of an aircraft from holding2(right).

Each transition has its own *precondition*. A transition can occur only when its precondition is satisfied. We say that a transition is *enabled* at a particular state of the model if its precondition is satisfied in that state.

One interesting notion in the SATS concept that the precondition of some transitions refers to is the *potential number of aircraft*. The potential number of aircraft in the initiation area of side σ counts not only the *actual* number of aircraft in that area, but also the number of *potential aircraft* that may possibly come to the area σ if they miss the approach, that is, aircraft outside of that area that are assigned σ as its mahf. The potential number of aircraft is expressed by the function virtual as follows, where assigned(zone,side) is the function to calculate the number of aircraft assigned side in zone.

```
virtual(z:zone_map,side:Side): nat =
    length(z(holding3(side))) + length(z(holding2(side))) +
    length(z(lez(side))) + length(z(maz(side))) +
    assigned(z(holding3(opposite(side))),side) +
    assigned(z(holding2(opposite(side))),side) +
    assigned(z(lez(opposite(side))),side) +
    assigned(z(maz(opposite(side))),side) +
    assigned(z(base(right)),side)+assigned(z(base(left)),side)+
    assigned(z(intermediate),side) + assigned(z(final),side)
```

To help a reader's intuition toward why the protocol has the rules represented by the preconditions of the transitions, here we briefly present some of the safety properties of the model that we will prove.

We will prove upper bounds on the numbers of aircraft in the vertical and lateral initiation areas (holding2, holding3, and lez): there is at most one aircraft in each of these zones. Now a reader may easily understand, for instance, why it is reasonable that the precondition of entry and descend transitions checks the emptiness of the zone that an aircraft goes to.

On the other hand, a more complicated precondition is defined for other transitions: for example, some preconditions refer to the potential number of aircraft, or whether the leader of the moving aircraft is in a specific area of the logical zones. We have to make use of these more complicated preconditions in order to prove the bound on the number of aircraft in some specific zone such as maz. This complication comes from the fact that, the transition representing a missed approach does not have a "guard" in a precondition that prevents the transition from being performed. This is quite reasonable, considering the real system: an aircraft cannot just assume some specific condition that prevents it from missing the approach. For this reason, some of the main properties we will prove do not immediately follow from the preconditions of the transitions, and thus we need a more intelligent way to prove them.

We present an IOA code for the SATS aircraft landing protocol in the following. It is actually described in the subset of the timed I/O automata specification language [6]. It imports a vocabulary called SatsVocab, which appear in the extended paper [5]. The vocabulary defines types and auxiliary functions that the automaton definition uses. In this paper, we give an informal description of these types and functions. The functions in_queue?(a,q) and on_zone?(q,a) are predicates that checks if aircraft a is in q. We just have two predicates to differentiate zones and sequences, which are intrinsically same in our model. We use on_approach?(a) to check if aircraft a is on the approach, and use on_approach?(side) to check if there is an aircraft assigned side in the approach area. The predicate on_zones?(a) is to check if aircraft a is in the operation area.

Here, we examine some important transitions to prove the main properties.

VerticalEntry: A newly entering aircraft is assigned its mahf from the system. As we explained before, the assignment is determined according to nextmahf (see the definition of the function aircraft). Also, a unique ID is given to a new aircraft when it enters the system. The uniqueness of its ID is guaranteed by the part of the precondition that is universally quantified. The precondition also checks the condition on the potential number of aircraft in the initiation area of the side where the new aircraft enters (virtual($side$)), as well as the emptiness of some zones. In a real system, this information is given by the Airport Management Module, which typically resides at the airport ground.

LateralEntry: It has a definition analogous to VerticalEntry. Note, however, that the precondition checks if the value of virtual($side$) is zero. It implies that, in the state of the model that this transition is enabled, there is no aircraft in that area, and also no aircraft assigned $side$ as its mahf outside of the area.

VerticalApproachInitiation: An aircraft initiates the approach from holding2 by this transition. Note that the precondition checks if the moving aircraft is either the first aircraft of the landing sequence (first_in_seq?(a)), or its leader aircraft has already initiates the approach (that is, it is in the approach area: on_approach?(leader(a,landing_seq))). This precondition is used as the "threshold" that delays the final approach initiation to the ground until when the safe separation of the aircraft in the system is guaranteed.

LateralApproachInitiation: The transition is different from VerticalApproachInitiation, in that it is always enabled whenever lez is not empty. Nevertheless, the aircraft can directly proceed to base only when specific conditions, which are equivalent to the precondition of VerticalApproach- Initiation, are met. Otherwise, the aircraft first moves to holding2.

MissedApproach: This transition is enabled whenever final is not empty. It reflects that there is no "guard" that prevents an aircraft from missing the approach, as discussed before. A missed aircraft gets reassigned its mahf according to nextmahf (see the definition of the function reassign), and is added to one of the maz zones according to its mahf before the reassignment. In the landing sequence, the aircraft is removed from the head of the sequence, and added to the end of it with the reassignment. The variable nextmahf is flipped in this case as well, so that the alternate assignment will be preserved even in case some aircraft miss the approach.

automaton SATS
imports SatsVocab

signature
   internal
        VerticalEntry(ac:Aircraft, id:ID, $side$:Side),
        LateralEntry(ac:Aircraft, id:ID, $side$:Side),
        HoldingPatternDescend(ac:Aircraft,$side$:Side),
        VerticalApproachInitiation(ac:Aircraft,$side$:Side),
        LateralApproachInitiation(ac:Aircraft,$side$:Side),
        Merging(ac:Aircraft,$side$:Side),
        Exit(ac:Aircraft),
        FinalSegment(ac:Aircraft),
        Landing(ac:Aircraft),
        Taxiing(ac:Aircraft),
        MissedApproach(ac:Aircraft),
        LowestAvailableAltitude(ac:Aircraft,$side$:Side)

states
    zones : zone_map, % mapping from a zone name to a zone
    nextmahf : Side, % Next missed approach holding fix
    landing_seq : queue % landing sequence is defined as a queue
    initially
        zones = initialZones $\wedge$
        nextmahf = right $\wedge$
        landing_seq = empty

   let
        %% access to the state components
        holding3($side$: Side) = zones[holding3($side$)];
        holding2($side$: Side) = zones[holding2($side$)];
        lez($side$: Side) = zones[lez($side$)];
        maz($side$: Side) = zones[maz($side$)];
        base($side$: Side) = zones[base($side$)];
        intermediate = zones[intermediate];
        final = zones[final];
        runway = zones[runway];

        %% first aircraft in the landing sequence?
        first_in_seq?(a:Aircraft) = (a = first(landing_seq));

        %% definig functions on a zone_map as functions on a state
        on_approach?(a:Aircraft) = on_approach?(zones, a);
        on_approach?($side$:Side) = on_approach?(zones,$side$);
        actual($side$:Side) = actual(zones,$side$);
        virtual($side$:Side) = virtual(zones,$side$);

        %% new aircraft
        aircraft($side$:Side, id_-:ID) = [IF empty?(landing_seq) THEN $side$ ELSE nextmahf, id_-];

        %% reassign aircraft
        reassign(a:Aircraft) = set_mahf(a, IF empty?(landing_seq) THEN a.mahf ElSE nextmahf);

        %% the first aircraft of z_from moves to z_to in $zones\_$
        move(z_from, z_to: z_name, $zones\_$: zone_map | $z\_from \neq z\_to \wedge \neg$ empty?(z_from)) =
            assign(assign($zones\_$, z_to, add($zones\_[z\_to]$, first($zones\_[z\_from]$))),
                z_from, rest($zones\_[z\_from]$))

        %% new aircraft enters a zone
        enter(z_enter: z_name, $side$:Side, id:ID, $zones\_$:zone_map) =
            assign($zones\_$, z_enter, add(zones[z_enter], aircraft($side$,id)));

transitions

internal VerticalEntry($a, id, side$)
pre virtual($side$) < 2 $\wedge$
    $\neg$on_approach?($side$) $\wedge$
    empty?(maz($side$)) $\wedge$
    empty?(lez($side$)) $\wedge$
    empty?(holding3($side$)) $\wedge$
    a = aircraft($side,id$) $\wedge$
    $\forall$ac: Aircraft
    ((on_zones?(ac) $\vee$
        in_queue?(ac, landing_seq) $\vee$
        on_zone?(runway, ac)) $\Rightarrow$ ac.id $\neq id$)
eff zones := enter(holding3($side$),$side,id$,zones);
    landing_seq := add(landing_seq, a);
    nextmahf := opposite(a.mahf);

internal LateralEntry($a, id, side$)
pre virtual($side$) = 0 $\wedge$
    a = aircraft($side,id$) $\wedge$
    $\forall$ac: Aircraft
    ((on_zones?(ac) $\vee$
        in_queue?(ac, landing_seq) $\vee$
        on_zone?(runway, ac)) $\Rightarrow$ ac.id $\neq id$)
eff zones := enter(lez($side$),$side,id$,zones);
    landing_seq := add(landing_seq,a);
    nextmahf := opposite(a.mahf);

internal HoldingPatternDescend($a, side$)
pre $\neg$(empty?(holding3($side$))) $\wedge$
    a = first(holding3($side$)) $\wedge$
    empty?(holding2($side$))
eff zones:=
    move(holding3($side$),holding2($side$),zones)

internal VerticalApproachInitiation($a, side$)
pre $\neg$(empty?(holding2($side$))) $\wedge$
    a = first(holding2($side$)) $\wedge$
    length(base(opposite($side$))) $\leq$ 1 $\wedge$
    (first_in_seq?(a) $\vee$
        on_approach?(leader(a,landing_seq)))
eff zones :=
    move(holding2($side$),base($side$),zones)

internal LateralApproachInitiation($a, side$)
pre $\neg$(empty?(lez($side$))) $\wedge$
    a = first(lez($side$))
eff IF length(base(opposite($side$))) $\leq$ 1 $\wedge$
        (first_in_seq?(a) $\vee$
        on_approach?(leader(a,landing_seq)))
    THEN
        zones :=
        move(lez($side$),base($side$),zones)
    ELSE
        zones :=
        move(lez($side$),holding2($side$),zones)
    FI

internal Merging($a, side$)
pre $\neg$(empty?(base($side$))) $\wedge$
    a = first(base($side$)) $\wedge$
    (first_in_seq?(a) $\vee$
    on_zone?(intermediate,
        leader(a,landing_seq)) $\vee$
    on_zone?(final,leader(a,landing_seq)))
eff zones := move(base($side$),intermediate,zones)

internal Exit(a)
pre $\neg$(empty?(intermediate)) $\wedge$
    $\neg$(empty?(landing_seq)) $\wedge$
    a = first(intermediate) $\wedge$
    first_in_seq?(a)
eff zones:=
    assign(zones,intermediate,rest(intermediate));
    landing_seq := rest(landing_seq)

internal FinalSegment(a)
pre $\neg$(empty?(intermediate)) $\wedge$
    a = first(intermediate)
eff zones := move(intermediate, final, zones)

internal Landing(a)
pre $\neg$(empty?(final)) $\wedge$
    $\neg$(empty?(landing_seq)) $\wedge$
    a = first(final) $\wedge$
    empty?(runway)
eff zones := move(final,runway,zones);
    landing_seq := rest(landing_seq);

internal Taxiing(a)
pre $\neg$(empty?(runway)) $\wedge$
    a = first(runway)
eff zones:= assign(zones, runway, rest(runway));

internal MissedApproach(a)
pre $\neg$(empty?(final)) $\wedge$
    $\neg$(empty?(landing_seq)) $\wedge$
    a = first(final)
eff zones:= assign(zones, final, rest(final));
    zones:= assign(zones, maz(a.mahf),
        add(maz(a.mahf),reassign(a)));
    landing_seq :=
        add(rest(landing_seq),reassign(a));
    nextmahf := opposite(reassign(a).mahf);

internal LowestAvailableAltitude($a, side$)
pre $\neg$(empty?(maz($side$))) $\wedge$
    a = first(maz($side$))
eff IF empty?(holding3($side$)) $\wedge$
        empty?(holding2($side$))
    THEN
        zones :=
        move(maz($side$),holding2($side$),zones)
    ELSE
        IF empty?(holding3($side$)) THEN
            zones :=
            move(maz($side$),holding3($side$),zones)
        ELSE
            zones :=
            move(maz($side$),holding3($side$),
            move(holding3($side$),holding2($side$),
            zones))
        FI
    FI

3   The Main Properties

In this section, we present the main properties that represents the safe separation of aircraft. There are seven properties taken from the original paper [2]. In PVS, each property is expressed as a predicate over the states, and is declared as an invariant as follows:

| `Invariant_#: LEMMA ( FORALL (s:states): reachable(s) => Inv#(s));` |

where `Inv#` is the predicate that expresses the property, and # is replaced by the actual number of the property. In the following, we describe the seven properties, along with the corresponding predicates in PVS. The predicate reachable(s) checks if s is a reachable state of the system.

Property 1: The total number of aircraft in the operation area (represented by arrival_op; a formal definition is in [5]) is *at most four.*

| `Inv1(s:states):bool = arrival_op(s) <= 4` |

Property 2: The total number of aircraft in each initiation area is *at most two.*

| `Inv2(s:states):bool = FORALL (side:Side): actual(s,side) <= 2` |

Property 3: The number of aircraft in each vertical holding fix (holding2 and holding3 of each side) is *at most one.*

| `Inv3(s:states):bool = FORALL (side:Side):`
| `    length(holding3(side,s)) <= 1 AND length(holding2(side,s)) <= 1` |

Property 4: The number of aircraft on a missed approach zone (maz(right) and maz(left), respectively) is *at most two.*

| `Inv4(s:states):bool = FORALL (side:Side): length(maz(side,s)) <= 2` |

Property 5: The number of aircraft on a lateral entry zone (lez(right) and lez(left), respectively) is *at most one.*

| `Inv5(s:states):bool = FORALL (side:Side): length(lez(side,s)) <= 1` |

Property 6: If a lateral entry zone of side σ (lez(σ)) is not empty, holding2(σ), holding3(σ), and maz(σ) are all empty.

| `Inv6(s:states):bool = FORALL (side:Side):`
| `    NOT(empty?(lez(side,s))) IMPLIES empty?(holding2(side,s)) AND`
| `                                     empty?(holding3(side,s)) AND`
| `                                     empty?(maz(side,s))` |

Property 7: The total number of aircraft assigned to one side as their mahf in the operation area (represented by assigned2fix; a formal definition is in [5]) is *at most two.*

| `Inv7(s:states):bool = FORALL (side:Side): assigned2fix(s,side)<=2` |

4   Proof of the Properties

Almost all properties are proved by induction over steps of the abstract model (the length of the sequence of transitions the model ever takes), some of which need to be strengthened to make an inductive proof work.

It turns out that some properties depend on other properties, and thus we have to prove them in such an order that a proof of each property just depends on the properties that have been proved. Because of this, the order of the proof in this section does not exactly match the numbering of the properties.[3]

4.1 Properties Part 1: Properties That Can Be Proved Without a Strengthening

In this subsection, we prove the properties that can be proved straightforwardly by induction without strengthening them (Properties 1, 7, and 5).

Theorem 1. (Property 1) *For any reachable state of the abstract model, the number of aircraft in the operation area is at most four.*

Proof. By induction. The base case is easy to prove.

[Induction step]: From the induction hypothesis, the number of aircraft in the operation area is at most four in the pre state. Two transitions, VerticalEntry and LateralEntry, add an aircraft to the operation area.

First, consider the case that VerticalEntry(side) is performed. If the number of aircraft in the area is strictly less than four in the pre state, the condition holds since the transition just adds one aircraft to the area. Now suppose the number of aircraft in the area is exactly four in the pre state. From the fact that the assignments of the mahf alternate in the landing sequence, it follows that there are exactly two aircraft assigned to each side. It implies that the value of virtual(side) is at least two in the pre state considering that, from the definition of virtual, the value is always more than or equal to the number of aircraft assigned σ. This contradicts virtual(side)¡2 from the precondition.

In the case that LateralEntry(side) is performed, we can prove the condition analogously to the case of VerticalEntry(side) using the fact that the transition checks if the value of virtual(side) is zero.

Theorem 2. (Property 7) *For any reachable state of the abstract model and a side σ, the number of aircraft on the operation area assigned σ as their mahf is at most two.*

Proof. From theorem 1 (Property 1), the number of aircraft in the operation area is at most four. Since the aircraft get alternate assignments, the number of assignments to one side is at most two.

Theorem 3. (Property 5) *For any reachable state of the abstract model and a side σ, the number of aircraft on $lez(\sigma)$ zone is at most one.*

Proof. By induction. We prove it for an arbitrary side σ. The base case is easy.

[Induction step]: From the induction hypothesis, the number of aircraft in $lez(\sigma)$ is at most one. The only transition that increases the number of aircraft in the zone is LateralEntry(σ). From the precondition of it, the value of virtual(σ) is zero. It implies that there is no aircraft in $lez(\sigma)$ before the transition. Thus the bound holds after the transition.

---

[3] Since we did not know what the order of the proof should be when we defined these properties in PVS, we just listed the properties in the order as appear in this paper. Though we could have re-numbered the properties so that it matches up the order of the proof, in order to maintain the consistency with the code in PVS, we numbered them in the same order as the code.

4.2   Blocking of Aircraft

In order to prove the rest of the properties, we have to strengthen them using a notion of *blocking of aircraft* introduced in this subsection. To see an example of why an inductive proof of the properties does not work without a strengthening, let us consider Property 2. As we mentioned in Section 2.5, there is no "guard" to prevent an aircraft from missing the approach (MissedApproach is enabled whenever the final zone is not empty). Thus if there are already two aircraft in the right initiation area, for example, and there is an aircraft assigned right in final, the bound would be violated by the MissedApproach transition.

One might consider strengthening the condition using the *potential number* of aircraft introduced in Section 2, instead of using the actual number of aircraft. Since the potential number is always greater than or equal to the actual number, we could prove the property by proving the bound on the potential number. However, this approach would not work, since the potential number *can* exceed two in some reachable states, as depicted in Figure 5. In the state depicted in the figure, the potential number of aircraft in the right initiation area is *three*.

Even if the potential number of aircraft exceeds two, the above scenario would not jeopardize Property 2. The potentially problematic scenario is that *c* initiates and misses the approach after the situation in the figure. However, this scenario would not happen because aircraft *c* has the leader aircraft *b*. From this fact and the rule of the approach initiation, the leader *b* has to leave the right initiation area *before* *c* initiates the approach. In other words, the approach initiation of aircraft *c* is "*blocked*" until *b* initiates the approach. This example leads to a notion of *blocking* of aircraft. That is, if all aircraft in the left side are either assigned left, or are preceded by some other aircraft *b* in the landing sequence, no aircraft assigned right can initiate the approach from the left side until the blocking aircraft *b* initiates the approach.

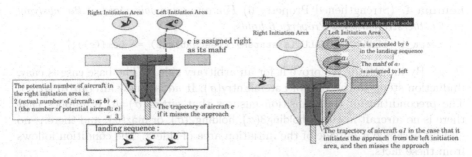

Fig. 5. The potential number of aircraft on the right initiation area is more than two

Fig. 6. The left initiation area is blocked by the first aircraft of lez(right)

The formal definition of blocking of aircraft in PVS is as follows, where precedes?(a,b,q) checks if aircraft a precedes aircraft b in sequence q, and on?(side,a,s) checks if aircraft a is in the initiation area of side in state s.

The first predicate represents the blocking condition between two aircraft (a is blocked by b), and the second predicate represents the blocking condition that implies all aircraft assigned side in the initiation area of the opposite side of side cannot initiate the approach until the blocking aircraft b initiates the approach. See Fig. 6 for an example of the blocked initiation area.

```
blocked_by?(a,b:Aircraft, side:Side, s:states):bool =
    mahf(a) = opposite(side) OR
    precedes?(b, a, landing_seq(s))
blocked_opposite_side?(b:Aircraft, side:Side, s:states):bool =
    Forall (a:Aircraft):
        on?(opposite(side),a,s) IMPLIES blocked_by?(a,b,side,s)
```

4.3   Properties Part 2: Strengthening Property 6

In this subsection, we strengthen Property 6 using the blocking condition defined in the previous subsection. We also presents a proof sketch of the strengthened property.

Consider proving Property 6 by induction for an arbitrary side σ. We have to ensure that there is no aircraft assigned σ in the approach area, since otherwise, one missed approach would violate the condition. Now in turn, to prove this condition, we have to guarantee that no aircraft assigned σ will initiate the approach when lez($sigma$) is not empty. Thus we need a blocking condition to hold in order to prevent such an approach initiation from the opposite side of σ. From the above discussion, we strengthen Property 6 as follows.

```
Lem1(s:states):bool = FORALL (side:Side):
    NOT (empty?(lez(side,s))) IMPLIES
            empty?(holding2(side,s)) AND empty?(holding3(side,s)) AND
            empty?(maz(side,s)) AND
            NOT on_approach?(s,side) AND
            blocked_opposite_side?(first(lez(side,s)),side,s)
```

Lemma 4. (Strengthened Property 6) *For any reachable state of the abstract model, the strengthened Property 6 holds.*

```
Lemma_1: LEMMA ( FORALL (s:states): reachable(s) => Lem1(s));
```

Proof. By induction. We prove it for an arbitrary side σ. The base case is easy. [Induction step]: In the case of LateralEntry(σ): It adds a new aircraft to lez(σ). The precondition of the transition ensures that virtual(σ)=0. It implies that there is no aircraft in either holding3(σ), holding2(σ), or maz(σ), and there is no aircraft assigned σ outside of the initiation area of side σ. The condition follows from these facts.

In the case of VerticalEntry(σ): The precondition checks if lez(σ) is empty. Thus the transition is disabled when lez(σ) is not empty.

In the case of MissedApproach(σ): From the induction hypothesis, all aircraft in the approach area are assigned opposite(σ). Thus the missed aircraft goes to maz(opposite(σ)), and hence maz(σ) is not affected by the transition.

In the case of VerticalApproachInitiation(opposite(σ)): The initiation area of opposite(σ) is blocked in the pre state. It follows that the aircraft that initiates the approach must be assigned opposite(σ), since otherwise it violates the order of the approach initiation. Thus NOT on_approach? is preserved.

The rest of the cases are easy to prove, using some auxiliary lemmas that state that the blocking condition is preserved by some specific transitions. (See [5] for more details).

4.4 Properties Part 3: The Key Lemma, and the Remaining Properties

In this section, we present a key lemma to prove the rest of the main properties. The lemma has the longest and most complex statement, and the proof of it is also complicated because of the substantial number of case analyses and discussions on the blocking condition. It consists of nine conditions, where two of them are from main properties, Properties 3 and 4, and the remaining seven conditions construct case analyses of the blocking situation. The formal description of the lemma appears in the next page.

The condition on each of these cases has a form analogous to the strengthened Property 6 proved in the previous subsection. Indeed, they are from the same philosophy: Consider proving Property 3 – the number of aircraft in one maz zone is at most two – by induction. Analogous to Property 6, when there are already two aircraft in maz(σ) for side σ, we have to guarantee that there is no aircraft assigned σ in the approach area, since otherwise one missed approach would violate the bound. Now, to ensure the above fact, we need a blocking condition for the initiation area of the opposite side of σ. The conditions from this discussion are represented in Case 1 of the lemma.

In the strengthened Property 6, we only have to consider one situation, as opposed to the multiple (seven) cases in this lemma. This is because the number of aircraft in lez increases just by LateralEnty, and this transition has a strict examination of the safe separation in its precondition: the potential number of aircraft in the side of entry must be zero. As we saw in the proof sketch of the strengthened Property 6, this precondition directly implies the required blocking condition.

In contrast, the number of aircraft in maz increases by MissedApproach, and as we have stated, this transition has no "guard" in its precondition to examine the current situation. It implies that we need an analogous blocking condition to hold in the pre state before MissedApproach is preformed. For this purpose, we need Case 2, which has a form analogous to Case 1, but represents the situation just before the number of aircraft in maz gets two by MissedApproach. Analogously, we need more cases to support Case 2, and then new cases to supports those cases, and so on. This iteration of finding cases ends when we reach a point where where we can guarantee the blocking condition in one case from another case that has been discovered, or from other properties that have been proved.

Following the above strategy, we constructed the seven cases, all of which depend on each other: we need some of the seven cases or two properties as an induction hypothesis to prove every single case. This is why the seven cases and two properties are defined as one lemma, and are proved together at the same time. Note that the blocking aircraft differs depending on the cases. That is, different cases uses the blocking aircraft in different positions. This represents the fact that the blocking aircraft can move by the transition, and thus we have to match up the blocking aircraft between the pre and post state.

```
%% case 1: two aircraft are in maz
Lem2_case1(s:states,side:Side):bool =
    length(maz(side,s))=2 IMPLIES
        empty?(holding2(side,s)) AND empty?(holding3(side,s)) AND
        NOT on_approach?(s,side) AND
        LET a1 = first(maz(side,s)) IN        %% first aircraft in maz
        LET a2 = first(rest(maz(side,s))) IN  %% second aircraft in maz
        LET a  = IF mahf(a1) = side THEN a2 ELSE a1 ENDIF IN
        blocked_opposite_side?(a,side,s)
%% case 2: one aircraft is in maz and some aircraft assigned 'side' are on approach.
Lem2_case2(s:states,side:Side):bool =
    length(maz(side,s))=1 AND on_approach?(s,side) IMPLIES
        assigned_approach(s,side) <= 1 AND
        LET a1 = first(maz(side,s)) IN
        blocked_opposite_side?(a1,side,s)
%% case 3: one aircraft is in maz and some aircraft are in holding2/3
Lem2_case3(s:states,side:Side):bool =
    length(maz(side,s))=1 AND
    (NOT (empty?(holding2(side,s))) OR NOT (empty?(holding3(side,s))))
        IMPLIES
        length(holding2(side,s)) + length(holding3(side,s)) <= 1 AND
        NOT on_approach?(s,side) AND
        LET a1 = IF NOT (empty?(holding2(side,s))
                    THEN first(holding2(side,s))
                    ELSE first(holding3(side,s)) ENDIF IN
        LET a2 = first(maz(side,s)) IN
        LET a  = IF mahf(a1) = side THEN a2 ELSE a1 ENDIF IN
        blocked_opposite_side?(a,side,s)
%% case 4: some aircraft assigned 'side' are on approach, and
%%         some aircraft are in hoding2/3.
Lem2_case4(s:states,side:Side):bool =
    (NOT (empty?(holding2(side,s))) OR NOT (empty?(holding3(side,s)))) AND
    on_approach?(s,side)
        IMPLIES
        length(holding2(side,s)) + length(holding3(side,s)) <= 1 AND
        empty?(maz(side,s)) AND
        assigned_approach(s,side) <= 1 AND
        LET a1 = IF NOT (empty?(holding2(side,s))
                    THEN first(holding2(side,s))
                    ELSE first(holding3(side,s)) ENDIF IN
        blocked_opposite_side?(a1,side,s)
%% case 5: both holding2 and holding3 are not empty.
Lem2_case5(s:states,side:Side):bool =
    (NOT (empty?(holding2(side,s))) AND NOT (empty?(holding3(side,s)))) IMPLIES
        empty?(maz(side,s)) AND
        NOT on_approach?(s,side) AND
        LET a1 = first(holding2(side,s)) IN
        LET a2 = first(holding3(side,s)) IN
        LET a  = IF mahf(a1) = side THEN a2 ELSE a1 ENDIF IN
        blocked_opposite_side?(a,side,s)
%% case 6: there is an aircraft that is assigned 'side' and is not blocked
%%         in the opposite side, and some aircraft are in h2/h3
Lem2_case6(s:states,side:Side):bool =
    LET a1 = IF NOT (empty?(holding2(side,s)))
                THEN first(holding2(side,s))
                ELSE first(holding3(side,s)) ENDIF IN
    (NOT (empty?(holding2(side,s))) OR NOT (empty?(holding3(side,s)))) AND
    ac_ready_to_approach?(side,s)
        IMPLIES
        length(holding2(side,s)) + length(holding3(side,s)) <= 1 AND
        empty?(maz(side,s)) AND
        NOT on_approach?(s,side) AND
        blocked_except_for_one?(a1,side,s)
%% case 7: there is an aircraft that is assigned 'side' and is not blocked
%%         in the opposite side, and one aircraft is in maz
Lem2_case7(s:states,side:Side):bool =
    LET a1 = first(maz(side,s)) IN
    length(maz(side,s))=1 AND
    ac_ready_to_approach?(side,s)
        IMPLIES
        blocked_except_for_one?(a1,side,s)
%% Lemma 2: combination of seven cases, and invariants 3 and 4.
Lem2(s:states):bool =
    FORALL (side:Side):
        Inv3(s) AND Inv4(s) AND Lem2_case1(s,side) AND
        Lem2_case2(s,side) AND Lem2_case3(s,side) AND Lem2_case4(s,side) AND
        Lem2_case5(s,side) AND Lem2_case6(s,side) AND Lem2_case7(s,side)
```

We use new auxiliary predicates blocked_except_for_one? and ac_ready_to_app-roach?. We do not have a space to present a definition, but it appears in [5].

Lemma 5. (The key lemma) *For any reachable state of the abstract model, the lemma introduced in this subsection holds.*

The complete proof appears in [5]. Due to the substantial amount of the case analyses, the length of the proof becomes as long as ten pages. We followed a way analogous to the proof of Lemma 4. As opposed to Lemma 4, however, we have to be careful about matching the blocking aircraft as stated before.
Now we prove Property 2 using Lemma 5.

Theorem 6. (Property 2) *For any reachable state of the abstract model and side σ, the number of aircraft in one initiation area is at most two.*

Proof. Suppose there are more than two aircraft in one initiation area. For any possible position of these aircraft, it violates either Property 3, 4, 5, or 6, or Case 1 or 3 of Lemma 5. This is a contradiction.

5 Conclusions and Future Work

In this paper, we first reconstructed the mathematical model of an aircraft landing protocol presented in [2], using the I/O automata framework. Though the protocol is complex, the IOA code we gave has a manageable form. Using the reconstructed model, we verified some safe separation properties of aircraft in the Self Controlled Area. All proofs of the properties have been rigorously checked using PVS. We found that using a mechanical prover is very helpful in managing a large proof for a moderately complex system such as ours.

The model in the paper is a discrete model in that the airspace and every movement of the aircraft are discretized. Using this model, we can verify the safe separation of aircraft in terms of the bound on the number of aircraft in a specific discretized area. However, to examine properties that involve more realistic dynamics of aircraft, such as the spacing between aircraft, we need a more precise modeling of the aircraft kinematics and the geometry of the airport. A continuous model, such as the one presented in [7], is suitable to deal with such properties. We are constructing a continuous model that more realistically reflects the dynamics of the aircraft than the model in [7]. We will also explore if the results in this work can carry over to the new model using a refinement.

References

1. T.Abbott, Jones, K., Consiglio, M., Williams, D., Adams, C.: Small Aircraft Transportation System, High Volume Operation concept: Normal operations. Technical Report NASA/TM-2004-213022, NASA Langley Research Center, NASA LaRC,Hampton VA 23681-2199, USA (2004)
2. Dowek, G., Muñoz, C., Carreño, V.: Abstract model of the SATS concept of operations: Initial results and recommendations. Technical Report NASA/TM-2004-213006, NASA Langley Research Center, NASA LaRC,Hampton VA 23681-2199, USA (2004)
3. Lynch, N.A.: Distributed Algorithms. Morgan Kaufmann Publishers Inc. (1996)

4. Owre, S., Rushby, J.M., Shankar, N.: PVS: A prototype verification system. In Kapur, D., ed.: 11th International Conference on Automated Deduction (CADE). Volume 607 of Lecture Notes in Computer Science., Saratoga, NY (1992) 748 – 752
5. Umeno, S.: Proving safety properties of an aircraft landing protocol using timed and untimed I/O automata: a case study. Master's thesis, Massachusetts Institute of Technology, Cambridge, MA (2006)
6. Garland, S.: TIOA User Guide and Reference Manual. (2005)
7. Muñoz, C., Dowek, G.: Hybrid verification of an air traffic operational concept. In: Proceedings of IEEE ISoLA Workshop on Leveraging Applications of Formal Methods, Verification, and Validation, Columbia, Maryland (2005)

Validating the Microsoft Hypervisor
(Abstract)

Ernie Cohen

Microsoft Corporation
Redmond, USA

Efforts to validate the Microsoft Hypervisor – a low-level program that partitions a real MP machine into a a number of virtual MP pachines – has led to some interesting formal methods developments. We'll survey some of these, including

- new algorithms for "optimal" stateless search and symbolic stateless search;
- techniques to make stateless search practical for shared memory programs, including efficient shared memory instrumentation and optimal trace replay using breakpoints;
- new techniques for model-based test generation, including the use of symbolic execution to eliminate redundancy and methods to handle invisible internal nondeterminism;
- formal models of the x86/x64 TLB and cache systems;
- verification of algorithms for efficient MP TLB virtualization, which has uncovered subtle design bugs;
- formal analyses of memory sharing between mutually distrustful partitions, which has revealed some surprising cache attacks;
- techniques for eliminating inductive constructs in first-order verification;
- techniques for specifying and reasoning about C code.

J. Misra, T. Nipkow, and E. Sekerinski (Eds.): FM 2006, LNCS 4085, p. 81, 2006.
© Springer-Verlag Berlin Heidelberg 2006

Interface Input/Output Automata

Kim G. Larsen[1], Ulrik Nyman[1], and Andrzej Wąsowski[2,*]

[1] Department of Computer Science, Aalborg University
{kgl, ulrik}@cs.aau.dk
[2] Computational Logic and Algorithms Group, IT University of Copenhagen
wasowski@itu.dk

Abstract. Building on the theory of interface automata by de Alfaro and Henzinger we design an interface language for Lynch's I/O automata, a popular formalism used in the development of distributed asynchronous systems, not addressed by previous interface research. We introduce an explicit separation of assumptions from guarantees not yet seen in other behavioral interface theories. Moreover we derive the composition operator systematically and formally, guaranteeing that the resulting compositions are always the weakest in the sense of assumptions, and the strongest in the sense of guarantees. We also present a method for solving systems of relativized behavioral inequalities as used in our setup and draw a formal correspondence between our work and interface automata.

1 Introduction

A suitably expressive interface language lies at the very center of any component-oriented development framework. Interfaces are abstractions of components, carrying all essential information necessary to establish cross-component compatibility. Instead of reasoning about components directly, one typically examines compatibility of their interfaces, while the adherence of a particular implementation to its interface is tested separately. This, not only allows for independent development of components, but also by introducing compositionality helps to combat the state space explosion problem in various automatic analyses.

Type annotations, type checking, and type inference have traditionally been used to decide compatibility of components soundly with respect to memory safety. However, static type correctness in this traditional sense fails to guarantee more elaborate properties, like correctness of communication, or deadlock freeness. This observation has inspired a long line of research on behavioral type systems and behavioral interface languages suitable for specification of highly trusted computer systems (see [1,2,3,4] and references therein for examples).

We follow de Alfaro and Henzinger [5,6] in studying an automata based interface language, or *interface automata*. Unlike them however, we explicitly separate, in the interface description, the assumptions that a component may make

---

* Partly supported by Center for Embedded Software Systems (CISS) in Aalborg.

J. Misra, T. Nipkow, and E. Sekerinski (Eds.): FM 2006, LNCS 4085, pp. 82–97, 2006.
© Springer-Verlag Berlin Heidelberg 2006

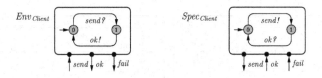

Fig. 1. $Client = (Env_{Client}, Spec_{Client})$

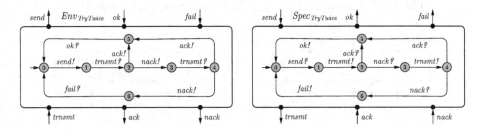

Fig. 2. $TryTwice = (Env_{TryTwice}, Spec_{TryTwice})$

about its use from the guarantees that it needs to commit to. Assumptions describe the possible behaviors of the component's external environment, while guarantees describe the possible behaviors of the component itself.

Each interface in our theory consists of two I/O automata. The first, called the *environment*, represents assumptions. The second, called the *specification*, describes guarantees. Figure 1 shows an interface for a *Client* component consisting of the automata Env_{Client} and $Spec_{Client}$. The arrows incoming to or outgoing from the box surrounding each of the automata visualize their static types, or *signatures*. The environment Env_{Client} specifies that even though the static type does allow a *fail* action, the emission of this action is disallowed for all compliant execution environments. The only legal input is *send*. One can still use the *Client* component in a context that syntactically permits *fail*, but the behavior of the *Client* is only guaranteed in environments that do not fail.

Alfaro and Henzinger model assumptions about the use of a component by the interface's inabilities to receive inputs. The output transitions of the very same interface automaton describe its guarantees. Since we separate the two, we alleviate the need for blocking. Our automata are *input enabled*—accepting any input from their signature in every state. In order to avoid clutter we usually do not draw loop transitions, which correspond to ignoring an input. There is one such implicit transition $1 \xrightarrow{send?} 1$ in Env_{Client} and three in $Spec_{Client}$.

Two interfaces can be combined into a composite interface, describing a new set of assumptions and guarantees. Interface *TryTwice*, presented in Fig. 2 can be composed with *Client*. The two components do not form a closed system, but are intended for use together with a further unspecified *LinkLayer* component.

Composition of interfaces is a central construction in any interface theory. One of our contributions is that the composition is derived systematically: we formally state requirements for it in the form of a system of inequalities, and derive a

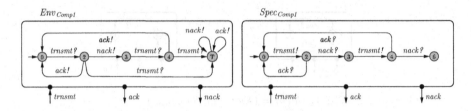

Fig. 3. $(Env_{TryTwice}, Spec_{TryTwice})|(Env_{Client}, Spec_{Client}) = Comp1$

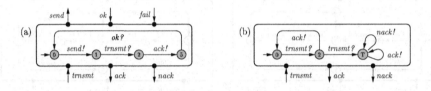

Fig. 4. (a) The environment Env_{NoNack} and (b) the environment Env_{Comp2}

result of the composition as a maximal solution of this system. Consequently properties of the composition hold by construction.

Figure 3 shows the interface resulting from composing *Client* and *TryTwice*. Later we shall explain how it has been computed. Now observe that any component legally interacting with this new interface may not send a *nack* twice in response to the *transmt* request—a simple consequence of the fact that this would make *TryTwice* respond with a *fail* to *Client*, violating the assumptions of the latter. The additional state T manifests the fact that the computed environment expresses the weakest assumptions. It allows receiving arbitrary behavior after a second *transmt* in a row, because any compliant implementation would never send it, and thus would never be affected by the subsequent behaviour.

An advantage of separating assumptions from guarantees is that one of the automata can be changed without affecting the other. Thus the same guarantees can be used for multiple interfaces. In [7] we have argued that this is useful for modeling software product lines: a family of component variants may be specified using a single specification (guarantee) and multiple environmental restrictions (assumptions). An advanced compiler may use the assumptions to derive specialized versions of the component from the same source code. Let us illustrate this with an example. Figure 4a gives an alternative environment Env_{NoNack} for the $Spec_{TryTwice}$ specification. This environment disallows the sending of a *nack* as a response to a *trnsmt* request. Any implementation of *TryTwice* is also an implementation of $(Env_{NoNack}, Spec_{TryTwice})$. If it is only used in Env_{NoNack}, then it could be automatically specialized to these specific circumstances. The error handling code could be removed as it is not needed in such a context. The composition $Comp2 = (Env_{NoNack}, Spec_{TryTwice})|(Env_{Client}, Spec_{Client})$ has exactly the same specification part as the *Comp1* composition. The resulting environment Env_{Comp2} (Fig. 4b) disallows the generation of the *nack* input even though the static type permits this.

As we have also argued in [7] the separation supports a simple declarative style of modeling assumptions: simple properties can be modeled as standalone automata and combined using the process algebraic operators of sum and product, corresponding to disjunction and conjunction of properties respectively.

An interesting theoretical side effect of our exposition, is an informal correspondence drawn between blocking and non-blocking interface theories. A single blocking interface automaton of [5] expresses both the assumptions of a component and its commitments. When a blocking interface automaton is unable to accept an input, it effectively assumes that any compatible environment will never provide it. In the theory for non-blocking systems the interfaces are composed of two non-blocking automata, and the same effect is achieved by explicitly using one of the automata for describing the permissible behavior of the surroundings.

The paper develops as follows. Section 2 defines I/O automata and interfaces. Section 3 discusses refinement of interfaces. The most central section, Section 4, is devoted to composition, while a more technical section, Section 5, is devoted to systems of inequalities used in section 4 and is a contribution in itself. But reading it is not essential for appreciating our interface theory. Section 6 draws a correspondence between interface automata and our interfaces, while section 7 discusses other related work. We conclude in section 8. A particularly interested reader can find the proofs of all our claims in an upcoming BRICS report.

2 I/O Automata and Their Interfaces

Definition 1. *An I/O automaton $S=(states_S, start_S, in_S, out_S, int_S, steps_S)$ is a 6-tuple, where $states_S$ is a set of states, $start_S \in states_S$ is an initial state, in_S is a set of input actions, out_S a set of output actions, and int_S is a set of internal actions. All of the action sets are mutually disjoint. We abbreviate $ext_S = in_S \cup out_S$ and $act_S = ext_S \cup int_S$. Then $steps_S \subseteq states_S \times act_S \times states_S$ is the set of transitions. I/O automata are input enabled: for every state s and any action $i \in in_S$ there exists a state s' and a transition $(s, i, s') \in steps_S$.*

We write $q \xrightarrow{a}_S q'$ if $(q, a, q') \in steps_S$. We often explicitly suffix external actions with direction of communication writing $q \xrightarrow{a!}_S q'$ if $a \in out_S$, and $q \xrightarrow{a?}_S q'$ if $a \in in_S$. Notice that the labels $a!$ and $a?$ still denote exactly the same action, and we can drop the suffixes whenever the direction of communication is irrelevant. We write $q \xrightarrow{a}_{/\!\!\!\!\!\!\!}$, meaning that there is no q' such that $q \xrightarrow{a} q'$.

Definition 2. *An execution of an I/O-automaton S starting in a state q^0 is a finite sequence of labels $q^0, a_0, q^1, a_1, q^2, a_2, \ldots, q^{n-1}, a_{n-1}, q^n$ such that all q^i's are members of $states_S$, all a_i's are members of act_S and for every $k = 0 \ldots n-1$ it is the case that $q^k \xrightarrow{a_k}_S q^{k+1}$. A trace σ of S is an execution ψ of S starting in the initial state, with all the states and internal actions deleted: $\sigma = \psi \restriction ext_S$, where $\psi \restriction X$ denotes a sequence created from ψ by removing symbols that are not in set X. The set of all traces of automaton S is denoted Trs_S.*

Two I/O-automata S_1 and S_2 are *syntactically composable* if their input and output sets do not overlap and their internal actions are not shared: $in_{S_1} \cap in_{S_2} =$

$outs_{S_1} \cap outs_{S_2} = ints_{S_1} \cap acts_{S_2} = acts_{S_1} \cap ints_{S_2} = \emptyset$. Two syntactically composable automata $S_1 = (states_{S_1}, starts_{S_1}, in_{S_1}, outs_{S_1}, ints_{S_1}, steps_{S_1})$ and $S_2 = (states_{S_2}, starts_{S_2}, in_{S_2}, outs_{S_2}, ints_{S_2}, steps_{S_2})$ can be composed into a single product automaton $S = S_1|S_2$, where $S = (states_S, starts_S, in_S, outs_S, ints_S, steps_S)$ and $states_S = states_{S_1} \times states_{S_2}$, $starts_S = (starts_{S_1}, starts_{S_2})$, $in_S = in_{S_1} \cup in_{S_2} \setminus outs_{S_1} \setminus outs_{S_2}$, $outs_S = outs_{S_1} \cup outs_{S_2} \setminus in_{S_1} \setminus in_{S_2}$, $ints_S = ints_{S_1} \cup ints_{S_2} \cup (exts_{S_1} \cap exts_{S_2})$, and $steps_S$ are defined by the following rules:

$$\text{if } q_1 \xrightarrow{a}_{S_1} q'_1 \text{ and } a \in acts_{S_1} \setminus acts_{S_2} \text{ then } (q_1, q_2) \xrightarrow{a}_{S_1|S_2} (q'_1, q_2)$$
$$\text{if } q_2 \xrightarrow{a}_{S_2} q'_2 \text{ and } a \in acts_{S_2} \setminus acts_{S_1} \text{ then } (q_1, q_2) \xrightarrow{a}_{S_1|S_2} (q_1, q'_2)$$
$$\text{if } q_1 \xrightarrow{a}_{S_1} q'_1 \text{ and } q_2 \xrightarrow{a}_{S_2} q'_2 \text{ then } (q_1, q_2) \xrightarrow{a}_{S_1|S_2} (q'_1, q'_2)$$

In practice unreachable states may be removed from the product, without affecting the results presented below.

Our composition (same as in [6]) differs from the standard I/O automata composition in that it applies hiding immediately. It is equivalent with the standard composition as long as each action is only shared by at most two components.

We define an interface model to be a pair (E, S) of I/O automata:

Definition 3. *A pair of I/O automata (E, S) is an interface if $E|S$ is a closed system, i.e. $in_E = outs$ and $out_E = in_S$.*

The environment automaton E drives the specification automaton S. Any implementation I of S must conform to S as long as it is receiving input that conforms to E. The behavior of I on sequences of inputs that cannot be provided by E is not constrained. We formalize this using relativized refinement:

Definition 4. *An I/O automaton I implements an interface (E, S), written $E \models I \leqslant S$, iff $out_I = outs$ and $in_I = in_S$ and $Tr_E \cap Tr_I \subseteq Tr_S$.*

3   Refinement of Interfaces

We establish a hierarchy on interfaces in order to quantify their generality.

Definition 5. *Let (E_1, S_1) and (E_2, S_2) be two interfaces with the same signatures. We will say that (E_1, S_1) is a stronger interface than (E_2, S_2), written $(E_1, S_1) \preceq (E_2, S_2)$, if (E_1, S_1) has less implementations than (E_2, S_2), so for any I/O automaton I: $E_1 \models I \leqslant S_1$ implies $E_2 \models I \leqslant S_2$.*

The refinement of interfaces can be seen as a subtyping relation in a behavioral type system for components. In such an interpretation we would say that (E_1, S_1) is a subtype of (E_2, S_2). We propose several simple sound characterizations of the above refinement that are useful in making proofs:

Theorem 1. *Let (E_1, S_1), (E_2, S_2) be interfaces with identical signatures. Then*

1. *$Tr_{E_1} \cap Tr_{S_1} = Tr_{E_2} \cap Tr_{S_2}$ implies $(E_1, S_1) \preceq (E_2, S_2)$ and $(E_2, S_2) \preceq (E_1, S_1)$*
2. *$Tr_{E_2} \subseteq Tr_{E_1} \wedge Tr_{S_1} \subseteq Tr_{S_2}$ implies $(E_1, S_1) \preceq (E_2, S_2)$*
3. *$Tr_{E_1} \setminus Tr_{S_1} \supseteq Tr_{E_2} \setminus Tr_{S_2}$ implies $(E_1, S_1) \preceq (E_2, S_2)$*

The above characterizations are convenient in establishing subtyping relations among interfaces in many concrete cases. However none of them are complete. The refinement of interfaces can be characterized in a sound and complete manner using a notion of tests that resembles failure traces of Hoare [8], but determinized, relativized with respect to the environment, and suffix closed.

Definition 6. *The set of conformance tests of interface* (E, S) *is defined as:*

$$test_{(E,S)} = \{\sigma \cdot a \mid \sigma \in Tr_E \cap Tr_S, \ \sigma \cdot a \in Tr_E \setminus Tr_S\} \cdot ext_E^* \ ,$$

where X^* *denotes the set of all finite sequences over alphabet* X.

Theorem 2. *Let* (E_1, S_1) *and* (E_2, S_2) *be two interfaces with identical signatures. Then* $test_{(E_1,S_1)} \supseteq test_{(E_2,S_2)}$ *iff* $(E_1, S_1) \preceq (E_2, S_2)$.

Without spelling out the details, we remark that a finite automaton, such that $test_{(E,S)}$ is its accepted language, can be computed in quadratic time, and can be used for testing containment in applications of the above theorem.

4   Interface Compositions

We would like to abstract compositions of components by compositions of their interfaces. For any two compatible interfaces (E_1, S_1) and (E_2, S_2) we should be able to derive an interface of their composition (E, S), the one that is implemented flawlessly by any two implementations of (E_1, S_1) and (E_2, S_2).

Two interfaces are *syntactically composable* if the I/O automata comprising them are pointwise syntactically composable. This guarantees that any components I_1 and I_2 implementing syntactically composable interfaces (E_1, S_1) and (E_2, S_2), are also syntactically composable. The question that we want to address is the *dynamic compatibility* of I_1 and I_2: can I_1 violate the environmental assumptions expressed in E_2? Can I_2 violate the assumptions in E_1?

We may be tempted to say that the composite interface is the composition of the interface parts: $(E, S) = (E_1|E_2, S_1|S_2)$. This construction, however, is unsound. It is possible to find two compliant implementations that, when composed together, violate (E, S). In order to arrive at a sound and complete notion of composition, we will state the requirements for the composite interface, and then derive the construction from them. The three requirements are: *independent implementability* [6], *mutal deadlock freeness*, and *associativity*.

Independent implementability means that (E, S) is such, that the implementations of (E_1, S_1) and (E_2, S_2) can be developed independently of each other, and their composition will implement the composition of their interfaces:

$$\text{For all } I_1, I_2. \ E_1 \models I_1 \leqslant S_1 \text{ and } E_2 \models I_2 \leqslant S_2 \text{ implies } E \models I_1|I_2 \leqslant S \ . \quad (1)$$

Mutual deadlock freeness means that any two correct implementations, when composed and embedded in an environment that obeys the assumptions of E, will not violate each other's assumptions:

For all $I_1, I_2. E_1 \models I_1 \leqslant S_1$ and $E_2 \models I_2 \leqslant S_2$

$$\text{implies } I_1 \models E|I_2 \leqslant E_1 \text{ and } I_2 \models E|I_1 \leqslant E_2 \ . \quad (2)$$

You may find it useful to refer to the flowgraph on Fig. 5a, while studying the above rule. Observe that in the composed system I_1 is indeed the environment in which $E|I_2$ operates. The composition $E|I_2$ is also the environment for I_1 and it is supposed not to violate any of the assumptions expressed in E_1.

Finally, associativity means that in whatever order compositions are applied, they give rise to equivalent interfaces:

$$((E_1, S_1) \,|\, (E_2, S_2)) \,|\, (E_3, S_3) \preceq (E_1, S_1) \,|\, ((E_2, S_2) \,|\, (E_3, S_3))$$
$$(E_1, S_1) \,|\, ((E_2, S_2) \,|\, (E_3, S_3)) \preceq ((E_1, S_1) \,|\, (E_2, S_2)) \,|\, (E_3, S_3) \ . \quad (3)$$

A disadvantage of the above requirements is that they are not constructive. They rely on quantification over all implementations, which makes them useless for computing the composition. Fortunately the quantification can be eliminated. The following theorem reduces the property of mutual deadlock freeness of all implementations to mutual deadlock freeness of the interfaces being composed:

Theorem 3. *Any environment E fulfills the requirement (2) iff it fulfills the following condition:*

$$S_1 \models E|S_2 \leqslant E_1 \text{ and } S_2 \models E|S_1 \leqslant E_2 \ . \quad (4)$$

The above reduction is very fortunate, as (4) also implies independent implementability with the choice of the guarantees component to be $S_1|S_2$:

Theorem 4. *Let (E_1, S_1) and (E_2, S_2) be syntactically composable interfaces, and E be an environment I/O automaton satisfying property (4). Then for all I_1 and I_2 such that $E_1 \models I_1 \leqslant S_1$ and $E_2 \models I_2 \leqslant S_2$ we have $E \models I_1|I_2 \leqslant S_1|S_2$.*

Consequently if we were able to find an environment E satisfying (4), then the interface $(E, S_1|S_2)$ would satisfy mutual deadlock freeness and independent implementability—a good candidate for the composition of environments. However, the environment satisfying (4) may not always exist. This is the case, if S_1 unconditionally, independently of E's behavior, violates the assumptions of S_2 expressed in E_2. In this case (E_1, S_1) and (E_2, S_2) are said to be *incompatible*.

Definition 7. *Interfaces (E_1, S_1), (E_2, S_2) are incompatible if there exists no I/O automaton E such that: $S_1 \models E|S_2 \leqslant E_1$ and $S_2 \models E|S_1 \leqslant E_2$.*

Figure 5b shows an interface *AlwaysFail*, which has a signature compatible with the signature of *Client*. Nevertheless the dynamic types of *Client* and *AlwaysFail* are incompatible in that they share only one nonempty trace, consisting of one step, and this trace ends in a deadlock.

In fact there typically exist many pairs (E, S) that satisfy all our requirements. For example an interface (M, U), consisting of a mute environment M never producing any outputs and a universal system specification U generating all possible traces, would satisfy the composition requirements of any two compatible interfaces. The interface (M, U) allows any implementation—it says that

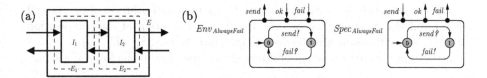

Fig. 5. (a) Flowgraph for a composition of (E_1, S_1) and (E_2, S_2). (b) *AlwaysFail*.

its implementations will behave in an arbitrary fashion (U), not allowing any external stimulation (M). Clearly, as a component interface, (M, U) is useless.

We should ensure that our composition operator produces the interface that carries over all the information available from its components. It must have the smallest possible set of implementations, while still satisfying all our requirements. Similarly, it must maximize the set of components compatible with it (as opposed to the set of components implementing it). We shall call this optimal interface *the most general*. Intuitively to achieve this optimality we need an environment E satisfying the requirements such that it is maximal with respect to trace inclusion. By increasing the set Tr_E we make it easier for components to be compatible with our interface. Similarly we make it harder to implement the composite interface, as increasing the set of traces of E decreases the assumptions that an implementation can make. The following theorem says that such a maximal E always exists for compatible interfaces:

Theorem 5. *Let (E_1, S_1) and (E_2, S_2) be two syntactically composable interfaces. If there exists an I/O automaton E enjoying property (4) then there also exists a maximal such environment with respect to trace inclusion.*

Theorem 6. *The composition operator mapping interfaces (E_1, S_1) and (E_2, S_2) to $(E, S_1|S_2)$, where E is the maximal solution of (4), is associative.*

Theorems 5–6 together with our earlier observations suggest that the interface $(E, S_1|S_2)$, where E is this maximal solution of equations (4), is even more likely to be the most general interface that we are searching for. A maximal solution of (4) can be found algorithmically for finite state interfaces. Section 5 describes a method that can be used for this purpose.

As increasing the environment E makes the interfaces more general, so does decreasing the specification S (within the limits set by the requirements). For any particular selection of E satisfying (1), no S can be smaller (relative to E) than $S_1|S_2$, because S_1 and S_2 themselves are valid implementations. So $S_1|S_2$ is the smallest possible specification of the composite interface with respect to any particular choice of E. This observation can be generalized to a claim that $(E, S_1|S_2)$ is the most general interface possible:

Theorem 7. *Let (E_1, S_1), (E_2, S_2) be interfaces. Let E be the maximal solution to (4) and let (E', S') satisfy independent implementability and mutual deadlock freeness. If (E', S') is compatible with (E'', S'') then also $(E, S_1|S_2)$ is compatible with (E'', S'').*

Having concluded that $(E, S_1|S_2)$, where E is a maximal solution of (4), is well defined and the most general, we can use it as a definition of the composition operator. We will denote this composite interface by $(E_1, S_1)|(E_2, S_2)$.

Furthermore our composition of interfaces is complete in the following sense

Theorem 8. *For compatible interfaces* (E_1, S_1), (E_2, S_2) *and any* (E', S') *satisfying independent implementability and mutual deadlock freeness:*

$$(E_1, S_1)|(E_2, S_2) \preceq (E', S') .$$

We remark that our composition would not be complete if we only required independent implementability. It seems likely from the work presented in [9] that it is indeed impossible, for our setting, to be complete in the above sense using only independent implementability. Similarly we would not be complete if we only required mutual deadlock freeness, simply because it does not restrict the S component, which can then be taken to be mute, likely yielding a smaller interface than ours. Still our composition is sound and complete with respect to both requirements combined. Requirements (2) and (3) have been introduced solely for their inherent usefulness. Their interplay guaranteeing soundness and completeness is a pleasant side effect.

Definition 8. *Let* (E_1, S_1), (E_2, S_2) *be syntactically composable interfaces. Their composition, denoted* $(E_1, S_1)|(E_2, S_2)$, *is an interface* $(E, S_1|S_2)$, *where* E *has the same signature as* $E_1|E_2$, *and is a maximal solution of (4).*

The operator of Def. 8 is associative, supports independent implementability and mutual deadlock freeness, and produces the most general interfaces.

5   Solving Behavioral Inequalities

Computing compositions of interfaces requires a method for finding solutions of systems of relativized linear inequalities. In particular we are interested in systems of inequalities of the following form:

$$\mathcal{C}(E) : \begin{cases} P_1 \models E|S_1 \leqslant F_1 \\ \quad \vdots \\ P_m \models E|S_m \leqslant F_m \end{cases} \tag{5}$$

where $\{P_i\}_{i=1..m}$, $\{S_i\}_{i=1..m}$ and $\{F_i\}_{i=1..m}$ are states of the three I/O automata P, S and F and E is a single unknown automaton. We are interested in finding a greatest such E with respect to $\leqslant$, or in reporting incompatibility between components, if no solutions exist. Since in (4) various components of inequalities come from separate automata, in order to apply the method below we need to construct three automata P, S and F as the disjoint unions of the automata that appear in the given place of the constraints in (4). We introduce three convenient mapping functions *in*, *out* and *ext* which from a state of the two automata F and S return respectively the set of input, output or external actions of the automata that this state originates from in the disjoint union computation. We will use them in the algorithm below to recover some of the signature information lost by making the disjoint union.

For simplicity of exposition we shall also assume that all I/O automata involved in the systems are deterministic. Otherwise they can be determinized without loss of information, as long as our refinement criterion is based on language inclusion. This assumption is not inherent to the method, though.

We should now state a property similar to Theorem 5, but formulated for systems of inequalities in general. We expand it to any number of constraints and do not require that all the I/O automata come from the same interfaces.

Theorem 9. *Let $\mathcal{C}(E)$ be a finite system of relativized inequalities:*

$$\mathcal{C}(E) \ : \ \begin{cases} P_1 \models E|S_1 \leqslant F_1 \\ \qquad \vdots \\ P_m \models E|S_m \leqslant F_m \end{cases}$$

If $\mathcal{C}(E)$ has a solution (an I/O automaton satisfying all the constraints), then $\mathcal{C}(E)$ also has a greatest solution with respect to trace set inclusion.

We begin with constructing a *modal transition system* [10] corresponding to $\mathcal{C}(E)$, and then choose a maximal solution from its states and transitions. From our perspective modal transition systems are automata with two transition relations $\rightarrow_{may}$ and $\rightarrow_{must}$.

Definition 9. *A modal transition system is a quadruple $\mathcal{S} = (Q, A, \rightarrow_{may}, \rightarrow_{must})$, where Q is a set of systems of constraints (states), A is a set of actions, $\rightarrow_{may} \subseteq Q \times A \times Q$ is the may transition relation, and $\rightarrow_{must} \subseteq Q \times A \times Q$ is the must transition relation, $\rightarrow_{must} \subseteq \rightarrow_{may}$.*

Systems of relativized inequalities can be seen as sets of constraint triples $\{(P_1, S_1, F_1), \ldots, (P_m, S_m, F_m)\}$ over the solution E. The constraints evolve when any of their components, including the unknown E, takes an action. This evolution comprises not only state changes of the I/O automata, but also removing and introducing constraints. Legal actions of the unknown component E in any of its states are dependent on the states of the constraints—on what all the P_i's, S_i's and all the F_i's can do. This is why we label states of our modal transition systems with systems of inequalities (sets of constraints). All the steps that are allowed by the constraints, but are not strictly required (like a possibility to produce an output) should give rise to *may* transitions in the modal transition system. While all the steps that are strictly required (like input actions enforced by input-enabledness) give rise to corresponding *must* transitions.

Formally three I/O automata P, S, F induce a modal transition system $\mathcal{E} = (Q, A_0, \rightarrow_{may}, \rightarrow_{must})$, where elements of Q are sets of constraints over states of P, S and F, enriched with a distinct primitive constraint FALSE denoting an empty set of solutions. The initial state A_0 is equal to the set $\{(P_1, S_1, F_1), \ldots, (P_m, S_m, F_m)\}$ of initial constraints, and the transition relations are defined according to the following rules:

$E \xrightarrow{a!}_{may} E'$ if and only if both of the following rules are satisfied:

For all $(P, S, F) \in E$ such that $a \in out_E \setminus in_S$
   If $\exists F'. F \xrightarrow{a!} F'$ and $\exists P'. P \xrightarrow{a} P'$ then $(P', S, F') \in E'$
   Else if $\exists P'. P \xrightarrow{a?} P'$ and $F \xnrightarrow{a!}$ then FALSE $\in E'$

For all $(P, S, F) \in E$ and all S' such that $a \in out_E \cap in_S$
   If $S \xrightarrow{a?} S'$ also $(P, S', F) \in E'$

$E \xrightarrow{a?}_{must} E'$ and $E \xrightarrow{a?}_{may} E'$ iff both of the following rules are satisfied:

For all $(P, S, F) \in E$ and all F' such that $a \in in_E \setminus out_S$
   If $F \xrightarrow{a?} F'$ and $P \xrightarrow{a!} P'$ then $(P', S, F') \in E'$
For all $(P, S, F) \in E$ such that $a \in in_E \cap out_S$
   If $S \xrightarrow{a!} S'$ then $(P, S', F) \in E'$

Each state $E \in Q$ of $\mathcal{E}$ is minimal such that it satisfies the above transition rules *and* the following *closure rules*:

For all $(P, S, F) \in E$ and $a \in ext_S \cap ext_F$
   If $\exists S'. S \xrightarrow{a} S'$ and $\exists F'. F \xrightarrow{a} F'$ and $\exists P'. P \xrightarrow{a} P'$
   then also $(P', S', F') \in E$.
For all $(P, S, F) \in E$ and $a \in ext_S \cap ext_F$
   If $S \xrightarrow{a!} S'$ and $F \xnrightarrow{a!}$ and $\exists P'. P \xrightarrow{a?} P'$ then FALSE $\in E$.

The two *may* rules discuss E making an output transition concerning an external output, or an internal communication with S respectively. The *must* rules state that E needs to accept all the inputs from the outside and from S respectively. Finally the closure rules allow S to advance without any interference with E on its own external actions. Whenever there is a possibility of violation of the relativized trace inclusion, we add false to the target state of E, hinting that E should not be allowed to make that step.

Definition 10. *The state consistency relation S over a modal transition system $\mathcal{E} = (Q, A, \rightarrow_{may}, \rightarrow_{must})$ is the maximal subset of Q such that if $E \in S$ then FALSE $\notin E$ and whenever $E \xrightarrow{a}_{must} E'$ then $E' \in S$.*

Definition 11. *A consistent set of transitions T of a modal transition system $\mathcal{E} = (Q, A, \rightarrow_{may}, \rightarrow_{must})$ with respect to consistency relation S is a maximal subset of $\rightarrow_{may}$, where whenever $(s, a, s') \in T$ then $s \in S$ and $s' \in S$.*

Theorem 10. *Let $\mathcal{C}(E)$ be a system of inequalities as required above, and $\mathcal{E} = (Q, A, \rightarrow_{may}, \rightarrow_{must})$ be the modal transition system induced by $\mathcal{C}$. Then the maximal solution of $\mathcal{C}(E)$ is an I/O automaton E such that its set of states $states_E$ is a maximal consistency relation over $\mathcal{E}$,*

$$start_E = \{(F_1, S_1), ..., (F_m, S_m)\},$$

$$in_E = \bigcup_{i=1}^{m} (in_{F_i} \setminus in_{S_i}) \cup \bigcup_{i=1}^{m} (out_{S_i} \setminus out_{F_i})$$

$$out_E = \bigcup_{i=1}^{m} (out_{F_i} \setminus out_{S_i}) \cup \bigcup_{i=1}^{m} (in_{S_i} \setminus in_{F_i}),$$

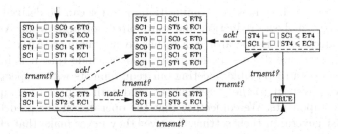

Fig. 6. The resulting modal transition system for the computation of Env_{Comp1}

and its set of transitions $step_E$ is a maximal consistent set of transitions of $\mathcal{E}$ with respect to $states_E$. If the maximal state consistency relation of $\mathcal{E}$ is empty then $\mathcal{C}$ has no solutions.

The set $\mathcal{S}$ can be found by a simple maximal fixpoint computation. In practice the consistency of the initial state may be decided in a local fashion without constructing the entire modal transition system.

Figure 6 shows the consistent part of the modal transition system induced by $(Env_{TryTwice}, Spec_{TryTwice})|(Env_{Client}, Spec_{Client})$. It can then be minimized in order to obtain Env_{Comp1}, shown in Fig. 3. Similarly $Spec_{Comp1}$ from Fig. 3 has been obtained by minimizing $Spec_{TryTwice} \mid Spec_{Client}$.

6 Interface Automata

The relation of our theory to interface automata [5,6] requires special attention, as we address several issues of that work; most importantly the representation of assumptions and guarantees within a single automaton. We clearly separate assumptions from guarantees, and the pairs of assumptions and guarantees can be constructed independently. In [6] Alfaro and Henzinger discuss static Assume/Guarantee interfaces featuring a similar split, however they do not persue the idea to the dynamic case.

In a larger perspective our work can be seen as a study of building interface theories as such: starting with a selection of the building blocks, going through requirements analysis, deriving the composition operator, and studying its generality. Let us review this process briefly. We begin with selecting important ingredients such as a component model, an interface model, an implementation relation and a refinement relation. The particular choice of input-enabled systems and (relativized) trace inclusion is not crucial for our developments. In fact we believe that a similar theory can be built using (relativized) simulation, or for timed automata. We choose I/O automata and trace inclusion because they are very different from Alfaro and Henzinger's interface automata, so we incidentally provide a component theory for a different community—the I/O automata community. At the same time our choice challenges some opinions expressed in [5,6] that building such a theory, especially supporting contravariant refinement, is impossible using language inclusion criteria or in a non-blocking setting.

Furthermore we show how the composition operator can be derived from requirements (by analysis, reduction and automated solving), while Alfaro and Henzinger introduce this operator in a rather ad hoc manner. After having derived our operator we discuss its generality, and conclude that it is indeed the most general operator possible, meeting our requirements with respect to trace inclusion, with respect to the $\preceq$ refinement, and with respect to compatibility with other components. We conjecture that the operator of our predecessors is also the most general in their setting, however they never make that claim.

Let us now draw a formal correspondance between the two interface theories.

Definition 12 (after [6]). *An interface automaton is a six-tuple $S = (states_S, start_S, in_S, out_S, int_S, steps_S)$, where $states_S$ is a finite set of states, $start_S \in states_S$ is an initial state, in_S, out_S, and int_S are three pairwise disjoint sets of input, output, and internal actions respectively, and $steps_S \subseteq states_S \times acts \times states_S$ is an input-deterministic transition relation, with $acts = in_S \cup out_S \cup int_S$.*

Notice that the transition relation of interface automata may be non input-enabled. Syntactic composability of interface automata is governed by the same rule as the composability of I/O automata, defined on p. 85. The composed interface is computed by taking a product of the two automata, and removing from it all *incompatible states*. A state of the product is an *error state* if one of its components can produce a shared output, that the other is unable to receive. A state of the product is *incompatible* if it can reach an error state by an execution over internally controllable transitions (transitions labeled with actions from: $int_{S_1|S_2} \cup out_{S_1|S_2}$).

Definition 13. *Two syntactically composable interface automata S_1 and S_2 are compatible iff removing all incompatible states from their product leaves an interface automaton with a non-empty set of reachable states.*

The function *unzip* defined below translates an interface automaton to an I/O automaton interface. If A is an interface automaton then $unzip_A := (E, S)$, where $states_S = states_E = states_A \cup \{T\}$, $start_S = start_E = start_A$, $in_S = out_E = in_A$, $out_S = in_E = out_A$, $int_S = int_E = int_A$. The transition relations of E and S are created from the transition relation of A by making it input-enabled on the respective input sets:

$$steps_E = steps_A \cup \{(s, a, T) | s \in states_A, a \in in_E, s \xrightarrow{a}\!\!\!\!\!/\,_A\}$$

$$steps_S = steps_A \cup \{(s, a, T) | s \in states_A, a \in in_S, s \xrightarrow{a}\!\!\!\!\!/\,_A\}$$

Theorem 11. *If A_1 and A_2 are two compatible interface automata, then $unzip_{A_1}$ and $unzip_{A_2}$ are compatible I/O automata interfaces.*

The *zip* function is a reverse of *unzip*: it translates an I/O automata interface into a single interface automaton, by computing the product of the two parts using the classic algorithm [11, chpt. 4.2] from automata theory: $zip_{(E,S)} := A$, where $states_A = states_E \times states_S$, $start_A = (start_E, start_S)$, $in_A = in_S$, $out_A = out_S$, $int_A = int_S \cup int_E$, and $steps_A = \{((s, e), a, (s', e')) | s \xrightarrow{a} s' \text{ and } e \xrightarrow{a} e'\}$.

Theorem 12. *If (E_1, S_1), (E_2, S_2) are compatible deterministic I/O automata interfaces, then $zip_{(E_1,S_1)}$, $zip_{(E_2,S_2)}$ are compatible interface automata.*

The fact that our compatibility only implies compatibility in the interface automata sense for unzippings of deterministic interfaces is not surprising. It is actually expected, due to the very different nature of the refinement relations used in the two theories: trace inclusion and alternating simulation [12].

Alfaro and Henzinger choose alternating simulation to support contravariant treatment of inputs and outputs. We stress that input-enabledness and relativized trace inclusion already guarantee contravariant treatment of behaviors in a very similar spirit. Still our theory somewhat strictly requires that implementations of an interface have precisely the same sort as their interfaces, so it is technically not possible to substitute a richer component in place of a simpler one, if they are the same on shared functionality. We stress that this deficiency is not inherent, while it simplifies the presentation. Contravariant signature extensions can be easily realized with relativized trace inclusion in the input-enabled setting. Instead of requiring $in_I = in_S$ and $out_I = out_S$ in Def. 3, insist on $in_S \subseteq in_I$ and $out_I \subseteq out_S$. In fact the only significant change required in later developments is the addition of a side condition to the independent implementability rule:

$$\forall I_1, I_2. E_1 \models I_1 \leqslant S_1 \text{ and } E_2 \models I_2 \leqslant S_2 \text{ and}$$

$$in_{I_1} \cap out_{S_2} \subseteq in_{S_1} \text{ and } in_{I_2} \cap out_{S_1} \subseteq in_{S_2} \text{ implies } E \models I_1|I_2 \leqslant S \ . \quad (6)$$

This is the very same side condition that Alfaro and Henzinger add to independent implementability in order to support contravariant signature extensions. It ensures that even though the implementation allows additional inputs, it will only be used as described in this interface. The other components will not communicate with it on these additional inputs.

7   Other Related Work

Our work relates directly to the original version of interface automata [5,6], which was later extended with time and resource information in [13] and [14]. To strengthen the case, we have used some examples from [6] adapting them to our framework, and aligned the terminology with [5,6] as much as possible. Another approach to compatibility for blocking-services is taken by Rajamani and Rehof in [2] targeting compatibility of web services. We work in the input-enabled asynchronous setting of I/O-automata [15], which is semantically closer to implementations of embedded systems. To the best of our knowledge similar properties have not been studied in the I/O automata community yet.

The notion of relativized refinement and equivalence, or more precisely simulation and bisimulation, is due to Larsen [16,17]. It was so far applied in the setting of protocol verification [18], automatic testing [19] and modeling software product lines [7]. Here we adapt it to a language inclusion based refinement.

The general method of solving systems of behavioral equations using disjunctive modal transition systems and bisimulation as a requirement was published in [20]. The method presented in section 5 is an adaptation of this earlier work to an input-enabled setting and language-inclusion based refinement. The original method does not assume determinism of processes in the system of constraints.

The preliminary version of this paper [21] featured a stronger definition of mutual deadlock freeness: $E|S_1 \leqslant E_2$ and $E|S_2 \leqslant E_1$. Being stronger, this formulation also implies independent-implementability, but it rules out many useful compositions as incompatible. The relativized version proposed here (2) is weaker, but still strong enough to imply independent implementability. As we have seen in the previous section, it behaves reasonably allowing roughly the same kind of compatible interfaces as interface automata. The present paper, completely rewritten, reworks the theory with this new characterization, adding associativity, refinement of interfaces, a new method for solving systems of inequalities, contravariant signature extension, and the correspondence to interface automata.

8 Conclusion

We have proposed an interface theory for distributed networks of asynchronous components modeled as I/O automata. The characteristic feature of our interfaces is an explicit separation of assumptions from guarantees. Apart from the usual engineering advantages offered by such a separation of concerns, it also allows modeling of families of interfaces implemented by software product lines.

We demonstrated that it is possible to build a reasonably behaved interface theory in an input-enabled setting, with language inclusion as refinement. We emphasize that our derivation of interface composition is systematic: we state requirements for composition and reduce the problem to finding a solution of a corresponding system of behavioral inequalities. We also discuss the generality of the constructed interface, concluding that it exhibits the weakest assumptions and the strongest guarantees that are possible with our requirements. Finally we describe a method for solving systems of inequalities arising in our setup and draw a formal correspondence between the present work and interface automata.

References

1. Igarashi, A., Kobayashi, N.: A generic type system for the pi-calculus. In: POPL 2001, ACM Press (2001)
2. Rajamani, S.K., Rehof, J.: Conformance checking for models of asynchronous message passing software. In Brinksma, E., Larsen, K.G., eds.: 14th International Conference on Computer Aided Verification (CAV). Volume 2404 of Lecture Notes in Computer Science., Copenhagen, Denmark, Springer-Verlag (2002) 166–179
3. Lee, E.A., Xiong, Y.: A behavioral type system and its application in Ptolemy II. Formal Aspects of Computing Journal (2004) Special issue on Semantic Foundations of Engineering Design Languages.
4. Lee, E.A., Zheng, H., Zhou, Y.: Causality interfaces and compositional causality analysis. [22]

 5. Alfaro, L., Henzinger, T.A.: Interface automata. In: Proceedings of the Ninth Annual Symposium on Foundations of Software Engineering (FSE), Vienna, Austria, ACM Press (2001) 109–120

 6. Alfaro, L., Henzinger, T.A.: Interface-based design. In: In Engineering Theories of Software Intensive Systems, proceedings of the Marktoberdorf Summer School, Kluwer Academic Publishers (2004)

 7. Larsen, K.G., Larsen, U., Wąsowski, A.: Color-blind specifications for transformations of reactive synchronous programs. In Cerioli, M., ed.: Proceedings of FASE, Edinburgh, UK, April 2005. LNCS, Springer-Verlag (2005)

 8. Hoare, C.: Communicating Sequential Processes. International Series in Computer Science. Prentice Hall (1985)

 9. Maier, P.: Compositional circular assume-guarantee rules cannot be sound and complete. In Gordon, A., ed.: Foundations of Software Science and Computational Structures: 6th International Conference, FOSSACS 2003. Volume 2620 of Lecture Notes in Computer Science, Springer-Verlag (2003) 343–357

10. Larsen, K.G., Thomsen, B.: A modal process logic. In: LICS, IEEE Computer Society (1988) 203–210

11. Hopcroft, J.E., Motwani, R., Ullman, J.D.: Introduction to Automata Theory, Languages and Computation. 2nd edn. Addison-Wesley (2001)

12. Alur, R., Henzinger, T.A., Kupferman, O., Vardi, M.: Alternating refinement relations. In Sangiorgi, D., de Simone, R., eds.: Proceedings of the Ninth International Conference on Concurrency Theory (CONCUR'98). Volume 1466 of Lecture Notes in Computer Science., Springer-Verlag (1998) 163–178

13. Alfaro, L., Henzinger, T., Stoelinga, M.I.A.: Timed interfaces. In Sangiovanni-Vincentelli, A., Sifakis, J., eds.: EMSOFT 02: Proc. of 2nd Intl. Workshop on Embedded Software. Lecture Notes in Computer Science, Springer (2002) 108–122

14. Chakabarti, A., de Alfaro, L., Henzinger, T.A., Stoelinga, M.I.A.: Resource interfaces. In Alur, R., Lee, I., eds.: EMSOFT 03: 3rd Intl. Workshop on Embedded Software. Lecture Notes in Computer Science, Springer (2003)

15. Lynch, N.: I/O automata: A model for discrete event systems. In: Annual Conference on Information Sciences and Systems, Princeton University, Princeton, N.J. (1988) 29–38

16. Larsen, K.G.: Context Dependent Bisimulation Between Processes. PhD thesis, Edinburgh University (1986)

17. Larsen, K.G.: A context dependent equivalence between processes. Theoretical Computer Science 49 (1987) 184–215

18. Larsen, K.G., Milner, R.: A compositional protocol verification using relativized bisimulation. Information and Computation 99 (1992) 80–108

19. Larsen, K.G., Mikucionis, M., Nielsen, B.: Online testing of real-time systems using UPPAAL. In: Formal Approaches to Testing of Software (FATES), Linz, Austria. September 21, 2004. Volume 1644 of Lecture Notes in Computer Science, Springer-Verlag (2005)

20. Larsen, K.G., Xinxin, L.: Equation solving using modal transition systems. In: Fifth Annual IEEE Symposium on Logics in Computer Science (LICS), 4–7 June 1990, Philadelphia, PA, USA. (1990) 108–117

21. Larsen, K.G., Nyman, U., Wąsowski, A.: Interface input/output automata: Splitting assumptions from guarantees. [22]

22. Hermanns, H., Rehof, J., Stoelinga, M.I.A., eds.: Workshop Procedings FIT 2005: Foundations of Interface Technologies. ENTCS, Elsevier Science Publishers (2005)

Properties of Behavioural Model Merging

Greg Brunet[1], Marsha Chechik[1], and Sebastian Uchitel[2]

[1] Department of Computer Science, University of Toronto,
Toronto, Ontario, Canada M5S2E4
{gbrunet, chechik}@cs.toronto.edu
[2] Department of Computing, Imperial College,
180 Queen's Gate, London, SW7 2RH UK
s.uchitel@doc.ic.ac.uk

Abstract. Constructing comprehensive operational models of intended system behaviour is a complex and costly task. Consequently, practitioners adopt techniques that support partial behaviour decription such as scenario-based specifications, and focus on elaborating these descriptions iteratively. In previous work, we show how this process can be formally supported by Modal Transition Systems (MTSs), observational refinement, and model merging. In this paper, we study a number of properties of merging MTSs and give insights on the implications these results have on engineering and reasoning about behaviour models. We illustrate the utility of our results on a case study.

1 Introduction

Although state-based behaviour modelling and analysis has been shown to be successful in uncovering subtle design errors, adoption by practitioners has been slow. Partly, this is due to the difficulty of constructing behavioural models – this task requires considerable expertise in modelling notations that developers often lack. In addition, and perhaps more importantly, the benefits of model analysis appear *after* comprehensive behavioural models have been built: classical state-based modelling approaches are generally not suited for providing early feedback, when system descriptions are still partial.

The problem is that state-based models, e.g., labelled transition systems (LTSs) [16], are assumed to be complete descriptions of the system behaviour up to some level of abstraction, i.e., the state machine is assumed to completely describe the system behaviour with respect to a fixed alphabet of actions. This completeness assumption is limiting, particularly if state-based modeling is to be adopted in iterative development processes [2], processes that adopt use-case and scenario-based specifications (e.g., [6]), or that are viewpoint-oriented [12].

In such development contexts, a more appropriate type of state-based model is one in which currently unknown aspects of behavior are explicitly modelled, distinguishing between positive, negative and unknown behaviours. Positive behaviours are those the system is expected to exhibit; negative behaviours are those the system is expected to never exhibit; unknown behaviours could become positive or negative, but the choice has not yet been made. State-based models that

J. Misra, T. Nipkow, and E. Sekerinski (Eds.): FM 2006, LNCS 4085, pp. 98–114, 2006.
© Springer-Verlag Berlin Heidelberg 2006

distinguish between these kinds of behaviour are referred to as *partial behavioural models*. A number of such models exist and promising results on their use to support incremental modelling and viewpoint analysis has been reported (e.g. Partial Labelled Transition Systems (PLTSs) [28], Modal Transition Systems (MTSs) [20,27], Mixed Transition Systems [8] and multi-valued Kripke structures [5]).

Our work focuses on MTSs. These models have been studied in depth (e.g. [20,15]) and are equipped with a notion of refinement that captures the idea of elaboration of a partial description into a more comprehensive one, in which some knowledge about the unknown behaviour of the system has been gained and modeled as either positive or negative behavior.

A logical extension to the notion of refinement is that of *model merging* — a process that allows integration of what is known about the behaviour of a system as modelled by different MTSs. Model merging supports putting together partial behavioural descriptions of the same system but given from two different perspectives, possibly by different stakeholders with different viewpoints [12], describing different, yet overlapping, aspects of the same system.

In our previous work [27], we introduce the notion of merging and argue that the core concept underlying model merging is that of common observational refinement. Note that composition of behavioural models is not a novel idea (e.g. [23]); however, focus has been on *parallel* composition which describes how two *different* components work together. In the context of model elaboration, we are interested in composing two partial descriptions of the *same* component to obtain a more elaborate version of both original partial descriptions.

In this paper, we aim to provide the necessary support for using merge in practice by answering several fundamental questions: When can two systems be merged? When is merge unique (i.e., when can the merging process be automated)? What kinds of properties are preserved in a merge? How can complex models be merged?

The rest of this paper is organized as follows. After reviewing the background material in Section 2, we provide, in Section 3, conditions for existence and uniqueness of merge. We study algebraic properties of merging in Section 4, both for the case when a unique merge exists and for the case when it yields one of several possible merges, and apply results of this paper to a case study in Section 5. We conclude with a discussion, summary, and directions for future research in Section 6. Proofs of the results in this paper are available in [3].

2 Background

In this section, we briefly review definitions of MTSs, define a 3-valued counterpart to weak μ-calculus, review definitions of merge, and fix the notation. For detailed explanations and discussion, refer to [27,3].

2.1 Transition Systems

We use the standard notion of labelled transition systems (LTS) and their extensions, modal transition systems (MTSs), which capture partial behavior.

Definition 1. *Let* States *be a universal set of states,* Act *be a universal set of observable action labels, and* $Act_\tau = Act \cup \{\tau\}$. *An LTS is a tuple* $P = (S, L, \Delta, s_0)$, *where* $S \subseteq$ States *is a finite set of states,* $L \subseteq Act_\tau$ *is a set of labels,* $\Delta \subseteq (S \times L \times S)$ *is a transition relation, and* $s_0 \in S$ *is the initial state. We use* $\alpha P = L \setminus \{\tau\}$ *to denote the communicating alphabet (vocabulary) of* P.

Definition 2. *An MTS* M *is a structure* $(S, L, \Delta^r, \Delta^p, s_0)$, *where* $\Delta^r \subseteq \Delta^p$, (S, L, Δ^r, s_0) *is an LTS representing* required *transitions of the system and* (S, L, Δ^p, s_0) *is an LTS representing its* possible *(but not necessarily required) transitions. We use* $\alpha M = L \setminus \{\tau\}$ *to denote the communicating alphabet of* M.

Given an MTS $M = (S, L, \Delta^r, \Delta^p, s_0)$, M has a required transition on ℓ (denoted $M \xrightarrow{\ell}_r M'$) if $M' = (S, L, \Delta^r, \Delta^p, s_0')$ and $(s_0, \ell, s_0') \in \Delta^r$. Similarly, M has a maybe transition on ℓ ($M \xrightarrow{\ell}_m M'$) if $(s_0, \ell, s_0') \in \Delta^p - \Delta^r$. $M \xrightarrow{\ell}_p M'$ means $(s_0, \ell, s_0') \in \Delta^p$. For an MTS M, M_n denotes changing the initial state to n. For $\gamma \in \{r, p\}$, we write $M \xRightarrow{\epsilon}_\gamma M'$ to denote $M(\xrightarrow{\tau}_\gamma)^* M'$, and $M \xRightarrow{\epsilon}_m M'$ to denote $M(\xRightarrow{\epsilon}_p)(\xrightarrow{\tau}_m)(\xRightarrow{\epsilon}_p)M'$, i.e., there is at least one maybe transition on τ. For $\ell \neq \tau$ and $\gamma \in \{r, p\}$, we write $M \xRightarrow{\epsilon}_\gamma M'$ to denote $M(\xRightarrow{\epsilon}_\gamma)(\xrightarrow{\ell}_\gamma)(\xRightarrow{\epsilon}_\gamma)M'$, and $M \xRightarrow{\epsilon}_m M'$ to denote $M(\xRightarrow{\epsilon}_m)(\xrightarrow{\ell}_p)(\xRightarrow{\epsilon}_p)M'$ or $M(\xRightarrow{\epsilon}_p)(\xrightarrow{\ell}_m)(\xRightarrow{\epsilon}_p)M'$, i.e., the maybe transition precedes or is on ℓ along the path from M to M'. For $\ell \in Act_\tau$, let $\hat{\ell} = \ell$ if $\ell \neq \tau$ and $\hat{\ell} = \epsilon$ if $\ell = \tau$. For $\gamma \in \{r, m, p\}$ and $\ell \in Act_\tau$, we often write $s \xrightarrow{\ell}_\gamma s'$ to mean $M_s \xrightarrow{\ell}_\gamma M_{s'}$ and similarly for $\Rightarrow_\gamma$. Transitions on the thick arrow $\Rightarrow_\gamma$ are referred to as *observable* transitions.

Figure 3 depicts two MTS models, $\mathcal{A}$ and $\mathcal{B}$. The initial state of an MTS is labeled 0, unless stated otherwise, and maybe transitions are denoted with a question mark following the label, and transitions on sets are short for a single transition on every element of the set. Note that all transitions in model $\mathcal{B}$ are required transitions, and is thus an LTS as well.

We capture the notion of elaboration of a partial description into a more comprehensive one using *observational refinement*:

Definition 3. N *is an* observational refinement *of* M, *written* $M \preceq_o N$, *if* $\alpha M = \alpha N$ *and* (M, N) *is contained in some refinement relation* $R \subseteq \wp \times \wp$ *for which the following holds for all* $\ell \in Act_\tau$:

$$1. (M \xrightarrow{\hat{\ell}}_r M') \implies (\exists N' \cdot N \xRightarrow{\hat{\ell}}_r N' \wedge (M', N') \in R)$$
$$2. (N \xrightarrow{\ell}_p N') \implies (\exists M' \cdot M \xRightarrow{\hat{\ell}}_p M' \wedge (M', N') \in R)$$

For example, $\mathcal{A} \preceq_o \mathcal{B}$ (see Figure 3) because $\mathcal{B}$ preserves the required behaviour of $\mathcal{A}$, and $\mathcal{A}$ can simulate the possible behaviour of $\mathcal{B}$.

In this paper, we use refinement to mean observational refinement, unless otherwise stated. Two models are *observationally equivalent* ($\equiv_o$) if they refine each other. We denote by $M@X$ the result of restricting αM to X, i.e., replacing actions in $Act \setminus X$ with τ and reducing αM to X.

$$\text{TD } \frac{M \xrightarrow{\ell}_r M'}{M\|N \xrightarrow{\ell}_r M'\|N} \ell \notin \alpha N \qquad \text{MT } \frac{M \xrightarrow{\ell}_m M', \; N \xrightarrow{\ell}_r N'}{M\|N \xrightarrow{\ell}_m M'\|N'} \ell \neq \tau \qquad \text{MD } \frac{M \xrightarrow{\ell}_m M'}{M\|N \xrightarrow{\ell}_m M'\|N} \ell \notin \alpha N$$

$$\text{TT } \frac{M \xrightarrow{\ell}_r M', \; N \xrightarrow{\ell}_r N'}{M\|N \xrightarrow{\ell}_r M'\|N'} \ell \neq \tau \qquad \text{MM } \frac{M \xrightarrow{\ell}_m M', \; N \xrightarrow{\ell}_m N'}{M\|N \xrightarrow{\ell}_m M'\|N'} \ell \neq \tau$$

Fig. 1. Rules for parallel composition

Definition 4. *Let M and N be MTSs where $M = (S_M, L_M, \Delta^r_M, \Delta^p_M, s_{0M})$ and $N = (S_N, L_N, \Delta^r_N, \Delta^p_N, s_{0N})$. Then parallel composition ($\|$) is a symmetric operator such that $M\|N$ is an MTS ($S_M \times S_N$, $L_M \cup L_N$, Δ^r, Δ^p, (s_{0M}, s_{0N})), where Δ^r and Δ^p are the smallest relations that satisfy the rules given in Figure 1.*

2.2   The Logic $\mathcal{L}^w_\mu$

While shown in [15] to characterize strong refinement, the 3-valued counterpart to μ-calculus ($\mathcal{L}_\mu$) [17] is not well-suited for describing the observable behaviour of an MTS and does not characterize *observational* refinement, because it makes no distinction between an observable action and τ. Instead, we define a 3-valued extension of *weak μ-calculus* ($\mathcal{L}^w_\mu$), which does make such a distinction. The 2-valued version of this logic has been shown to be a useful logic for expressing properties of LTSs in [26].

3-valued $\mathcal{L}^w_\mu$ enables a formula to evaluate to **t** (*true*), **f** (*false*), or $\perp$ (*maybe*). For a set of fixed point variables *Var*, $a \in Act_\tau$ and $Z \in Var$, an $\mathcal{L}^w_\mu$ formula ϕ has the grammar $\phi \triangleq \mathbf{t} \mid \mathbf{f} \mid \perp \mid Z \mid \neg\phi \mid \phi \wedge \phi \mid \phi \vee \phi \mid \langle a \rangle_o \phi \mid [a]_o \phi \mid \mu Z.\phi \mid \nu Z.\phi$, where $\langle a \rangle_o$ and $[a]_o$ are the *next* operators with intended meanings "exists a next state reachable via an observable transition on a" and "for all next states reachable via an observable transition on a", respectively. We write $\phi(Z)$ to denote a formula that might contain free occurrences of the variable Z. μ and ν represent the least and greatest fixed points, respectively.

Let ϕ be a formula in $\mathcal{L}^w_\mu$, $M = (S_M, L_M, \Delta^r_M, \Delta^p_M, s_0)$ be an MTS, and $e_1, e_2 :$ *Var* $\rightarrow \mathcal{P}(S_M)$ be *environments* mapping fixed point variables to sets of states. $[\![\phi]\!]^\top_{e_1}$ ($[\![\phi]\!]^\perp_{e_2}$) denotes the set of states in M where ϕ is *true* (*false*). The set of states where ϕ is *maybe* is then $S_M \backslash ([\![\phi]\!]^\top_{e_1} \cup [\![\phi]\!]^\perp_{e_2})$ (i.e., ϕ is not *true* or *false*).

Definition 5. (3-valued Semantics of $\mathcal{L}^w_\mu$) *For an MTS M, a formula ϕ in $\mathcal{L}^w_\mu$, and environments e_1 and e_2, $[\![\phi]\!]^\top_{e_1} \subseteq S_M$ and $[\![\phi]\!]^\perp_{e_2} \subseteq S_M$ are defined as shown in Figure 2, where $a \in Act_\epsilon$, and $e_i[Z \rightarrow S]$ is the same environment as e_i except it maps Z to S.*

$\phi_1 \vee \phi_2$, $[a]_o \phi$ and $\nu Z.\phi(Z)$ are defined through negation: $\phi_1 \vee \phi_2 = \neg\phi_1 \wedge \neg\phi_2$, $[a]_o \phi = \neg\langle a \rangle_o \neg\phi$, and $\nu Z.\phi(Z) = \neg\mu Z.\phi(\neg Z)$. The value of ϕ in M is its value in the initial state. We omit the environments from $[\![\phi]\!]^\top$ and $[\![\phi]\!]^\perp$ to mean that e_1 and e_2 map every Z in *Var* to $\emptyset$ and S_M, respectively.

For example, the property $\langle a \rangle_o \mathbf{t}$ (which expresses the ability to perform an *observable* transition on a) evaluates to *true* in both $\mathcal{A}$ and $\mathcal{B}$ in Figure 3, even

$$\begin{array}{ll}
[\![\mathbf{t}]\!]_{e_1}^\top \triangleq S_M & [\![\varphi \wedge \psi]\!]_{e_1}^\top \triangleq [\![\varphi]\!]_{e_1}^\top \cap [\![\psi]\!]_{e_1}^\top \\
[\![\mathbf{t}]\!]_{e_2}^\bot \triangleq \emptyset & [\![\varphi \wedge \psi]\!]_{e_2}^\bot \triangleq [\![\varphi]\!]_{e_2}^\bot \cup [\![\psi]\!]_{e_2}^\bot \\
[\![\bot]\!]_{e_1}^\top \triangleq \emptyset & [\![\langle a \rangle_o \phi]\!]_{e_1}^\top \triangleq \{s \in S_M \mid \exists s' \in S_M \cdot (s \xRightarrow{a}_r s' \wedge s' \in [\![\phi]\!]_{e_1}^\top)\} \\
[\![Z]\!]_{e_1}^\top \triangleq e_1(Z) & [\![\langle a \rangle_o \phi]\!]_{e_2}^\bot \triangleq \{s \in S_M \mid \forall s' \in S_M \cdot (s \xRightarrow{a}_p s' \Rightarrow s' \in [\![\phi]\!]_{e_2}^\bot)\} \\
[\![Z]\!]_{e_2}^\bot \triangleq e_2(Z) & [\![\mu Z.\phi(Z)]\!]_{e_1}^\top \triangleq \cap \{S \subseteq S_M \mid [\![\phi]\!]_{e_1[Z \to S]}^\top \subseteq S\} \\
[\![\neg \phi]\!]_{e_1}^\top \triangleq [\![\phi]\!]_{e_2}^\bot & [\![\mu Z.\phi(Z)]\!]_{e_2}^\bot \triangleq \cap \{S \subseteq S_M \mid [\![\phi]\!]_{e_2[Z \to S]}^\bot \subseteq S\}
\end{array}$$

Fig. 2. 3-valued semantics of $\mathcal{L}_\mu^w$

though the transition on a in $\mathcal{B}$ is preceded by a τ. Additionally, the property $[a]_o \langle b \rangle_o \mathbf{t}$ evaluates to *maybe* in $\mathcal{A}$ because $\mathcal{A}_0 \xrightarrow{a}_r \mathcal{A}_1$ is the only transition on a from the initial state and $\mathcal{A}_1 \xrightarrow{b}_m \mathcal{A}_1$ is the only transition on b from $\mathcal{A}_1$.

The logic $\mathcal{L}_\mu^w$ characterizes observational refinement. In the 3-valued world, this means that an MTS M is refined by an MTS N if and only if all *true* and *false* $\mathcal{L}_\mu^w$ properties in M are preserved in N.

Theorem 1. *If M and N are MTSs with $\alpha M = \alpha N$, then:*
$$M \preceq_o N \Leftrightarrow \forall \phi \in \mathcal{L}_\mu^w \cdot (s_{0M} \in [\![\phi]\!]^\top \Rightarrow s_{0N} \in [\![\phi]\!]^\top) \wedge (s_{0M} \in [\![\phi]\!]^\bot \Rightarrow s_{0N} \in [\![\phi]\!]^\bot)$$

Finally, if M is an LTS, the semantics in Definition 5 reduces to the standard 2-valued semantics in [26].

2.3   Merging Models

The intuition behind merge is to find a more precise system by combining what is known from two partial descriptions of that system. This is a process aimed at finding a common *observational* refinement, and may require human intervention [27]. We review this process below.

Definition 6. *An MTS P is a* common refinement (CR) *of MTSs M and N if $\alpha P \supseteq (\alpha M \cup \alpha N)$, $M \preceq_o P@\alpha M$ and $N \preceq_o P@\alpha N$.*

We denote the set of CRs of models M and N by $\mathcal{CR}(M, N)$. Two MTSs, M and N, are *consistent* iff $\mathcal{CR}(M, N) \neq \emptyset$. For example, models $\mathcal{G}$ and $\mathcal{H}$ over

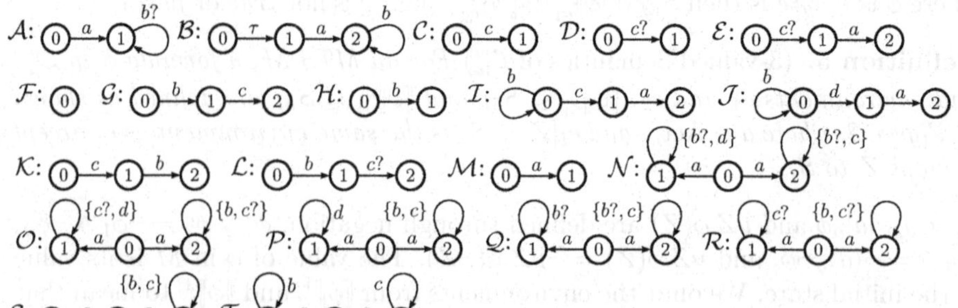

Fig. 3. Example MTSs

the vocabulary $\{b, c\}$ in Figure 3 are inconsistent because $\mathcal{H}$ proscribes the observable trace bc, whereas $\mathcal{G}$ requires it.

In [27], it is argued that the merged model should not introduce unnecessary behaviours, and is therefore based on finding a *minimal common refinement*:

Definition 7. *An MTS P is a* minimal common refinement (MCR) *of MTSs M and N if $P \in CR(M, N)$, $\alpha P = \alpha M \cup \alpha N$, and there is no MTS $Q \not\approx_o P$ such that $Q \in CR(M, N)$ and $Q@\alpha P \preceq_o P$.*

Let $\mathcal{MCR}(M, N)$ be the set of all MCRs of M and N. The *merge* of two consistent MTSs M and N, written $M + N$, is *one* of the models in $\mathcal{MCR}(M, N)$. Therefore, by Theorem 1, merge preserves all *true* and *false* $\mathcal{L}_\mu^w$ properties. Additionally, if there are several MCRs (see Section 3), merging involves a choice of the most appropriate one, which requires human intervention [27].

3 Existence and Uniqueness of Merge

In this section, we give practical conditions for existence and uniqueness of merge. If the latter condition is satisfied, the merge process can be fully automated.

Existence. Since merge is based on observational refinement, by Theorem 1, consistent systems over the *same* vocabulary should agree on all concrete behaviours, i.e., there should be no $\mathcal{L}_\mu^w$ property that is *true* in one system and *false* in the other (a *distinguishing* property).

Theorem 2. *If M and N are MTSs with $\alpha M = \alpha N$, then:*
$$CR(M, N) \neq \emptyset \Leftrightarrow (\nexists \phi \in \mathcal{L}_\mu^w \cdot s_{0M} \in [\![\phi]\!]^\top \wedge s_{0N} \in [\![\phi]\!]^\perp)$$

Distinguishing properties can be used as a form of feedback when two systems are inconsistent. For example, the property $\langle b \rangle_o \langle c \rangle_o t$ is *true* in $\mathcal{G}$ and *false* in $\mathcal{H}$, and $\mathcal{G}$ and $\mathcal{H}$ are inconsistent.

Models with *different* vocabularies must be first restricted to the shared vocabulary, but a property that distinguishes between the restricted versions of two inconsistent systems does not always exist (i.e., inconsistencies may be caused by non-shared actions). For example, $\mathcal{I}$ and $\mathcal{J}$ (see Figure 3) with $c \notin \alpha \mathcal{J}$ and $d \notin \alpha \mathcal{I}$ are inconsistent because $\mathcal{I}$ requires that b's are only proscribed after a c, whereas $\mathcal{J}$ requires that b's are only proscribed after a d. However, $\mathcal{I}@(\alpha \mathcal{I} \cap \alpha \mathcal{J})$ $= \mathcal{J}@(\alpha \mathcal{I} \cap \alpha \mathcal{J})$, and therefore no property distinguishes them by Theorem 2. Sufficient conditions for such properties to exist, and algorithms to check consistency and to construct distinguishing properties are given in [3]. Intuitively, the conditions require that following a non-shared action in one system (e.g., c in $\mathcal{I}$) does not lead to a state that is inconsistent with the other system that has not changed state (e.g., $\mathcal{I}_1$ is inconsistent with $\mathcal{J}_0$). This makes sense because the non-shared action is unobservable to the other system.

Uniqueness. When $|\mathcal{MCR}(M, N)| = 1$ (up to observational equivalence), the unique merge is called the *least common refinement* (LCR), denoted $\mathcal{LCR}_{M,N}$.

One way that multiple incomparable MCRs may exist is if there are several ways of merging behaviours that correspond to non-deterministic choices. For example, consider models Q and R in Figure 3 with vocabulary $\{a, b, c\}$. Both Q and R have two non-equivalent successors on a from the initial state, i.e., $Q \xrightarrow{a}_r Q_1$ and $Q \xrightarrow{a}_r Q_2$ such that $Q_1 \neq_o Q_2$, and similarly for R. However, both of Q_1 and Q_2 are consistent with R_1 and R_2. In particular, S is in $\mathcal{MCR}(Q, R)$ and corresponds to merging Q_1 with R_1, and Q_2 with R_2, whereas T corresponds to merging Q_1 with R_2, and Q_2 with R_1. Since $S \neq_o T$, $\mathcal{LCR}_{Q,R}$ does not exist. Sufficient conditions that restrict the existence of such choices, e.g., requiring that choices similar to those available with Q_1, Q_2, R_1, and R_2 lead to equivalent behaviours, have been given in [3] and are omitted here due to space limitations. The conditions are consequences of the modelling notation: non-deterministic choice could be abstracting different aspects of the system, and hence, choices could be composed in different ways, leading to multiple MCRs.

4   Algebraic Properties of Merge

In practice, merging is likely to be used in combination with refinement and parallel composition (for one such example, refer to Section 5). Therefore, it is essential to study *algebraic* properties of merge to guarantee that the overall process yields sensible results. For example, does the order in which various partial models are merged matter? Is it the same to merge two models and elaborate the result through refinement than to elaborate the models independently and then merge them? In this section, we aim to answer such questions. Specifically, we show that while the existence of multiple non-equivalent MCRs does not guarantee many of the properties that hold for the LCR case, the right choice of MCR among the possible merges can be made in order to guarantee particular algebraic properties, further emphasizing the need for human intervention in merge.

4.1   Properties of LCRs

Throughout this subsection, whenever we write $M + N$, we assume that M and N are consistent MTSs and $+$ results in $\mathcal{LCR}_{M,N}$.

Proposition 1. *For MTSs M, N, and P, the $+$ operator satisfies:*
1. *(Idempotency)* $M + M \equiv_o M$.
2. *(Commutativity)* $M + N \equiv_o N + M$.
3. *(Associativity)* $(M + N) + P \equiv_o M + (N + P)$.

A useful property of $+$ is monotonicity with respect to observational refinement: $(M \preceq_o P) \wedge (N \preceq_o Q) \Rightarrow M + N \preceq_o P + Q$. This allows for elaborating different viewpoints independently while ensuring that the properties of the original viewpoints put together still hold.

Proposition 2. (Monotonicity) *The operator $+$ is monotonic with respect to observational refinement.*

We now look at distributing parallel composition over merging. Assume that two stakeholders have developed partial models M and N of the intended behaviour of a component M. Each stakeholder will have verified that some required properties hold in a given context (other components and assumptions on the environment $P_1, \ldots, P_n$). It would be desirable if merging viewpoints M and N preserved the properties of both stakeholders under the same assumptions on the environment, i.e., in $(M + N) \parallel P_1 \parallel \cdots \parallel P_n$. This would be supported if $(M\|P_1\| \cdots \|P_n) + (N\|P_1\| \cdots \|P_n) \preceq_o (M + N)\|P_1\| \cdots \|P_n$; but unless some conditions are imposed on the model vocabularies, this property does not hold.

Example 1. Consider models $\mathcal{C}$, $\mathcal{D}$, and $\mathcal{F}$ in Figure 3 and assume that $\alpha\mathcal{F} = \emptyset$. $\mathcal{D} + \mathcal{F}$ is always equivalent to $\mathcal{D}$, and by rule MT in Figure 1, so is $(\mathcal{D} + \mathcal{F})\|\mathcal{C}$. On the other hand, $\mathcal{D}\|\mathcal{C}$ is equal to $\mathcal{D}$ and $\mathcal{F}\|\mathcal{C}$ is equal to $\mathcal{C}$, by rules MT and TD, respectively. It follows that $(\mathcal{F}\|\mathcal{C}) + (\mathcal{D}\|\mathcal{C})$ is equivalent to $\mathcal{C}$, and hence: $(\mathcal{F}\|\mathcal{C}) + (\mathcal{D}\|\mathcal{C}) \equiv_o \mathcal{C} \npreceq_o \mathcal{D} \equiv_o (\mathcal{F} + \mathcal{D})\|\mathcal{C}$.

The desired property fails due to the parallel composition of $\mathcal{F}$ and $\mathcal{C}$. Since c does not belong to $\alpha\mathcal{F}$, parallel composition does not restrict the occurrence of c when composing $\mathcal{F}$ with $\mathcal{C}$. However, this is methodologically wrong if we assume that $\mathcal{F}$ and $\mathcal{D}$ model the same component (which is reasonable because $\mathcal{F}$ and $\mathcal{D}$ are being merged). From $\mathcal{D}$, we know that the system modelled by $\mathcal{F}$ can communicate over c. Hence, c should be included in $\alpha\mathcal{F}$; otherwise, the communicating interface between the components modelled by $\mathcal{F}$ and $\mathcal{C}$ is under-specified. Therefore, when composing two partial models in parallel, the entire interface through which the corresponding system components communicate should be in the alphabet of their partial descriptions. We therefore require that $\alpha P \subseteq \alpha M \cap \alpha N$, where $P = P_1\| \cdots \|P_n$, for distributivity to hold.

Proposition 3. (Distributivity) *If M, N, and P are MTSs such that $\alpha P \subseteq \alpha M \cap \alpha N$, then: $(M\|P) + (N\|P) \preceq_o (M + N)\|P$.*

The other direction of Proposition 3 does not hold: $(M + N)\|P \npreceq_o (M\|P) + (N\|P)$. This makes sense, as the composition of M with P may restrict the behaviours of M, for instance, making certain states of M unreachable. It is possible that $M\|P + N\|P$ does not refine $(M + N)\|P$ because inconsistencies are caused by those states of M that are unreachable in $M\|P$.

Example 2. Assume that models $\mathcal{D}$, $\mathcal{E}$, and $\mathcal{F}$ in Figure 3 are over the vocabulary $\{a, c\}$. Models $\mathcal{D}$ and $\mathcal{E}$ are consistent and their LCR is $\mathcal{F}$. So, $(\mathcal{D} + \mathcal{E})\|\mathcal{D} \equiv_o \mathcal{F}$ by the rules in Figure 1. On the other hand, $\mathcal{D}\|\mathcal{D} = \mathcal{D}$ and $\mathcal{E}\|\mathcal{D} = \mathcal{D}$, and therefore by Idempotency, $\mathcal{D}\|\mathcal{D} + \mathcal{E}\|\mathcal{D} \equiv_o \mathcal{D}$. Since $\mathcal{F} \npreceq_o \mathcal{D}$, the result follows.

In Example 2, $\mathcal{D}$ and $\mathcal{E}$ have a disagreement on a after following the maybe transitions on c, which results in the merge $\mathcal{F}$. The source of this disagreement is removed upon composing both $\mathcal{D}$ and $\mathcal{E}$ with $\mathcal{D}$, because $\mathcal{D}$ restricts the behaviour of $\mathcal{E}$ on a. The merge of $\mathcal{D}\|\mathcal{D}$ and $\mathcal{E}\|\mathcal{D}$ therefore allows more behaviours, and does not refine $(\mathcal{D} + \mathcal{E})\|\mathcal{D}$.

4.2   Properties of MCRs

In this subsection, we present algebraic properties of $+$ without assuming the existence of the LCR. The algebraic properties are therefore stated in terms of sets and the different choices that can be made when picking an MCR. Idempotence is the only property in Section 4.1 that still holds, since an LCR always exists between a system and itself. The rest of the properties discussed in Section 4.1 require some form of weakening.

Commutativity does not hold in general: if M and N are any two MTSs that have at least two different MCRs, then certainly not every $M+N$ is equivalent to every $N+M$. On the other hand, $\mathcal{MCR}(M, N)$ is always equal to $\mathcal{MCR}(N, M)$, and therefore the same MCR can be chosen.

Proposition 4. (Commutativity) $\mathcal{MCR}(M, N) = \mathcal{MCR}(N, M)$.

Associativity fails for the same reason that commutativity fails. The strongest form of associativity in terms of sets is:

$$\forall A \in \mathcal{MCR}(M, N) \cdot \forall B \in \mathcal{MCR}(N, P) \cdot \mathcal{MCR}(A, P) = \mathcal{MCR}(M, B)$$

The following example shows that this form does not hold in general.

Example 3. Consider models $\mathcal{C}$, $\mathcal{H}$, and $\mathcal{M}$ in Figure 3 and assume that $\alpha\mathcal{C} = \{c\}$, $\alpha\mathcal{H} = \{b\}$, and $\alpha\mathcal{M} = \{a\}$. Model $\mathcal{K}$ is in $\mathcal{MCR}(\mathcal{C}, \mathcal{H})$, and there is no $D \in \mathcal{MCR}(\mathcal{M}, \mathcal{C})$ such that $\mathcal{MCR}(\mathcal{K}, \mathcal{M}) = \mathcal{MCR}(\mathcal{H}, D)$.

In Example 3, $\mathcal{K}$ requires that action c precedes action b in every trace, and therefore so does every MCR of $\mathcal{K}$ and $\mathcal{M}$, since neither b nor c is in $\alpha\mathcal{M}$. However, because b is not in $\alpha\mathcal{M}$ or $\alpha\mathcal{C}$, for every D in $\mathcal{MCR}(\mathcal{M}, \mathcal{C})$, there is an MCR of $\mathcal{H}$ and D such that action c follows action b. Hence, $\mathcal{MCR}(\mathcal{K}, \mathcal{M}) \neq \mathcal{MCR}(\mathcal{H}, D)$ for *any* D in $\mathcal{MCR}(\mathcal{M}, \mathcal{C})$. In fact, Example 3 shows that there exists M, N, and P such that: $\exists A \in \mathcal{MCR}(M, N) \cdot \forall B \in \mathcal{MCR}(N, P) \cdot \mathcal{MCR}(A, P) \neq \mathcal{MCR}(M, B)$. Therefore, set equality of $\mathcal{MCR}(A, P)$ and $\mathcal{MCR}(M, B)$ for associativity is not possible. Additionally, it can be shown that fixing both A in $\mathcal{MCR}(M, N)$ and B in $\mathcal{MCR}(N, P)$ is unreasonable, as it may force incompatible decisions to be made when merging A with P and M with B [3]. Instead, the following proposition outlines two forms of associativity, without set equality, that fix some A in $\mathcal{MCR}(M, N)$ or some B in $\mathcal{MCR}(N, P)$, but not both.

Proposition 5. (Associativity) If M, N, and P are MTSs, then:

1. $\forall A \in \mathcal{MCR}(M, N) \cdot \exists B \in \mathcal{MCR}(N, P) \cdot (\mathcal{MCR}(A, P) \cap \mathcal{MCR}(M, B) \neq \emptyset)$,
2. $\forall B \in \mathcal{MCR}(N, P) \cdot \exists A \in \mathcal{MCR}(M, N) \cdot (\mathcal{MCR}(A, P) \cap \mathcal{MCR}(M, B) \neq \emptyset)$,

where $\mathcal{CR}(A, P) \neq \emptyset$ and $\mathcal{CR}(M, B) \neq \emptyset$.

Condition (1) in Proposition 5 says that for any $M+N$, there exists some $N+P$ such that the same MCR for $(M + N) + P$ and $M + (N + P)$ can be selected. Condition (2) is analogous to condition (1) with the roles of $M + N$ and $N + P$ reversed. Note that Proposition 5 reduces to Proposition 1 if all sets of MCRs are singletons (up to equivalence).

Monotonicity is also disrupted by multiple MCRs. It is not expected that any choice of $M + N$ is refined by any choice of $P + N$ when M is refined by P, because incompatible decisions may be made in the two merges. Rather, there are two desirable forms of monotonicity: (1) whenever $M + N$ is chosen, some $P + N$ can be chosen such that $P + N$ refines $M + N$; and (2) whenever $P + N$ is chosen, then some $M + N$ can be chosen such that $P + N$ refines $M + N$. Form (1) does not hold, as the following example shows.

Example 4. Models $\mathcal{D}$ and $\mathcal{H}$ in Figure 3 with $\alpha\mathcal{D} = \{c\}$ and $\alpha\mathcal{H} = \{b\}$ are consistent, and their merge $\mathcal{D} + \mathcal{H}$ may result in model $\mathcal{K}$. Also, $\mathcal{D} \preceq_o \mathcal{F}$ (assuming that $\alpha\mathcal{F} = \{c\}$) and models $\mathcal{F}$ and $\mathcal{H}$ are consistent. However, $\mathcal{LCR}_{\mathcal{F},\mathcal{H}}$ is equivalent to $\mathcal{H}$ over $\{b, c\}$, and since $\mathcal{H} \npreceq_o \mathcal{K}$, no MCR of $\mathcal{F}$ and $\mathcal{H}$ that refines $\mathcal{K}$ can be chosen.

Form (1) fails because there are two choices of refinement being made. On the one hand, by picking a minimal common refinement for M and N over others, we are deciding over incompatible refinement choices. On the other hand, we are choosing how to refine M into P. These two choices need not be consistent, leading to failure of monotonicity. This tells us that choosing an MCR adds information to the merged model, which may be inconsistent with evolutions of the different viewpoints that are represented by the models being merged. Form (2) always holds, as stated below.

Proposition 6. (Monotonicity) *If M, N, P, and Q are MTSs, then:*

$$M \preceq_o P \wedge N \preceq_o Q \Rightarrow \forall B \in \mathcal{MCR}(P, Q) \cdot \exists A \in \mathcal{MCR}(M, N) \cdot A \preceq_o B$$

Thus, once $P + Q$ is chosen, there always exists some $M + N$ that it refines, and so the properties of M and N are preserved in $P + Q$. Note that if $\mathcal{MCR}(M, N)$ is a singleton set, Proposition 6 reduces to Proposition 2, as expected. In practical terms, this means that if the various viewpoints are still to be elaborated, the results of reasoning about one of their possible merges (picked arbitrarily) are not guaranteed to carry through once the viewpoints have been further refined.

We now address distributivity in the context of multiple MCRs. Similar to monotonicity, there are two desirable forms of this property: (1) given any A in $\mathcal{MCR}(M\|P, N\|P)$, there is some B in $\mathcal{MCR}(M, N)$ such that A is refined by $B\|P$; and (2) given any B in $\mathcal{MCR}(M, N)$, there is some A in $\mathcal{MCR}(M\|P, N\|P)$ such that A is refined by $B\|P$. Form (1) does not hold, as the following example shows.

Example 5. Consider models $\mathcal{F}$, $\mathcal{N}$, $\mathcal{O}$, $\mathcal{P}$, $\mathcal{Q}$, $\mathcal{R}$, $\mathcal{S}$, and $\mathcal{T}$ in Figure 3 and assume that $\alpha\mathcal{F} = \{d\}$, and the rest have vocabulary $\{a, b, c, d\}$. By the rules in Figure 1, $\mathcal{N}\|\mathcal{F} = \mathcal{Q}$ and $\mathcal{O}\|\mathcal{F} = \mathcal{R}$, and furthermore, $\mathcal{T}$ is in $\mathcal{MCR}(\mathcal{Q}, \mathcal{R})$. On the other hand, $\mathcal{LCR}_{\mathcal{N},\mathcal{O}}$ is $\mathcal{P}$, and $\mathcal{P}\|\mathcal{F} = \mathcal{S}$, which is not a refinement of $\mathcal{T}$.

In the previous example, $\mathcal{LCR}_{\mathcal{N},\mathcal{O}}$ exists because the required transitions on d in these models restrict the choices that can be made with respect to combining the non-determinism on action a: ($\mathcal{N}_1$ and $\mathcal{O}_1$) and ($\mathcal{N}_2$ and $\mathcal{O}_2$) are consistent, but neither ($\mathcal{N}_1$ and $\mathcal{O}_2$) nor ($\mathcal{N}_2$ and $\mathcal{O}_1$) are consistent. Upon composing with

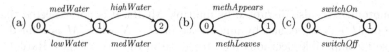

Fig. 4. The MTSs for (a) *WaterLevelSensor*, (b) *MethaneSensor*, and (c) *Pump*

$\mathcal{F}$, the source of the inconsistencies between ($\mathcal{N}_1$ and $\mathcal{O}_2$) and ($\mathcal{N}_2$ and $\mathcal{O}_1$) is removed, and consequently, $\mathcal{LCR}_{\mathcal{N}\|\mathcal{F},\mathcal{O}\|\mathcal{F}}$ does not exist. In particular, similar to Example 2 in Section 4.1, parallel composition may remove inconsistencies between M and N, allowing for more common refinements of $M\|P$ and $N\|P$.

On the other hand, Form (2) holds, and is of particular utility when elaborating models from different viewpoints (see Section 5).

Proposition 7. (Distributivity) *If M, N, and P are such that $\alpha P \subseteq \alpha M \cap \alpha N$, then:* $\forall B \in \mathcal{MCR}(M, N) \cdot \exists A \in \mathcal{MCR}(M\|P, N\|P) \cdot A \preceq_o B\|P$.

In this subsection, we showed that when $+$ does not necessarily produce an LCR, most properties studied in Section 4.1 fail to hold. Intuitively, the existence of inequivalent MCRs implies that merging involves a choice that requires some form of human intervention: a choice which is loaded with domain knowledge. This impacts the results on algebraic properties when moving from LCRs to MCRs. However, we have shown that the right choices of MCRs can be made in order to guarantee particular algebraic properties.

5   A Case Study: The Mine Pump

In this section, we show how our results support elaboration of partial models for a mine pump case study [18].

Overview. A pump controller is used to prevent the water in a mine sump from passing some threshold, and hence flooding the mine. To avoid the risk of explosion, the pump may only be active when there is no methane gas present in the mine. The pump controller monitors the water and methane levels by communicating with two sensors. In addition, the pump is equipped with a danger light that is intended to reflect the presence of methane in the sump.

We model the mine pump with four components: *WaterLevelSensor*, *MethaneSensor*, *PumpControl*, and *Pump*. The complete system, *MinePump*, is the parallel composition of these components, namely (*PumpControl* $\|$ *Pump* $\|$ *MethaneSensor* $\|$ *WaterLevelSensor*).

WaterLevelSensor models the water sensor and includes assumptions on how the water level is expected to change between low, medium, and high. *MethaneSensor* keeps track of whether methane is present in the mine, and *Pump* models the physical pump that can be switched on and off. For simplicity, we assume to have complete knowledge for these descriptions and hence model them with LTSs depicted in Figure 4, where initially the water is low, the pump is off, and no methane is present.

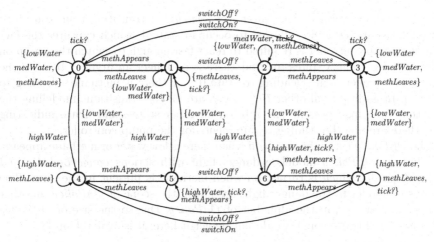

Fig. 5. The MTS for *OnPolicy*

PumpControl describes the controller that monitors water and methane levels, controls the pump in order to guarantee the safety properties of the pump system, and also maintains the status of the danger light according to the methane level. This informal description leaves open the exact water level at which to turn the pump on and off. For example, the pump could be turned on when there is high water or possibly when the water is not low, (e.g., at a medium level). The pump could be turned off when there is low water or possibly when the water is not high.

Partial Behaviour Models. We assume that there are two stakeholders for the pump controller: one with the knowledge of when the pump should be on (referred to as the on policy) and another with knowledge of when the pump should be off (referred to as the off policy).

The MTS models used to describe the policies for the pump controller use an event labelled *tick*, which models the passage of time units as kept by a global clock. All components whose behaviour is timed synchronize to this event. This corresponds to a standard approach to modelling discrete time in event-based formalisms [22]. Modelling time is required for systems such as the mine pump, where urgency of certain events, such as switching the pump off to avoid an explosion, must be captured.

Consider the *OnPolicy* model (Figure 5) provided by one of the stakeholders. This model attempts to describe how the pump controller will ensure that the pump is on in order to satisfy the safety requirements for the mine. To do so, the controller keeps track of the water level and methane presence information provided by the various sensors. States 4 to 7 and 0 to 3 are those in which the water level is high and not high, respectively, while states {1, 2, 5, 6} and {0, 3, 4, 7} are those in which methane is present and not present, respectively.

The on policy requires the pump controller to switch the pump on when there is high water and no methane present (see transition labelled *switchOn* from state 4 to state 7), and leaves the possibility open for turning the pump on when there is medium water or low water (see *switchOn?* transition from state 0 to state 2). Event *tick* is not allowed to occur in state 4, which captures the fact that the pump controller is required to react fast enough to switch the pump on before the time unit expires (or that there is no longer an urgency because the water is no longer high – leading to state 0 – or there is methane – leading to state 5). In addition, all other *tick* events are maybe transitions modelling the fact that time may pass at any rate on all other states, and hence indicating that there are no other timing requirements for the pump controller.

The *OffPolicy* turns the pump off when there is low water or methane appears. In addition, *OffPolicy* models a danger light with actions *dangerLightOn* and *dangerLightOff*, which is turned on when methane is present in the mine. The actions that refer to the danger light are not in the scope of *OnPolicy*; in other words, they are not in the alphabet of *OnPolicy*. Due to the size of *OffPolicy* (16 states, 112 transitions), we do not depict it here; it is available in [3].

Properties. We consider four properties that stakeholders expect their models to satisfy, but due to lack of space omit their formalization in $\mathcal{L}_\mu^w$. The first two properties (Φ_1 and Φ_2) are expected to be satisfied by both policies. Φ_1 states that the pump should only be turned on if it is off and similarly, Φ_2 states that the pump should only be turned off if it is on. These two properties necessitate including both *switchOn* and *switchOff* in the scope of *OnPolicy* and *OffPolicy*. In addition, the stakeholder for the on policy expects that when there is high water and no methane, the pump should be on (Φ_3), while the stakeholder for the off policy expects that if there is low water or methane present, the pump should be off (Φ_4).

It is possible to show that both $MinePump_1$ and $MinePump_2$ satisfy properties Φ_1 and Φ_2 and additionally, $MinePump_1$ satisfies Φ_3 and $MinePump_2$ satisfies Φ_4. As *OnPolicy* leaves the off policy open by modelling possibilities for turning the pump off with maybe behaviour, and similarly, *OffPolicy* leaves the on policy open, properties Φ_3 and Φ_4 evaluate to *maybe* in $MinePump_2$ and $MinePump_1$, respectively.

Merge. Given the results presented above, we claim that the system model resulting from the merged policies and models for the environment satisfy all requirements, i.e. (*OnPolicy* + *OffPolicy*) ‖ *WaterLevelSensor* ‖ *MethaneSensor* ‖ *Pump* satisfies Φ_1, Φ_2, Φ_3, and Φ_4. The argument is as follows.

Using the consistency algorithm in [3], *OnPolicy* and *OffPolicy* can be shown to be consistent, and hence the full pump controller can be defined as *PumpControl* = *OnPolicy* + *OffPolicy*. Additionally, the alphabet restrictions in Proposition 7 are satisfied by $MinePump_1$ and $MinePump_2$, and therefore there exists a merge of $MinePump_1$ and $MinePump_2$ that is refined by *MinePump*. Hence, by definition of merge and Theorem 1, properties Φ_1, Φ_2, Φ_3, and Φ_4 hold in *MinePump*. In particular, the *maybe* properties Φ_3 and Φ_4 of $MinePump_1$ and $MinePump_2$ become *true* properties of *MinePump*, which corresponds to the on and off policies being refined into concrete behaviours in the merge.

The above reasoning did not rely on the fact that the LCR of *OnPolicy* and *OffPolicy* exists. Existence of the LCR does guarantee that the merge of the policies can be built automatically using the algorithms reported in [3].

In addition, by Proposition 7, the properties of the compositions *MinePump₁* and *MinePump₂* are preserved in addition to those of *OnPolicy* and *OffPolicy*. This is important as some relevant properties may only hold under certain assumptions on the environment. In this case study, *OnPolicy* could easily be modified to be under-specified enough so as not to satisfy Φ_1 without the assumption (modelled in *WaterLevelSensor*) that water levels cannot jump directly from low to high without going through medium.

Now suppose that further information regarding the on and off policies becomes available, e.g., that the pump controller should try to keep the pump off as much as possible while satisfying existing requirements. This means that the pump should only be switched on when the water is high and should be switched off as soon as the water is no longer high. By monotonicity (Proposition 6), we know that rather than being forced to elaborate the merged model *MinePump* or *PumpControl*, we can effectively refine the two original policies into *OnPolicy'* and *OffPolicy'* and then merge them with the guarantee that in the final model ((*OnPolicy'* + *OffPolicy'*) ‖ *Pump* ‖ *MethaneSensor* ‖ *WaterLevelSensor*) all required properties still hold.

Conclusion. In this section, we have exemplified several of the properties of merge discussed in this paper. Specifically, we showed that we can start from partial models from different stakeholders, each satisfying certain system requirements (possibly under some assumptions on the environment), and elaborate through refinement, merge and parallel composition a system model that preserves the properties of the initial viewpoints.

6 Conclusions

In this section, we summarize the paper, compare our work with related approaches, and discuss directions for future research.

Summary. Merging is a process based on finding a common observational refinement of consistent systems [27], and therefore preserves weak μ-calculus properties of the original systems. In this paper, we studied fundamental questions related to using merge in practice. In particular, we showed that existence of merge is characterized by weak μ-calculus properties and can be decided algorithmically, and described conditions for uniqueness, which are essential for automating merge. Together with several algebraic properties (both in the case when the LCR exists and when merge results in one of several MCRs), our results provide the necessary support for merging complex systems, such as those involving the parallel composition of several components, as demonstrated in the case study.

Related Work. Explicit partiality corresponds naturally to the lack of information at modelling time [9] or to the loss of information due to abstraction [4,8,14,25].

State-machine formalisms have been extended to allow partiality in states (e.g., Partial Kripke Structures (PKs) [4]), transitions (e.g., MTSs [21], Mixed Transition Systems [8]), or both (e.g., Generalized KMTSs [25]). In all these formalisms, properties that are preserved in a more defined model have been identified, e.g. Hennessy-Milner logic for MTSs [21], 3-valued CTL for PKs, and 3-valued μ-calculus for KMTSs [14].

The approaches closest to ours are those of Larsen et al. [19,20] and Huth et al. [13,14]. [20] introduced an operator with a behaviour similar to our merge (called *conjunction*), but defined only for MTSs over the same vocabulary with no τ transitions, and for which there is an *independence relation* (at which point the LCR exists). Although not studied in depth, the operators in [20,19] are based on strong refinement. We have shown that the existence of multiple MCRs introduces a number of subtle issues for a similar operator based on observational refinement. Extensions to MTSs have been proposed to guarantee uniqueness of merge and generalization (e.g. [19,14]). The price paid is more complicated modelling frameworks which engineers may not adopt as easily, and hence we focus on MTSs. In addition, non-uniqueness of merge can be seen as an opportunity for elicitation, validation, and negotiation of partial descriptions. Finally, Hussain and Huth [13] study the problem of finding a common (strong) refinement between multiple MTS, but focus on the complexity of the relevant model-checking problems rather than engineering issues (e.g., existence, uniqueness and algebraic properties). Our models are more general in that we allow τ transitions and different alphabets, but less general in that the work in [13] handles hybrid constraints between the models.

Our work focuses on merging models that describe only the *observable* behaviour of a system, and thus simulation-like relations are central to merging. Other approaches to merging descriptions exist, but the models being merged include state information [9,24,5,29,11,1] and consequently other notions of preservation may apply, such as isomorphism [9,24].

An alternative to partial operational descriptions, on which we focus, is the use of declarative specifications. For instance, classical logics are partial and support merging as the conjunction of theories. Similarly, Live Sequence Charts [7] support merging through logical conjunction, as each chart can be interpreted as a temporal logic formula. We believe that our approach is more suitable for exploration and validation of unknown behaviours, since explicit reasoning about such behaviours is an integral part of our merging process.

Future Work. The long-term goal of our work is to provide automated support for creating, merging and elaborating partial behavioural models, as well as enabling users to choose the desired merge from the set of possible minimal common refinements. In the near future, we plan to conduct additional case studies, and produce implementations of the merge algorithms found in [3]. In addition, since weak μ-calculus is expressive but can be subtle to use, we plan to extend the logic Fluent LTL (FLTL) [10], which is a simple language for expressing complex temporal properties of LTSs, to reasoning about partial models and use it as the specification language in our framework.

Acknowledgements. The work was partially funded by EPSRC grant PBM EP/C541138 and NSERC. We thank Shiva Nejati for finding interesting counterexamples to our claims.

References

1. T. Ball, V. Levin, and F. Xie. "Automatic Creation of Environment Models via Training". In *TACAS'04*, volume 2988 of *LNCS*, pages 93–107, 2004.
2. B. Boem and R. Turner. *Balancing Agility and Discipline: A Guide for the Perplexed*. Person Education, 2004.
3. G. Brunet. "A Characterization of Merging Partial Behavioural Models". Master's thesis, University of Toronto, Department of Computer Science, January 2006.
4. G. Bruns and P. Godefroid. "Model Checking Partial State Spaces with 3-Valued Temporal Logics". In *CAV'99*, volume 1633 of *LNCS*, pages 274–287, 1999.
5. M. Chechik, B. Devereux, S. Easterbrook, and A. Gurfinkel. "Multi-Valued Symbolic Model-Checking". *ACM TOSEM*, 12(4):1–38, October 2003.
6. CREWS. "Cooperative Requirements Engineering With Scenarios", 1999.
7. W. Damm and D. Harel. "LSCs: Breathing Life into Message Sequence Charts.". *FMSD*, 19(1):45–80, 2001.
8. D. Dams, R. Gerth, and O. Grumberg. "Abstract Interpretation of Reactive Systems". *ACM TOPLAS*, 2(19):253–291, 1997.
9. S. Easterbrook and M. Chechik. "A Framework for Multi-Valued Reasoning over Inconsistent Viewpoints". In *ICSE'01*, pages 411–420, 2001.
10. D. Giannakopoulou and J. Magee. "Fluent Model Checking for Event-Based Systems". In *ESEC/FSE'03*, pages 257–266, 2003.
11. S. Horwitz, J. Prins, and T. Reps. "Integrating Noninterfering Versions of Programs.". *ACM TOPLAS*, 11(3):345–387, 1989.
12. A. Hunter and B. Nuseibeh. "Managing Inconsistent Specifications: Reasoning, Analysis and Action". *ACM TOSEM*, 7(4):335–367, 1998.
13. A. Hussain and M. Huth. "On Model Checking Multiple Hybrid Views". In *1st Int. Symp. on Leveraging Applications of FMs*, pages 235–242, 2004.
14. M. Huth, R. Jagadeesan, and D. Schmidt. "A Domain Equation for Refinement of Partial Systems". Submitted, 2002.
15. M. Huth, R. Jagadeesan, and D. A. Schmidt. "Modal Transition Systems: A Foundation for Three-Valued Program Analysis". In *ESOP'01*, volume 2028 of *LNCS*, pages 155–169, 2001.
16. R. Keller. "Formal Verification of Parallel Programs". *Communications of the ACM*, 19(7):371–384, 1976.
17. D Kozen. "Results on the Propositional μ-calculus". *TCS*, 27:334–354, 1983.
18. J. Kramer, J. Magee, and M. Sloman. "CONIC: an Integrated Approach to Distributed Computer Control Systems". *IEE Proceedings*, 130(1):1–10, 1983.
19. K. Larsen and L. Xinxin. "Equation Solving Using Modal Transition Systems". In *LICS'90*, pages 108–117, 1990.
20. K. G. Larsen, B. Steffen, and C. Weise. "A Constraint Oriented Proof Methodology based on Modal Transition Systems". In *TACAS'95*, LNCS, pages 13–28, 1995.
21. K.G. Larsen and B. Thomsen. "A Modal Process Logic". In *LICS'88*, pages 203–210, 1988.
22. J. Magee and J. Kramer. *"Concurrency - State Models and Java Programs"*. John Wiley, 1999.

23. R. Milner. *Communication and Concurrency.* Prentice-Hall, New York, 1989.
24. M. Sabetzadeh and S.M. Easterbrook. "Analysis of Inconsistency in Graph-Based Viewpoints: A Category-Theoretic Approach". In *ASE'03*, pages 12–21, 2003.
25. S. Shoham and O. Grumberg. "Monotonic Abstraction-Refinement for CTL". In *TACAS'04*, volume 2988 of *LNCS*, pages 546–560, 2004.
26. C. Stirling. "Modal and Temporal Logics for Processes". In *VIII Banff Conf. on Logics for Concurrency : Structure Versus Automata*, pages 149–237, 1996.
27. S. Uchitel and M. Chechik. "Merging Partial Behavioural Models". In *FSE'04*, pages 43–52, 2004.
28. S. Uchitel, J. Kramer, and J. Magee. "Behaviour Model Elaboration using Partial Labelled Transition Systems". In *ESEC/FSE'03*, pages 19–27, 2003.
29. J. Whittle and J. Schumann. "Generating Statechart Designs from Scenarios". In *ICSE'00*, pages 314–323, 2000.

Automatic Translation from *Circus* to Java

Angela Freitas and Ana Cavalcanti

Department of Computer Science
University of York, UK

Abstract. *Circus* is a combination of Z and CSP that supports the development of state-rich reactive systems based on refinement. In this paper we present *JCircus*, a tool that automatically translates *Circus* programs into Java, for the purpose of animation and simulation. It is based on a translation strategy that uses the JCSP library to implement some of the CSP constructs of *Circus*. The tool generates a simple graphical interface; we present a simple example to demonstrate the translation strategy, and the execution of the resulting program. We discuss the class `GeneralChannel`, which we designed to support the implementation of multi-synchronisation. We also discuss our improvements to the translation strategy, some limitations of the tool, and our approach to prove the correctness of the multi-synchronisation protocol.

1 Introduction

Circus [1] is a combination of the Z notation [2], the process algebra CSP [3], and Djikstra's language of guarded commands. It is a unified language for specification and design of state-rich reactive systems. In general terms, data requirements are expressed with Z schemas, and behavioural aspects are expressed using Z, CSP and the guarded commands. *Circus* also includes a refinement calculus, which allows stepwise development of programs. The semantics of *Circus* is based on the Unifying Theories of Programming [4], a relational model that unifies programming theories across many different paradigms.

Circus supports specifications of systems at various levels of abstraction. In [5], a complete development strategy supported by *Circus* is presented. Starting from an abstract *Circus* specification, refinement laws are gradually applied in order to reach a concurrent implementation in which all schemas used to describe operations are refined to commands and CSP actions. Afterwards, a translation strategy is applied to generate a Java implementation. The JCSP library [6] is used for implementation of some CSP primitives in Java.

Unlike the refinement calculus, which requires human expertise to be applied, the translation strategy can be automated. Tool support is important to save effort and avoid human errors that are typical of the activity of writing code.

This paper describes *JCircus*, a tool that implements the translation strategy from *Circus* to Java. It receives as input a *Circus* program written in LATEX

J. Misra, T. Nipkow, and E. Sekerinski (Eds.): FM 2006, LNCS 4085, pp. 115–130, 2006.
© Springer-Verlag Berlin Heidelberg 2006

markup based on that adopted for the Z Standard [7], and produces a Java program that implements the program. *JCircus* translates concrete *Circus* programs, that is, those in which specification statements and Z schemas are not used in action definitions. The strategy covers a large subset of concrete *Circus*, including generic processes and some CSP replicated operators. Due to limitations in the JCSP library, however, the protocols and data structures used in the implementation impose restrictions on the input programs.

JCSP does not implement multi-synchronisation, that is, synchronisation involving three or more processes. As *Circus* includes this feature, the translation strategy makes use of a protocol that implements multi-synchronisation. For *JCircus* we designed the class `GeneralChannel` that represent channels; it encapsulates the protocol, in the case of channels involved in multi-synchronisation. This class can be regarded as an extension of JCSP, as its use is not restricted to Java implementations of *Circus* programs.

The main purpose of *JCircus* is to provide animation for *Circus* programs; for that, it also provides a simple graphical interface for execution of the generated programs. We do not have efficiency as a primary concern, but rather, correctness: we have formally verified part of the translation strategy, namely, the multi-synchronisation protocol.

In the next section we give a brief introduction to *Circus* and in Section 3 we present the JCSP library. In Section 4, we present *JCircus* and the translation strategy with a simple example, and we also present the class `GeneralChannel`. In Section 5, we discuss our improvements to the strategy, some errors that were found in the original strategy, the limitations of *JCircus*, and our approach to prove its correctness. In Section 6, we draw conclusions and discuss some directions of future work.

2   *Circus*

In *Circus*, just as in CSP, a system is regarded as a process. However, in *Circus* a process may contain an internal state, which is described using the schema constructs of Z. The state of a process is encapsulated; channels are the only means of communication between a process and its environment.

Like a Z specification, a *Circus* program is formed by a sequence of paragraphs. We use a small example of a program that calculates the greatest common divisor (GCD) between two natural numbers (Figure 1) to explain some of the main constructs of *Circus*.

Our example begins with the declaration of two channels that communicate natural numbers. The channel *in* receives two numbers, in sequence, and the channel *out* outputs their GCD.

A process declaration gives its name and a process definition. The most basic form of process definition specifies the state of the process, a sequence of process paragraphs, and a nameless main action which describes the behaviour of the process. All these are delimited by the keywords **begin** and **end**.

channel *in*, *out* : ℕ

process *GCD_Euclidean* ≙ **begin**
  state *GCDState* ≙ [*a*, *b* : ℕ]
  InitState ≙ *x*, *y* : ℕ • *a*, *b* := *x*, *y*
  UpdateState ≙ *a*, *b* := *b*, *a* **mod** *b*
  GCD ≙ μ *X* • **if** *b* = 0 → *out*!*a* → *Skip*
                     ⫿ *b* ≠ 0 → *UpdateState*; *X*
                     fi
  • *in*?*x* → *in*?*y* → *InitState*(*x*, *y*); *GCD*
end

channel *gcd*, *sum*
channel *read*, *write* : ℕ

process *SumOrGCD* ≙ (*GCD_Euclidean* ⟦ ⦃ *in*, *out* ⦄ ⟧ *GCDClient*) \ ⦃ *in*, *out* ⦄

process *GCDClient* ≙ **begin**
  ReadValue ≙ *read*?*x* → *read*?*y* → *ChooseOper*(*x*, *y*)
  ChooseOper ≙ *x*, *y* : ℕ •
    gcd → *in*!*x* → *in*!*y* → *out*?*r* → *write*!*r* → *Skip*
    □
    sum → *write*!(*x* + *y*) → *Skip*
  • μ *X* • *ReadValue*; *X*
end

Fig. 1. Concrete *Circus* program for calculation of the GCD

In our example, we declare a process *GCD_Euclidean* which has its state described by the schema *GCDState*; it contains two components, *a* and *b*, which are initialised with the numbers for which we want to calculate the GCD. The following definitions in the basic process describe actions. The initialisation operation is *InitState*, which defines a parametrised action that takes *x* and *y* as input, and assign them to *a* and *b*. The action *UpdateState* updates the values of the state components in each iteration of the calculation of the GCD. The recursive action *GCD* implements the Euclidean algorithm for calculation of the GCD. When *b* ≠ 0, it recurses; if *b* = 0, then the GCD is output. The basic action *Skip* terminates without communicating values or changing the state.

The main action describes the behaviour of the process. It receives two inputs through channel *in*, initialises the state with these values, and then calls *GCD*.

A process definition like that of *GCD_Euclidean* uses Z and CSP constructs to define the state and the behaviour of the process. It is also possible to define processes in terms of others previously defined, using the CSP operators for sequence, external choice, internal choice and parallelism, among others. The process *SumOrGCD* is a parallel composition of the processes *GCD_Euclidean* and *GCDClient*. They communicate via *in* and *out*, which are hidden; this means that the environment cannot see communications that occur through them.

The process *GCDClient* is recursive: in each iteration, it reads values x and y from a channel *read*, and passes them to the parametrised action *ChooseOper*, which offers a choice between the sum and the greatest common divisor operations. The external choice operator is as in CSP: it offers the environment a choice between two or more actions. If the GCD operation is chosen, it delegates to process *GCD_Euclidean* the calculation of the greatest common divisor; communication occurs through channels *in* and *out*. Otherwise, it outputs on *write* the summation of the two values.

In Section 4, we discuss the translation of this example to Java using *JCircus*. More details on *Circus* can be found in [8].

3   JCSP

The translation strategy makes use of the JCSP library to implement many of the CSP constructs used by *Circus*. The library provides a simplified way to program concurrency in Java without having to deal directly with the Java primitives.

In JCSP, a process is a class that implements the interface `CSProcess`, which defines only the method `public void run()`. The implementation must encode in this method the behaviour of the process.

JCSP also defines interfaces for channels: `ChannelInput` is the interface for input channels and defines the method `read`; `ChannelOutput` is the interface for output channels and defines the method `write`; `Channel` extends both `Channel Input` and `ChannelOutput` and is used for channels which are not specified as input or output channels. The implementations for channels are the classes `One2OneChannel`, `One2AnyChannel`, `Any2OneChannel` and `Any2AnyChannel`. The appropriate implementation to be used when creating a channel depends on whether there are one or more possible readers and writers for the channel.

Synchronisation in JCSP is not in exact correspondence with the original concept in CSP. Despite being possible to have more than one process that read or write on a channel, only one pair of processes can synchronise at each time; this model is similar to that of occam [9]. Thus, multi-synchronisation, that is, three or more processes synchronising on a single communication, which is allowed in CSP, is not directly supported by JCSP. To solve this problem, the translation strategy implements a protocol for multi-synchronisation.

The class `Alternative` implements the external choice operator. Its constructor takes an array of channels that may be selected. The implementation of the alternation requires that only input channels that have at most one reader participate. The method `select()` waits for one or more channels to become ready to communicate, makes an arbitrary choice between them, and returns the index of the selected channel.

Parallelism is implemented by class `Parallel`, which implements `CSProcess`. The constructor takes an array of `CSProcesses`, which are the processes that compose the parallelism. The method `run` executes all processes in parallel and terminates when all processes terminate. Differently from CSP, it is not possible to choose the channels on which the processes synchronise; in JCSP, they synchronise on all channels that they have in common.

The CSP constructors *Skip* and *Stop* are implemented by the classes Skip and Stop, respectively. JCSP includes also implementations for other features that are not available in CSP, such as barrier synchronisation, timers and process managers, among others, and extensions for the java.awt library that provide channel interfaces for graphical components. For details, see [6].

4   JCircus

The translator from *Circus* to Java is an implementation of the translation strategy that was originally described in [5]. The strategy defines rules for translation of each construct of *Circus*. Translation is carried out by the recursive application of the translation rules, following the syntactic structure of the program. We proposed some adaptations to the original translation strategy, which we discuss later on in this section and in Section 5. The complete reference to the rules implemented in *JCircus* can be found in [10].

JCircus translates a concrete *Circus* program (written in LATEX markup) into a Java program that implements the specification. It requires from the user: the path of the input file, the name of the project (which will be the name of the Java package for the program), and the output path. Before translation, the tool performs parsing and typechecking, and verifies if the specification meets the requirements for translation.

For each process definition in the input file, the tool asks if the user wants to create a main class for it. For a process X, this class is called Main_X, and it is the starting point for the execution of the process. It implements a parallel composition of the process and a graphical interface that simulates its environment. A batch file Run_X.bat is also created; it contains commands to compile the project and run the class Main_X using JDK [11].

4.1   The Translation Strategy

The translation consists of two phases. The first phase collects information about types and channels: the free types defined in the program, the channels used by each process, how they are used (for input or output), and whether they are hidden or not. The second phase uses this information to generate the Java code; it is basically an application of the translation rules.

Figure 2 shows as an example the rule for translation of a process declaration. The function $[\![\,]\!]^{ProcDecl}$ is applied to a process declaration (ProcDecl) and takes as parameter the name of the project (N). Each process declaration is translated to a Java class that implements the interface CSProcess, and has the same name as the process. The body of the class is translated with the rule for process definition (ProcDef), which we omit here. This rule introduces the attribute declarations, the constructor, and the implementation of the method run.

Figure 3 shows the class GCD_Euclidean (without package and import declarations), which results from the translation of the process *GCD_Euclidean*. Its private attributes are the channels that this class uses: *in* and *out*. As they are not

Rule A.1 *Process declaration*

$\|[\_]\|^{ProcDecl}$: ProcDecl $\twoheadrightarrow$ N $\twoheadrightarrow$ JCode
$\|[\,$**process** $P \mathrel{\widehat{=}} ProcDef\,]\|^{ProcDecl}\ proj =$
    package $proj$.processes;
    import java.util.*;
    import jcsp.lang.*;
    import $proj$.axiomaticDefinitions.*;
    import $proj$.typing.*;
    public class P implements CSProcess { $\|[\,ProcDef\,]\|^{ProcDef}$ P }

Fig. 2. Translation rule

hidden in the declaration of the process, they are taken as input by the constructor of the class. The channels are implemented by the class GeneralChannel. The use of this class was one of the modifications to the original strategy, which used the Any2OneChannel class provided by JCSP instead.

The translation of the process definition gives the implementation of the method run (Figure 3, lines 6-47) of the class. In our example, it is a definition of a basic process, which is translated to a call to the method run of an anonymous instantiation of CSProcess (lines 7-46).

The anonymous instantiation of CSProcess declares the state components as private attributes. Since an action cannot be referenced outside the process where it is defined, action definitions are translated as private methods.

The parametrised action definition *InitState* yields a parametrised method with the same name. The *Circus* multiple assignment is translated to a sequence of Java assignments. The implementation of the multiple assignment in action *UpdateState* needs auxiliary variables because variable a is being updated and used within the same assignment.

The definition of the action *GCD* uses the recursive operator μ; the translation defines an inner class I_0. The translation of the recursive action yields the declaration (lines 18-34), initialisation (line 35), and execution (line 36) of the method run of this class. It implements CSProcess, and its method run contains the implementation of the body of the recursion. In the places where a recursive call is made, there is a new instantiation and execution of I_0 (lines 28-29).

The main action of the basic process is translated as the body of the method run for the anonymous class that implements it (lines 39-44). In our example, we have two inputs on channel *in*, a call to *InitState*, and a call to *GCD*.

Figure 4 shows the translation of the process *SumOrGCD*. It is a parallel composition of two other processes; so, its attributes are the channels used by each of them. However, since *in* and *out* are hidden in this process, they are not taken by the constructor, instead, they are created there.

The constructor of the class GeneralChannel takes an Any2OneChannel and an object of type ChannelInfo. This class is a mapping that associates a process name with an integer, that indicates if the instance of the channel is used

```
public class GCD_Euclidean implements CSProcess {                        (1)
  private GeneralChannel in, out;                                        (2)
  public GCD_Euclidean(GeneralChannel in, GeneralChannel out) {          (3)
    this.in = in;     this.out = out;                                    (4)
  }                                                                      (5)
  public void run () {                                                   (6)
    (new CSProcess() {                                                   (7)
      private CircusNumber a, b;                                         (8)
      private void InitState(CircusNumber x, CircusNumber y) {           (9)
        a = x;     b = y;                                               (10)
      }                                                                 (11)
      private void UpdateState() {                                      (12)
        CircusNumber aux_a = b;                                         (13)
        CircusNumber aux_b = a.mod(b);                                  (14)
        a = aux_a;     b = aux_b;                                       (15)
      }                                                                 (16)
      private void GCD() {                                              (17)
        class I_0 implements CSProcess {                                (18)
          public I_0() {}                                               (19)
          public void run() {                                           (20)
            if ((b.getValue() ==                                        (21)
                (new CircusNumber(0)).getValue())) {                    (22)
              out.write(a);                                             (23)
              (new Skip()).run();                                       (24)
            } else if (b.getValue() !=                                  (25)
                (new CircusNumber(0)).getValue()) {                     (26)
              UpdateState();                                            (27)
              I_0 i_0_0 = new I_0();                                    (28)
              i_0_0.run();                                              (29)
            } else {                                                    (30)
              while(true){}                                             (31)
            };                                                          (32)
          }                                                             (33)
        }                                                               (34)
        I_0 i_0_0 = new I_0();                                          (35)
        i_0_0.run();                                                    (36)
      }                                                                 (37)
      public void run() {                                               (38)
        { CircusNumber x = (CircusNumber) in.read();                    (39)
          { CircusNumber y = (CircusNumber) in.read();                  (40)
            InitState(x, y);                                            (41)
            GCD();                                                      (42)
          }                                                             (43)
        }                                                               (44)
      }                                                                 (45)
    }).run();                                                           (46)
  }                                                                     (47)
}                                                                       (48)
```

Fig. 3. Translation of process *GCD_Euclidean*

```
public class SumOrGCD implements CSProcess {

  private GeneralChannel  gcd, read, sum, write, in, out;
  public SumOrGCD(GeneralChannel gcd, GeneralChannel read,
                          GeneralChannel sum, GeneralChannel write) {
    this.gcd = gcd;
    this.read = read;
    this.sum = sum;
    this.write = write;

    ChannelInfo inf_in = new ChannelInfo();
    inf_in.put("GCDClient", new Integer(0));
    inf_in.put("GCD_Euclidean", new Integer(1));
    this.in = new GeneralChannel(new Any2OneChannel(),inf_in,"SumOrGCD");

    ChannelInfo ch_out = new ChannelInfo();
    inf_out.put("GCDClient", new Integer(1));
    inf_out.put("GCD_Euclidean", new Integer(0));
    this.out = new GeneralChannel(new Any2OneChannel(),inf_out,"SumOrGCD");
  }
  public void run(){
    new Parallel(new CSProcess[] {
      new GCDClient(new GeneralChannel(gcd, "GCDClient"),
                        new GeneralChannel(in, "GCDClient"),
                        new GeneralChannel(out, "GCDClient"),
                        new GeneralChannel(read, "GCDClient"),
                        new GeneralChannel(sum, "GCDClient"),
                        new GeneralChannel(write, "GCDClient")),

      new GCD_Euclidean(new GeneralChannel(in,"GCD_Euclidean"),
                        new GeneralChannel(out,"GCD_Euclidean"))
    }).run();
  }
}
```

Fig. 4. Translation of process *SumOrGCD*

as an input (1) or an output (0) channel. In our example, channel *in* is used for input by the process *GCD_Euclidean* and for output by the process *GCDClient*; the channel *out* is used for output by *GCD_Euclidean* and for input by *GCDClient*. The constructor also takes the name of the process that is using the instance of the channel; in our case, the process *SumOrGCD*.

The body of the method run contains the translation of the parallelism, which uses the class Parallel of JCSP. As said before, the constructor of Parallel takes an array of CSProcesses; in this case, instances of GCD_Euclidean and GCDClient. Their constructors take the channels used by each process. We construct new instances of the channels based on the ones that we already have, changing only one attribute: the name of the process.

4.2   Running the Program Generated by *JCircus*

Besides the classes specified by the translation strategy, *JCircus* also generates a simple graphical interface to simulate the execution of a process. For a process X, this class is called `Gui_X`; it represents the environment that interacts with the process. It is a Java Swing frame, with buttons and fields to represent the interface of the process to its environment, namely, the channels that the process uses and are not hidden. The state, hidden channels, and internal operations are not visible by the environment. The graphical interface is also an implementation of a `CSProcess`. It runs in parallel with the class that represents the process.

Figure 5 shows the graphical interface for the process *GCD_Euclidean*. This process uses only two channels: the input channel *in* and the output channel *out*, and both communicate natural numbers. In the text fields next to the buttons, we can type values for the input channels or visualise the values communicated through the output channels.

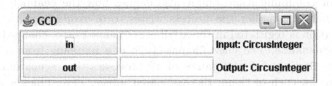

Fig. 5. GUI for process *GCD*

When we run the class `Main_GCD_Euclidean`, the screen presented in Figure 5 is shown. The program waits for a synchronisation on channel *in*, as this is the first communication in which the process *GCD_Euclidean* can engage. As this is an input channel, we must type in the first text field the input value, which is the first of the pair of numbers for which we want to calculate the *GCD*. After entering the value, we press the button in; this represents the synchronisation on channel *in*. The generated program does not perform parsing or type checking. It expects that the values entered by the user are well-formed and well-typed.

Once the first number has been entered, the program waits for the second communication through channel *in*. After that, the program calculates the GCD and waits for synchronisation on the channel *out*. When we press the button out, the GCD appears in the text field just next to it.

4.3   The Class `GeneralChannel`

The original translation strategy used the class `Any2OneChannel` from the JCSP library to implement a simple synchronised channel, that is, a channel on which at most two processes synchronise. This class implements the interface `Channel` which defines methods `read` and `write`. Every synchronisation is point-to-point; it occurs by monitor synchronisation when one reference calls `read` and the other calls `write`. Multi-synchronisation is not directly supported by JCSP.

To allow the implementation of processes that use multi-synchronisation, the original translation strategy makes use of a protocol: for each channel involved in a multi-synchronisation, there is a controller process running in parallel with the system, and this process manages the requests for multi-synchronisation on the channel it controls. The communication between the controller and each process is done via simple synchronisations. Basically, each channel c is replaced by an array of `Any2OneChannels` `from_c`, which the controller uses to communicate with their clients, and an `Any2OneChannel` channel `to_c`, which is shared by the clients to send messages to the controller.

We have designed a class `GeneralChannel` to provide an abstraction for channels irrespectively of their use in multi-synchronisations. This class encapsulates the data necessary for the implementation of multi-synchronisation; it contains an array of `Any2OneChannels` `from` and one `Any2OneChannel` `to`. If the instance of the channel is not involved in a multi-synchronisation, the channel `to` is used, and the array `from` is ignored.

An object of class `GeneralChannel` contains not only the data necessary to implement communication, but it also defines how the channel is used by a process, that is, whether the process writes to or reads from the channel. This information is registered in the attributes `ChannelInfo channelInfo` and `String processName`. The class `ChannelInfo` is a mapping from `Strings` to integers. The `Strings` are the names of all processes that synchronise on the channel, and, for each of them, the associated integer determines whether the channel is used for writing or reading. The attribute `String processName` records the name of the process that uses the instance of the channel. By looking up `processName` in `channelInfo`, the constructor sets up the attribute `int rw`, which holds 0 if this instance is used for writing, and 1 if it is used for reading.

The class `GeneralChannel` has three constructors: one for channels used in simple communications, one for channels involved in multi-synchronisations, and one that constructs a channel from another `GeneralChannel`, changing only the process name. The last one is used when calling the constructor within a compound process' class; for example, the instantiation of `GCDClient` and `GCD_Euclidean` in Figure 4. When using this constructor, the status `rw` is properly set for the new `GeneralChannel` instance, according to the new `processName`. The signatures of the constructors are presented in Figure 6.

Like the class `Any2OneChannel`, the class `GeneralChannel` defines methods `read` and `write`. In the case of a channel that is not involved in a multi-synchronisation, the implementation just calls the method `read` or `write` of the channel `to`; in the case of a channel involved in multi-synchronisation, these methods contain an implementation of the protocol for the appropriate case.

Besides the methods `read` and `write`, the class `GeneralChannel` also defines the method `synchronise`. It is used in the translation of channels that do not communicate values, as channels *gcd* and *sum* in our example (these channels do not contain input (?) or output (!) fields). Since, in JCSP, the synchronisations are point-to-point, it is necessary to always define a reader and a writer. In our

```
/* Constructor for multi-synchronisation */
public GeneralChannel (Any2OneChannel to, Any2OneChannel[] from,
        ChannelInfo channelInfo, String procName) { ... }

/* Constructor for single-synchronisation */
public GeneralChannel (Any2OneChannel[] from,
        ChannelInfo channelInfo, String procName) { ... }

/* Constructs a new instance of a channel, changing the processName */
public GeneralChannel (GeneralChannel gc, String procName) { ... }
```

Fig. 6. Constructors of `GeneralChannel`

implementation we use the method `synchronise`, so that we do not have to determine if a channel should be read or written, in a particular process.

To determine if a channel is used as a reader or a writer in one process requires inspecting the uses of the process. In the example below we have three processes A, B, and C that execute an event c. These processes are combined in parallel, two at a time in the processes *ParAB*, *ParBC* and *ParAC*.

> **process** $A \mathrel{\widehat{=}}$ **begin** $\bullet\ c \rightarrow Skip$ **end**
> **process** $B \mathrel{\widehat{=}}$ **begin** $\bullet\ c \rightarrow Skip$ **end**
> **process** $C \mathrel{\widehat{=}}$ **begin** $\bullet\ c \rightarrow Skip$ **end**

> **process** $ParAB \mathrel{\widehat{=}} A \,\|[\, \{\!|\ c\ |\!\} \,]\|\, B$
> **process** $ParAC \mathrel{\widehat{=}} A \,\|[\, \{\!|\ c\ |\!\} \,]\|\, C$
> **process** $ParBC \mathrel{\widehat{=}} B \,\|[\, \{\!|\ c\ |\!\} \,]\|\, C$

If we determine, for instance, that channel c will be a reader in process A and a writer in process B (for the parallelism *ParAB*), then we would not be able to determine the role of channel c in process C; *ParAC* would require that it was a writer, and *ParBC* would require it to be a reader.

In our solution, the communications on channel c are translated using the method `synchronise`, whose implementation is presented in Figure 7. The attribute `rw` is set in the constructor of the `GeneralChannel`, as explained before, according to the mapping in the `ChannelInfo` objects, which are initialised in

```
public Object synchronise(Object x) {
    Object r = null;
    if (this.rw == GeneralChannel.READ)
        r = this.read();
    else
        this.write(x);
    return r;
}
```

Fig. 7. Implementation of method `synchronise`

the classes `Main_ParAB`, `Main_ParAC` and `Main_ParBC`, with specific mappings for each parallelism.

5 Discussions

Our main contribution to the original translation strategy was the class introduced in the last section, `GeneralChannel`. In this section, we discuss other improvements to the original translation strategy, including the correction of an error related to parallelism of actions. Furthermore, we discuss the limitations of *JCircus* and our approach for validating the multi-synchronisation protocol.

5.1 Translation of *Circus* types

The treatment of types in *JCircus* is different from that in the original proposal, in which free types and special forms of abbreviation are translated to classes that represent types. The forms of abbreviation considered were those that defined sets in terms of at most one other set, by extending or restricting its elements; that is, they could have the form $TName_{exp} == TName \cup \{V_1, \ldots, V_m\}$ or $TName_{exp} == TName \setminus \{V_1, \ldots, V_n\}$. For instance, the following example is taken from a case study presented in [8].

$$Mode ::= automatic \mid manual \mid disabled$$
$$SwitchMode == Mode \setminus \{disabled\}$$

In the original translation strategy, these definitions yield two classes: `Mode`, which defines constants `final int automatic = 0`, `final int manual = 1`, and `final int disabled = 2`; and `SwitchMode`, which extends `Mode` and defines a constant `int final MAX = 1`, that restricts the values that it can assume.

We found this approach inappropriate because the notion of type here does correspond to the *Circus* type system, which follows that of Z: *SwitchMode* does not introduce a new type. It actually defines a set; a variable declared as, for instance, **var** x : *SwitchMode* actually has type *Mode*. The treatment of types in the original translation strategy could result in a situation in which a correctly typed *Circus* program would result in a Java program that does not compile.

In the implementation of *JCircus*, we opted for following the *Circus* type system to have a 1-1 mapping between *Circus* types and Java classes that represent types. At the moment, we implement only free types and the basic type $\mathbb{A}$; we do not treat compound types yet, which is left as future work. Each free type definition generates a class that represents that type, and abbreviations are not considered. The basic type $\mathbb{A}$, defined in the Z Standard to represent number types, is implemented using class `CircusNumber`, but we have another restriction here, since at the moment this class only implements a subset of $\mathbb{A}$: the set of integer numbers. Although in a *Circus* specification a number variable can hold a value from an infinite set, in a programming language, like Java, we have finite memory, which restricts the actual ranges that can be represented.

5.2 Parallelism of Actions

We found a mistake regarding the translation of action parallelism. Action parallelism is different from process parallelism because the former requires the definition of the set of variables that each parallel action can modify; we call this set a partition. For process parallelism, there is no such concern, since each process can access only its own data. The semantics of action parallelism defines that each parallel action deals with copies of the local variables, and at the end of the parallelism, the original variables are updated with the values of their respective copies from the actions where they appear in the partition. In this way, concerns about shared access to the state by the parallel actions are avoided.

The original translation strategy did not reflect this semantics when one of the parallel actions contained an action call. In this situation, the action call, which was translated as a method call, would update the original values, instead of the copy. Our solution was to change the translation of an action call that occurs within a parallelism; it is translated using an inner class (that implements CSProcess) that declares as attributes copies of the local variables. The translation consists of instantiation and execution of this class, and update of the values of the original variables at the end.

5.3 Limitations

The implementation of *JCircus* also helped us to identify some requirements that were not explicitly stated in the original translation strategy. We describe three of them here. First, synchronisation on channels must always involve the same number of processes, and the same processes. So, this is not allowed.

process $P_1 \mathrel{\widehat{=}}$ **begin** $\bullet\ c \rightarrow Skip$ **end**
process $P_2 \mathrel{\widehat{=}}$ **begin** $\bullet\ c \rightarrow Skip$ **end**
process $P_3 \mathrel{\widehat{=}}$ **begin** $\bullet\ c \rightarrow Skip$ **end**

process $P \mathrel{\widehat{=}} (((P_1 \, [\![\, \{\!| \ c \ |\!\} \,]\!] \, P_2) \, [\![\, \{\!| \ c \ |\!\} \,]\!] \, P_3); \ (P_1 \, [\![\, \{\!| \ c \ |\!\} \,]\!] \, P_2)) \setminus \{\!| \ c \ |\!\}$

Process P is a sequential composition; the first process is a parallelism of three processes P_1, P_2 and P_3, synchronising on c; the second is a parallelism of P_1 and P_2, synchronising on c. So, in the first parallelism, channel c is involved in a multi-synchronisation, whereas in the second one, it is not. This cannot occur; the channel c is instantiated in the constructor of class P, and the settings regarding multi-synchronisation must hold for the whole implementation of process P.

The second limitation we discuss here also involves parallelism. Because the implementation of class GeneralChannel uses the name of the processes involved to determine how each process uses the channel, there cannot be repeated copies of a processes in a parallelism, or parallelism of anonymous processes, like in the following examples.

process $P \mathrel{\widehat{=}} A \, [\![\, \{\!| \ \dots \ |\!\} \,]\!] \, A$
process $Q \mathrel{\widehat{=}}$ **begin** $\dots$ **end** $[\![\, \{\!| \ \dots \ |\!\} \,]\!]$ **begin** $\dots$ **end**

However, this is not a serious restriction, which can be solved by redefining the processes with new names. This rewriting could be automatically done by *JCircus*, and this is one of the improvements that are planned for future versions.

The third limitation is that the situation in which a channel is used for reading and for writing by the same process is not allowed. The reason is the design of the class `GeneralChannel`, already discussed; it requires that the role of a channel is uniquely determined in each process where it is used.

These and other limitations are recognised and documented as restrictions on the input specification. They are also checked by *JCircus*; it gives an error message in the case that the input program violates one of these restrictions.

5.4   Verification of the Multi-synchronisation Protocol

In order to have a useful tool, we are concerned not only with the correct implementation of the translation rules, but also with a guarantee that the rules themselves are correct. A complete proof of soundness for the translation strategy requires a formal semantics for Java, and a mapping from the *Circus* semantics. With that, we could prove that the semantics of every *Circus* program is in correspondence with the semantics of the Java program obtained with the translation. This, however, is by no means a simple task. We have proposed a smaller step to bridge the gap between *Circus* and Java: to model the JCSP constructs and the Java programs in *Circus* itself, and use the *Circus* refinement calculus to prove that the translation rules are refinement laws. We used this approach to tackle the verification of the algorithm for multi-synchronisation.

We were inspired by the work on [12] which considers a simple form of multi-synchronisation. It is verified to be equivalent to another model that uses only simple synchronisations. We have used a similar approach to verify a more complex type of multi-synchronisation, where the channel takes part in an external choice. We proposed a *Circus* model for this kind of multi-synchronisation; then we proposed a *Circus* model for the multi-synchronisation protocol, and proved, using the refinement calculus of *Circus* that the multi-synchronisation is refined by our model of the implementation. The model is very close to the implementation and improves our confidence in it.

The approach taken for carrying out the refinement consists in refining the specification to an action system; transforming the implementation model into another action system; and then proving that the action systems are equivalent. An action system is a type of recursive process whose execution is controlled by a local variable which determine which events that are enabled in each iteration. We have used equality or refinement rules in each step of the transformation.

6   Conclusions

We have described *JCircus*, a tool that implements a translation strategy from *Circus* to Java. *JCircus* was developed in Java itself, and the translator module amounts to about 10000 lines of code. We have followed a structured approach for design and testing, and the project is documented in UML.

JCircus was implemented using the CZT framework [13], an open-source Java framework for the ISO Z Standard and extensions. It has been recently extended to support *Circus*. The framework provides, among other things, a Java library for abstract syntax trees, basic tools like parsers, type checkers and printers, and an interchange format, based on XML, for representing specifications. The use of the CZT framework allows future integration with other tools for *Circus* that use the same framework. Currently, we have a parser and a type checker [14] for *Circus*, that *JCircus* already uses, and a prototype model checker for *Circus* [15]. A long-term goal of the *Circus* group is to provide an integrated environment that supports development using *Circus*. *JCircus* is available at http://www.cs.york.ac.uk/circus/jcsp/freitas-msc/, where we can also find examples of translations.

Some previous work on translation tools are a translator from a subset of CSP into Handel-C [16], and a translator of CSP to Java and C code [17]. The latter also uses libraries that implement CSP operators in a programming language. Their strategy is similar to ours, however, we have the translation rules formalised and we cover a broader range of CSP operators. As far as we know, there is no other translator for *Circus*.

Another distinguishing feature of our work is the generation of the graphical interface. It is an additional functionality provided by *JCircus* and is not formalised by the translation rules. It makes the execution of the program generated immediately available, and is appropriate for the rapid prototyping of *Circus* programs. The classes that capture the behaviour of each of the processes, however, can be used in other contexts, where, for example, an interface that is more specific to the application is implemented.

JCircus can translate some interesting examples, but the work is far from complete. There are still some features that need to be implemented to make the tool more useful. Some *Circus* constructs are not supported by our tool because we do not have a robust parser yet. However, the translation rules are all implemented. The CZT project is currently working on a new parser for *Circus*, which extends the existing Z parser. When this parser is done, the translation of the constructs which are not currently supported will become available.

One important extension is the provision of implementation of compound *Circus* types, and number types other than integers in the CircusNumber class. Implementation of more types will make the tool available for translation of a larger range of programs. Another piece of future work is the investigation of new implementations for the external choice and parallelism that avoid the limitations of classes Alternative and Parallel of JCSP. The limitations described in Section 5.3 also make an interesting topic for future research.

Acknowledgements

The authors thank Marcel Oliveira for extensive discussion about the translation strategy; Leo Freitas for discussion about the design of *JCircus*; and Manuela Xavier, who implemented the typechecker which is part of *JCircus*. This work has been partially funded by the Royal Society and QinetiQ.

References

1. J. C. P. Woodcock and A. L. C. Cavalcanti. A Concurrent Language for Refinement. In *5th Irish Workshop on Formal Methods*, 2001.
2. J. C. P. Woodcock and J. Davies. *Using Z - Specification, Refinement, and Proof.* Prentice-Hall, 1996.
3. C. A. R. Hoare. *Communicating Sequential Processes.* Prentice-Hall, 1985.
4. C. A. R. Hoare and J. He. *Unifying Theories of Programming.* Prentice-Hall, 1998.
5. M. V. M. Oliveira. *A Refinement Calculus for Circus.* PhD thesis, Department of Computer Science, The University of York, 2005.
6. P. H. Welch. Process Oriented Design for Java: Concurrency for All. In *International Conference on Parallel and Distributed Processing Techniques and Applications (PDPTA 2000)*, 2000.
7. Z Standards Panel. Formal Specificationn - Z Notation - Syntax, Type and Semantics — Consensus Working Draft 2.6, 2000. At http://www.cs.york.ac.uk/~ian/zstan/.
8. M. V. M. Oliveira, A. L. C. Cavalcanti, and J. C. P. Woodcock. Refining Industrial Scale Systems in *Circus*. In *Communicating Process Architectures*, 2004.
9. The occam archive. At http://vl.fmnet.info/occam/.
10. A. Freitas. From *Circus* to Java: Implementation and Verification of a Translation Strategy. Master's thesis, Department of Computer Science, The University of York, 2005.
11. Java Development Kit. http://java.sun.com/javase/.
12. J. C. P. Woodcock. Using *Circus* for Safety-Critical Applications. In *VI Brazilian Workshop on Formal Methods*, 2003.
13. P. Malik and M. Utting. CZT: A Framework for Z Tools. In *5th International Conference of Z and B Users (ZB 2005)*, 2005.
14. M. Xavier. Definição Formal e Implementação do Sistema de Tipos para a Linguagem *Circus*. Master's thesis, Centro de Informática, Universidade Federal de Pernambuco, Brazil, 2006. To be submitted.
15. L. Freitas. *Model checking Circus.* PhD thesis, Department of Computer Science, The University of York, 2005.
16. J. D. Phillips and G. S. Stiles. An Automatic Translation of CSP to Handel-C. In *Communicating Process Architectures*, 2004.
17. V. Raju, L. Rong, and G. S. Stiles. Automatic Conversion of CSP to CTJ, JCSP, and CCSP. In *Communicating Process Architectures*, 2003.

Quantitative Refinement *and* Model Checking for the Analysis of Probabilistic Systems

A.K. McIver

Dept. Computer Science, Macquarie University, NSW 2109 Australia
anabel@ics.mq.edu.au

Abstract. For standard (ie non-probabilistic) systems of reasonable size, correctness is analysed by simulation and/or model checking, possibly with standard program-logical arguments beforehand to reduce the problem size by abstraction.

For probabilistic systems there are model checkers and simulators too; but probabilistic program logics are rarer. Thus e.g. model checkers face more severe exposure to state explosion because "front-end" probabilistic abstraction techniques are not so widely known [18].

We formalise probabilistic refinement of action systems [3] in order to provide just such a front end, and we illustrate with the probabilistic model checker PRISM [21] how it can be used to reduce state explosion. The case study is based on a performance analysis of randomised backoff in wireless communication [1].

Keywords: Probabilistic abstraction and refinement, structured specification and analysis of performance, probabilistic model checking.

1 Introduction

The analysis of performance properties of systems requires a quantitative assessment of behaviour, and currently there are two major styles of quantitative verification.

Probabilistic model checking links a "programming" language (for describing the system operationally) with a "logical" language (for describing the desired properties). The latter is usually a form of probabilistic temporal logic expressing e.g. "with probability p the system will eventually establish G". The model checker checks automatically whether the former satisfies the latter.

Proof-based methods, on the other hand, are more general in principle but harder to use in practice. For them, the link between the operational description and the desired properties is made by a formal proof; but the proof is not provided automatically — it must be figured out (by a human).

Although our main focus is on proof, our aim is to combine the two in a way that takes the best from each, and avoids many of their individual limitations. We use the proof-based methods to analyse only *part* of the system, concentrating on exposing a high-level abstraction which preserves the properties of interest. We take this as far as we can, for the more we abstract the smaller the state

J. Misra, T. Nipkow, and E. Sekerinski (Eds.): FM 2006, LNCS 4085, pp. 131–146, 2006.
© Springer-Verlag Berlin Heidelberg 2006

space will be; but when the details begin to bite, making continued progress with proof either difficult or impossible, we switch over to model checking — and just push the button.

The key for the abstraction is "preserves the properties of interest". For this we use *action systems* [3,23,9] enhanced with probability based on a (sequential) probabilistic program logic [18]. Action systems are sufficiently general to connect the sequential program logic, and its probabilistic programming language pCSP [19], to the modelling language used by probabilistic model checkers such as PRISM [14].

Our contributions are as follows

1. *An extension of probabilistic action systems* of Morgan [19] to include synchronisation (Sec. 3.1), hiding (Sec. 3.2) and property-preserving refinement (Sec. 3.3);
2. *Proof rules for probabilistic refinement* in the context of hiding, extending those used in standard frameworks [7] (Sec. 3);
3. *A mapping* from a subset of action systems to PRISM's modelling language, allowing quantitative specifications to be verified using PRISM (Sec. 4);

The contributions are illustrated by a small case study (Sec. 5), demonstrating how the probabilistic backoff procedure used in wireless communication may be developed in a stepwise fashion, appealing to model checking to investigate detailed performance issues. Our experiments using the PRISM model checker indicate that the technique of probabilistic refinement can substantially reduce the state space overhead, whilst maintaining the integrity of the performance analysis in subsequent refinements, without the need for further model checking. Finally we note that all proofs of lemmas are available elsewhere [1].

The notational conventions used are as follows. Function application is represented by a dot, as in $f.x$. We use an abstract state space S, and denote the set of discrete probability distributions over S by $\overline{S}$ (that is the sub-normalised functions from S into the real interval $[0,1]$, where function f is sub-normalised if $\sum_{s:\ S} f.s \leq 1$). Given predicate *Pred* we write $[Pred]$ for the *characteristic* function mapping states satisfying *Pred* to 1 and to 0 otherwise, punning 1 and 0 with "True" and "False". The $(p, 1-p)$-weighted average of distributions d and d' is denoted $d\ _p\!\oplus d'$.

2   Probabilistic Guarded Commands

When programs incorporate probability, their properties can no longer be guaranteed "with certainty", but only "up to some probability". For example the program

$$coin \quad \hat{=} \quad b := \mathsf{T} \ _{2/3}\!\oplus \ b := \mathsf{F} \ , \tag{1}$$

sets the Boolean-valued variable b to T only with probability 2/3 — in practice this means that if the statement were executed a large number of times, and the

---

[1] http://www.comp.mq.edu.au/~anabel/

final values of b tabulated, roughly $2/3$ of them would record b having been set to T (up to well-known statistical confidence [8]).

The language pGCL and its associated *quantitative logic* [18] were developed to express such programs and to derive their probabilistic properties by extending the classical assertional style of programming [20]. Programs in pGCL are modelled (operationally) as functions (or transitions) which map *initial states* in S to (sets of) probability distributions over *final states* — the program at (1) for instance has a single transition which maps any initial state to a (single) final distribution; we represent that distribution as a function d, evaluating to $2/3$ when $b = \mathsf{T}$ and to $1/3$ when $b = \mathsf{F}$.

Since properties are now quantitative we express them via a logic of *real-valued functions*, or *expectations*. For example the property "the final value of b is T with probability $2/3$" can be expressed as the *expected value* of the function $[b = \mathsf{T}]$ with respect to d [8], which evaluates to $2/3 \times 1 + 1/3 \times 0 = 2/3$.

Direct appeal to the operational semantics quickly becomes impractical for all but the simplest programs — better is the equivalent transformer-style semantics which obtained by rationalising the above calculation in terms of expected values rather than transitions, and the explanation runs as follows. Writing $\mathcal{E}S$ for the set of all (non-normalised) functions from S to $[0, 1]$, which we call the set of *expectations*, we say that the expectation $[b = \mathsf{T}]$ has been transformed to the expectation $2/3$ by the program *coin* (1) above so that they are in the relation "$2/3$ is the expected value of $[b = \mathsf{T}]$ with respect to the *coin*'s result distribution". More generally given a program *Prog*, an expectation E in $\mathcal{E}S$ and a state $s \in S$, we define wp.*Prog.E.s* to be the expected value of E with respect to the result distribution of program *Prog* if executed initially from state s [18]. We say that wp.*Prog* is the *expectation transformer* relative to *Prog*. In our example that allows us to write

$$2/3 \;\equiv\; \mathsf{wp}.(b := \mathsf{T}\,{}_{2/3}\!\oplus b := \mathsf{F}).[b = \mathsf{T}]\;.$$

In the case that *nondeterminism* is present, execution of *Prog* results in a *set* of possible distributions and we modify the definition of wp to take account of this — indeed we define wp.*Prog.E.s* so that it delivers the *least*-expected value with respect to all distributions in the result set. The transformers [18] give rise to a complete characterisation of probabilistic programs with nondeterminism, and they are sufficient to express many performance-style properties, including the probability that an event occurs [18], the expected time that it occurs [18], and long-run average of the number of times it occurs over many repeated executions of the system [16].

In Fig. 1 we set out the semantics for pGCL, a variation of Dijkstra's GCL with several extensions and modifications, all of which are labelled by (†). They are miracles, probability and "unguarded iteration" [4], the last representing a looping program which can iterate for an indeterminate length of time, a behaviour typifying reactive systems. All the programming features have been defined previously elsewhere, and (apart from probabilistic choice) have interpretations which are merely adapted to the real-valued context. For example nondeterminism, as explained above, is interpreted *demonically* and can be thought of as being resolved by a "minimal-seeking demon", providing guarantees on all program behaviour, such as is expected for total correctness. *Probabilistic choice*, on the other hand, selects the operands at random with weightings determined by the probability parameter p.

In addition to the definitions in Fig. 1 we will use the function gd which, applied to a command, defined the states from which the command is enabled.

$$gd.C \quad \hat{=} \quad (1 - \mathsf{wp}.C.0) , \tag{2}$$

so that when applied to a command of the form $G \rightarrow Prog$ returns $[G]$; we also refer to $Prog$ in $G \rightarrow Prog$ as its *body*. Given a family $\mathcal{I}$ of commands we write $\|_{i:\mathcal{I}} C_i$ for the generalised (nondeterministic) choice over the family, and $\sum_{i \in \mathcal{I}} C_i @ p_i$ for the generalised probabilistic choice (where $\sum_{i \in \mathcal{I}} p_i = 1$). Similarly for variable v we write $n :\in Pred$ for the generalised nondeterministic choice over any value from its type that satisfies the predicate *Pred*.

We say that a command is *normal* if it is of the form of a generalised probabilistic choice over standard (non-probabilistic) commands F_i, i.e. of the form $\sum_{i \in \mathcal{I}} F_i @ p_i$, where $\sum_{i \in \mathcal{I}} p_i \leq 1$. We shall need to be able to compose the effect of "running" commands simultaneously, and the next definition sets out how to do it.

Definition 1. *Given normal guarded commands $C \hat{=} G \rightarrow Prog$ and $C' \hat{=} G' \rightarrow Prog'$, we define their* composition *as follows.*

$$C \otimes C' \quad \hat{=} \quad (G \wedge G') \rightarrow \sum_{(i,j) \in I \times J} (F_i \otimes F'_j) @(p_i \times p'_j) ,$$

where $Prog = \sum_{i \in I} F_i @ p_i$ and $Prog' = \sum_{j \in J} F'_j @ p'_j$, and $\mathsf{wp}.F \otimes F'$ is given by the fusion *operator of Back and Butler [4]. In the case that F and F' operate over distinct state spaces (as in our case study), $F \otimes F'$ is equivalent to $F \; ; \; F'$.*

We end this section with a list of some nice features and idioms of pGCL.

• Unguarded iteration satisfies the equation it C ti = skip $\|$ C; (it C ti), expressing the fact that termination may occur at any time.

• Following from above, it magic ti = skip $\|$ magic ; (it magic ti) = skip.

• When C is a guarded command $G \rightarrow Prog$, the expression

$$\mathsf{wp}.(\text{it } C \text{ ti}).1 , \tag{3}$$

is the greatest guaranteed probability that the command (if executed) must establish $\neg G$ eventually. If this is 1 at any state, it means that the demon is obliged to terminate after a finite number of executions of C (with probability 1) to minimise the risk of a miracle; if it is 0 however it means that C may be executed forever, without ever establishing $\neg G$.

For example when G is "$(n > 0)$", and *Prog* is "$n := n + 1$", then (3) is the (standard) $[n \leq 0]$, since when n is greater than 0, the command can increase n indefinitely, and when n is less than 0 the interior command cannot execute

skip	wp.skip.$E \triangleq E$,
abort	wp.abort.$E \triangleq 0$,
magic(†)	wp.magic .$E \triangleq 1$,
assignment	wp.$(x := f).E \triangleq E[x := f]$,
sequential composition	wp.$(r; r').E \triangleq$ wp.r.(wp.$r'.E$) ,
probabilistic choice(†)	wp.$(r \,_p\!\oplus r').A \triangleq p \times$ wp.$r.E + (1{-}p) \times$ wp.$r'.E$,
nondeterministic choice	wp.$(r \mid r').A \triangleq$ wp.$r.E \sqcap$ wp.$r'.E$, where $\sqcap$ is pointwise minimum,
Boolean choice	wp.(if G then r else r').$E \triangleq [G] \times$ wp.$r.E + [\neg G] \times$ wp.$r'.E$,
Guarded command	wp.$(G \rightarrow r).E \triangleq [G] \times$ wp.$r.E + [\neg G]$,
Unguarded iteration(†)	wp.(it r ti).$E \triangleq (\mu X \bullet E \sqcap$ wp.$r.X)$.

E is an expectation in $\mathcal{E}S$, and f is a function of the state. The real p is restricted to lie between 0 and 1, and the term $(\mu X \ldots)$ refers to the least fixed point with respect to $\leq$, which we lift to real-valued functions; it is guaranteed to exist since the expectations form a complete partial order. Commands labelled † are extensions of the standard pGCL. Commands are ordered using *refinement*, so that more refined programs improve probabilistic results, thus

$$P \sqsubseteq Q \quad \textit{iff} \quad (\forall E \in \mathcal{E}S \cdot \text{wp}.P.E \leq \text{wp}.Q.E) .$$

Fig. 1. Structural definitions of wp for pGCL with miracles and unguarded iteration

even once. On the other hand if *Prog* is "$n := n + 1 \,_{2/3}\!\oplus n := n - 1$" (and G remains "$(n > 0)$"), then solving the fixed point equation (for the least solution) tells us that (3) is $1/2$ evaluated at "$n = 1$", implying that there is only $1/2$ chance that the command must establish $(n \leq 0)$ if iterated indefinitely. (And indeed the larger the initial value of n, the more likely is it that the command may be iterated forever, without incurring a miracle at all.[2])

- $gd.C \times$ wp.$C.post$ selects the greatest guaranteed expected value of *post* from initially enabled states.
- We write $\langle G \rangle$ for the "coercion" $G \rightarrow$ skip, the command which behaves like magic if G does not hold. Similarly we use $\{G\}$ for its dual, if G then skip else abort, the "assertion", which behaves like skip if G holds, and aborts if it doesn't. We say that a command C terminates, or is *total* if wp.$C.1 = 1$.

3 Probabilistic Action Systems

Action systems [3] are a "state-based" formalism for describing so-called reactive systems, *viz.* systems that may execute indefinitely. Although others [9,23] have added probability to action systems, our work is most closely related to Morgan's version of labelled probabilistic action systems [19], which we extend in various ways described below.

---

[2] See [18], page 287 for a wp-proof of this fact: it is an example of the asymmetric random walk.

A (probabilistic) action system consists of a (finite) set of labelled guarded commands, together with a distinguished command called an initialisation. An action system is said to *operate* over a state space S, meaning that the variables used in the system define its state space. Operationally an action system first executes its initialisation, after which any labelled action may "fire" if its guard is true by executing its body. Actions may continue to fire indefinitely until all the guards are false. If more than one guard is true then any one of those actions may fire, nondeterministically. We reserve the label τ for "hidden" actions, discussed later in Sec. 3.2.

In Fig. 2 we set out a small example of a probabilistic action system *Walker* which operates over the state defined by its variable n. First n is set nondeterministically either to -1 or 1, and then action a or b fires depending on whether n is greater than or less than 0, terminating if n is ever set to 0 (which, incidently, occurs with probability 1). In terms of actions, *Walker* executes alternately a string of a's or b's, whose frequency is determined by the probabilistic transitions.

$$Walker \; \hat{=} \; \left(\begin{array}{l} \textbf{var } \mathsf{n} : \mathbb{Z} \\ \textbf{initially } n :\in \{-1, 1\} \\ a : \; (n > 0) \; \rightarrow \; n := n + 1 \;\; _{1/3}\oplus \;\; n := n - 2 \\ b : \; (n < 0) \; \rightarrow \; n := n + 2 \;\; _{2/3}\oplus \;\; n := n - 2 \end{array} \right)$$

Fig. 2. A random walker with actions

For action system P and label a we write P_a for the generalised choice of all actions labelled with a, and P_i for its initialisation. In the case that P has no a action we define P_a to be magic . The set of non-τ labels (labelling actions in P) is denoted $\alpha.P$, and called P's *alphabet*. The semantics of an action system is given by pGCL set out at Fig. 1, so that, for example, $gd.(P_a) \times \mathsf{wp}.P_a.E$ is the greatest guaranteed expected value of E from execution of P_a.

We use the action labels in two important ways — the first is to define *synchronisation* and the second is to define *refinement* of action systems. We deal with both below.

3.1 Synchronising Actions

We define synchronisation so that all action systems participating in a parallel composition simultaneously fire their choice-shared actions together — in this mode the nondeterminism (arising from possibly overlapping guards) is resolved first, followed by any probability in the bodies. All other actions fire independently, interleaving with any others.

Definition 2. *Given normal action systems P and Q and subset A of actions (not containing τ), we define their parallel composition $P\|_A Q$ as follows.*

1. $P\|_A Q$ *operates over the union of the two state spaces, and* $\alpha.(P\|_A Q) = \alpha.P \cup \alpha.Q$;
2. $(P\|_A Q)_i \; \hat{=} \; P_i \otimes Q_i$;
3. $(P\|_A Q)_b \; \hat{=} \; P_b \parallel Q_b$, *for* $b \notin A$;
4. $(P\|_A Q)_a \; \hat{=} \; \parallel_{\{P^a \in P, Q^a \in Q\}} P^a \otimes Q^a$ *for* $a \in A$, *where* P^a *and* Q^a *are the individual a-labelled actions belonging to* P *and* Q *respectively.*

Note that the normality is preserved by Def. 2.

3.2 Hiding Actions

Our notion of abstraction is founded on the use of τ to indicate actions which are hidden *viz.* those actions that execute so-to-speak "behind the scenes". The idea is to imagine an observer of the system judging its behaviour only on the passage of non-τ-labelled actions. Thus he does not notice the actual firing of the τ actions, according any state change they may induce instead to the actions he has witnessed. The next definition sets out the details.

Definition 3. *Given a labelled action system* P, *and a set of labels* H, *we define the action system* $P \backslash H$ *as follows:* [3]

1. $P \backslash H$ *operates over the same state space as* P, *and* $\alpha.(P \backslash H) \hat{=} (\alpha.P) - H$;
2. $(P \backslash H)_a \hat{=} P_a$, *if* $a \notin H$;
3. $(P \backslash H)_\tau \hat{=} P_\tau \parallel (\parallel_{h \in H} P_h)$.

Thus *Walker*$\backslash\{b\}$ is the action system in which the only "observed actions" are a's. In between any a-action, an arbitrary number of the (now) hidden b-actions may be executed unobserved, but because wp.(it *Walker$_b$* ti).1 $= 1$, only finitely many can occur between every a action.[4] On the other hand Def. 3 forces hidden actions to fire in the case that *only* hidden actions are enabled.

3.3 Action Refinement

The ability to compare programs' behaviour is the mainstay of specification and refinement, and when used in conjunction with hiding is crucial for step-wise development of correct systems. Even though refinements normally contain more detail (and are thus more complicated) than the specifications from which they are derived, refinement ensures that they satisfy at least as many properties. Here we set out a formal treatment of property-preserving refinement (including quantitative properties) together with the principles underlying its definition.

In standard state-based programs, the refinement relation is applied to "the complete execution of the program". In this context however, there is no natural notion of "complete execution", as many actions may need to be fired to achieve some goal. Here we combine the principles of event-based formalisms

---

[3] This definition is similar to Butler and Morgan's definition [4] in terms of refinement.
[4] It is possible to introduce "divergence" after hiding — a situation in which hidden actions may iterate indefinitely, and which is equivalent to abortion — however we do not discuss that here.

(such as *Event B* [2]) and the probabilistic state-based approach to define a relation between probabilistic action systems in which the labels determine the observable behaviour. Our definition of refinement next compares the behaviour of observable — i.e. labelled — events, event-by-event. [5]

Definition 4. *Let P and Q be action systems operating over the same state spaces. We say that P is* refined by Q, *or $P \preceq Q$, if* [6]

  1. P_i ; it P_τ ti $\sqsubseteq Q_i$; it Q_τ ti
  2. it P_τ ti ; P_a ; it P_τ ti $\sqsubseteq$ it Q_τ ti ; Q_a; it Q_τ ti, for each $a \in \alpha.Q$,

where $\sqsubseteq$ is defined at Fig. 1 above.

For example, we see that $Walker\backslash\{b\} \preceq ReflectingWalk$ (where *ReflectingWalk* is defined in Fig. 3) since the effect of an arbitrary number of hidden actions in $Walker\backslash\{b\}$ (formerly the b actions) is summarised by the single τ event in *ReflectingWalk*. (Recall that hidden actions are forced to execute until a visible event is enabled.)

3.4   Property Preservation

The significance of a refinement relation is that it preserves properties, and in this section we set out how to define and test quantitative properties, and show that they are preserved by Def. 4. Our approach is via a small testing language in the style of concurrent logics [6], the key idea being that investigating a test is simpler than investigating all behaviours of a program in all contexts. In this case an action system is tested by incorporating it in a special testing program which can only do three things: either it aborts, exhibits a miracle or terminates in a valid state. Only in the latter case does the action system pass the test. Thus algorithms which implement the test then only need check for termination.

Definition 5. *Given an alphabet A we define a test T as follows.*

$$T \;\; \hat{=} \;\; \{G\} \mid \langle G \rangle \mid T;T \mid \;\; \|_{a \in K} a \mid \text{it } T \text{ ti} ,$$

where a is any label in A, and G and K are constant symbols.

A test t is to be understood in the context of an interpretation (set out at Def. 6 below) in which the labels correspond to the execution of actions in a given action system (effectively procedure calls), and the constants correspond to predicates over the variables (G), or subsets of actions (K). Thus tests specify sequences of labelled actions and named conditions corresponding to complex temporal formulae which may or may not be satisfied by particular instances of action systems. Our testing language is expressive enough to capture some important

---

[5] Compare the definition of state-based data-refinement [12].

[6] Note that hidden actions cannot be compared directly since in some cases one action system might not have hidden actions, whilst the other might.

classes of properties sufficient to make our connection to model checking "reachability" results. For example the property "predicate B holds until G does" can be specified by

$$B \triangleright G \;\; \hat{=} \;\; \text{it } \langle \neg G \rangle \; ; \; (\; \|_{a:\,A} a) \text{ ti } ; \; \langle G \vee \neg B \rangle \; ; \; \{G\} \; . \tag{4}$$

To see that observe that if $\neg G \wedge B$ holds (for a particular interpretation), the minimal-seeking nature of the nondeterminism will force it to fire any enabled action rather than terminate the iteration, since in that case execution of the coercion $\langle G \vee \neg B \rangle$ will result in a miracle. Similarly if $\neg G \wedge \neg B$ holds the demon will jump out of a loop resulting in a following abort (execution of $\{G\}$), but if G holds, the demon chooses between either a miracle or simply to terminate, the latter being the better option. [7]

Next we can interpret a test over an action system P simply by instantiating each label a by P_a, factoring in the initialisation and the hidden events, in the latter case by allowing an arbitrary number of hidden events to come before or after any visible event.

Definition 6. *For action system P such that $\alpha.P \subseteq A$, we interpret a test t over P as the pGCL program $\{t\}^{\mathcal{V}}_P$ (defined below), where $\mathcal{V}$ maps constants G to predicates over S, and constants K to finite, nonempty subsets of actions from A.*

$$\{t\}^{\mathcal{V}}_P \;\; \hat{=} \;\; P_i \; ; \; \text{it } P_\tau \text{ti } ; \; \|t\|^{\mathcal{V}}_P \;, \text{where}$$

$$\|t\|^{\mathcal{V}}_P \;\; \hat{=} \;\; \begin{cases} \{\mathcal{V}.G\} \text{ or } \langle \mathcal{V}.G \rangle & , \text{if } t = \{G\} \text{ or } \langle G \rangle \\ \|t'\|^{\mathcal{V}}_P \; ; \; \|t''\|^{\mathcal{V}}_P & , \text{if } t = t'; t'' \\ \|_{a \in \mathcal{V}.K}(\text{it } P_\tau \text{ti } ; \; P_a \; ; \; \text{it } P_\tau \text{ti}) & , \text{if } t = \|_{a \in K} a \\ \text{it } \|t'\|^{\mathcal{V}}_P \text{ ti} & , \text{if } t = \text{it } t' \text{ ti} \;. \end{cases}$$

We can now prove our property-preserving character of refinement, which tells us that properties expressed in the wp-style are all preserved.

Lemma 1. *If action systems $P \preceq Q$ then for any test t and any $\mathcal{V}$ mapping as in Def. 6, we have that $\{t\}^{\mathcal{V}}_P \sqsubseteq \{t\}^{\mathcal{V}}_Q$.*

$$ReflectingWalk \;\hat{=}\; \left(\begin{array}{l} \textbf{var } n : \mathbb{Z} \\ \textbf{initially } n :\in \{-1, 1\} \\ a : (n > 0) \rightarrow \; n := n + 1 \; _{1/3}\oplus n := n - 2 \\ \tau : (n < 0) \rightarrow \text{if } (\text{odd}.n) \text{ then } n := 1 \text{ else } n := 0 \end{array} \right)$$

Fig. 3. A walker with a reflecting barrier

---

[7] Note that this explanation is valid only when the action system always has some action enabled — in the simple case of magic for example, the miracle will automatically "guarantee" success.

Thus (abusing notation so that constants stand for themselves) Def. 6 tells us that $\mathsf{wp}.\{|(n < 0) \triangleright (n = 1)|\}^{\mathcal{V}}_{Walker}.[n = 1]$, computes the chance that n becomes 1, after being negative by iterating the actions of *Walker*, in this case it is only possible if n is initially negative and odd. Moreover Lem. 1 ensures that this result applies to *ReflectingWalk* as well, a fact easily checked by inspecting Fig. 3.

3.5   Changing Variables

In many cases, as systems are developed, we need to introduce new variables. To deal with this we use the technique familiar to the treatment of standard datatypes with named operations [7]. We partition the state space between "global" and "local" variables — the idea is that two action systems having different state spaces can still be compared by looking at their respective properties restricted to their *shared* global state. [8] As for datatypes we are then able to match corresponding execution paths using a "simulation" function which converts P's "local state" into Q's, so that the refinement relation Def. 4 thus applies.

Definition 7. *Given action systems P and Q with global variables g, and local variables a and c respectively, we say that $P \preceq_g Q$, or Q refines P with respect to g if there is a standard (i.e. non-probabilistic), non-miraculous and terminating simulation program rep, mapping variables a to c such that*

1. P_i ; rep $\quad \sqsubseteq \quad Q_i$;
2. P_a ; rep $\quad \sqsubseteq \quad$ rep ; Q_a ,   for $a \in \alpha.Q$
3. (it P_τ ti) ; rep $\quad \sqsubseteq$ rep ; (it Q_τ ti);
4. $\mathsf{skip}_g \quad \sqsubseteq \quad$ rep ; skip_g;

where skip_g is a special "do nothing" program which projects the state onto that defined by the global variables g.

If P_τ is magic , the third condition of Def. 7 (normally) reduces to a proof of termination for the iteration — this can be done using *probabilistic variants*, discussed elsewhere [18].

The next lemma sets out our property-preservation criterion.

Lemma 2. *Given action systems P and Q with shared (global) variables g, any test t, and mapping $\mathcal{V}$ mapping any constants G in t to predicates over g, then if $P \preceq_g Q$ we must have also that $\{|t|\}^{\mathcal{V}}_P$; $\mathsf{skip}_g \quad \sqsubseteq \quad \{|t|\}^{\mathcal{V}}_Q$; skip_g.* [9]

In this section we set out how to prove property-preserving refinements. In the next section we discuss how those properties may be verified using probabilistic model checking.

---

[8] If they do not share any global state — an unusual situation — then condition 4 in Def. 7 is the same as saying that *rep* must terminate.

[9] In the special case that P's local variables are mapped to Q's local variables, we may express a test more conveniently using local state, and the results interpreted over P will still apply to Q provided all the constants G are related by *rep* in the two interpretations.

4   Probabilistic Model Checking

The PRISM model checker [14] comprises a system description language together
with a property specification language based on probabilistic temporal logic. Although the operational interpretation (including the definition of synchronisation
and hiding) are semantically identical to deterministic normal action systems,
PRISM does not have a facility for refinement in the style set out here. In terms
of a specification and refinement task, Lem. 3, next, shows how we can appeal
to PRISM as an "oracle" to compute quantitative properties which by Lem. 2
will be preserved for all subsequent refinements. [10]

Lemma 3. *Given deterministic normal action systems $P_1, \ldots P_n$, we have that*

$$\mathsf{wp}.\{|(B \triangleright G)|\}^{\mathcal{V}}_P.[G].s_0 \quad = \quad [\mathcal{V}.B \; \mathcal{U} \; \mathcal{V}.G] \;,$$

*where $(B \triangleright G)$ is defined at (4), $P \triangleq P_1\|_A \ldots \|_A P_n$, A is the union of the
alphabets of the P_i, and the PRISM formula $[\mathcal{V}.B \; \mathcal{U} \; \mathcal{V}G]$ is interpreted as "the
least probability that $\mathcal{V}.B$ holds until until $\mathcal{V}.G$" does relative to P from intial
s_0.* [11]

5   A Stepwise Development of Probabilistic Backoff

In this section we develop a small case study based on the probabilistic backoff
procesdure of the IEEE 802.11 standard for wireless communication [1].

5.1   Two Senders and a Receiver

We begin with a very simple specification of part of a network consisting of two
"sending stations" and one "receiver", given by

$$Network_0 \quad \triangleq \quad Sender_A \;\|_A\; Receiver_{AB} \;\|_A\; Sender_B \;,$$

where the definitions of the sender and receiver are set out in Fig. 4, and $\mathcal{A}$ is
the set of all labelled events. This very straightforward specification depicts a
scenario in which senders A and B both need to send messages to a receiver,
who alternately listens, and then acknowledges any message which arrives safely.
Although in reality there may be collisions, and message loss, due to shared
channels those details are not included, since the intention is that "in the end"
both senders should send their messages intact. The $Network_0$ comprises a single
action system, which nondeterministically delivers a message first from one of the
senders, and then from the other in some order. Amongst the facts that may be
proved about this system is that an acknowledgement cannot precede a sending
event, by investigating formula $[(\neg s_a = wait \wedge \neg s_a = sent) \; \mathcal{U} \; (\neg s_a = sent)]$ using
PRISM. [12]

---

[10] Note the conventions relating to "local" and global" variables within PRISM differ
from ours.

[11] A similar result holds for "the greatest probability".

[12] Normally this safety property requires a greatest fixed point, however since s_a eventually satisfies *sent* or *wait* the least fixed point is valid.

$Sender_A \;\hat{=}$

$$\left(\begin{array}{l}\textbf{var } s_a: \{wait, sent, recv\} \\ \textbf{initially } s_a := wait \\ send_a : (s_a = wait) \rightarrow s_a := sent \\ ack_a : \;\;(s_a = sent) \rightarrow s_a := recv \end{array}\right)$$

$Receiver_{AB} \;\hat{=}$

$$\left(\begin{array}{l}\textbf{var } r: \{listen, ack\} \\ \textbf{initially } r := listen \\ send_a : (r = listen) \rightarrow r := ack \\ ack_a : \;\;(r = ack) \rightarrow r := listen \\ send_b : (r = listen) \rightarrow r := ack \\ ack_b : \;\;(r = ack) \rightarrow r := listen \end{array}\right)$$

Fig. 4. A sender and a receiver

5.2 Introducing Collisions

Next we introduce the possibility of collisions, indicating that both senders attempt to send over a shared "channel" at the same time. To do this we introduce an action system $Channel_{AB}$ depicted in Fig. 5 to model the shared channel, and augment the senders with a new event *"clash"*. the channel can be blocked — indicating that two senders try to use it at the same time — or clear; but can only be blocked for a limited time, since the probabilistic choice ensures that event *clash* may only occur for a finite number of times. As we're interested in the expected number of times the clashing event occurs before one of the senders' messages gets through, we include a variable t whose only purpose is to count clashing events. The intermediate

$Sender'_A \;\hat{=}$

$$\left(\begin{array}{l}\textbf{var } s_a: \{wait, sent, recv\} \\ \textbf{initially } s_a := wait \\ send_a : (s_a = wait) \rightarrow s_a := sent \\ ack_a : \;\;(s_a = sent) \rightarrow s_a := recv \\ clash : \textsf{skip} \end{array}\right)$$

$Channel_{AB} \;\hat{=}$

$$\left(\begin{array}{l}\textbf{var } c: \{block, clear\}, \; t: \{0 \dots T\} \\ \textbf{initially } c := block \; ; \; t := 0 \\ clash : (c = block) \rightarrow t := t + 1; \textsf{skip} \;_p\oplus c := clear \end{array}\right)$$

Fig. 5. Adding a clashing event and a channel

$$Network_1 \quad \hat{=} \quad Sender'_A \;||_A\; Receiver_{AB} \;||_A\; Sender'_B \;||_{\{clash\}}\; Channel_{AB} \;,$$

does not include the precise details of the mechanism employed to clear the channel, but only the overall effect *viz.* that it does indeed clear. Our first task is to show that $Network_1$ is a refinement of $Network_0$.

Lemma 4

$$Network_0 \quad \preceq_g \quad Network_1 \setminus \{clash\} \;,$$

where g represents the variables s_a, t and r.

Proof. Use the function rep $\hat{=}$ c :$\in$ {block, clear} ; t :$\in$ {0, ..., N}, noting that it distributes through any guard since it is standard so that the comment after Def. 7 applies, and this we only need prove the termination of (it $Network_1 \setminus \{clash\}$ ti). *But from Def. 3*

$$(Network_1 \setminus \{clash\})_\tau = (Channel_{AB})_{clash} ,$$

and it ($Channel_{AB\,clash}$) ti *must terminate with probability* 1, *a fact that can be checked using a probabilistic variant [18].*

Lem. 4 together with Lem. 2 imply that the properties verified for $Network_0$ still hold of $Network_1$, and we do not need to check them again directly. Moreover at this point it is possible to obtain some indication of the performance of the system by analysing $Network_1$. For example we can estimate the expected number of clashes by investigating the various probabilities that the two senders are both in the state *sent*, and t is set to a specific integer. To do this we model check the property "$[\neg(s_a = sent \wedge s_b = sent) \mathcal{U} (t \leq n)]$". The expected number of clashes may then be derived from these probabilities.

5.3 Probabilistic Backoff

Our final refinement is to introduce the randomised backoff procedure in each sender. When each process detects that it is in collision with another — again the details of how they do this have been suppressed — it sets its "backoff counter" to some random number and then counts down. As there is a good chance that the two backoff counters will be set to different values, the implication is that one of the senders will try to re-send at a time when the other is still "counting down", thus breaking the deadlock.

$RandSender_A \hat{=}$

$$\begin{pmatrix} \textbf{var } s_a: \{wait, sent, recv\}, \ bc_a: \{0 \ldots N\} \\ \textbf{initially } s_a := wait; \ bc_a := 0 \\ send_a : (s_a = wait) \rightarrow s_a := sent \\ ack_a : (s_a = sent) \rightarrow s_a := recv \\ clash : (bc_a = 0 \wedge s_a = wait) \rightarrow flip(bc_a) \\ tick : (bc_a > 0) \rightarrow bc_a := bc_a - 1 \\ tick : (bc_a = 0 \wedge s_a \neq wait) \rightarrow \text{skip} \end{pmatrix}$$

$Channel'_{AB} \hat{=}$

$$\begin{pmatrix} \textbf{var } t: \{0, \ldots, T\} \\ \textbf{initially } t := 0 \\ clash : t := t + 1 \end{pmatrix} ,$$

where $flip(x)$ sets the value of variable x to be n with probability $1/r^{n+1}$, if $n < N$, and to N with probability $1 - (1/r)^N$.

Fig. 6. A sending station with a backoff procedure, and channel to count clashes

The new system,

$$Network_2 \quad \hat{=} \quad RandSender_A \parallel_{A'} Receiver_{AB} \parallel_{A'} RandSender_B ,$$

is the parallel composition of the three components, this time synchronising on the all events given by $\mathcal{A}' \mathrel{\hat=} \mathcal{A} \cup \{clash, \quad tick\}$; we show that it is a refinement of $Network_1$.

Lemma 5

$$Network_1 \quad \preceq_g \quad Network_2 \backslash \{tick\} \,,$$

where g represents s_a, t and r.

Proof. We use rep $\hat=$ if ($c = clash$ then $(bc_a, bc_b :\in (bc_a = bc_b))$ else $(bc_a, bc_b :\in (bc_a \neq bc_b))$, and the argument now follows as for Lem. 4, noting that the probabilities when $bc_a = bc_b$ after the execution of flip(bc_a) and flip(bc_a) must add up to p, a condition which induces a relation between p and r, i.e. $p = \sum_{i<N} r^{2(i+1)} \times (1-r)^2 + (1-r)^{2N}$. Finally we must use Def. 2 to separate the single actions representing the synchronisation of clash and tick into actions residing in $RandSender_A$ and $RandSender_B$.

We end by noting that the facts gathered about $Network_0$ and $Network_1$ — that no acknowledgement may be sent before a send event, and the expected number of times that the senders try to send at the same time — still apply to $Network_2$, without the need for any further checks.

5.4   Experimental Results

Our experiments with PRISM implementations of examples of the above small systems demonstrate the large increase in model size with later refinements, thus abstraction of this kind may be thought of as easing state space explosion. For example with N set to 5 and T set to 100, the PRISM model for $Network_1$ consisted of 1608 states and 2009 transitions, whilst the PRISM model for $Network_2$ consisted of 20,008 states and 39,611 transitions. In a more realistic case study in which we include timing constraints we expect the increase to be greater still.

6   Comparisons with Other Work and Research Directions

Our contribution can be viewed as the first step towards a fully integrated system in which developers may use automation to explore (to some extent) the quantitative performance of their design decisions at early stages in their development. Just as we have come to expect from a development based on qualitative properties alone, the formal refinement relation ensures that the integrity of performance analysis is preserved as the system matures. Whilst our results show that model checking does not need to be used again once the specified performance property has been verified of an abstract system, the refinement process may continue in principle all the way to the code level. More experience is needed to decide when best to use the model checking results within a development.

Research in the modelling and evaluation of system performance has primarily focussed on process algebra such as PEPA [11] and TIPP [10] and Stochastic Petri nets [15]. These approaches allow specification of delays, which are realised by exponential distributions in a Markov Process simulation. Equivalence between processes — where it is available — is via various weak and strong bisumulations, and indeed our use of *rep* is similar to Hillston's propert-preserving weak bisimulations. However none of these cases can the performance properties be transferred *directly* to the code level, in a structured manner as they can with the specification/refinement paradigm presented here.

Other approaches using probabilistic action systems include Sere and Troubitsyna [23] and Hallerstede [9]. In the former case hiding is not available, whilst the latter models an action system as a Markov Decision Process with specified rewards. Mechanised tool support automates the selection of a refinement which guarantees the optimal cost with respect to the "long-run average". Although the system allows refinement, equality between action systems is necessary to preserve the integrity of the properties in more refined systems. In contrast the approach we have taken is closer to the normal refinement style, in which the value of worst-case properties increases up the refinement order; moreover best case-properties can also be ordered via refinement to prove worst case upper bounds, and are investigated elsewhere [5]. We note that our theory founded on expectations gives access to probabilities, expected times [18] and long-run averages [16], though more work is required for tools to compute the latter property directly.

The use of simulations for probabilistic systems has been studied by others, most notably Segala [22] using probabilistic automata; there are also many extensions of process algebras to include probability [13]. However, these approaches tend to deal directly with operational features of systems, compared to this work whose domain-theoretical basis exposes the (standard) mathematical structures underlying the probabilistic and nondeterministic features of the semantics. In particular this approach establishes straightforwardly the definitions of the associated quantitative transformer logic, allowing us to address the practical goal of preservation of system properties. Stepwise developments of wireless-like protocols have been carried out by Stoelinga [24].

Future work will explore the use of annotating programs with delays and other performance criteria, and developing tool support for the proof of program refinements.

References

1. IEEE 802.11 standard. http://grouper.ieee.org/groups/802/11/main.html.
2. J.-R. Abrial. Extending *B* without changing it (for developing distributed systems). In H. Habrias, editor, *First Conference on the B Method*, pages 169–190. Laboratoire LIANA, L'Institut Universitaire de Technologie (IUT) de Nantes, November 1996.
3. R.-J.R. Back. A calculus of refinements for program derivations. *Acta Informatica*, 25:593–624, 1988.
4. M.J. Butler and C.C. Morgan. Action systems, unbounded nondeterminism and infinite traces. *Formal Aspects of Computing*, 7(1):37–53, 1995.
5. O. Celiku and A. McIver. Cost-based analysis of probabilistic programs mechanised in HOL. *Nordic Journal of Computing*, 2004.

6. M. de Nicola and M. Hennessy. Testing equivalence for processes. *Theoretical Computer Science*, 34, 1984.

7. P.H.B. Gardiner and C.C. Morgan. Data refinement of predicate transformers. *Theoretical Computer Science*, 87:143–62, 1991.

8. G.R. Grimmett and D. Welsh. *Probability: an Introduction*. Oxford Science Publications, 1986.

9. S. Hallerstede and M. Butler. Performance analysis of probabilistic action systems. 2005.

10. H. Hermanns, U. Herzog, U. Klehmet, V. Mertsiotakis, and M. Siegle. Compositional performance modelling with the tipp tool. *Performance Evaluation*, 39:5–35, 2000.

11. J. Hillston. *A Compositional Approach to Performance Modelling*. Cambridge University Press, 1996.

12. C.A.R. Hoare, Jifeng He, and J.W. Sanders. Prespecification in data refinement. *Inf. Proc. Lett.*, 25(2):71–6, May 1987.

13. B. Jonsson, K.G. Larsen, and Wang Yi. Probabilistic extensions of process algebras. *Handbook of Process Algebras*, (1):685–710, 2001.

14. M. Kwiatkowska, G. Norman, and D.Parker. Probabilistic symbolic model checking with PRISM: A hybrid approach. 2002. Accepted for TACAS 2002.

15. M. Ajmone Marsan, Gianfranco Balbo, Gianni Conte, Susanna Donatelli, and Giuliana Franceschinis. *Modelling with generalised stochastic petri nets*. Wiley, New York, 1995.

16. A.K. McIver. A generalisation of stationary distributions, and probabilistic program algebra. In Stephen Brookes and Michael Mislove, editors, *Electronic Notes in Theo. Comp. Sci.*, volume 45. Elsevier, 2001.

17. A.K. McIver and C.C. Morgan. Results on the quantitative μ-calculus $qM\mu$. To appear in *ACM TOCL*, 2004.

18. Annabelle McIver and Carroll Morgan. *Abstraction, Refinement and Proof for Probabilistic Systems*. Technical Monographs in Computer Science. Springer Verlag, New York, 2004.

19. C.C. Morgan. Of probabilistic Wp and CSP. *25 years of CSP*.

20. C.C. Morgan. *Programming from Specifications*. Prentice-Hall, second edition, 1994.

21. PRISM. Probabilistic symbolic model checker. www.cs.bham.ac.uk/~dxp/prism.

22. Roberto Segala. *Modeling and Verification of Randomized Distributed Real-Time Systems*. PhD thesis, MIT, 1995.

23. Kaisa Sere and Elena Troubitsyna. Probabilities in action systems. In *Proc. of the 8th Nordic Workshop on Programming Theory*, 1996.

24. Mariëlle Stoelinga and Frits Vaandrager. Root contention in IEEE 1394. *Lecture Notes in Computer Science*, 1601:53–74, 1999.

Modeling and Validating Distributed Embedded Real-Time Systems with VDM++

Marcel Verhoef[1,*], Peter Gorm Larsen[2], and Jozef Hooman[3]

[1] Chess Information Technology and Radboud University Nijmegen, NL
[2] Engineering College of Aarhus, Denmark
[3] Embedded Systems Institute and Radboud University Nijmegen, NL
Marcel.Verhoef@chess.nl, pgl@iha.dk, hooman@cs.ru.nl

Abstract. The complexity of real-time embedded systems is increasing, for example due to the use of distributed architectures. An extension to the Vienna Development Method (VDM) is proposed to address the problem of deployment of software on distributed hardware. The limitations of the current notation are discussed and new language elements are introduced to overcome these deficiencies. The impact of these changes is illustrated by a case study. A constructive operational semantics is defined in VDM++ and validated using VDMTOOLS. The associated abstract formal semantics, which is not specific to VDM, is presented in this paper. The proposed language extensions significantly reduce the modeling effort when describing distributed real-time systems in VDM++ and the revised semantics provides a basis for improved tool support.

1 Introduction

The complexity of embedded systems is rapidly increasing; they are becoming distributed almost by default, for example due to the System-on-Chip design philosophy which is often used nowadays. Safety-critical applications have traditionally been federated, meaning that each "function" has its own CPU with minimal interconnections to other functions in the system. This approach is expensive and for some application areas, such as the automobile industry, it is no longer economically viable to do so. The current trend is rather to combine functions together on the same processing unit and then distribute their operation between a number of networked fault-tolerant processors in order to reduce cost. It is not hard to imagine that finding the "right" deployment of functionality over such a distributed architecture, that meets all the imposed system-level requirements, is quite a challenging problem.

It is natural to advocate the use of formal techniques in this application area in order to cope with this complexity and indeed a large body of knowledge exists on their use. Most formal techniques however, are not able to deal with

---

* This work has been carried out as part of the Boderc project under the responsibility of the Embedded Systems Institute. This project was partially supported by the Netherlands Ministry of Economic Affairs under the Senter TS program.

J. Misra, T. Nipkow, and E. Sekerinski (Eds.): FM 2006, LNCS 4085, pp. 147–162, 2006.
© Springer-Verlag Berlin Heidelberg 2006

the combination of complex behavior, timing, concurrency and in particular distribution in a flexible and intuitive way. Tool support often does not scale very well to the size of problems faced by industry. System development lead times remain substantial, even if formal methods can be usefully applied.

The Vienna Development Method (VDM) has been used in several large-scale industrial projects [1,2,3,4]. Their success was very much due to the solid formal basis of the notation and the availability of robust and commercial grade tools. However, not much is known about the application of VDM in the area of distributed real-time embedded systems. In earlier work [5], we reported that it is very hard to describe such systems in VDM. The language is not sufficiently expressive and important tool features are missing to analyze such models.

The aim of this paper is to make VDM++ better suited for describing distributed embedded real-time systems and to enable the design space exploration as mentioned before. In Sect. 2, an overview of the notation and the existing timed extension is presented. The limitations experienced in our earlier work are summarized and we introduce the main proposed adaptations: the addition of deployment and asynchronous communication. A small case study is presented in Sect. 3 that demonstrates the impact of the proposed changes. In Sect. 4, we define an abstract formal semantics of the extended language and discuss how the semantics has been validated. Finally, in Sections 5 and 6 we present related work and we discuss the results achieved.

2   An Overview of the VDM Notation

VDM++ is an object-oriented and model-based specification language with a formally defined syntax, static and dynamic semantics. It is a superset of the ISO standardized notation VDM-SL [6]. VDM++ was originally designed in the ESPRIT project AFRODITE and it was subsequently improved and tools were implemented by IFAD. Different VDM dialects are supported by industry strength tools, called VDMTOOLS, which are currently owned and further developed by CSK [1]. A timed extension to VDM++ was delivered as part of the VICE project: "VDM++ In a Constrained Environment" [7].

The dynamic semantics of an executable subset of VDM++ is provided as a constructive operational semantics specified in VDM-SL which is roughly 500 pages including informal explanation [8]. The core of this specification is an abstract state machine which is able to execute a set of formally defined primitive instructions. Special functions are supplied to "compile" each abstract syntax element into such a sequence of instructions. The dynamic semantics specification is executable and can be validated using VDMTOOLS. The test suite contains several thousand test cases which are also used to verify the implementation. The industrial success of VDMTOOLS is, for a large part, due to excellent conformance of the tool to the formally defined operational semantics and the round-trip engineering with UML.

---

[1] *http://www.csk.com/support_e/vdm/*

For an in-depth presentation of the language and supporting tools [2] see [3]. We provide an overview in Sect. 2.1 and introduce the timed extensions in Sect. 2.2. The limitations of these extensions are discussed in Sect. 2.3 and we present our proposed language modifications in Sect. 2.4.

2.1 The Basic VDM++ Notation

In VDM++, a model consists of a collection of class specifications. We distinguish active and passive classes. Active classes represent entities that have their own thread of control and do not need external triggers in order to work. In contrast, passive classes are always manipulated from the thread of control of another active class. We use the term object to denote the instance of a class. More than one instance of a class might exist. An instance is created using the *new* operator, which returns an object reference. A class specification has the following components:

Class header: The header contains the class name declaration and inheritance information. Both single or multiple inheritance are supported.

Instance variables: The state of an object consists of a set of typed variables, which can be of a simple type such as *bool* or *nat*, or complex types such as sets, sequences, maps, tuples, records and object references. The latter are used to specify relations between classes. Instance variables can have invariants and an expression to define the initial state.

Operations: Class methods that may modify the state can be defined implicitly, using pre- and postcondition expressions only, or explicitly, using imperative statements and optional pre- and postcondition expressions.

Functions: Functions are similar to operations except that the body of a function is an expression rather than an imperative statement. Functions are not allowed to refer to instance variables, they are pure and side-effect free.

Synchronization: Operations in VDM++ are re-entrant and their invocation is defined with synchronous (rendez-vous) semantics. It is possible to constrain the execution of an operation by specifying a permission predicate [9]. A permission predicate is a Boolean expression over so-called history counters that acts as a guard for the operation, for example to express mutual exclusion. History counters are maintained per object to count the number of requests, activations and completions per operation.

Thread: A class can be made "active" by specifying a thread. A thread is a sequence of statements which are executed to completion at which point the thread dies. The thread is created whenever the object is created but the thread needs to be started explicitly using the *start* operator. It is possible to specify threads that never terminate.

2.2 The Existing Timed Extension to VDM++

In the VICE project [7], time was added by assigning a user-configurable default duration to each basic language construct. Whenever a statement is evaluated by

---

[2] Many examples and free tool support can be found at *http://www.vdmbook.com*

the interpreter, the global notion of time is increased by the specified amount. In this way, it was possible to simulate the timed behavior of a program running on a single processor. In addition, the user can specify the task switch overhead and the scheduling policy used. The duration statement was added to the language, with the concrete syntax *duration(d) IS*, which implies that all statements in *IS* are executed instantaneously and then time is increased by *d* time units. The duration statement is used to override the default execution time for *IS*. Furthermore, the periodic statement was introduced, with the concrete syntax *periodic(d)(Op)*. This statement can only be used in the thread clause to denote that operation *Op* is called periodically every *d* time units.

2.3   The Limitations of Timed VDM++

In previous work [5], we assessed the suitability of timed VDM++ for distributed real-time embedded systems. We list the most important problems here.

1. Operations in VDM++ are synchronous; calls are either blocked on a permission predicate (guard) or executed in the context of the thread of control of the caller. The caller has to wait until the operation is completed before it can resume. This is very cumbersome when embedded systems are modeled. These systems are typically reactive by nature and asynchronous. An event loop can be specified to describe this, but the complexity of the model is increased and analysis of the model becomes harder.

2. Timed VDM++ supports a uni-processor multi-threading model of computation which means that at most one thread can claim the processor and only this active thread can push time in the model forward. This is insufficient for describing embedded systems because 1) they are often implemented on a distributed architecture and 2) these systems need to be described in combination with their environment. The subsystems and the environment are independent and therefore need their own notion of time which requires a multi-processor multi-threading model of computation.

3. The duration statement in timed VDM++ denotes a time penalty that is independent of the resource that executes the statement. When deployment is considered, it is essential to also be able to express time penalties that are relative to the capacity of the computation resource. Furthermore, there should be an additional time penalty that reflects the message handling between two computation resources whenever a remote operation call is performed.

2.4   Proposed Changes

Our aim is to minimize the impact on the existing language as much as possible. Ideally, we want to remain backwards compatible in order to reuse existing models and tools. Therefore, we have not considered to merge VDM++ with other techniques. Informally, we propose the following changes:

1. The semantics of timed VDM++ is based on the assumption that at most one thread can push time forward in the model. We propose a richer semantics in which this limitation is removed. Any thread that is running on a computation resource or any message that is in transit on a communication resource can cause time to elapse. Models that contain only one computation resource are compatible to models in timed VDM++.
2. The suggestion is to introduce the *async* keyword in the signature of an operation to denote that an operation is asynchronous. The caller shall no longer be blocked, it can immediately resume its own thread of control after the call is initiated. A new thread is created and started immediately to execute the body of the asynchronous operation.
3. A collection of special predefined classes, *BUS* and *CPU*, are made available to the specifier to construct the distributed architecture in his model. The *system* class is used to contain such an architecture model. User-defined classes can be instantiated and deployed on a specific *CPU* in the model. The communication topology between the computation resources in the model can be described using the *BUS* class.
4. The *duration* statement is kept intact to specify time delays that are independent of the system architecture. In addition, we introduce the *cycles* statement, with a similar concrete syntax, to denote a time delay that is relative to the capacity of the resource. The time delay incurred by the message transfer over the *BUS* can be made dependent of the size of the message being transfered, which is a function of the parameter values passed to the operation call.

We will demonstrate the impact of these changes in Sect. 3 using a small case study and in Sect. 4 we present the semantics of the main extensions.

3 Modeling an In-Car Radio Navigation System

In previous work [10,11], we have studied the design of an in-car radio navigation system. Such an infotainment system typically executes several concurrent software applications that share a common, and often distributed, hardware platform. Each application has individual requirements that need to be met and the question is whether all requirements can be satisfied when a particular architecture is chosen. We present a VDM++ model of the distributed in-car radio navigation system using the suggested language improvements. We have focused on modeling the non-functional performance aspects because these will highlight the impact of the language changes most prominently. The case study aims to demonstrate that it is easy to describe distributed architectures and the associated deployment of functionality onto it. The model presented here reflects one of the proposals that was considered during the design, consisting of three processing units connected through an internal communication bus. We use the terms application and task to informally describe the case study. An overview is presented in Fig. 1.

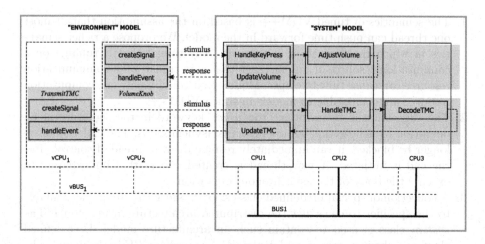

Fig. 1. Informal overview of the case study

Two applications are running on the system: *ChangeVolume* and *ProcessTMC*. Each application consists of three individual tasks. The *ChangeVolume* application, represented by the top right gray box, controls the volume of the radio. The task `HandleKeyPress` takes care of all user interface input handling, `AdjustVolume` modifies the volume accordingly and `UpdateVolume` displays the new volume setting on the screen. The *ProcessTMC* application, indicated by the bottom right gray box in Fig. 1, handles all Traffic Message Channel (TMC) messages. TMC messages arrive at the `HandleTMC` task where they are checked and forwarded to the `DecodeTMC` task to be translated into human readable text which is displayed on the screen by the `UpdateTMC` task.

Two additional applications represent the environment of the system: *VolumeKnob* and *TransmitTMC*. The former is used to simulate the behavior of a user turning the volume knob at a certain rate and the latter is used to simulate the behavior of a radio station that transmits TMC messages. Both applications inject stimuli into the system (`createSignal`) and observe the system response (`handleEvent`).

In the remainder of this section, we will present how applications and tasks from the informal case study description relate to classes, operations and threads in VDM++. Furthermore, we will show how distributed architectures are described and how objects are deployed. We present the environment model in more detail in Sect. 3.1 and the system model in Sect. 3.2.

3.1   The Environment Model

In our case study, there are two environment applications. Each application is represented by a class, the tasks are represented by operations in that class. An instance of the class is automatically deployed on an implicit computation resource, denoted by the dashed boxes in Fig. 1. Environment applications operate in parallel to the system and independent of each other. Execution of an environment application does *not* affect the notion of time in other environment or system applications. Environment applications communicate with the system applications over an implicit communication resource that connects all computation resources in the model.

Typical system-level temporal and timing properties can be specified over the interface between the environment and the system model. Informal examples of these requirements are: *"The order of the VolumeKnob stimuli is preserved by the output response sequence of the system."* and *"For each HandleTMC stimulus, the maximum allowed response time shall be less than 1000 time units."*. These requirements can be modeled using standard VDM++ constructs. The TransmitTMC class is presented in Fig. 2.

```
class TransmitTMC
instance variables
  static private id : nat := 0;
  protected e2s : map nat to nat := {|->};
  protected s2e : map nat to nat := {|->}

operations
  getNum: () ==> nat
  getNum () == ( dcl res : nat := id; id := id + 1; return res );

  async public handleEvent : nat ==> ()
  handleEvent (pev) == s2e := s2e munion {pev |-> time}
  post forall idx in set dom s2e & s2e(idx) - e2s(idx) <= 1000;

  createSignal : () ==> ()
  createSignal () ==
    ( dcl num : nat := getNum(); e2s := e2s munion {num |-> time};
      RadNavSys'radio.HandleTMC (num) )

thread periodic (1000) (createSignal)
sync mutex(getNum)

end TransmitTMC
```

Fig. 2. The *TransmitTMC* class

Two instance variables are maintained to log the stimuli (*e2s*) and the responses (*s2e*). These variables are mappings from a unique natural number provided by the operation getNum, to identify each stimulus, to another natural number that represents the time at which the event was recorded. The *time* keyword provides access to the "wall clock" of the interpreter whenever the model is executed. A TMC event is inserted into the system by the periodic thread createSignal every 1000 time units by calling the asynchronous operation HandleTMC of the *Radio* class shown in Fig. 3. The operation handleEvent is called by the system at the end of the UpdateTMC operation (not shown here), indicating that the event was completely processed by the *ProcessTMC* application. The worst-case response time requirement is encoded as a postcondition to the **handleEvent** operation. The postconditions are checked when the model is simulated. Whenever the postcondition is false, the interpreter will stop and the state of the system can be inspected to determine the cause of the problem. Other timeliness requirements can be specified in a similar way.

3.2   The System Model

In the system model of our example, there are two independent applications that consist of three tasks each. Tasks can either be triggered by external stimuli or by receiving messages from other tasks. A task can also actively acquire or provide information by periodically checking for available data on an input source or delivering new data to an output source. All three notions of task activation are supported by our approach. Note that task activation by external stimuli can be used to model *interrupt handling*. The **HandleKeyPress** and **HandleTMC** tasks belong to this category. The other tasks in our system model are message triggered. We already used periodic task activation in the environment model (**createSignal**).

```
class Radio
operations
  async public AdjustVolume : nat ==> ()
  AdjustVolume (pno) ==
    ( duration (150) skip; RadNavSys 'mmi.UpdateVolume (pno) );

  async public HandleTMC : nat ==> ()
  HandleTMC (pno) ==
    ( cycles (1E5) skip; RadNavSys 'navigation.DecodeTMC (pno) )
end Radio
```

Fig. 3. The *Radio* class

Application tasks are modeled by asynchronous operations in VDM++. Fig. 3 presents the definition of **AdjustVolume** and **HandleTMC**, which are grouped together in the *Radio* class. We use the *skip* statement for illustration purposes here, it can be replaced with an arbitrary complex statement to describe the actual system function that is performed, for example changing the amplifier volume set point. Note that **AdjustVolume** uses the *duration* statement to denote that a certain amount of time expires independent of the resource on which it is deployed. The duration statement now states that changing the set point always takes 150 time units. For illustration purposes, **HandleTMC** uses the *cycles* statement to denote that a certain amount of time expires relative to the capacity of the computation resource on which it is deployed. If this operation is deployed on an resource that can deliver 1000 cycles per unit of time then the delay (duration) would be 1E5 divided by 1000 is 100 time units. A suitable unit of time can be selected by the modeler.

A special class called *CPU* is provided to create computation resources in the system model. Each computation resource is characterized by its processing capacity, specified by the number of available cycles per unit of time, the scheduling policy that is used to determine the task execution order and a factor to denote the overhead incurred per task switch. For this case study, fixed priority preemptive scheduling with zero overhead is used, although our approach is not restricted to any policy in particular.

```
system RadNavSys
    instance variables
        -- create the application tasks
        static public mmi  := new MMI();
        static public radio  := new Radio();
        static public navigation := new Navigation();

        -- create CPU (policy, capacity, task switch overhead)
        CPU1 : CPU := new CPU(<FP>, 22E6, 0);
        CPU2 : CPU := new CPU(<FP>, 11E6, 0);
        CPU3 : CPU := new CPU(<FP>, 113E6, 0);

        -- create BUS (policy, capacity, message overhead, topology)
        BUS1 : BUS := new BUS(<FCFS>, 72E3, 0, {CPU1, CPU2, CPU3})

    operations
        -- the constructor of the system model
        public RadNavSys: () ==> RadNavSys
        RadNavSys () ==
            ( CPU1.deploy(mmi);           -- deploy MMI on CPU1
              CPU2.deploy(radio);         -- deploy Radio on CPU2
              CPU3.deploy(navigation) )   -- deploy Navigation on CPU3
    end RadNavSys
```

Fig. 4. The top-level system model for the case study

A special class *BUS* is provided to create communication resources in the system model. A communication resource is characterized by its throughput, specified by the number of messages that can be handled per unit of time, the scheduling policy that is used to determine the order of the messages being exchanged and a factor to denote the protocol overhead. The granularity of a message can be determined by the user. For example, it can represent a single byte or a complete Ethernet frame, whatever is most appropriate for the problem under study. For this case study, we use First Come First Served scheduling with zero overhead, but again the approach is not restricted to any policy in particular. An overview of the VDM++ system model is presented in Fig. 4.

4   Abstract Operational Semantics

In this section we formalize the semantics of the proposed changes to VDM++, as described in Sect. 2.4. To highlight the main changes and modifications, an abstract basic language which includes the new constructs is defined in Sect. 4.1. We describe the intended meaning and discuss the most important issues that had to be addressed when formalizing this. In Sect. 4.2, a formal operational semantics is defined. Validation of this semantics is discussed in Sect. 4.3.

4.1   Syntax

We abstract from many aspects and constructs in VDM++ and assume given definitions of classes, including explicit definitions of synchronous and asynchronous operations. It is assumed that these definitions are compiled into a sequence of instructions. We abstract from most local, atomic instructions (such as assignments) and consider only the *skip* instruction. Let d denote a nonnegative time value, and let *duration* (d) be an abbreviation of *duration(d) skip*. Assume that, for an instruction sequence *IS*, the statement *duration(d) IS* is translated into *IS ˆ duration(d)*, where internal durations inside *IS* have been removed and the "ˆ" operator concatenates the duration instruction to the end of a sequence. The concatenation operation is also used to concatenate sequences and to add an instruction to the front of the sequence. Functions *head* and *tail* yield the first element and the rest of the sequence, resp., and $\langle\rangle$ denotes the empty sequence. Let *ObjectId* be the set of object identities, with typical element *oid*. *Operation* denotes the set of operations, with typical element *op*. The predicate *syn?(op)* is true iff the operation is synchronous. The syntax of the instructions is defined by:

Instr.	$I ::= skip \mid call(oid, op) \mid duration(d) \mid periodic(d)\ IS$
Instr. Seq.	$IS ::= \langle\rangle \mid I \,\hat{}\, IS$

These basic instructions have the following informal meaning:

- *skip* represents a local statement which does not consume any time.
- *call(oid, op)* denotes a call to an operation *op* of object *oid*. Depending on the *syn?* predicate, the operation can be synchronous (i.e., the caller has to wait until the execution of the operation body has terminated) or asynchronous (the caller may continue with the next instruction and the operation body is executed independently). There are no restrictions on re-entrance here, but in general this can be restricted by permission predicates as discussed in Sect. 2.1. These are not considered here, also parameters are ignored.
- *duration(d)* represents a time progress of d time units. When d time units have elapsed the next statement can be executed. As shown in Sect. 3.2, *cycles(d)* can be expressed as a duration statement.
- *periodic(d) IS* leads to the execution of instruction sequence *IS* each period of d time units.

To formalize deployment, assume given a set of nodes *Node* and a function *node* which gives for each object identity *oid* its processor, denoted *node(oid)*. Furthermore, assume given a set of links, defined as a relation between nodes *Link = Node × Node*, to express that messages can be transmitted from one node to another via a link. In the semantics described here we assume, for simplicity, that a direct link exists between each pair of communicating nodes. Note that *CPU* and *BUS*, as used in the radio navigation case study, are concrete examples of a node and a link.

The formalization of the precise meaning of the language described above raises a number of questions that have to answered and on which a decision has to be taken. We list the main points:

- How to deal with the combination of synchronous and asynchronous operations, e.g. does one has priority over the other, how are incoming call request recorded, is there a queue at the level of the node or for each object separately? We decided for an equal treatment of both concepts; each object has a single FIFO queue which contains both types of incoming call requests.
- How to deal with synchronous operation calls; are the call and its acceptance combined into a single step and does it make a difference if caller and callee are on different nodes? In our semantics, we distinguish between a call within a single node and a call to an operation of an object on another node.

  For a call between different nodes, a call message is transferred via a link to the queue of the callee; when this call request is dequeued at the callee, the operation body is executed in a separate thread and, upon completion, a return message is transmitted via the link to the node of the caller.

  For a call within a single node, we have made the choice to avoid a context switch and execute the operation body directly in the thread of the caller. Instead, we could have placed the call request in the queue of the callee.
- Similar questions hold for asynchronous operations. On a single node, the call request is put in the queue of the callee, whereas for different nodes the call is transferred via a link. However, no return message is needed and the caller may continue immediately after issuing the call.
- How are messages between nodes transferred by the links? In principle, many different communication mechanisms could be modeled. As a simple example, we model a link by a set of messages which include a lower and an upper bound on message delivery. For a link l, let $\delta_{min}(l)$ and $\delta_{max}(l)$ be the minimum and maximum transmission time. It is easy to extend this and make the transmission time dependent of, e.g., message size and link traffic.
- How to deal with time, how is the progress of time modeled? In our semantics, there is only one global step which models progress of time on all nodes. All other steps do not change time; all assumptions on the duration of statements, context switches and communications have to be modeled explicitly by means of duration statements.
- What is the precise meaning of *periodic(d) IS* if the execution of *IS* takes more than d time units? We decided that after each d time units a new thread is started to ensure that every d time units the *IS* sequence can be

executed. Of course, this might potentially lead to resource problems for particular applications, but this will become explicit during analysis.

4.2 Formal Operational Semantics

The aim of the operational semantics is to define the execution of the language defined in Sect. 4.1. To capture the state of affairs at a certain point during the execution, we introduce a *configuration* (Def. 1). Next we define the possible steps from one configuration to another, denoted by $C \longrightarrow C'$ where C and C' are configurations (Def. 3). This finally leads to a set of runs of the form $C_0 \longrightarrow C_1 \longrightarrow C_2 \longrightarrow \ldots$ (Def. 8).

To focus on the essential aspects, we assume that the set of objects is fixed and need not be recorded in the configuration. However, object creation can be added easily, see e.g. [12]. Let *Thread* be a set of thread identities; each thread i is related to one object, denoted by o_i. This also leads to the deployment of threads: $node(i) = node(o_i)$. Finally, we extend the set of instructions *Instruction* with an auxiliary statement $return(i)$. This statement will be added during the executing at the end of the instruction sequence of a synchronous operation which has been called by thread i.

Definition 1 (Configuration). A *configuration* C contains the following fields:

- *instr* : *Thread* $\rightarrow$ *seq*[*Instruction*] which is a function which assigns a sequence of instructions to each thread.
- *curthr* : *Node* $\rightarrow$ *Thread* yields for each node the currently executing thread.
- *status* : *Thread* $\rightarrow$ {*dormant, alive, waiting*} to denote the status of threads.
- q : *ObjectId* $\rightarrow$ *queue*[*Thread* $\times$ *Operation*] records for each object a FIFO queue of incoming calls, together with the calling thread (needed for synchronous operations only).
- *linkset* : *Link* $\rightarrow$ *set*[*Message* $\times$ *Time* $\times$ *Time*] records the set of the incoming messages for each link, together with lower and upper bound on delivery. A message may denote a call of an operation (including calling thread and called object) or a return to a thread.
- *now* : *Time* to denote the current time.

For a configuration C, we use the notation $C(f)$ to obtain its field f, such as $C(instr)$. For a FIFO queue, functions *head* and *tail* yield the head of the queue and the rest, respectively; *insert* is used to insert an element and $\langle\rangle$ denotes the empty queue. For sets we use *add* and *remove* to insert and remove elements. We use $exec(C, i)$ as an abbreviation for $C(curthr)(node(i)) = i$ to express that thread i is executing on its node. Let $fresh(C, oid)$ yield a fresh, not yet used, thread identity (so with status *dormant*) corresponding to object *oid*. To express modifications of a configuration, we define the notion of a variant.

Definition 2 (Variant). The *variant* of a configuration C with respect to a field f and value v, denoted by $C[\, f \mapsto v\,]$, is defined as

$$(C[\, f \mapsto v\,])(f') = \begin{cases} v & \text{if } f' = f \\ C(f') & \text{if } f' \neq f \end{cases}$$

Similarly for parts of the fields, such as $instr(i)$.

Steps have been grouped into several definitions, leading to the following overall definition of a step.

Definition 3 (Step). $C \longrightarrow C'$ is a *step* iff it corresponds to the execution of an instruction (Def. 4), a context switch (Def. 5), the delivery of a message by a link (Def. 6), or the processing of a message from a queue (Def. 7).

Definition 4 (Execute Instruction). A step $C \longrightarrow C'$ corresponds to the execution of an instruction iff there exists a thread i such that $exec(C, i)$ and $head(C(instr)(i))$ is one of the following instructions:

- *skip*: Then the new configuration equals the old one, except that the skip instruction is removed from the instruction sequence of i, that is,
  $C' = C[\, instr(i) \mapsto tail(C(instr)(i))\,]$
- *call(oid, op)*: Let IS be the explicit definition of operation op of object oid. If caller and callee are on the same node, i.e. $node(i) = node(oid)$ and $syn?(op)$ then IS is executed directly in the thread of the caller, i.e.,
  $C' = C[\, instr(i) \mapsto IS\hat{\ } tail(C(instr)(i))\,]$
  Otherwise, if not $syn?(op)$, we add the pair (i, op) to the queue of oid, i.e.,
  $C' = C[\, instr(i) \mapsto tail(C(instr)(i)), \ q(oid) \mapsto insert((i, op), C(q)(oid))\,]$
  If $node(i) \neq node(oid)$ and link l connects the nodes, then the call is transmitted via l, so added to the linkset. If $syn?(op)$, thread i becomes *waiting*:
  $C' = C[\, instr(i) \mapsto tail(C(instr)(i)), \ status(i) \mapsto waiting,$
  $\qquad\qquad linkset(l) \mapsto insert(m, C(linkset)(l))\,]$
  where $m = (call(i, oid, op), C(now) + \delta_{min}(l), C(now) + \delta_{max}(l))$. Similarly for asynchronous operations, except that then the status of i is not changed.
- *duration(d)*: To allow progress of time, we require that all threads that are *alive* and have a non-empty instruction sequence can only perform a duration. Then time may progress with t time units if $C(now) + t$ is smaller or equal than all upper bounds of messages in link sets and t is smaller or equal than all durations that are at the head of an instruction sequence of some thread. To ensure progress of time (and to avoid Zeno behavior) we choose the largest t satisfying these conditions. Durations in instruction sequences are modified by the following definition which yields a new function from threads to instruction sequences:
  $NewDuration(C, t) = \lambda i : \text{if } head(C(instr)(i)) = duration(d_i)$
  $\qquad\qquad\qquad \text{then if } d_i - t = 0 \text{ then } tail(C(instr)(i))$
  $\qquad\qquad\qquad\qquad \text{else } duration(d_i - t)\hat{\ } tail(C(instr)(i))$
  $\qquad\qquad\qquad \text{else } C(instr)(i).$
  $C' = C[\, instr \mapsto NewDuration(C, t), \ now \mapsto C(now) + t\,]$
- *periodic(d) IS*: In this case, IS is added to the instruction sequence of thread i and a new thread $j = fresh(C, o_i)$ is started which repeats the periodic instruction after a duration of d time units, i.e.
  $C' = C[\, instr(i) \mapsto IS, \ instr(j) \mapsto duration(d)\hat{\ } periodic(d)\ IS,$
  $\qquad\qquad status(j) \mapsto alive\,]$
- *return(j)*: Then we have $node(i) \neq node(j)$ and the return is transmitted via the link l which connects the nodes, i.e.,

$C' = C[\ instr(i) \mapsto tail(C(instr)(i)),\ linkset(l) \mapsto insert(m, C(linkset)(l))\ ]$
where $m = (return(j), C(now) + \delta_{min}(l), C(now) + \delta_{max}(l))$

Definition 5 (Context Switch). A step $C \longrightarrow C'$ corresponds to a context switch iff there exists a thread i which is not running, i.e. $\neg exec(C, i)$, and also not dormant or waiting, i.e. $C(status)(i) = alive$. Then i becomes the current thread and a duration of δ_{cs} time units is added to represent the context switching time:
$C' = C[\ instr(i) \mapsto duration(\delta_{cs}) \hat{\ } C(instr)(i),\ curthr(node(i)) \mapsto i\ ]$

Definition 6 (Deliver Link Message). A step $C \longrightarrow C'$ corresponds to the message delivery by a link iff there exists a link l and a triple (m, lb, ub) in $C(linkset)(l)$ with $lb \leq C(now) \leq ub$. There are two possibilities for message m:

- $call(i, oid, op)$: Insert the call in the queue of object oid:
  $C' = C[\ q(oid) \mapsto insert((i, op), C(q)(oid)),$
  $\qquad\qquad linkset(l) \mapsto remove((m, lb, ub), C(linkset)(l))\ ]$
- $return(i)$: Wake-up the caller, i.e.
  $C' = C[\ status(i) \mapsto alive,\ linkset(l) \mapsto remove((m, lb, ub), C(linkset)(l))\ ]$

Definition 7 (Process Queue Message). A step $C \longrightarrow C'$ corresponds to the processing of a message from a queue iff there exists an object oid with $head(C(q)(oid)) = (j, op)$. Let $j = fresh(C, oid)$ be a fresh thread and IS be the explicit definition of op. Then if the operation is synchronous, i.e. $syn?(op)$, then we start a new thread with IS followed by a return to the caller:
$C' = C[\ instr(j) \mapsto IS \hat{\ } return(j),\ status(j) \mapsto alive,\ q(oid) \mapsto tail(C(q)(oid))\ ]$
Similarly for an asynchronous call, where no return instruction is added:
$C' = C[\ instr(j) \mapsto IS,\ status(j) \mapsto alive,\ q(oid) \mapsto tail(C(q)(oid))\ ]$

Definition 8 (Operational Semantics). The operational semantics of a specification in the language of Sect. 4.1 is a set of execution sequences of the form $C_0 \longrightarrow C_1 \longrightarrow C_2 \longrightarrow \ldots$, where each pair $C_i \longrightarrow C_{i+1}$ is a step (Def. 3) and the initial configuration C_0 satisfies a number of constraints, such as: initially no thread has status $waiting$, all current threads are $alive$, the auxiliary instruction $return$ does not occur in any instruction sequence, and all queues and link sets are empty.

Observe that in the current semantics the threads that may execute are chosen non-deterministically. By introducing fairness constraints, or a particular scheduling strategy such as round robin or priority-based pre-emptive scheduling, the set of execution sequences can be reduced. Another reduction can be obtained by the use of permission predicates.

4.3   Validation

The formal operational semantics has been validated by formulating it in the typed higher-order logic of the verification system PVS [3] and verifying properties about it using the interactive theorem prover of PVS.

---

[3] PVS is freely available, see *http://pvs.csl.sri.com/*. The PVS files and all VDM++ models are available on-line at *http://www.cs.ru.nl/~marcelv/vdm/*

In fact, the formal operational semantics presented in this paper is based on a much larger constructive (and therefore executable) operational semantics of the extended language, which has been specified in VDM++ itself. This "bootstrapping" approach allows us to interpret models written in the modified language by symbolic execution of its abstract syntax in the constructive operational semantics model using the existing and unmodified VDMTOOLS.

A large collection of test cases has been created to observe the behavior of each new language construct and we are fairly confident that the proposed language changes are consistent. The constructive operational semantics is currently approximately 100 pages including the test suite. It can be used as a specification to implement the proposed language changes in VDMTOOLS.

5   Related Work

In the context of UML, there is related work [13,12] about the precise meaning of active objects, with communication via signals and synchronous operations, and threads of control. In [13] a labeled transition system has been defined using the algebraic specification language CASL, whereas [12] uses the specification language of the theorem prover PVS to formulate the semantics. Note that UML 2.0 adopts the run-to-completion semantics, which means that new signals or operation calls can only be accepted by an object if it cannot do any local action, i.e., it can only proceed by accepting a signal or call. Hence, the number of threads is more restricted than in the VDM++ semantics described here. In addition none of these works deal with deployments. The related work that comes closest here is the UML Profile for Schedulability, Performance and Time, and research on performance analysis based on this profile [14].

6   Concluding Remarks

We propose an extension of VDM++ to enable the modeling of distributed real-time embedded systems. These language extensions allows us to experiment with different deployment strategies at a very early stage in the design. On the syntactic level, the changes seem minor but they make a big difference. The model of the in-car navigation system presented in this paper is significantly smaller than the model that was created earlier with timed VDM++. Moreover, the new model covers a much larger part of the problem domain. We believe that important system properties can be validated in a very cost-effective way if these features are implemented in VDMTOOLS.

A constructive operational semantics was defined for a language subset to prototype and validate the required improvements in the semantics. The changes are substantial but they still fit the general framework of the full VDM++ dynamic semantics. Furthermore, a generalized abstract operational semantics, that is not specific to VDM, is presented in this paper as a result.

One might argue that VDM and therefore this work, is not very relevant for distributed real-time embedded systems. We believe that this is not true. The

Japanese company CSK, which has recently bought the intellectual property rights to VDMTOOLS, is targeting this market in particular and they have already expressed their interest in our results. For example, we were granted access to the company confidential dynamic semantics specification. Furthermore, we hope that the availability of free VDM tools and the recently published book [3] will revitalize the VDM community.

Acknowledgments. The authors wish to thank the anonymous reviewers, Søren Christensen,John Fitzgerald, Finn Overgaard Hansen, Shin Sahara and Evert van de Waal for their valuable comments and support when writing this paper.

References

1. Van den Berg, M., Verhoef, M., Wigmans, M.: Formal Specification of an Auctioning System Using VDM++ and UML – an Industrial Usage Report. In Fitzgerald, J., Larsen, P.G., eds.: VDM in Practice. (1999) 85–93
2. Hörl, J., Aichernig, B.K.: Validating Voice Communication Requirements using Lightweight Formal Methods. IEEE Software **13-3** (2000) 21–27
3. Fitzgerald, J., Larsen, P.G., Mukherjee, P., Plat, N., Verhoef, M.: Validated Designs for Object–oriented Systems. Springer (2005)
4. Kurita, T., Oota, T., Nakatsugawa, Y.: Formal Specification of an IC for Cellular Phones. In: Proceedings of Software Symposium 2005, Software Engineering Association of Japan (2005) 73–80 (in Japanese)
5. Verhoef, M.: On the Use of VDM++ for Specifying Real-time Systems. Proc. First Overture Workshop (2005)
6. Andrews, D. J., Larsen, P. G., Hansen, B. S., Brunn, H., Plat, N., Toetenel, H., Dawes, J., Parkin, G. and others: Vienna Development Method – Specification Language – Part 1: Base Language. ISO/IEC 13817-1 (1996)
7. Mukherjee, P., Bousquet, F., Delabre, J., Paynter, S., Larsen, P.G.: Exploring Timing Properties Using VDM++ on an Industrial Application. In Bicarregui, J., Fitzgerald, J., eds.: The Second VDM Workshop. (2000)
8. Larsen, P.G., Lassen, P.B.: An Executable Subset of Meta-IV with Loose Specification. In: VDM '91: Formal Software Development Methods, Springer LNCS 551 (1991) 604–618
9. Lano, K.: Logic Specification of Reactive and Real-time Systems. Journal of Logic and Computation **8-5** (1998) 679–711
10. Wandeler, E., Thiele, L., Verhoef, M., Lieverse, P.: System Architecture Evaluation Using Modular Performance Analysis – A Case Study. Software Tools for Technology Transfer, Springer (2006) (to appear)
11. Hendriks, M., Verhoef, M.: Timed Automata Based Analysis of Embedded System Architectures. In: Proc. WPDRTS'06. IEEE (2006)
12. Hooman, J., van der Zwaag, M.: A Semantics of Communicating Reactive Objects with Timing. Software Tools for Technology Transfer **8-2** Springer (2006) 97–112
13. Reggio, G., Astesiano, E., Choppy, C., Hussmann, H.: Analysing UML Active Classes and Associated Statecharts - a Lightweight Formal Approach. In: Fundamental Approaches to Software Engineering, Springer LNCS 1783 (2000) 127–146
14. Bennet, A., Field, A.J., Woodside, M.C.: Experimental Evaluation of the UML Profile for Schedulability, Performance and Time. In: UML2004 – The Unified Modeling Language, Springer LNCS 3273 (2004) 143–157

Towards Modularized Verification of Distributed Time-Triggered Systems[*]

Jewgenij Botaschanjan[1], Alexander Gruler[1], Alexander Harhurin[1], Leonid Kof[1], Maria Spichkova[1], and David Trachtenherz[2]

[1] Institut für Informatik, TU München,
Boltzmannstr. 3, D-85748, Garching bei München, Germany
{botascha, gruler, harhurin, kof, spichkov}@in.tum.de
[2] BMW Group Research and Technology,
Hanauer Strasse 46, D-80992, München, Germany
David.Trachtenherz@bmw.de

Abstract. The correctness of a system according to a given specification is essential, especially for safety-critical applications. One such typical application domain is the automotive sector, where more and more safety-critical functions are performed by largely software-based systems.

Verification techniques can guarantee correctness of the system. Although automotive systems are relatively small compared to other systems (e.g. business information systems) they are still too large for monolithic verification of the system as a whole.

Tackling this problem, we present an approach for modularized verification, aiming at time-triggered automotive systems. We show how the concept of tasks, as used in current automotive operating systems, can be modeled in a CASE tool, verified and deployed. This results in a development process facilitating verification of safety-critical, real-time systems at affordable cost.

1   Introduction

Together with the growing functionality offered by today's distributed reactive systems, the associated complexity of such systems is also dramatically increasing. Taking into account that the vast majority of the functionality is realized in software, the need for appropriate design and verification support becomes obvious.

A prime example for this trend is the current situation in the automotive domain. Here, a premium class car contains up to 70 electronic control units (ECUs) which are responsible for all kinds of applications: infotainment (like navigation and radio), comfort (power windows, seat adjustment, etc.), control of technical processes (motor control, ABS, ESP), and much more. Consequently, the amount of associated software is enormous – with the tendency to further increase in the future.

With the trend going towards drive-by-wire, the software becomes responsible for safety-critical functions, like steer-by-wire and brake-by-wire. The state-of-the-art method of quality assurance, namely testing, is not sufficient in the case of safety-relevant

---

[*] This work was partially funded by the German Federal Ministry of Education and Technology (BMBF) in the framework of the Verisoft project under grant 01 IS C38. The responsibility for this article lies with the authors.

J. Misra, T. Nipkow, and E. Sekerinski (Eds.): FM 2006, LNCS 4085, pp. 163–178, 2006.
© Springer-Verlag Berlin Heidelberg 2006

functions: Testing can solely show the absence of bugs in a finite number of standard situations. However, it can never *guarantee* the software correctness. Formal verification is a better choice in this case, as it can *guarantee* that the software satisfies its specification.

Unfortunately, current verification techniques for reactive systems suffer from some problems: Firstly, in order to prove the correctness of a system, both the application logic itself as well as its infrastructure (operating system and communication mechanisms) have to be verified. This results in an overall verification effort which cannot be mastered by verifying the system as a whole.

Secondly, there is no continuous verification technique: While current CASE tools typically used for automotive software development (like MATLAB/Simulink [1], Rose RT [2], AutoFOCUS [3]) allow modeling of the functionality and structure of a real-time system, they do not provide an explicit deployment concept. However, without deployment support it makes no sense to verify properties on the application model, since they do not necessarily hold after deployment.

To tackle these problems we introduce a task concept for the model-based development of distributed real-time systems, which allows modularized verification while preserving verified properties for the model after deployment. Together, this results in a continuous methodological support for development of verified automotive software.

We show the feasibility of our concepts on a case study. We demonstrate that embedding of tasks into a realistic environment, such as a time-triggered bus and a time-triggered operating system, does not violate the verified properties.

The remainder of this paper is organized as follows: Section 2 introduces the case study used as a continuous example throughout the whole paper. Sections 3 and 4 present the deployment platform (FlexRay Communication Protocol [4] and OSEK-time OS [5]) and the CASE tool AutoFOCUS [3], used to specify the case study as a task model. Sections 5 and 6 are the technical core of the paper: They show how the tasks should be constructed in order that they are deployable without any loss of verified properties. Section 7 gives an overview of related work and, finally, Section 8 summarizes the whole paper.

2 Case Study: Emergency Call (eCall)

To demonstrate the introduced ideas we use an automated emergency call as a running example throughout this paper. According to the proposal by the European Commission [6], such an automated emergency call should become mandatory in all new cars as of 2009. The application itself is simple enough to be sketched in a few paragraphs, but it still possesses typical properties of automotive software. By this we mean that it is a safety-critical application distributed over several electronic control units (ECUs), whose correct functionality not only depends on the correctness of the application itself but also on the correctness of a real-time OS and a real-time bus.

We model the eCall as a system consisting of 3 sub-systems, namely: a GPS navigation system, a mobile phone, and the actual emergency call application. External information (e.g. the crash sensor, the GPS signals) is considered to be a part of the environment. According to [6], these components interact as follows: The navigation system sends periodically the vehicle's coordinates to the emergency call application so that it always possesses the latest coordinates. The crash sensor sends periodically the current crash status to the emergency call application. If a crash is detected, the emergency call application initiates the eCall by prompting the mobile phone to establish a connection to the emergency center. As soon as the mobile phone reports an open connection, the application transmits the coordinates to the mobile phone. After the coordinates have been successfully sent, the application orders the mobile phone to close the connection. The emergency call is finished as soon as the connection is successfully closed. If the radio link breaks down during the emergency call, the whole procedure is repeated from the initiation step.

3 Deployment Platform

In order to master the inherent complexity of automotive systems, industry came up with a number of standards, based on the *time-triggered paradigm* [7]. They allow realization of distributed systems with predictable time behavior, and thus can be considered as an appropriate deployment target for safety-critical real-time systems.

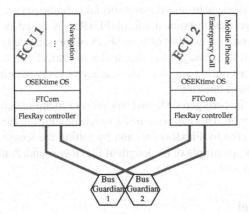

Fig. 1. Target Deployment Platform Architecture

In a time-triggered system actions are executed at predefined points in time. In particular, using time-triggered operating systems (VxWorks [8], QNX [9], OSEKtime [10]), the execution of application processes is statically scheduled, and by applying time-triggered communication protocols (TTP/C [11], TTCan [12], FlexRay [13]), the communication schedule becomes static as well. Further on, time-triggered communication protocols provide, using time synchronization, a global time base to the distributed communication partners. By this a combination of time-triggered OS and network allows realization of a deterministic system behavior with guaranteed response times.

The target deployment platform of the presented work is a network of ECUs connected by a FlexRay bus with a multiple-star topology and with OSEKtime OS running on every node (see [14] for details). Fig. 1 shows a possible deployment of the three tasks from the eCall study on two ECUs.

OSEKtime. OSEKtime OS is an OSEK/VDX [10] open operating system standard of the European automotive industry [5]. The OSEKtime OS supports static cyclic scheduling. In every round the dispatcher activates a process at the point of time specified in the scheduling table. If another process is running at this time, it will be preempted until the completion of the activated process. OSEKtime also monitors the deadlines of the processes. In the case of deadline violation an error hook is executed.

FTCom [15] is the OSEKtime fault-tolerant communication layer that provides a number of primitives for interprocess communication and makes task distribution transparent. Messages kept in FTCom are uniquely identified by their IDs. For every message ID FTCom realizes a buffer of length one. Application processes can send or receive messages with certain IDs using communication primitives offered by FTCom. However, they are not aware of the location of their communication partners, i.e. whether they communicate locally or through a bus.

FlexRay. FlexRay [4,16,17] is a communication protocol for safety critical real-time automotive applications, that has been developed by the FlexRay Consortium [13]. It is a static time division multiplexing network protocol and supports fault-tolerant clock synchronization via a global time base. The drifting clocks of FlexRay communication partners are periodically synchronized using special sync messages.

The static message transmission mode of FlexRay is based on *rounds*. FlexRay rounds consist of a constant number of time slices of the same length, so called *slots*. A node can broadcast its messages to other nodes at statically defined slots. At most one node can broadcast during any slot. The latency of every message transmission is bounded by the length of one slot.

A combination of time-triggered OS and bus allows synchronization of the computations and communication. This can be done by synchronizing the local ECU clock with the global time delivered by FlexRay bus and by setting the length of the OSEKtime dispatcher round to be a multiple of the length of FlexRay round. A unit of computation is then also a FlexRay slot.

4   Logical Model

AutoFOCUS is a CASE tool for graphical specification of reactive systems. The tool has a formal time-synchronous operational semantics. With its graphical specification language AutoFOCUS supports different views on the system, namely structure, behavior, interaction and data-type view. This section gives a very short introduction to Auto-FOCUS. A more detailed description of AutoFOCUS and its diagram types can be found in [18].

Structural View: System Structure Diagrams (SSDs). A system in AutoFOCUS is modeled by a network of components C, denoted as rectangles (cf. Fig. 2, where the task model of the eCall application is shown). The communication interface of a component $c \in C$ is defined by a set of typed directed *ports* P_c. There are *input* and *output* ports, represented by empty and solid circles, respectively. The components communicate via typed channels, which connect input and output port pairs of matching types. An output port can be a source of several channels, while an input port can be a sink of at

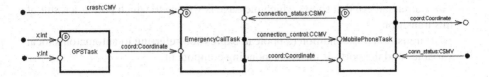

Fig. 2. The Component Architecture of the eCall Study

most one. A component can be refined by a further component network. This results in a hierarchical order of SSDs. The leaf components in the hierarchy have an assigned behavior, described by *State Transition Diagrams*.

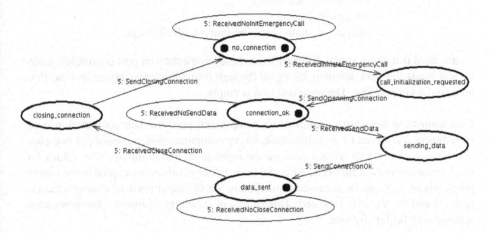

Fig. 3. State Transition Diagram of the *Mobile Phone* Logic Component

Behavior View: State Transition Diagrams (STDs). The behavior of a leaf component is defined by an extended I/O automaton. It consists of a set of *control states*, *transitions*, and *local variables* (cf. Fig. 3). Black dots on the left of the states denote initial states, black dots on the right denote idle states[1]. ("5" on the transition labels denotes the transition priority and is unimportant in the context of our application.)

An STD automaton $\mathcal{A}$ is completely defined by its set of control states S, the set of local variables V, the initial state $s_0 \in S$, and the transition relation δ. A transition, denoted by

$$(s_1 \xrightarrow{pre:in:out:post} s_2) \in \delta(\mathcal{A}), \text{ for } s_1, s_2 \in S,$$

consists of four elements:

- *pre*, transition precondition (a boolean expression referring to automaton's local variables and the ports of the corresponding component)
- *in*, input pattern that shows which message must be available on which port in order that the transition is triggered

---

[1] Idle states will be defined below, see Sect. 5.2.

- *out*, output pattern that shows which message is written to which port as a result of this transition
- *post*, transition postcondition (a boolean expression referring to automaton's local variables and the ports of the corresponding component)

A transition can be triggered in the state s_1 if the input ports specified in the input pattern *in* have received the necessary input messages and the precondition *pre* is satisfied. The transition outputs data to output ports specified in *out*, changes the local variables according to the postcondition *post*, and puts the automaton into the state s_2.

For example, the transition with label ReceivedNoCloseConnection from Figure 3 has the form:

> (x != close_connection):
> connection_control?x:
> connection_status!data_sending_ok,idle!Present:

It is fired if it gets a signal different from close_connection on port connection_control and sends the data_sending_ok signal through port connection_status and the Present signal via port idle. The postcondition is empty.

Communication Semantics. AutoFOCUS components perform their computation steps simultaneously, driven by a global clock. Every computation step consists of two phases: First, a component reads values on the input ports and computes new values for local variables and output ports. After the time tick new values are copied to the output ports, where they can be accessed immediately via the input ports of connected components and the cycle is repeated. This results in a *time-synchronous* communication scheme with buffer size one.

5 Deployment

An automotive system is distributed over several communicating electronic control units (ECUs). In the early design stages it is simpler to model application logic without considering timing properties and future deployment. Pure functionality modeling results in systems that have to be deployed manually and after deployment can show wrong behavior or violate timing constraints.

In this section we motivate and describe the AutoFOCUS Task Model (*AFTM*), which will be used for (semi-)automatic verification of time–triggered systems. Here, we introduce a framework enabling modeling and deployment of tasks. The framework architecture ensures that the properties verified for the logical model are preserved after deployment. This results in a verified automotive system, provided that the infrastructure (OS/bus) is verified. For these purposes the framework [14] for automotive systems with the formalized and verified OSEKtime OS and the FlexRay protocol can be used. This verification framework is developed in the automotive part of the Verisoft project [19,20].

5.1 Design Process

The AutoFOCUS Task Model is designed to be an integral part of a model-based development process. The prerequisite for this process is a formal specification of the desired system. The envisioned process produces the following artifacts:

- The AutoFOCUS model (see also Section 4) represents the application logic (functionality) without incorporating any deployment information. It is the basis for the AutoFOCUS task model.
- The AutoFOCUS Task Model is an extension of the AutoFOCUS model, targeting at future deployment to a time-triggered platform. This model is verified against the given specification.
- C0 code[2] is generated from the AFTM. This code is the basis for the estimation of the worst case execution times (WCETs) that are needed for scheduleability analysis (see Section 6.1). WCETs can be estimated, given a compiled C program and the processor the program runs on [23]. The behavioral equivalence between C0 code and the automaton it was generated from must be proven. This proof can be done, for example, by the means of translation validation [24]:
  - Every transition of an AutoFOCUS automaton is annotated with a pre- and a postcondition.
  - The piece of code, generated from a particular transition, can be annotated with the same pre- and postconditions as the transition itself.
  - Finally, we verify that the pre- and postconditions hold for the generated code.
- For the deployment and scheduling the decision must be taken which tasks run on which ECUs. The schedules both for every ECU and for the communication bus must be also constructed. The schedules have to take into account casual dependencies of the tasks, the WCETs and the real-time requirements (e.g. specified response times).
  At the moment we do not construct schedules but only check existing schedules for correctness. Construction of schedules is a part of our future work.

In that way we obtain a continuous model-based development process, ranging from high-level system design to verified deployed code.

5.2 AutoFOCUS Task Model (AFTM)

An AutoFOCUS task model is obtained from AutoFOCUS model components through encapsulation – Fig. 4 shows an AFTM task originating from an AutoFOCUS component app_logic. A task may contain a single component or a network consisting of several components – it is then treated as a product automaton (see *Behavior View* in Sect. 4). The transformation from an AutoFOCUS model into an AutoFOCUS task model is performed manually at the moment, but it is planned to extend the tool AutoFOCUS in order to automate this transformation.

---

[2] The language C0 [21] is a Pascal-like restriction of C that is similar to MISRA C [22]. In safety critical applications it is feasible to use C in some restricted way to have less error-prone programming style.

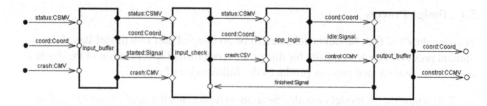

Fig. 4. AutoFOCUS task model of EmergencyCallTask

An AutoFOCUS task model consists of a set $\mathcal{T}$ of *tasks* T_i with $i \in \{1, \ldots, m\}$ for an arbitrary but constant m and a set of directed channels between them. We denote by $Pred, Succ : \mathcal{T} \rightarrow \mathcal{P}(\mathcal{T})$ the functions indicating data flow between tasks: $T_j \in Succ(T_i)$ means that there is a channel going from T_i to T_j and $T_j \in Pred(T_i)$ denotes a channel going from T_j to T_i.

Every component in an AutoFOCUS model runs continuously, whereas the execution of a reactive system is an infinite sequence of finite computations started by the OS scheduler and terminating with a special exit() system call. To match this computation model, we introduce in AFTM the notion of finite computations through *idle states*. An idle state is a state of the original logic component (or component network), where the computation can continue only after having received new input. In contrast to idle states, *non-idle* states are allowed to have outgoing transitions only without requiring any input. Thereby the set of control states is partitioned into two disjoint subsets:

$$S_{idle} = \{s \mid s \in S \wedge \forall (s \xrightarrow{pre:in:out:post} s') \in \delta(\mathcal{A}).\ in \neq \emptyset\} \tag{1}$$

$$S_{non\_idle} = \{s \mid s \in S \wedge \forall (s \xrightarrow{pre:in:out:post} s') \in \delta(\mathcal{A}).\ in = \emptyset\} \tag{2}$$

An AFTM task computation is a finite sequence of state transitions leading from an idle state to some other idle state:

$$c(val(P_c), s_0) = s_0 \xrightarrow{pre_1:in:out_1:post_1} s_1 \xrightarrow{pre_2:\emptyset:out_2:post_2} \ldots$$
$$\xrightarrow{pre_{n-1}:\emptyset:out_{n-1}:post_{n-1}} s_{n-1} \xrightarrow{pre_n:\emptyset:out_n:post_n} s_n \tag{3}$$

where $s_0, s_n \in S_{idle}$, $s_1, \ldots, s_{n-1} \in S_{non\_idle}$, $(s_{i-1} \xrightarrow{pre_i:in_i:out_i:post_i} s_i) \in \delta(\mathcal{A})$ for all $i \in \{1, \ldots, n\}$, and $val(P_c)$ denotes the valuation of the component's ports. This linkage between target platform task runs and AFTM task computations is also utilized for timing analysis (cf. Sect. 6.2).

In the *Mobile Phone* logic component STD (Fig. 3, page 167) the states no_connection, connection_ok and data_sent are idle. An example of the finite computations that can be performed by this automaton is connection_ok $\rightarrow$ sending_data $\rightarrow$ data_sent.

Upon reaching an idle state the encapsulated component of a task always sends a signal through a dedicated idle port:

$$\forall (s_1 \xrightarrow{pre:in:out:post} s_2) \in \delta(\mathcal{A}) : (s_2 \in S_{idle} \Leftrightarrow (\text{idle!Present}) \in out) \tag{4}$$

A distributed time-triggered system usually does not guarantee the simultaneous presence of all required input signals because of delays. As an AFTM task may start only when all required input data are available we introduce an *input check* for every task – it forwards the inputs and thus allows the task to start only after all required inputs have arrived and the task is not running, i.e. it is in an idle state.

We introduce two kinds of input checks: OR and AND. An OR-task T can start when at least one input from any task $T_i \in Pred(T)$ has arrived. For instance the EmergencyCallTask task on Fig. 2 is activated either to store new coordinates from the GPSTask or to perform an emergency call after having received a crash signal. The idea behind the AND-check is that the task can start only when all the inputs are available. For instance, the GPSTask (Fig. 2) may first start when both coordinate inputs x and y have arrived.

The input checks get their inputs solely from the *input buffers* (see e.g. input_buffer component in Fig. 4). These buffers store the arriving data as long as the tasks cannot process them. After the data gathered by the buffer has passed the input check, the input check sends the started signal to the buffer. Thereupon the input buffer is flushed and starts gathering a new data set. This simulates the behavior of the FTCom, which is used for task communication on the deployment platform (cf. Sect. 3).

The *output buffer* is necessary to assure well-defined points in time for communication and thus to make communication behavior predictable. The output buffer stores the outputs of the application logic and forwards them to the environment on receiving the idle signal. After that the output buffer is flushed and forwards the idle signal to the input check, indicating the completion of the task computation.

The introduced concepts of input checks and input/output buffers, as well as idle states, allow correct deployment on a distributed platform running with OSEKtime/Flex-Ray (cf. Sect. 3). The AFTM properties facilitating deployment are in particular the following: it models the behavior of the FTCom communication layer, it supports the notion of finite computations as suitable for time-triggered systems, it reads the input data at the beginning and communicates the results at the end of the computation, thus facilitating scheduling and modular verification.

5.3   Code Generation

To run a task on a real system the representation of the model as code in some executable language is needed (e.g., for the automotive domain C code is usually used). Out of the AFTM the corresponding C code (more precisely: C0 code) can be generated in a strict schematical way.

In the presented approach properties of a task are proven for the corresponding AFTM since this is more effective than verifying the generated C0 code. The equivalence of AFTM and C0 guarantees that the verified properties for the AFTM also hold for the C0 code. This equivalence can easily be proven using translation validation [24].

6   Verification

In the previous sections we have described how an AutoFocus component model can be packed into an AFTM. This section shows how the AFTM and the deployed system, based on AFTM, can be verified. The verification is accomplished in several steps: First, the AutoFOCUS model, packed into AFTM, is verified. This can be done, as the SMV model checker [25] is integrated with AutoFOCUS [26]. Then, it is necessary to show that the properties verified for the AutoFOCUS model remain valid in the deployed model. Formally, let $Model_{AFTM}$ denote the AutoFOCUS Task Model, $Model_{depl}$ the deployed model, and P the specification (a set of LTL properties). Then, the accomplishment of this procedure results in the following property.

$$(Model_{AFTM} \vDash P) \Rightarrow (Model_{depl} \vDash P) \tag{5}$$

The prerequisite for the fulfillment of this formula is that $Model_{AFTM}$ is a valid instance of the AFTM, as described in Sect. 5.2. This is discussed in Sect. 6.1. Sect. 6.2 shows that AFTM constraints, together with certain scheduling constraints put on the deployed system, imply behavioral equivalence between $Model_{AFTM}$ and $Model_{depl}$. Behavioral equivalence, in turn, provides the desired correctness of the deployed system, given that $Model_{AFTM}$ was verified.

6.1 Task and System Properties

To ensure the validity of a particular AutoFOCUS task model, certain properties have to be proven. First, it must be shown for every component network, deployed to one task, that all states in its product automaton that are marked as *idle* satisfy Formula 1. All the remaining states must satisfy Formula 2 (see page 170). These are purely syntactic checks on the AutoFOCUS task product automaton.

In the eCall example the automaton of the mobile phone component as shown in Fig. 3 (page 167) has three idle states (no_connection, connection_ok and data_send). In these states new inputs from the Emergency Call task and the radio link status are expected respectively. The remaining states are non-idle, thus, the transitions from these states are not allowed to access the input ports.

The second property to be verified is that every task sends a special idle signal before entering an idle state. This signal is needed in AFTM to affect input_check and output_buffer components (see Sect. 5.2). Formally it must be verified that Formula 4 holds for every transition.

Finally, it is necessary to verify that every sequence of transitions starting in an idle state always reaches some idle state within a finite number of steps. The first two properties are simply syntactic checks on the model, while the last one can be verified via model checking. To verify the last property, it is possible to use the SMV back end of the tool AutoFOCUS.

6.2 Timing Properties

Timing properties ensure the equivalence of the data flow dependencies imposed by the AFTM channels and the task dependencies in the deployed system. The prerequisite for every timing analysis technique are the estimates for BCET/WCET for every task. In our setting these are minimal/maximal execution times between any pair of idle states. The estimation can be done e.g. using the static analysis techniques by AbsInt [23].

The task running time expressed in the logical time base of the deployment architecture (number of slots) is then obtained by dividing the BCET/WCET estimates by the slot length:

$$b^{slot} = \left\lceil \frac{bcet}{|slot|} \right\rceil, w^{slot} = \left\lceil \frac{wcet}{|slot|} \right\rceil \tag{6}$$

The assumption is that no two tasks (on the same ECU) can run in the same slot. By this, the logical running times of a task T which can be used in the scheduleability analysis lie within $[b^{slot}(T), \dots, w^{slot}(T)]$. Thus, in the remainder of this section the notion of logical time is used in the scheduling constraints.

We describe the deployment of the system by the following definitions for arbitrary tasks $T_i, T_j \in \mathcal{T}$. The set of relative start times[3] is denoted by $start(T_i)$. W.l.o.g. we assume that $start(T_k) \neq \emptyset$ for all $T_k \in \mathcal{T}$. Let the predicate $ecu(T_i, T_j)$ denote the deployment of tasks on the same ECU. The messages produced by a task are sent through FlexRay in slots from the set $send(T_i)$[4]. Finally, the number of slots in the OS round is denoted by $|round|$.

The scheduleability analysis for the given technical infrastructure lies beyond the scope of this paper, however, the obtained scheduling tables have to be checked for their correctness for the given AFTM. We say a scheduling table to be correct, if the following properties hold.

Communication Jitter. In order to make the bus communication deterministic, the Flex-Ray slots reserved for the messages produced by a task T, must not lie within the following interval (see Fig. 5):

$$\forall s \in start(T) : \forall ss \in send(T) : ss \notin (s + b^{slot}(T), s + w^{slot}(T)]$$

In the case of a local communication, the consuming task T_2 must not be started before the WCET of its producing counterpart T_2 passes:

$$ecu(T_1, T_2) \wedge T_1 \in Pred(T_2) \Rightarrow$$
$$\forall s_1 \in start(T_1), s_2 \in start(T_2) : s_2 \notin (s_1 + b^{slot}(T_1), s_1 + w^{slot}(T_1)]$$

These properties allow us to define the *transport time* function tr. For a given pair of tasks T_1 and T_2 with $T_1 \in Pred(T_2)$ and a start time $s_1 \in start(T_1)$, $s_1 + tr(T_1, s_1, T_2)$ is the minimal time after which T_2 is allowed to access the messages produced by T_1 when T_1 is started at time s_1. An earlier access would violate the above properties. For the *local communication*, i.e., $ecu(T_1, T_2)$ holds, this time is $w^{slot}(T_1)$. Otherwise, $tr(T_1, s_1, T_2)$ is the longest distance to the next sending slot from $send(T_1)$, which transports data that T_2 is interested in, plus 1 slot for the transportation itself. The last case is illustrated in Fig. 6. Due to the above constraints, for any fixed triple of parameters the value of tr is constant.

Control & Data Flow. The start times of tasks have to respect the data and control flow relations between them. We constraint starts/terminations allowed to occur between

---

[3] A task can be started several times per OS round.
[4] Note that the set can be empty if the task sends its results only locally.

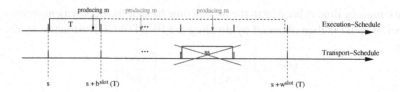

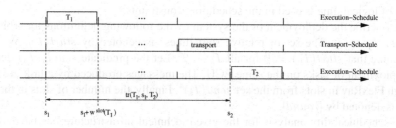

Fig. 5. Constrained Transport Times

Fig. 6. Allowed Start Time

any pair of subsequent executions of a task T. For that purpose we define the following sets and predicates on them: For a task T let $start^{\perp}(T) = start(T) \cup \{-1\}$ and $start^{\top}(T) = start(T) \cup \{|round| + \min start(T)\}$. The value -1 denotes a fictitious start time smaller than any actual start time of T. The additional value of $start^{\top}(T)$ defines the first T's start in the next round. Obviously, it will be greater than any number in $start(T)$. Then for a given start time $s \in start^{\perp}(T)$ we denote T's next start time by $next(T, s) = s'$, with a *minimal* s', such that $s' \in start^{\top}(T)$ and $s' > s$. Further on, for a given start time $s \in start^{\top}(T)$ we define T's previous start time by $prev(T, s) = s'$, with a *maximal* s', such that $s' \in start^{\perp}(T)$ and $s' < s$.

Using the definitions from above, we can now formulate scheduling constraints for the both kinds of input check semantics. The AND-task T which needs outputs from the tasks $T_1, \ldots, T_n$ demands, that these tasks must deliver their outputs between any pair of subsequent starts of T (see also Fig. 7).

$$\forall s \in start(T) : \forall T' \in Pred(T) : \exists s' \in start(T') :$$
$$prev(T, s) \leq s' + tr(T', s', T) < s$$

In the case of the OR-semantics for T, at least one of the tasks $T_1, \ldots, T_n$ has to deliver its outputs in this interval.

$$\forall s \in start(T) : \exists T' \in Pred(T) : \exists s' \in start(T') :$$
$$prev(T, s) \leq s' + tr(T', s', T) < s$$

No Data Loss. In the presented work we consider systems where no data loss is allowed. By this a message has to be consumed by corresponding tasks, before it will be overwritten. This implies the following relationship between two subsequent transports

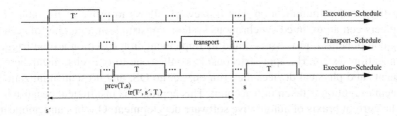

Fig. 7. Correct Data Flow

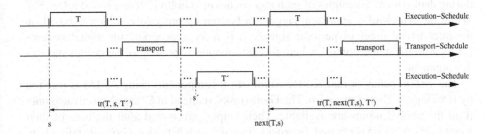

Fig. 8. No Data Loss

from any producing task T and the start times of the corresponding consumers (see also Fig. 8).

$$\forall s \in start(T) : \forall T' \in Succ(T) : \exists s' \in start^\top(T) :$$
$$s + tr(T, s, T') < s' \leq next(T, s) + tr(T, next(T, s), T')$$

Additionally to the above timing constraints, the response times, which are an important part of the specification of real-time systems, have to be checked. Since the task running and transport times are calculable as described above, the response times can be easily estimated.

The positive accomplishment of the above proof obligations guarantees the correctness of deployment. Thus, the resulting system will work correctly within the assumed environment.

7 Related Work

In this paper we presented a concept for separate verification of application logic and infrastructure. The necessity of the separation of functionality and infrastructure verification is also argued for by Sifakis et al. [27]. They introduce a formal modeling framework and a methodology, addressing the analysis of correct deployment and timing properties. The extention in our task concept is the explicit modeling of task dependencies and explicit statements about task activation conditions.

There also exist other approaches for the verification of distributed real-time software. J. Rushby in [28] has presented a framework for a systematic formal verification of time–triggered communication. His framework allows to prove a simulation relationship between an untimed synchronous system, consisting of a number of communicating components ("processors") and its implementation based on a time-triggered communication system. His approach considers only a one-to-one relationship between components and physical devices they run on, i.e. no OS, and no sequentialization of component execution is taken into account. This approach is insufficient because it neglects the current praxis of automotive software development: OS, bus and application logic are developed by different suppliers and therefore should be treated separately.

There are also constructive approaches, trying to keep the properties of the models during deployment. Examples of such approaches are Giotto [29] and AutoMoDe [30]. While the AutoMoDe approach suggests a bottom-up procedure, which is based on the inter-arrival times of periodic signals, it is more appropriate for digital systems for measurement and control, where this information is present at the design stage of development.

The system behavior realized for AutoFOCUS components using AFTM is inspired by Henzinger's Giotto approach. The Giotto tasks, realized in C, are also activated only if all the needed inputs are available. Their outputs are issued after the time of their worst case execution is elapsed. In order to provide such behavior, Giotto installs a low-level system driver, called *E-machine*, which takes over the role of input and output check during the run-time. For this setting the construction of schedules was proven to be polynomial in [31]. However, in contrast to the presented approach, the data and control flow, which serves as an input for schedule synthesis, are extracted in a rather *ad hoc* manner, e.g. it cannot be proven, that they correspond to the actual behavior of the C-code tasks. Furthermore, no additional middleware like the E-machine is needed in the presented work.

As noted in [32], in the CASE tools typically used for model-based software development in the automotive domain, like MATLAB/Simulink [1], Rose RT [2], Auto-FOCUS [3], there is no explicit deployment concept. In other tools, like ASCET-SD [33] or Cierto VCC [34], there is an ability to build a deployment model for one ECU only. However these tools allow the modeling of the systems only on a very low level of abstraction. The application of such tools in the early design phases would lead to unnecessary over-specification.

8   Conclusion

The task-based application model is simple enough to be verified using automated verification techniques such as model checking and robust enough to be deployed without violation of the verified properties. The special task construction using message buffering and input checks assures that the task behavior remains the same even after deployment. Thus, the properties verified for the pure task-based system remain valid for the deployed system.

It is important that in the presented approach the operating system and the communication bus are verified separately from the application logic. The verification tasks interact in the assumption/guarantee way: for the application verification we assume a certain behavior of the infrastructure and for the infrastructure we verify that it guarantees the assumed properties. This reduces the complexity of verification and results in a completely verified system. The separation of functional and timing properties brings additional reduction of the verification effort.

The only piece missing to provide a pervasively verified time-triggered system is the verified infrastructure (OS/bus) providing the properties that the application layer (deployed AFTM) relies on. Such a verified infrastructure is being developed in the Verisoft project [19]. In the context of this project the methodology presented in this paper will also be applied to the emergency call application [6] to achieve a proof-of-concept pervasive verification of an automotive system.

References

1. The MathWorks. http://www.mathworks.com (18.05.2006)
2. IBM Rational Rose Technical Developer. http://www-306.ibm.com/software/awdtools/developer/technical/ (18.05.2006)
3. AutoFocus. http://autofocus.in.tum.de/ (18.05.2006)
4. FlexRay Consortium: FlexRay Communication System - Protocol Specification - Version 2.0. (2004)
5. OSEK/VDX: Time-Triggered Operating System - Specification 1.0. (18.05.2006)
6. European Commission (DG Enterprise and DG Information Society): eSafety forum: Summary report 2003. Technical report, eSafety (2003)
7. Kopetz, H., Grünsteidl, G.: TTP — a protocol for fault-tolerant real-time systems. Computer 27(1) (1994) 14–23
8. VxWorks: A Realtime Operating System (RTOS). http://www.windriver.com (18.05.2006)
9. QNX: A Realtime Operating System (RTOS). http://www.qnx.com (18.05.2006)
10. OSEK/VDX. http://www.osek-vdx.org (18.05.2006)
11. TTP/C. http://www.vmars.tuwien.ac.at/projects/ttp/ttpc.html (18.05.2006)
12. TTCan: Time Triggered Communication on CAN. http://www.ttcan.com (18.05.2006)
13. FlexRay Consortium. http://www.flexray.com (18.05.2006)
14. Botaschanjan, J., Kof, L., Kühnel, C., Spichkova, M.: Towards Verified Automotive Software. In: ICSE, SEAS Workshop, St. Louis, Missouri, USA (2005)
15. OSEK/VDX: Fault-Tolerant Communication - Specification 1.0. http://portal.osek-vdx.org/files/pdf/specs/ftcom10.pdf (18.05.2006)
16. FlexRay Consortium: FlexRay Communication System - Bus Guardian Specification - Version 2.0. (2004)
17. FlexRay Consortium: FlexRay Communication System - Electrical Physical Layer Specification - Version 2.0. (2004)
18. Huber, F., Schätz, B., Einert, G.: Consistent Graphical Specification of Distributed Systems. In: Industrial Applications and Strengthened Foundations of Formal Methods (FME'97). Volume 1313 of LNCS., Springer Verlag (1997) 122–141
19. Verisoft Project. http://www.verisoft.de (18.05.2006)
20. Verisoft–Automotive Project. http://www4.in.tum.de/verisoft/automotive (18.05.2006)
21. Leinenbach, D., Paul, W., Petrova, E.: Towards the Formal Verification of a C0 Compiler. In: 3rd International Conference on SEFM, Koblenz, Germany (2005) 2–12

22. The Motor Industry Software Reliability Association (MISRA): Guidelines for the Use of the C Language in Critical Systems. Motor Industry Research Association (MIRA), Ltd., UK. (18.05.2006)
23. AbsInt Angewandte Informatik GmbH. Worst-Case Execution Time Analyzers. http://www.absint.com/profile.htm (18.05.2006)
24. Pnueli, A., Siegel, M., Singerman, E.: Translation validation. In: Tools and Algorithms for the Construction and Analysis of Systems. Volume 1384 of LNCS. (1998) 151–166
25. Cimatti, A., Clarke, E.M., Giunchiglia, E., Giunchiglia, F., Pistore, M., Roveri, M., Sebastiani, R., Tacchella, A.: NuSMV 2: An open source tool for symbolic model checking. In: Proceedings of CAV 2002, Copenhagen, Denmark (2002) 359–364
26. Wimmel, G., Lötzbeyer, H., Pretschner, A., Slotosch, O.: Specification based test sequence generation with propositional logic. Journal of STVR: Special Issue on Specification Based Testing (2000) 229–248
27. Sifakis, J., Tripakis, S., Yovine, S.: Building models of real-time systems from application software. Proceedings of the IEEE 91(1) (2003) 100–111
28. Rushby, J.: Systematic formal verification for fault-tolerant time-triggered algorithms. In: Dependable Computing for Critical Applications—6. Volume 11., IEEE Computer Society (1997) 203–222
29. Henzinger, T.A., Horowitz, B., Kirsch, C.M.: Giotto: A time-triggered language for embedded programming. Proceedings of the IEEE 91 (2003) 84–99
30. Bauer, A., Romberg, J.: Model-Based Deployment in Automotive Embedded Software: From a High-Level View to Low-Level Implementations. In: Proceedings of MOMPES, satelite of ACSD'04, Hamilton, Canada (2004) 93–106
31. Henzinger, T.A., Kirsch, C.M., Majumdar, R., Matic, S.: Time-safety checking for embedded programs. In: EMSOFT. (2002) 76–92
32. Braun, P., Broy, M., Cengarle, M.V., Philipps, J., Prenninger, W., Pretschner, A., Rappl, M., Sandner, R. In: The automotive CASE. Wiley (2003) 211 – 228
33. ASCET-SD. http://de.etasgroup.com/products/ascet (18.05.2006)
34. Cadence Cierto VCC. http://www.cadence.com (18.05.2006)

A Story About Formal Methods Adoption by a Railway Signaling Manufacturer

Stefano Bacherini[2], Alessandro Fantechi[1],
Matteo Tempestini[2], and Niccolò Zingoni[2]

[1] Università degli Studi di Firenze, Dipartimento di Sistemi e Informatica
[2] General Electric Transportation Systems
fantechi@dsi.unifi.it, Stefano.Bacherini@trans.ge.com,
Matteo.Tempestini@ge.com, Niccolo.Zingoni@ge.com

Abstract. This paper reports the story of the introduction of formal methods in the development process of a railway signaling manufacturer. The first difficulty for a company is due to the many different formal methods proposals around; we show how this difficulty has been addressed and how the choice of a reference formal specification notation and of the related tools has been driven by many external factors related to the specific application domain, to the company policies, to european regulations. Cooperation with University has been fundamental in this process, which is now at the stage in which internal acceptance of the chosen formalisms and tools is established.

1 Introduction

Railway signaling has been often considered as one of the most successful areas for the industrial application of formal methods, reporting many success stories.

There are two main reasons for this success. On the one hand, railway signaling has always generated the interest of formal methods researchers: its safety requirements with the implied need to avoid any kind of errors, the discrete nature of typical control computations and the absence of very hard real-time constraints, have made it a promising application field, in which the different formal specification and verification techniques can be conveniently applied. On the other hand, railways have always had a very strong safety culture, based on simple fail-safe principles. In electromechanical equipments, used in most signaling systems before the introduction of computers, gravity was used to bring a system to the fail-safe state (e.g. all signals to red) in any occurrence of a critical event. On the other hand, the impossibility of predicting in general the effects of the occurrence of faults in computer-based equipment, has long delayed the acceptance of computer-controlled signaling equipment by railway companies. The employment of very stable technology and the quest for the highest possible guarantees have been key aspects for the adoption of computer-controlled equipment in railway applications. Formal proof, or verification, of safety has been therefore seen as a necessity.

J. Misra, T. Nipkow, and E. Sekerinski (Eds.): FM 2006, LNCS 4085, pp. 179–189, 2006.
© Springer-Verlag Berlin Heidelberg 2006

In this paper, we offer some insight into the actual industrial usage of formal methods in this field, describing the experience of a railway signalling company, namely the railway signaling division of General Electric Transportation Systems (GETS), confronted with the need to adopt formal specification and development techniques in the development cycle of safety-related equipment.

We will see how the choice of which formalism and tool to adopt inside the company development cycle has been influenced by several factors. The choice is indeed not easy: there are many notations, methods, and (prototypal) tools originating from the academia, which however lack industrial strength in terms of tool stability, documentation and user support. On the other hand, there are very few technically sound methods and tools coming from industry. Indeed, the combination of several external factors, such as specific characteristics of the application domain, the general company policies, the european safety regulations, and the trends over the last years of the main actors of the application domain (namely, railway operators, railway infrastructure owners, railway signalling industries), has actually facilitated the choice, narrowing the range of preferred formalisms and tools.

In section 2, the EN50128 guidelines by the European Committee for Electrotechnical Standardization regarding the development of software for railway signaling are discussed, with regards to the adoption of formal specification techniques. Section 3 reports more information of the recent evolution of the context in which GETS operates. Section 4 discusses some first experiments that have been conducted in cooperation with academy in order to correctly address the issue. Section 5 discusses the choice made by GETS to adopt Stateflow of the Matlab environment as the reference formalism and tool.

2   CENELEC Guidelines

The EN50128 guidelines [6], issued by the European Committee for Electrotechnical Standardization (CENELEC), address the development of "Software for Railway Control and Protection Systems", and constitute the main reference for railway signaling equipment manufacturers in Europe, with their use spreading to the other continents and to other sectors of the railway (and other safety-related) industry.

The EN50128 document is part of a series of documents regarding the safety of railway control and protection systems, in which the key concept of Software Safety Integrity Level (SWSIL) is defined. One of the first steps indicated by these guidelines in the development of a system is to define a Safety Integrity Level (SIL) for each of its components, on the basis of the level of risk associated, by means of a risk assessment process. Assigning different SILs to different components helps to concentrate the efforts (and therefore the production costs) on the critical components. The SILs range from 4 (very high), to 1 (low), and 0 (not safety-related).

The EN50128 guidelines dictate neither a precise development methodology for software, nor any particular programming technique, but they classify a wide range of commonly adopted techniques in terms of a rating (from "Forbidden" to "Highly Recommended" and "Mandatory") with respect to the established SIL of the component. Formal methods (in particular CCS, CSP, HOL, LOTOS, OBJ, Temporal Logic, VDM, Z and B are cited as examples) are rated as highly recommended for the specification of systems/components with the higher levels of SIL. Formal proof is also highly recommended as a verification activity. Anyway, formal techniques are not classified as mandatory, since alternative, more traditional techniques are also accepted. We should notice however that this is the first time (the first edition of EN50128 dates back to 1994) that a strong indication about the usage of formal methods appears in standard guidelines.

Indeed, despite CENELEC directives and success stories, formal methods have not permeated the whole railway signaling industries, where much software is still written in traditional ways. This is due to the investments needed to build up a formal methods culture, and to the high costs of commercial support tools. Moreover, equipment can conform to CENELEC without applying formal methods. Verification by thorough testing can be claimed compliant to EN50128. But relying only on traditional testing shifts an enormous effort (usually more than 50% of the total development effort) on the shoulders of the testing department. This becomes a risk for a company that is more and more required by the market to be CENELEC compliant. Indeed, since testing activities are performed in late phases of product life cycle, bugs detection and fixing activities imply reviews of early phases with, consequently, high costs and stretched time. The only solution is to shift back the effort to the design team, by introducing formal methods in the specification and design phases. This is why the railway signalling division of General Electric Transportation Systems (GETS) has taken the decision to adopt formal methods in the development cycle of SIL 4 equipments.

3   The Context

Historically, the ancestors of GETS, similarly to many railway industries all over Europe, had a strict collaboration with Italian State railways. The design of new equipment were carried on as a single team between the railway operator and the equipment providers. The evolution and liberalization of the European market has clearly separated the roles of the operator, which issues equipment specifications, and providers, which implement the specification, but also needs to produce addressing the global market. Hence the specification themselves have gained more importance, in particular with respect to the possibility to have unambiguous, formally specified, specifications.

Indeed, this new trend has become evident inside a joint project between Politecnico di Milano and Italian State Railway FS, Infrastructure Department (which recently became Rete Ferroviaria Italiana S.p.A.). The purpose of the project was to define procedures and rules for managing software procurement for safety-critical signaling equipment [8]. One of the aims of the project was to select and classify formal methods that were sufficiently mature for industrial usage, were supported by automated tools, and were likely to gain acceptance by average engineers, both in the railway and computer technology domains.

One of the indications emerging from this project was that Statecharts [11] and SDL [5] were perceived as the most suitable formalisms according to various parameters, including those cited above.

Another event to be noted is the launching of the Eurointerlocking project by a consortium among the main European infrastructure companies, with the aim of developing a standard interlocking system at a European level, with the purpose to reduce costs, by means of use of standardized components and standardized interlocking rules. Inside Eurointerlocking, we can cite the interesting EIFFRA (Euro-Interlocking Formalised Functional Requirements Approach) activity [13], where, together with an attention to textual requirements, and requirement management tools, such as Telelogic DOORS, model-based requirements are addressed, by proposing UML [19] state diagrams and Statecharts to describe the behaviour, and OCL [20] to describe properties of the interlocking systems.

We can also mention another experience inside Eurointerlocking, by SNCF-RFF, which has modeled their national (relay based) interlocking logic principles using Statecharts and Statemate [15].

In conclusion, the trend that we can note within the railway signaling field is towards state machine - based formalisms, such as SDL and Statecharts, the latter in their various dialects (UML, Statemate, etc...). The graphical syntax and the availability of commercial support tools are considered as positive discriminant factors.

4   The Experiments

GETS has addressed the problem of introducing formal methods in its development process by contacting experts at University of Florence. Collaboration with the Faculty of Engineering of the University of Florence was indeed a tradition, already established on mechanics and electronics. Facing the problem of addressing software certification along CENELEC guidelines, and given that exhaustive testing, possible on the small software systems of the beginnings, was no more viable, GETS has asked to the University experts to establish a common project of technology transfer about formal methods.

The project has followed the indications of the already cited RFI procurements guidelines [8] . In particular some first experiments, have been attempted, modeling in SDL some already produced systems [1,7], with specific attention to the issues of validation coverage [2] and of code generation [3].

Though modelling with SDL allowed a formal methods culture to start to consolidate inside GETS, it was not felt that this was the definitive choice, both for some difficulties emerged with the language itself (the asynchronous nature of communication, inherited by the original mission of SDL to describe communication protocols, and some other characteristics of the messages management have been perceived as difficulties by the designers) and for the not clear future of the language and its support tools, which were going to be merged into the UML 2.0 world.

Following the trends that have been noted in the international railway signalling arena, mainly inside the Eurointerlocking effort, later experiments have switched to Statecharts, at first in their Statemate dialect. At that time, it seemed that also the major GETS client, namely RFI, was inclined to use Statemate Statecharts for drawing their systems specifications. The experiments consisted in the formal specification of a railway signalling system for the objects detection in level crossing areas. The system, named PAI-PL, was developed and homologated SIL 4 by GETS using a customer paper based requirements specification. During the experiment, that specification was translated in a Statemate model and analysed using the related model checker tools. The results showed both that formal methods could be used in specification activities and that could also permit to find mistakes or ambiguous aspects in requirements. Nevertheless after some time, and a quite dense dialog with RFI, it has appeared that no clear decision had already been taken, and that the railway infrastructure company was not ready to abandon its traditional way of developing specifications in favour of formal statecharts specification. This is also because, GETS apart, most of the others signalling companies did not replied positively to formal methods quest by RFI.

The choice of the formal method and support tools were now back in the hands of GETS. The experience acquired on Statecharts indicated that a natural candidate tool to acquire was ILogix Statemate tool [12]. At this point, however, other factors, mostly related to costs, have been taken in consideration. We should recall that the quest for the adoption of a formal method for the specification of systems were coming mainly from the V&V department. Inside the company the high investment needed to acquire the tools would have been therefore not shared among all the departments. Design departments were more keen to adopt instead more flexible tools that could aid several aspects of the design, and not only the specification by statecharts of the "discrete" behaviour of a system.

5   The Choice of Stateflow

An attractive competitor appeared on the scene, in the form of the Stateflow component [16] of the Matlab modeling environment [17] . Indeed Stateflow statecharts share most of the characteristics of other dialects of statecharts, but their semantics have some restrictions, especially in comparison with that described in [11]. Indeed, Statemate semantics is based on three different views (behavioural, functional and structural) of a system, which are related to three corresponding charts (statecharts, activity-charts and module-charts) in a model. Instead, Stateflow semantics permits to represent only the behavioural view, while there is no special formalism to represent the other ones. These and the interactions with the behavioural view can be partially and sometimes with difficulty made up using Simulink formalism. It is in particular a very hard task to develop a model compound by nested functional and behavioural blocks.

From the behavioural point of view, the most peculiar characteristic of State-flow semantics is the use of the "clockwise rule" to evaluate the transitions from the same state. If no user-defined priority rule is given, transitions from the same state are ordered first on the form of their guards (transitions guarded by an event are evaluated before those guarded only by a condition, and unguarded transitions come last): remaining unordered transitions from the state (i.e. sharing the same form of the guards) are ordered by their graphical appearance: the first transition is the one whose arc starts closest to the upper left corner of the source state, and the others follow clockwise. We refer to [10] for a complete formal description of Stateflow semantics. The clockwise rule has two main implications:

- the Stateflow semantics is completely deterministic, since outgoing transitions are always deterministically ordered. The problem is that determinism in some intricate cases (e.g. involving overlapping boolean conditions) cannot be immediately perceived by the user, who naturally considers them as non-deterministic. On the other hand, while Statemate or other statecharts tools are able to identify (statically or by model-checking) possible sources of nondeterminism, this is not possible in Stateflow, where such critical situations perceived by the user as nondeterministic, are actually resolved only at simulation time.
- porting specifications from Statemate or UML Statecharts to Stateflow and vice-versa (by simple manual redrawing or by some import/export tool through a XML/XMI format) is not immediate, and care should be taken that the intended meaning of the specifications is preserved during the porting.

We can observe however that the delays of the major client in adopting formal specifications, referred in the previous sections, have moved the focus away from waiting for specifications from the client, towards the proprietary production and use of specifications, for a later sharing with and approval by the client. Hence, the issue of porting has no more been considered crucial for GETS.

The semantic disadvantages of Stateflow had their counterpart in the possibility offered by Matlab, and by lots of tools compatible with Matlab and Simulink environment, of modelling and simulating several aspects of a system: this possibility was felt as very attractive by many groups inside the design department. Moreover, Matlab was already widely used at corporate level, so that knowledge about it could be easily retrieved over the corporation intranet. Again, several modeling experiments were started, which allowed a better knowledge of the peculiar characteristics of Stateflow. In Figure 1, the main statechart extracted by the model of the already cited PAI-PL system is shown; actually, the represented states are phases of the execution of the system, defined in conformance with the customer requirement specification, and are hierarchically subdivided in lower level statecharts.

The experiments have shown the capability of Stateflow to formally describe the behaviour of a system, allowing simulation and integration in a complete model of the system. The experiments have actually revealed the semantic

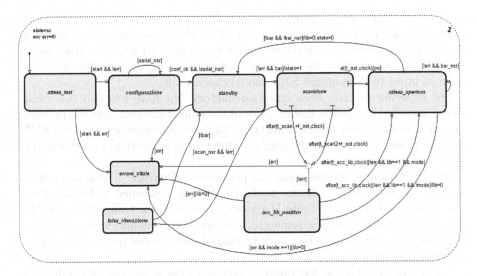

Fig. 1. The Stateflow model of PAI-PL phases

problems that plague Stateflow, but the expected advantages were valued as positively counterbalancing the negative aspects; hence, a decision to adopt Stateflow was taken.

For the first time, Stateflow was actually adopted in the design of a new system, while previous experiments were mainly playing with the specifications of systems already in production. The tool was successfully used to formally define the high levels requirements of this new system and to share the specification with the customer. A more detailed model was developed to define the software requirements of the system and used to design and write down some functions of the application code. Moreover the model was used to carry out functional system tests and to identify corner-case scenarios.

Currently, the use of Matlab has still to become widespread inside the company, and this is planned to occur incrementally on a project by project base. The collaboration with University is still active, and is now focused over the added value that can be obtained from Stateflow specifications, in terms of early validation (through model checking), test case generation and code generation These are listed in order of priority for GETS: namely, first guaranteeing an early validation of Stateflow models, then guaranteeing the consistency between developed code and the model by means of high coverage testing, and last investigating the possibility of automating the code generation from the Stateflow model.

5.1 Model Checking over Stateflow Specifications

Model checking the Stateflow specifications in search of inaccuracies or to guarantee the exhaustiveness of their verification and the compliance with customer requirements is the first goal for our research activity. Actually, several experiments have already been carried on, using SF2SMV [14], a conversion tool developed at Carnegie Mellon University under a contract of the locomotive branch of GETS. The tool allows to convert a Stateflow specification so that it can be given as input to the popular SMV model checker [18].

The experiments have been quite satisfactory, but have revealed two weaknesses, namely the missing maintenance of the conversion tool, and the problem (common to any other format translator) that counterexamples given by SMV must be traced by hand on the original Stateflow specification, and this is certainly a not immediate step.

We are currently investigating the possibility of writing a translator from Stateflow to the UMC on the fly model checker [9], developed at ISTI in Pisa, which takes as input UML State Diagrams. Obviously, the translator should be able to encode the Stateflow semantics into the UML semantics. In return, we are confident to obtain a better back tracing of counterexamples to the original Stateflow specification.

An alternative that is also taken in consideration is the use of commercial model checkers for Stateflow specifications, such as TNI's SCB and OSC's Embedded Validator. An evaluation of such tools is also planned.

5.2   Test Case Generation from Stateflow Specifications

The model developed in GETS allowed to identify corner-case scenarios of software behaviour and to adopt them as test cases during real system testing. Nevertheless the tests were not collected with a formal methodology that permits to measure the coverage of the model, but were identified during model simulation activities with the only purpose of defining software requirements. Therefore it was impossible both to evaluate the correctness of the model and to completely test the conformance of the real system to the software requirements through the model. These two aspects showed the need to develop a test case generation strategy. Indeed a test generation tool can help the user, together with a model checking activity, in the model validation; moreover, it can be used to strengthen the relations between the model and the software: this can be done by testing the same scenario on the model and the system and comparing the outputs. The purpose is to reduce the time to define the test cases and increase the detection of corner case scenarios. Therefore test case generation can be used to reduce the execution time of the functional tests. For this purpose automatic procedures, such as parallel execution of the model and the system with outputs comparison, will be investigated. An analysis of test generation tools as TNI's STB or T-VEC's Test Generation for Simulink is also planned.

5.3   Code Generation from Stateflow Specifications

Automatic code generation is usually considered as a natural output of a software formal specification because it can be easily obtained from a model using a proper tool. This is true in several application domains, but not in railways, where code generation is viewed not less suspiciously than formal methods. Indeed railways safety-related systems are based upon architectures designed with safety more than performance targets in mind. Moreover, the operating software is wrote down mainly to satisfy testing, synchronization and other safety issues. Therefore, the application software needs to be written down following strict constraints, to be seamlessly integrated with the hardware and the operating software. Integration can be very hard, using the code generated from a model: evaluating and understanding how much hard is the object of future work. The evaluation could be done starting with a simple model and analysing the code generated with tools such as ADI's Beacon for Simulink/Stateflow, to understand which language structures it uses and how readable and "linked" to the model it is.The idea is that only using a special precaution during the model development is possible to generate a usable code that can be successfully integrated with the existing one. If the experiment gives good results, the code generation could be used for development of some application functions. For these functions, the effort could be shifted in the early phases of software life cycle (the model development) and most bugs could be fixed during model validation (test generation and model checking). Of course this will not replace standard software testing activities, but will reduce the time of the software life cycle and will guarantee the conformance of the software developed to the model used as software requirements specification.

6   Lessons Learned and Conclusions

The industrial acceptance of formal methods has always been difficult; though many success stories are reported, formally developed software is still a small percentage of the overall installed software. Application domains where safety is a major concern are the ones where industrial formal method applications are more easily found; in particular, railway signaling is considered one of the most successful area of formal methods diffusion. However, the choice among so many different formal methods proposals is not an easy task for a company; the risk of early choices of methods that are not suitable or are not widely accepted by the company departments is high. The experience we have reported has profited of many enabling factors that have in the end facilitated the choice:

- collaboration with academic experts;
- no time–to–market pressure (due to the longer time span of projects w.r.t. other application domains), which has allowed a long experimental phase before selection;
- European regulations asking for formal methods;
- a market evolution pushing for formal methods adoption;
- indications from the major clients about the preferred formalisms for specification.

However, even in this favourable setting for the growth of a formal method culture and in spite of standard and customers indications, the choice was still not easy. Cost factors and company policies necessarily have driven, or even imposed, the choice. In the story we have told, the final choice of Stateflow has on one side followed a trend that has recently emerged in railway signaling, that is, a shift towards behavioral, state-machine based formalisms; on the other hand, this choice was favoured by the industrial quest for formalisms supported by commercial integrated environments, which have a broader scope of application. Tools that give the ability of simulating and model-checking specifications, and of generating code from them provide an interesting added value. The current stage of the adoption of Stateflow in GETS is that the tool is being used for specification and simulation in several new projects. Still more experiments are needed to better evaluate benefits and deficiencies of using model-checking, test case generation and code generation in GETS'products life cycle, and to choose industrial-strength tools offering such functionalities. Hence, it is too early to draft a final balance of the experience: the return of the ongoing analysis will actually be seen in several years.

References

1. S. Bacherini, S. Bianchi, L. Capecchi, C. Becheri, A. Felleca, A. Fantechi, E. Spinicci, *Modelling a railway signalling system using SDL*. In *Proceedings 4th Symposium on Formal Methods for Railway Operation and Control Systems (FORMS'03)*, Budapest. L'Harmattan Hongrie, 2003.
2. M. Banci, M. Becucci, A. Fantechi, E. Spinicci, Validation Coverage for a Component-based SDL model of a Railway Signalling System, Electr. Notes Theor. Comput. Sci. 116: 99-111 (2005).
3. M. Becucci, A. Fantechi, M Giromini, E. Spinicci "A Comparison between Hand-written and Automatic Generation of C Code from SDL using Static Analysis", Software: Practice&Experience, vol. 35, n 114, 2005, pp. 1317-1347.
4. G. Booch, J. Rumbaugh, and I. Jacobson. *The Unified Modeling Language User Guide*. Addison-Wesley, 1999.
5. J. Ellsberger, D. Hogrefe, and A. Sarma. *SDL - Formal Object-oriented Language for Communicating Systems*. Prentice Hall, 1997.
6. European Committee for Electrotechnical Standardization. EN 50128, Railway Applications Communications, Signaling and Processing Systems Software for Railway Control and Protection Systems, 2001.
7. A. Fantechi, E. Spinicci, *Modelling and Validating a Multiple-configuration railway signalling system using SDL*. Electronic Notes in Theoretical Computer Science 82 No. 6 (2003)
8. U. Foschi, M. Giuliani, A. Morzenti, M. Pradella, and P. San Pietro. The role of formal methods in software procurement for the railway transportation industry. In *Proceedings 4th Symposium on Formal Methods for Railway Operation and Control Systems (FORMS'03)*, Budapest. L'Harmattan Hongrie, 2003.
9. S. Gnesi, F. Mazzanti. "On the fly model checking of communicating UML State Machines" Second ACIS International Conference on Software Engineering Research Management and Applications (SERA2004), Los Angeles, USA, 5-7 May 2004.
10. G. Hamon, J. M. Rushby. An Operational Semantics for Stateflow. FASE 2004: 229-243, LNCS 2984

11. D. Harel. Statecharts: A visual formalism for complex systems. *Science of Computer Programming*, 8(3):231–274, 1987.
12. D. Harel, H. Lachover, A. Naamad, A. Pnueli, M. Politi, R. Sherman, A. Shtull-Trauring, M. Trakhtenbrot, *STATEMATE: A Working Environment for the Development of Complex Reactive Systems*, IEEE Transactions on Software Engineering, Vol. 16, N. 4, April 1990, pp. 403-414
13. N.H. König and S. Einer. The Euro-Interlocking formalized functional requirements approach (EIFFRA). In *Proceedings 4th Symposium on Formal Methods for Railway Operation and Control Systems (FORMS'03)*, Budapest. L'Harmattan Hongrie, 2003.
14. B. Krogh, C. Spencer, "Formal Verification of Stateflow Diagrams Using SMV", http://www.ece.cmu.edu/ webk/sf2smv/
15. P. Le Bouar. Interlocking SNCF functional requirements description. Euro-Interlocking Project, Paris, May 2003.
16. The Mathworks: Stateflow and Stateflow Coder, Users Guide. (2005)
17. The Mathworks: MATLAB 7 Users Guide. (2005)
18. K.L. McMillan. Symbolic Model Checking, Kluwer Academic Publishers, 1993.
19. Object Management Group, 1999, *Unified Modeling Language Specification, Version 1.5* http://www.omg.org/technology/documents/formal/uml.htm
20. J. Warmer and A. Kleppe. OCL: The constraint language of the UML. Journal of Object-Oriented Programming, 12(1):10–13,28, Mar. 1999.

Partially Introducing Formal Methods into Object-Oriented Development: Case Studies Using a Metrics-Driven Approach

Yujun Zheng[1,2], Jinquan Wang[1], Kan Wang[3], and Jinyun Xue[2,4]

[1] Systems Engineering Institute of Engineer Equipment, 100093 Beijing, China
uchengz@yahoo.com.cn
[2] Institute of Software, Chinese Academy of Sciences, 100080 Beijing, China
[3] Academy of Armored Force Engineering, 100072 Beijing, China
[4] College of Computer Information and Engineering, Jiangxi Normal University,
330027 Nanchang, China

Abstract. Among researchers and practitioners, there are disputations about whether, where, and to which degree formal methods worth their cost. Based on our experiences of industrial software projects over the last years, we develop an empirical approach of partially introducing formal methods into object-oriented software development. Once an initial architecture design is available, object-oriented metrics can be useful criteria for selecting core parts of software systems for formal treatment. Case studies of the application of our approach show that partially adopting formal methods could achieve a satisfying balance between investment and product quality in a cost-effective way.

1 Introduction

Formal methods use mathematically precise models to build software and hardware systems, and therefore offer the promise of overall improvement of software quality and reliability. Nevertheless, most companies have been unwilling to risk using formal methods in their software development, mainly on the grounds that:

- High introductory costs associated with training and use of formal methods;
- Theoretical and practical limits of formal methods [1];
- Mighty advances of other software engineering methods which also contribute greatly to software quality [2].

Since in most cases formal methods are not yet suitable for full-scale implementation of large systems, an alternative is to partially introduce them to where requirements justify their expense. Generally, formal methods can be cost-effective if their use is limited to core parts of systems, which should be selected under criteria of reliability, safety, availability, security, complexity, etc. However, such criteria are often ambiguous, interrelated, and difficult to be expressed numerically or accurately; therefore hard and fast rules do not exist on how to

J. Misra, T. Nipkow, and E. Sekerinski (Eds.): FM 2006, LNCS 4085, pp. 190–204, 2006.
© Springer-Verlag Berlin Heidelberg 2006

choose metrics, set baselines, and make decisions. Until now, other than providing some general principles (e.g., [3] and [4]), few research has been done to find a practicable and measurable solution for partially adopting formal development process.

The motivation for this paper derives from our experience on adopting formal methods into software development practices over the last four years. After a successful project full-implemented with the B-Method [5], the working group hoped that some other projects with much more limited resources could also benefit from formal techniques. Most of the projects would employ object-oriented development (OOD), in which we believed that the metrics of the initial architecture designs could provide meaningful information for deciding which parts of the system are worth the high cost of formal treatment. Thus we began to develop a metrics-driven approach of partially introducing formal methods into OOD. Our approach has become much more practicable after being tested and improved through several projects.

The paper is structured as follows: Section 2 provides an overview of our metrics-driven approach. Section 3 presents a case study of an experimental project in a classroom environment, whose main purpose is to demonstrate the feasibility of our approach. The next two case studies in Section 4 introduce the approach into industrial projects: a commercial management information system (MIS) and an embedded system. The last two case studies in Section 5 are projects dealing with software evolution, where we take full advantage of recorded metrics of the old systems. Section 6 concludes with some discussions. The definitions of metrics used in the paper are described in Appendix.

2   A Metrics-Driven Approach for Partially Adopting Formal Methods

In this section we describe the empirical approach for adopting formal methods into software development based on software quality metrics, an overview of which is provided by the flowchart in Fig. 1.

2.1   Project Assessment

The first step is to determine the applicability of formal methods in the software project. There are some principles and guidelines (e.g. in [6,7,8]) help to decide whether formal methods are useful for certain projects. In general, we should also carefully conduct investigations on the following aspects:

- Project content and history: Is the project from scratch, or an evolutionary one? Are there any parts of the software artifacts with high requirements of reliability, safety, availability, and security? Which experiences and lessons can be obtained from similar projects?
- Project goals: How important is the project to the organization? To what extent are reliability, quality, economics, and time to market of importance to the success of the project?

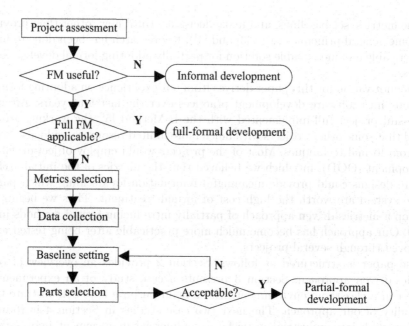

Fig. 1. The flowchart for adopting formal methods based on software quality metrics

- Alternatives: Are there alternative solutions such as using COTS (components off-the-shelves) and subcontracts that can effectively deal with the project requirements and risks?

Inevitably, the answers here are often highly influenced by the expectations and pre-requisite knowledge of the decision-makers. In Addition, contractual requirements may also play a key role in deciding whether a full-scale formal development is mandatory.

2.2   Metrics Selection and Data Collection

After making the decision of partial formal development, we need to choose quality models and metrics based on criteria including predictive validity, simplicity, and quality of assumption [9]. For evolutionary projects, capability of the models and accuracy of the metrics are very important, while in new projects predictability of the models is more crucial. In both conditions, we should also take data collection techniques and tools, and correlations between the metrics and the models into consideration.

Ideally, the more the metrics and the data, the more effective the application of formal methods will be. However, the effort and cost of data collection and analysis are by no means trivial undertakings in large projects, and hence the cost-effectivity is one of the major factors in metrics selection.

2.3   Candidate Parts Selection

To select core parts of a complex object-oriented system, we suggest a "de-escalatory" policy. That is, the selection process can be further divided into the following sub-steps:

1. Along with analysis and design, pick out crucial components (if any exists) whose failures may cause significant losses or catastrophic results.
2. Apply metrics to the remaining components to select candidates for formal treatment.
3. Penetrate into the remaining components and apply metrics to select candidate classes for formal treatment.
4. Penetrate into the remaining classes and apply metrics to select candidate methods for formal treatment.

Here the last sub-step may be omitted if the initial design is not detailed enough or it is too difficult to collect data relevant to method overriding and invocation.

Finally, we should estimate the prospective cost, time, and other resources that would be consumed by the introduction of formal methods, and go back to adjust the baselines until affordable. There is no simple way to make an accurate estimate required for software development. Some algorithmic models such as the early design model and the post-architecture model of COCOMO II [10] can be adapted to produce estimates for formal development and compare different ways of investment (e.g., [11]). Since metrics selection and baseline setting may be largely based on intuition, the process is always iterative.

3   A Feasibility Study

To study the feasibility and effectiveness of our approach, we ran this case study in a classroom environment, which allows new concepts to be tested before using them with expensive developers from industry [12]. The project was a ticket-issuing system, developed by students from the Academy of Armored Force Engineering.

The experimentation consisted of three stages. At the first stage, under the guidance of the tutor, the class that had just completed two courses "Cleanroom Software Engineering" and "MIS Development with J2EE" carried out the OOD of the system, the result of which contained 46 classes: 35 classes to be developed from scratch and 11 classes can be found in the standard library.

For 35 application-specific classes, we collected their design metrics of coupling, cohesion, and inheritance, which were taken from [13,14,15]. We then chose seven metrics to set baselines for selecting classes: those with any two metrics beyond (worse than) the baselines were considered with high complexity and/or reusability, and therefore were hypothesized to be worthwhile to apply formal methods, as summarized in Table 1.

At the second stage, the class was equally divided into three groups, which were then asked to implement the system independently: Group A developed all 35 classes using traditional (informal) object-oriented programming; Group B developed 9 selected classes with the formal method that they had just learned,

Table 1. Metrics applied and classes selected

Metrics	Baseline	Classes selected	Percentage
CBO	5	6	17.1%
LCOM	10	4	11.4%
NOC	5	2	5.7%
NOD	15	0	0
RFC	50	10	28.6%
SIX	0.8	7	20%
WMC	40	11	31.4%
Total	2 metrics beyond	9	25.7%

i.e., an approach of Cleanroom specification and design techniques combined with OO methodologies[1], and other 26 classes with traditional OO programming; Group C developed all 35 classes formally.

For each release of the system, we respectively performed a white-box testing, whose purpose was to collect static fault data (measured by DDKLOC), and a black-box testing, whose purpose was to collect dynamic fault data (measured by MTTF) of the system. The errors found by the white-box testing were then fed back to the corresponding groups for correction.

At the third stage, the three groups fulfilled the tasks of corrective maintenance; afterwards the white-box and black-box testing were performed again for the systems. The graph in Fig. 2 shows the comparative results of the experimentation including the time of development and maintenance, as well as the DDKLOC and MTTF metrics before and after the maintenance.

According to this study, in contrast to informal development, partial-formal development offered about a 2210% dynamic quality improvement (in MTTF) with only a 37% additional investment (in person-hours), which manifested that the formal method was effectively introduced to core parts of the system. At the same time, in contrast to partial-formal development, complete-formal development achieved about a 390% dynamic quality improvement, but with an 88% additional investment. Based on the comparison of informal, partial-formal and complete-formal development, we drew the conclusion that partially adopting formal development process could achieve a good, if not optimal, balance between investment and product quality.

Furthermore, the case study revealed another interesting aspect that we had not recognized at the beginning: Although the system with partial-formal development may still be far less quality than that with complete-formal development, in combined with intensive testing and corresponding corrective maintenance (mainly on those informally developed), partially adoption of formal methods may also be likely to achieve a quality level much closer to that of full-scale formal implementation. In this case study, the first release of Group B achieved

---

[1] That is, an object class without any implementation is first modeled as a black box, which is refined to a state box by introducing data implementation, and then refined to a clear box by introducing process implementation [16].

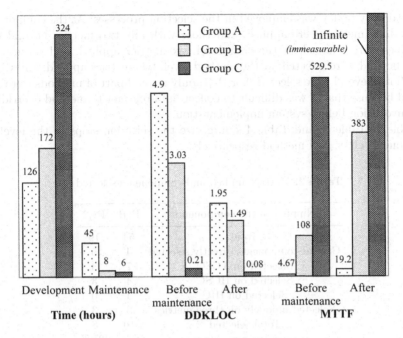

Fig. 2. Development efforts and product qualities of the three groups

only 20% of the dynamic quality of Group C, its second release finally achieved 72%, with only 56% of total time invested[2].

Inevitably, this case study was just a feasibility study that concerned with generating and testing some hypotheses about our approach and its usefulness. The selected metrics were used to measure the complexity and significance of classes, and some of them were also good indicators for prediction of fault-proneness [17,18], but their expressiveness was neither comprehensive nor persuasive. Nevertheless, the case study provided meaningful information as desired: our approach produced useful results that could be achieved in a cost-effective way.

4   Two Industrial Case Studies

After the feasibility study in the classroom environment, we introduced the approach into two industrial projects: one was a materiel management information system, namely Prj1, which employed the Cleanroom techniques and object-oriented specifications; the other was a ballistic computer system [19], namely Prj2, which employed the B- Method and Toolkit [5].

In comparison with the first experimental project, we implemented the metrics-driven approach for these two projects on a much larger scale. The metrics taken from [9,14,15,20] were applied to software elements from the component (program assemble) level to the method level. For both the case studies, the

---

[2] Here we did not take the testing time into consideration, which was believed to be trivial when using automatic tools.

de-escalatory policy was employed in the selection processes: At the component level, three metrics were applied, and those with any two metrics beyond the baselines were selected; at the class level, six metrics applied, and those with three beyond were selected; at the method level, two metrics applied, and those with both beyond were selected. For Prj1, only a small part of methods were analyzed because that it was difficult to collect data relevant to method overriding and invocation before system implementation.

Table 2, Table 3, and Table 4 summarize the selection steps at the level of component, class, and method respectively.

Table 2. Metrics applied and components selected

Number of the components	Prj1	Prj2
Total	54	19
Crucial components directly selected	4	5
Selected on TCSC	7	3
Selected on HCSC	4	3
Selected on HIC	4	0
Selected uniquely on three metrics	6	3
Total selected	10	8
Selection percentage	18.5%	42.1%

Table 3. Metrics applied and classes selected

Number of the classes	Prj1	Prj2
Total	762	340
Selected along with components	112	141
Selected on CBO	42	42
Selected on LCOM	48	15
Selected on NOC	23	10
Selected on NOD	26	18
Selected on RFC	44	17
Selected on ICHC	155	63
Selected uniquely on the six metrics	86	52
Total selected	198	193
Selection percentage	26%	56.8%

For both the projects, we respectively selected two other projects which were of similar domain and scale to compare their development effectiveness. Tow comparative projects for Prj1 (namely Prj1A and Prj1B) both employed informal program techniques. As illustrated in Fig. 3, through partially adopting formal methods, Prj1 achieved about a 1520% dynamical quality improvement over Prj1A and 520% over Prj1B, with only about a 33% additional cost over Prj1A and 113% over Prj1B, or at the expense of a 24% productivity loss to Prj1A and 53% to Prj1B.

Table 4. Metrics applied and methods selected

Number of the methods (K)	Prj1	Prj2
Total	13.5	26.8
Selected along with class	2.1	10.9
Selected on NOOM	3.6	1.3
Selected on ICHM	1.9	4.1
Selected uniquely on the two metrics	1.3	3.7
Total selected	3.4	14.6
Selection percentage	25.2%	54.5%

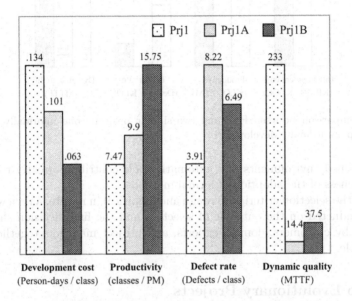

Fig. 3. Comparison between Prj1 and two similar projects informally developed

For Prj2, one of its comparative project (namely Prj2A) was informally developed, and the other (namely Prj2B) was complete-formally developed. As shown in Fig. 4, with nearly the same development cost and productivity, Prj2 achieved great quality improvement over Prj2A. However, the improvement of Prj2B over Prj2 was at the expense of a 77% additional cost and a 44% productivity loss.

Results of the case studies showed that our approach was successfully transferred form research phase to industry. Lessons learned from the studies included:

- High quality analysis and design should be taken as prerequisites to the application of our metrics-driven approach.
- For large projects, data collection and analysis are by no means trivial undertakings; therefore relevant resource consumed and consequent influence must be taken into consideration at the beginning of project planning.

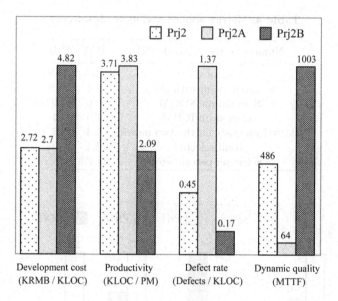

Fig. 4. Comparison between Prj2 and two similar projects, one informally and the other complete-formally developed

- Controlled environments and automatic tools contribute greatly to the effectiveness of the adoption of formal methods.
- Since the selection criteria are rough and empirical in nature, a review should be conducted on the outcome of selection and the final decision should be made by customers, domain experts, and project managers together when possible.

5   Two Evolutionary Projects

Rather than developed from scratch, the two case studies (namely Prj3 and Prj4) in this section dealt with software evolution projects, in which recorded metrics of system development and operation provided valuable information for selecting elements to apply formal methods. Evolutionary tasks mainly included adding and modifying functionalities, repairing software faults, and adapting interfaces to changed environment. Selected parts were re-developed using UML formalization and transformation [21].

Since data collection and analysis could be very expensive when analyzing a broader set of metrics, we employed a "two-round-election" strategy when applying the metrics. That is, we classified the baselines into two categories: one used to extensively select "potentially worthwhile" candidates, and the other used to eliminate "unworthwhile" candidates from first-round winners.

In the first round we extensively selected candidates with high failure rate or high complexity based on product quality metrics from [14,15,22], as summarized in Table 4. Afterwards, based on product, in process, and mainte-

Table 5. Summary of the first-round selection

Perspective	Item	Prj3	Prj4
Failure rate	Components selected on DDKLOC	7	5
	Components selected on MTTF	6	2
	Components selected on MTI	14	4
	Components selected uniquely	19	9
	Class selected with components	399	112
Complexity	Components selected on TCSC	18	6
	Components selected on HCSC	22	9
	Components selected on HIC	30	8
	Components selected uniquely	45	14
	Class selected with components	773	110
	Classes selected on WMC	528	106
	Classes selected on NOC	212	39
	Classes selected on RFC	135	21
	Classes selected on LCOM	165	24
	Classes selected uniquely	673	124
Total	Components selected	64	18
	Components selection percentage	27.1%	42.9%
	Classes selected	1845	346
	Classes selection percentage	39.4%	54.2%

nance quality metrics from [9,13,23], we stepwise eliminated candidates that featured low customer problems, minimal development efforts, and low maintenance efforts, as summarized in Table 5. A comparative analysis on quality before and after the evolutions is shown in Fig. 5.

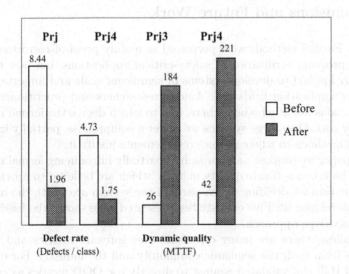

Fig. 5. Comparison of evolutionary effects on software quality

Table 6. Summary of the second-round selection

Perspective	Item	Prj3	Prj4
Customers	Components analyzed	10	4
	Components eliminated on PUM	2	2
	Components eliminated on PDC	4	2
	Components eliminated uniquely	5	3
	Class eliminated with components	139	39
Developers	Components analyzed	59	15
	Components eliminated on SPS	13	2
	Components eliminated on DRE	5	3
	Components eliminated uniquely	16	4
	Class eliminated with components	452	72
	Classes analyzed	1254	235
	Classes eliminated on SPS	365	33
	Classes eliminated on DRE	152	21
	Classes eliminated uniquely	440	39
Maintainers	Components analyzed	43	11
	Components eliminated on WBMI	6	3
	Components eliminated on WPDF	3	2
	Components eliminated on WRDI	4	2
	Components eliminated uniquely	8	3
	Class eliminated with components	182	50
Total	Components eliminated	29	10
	Components eliminated percentage	45.3%	55.6%
	Classes eliminated	1213	200
	Classes eliminated percentage	65.8%	57.8%

6   Conclusions and Future Work

Originally, Formal methods were perceived as mainly proof-of-correctness techniques for program verification of safety-critical applications, but now they are increasingly applied to develop systems of significant scale and importance and in all other application fields [24]. Among researchers and practitioners, there are disputations about whether, where, and to which degree the formal methods worth their cost. Over large systems we prefer a compromise: partially introducing formal methods to where project requirements justify it.

In this paper we propose an approach of partially introducing formal methods into OOD based on software quality metrics, which are believed to provide valuable information for deciding which parts of the system are worth the high cost of formal development. Five case studies presented have shown the feasibility of our metrics-driven approach.

Nevertheless, there are many criticisms over software metrics and statistical models from both the academic community and the industry. For example, Mayer and Hall [25] validated against to directly use OOD metrics as complexity metrics. In [26] Fenton and Neil also criticized multivariate statistical models produced in an attempt to find a single complexity metric that will account for defects. Although metrics applied in our case studies are elaborately selected and are believed to have strong relationships with complexity, fundamentality, and fault-proneness of software artifacts [27], it is still not reasonable to try to work out an all-around set of criteria.

As an empirical study, our approach needs to be tested and improved through further research on larger body of experimental data and more kinds of projects. Ongoing efforts include making the approach more firmly rooted in measurement theory (e.g., conducting false positives and false negatives analysis on the results of selection) and developing a cost-driven approach for introducing formal methods in projects with fixed budgets and schedules.

Acknowledgements

We are grateful to the Academy of Armored Force Engineering and in particular Dr. Zhang W. and Du J. for help in the formulation of the feasibility study.

References

1. Kneuper, R.: Limits of Formal Methods. Formal Aspects of Computing Vol. 9, No. 4 (1997) 379-394
2. Sommerville, I.: Software Engineering (7th Ed.). Addison-Wesley, Reading, MA (2004)
3. Mills, H.D., Dyer, M., and Linger, R.C.: Cleanroom Software Engineering, IEEE Software, Vol. 4, No. 5 (1987) 19-24
4. Vienneau, R.L.: A Review of Formal Methods, Software Engineering, (Eds. Dorfman, M.and Thayer, R.H.) IEEE Computer Society Press (1996) 181-192
5. Abrial, J.R.: The B-Book: Assigning Programs to Meanings. Cambridge University Press, Cambridge (1996)
6. Clarke, E.M. and Wing, J.M.: Formal Methods: State of the Art and Future Directions. CMU-CS-96-178, Carnegie-Mellon University, Pittsburgh, PA (1996)
7. Heitmeyer, C.L.: Developing High Quality Software with Formal Methods: What Else Is Needed? In Proceedings of 25th IFIP International Conference on Formal Techniques for Networked and Distributed Systems, Lecture Notes in Computer Sciences, Vol. 3731, Springer-Verlag, Berlin Heidelberg (2005) 13-19
8. Craigen, D., Gerhart, S., and Ralston, T.: An International Survey of Industrial Applications of Formal Methods. NIST GCR 93/626, National Technical Information Service, VA (1993)
9. Kan, S. H.: Metrics and Models in Software Quality Engineering (2nd Ed.). Addison-Wesley, Reading, MA (2003)
10. Boehm, B.: COCOMO II Definition Manual. Univ. of Southern California (1997) (Available at: http://sunset.usc.edu/research/COCOMOII)
11. Zheng, Y.J., Wang, K., and Xue, J.Y.: An Extension of COCOMO II for the B-Method. In Proceedings of 7th International Workshop on Economics-Driven Software Engineering Research, ACM Press, New York, NY (2006).
12. Shull, F., Carver J., and Travassos, G.H.: An Empirical Methodology for Introducing Software Processes. In Proceedings of European Software Engineering Conference, ACM Press, New York, NY (2001) 288-296

13. Barnard, J.: A New Reusability Metric for Object-Oriented Software. Software Quality Journal, Vol. 7, No. 1 (1998) 35–50
14. Chidamber, S.R. and Kemerer, C.F.: A Metrics Suite for Object-Oriented Design. IEEE Transactions on Software Engineering, Vol. 20, No. 6 (1994) 476-493
15. Lorenz, M. and Kidd, J.: Object-Oriented Software Metrics: A Practical Guide. Prentice-Hall, New York (1994)
16. Deck, M.: Cleanroom and Object-Oriented Software Engineering: A Unique Synergy. In Proceedings of 8th Annual Software technology Conference, Salt Lake City, UT (1996)
17. Andrews, A. and Stringfellow, C.: Quantitative Analysis of Development Defects to Guide Testing: A Case Study. Software Quality Journal, Vol. 9, No. 3 (2001) 195–214
18. Binkley, A.B. and Schach, S.R.: Prediction of Run-time Failures using Static Product Quality Metrics. Software Quality Journal, Vol. 7, No. 2 (1998) 141–147
19. Zhang, Z.Q., Zheng, Y.J., and Li H.Y.: B-Method based approach for designing ballistic computers. Computer Engineering and Design, Vol. 26, No. 12 (2005) 3295-3298
20. Bellin, D., Tyagi, M., and Tyler, M.: Object-Oriented Metrics: An Overview. In Proceedings of 1994 Conference on the Centre for Advanced Studies on Collaborative Research, IBM Press, Carlsbad, CA (1994)
21. Warmer, J. and Kleppe, A.: The Object Constraint Language: Precise Modeling with UML (2nd ed.). Addison-Wesley, Reading MA (2003)
22. Henry, S.M. and Kafura, D.: Software Structure Metrics Based on Information Flow. IEEE Transactions on Software Engineering, vol. 7, No. 5 (1981), 510-518.
23. Daskalantonakis, M.K.: A Practical View of Software Measurement and Implementation Experiences within Motorola, IEEE Transactions on Software Engineering, vol. 18, No. 11 (1992) 998-1010.
24. Gogolla, M.: Benefits and Problems of Formal Methods. In Proceedings of 9th Ada-Europe International Conference on Reliable Software Technologies. Lecture Notes in Computer Sciences, Vol. 3063. Springer-Verlag, Berlin Heidelberg (2004) 1–15
25. Mayer, T. and Hall, T.: A critical analysis of OO design metrics. Software Quality Journal, Vol. 8, No. 2 (1999) 97-110
26. Fenton, N.E. and Neil, M.: A Critique of Software Defect Prediction Models. IEEE Transactions on Software Engineering, Vol. 25, No. 2 (1999) 675-689
27. Briand, L.C., Wust, J., and Lounis, H.: Replicated Case Studies for Investigating Quality Factors in Object-Oriented Designs. Empirical Software Engineering, Vol. 6, No. 1 (2001) 11-58

Appendix: Definitions of the Metrics used in the Paper

Table 7. The definitions of quality metrics used in the paper

Name	Definition	Expression
CBO	Coupling between object classes	The number of other classes to which a class is coupled
DDKLOC	Delivered defects per thousand source lines code	$(N_D + N_F)/L$, where N_D denotes the number of known delivered defects, N_F the number of uniquely new defects found after release, and L the size (in KLOC)
DRE	Defect removal effectiveness	R/L, where R denotes the number of defects removed during the development phase, and L the number of defects latent in the product
HCSC	Hybrid component structural complexity	$\frac{\sum_{i=1}^{n}(S_i \times R_i)^2}{n}$, where n denotes the number of agent classes (act as both servers and clients) in the component, S the number of classes that consume the service of a class, and R the number of classes that provide services for the class.
HIC	Hybrid inheritance complexity	$\frac{\sum_{i=1}^{n}(B_i \times D_i)^2}{n}$, where n denotes the number of hierarchy trees in a component, B the number of levels of a given tree, and D the number of leaves in a given tree
ICHM	Information-flow-based cohesion of a method	$\sum_{i=1}^{n} H_i$, where n denotes the number of invocations of other methods of the same class, and H the number of parameters of the invoked method
ICHC	Information-flow-based cohesion of a class	$\sum_{i=1}^{n} I_i$, where n denotes the number of methods in a class, and I the Information-flow-based cohesion of a given method
LCOM	Lack of cohesion on methods of a class	The number of pairs of methods in a class using no attribute in common
MTTF	Mean time to failure	$H/(I+1)$, where H denotes the total CPU run hours, and I the number of (unique) software failures
MTI	Mean time to unplanned initial program loads	$\sum_{i=1}^{n} W_i \times (\frac{H_i}{I_i+1})$, where n denotes the number of delivered releases that data collection has been performed, H the total CPU run hours, W the weighting factor, and I the number of (unique) unplanned IPLs due to software failures
NOC	Number of children	The number of classes that directly inherit from a class
NOD	Number of descendents	The number of classes that directly or indirectly inherit from a class
NOOM	Number of overriding methods	The number of methods that directly override a method

continued on the next page

Table 7. (*continued*)

Name	Definition	Expression
PUM	Problems per user month	$\frac{\sum_{i=1}^{n}(D_i+P_i)}{n}$,where n denotes the number of delivered releases that data collection has been performed, D the number of true defects reported, and P the number of non-defect-oriented problems reported
PDC	Percent of dissatisfied customers	$(D+E)/N$, where N denotes the number of customers surveyed using a five-point scale (5-very satisfied, 4-satisfied, 3-neutral, 2-dissatisfied, 1-very dissatisfied), D and E the number of dissatisfied and very dissatisfied customers respectively
FC	Response for a class	$\sum_{i=1}^{n}(m_i+\sum_{j=1}^{m_i}C_j)$,where n denotes the number of message types the class can receive, m the number of methods executed in response to a given message, and C the number of methods directly called by a given method
SIX	Specialization index	NMO × DIT / (NMO + NMA + NMINH), where NMO denotes the number of methods overridden in a class, DIT the depth of the class in the inheritance tree, NMA the number of methods added, and NMINH the number of methods inherited
SPS	Software productivity on single element	L/T, where L denotes the size of the software element (in LOC), and T the development time (in PM)
TCSC	Traditional component structural complexity	$\frac{\sum_{i=1}^{n}R_i^2}{n}$,where n denotes the number of receiving classes in a component, and R the number of classes that consume the service of a given class
WBMI	Worst backlog management index	MIN($\frac{N_C}{N_A}$ × 100%),where N_C denotes the number of problems closed (during every month after release), and N_A the number of problem arrivals
WMC	Weighted methods per class	$\sum_{i=1}^{n}W_i$,where n denotes the number of methods in the class, and W the cyclomatic complexity of a given method
WPDF	Worst percent delinquent fixes	MAX($\frac{N_D}{N_S}$ × 100%),where N_D denotes the number of fixes delayed (during every month after release), and N_S the number of fixes delivered in a specified time
WRDI	Worst real-time delivery index	WRDI = MAX($\frac{N_D}{N_B+N_A}$ × 100%),where N_D denotes the number of fixes delayed (during every month after release), N_B the number of problems backlogged, and N_A the number of problem arrivals

Compositional Class Refinement in Object-Z

Tim McComb and Graeme Smith

School of Information Technology and Electrical Engineering
The University of Queensland
{tjm, smith}@itee.uq.edu.au

Abstract. Object-Z allows coupling constraints between classes which, on the one hand, facilitate specification at a high level of abstraction, but, on the other hand, make class refinement non-compositional. The consequence of this is that refinement is not practical for large systems. This paper overcomes this limitation by introducing a methodology for compositional class refinement in Object-Z. The key step is an equivalence transformation of an arbitrary Object-Z specification to one in which introduced constraints prohibit non-compositional refinements. The methodology also allows the constraints which couple classes to be refined yielding an unrestricted approach to compositional class refinement.

1 Introduction

The need for modularity and reuse in software development has led to the dominance of object-oriented programming languages in the software industry. The benefits of an object-oriented approach can also apply to formal software development. Formal languages such as Object-Z [8], OhCircus [1] and TCOZ [4] support notions of classes and inheritance facilitating the development of specifications which are readily understood and reasoned about in a modular fashion.

In Object-Z, operations in one class are able to restrict the outputs of operations in other classes with which they are composed. As discussed by Smith and Derrick [10], this allows a more abstract level of specification when modelling systems. In particular, consensus between objects can be readily specified independently of the protocol used to obtain it. This can lead to specifications which are both easier to understand and analyse.

As a result, however, if an object of an Object-Z class A exists in a specification X (denoted here by $X(A)$), and A is refined to a concrete class C, then the specification $X(C)$ is not necessarily a refinement of the specification $X(A)$ — class refinement is not compositional. The consequence of this is that refinement is impractical when dealing with large systems, as the process cannot be performed in a modular fashion.

This issue stems from a related issue in the Z specification language [11], upon which Object-Z is based. The existence of a refinement relationship between individual schemas in Z does not imply that refinement holds when the schemas are composed together. Constructs such as schema conjunction, for example, must be unfolded to form a single schema that may then be refined.

J. Misra, T. Nipkow, and E. Sekerinski (Eds.): FM 2006, LNCS 4085, pp. 205–220, 2006.
© Springer-Verlag Berlin Heidelberg 2006

The possible unfolding of such compositional operators is a sensible mitigation to this problem in Z, but in Object-Z this is not usually a plausible option. Object-Z classes encapsulate state and operations to form an abstract data type, and compositional operators may be used to compose operations within different classes. This feature is very useful for the purpose of specification, but prohibits the unfolding of operations to form a single, refineable operation because they may apply to different states. Furthermore, such unfolding would go against the desire for modular refinement.

The non-compositionality of class refinement in Object-Z is discussed by Derrick and Boiten [2]. They demonstrate that compositionality can be achieved under certain syntactic restrictions to the use of the language. However, they do not suggest that these restrictions be adopted for Object-Z as they would greatly inhibit the way Object-Z is used in practice.

The issue has also arisen in the context of integrating Object-Z and CSP [7,3,4,9] for the specification of concurrent systems. In most of this work [3,4,9], alternative semantics of Object-Z classes have been developed which disallow the external restricting of outputs to enable compositional class refinement.

In this paper, we present a methodology for compositional refinement in Object-Z that requires neither syntactic restrictions to the language, nor an alternative semantics of classes. The key step is an equivalence transformation of the specification to one in which individual classes can be refined compositionally. The transformation introduces constraints into class operations which prevent non-compositional refinements. It also isolates the constraints that couple classes together, and allows these coupling constraints to be refined independently of the classes, and hence independently of the operations whose composition is the cause of the coupling. This yields an unrestricted approach to compositional class refinement.

In Section 2, we provide an overview of class refinement in Object-Z. In Section 3, we motivate our work with an indicative example of where class refinement is not compositional. In Section 4, we present a simple approach to transforming Object-Z specifications to enable compositional class refinement. To overcome the restrictions imposed on refinement by this simple approach, we present a further transformation step in Section 5 which enables us to refine the coupling constraints between classes. We conclude with a discussion of the approach and future work in Section 6.

2   Class Refinement

The standard notion of class refinement used with Object-Z is data refinement. Values of the state variables of a class are regarded as being internal so that refinement can be used to change the representation of the state of a class. As with Z, there are two forms of simulation rules which are together complete, i.e., all possible refinements can be proved with a combination of the rules. In this paper, we consider the most common form, referred to as *downward simulation*. Adapting our approach to *upward simulation* is left as future work.

Downward simulation of Object-Z classes is defined as follows[1] [2]:

Definition 1. *An Object-Z class with state schema CState, initial state schema CInit and operations $COp_1 \ldots COp_n$ is a downward simulation of an Object-Z class with state schema AState, initial state schema AInit and operations $AOp_1 \ldots AOp_n$, if there is a retrieve relation R such that the following hold.*

Initialisation. $\forall\, CState \bullet CInit \Rightarrow (\exists\, AState \bullet AInit \wedge R)$
Applicability. $\forall\, AState;\ CState;\ ?AOp_i \bullet R \Rightarrow (pre\, AOp_i \Leftrightarrow pre\, COp_i)$
Correctness. $\forall\, AState;\ CState;\ CState';\ ?AOp_i;\ !AOp_i \bullet$
$\qquad\qquad R \wedge COp_i \Rightarrow (\exists\, AState' \bullet R' \wedge AOp_i)$

where i ranges over 1 to n, and $?AOp_i$ and $!AOp_i$ denote the declarations of inputs and outputs respectively of AOp_i (which must be the same as those of COp_i).

Note that the applicability condition does not allow the 'enabledness' of a refined operation to be either weakened or strengthened. This is because Object-Z possesses a *blocking semantics* where an operation's precondition (which determines whether or not it is enabled) acts as a guard; if it is false, the operation 'blocks', i.e., cannot occur, and the same must be true for any refinement.

3 Motivating Example

In this section, we introduce an example that does not allow for compositional refinement as defined by the downward simulation rules for refinement of Object-Z classes. Such examples arise due to the fact that conjunction can be used to combine operations from different classes. Conjunction manifests itself not only in the conjunction operator, but also in the parallel and sequential composition operators which are defined in terms of conjunction [8]. In each case, it is possible for both operation schemas to restrict a particular post-state variable. When there is unresolved non-determinism over such a post-state variable, refining one of the schemas may result in the conjunction becoming *false*.

3.1 Bargaining Example

Our example models the simple negotiation of a sale. In the specification below[2], the buyer has a certain amount of *cash* and is prepared to spend all of it, but the vendor will only sell at a price that is between the reserve price and the asking price (inclusively). The specification abstracts away the details of the negotiation process to leave the actual price paid as a non-deterministically chosen amount. This amount is implicitly agreed upon by both the vendor and the buyer via

---

[1] Note that the state variables of a schema S *after* each operation are denoted by S'.
[2] We assume some familiarity with Object-Z. Details of the notation can be found in [8].

the shared post-state variable *price!*. After the *Transaction*, the buyer's *cash* decreases as much as the vendor's *takings* increase; this is the price paid.

┌─ *Buyer* ──────────────────────────
│ ┌──────────────────────────────
│ │ *cash* : $\mathbb{N}$
│ └──────────────────────────────
│ ┌─ *Buy* ──────────────────────
│ │ $\Delta(cash)$
│ │ *price!* : $\mathbb{N}$
│ ├──────────────────────────────
│ │ *price!* $\leq$ *cash*
│ │ *cash'* = *cash* − *price!*
│ └──────────────────────────────
└────────────────────────────────────

┌─ *Vendor* ─────────────────────────
│ ┌──────────────────────────────
│ │ *takings, reserve, asking* : $\mathbb{N}$
│ └──────────────────────────────
│ ┌─ *Sell* ─────────────────────
│ │ $\Delta(takings)$
│ │ *price!* : $\mathbb{N}$
│ ├──────────────────────────────
│ │ *reserve* $\leq$ *price!* $\leq$ *asking*
│ │ *takings'* = *takings* + *price!*
│ └──────────────────────────────
└────────────────────────────────────

┌─ *Market* ───
│ ┌──
│ │ *buyer* : *Buyer*
│ │ *vendor* : *Vendor*
│ └──
│ *Transaction* $\hat{=}$ *buyer.Buy* $\wedge$ *vendor.Sell*
└──

The problem with refining class *Buyer* or *Vendor* is that such a refinement may render it impossible to select and agree upon a price – thus the precondition of the *Transaction* operation in *Market* becomes *false*. For example, consider $Vendor_1$ below as a refinement of *Vendor* and the question of whether $Market_1$ is a refinement of *Market*.

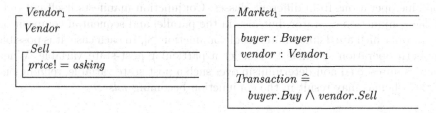

Here, $Vendor_1$ takes advantage of inheritance in Object-Z to derive its definition from *Vendor*. Inheritance is defined primarily in terms of conjunction in Object-Z [8], such that the state schema of $Vendor_1$ is exactly that of *Vendor*, but the operation *Sell*, since it appears in both $Vendor_1$ and *Vendor*, is interpreted as the conjunction of $Vendor_1.Sell$[3] and *Vendor.Sell*.

Since the vendor insists upon accepting only the asking price, the *Transaction* operation in $Market_1$ is not enabled when the buyer has only enough cash to meet the reserve price. Although the refinement of *Vendor* has not altered the precondition of *Sell*, the precondition of operation $Market_1.Transaction$ is stronger

───────────────────────────
[3] We use the notation *C.Op* to refer to the operation *Op* of class *C*.

than *Market.Transaction* in the case that *vendor.asking* $\neq$ *vendor.reserve*. We can observe this by calculating and comparing the preconditions[4].

> pre *Buyer.Buy* = *cash* $\in \mathbb{N}$
> pre *Vendor.Sell* = *reserve* $\in \mathbb{N} \wedge$ *reserve* $\leq$ *asking* $\wedge$ *asking* $\in \mathbb{N} \wedge$
>   *takings* $\in \mathbb{N}$
> pre *Market.Transaction* = pre *Buyer.Buy* $\wedge$ pre *Vendor.Sell* $\wedge$
>   *buyer.cash* $\geq$ *vendor.reserve*

> pre *Vendor$_1$.Sell* = pre *Vendor.Sell*
> pre *Market$_1$.Transaction* = pre *Buyer.Buy* $\wedge$ pre *Vendor$_1$.Sell* $\wedge$
>   *buyer.cash* $\geq$ *vendor.asking*

The predicate that couples the preconditions of the *Buy* and *Sell* operations in the precondition of *Transaction* relates the amount of cash the buyer has to the reserve and asking prices of the vendor. This is necessary because an agreement must be made over the binding of the post-state variable *price!*. Clearly when *vendor.asking* $\neq$ *vendor.reserve* the preconditions of *Market.Transaction* and *Market$_1$.Transction* differ; thus *Market* is not refined by *Market$_1$*.

4   Enabling Compositional Refinement

Throughout the remainder of this paper, given an operation A, say, we will let *AState* denote the state schema of A's class together with A's inputs, and *AState'* the state schema of A's class together with both A's inputs and outputs.

Suppose that we have the conjunction of operations $A \wedge B$ in an Object-Z specification, where A and B are from different classes (and hence operate on different states). If we refine A to C, under what circumstances is $C \wedge B$ not a refinement of $A \wedge B$?

When C is a downward simulation of A, via the correctness condition we have

$$\forall \textit{AState};\ \textit{CState};\ \textit{CState'} \bullet R \wedge C \Rightarrow (\exists \textit{AState'} \bullet R' \wedge A)$$

where R is the retrieve relation for the simulation.

Since $P \Rightarrow (\exists x \bullet P)$, it follows from this that

$$\forall \textit{AState};\ \textit{CState};\ \textit{CState'};\ \textit{BState};\ \textit{BState'} \bullet R \wedge C \wedge B \Rightarrow$$
$$(\exists \textit{AState'};\ \textit{BState'} \bullet R' \wedge A \wedge B)$$

Hence, correctness will always hold between $A \wedge B$ and $C \wedge B$.

When C is a downward simulation of A, via the applicability condition we have

$$\forall \textit{AState};\ \textit{CState} \bullet R \Rightarrow (\text{pre } A \Leftrightarrow \text{pre } C)$$

---

[4] In Object-Z the precondition is defined by existentially quantifying the post-state variables (outputs included) over the predicate of the operation [2].

which expands to [2]

$$\forall\, AState;\ CState \bullet R \Rightarrow ((\exists\, AState' \bullet A) \Leftrightarrow (\exists\, CState' \bullet C))$$

The applicability condition between $A \wedge B$ and $C \wedge B$ is

$$\forall\, AState;\ CState;\ BState \bullet R \Rightarrow$$
$$((\exists\, AState';\ BState' \bullet A \wedge B) \Leftrightarrow (\exists\, CState';\ BState' \bullet C \wedge B))$$

This follows from the above when $BState'$ does not overlap with $AState'$ and $CState'$. When there is overlap, as was the case in the example of Section 3, the applicability condition can fail.

By definition, state variables of distinct classes are themselves distinct [8], hence such an overlap is only possible over output variables. Since output variables cannot be added or removed under data refinement (since they are not part of the class's internal state), the output variables of $AState'$ will be identical to those of $CState'$. Hence, refinement of A to C can only fail to be compositional when A and B have shared output variables.

We require an approach that prevents us from performing refinements that will add constraints on shared outputs. Our methodology achieves this by equating such output variables to fresh shared input variables. Input variables are part of the precondition of an operation and hence constraints cannot be added to them during refinement. Consequently, constraints cannot be added to the output variables equated to them.

For each conjunction $A \wedge B$ in a specification, where A and B are from different classes, we begin by determining the common-named output variables in the operations[5]. Let the declaration of these output variables be denoted by $\vec{v}! : \vec{T}$.

We then introduce an operation Θ_{AB} which equates the shared output variables of A and B with fresh input variables $\vec{u}?$ (these do not appear in either A or B).

$$\Theta_{AB} \;\hat{=}\; [\, \vec{u}? : \vec{T};\ \vec{v}! : \vec{T} \mid \vec{v}! = \vec{u}? \,]$$

We then extend the class of operation A with an additional operation $A_B \;\hat{=}\; A \wedge \Theta_{AB}$. We similarly extend the class of operation B with an additional operation $B_A \;\hat{=}\; B \wedge \Theta_{AB}$.

The conjunction $A \wedge B$ is then replaced with the conjunction of the new operations, but with the fresh shared input variables hidden.

$$(A_B \wedge B_A) \setminus \{\vec{u}?\}$$

The hiding of the input variables makes this process an equivalence transformation.

Theorem 1. *Equivalence transformation*

$$(A_B \wedge B_A) \setminus \{\vec{u}?\} \equiv (A \wedge B)$$

---

[5] In a well-formed specification, such output variables will also necessarily have the same type [8].

Proof

$$(A_B \wedge B_A) \setminus \{\vec{u?}\}$$
$$\equiv \exists\, \vec{u?} : \vec{T} \bullet A_B \wedge B_A \qquad\qquad\qquad \text{definition of hiding [8]}$$
$$\equiv \exists\, \vec{u?} : \vec{T} \bullet A \wedge B \wedge \Theta_{AB} \qquad\qquad\qquad \text{operation definitions}$$
$$\equiv A \wedge B \wedge (\exists\, \vec{u?} : \vec{T} \bullet \Theta_{AB}) \qquad\qquad \text{since } \vec{u?} \text{ do not appear in } A \text{ and } B$$
$$\equiv A \wedge B \qquad\qquad\qquad\qquad \text{one-point rule } (\vec{v!} = \vec{u?})$$

∎

When an Object-Z specification is transformed in this manner, compositional class refinement is then possible.

Theorem 2. *Compositional refinement*

$$A_B \sqsubseteq C \qquad\qquad\qquad\qquad\qquad\qquad\qquad \text{under retrieve relation } R$$
$$\vdash$$
$$(A_B \wedge B_A) \setminus \{\vec{u?}\} \sqsubseteq (C \wedge B_A) \setminus \{\vec{u?}\} \qquad\qquad\qquad \text{under } R$$

Proof

Applicability: The downward simulation proof obligation for applicability is:

$$\forall\, AState;\ BState;\ CState \bullet$$
$$R \Rightarrow (\text{pre}\,((A_B \wedge B_A) \setminus \{\vec{u?}\}) \Leftrightarrow \text{pre}\,((C \wedge B_A) \setminus \{\vec{u?}\}))$$

For all pairs of states from *AState* and *CState* for which R does not hold, the quantified expression becomes true owing to the implication. For all other pairs of states (i.e., those where R holds), we need to show the following is true for all states from *BState*.

$$\text{pre}\,((A_B \wedge B_A) \setminus \{\vec{u?}\}) \Leftrightarrow \text{pre}\,((C \wedge B_A) \setminus \{\vec{u?}\})$$

Since $A_B \sqsubseteq C$, for pairs of states related by R the applicability condition gives us $\text{pre}\, A_B \Leftrightarrow \text{pre}\, C$ for all $\vec{u?} : \vec{T}$. Hence,

$$(\text{pre}\, A_B \wedge \text{pre}\, B_A) \setminus \{\vec{u?}\} \Leftrightarrow (\text{pre}\, C \wedge \text{pre}\, B_A) \setminus \{\vec{u?}\}$$

Therefore by Lemma 1 (see Appendix), we have

$$\text{pre}\,((A_B \wedge B_A) \setminus \{\vec{u?}\}) \Leftrightarrow \text{pre}\,((C \wedge B_A) \setminus \{\vec{u?}\})$$

∎

Correctness: The downward simulation proof obligation for correctness is:

$$\forall\, AState;\ BState;\ CState;\ BState';\ CState' \bullet$$
$$R \wedge (B_A \wedge C) \setminus \{\vec{u?}\} \Rightarrow (\exists\, AState' \bullet R' \wedge (B_A \wedge A_B) \setminus \{\vec{u?}\})$$

Since $A_B \sqsubseteq C$, the correctness condition gives us

$$\forall\, AState;\ CState;\ \vec{u?} : \vec{T};\ CState' \bullet R \wedge C \Rightarrow (\exists\, AState' \bullet R' \wedge A_B)$$

Since $P \Rightarrow (\exists x \bullet P)$,

$$\forall \mathit{AState}; \; \mathit{BState}; \; \mathit{CState}; \; \vec{u?} : \vec{T}; \; \mathit{BState'}; \; \mathit{CState'} \bullet$$
$$R \wedge B_A \wedge C \Rightarrow (\exists \mathit{AState'} \bullet R' \wedge A_B) \wedge (\exists \mathit{BState'} \bullet B_A)$$

Following the reasoning of Lemma 2 (see Appendix) with the fact that R' does not refer to variables of B_A,

$$\forall \mathit{AState}; \; \mathit{BState}; \; \mathit{CState}; \; \vec{u?} : \vec{T}; \; \mathit{BState'}; \; \mathit{CState'} \bullet$$
$$R \wedge B_A \wedge C \Rightarrow (\exists \mathit{AState'}; \; \mathit{BState'} \bullet R' \wedge A_B \wedge B_A)$$

Since $P \Rightarrow Q \Rightarrow (\exists x \bullet P) \Rightarrow (\exists x \bullet Q)$ and $\vec{u?}$ do not appear in R,

$$\forall \mathit{AState}; \; \mathit{BState}; \; \mathit{CState}; \; \mathit{BState'}; \; \mathit{CState'} \bullet$$
$$R \wedge (B_A \wedge C) \setminus \{\vec{u?}\} \Rightarrow (\exists \mathit{AState'}; \; \mathit{BState'} \bullet R' \wedge (B_A \wedge A_B) \setminus \{\vec{u?}\})$$

■

4.1 Example

The operation *Transaction* in *Market* is defined as the composition of *Buyer.Buy* and *Vendor.Sell*, which share the output variable *price!*. In Section 3.1 we attempted to refine *Transaction* but failed owing to the fact that the precondition is altered. We transform the operations *Buyer.Buy* and *Vendor.Sell* as described above. Our new specification (*Market$_2$*) is illustrated below, where the new operations have been named *TransactionBuy* and *TransactionSell*, and where the fresh input variable is *agreed?*.

```
┌─ Buyer₂ ──────────────────────────
│ Buyer
│ TransactionBuy ≙ Buy ∧
│   [ agreed? : ℕ | price! = agreed? ]
```

```
┌─ Vendor₂ ──────────────────────────
│ Vendor
│ TransactionSell ≙ Sell ∧
│   [ agreed? : ℕ | price! = agreed? ]
```

```
┌─ Market₂ ───────────────────────────────────────
│ buyer : Buyer₂
│ vendor : Vendor₂
│ ─────────────────────────────────────────────
│ Transaction ≙ (buyer.TransactionBuy ∧ vendor.TransactionSell) \ {agreed?}
```

When we calculate the preconditions for *TransactionBuy* and *TransactionSell* in this version of the specification, we find that they include constraints over the shared input variable *agreed?*, and the operations include similar constraints over the shared output variable *price!*.

$$\text{pre } Buyer_2.\,TransactionBuy = \text{pre } Buyer.Buy \wedge agreed? \in \mathbb{N} \wedge$$
$$agreed? \leq cash$$
$$\text{pre } Vendor_2.\,TransactionSell = \text{pre } Vendor.Sell \wedge agreed? \in \mathbb{N} \wedge$$
$$reserve \leq agreed? \leq asking$$

If we attempt to refine $Vendor_2$ in the same manner as $Vendor_1$ was proposed to refine $Vendor$ (refer to Section 3.1), by adding the constraint $price! = asking$ to $Vendor_2.\,TransactionSell$, we find now that this is prohibited as the precondition would be strengthened by the additional constraint on $agreed?$. In essence, the process of transforming the specification has restricted the possible refinements of the classes representing the buyer and vendor to only those allowable by their context.

5   Refinement of Coupling Constraints

Whilst the transformation of Section 4 enables compositional refinement, after the transformation we are forever restricting possible valid implementations (refinements) of the specification. This limitation was alluded to in the previous section: specifically, we cannot further narrow non-determinism over shared output variable bindings where previously such a refinement may have been possible. For instance, if a more generous vendor were substituted into the market example in Section 4.1 that insisted upon accepting only the reserve price, this would result in a valid compositional refinement. Since proving even this refinement would be impossible after the transformation, it is clearly too restrictive an approach.

To counteract this limitation we introduce a further transformation that results in a new operation $Coupling_{AB}$ for each conjunction $A \wedge B$, where A and B are in different classes. This operation is responsible for establishing the bindings for the fresh input variables in the composition. Two properties of $Coupling_{AB}$ are certainly crucial: it must be compositionally refineable itself; and it must not interfere with the fact that the operations are already compositionally refineable under Theorems 1 and 2. We define $Coupling_{AB}$ as the conjunction of the preconditions of the two respective operations after the first transformation. The inputs $\vec{u}?$ introduced by the first transformation, however, are renamed to outputs.

$$Coupling_{AB} \mathrel{\widehat{=}} [\,\text{pre } A_B \wedge \text{pre } B_A\,][\,\vec{u}!/\vec{u}?\,]$$

The Object-Z operator that facilitates the introduction of $Coupling_{AB}$ into the specification is the parallel composition operator ($\|$) [8]. This operator equates (through renaming) outputs in one operation with inputs in the other that share the same basename, and hides the equated variables. It is intended to model communication between the two operands. Given that the inputs $\vec{u}?$ are renamed to outputs, the parallel operator allows those outputs to be fed into the inputs of the composition we are working with:

Theorem 3. *Introduce coupling operation*

$$(A_B \wedge B_A) \setminus \{\vec{u?}\} \equiv Coupling_{AB} \parallel (A_B \wedge B_A)$$

Proof

$$
\begin{aligned}
&(A_B \wedge B_A) \setminus \{\vec{u?}\} \\
&\equiv ([\text{pre}\, A_B \wedge \text{pre}\, B_A] \wedge A_B \wedge B_A) \setminus \{\vec{u?}\} && Op \Rightarrow [\text{pre}\, Op] \\
&\equiv ([\text{pre}\, A_B \wedge \text{pre}\, B_A][\vec{u!}/\vec{u?}] \wedge (A_B \wedge B_A)[\vec{u!}/\vec{u?}]) \setminus \{\vec{u!}\} \\
&\equiv [\text{pre}\, A_B \wedge \text{pre}\, B_A][\vec{u!}/\vec{u?}] \parallel (A_B \wedge B_A) && \text{definition of parallel [8]} \\
&\equiv Coupling_{AB} \parallel (A_B \wedge B_A) && \text{definition of } Coupling_{AB}
\end{aligned}
$$

∎

Since $Coupling_{AB}$ is the conjunction of the preconditions of the operands involved in the original composition, and those preconditions were strengthened to include the constraints on the shared output variables, it represents the entirety of the coupling constraints of the two operands. The fact that the input variables $\vec{u?}$ which are affected by those constraints are renamed to output variables means that the coupling predicates may be strengthened via normal refinement processes, which is desirable. The parallel operator hides the communicating variables, and thus relaxes the requirement to explicitly hide them as mandated by Theorem 1. The $Coupling_{AB}$ operation is itself capable of being compositionally refined, and does not affect the ability of the other operations to be compositionally refined.

Theorem 4. *Compositionally refine coupling*

$$Coupling_{AB} \sqsubseteq C \qquad\qquad\qquad\qquad \text{under retrieve relation } R$$
$$\vdash$$
$$Coupling_{AB} \parallel (A_B \wedge B_A) \sqsubseteq C \parallel (A_B \wedge B_A) \qquad\qquad \text{under } R$$

Proof

Applicability: The downward simulation proof obligation for applicability is (noting that the pre-state of $Coupling_{AB}$ is $AState;\ BState$):

$$\forall AState;\ BState;\ CState \bullet$$
$$R \Rightarrow (\text{pre}\,(Coupling_{AB} \parallel (A_B \wedge B_A)) \Leftrightarrow \text{pre}\,(C \parallel (A_B \wedge B_A)))$$

For all pairs of states from $AState;\ BState$ and $CState$ for which R does not hold, the quantified expression becomes true owing to the implication. For all other pairs of states (i.e., those where R holds), we need to show the following is true.

$$\text{pre}\,(Coupling_{AB} \parallel (A_B \wedge B_A)) \Leftrightarrow \text{pre}\,(C \parallel (A_B \wedge B_A)))$$

Since $Coupling_{AB} \sqsubseteq C$, for pairs of states related by R the applicability condition gives us

$$\text{pre}\, Coupling_{AB} \Leftrightarrow \text{pre}\, C$$

Hence,

$$\text{pre } Coupling_{AB} \wedge \text{pre } Coupling_{AB} \Leftrightarrow \text{pre } C \wedge \text{pre } Coupling_{AB}$$

By definition of pre [2] and noting that the only post-state variables are $\vec{u}!$,

$$(\exists \vec{u}! : \vec{T} \bullet Coupling_{AB} \wedge Coupling_{AB}) \Leftrightarrow (\exists \vec{u}! : \vec{T} \bullet C \wedge Coupling_{AB})$$

By definition of $Coupling_{AB}$,

$$(\exists \vec{u}! : \vec{T} \bullet Coupling_{AB} \wedge [\text{pre } A_B \wedge \text{pre } B_A][\vec{u}!/\vec{u}?])$$
$$\Leftrightarrow$$
$$(\exists \vec{u}! : \vec{T} \bullet C \wedge [\text{pre } A_B \wedge \text{pre } B_A][\vec{u}!/\vec{u}?])$$

Let P' and Q' be the declarations of the post-state variables of A_B and B_A respectively. By the definition of pre [2],

$$(\exists \vec{u}! : \vec{T} \bullet Coupling_{AB} \wedge (\exists P' \bullet A_B \wedge \exists Q' \bullet B_A)[\vec{u}!/\vec{u}?])$$
$$\Leftrightarrow$$
$$(\exists \vec{u}! : \vec{T} \bullet C \wedge (\exists P' \bullet A_B \wedge \exists Q' \bullet B_A)[\vec{u}!/\vec{u}?])$$

By Lemma 2 (see Appendix),

$$(\exists \vec{u}! : \vec{T} \bullet Coupling_{AB} \wedge (\exists P'; \ Q' \bullet A_B \wedge B_A)[\vec{u}!/\vec{u}?])$$
$$\Leftrightarrow$$
$$(\exists \vec{u}! : \vec{T} \bullet C \wedge (\exists P'; \ Q' \bullet A_B \wedge B_A)[\vec{u}!/\vec{u}?])$$

Since variables declared in $P'; \ Q'$ do not appear in $Coupling_{AB}$ and C,

$$(\exists \vec{u}! : \vec{T}; \ P'; \ Q' \bullet Coupling_{AB} \wedge (A_B \wedge B_A)[\vec{u}!/\vec{u}?])$$
$$\Leftrightarrow$$
$$(\exists \vec{u}! : \vec{T}; \ P'; \ Q' \bullet C \wedge (A_B \wedge B_A)[\vec{u}!/\vec{u}?])$$

By the definition of $\parallel$ [8],

$$(\exists P'; \ Q' \bullet Coupling_{AB} \parallel (A_B \wedge B_A)) \Leftrightarrow (\exists P'; \ Q' \bullet C \parallel (A_B \wedge B_A))$$

By the definition of pre [2] (noting that $\vec{u}!$ is hidden by the parallel operator),

$$\text{pre}(Coupling_{AB} \parallel (A_B \wedge B_A)) \Leftrightarrow \text{pre}(C \parallel (A_B \wedge B_A)) \qquad \blacksquare$$

Correctness: The downward simulation proof obligation for correctness is (noting that the only post-state variables of $Coupling_{AB}$ and C are the outputs $\vec{u}!$):

$$\forall AState; \ BState; \ CState \bullet$$
$$R \wedge (C \parallel (A_B \wedge B_A)) \Rightarrow (\exists \vec{u}! : \vec{T} \bullet R' \wedge (Coupling_{AB} \parallel (A_B \wedge B_A)))$$

Since $Coupling_{AB} \sqsubseteq C$, the correctness condition gives us

$$\forall \, AState; \; BState; \; CState; \; \vec{u!} : \vec{T} \bullet R \wedge C \Rightarrow (\exists \, \vec{u!} : \vec{T} \bullet R' \wedge Coupling_{AB})$$

Hence,

$$\forall \, AState; \; BState; \; CState; \; \vec{u!} : \vec{T} \bullet$$
$$R \wedge C \wedge (A_B \wedge B_A))[\vec{u!}/\vec{u?}] \Rightarrow$$
$$(\exists \, \vec{u!} : \vec{T} \bullet R' \wedge Coupling_{AB}) \wedge (A_B \wedge B_A)[\vec{u!}/\vec{u?}]$$

Since $\vec{u!}$ do not appear free in R',

$$\forall \, AState; \; BState; \; CState; \; \vec{u!} : \vec{T} \bullet$$
$$R \wedge C \wedge (A_B \wedge B_A))[\vec{u!}/\vec{u?}] \Rightarrow$$
$$R' \wedge (\exists \, \vec{u!} : \vec{T} \bullet Coupling_{AB}) \wedge (A_B \wedge B_A)[\vec{u!}/\vec{u?}]$$

Since $(A_B \wedge B_A)[\vec{u!}/\vec{u?}] \Rightarrow Coupling_{AB}$ and $P \Rightarrow (\exists \, x \bullet P)$,

$$\forall \, AState; \; BState; \; CState; \; \vec{u!} : \vec{T} \bullet$$
$$R \wedge C \wedge (A_B \wedge B_A))[\vec{u!}/\vec{u?}] \Rightarrow$$
$$R' \wedge Coupling_{AB} \wedge (A_B \wedge B_A)[\vec{u!}/\vec{u?}]$$

Since $P \Rightarrow Q \Rightarrow (\exists \, x \bullet P) \Rightarrow (\exists \, x \bullet Q)$,

$$\forall \, AState; \; BState; \; CState \bullet$$
$$(\exists \, \vec{u!} : \vec{T} \bullet R \wedge C \wedge (A_B \wedge B_A))[\vec{u!}/\vec{u?}]) \Rightarrow$$
$$(\exists \, \vec{u!} : \vec{T} \bullet R' \wedge Coupling_{AB} \wedge (A_B \wedge B_A)[\vec{u!}/\vec{u?}])$$

Since $\vec{u!}$ do not appear free in R and R', by definition of $\|$ [8],

$$\forall \, AState; \; BState; \; CState \bullet$$
$$R \wedge (C \parallel (A_B \wedge B_A)) \Rightarrow R' \wedge (Coupling_{AB} \parallel (A_B \wedge B_A))$$

Since $P \Rightarrow Q \Rightarrow P \Rightarrow (\exists \, x \bullet Q)$,

$$\forall \, AState; \; BState; \; CState \bullet$$
$$R \wedge (C \parallel (A_B \wedge B_A)) \Rightarrow (\exists \, \vec{u!} : \vec{T} \bullet R' \wedge (Coupling_{AB} \parallel (A_B \wedge B_A)))$$

∎

Theorem 5. *Compositional refinement with coupling*

$A_B \sqsubseteq C_B$ under retrieve relation R

⊢

$Coupling_{AB} \parallel (A_B \wedge B_A) \sqsubseteq Coupling_{AB} \parallel (C_B \wedge B_A)$ under R

Proof

$Coupling_{AB} \parallel (A_B \wedge B_A)$

$\equiv (A_B \wedge B_A) \setminus \{\vec{u?}\}$ Theorem 3

$\sqsubseteq (C_B \wedge B_A) \setminus \{\vec{u?}\}$ Theorem 2

$\equiv Coupling_{CB} \parallel (C_B \wedge B_A)$ Theorem 3

Since $A_B \sqsubseteq C_B$, the applicability condition stipulates that $\text{pre} \, A_B \Leftrightarrow \text{pre} \, C_B$, therefore $Coupling_{CB} \equiv Coupling_{AB}$.

∎

5.1 Example

To demonstrate the effectiveness of introducing and performing refinements of a *Coupling* operation, we augment the *Transaction* operation from the *Market* example with the coupling operation *Bargain*.

Market3

> buyer : $Buyer_2$
> vendor : $Vendor_2$
>
> ---
> **Bargain**
> agreed! : $\mathbb{N}$
>
> ---
> $agreed! \leq buyer.cash$
> $vendor.reserve \leq agreed! \leq vendor.asking$
>
> ---
> $Transaction \;\hat{=}\; Bargain \;\|\; (buyer.TransactionBuy \;\wedge\; vendor.TransactionSell)$

Bargain is defined using the preconditions of the *Buy* and *Sell* operations, but the typing constraints are not included in the predicate of the operation because they are implicitly enforced in the declarations [8].

There is one problem that arises as a result of introducing the *Bargain* operation to the specification (and *Coupling* operations in general to any specification) — it necessitates direct access to state variables of external classes. This immediately prohibits future data refinements of any externally referenced variables in these classes [2]. The solution to this problem is to introduce a dedicated accessor operation, local to the external class, to insulate the state from this dependency. $Buyer_3$ and $Vendor_3$ include such operations[6].

Buyer3

> $Buyer_2$
> $GetCash \;\hat{=}\; \big[\, cash! : \mathbb{N} \mid cash! = cash \,\big]$

Vendor3

> $Vendor_2$
> $GetAsking \;\hat{=}\; \big[\, asking! : \mathbb{N} \mid asking! = asking \,\big]$
> $GetTakings \;\hat{=}\; \big[\, takings! : \mathbb{N} \mid takings! = takings \,\big]$
> $GetReserve \;\hat{=}\; \big[\, reserve! : \mathbb{N} \mid reserve! = reserve \,\big]$

We can now replace the references to the state variables with input variables to match the output variables of the accessor operations. Using parallel, we communicate the values of these variables into the *Bargain* operation.

---

[6] We take the view that the interface of a class can be widened under refinement [5].

$\boxed{\begin{array}{l} Market_4 \\ \hline \boxed{\begin{array}{l} buyer : Buyer_3 \\ vendor : Vendor_3 \end{array}} \\ \\ \boxed{\begin{array}{l} Bargain \\ \hline cash?, asking?, takings?, reserve? : \mathbb{N} \\ agreed! : \mathbb{N} \\ \hline agreed! \leq cash? \\ reserve? \leq agreed! \leq asking? \end{array}} \\ \\ Transaction \;\widehat{=}\; ((buyer.GetCash \wedge vendor.GetAsking \wedge vendor.GetTakings \\ \qquad \wedge \; vendor.GetReserve) \parallel Bargain) \parallel (buyer.Buy \wedge vendor.Sell) \end{array}}$

There is no possibility of compositionality problems arising through the introduction of these accessor operations, as these operations cannot possibly be refined. This is due to the fact that, by equating the output variable directly to a state variable, there is no non-determinism.

The refinement that was disallowed at the beginning of Section 5 can now be applied to *Bargain*; that is, the refinement where the vendor always acts generously by only accepting the reserve price.

$\boxed{\begin{array}{l} Market_5 \\ \hline Market_4 \\ Bargain \;\widehat{=}\; \lceil\, reserve? = agreed! \,\rceil \end{array}}$

Since this is a valid refinement of *Bargain*, our theory has shown that this will result in a valid refinement of the entire system.

6   Conclusion and Future Work

In this paper, we have introduced a methodology for compositional class refinement in Object-Z. In general, class refinement is not compositional due to the possibility of constraints on shared outputs when operations from different classes are conjoined. To overcome this, our methodology transforms an Object-Z specification into an equivalent one in which all class refinements are compositional.

The methodology considers only conjunction between operations from different classes. It is shown in [8], that all binary operation operators in Object-Z but one can be rewritten in terms of conjunction, or in terms of Z constructs which can be rewritten in terms of conjunction [11]. The exception is the choice operator. This operator does not cause compositionality problems, however, since it requires only one of the combined operations be satisfied for the entire operation itself to be satisfied. Hence, the methodology is general enough to use with any Object-Z specification.

Our goal is to combine the methodology with previous work on structurally transforming Object-Z specifications to resemble object-oriented designs [5,6]. The combination will enable us to refine Object-Z specifications to the exact structure of an object-oriented program; so that there is a direct mapping, not only between classes, but also between each operation in the specification and program. This will encourage refinement to a low-level of abstraction and make the final step from specification to code less error-prone.

References

1. A. Cavalcanti, A. Sampaio, and J. Woodcock. Unifying classes and processes. *Software and System Modelling*, 4(3):277–296, 2005.
2. J. Derrick and E. Boiten. *Refinement in Z and Object-Z, Foundations and Advanced Applications*. Springer-Verlag, 2001.
3. C. Fischer. CSP-OZ - a combination of CSP and Object-Z. In H. Bowman and J. Derrick, editors, *Formal Methods for Open Object-Based Distributed Systems (FMOODS'97)*, pages 423–438. Chapman & Hall, 1997.
4. B. Mahony and J.S. Dong. Timed Communicating Object Z. *IEEE Transactions on Software Engineering*, 26(2):150–177, 2000.
5. T. McComb. Refactoring Object-Z specifications. In M. Wermelinger and T. Margaria-Steffen, editors, *Fundamental Approaches to Software Engineering (FASE '04)*, volume 2984 of *Lecture Notes in Computer Science*, pages 69–83. Springer-Verlag, 2004.
6. T. McComb and G. Smith. Architectural design in Object-Z. In P. Strooper, editor, *Australian Software Engineering Conference (ASWEC '04)*, pages 77–86. IEEE Computer Society Press, 2004.
7. G. Smith. A semantic integration of Object-Z and CSP for the specification of concurrent systems. In J. Fitzgerald, C. Jones, and P. Lucas, editors, *Formal Methods Europe (FME'97)*, volume 1313 of *Lecture Notes in Computer Science*, pages 62–81. Springer-Verlag, 1997.
8. G. Smith. *The Object-Z Specification Language*. Advances in Formal Methods. Kluwer, 2000.
9. G. Smith and J. Derrick. Specification, refinement and verification of concurrent systems – an integration of Object-Z and CSP. *Formal Methods in System Design*, 18(3):249–284, 2001.
10. G. Smith and J. Derrick. Abstract specification in Object-Z and CSP. In C. George and Huaikou Miao, editors, *International Conference on Formal Engineering Methods (ICFEM 2002)*, volume 2495 of *Lecture Notes in Computer Science*, pages 108–119. Springer-Verlag, 2002.
11. J.M. Spivey. *The Z Notation: A Reference Manual*. Prentice Hall, 2nd edition, 1992.

Appendix

Lemma 1. *Distribution of pre*

$$pre\,((A_B \wedge B_A) \setminus \{\vec{u}?\}) \equiv (pre\ A_B \wedge pre\ B_A) \setminus \{\vec{u}?\}$$

Proof

Let P' and Q' be the declarations of the post-state variables of A_B and B_A respectively.

$$\text{pre}\,((A_B \wedge B_A) \setminus \{\vec{u?}\})$$

$\equiv \exists \vec{u?} : \vec{T} \bullet (\exists P';\ Q' \bullet A_B \wedge B_A) \qquad$ definition of pre [2] and hiding [8]

$\equiv \exists \vec{u?} : \vec{T} \bullet (\exists P' \bullet A_B) \wedge (\exists Q' \bullet B_A) \qquad\qquad$ Lemma 2

$\equiv (\text{pre}\,A_B \wedge \text{pre}\,B_A) \setminus \{\vec{u?}\} \qquad$ definition of pre [2] and hiding [8]

∎

Lemma 2. *Distribution of* $\exists$

$$\exists P';\ Q' \bullet A_B \wedge B_A \equiv (\exists P' \bullet A_B) \wedge (\exists Q' \bullet B_A)$$

where P' and Q' are the declarations of the post-state variables of A_B and B_A respectively.

Proof

Let S' and T' be the declarations of post-state variables of A_B and B_A respectively, other than the shared output variables $\vec{v!}$.

$\exists P';\ Q' \bullet A_B \wedge B_A$

$\equiv \exists \vec{v!} : \vec{T} \bullet \exists S';\ T' \bullet A_B \wedge B_A$

$\equiv \exists \vec{v!} : \vec{T} \bullet (\exists S' \bullet A_B) \wedge (\exists T' \bullet B_A)$

$\equiv (\exists P' \bullet A_B) \wedge (\exists Q' \bullet B_A) \qquad\qquad\qquad\qquad \vec{v!} = \vec{u?}$ in A_B and B_A

∎

A Proposal for Records in Event-B[*]

Neil Evans[1] and Michael Butler[2]

[1] AWE, Aldermaston, U.K.
[2] School of Electronics and Computer Science, University of Southampton, U.K.

Abstract. The B method is a well known approach to the formal specification and development of sequential computer programs. Inspired by action systems, the B method has evolved to incorporate system modelling and distributed system development. This extension is called Event-B. Even though several of the structuring mechanisms of the original B method are absent from Event-B, the desire to define and maintain structured data persists. We propose the introduction of records to Event-B for this purpose. Our approach upholds the refinement principles of Event-B by allowing the stepwise development of records too.

1 Introduction

The Praxis[1] case study of the RODIN project is a (subset of a) VDM development of an air traffic control display system (CDIS) undertaken by Praxis in 1992. One of the objectives of the case study is to drive the RODIN methodology, including Event-B itself [7]. CDIS is currently being redeveloped using Event-B and existing B tool support. The motivating feature of the case study is its size, and the challenge is to develop techniques for constructing large specifications in general so that the functionality of the overall system can be understood by everyone involved in a project of this kind (a criticism of the original CDIS specification).

Although the case study does not aim to construct a translation from VDM to Event-B, there are several advantages to preserving the VDM record structure. In particular, it serves to organise a vast amount of structured data. So it is worthwhile investigating how records (with arbitrary field types) can be incorporated in Event-B. More generally, however, we have identified the benefits of incorporating additional subtyping/inheritance-like properties of records to enable their stepwise development through refinement, and to allow better conceptual modelling during the early stages of an Event-B development. In order to address the challenges of CDIS, this allows us to start with a very abstract/generic view of the system and, through refinement, introduce airport-specific details later in the development. Hence, the project members can choose a suitable level of abstraction to view the system.

---

[*] This research was carried out as part of the EU research project IST 511599 RODIN (Rigorous Open Development Environment for Complex Systems) http://rodin.cs.ncl.ac.uk.
[1] Praxis High Integrity Systems Ltd., U.K.

J. Misra, T. Nipkow, and E. Sekerinski (Eds.): FM 2006, LNCS 4085, pp. 221–235, 2006.
© Springer-Verlag Berlin Heidelberg 2006

Our proposal does not require any changes to the semantics of Event-B, although we propose an extension to its syntax.

After we have given an introduction to Event-B, we give a brief overview of records (composites) in VDM. We then show how records can be modelled using existing B constructs, namely **SETS**, **CONSTANTS** and **PROPERTIES**. Along the way, we propose some syntactic sugar to make such definitions more succinct. Our intention is to incorporate this syntax into the Event-B language, thereby eliminating the need to define an unsugared version manually. We then introduce two forms of record refinement: record extension and record subtyping. An example is given to illustrate the use of record refinement in a development, which includes a novel use of record refinement to enable the interface extension of an event. Finally, we discuss other issues that arise from our approach. This example demonstrates the refinement techniques currently being used in the CDIS case study.

Note that open source tools supporting Event-B are currently under construction as part of the RODIN project. However, by writing stylised specifications, existing B tools such as Atelier B [3] and the B Toolkit [5] can be applied to Event-B specifications.

2   Event-B

An abstract Event-B specification comprises a static part called the *context*, and a dynamic part called the *machine*. The machine has access to the context via a **SEES** relationship. All sets, constants, and their properties are defined in the context. The machine contains all of the state variables. The values of the variables are set up using the **INITIALISATION** clause, and values can be changed via the execution of *events*. Ultimately, we aim to prove properties of the specification, and these properties are made explicit using the **INVARIANT** clause. The tool support generates proof obligations which must be discharged to verify that the invariant is maintained.

Events are specialised B operations [1]. In general, an event E is of the form

$$E \ \widehat{=} \ \textbf{WHEN} \ G(v) \ \textbf{THEN} \ S(v) \ \textbf{END}$$

where $G(v)$ is a Boolean guard and $S(v)$ is a generalised substitution (both of which may be dependent on state variable v)[2]. The guard must hold for the substitution to be performed (otherwise the event is *blocked*). There are three kinds of generalised substitution: *deterministic*, *empty*, and *non-deterministic*. The deterministic substitution of a variable x is an assignment of the form $x := E(v)$, for expression E, and the empty substitution is *skip*. The non-deterministic substitution of x is defined as

$$\textbf{ANY} \ t \ \textbf{WHERE} \ P(t,v) \ \textbf{THEN} \ x := F(t,v) \ \textbf{END}$$

Here, t is a local variable that is assigned non-deterministically according to the predicate P, and its value is used in the assignment of x via the expression F.

---

[2] The guard is omitted if it is trivially true.

Note that in this paper we abuse the notation somewhat by allowing events to be decorated with input and output parameters (and preconditions to type the input parameters) in the style of classical B [1].

In order to refine an abstract Event-B specification, it is possible to refine the model and context separately. Refinement of a context consists of adding additional sets, constants or properties (the sets, constants and properties of the abstract context are retained).

Refinement of existing events in a model is similar to refinement in the B method: a *gluing invariant* in the refined model relates its variables to those of the abstract model. Proof obligations are generated to ensure that this invariant is maintained. In Event-B, abstract events can be refined by more than one concrete event. In addition, Event-B allows refinement of a model by adding new concrete events on the proviso that they cannot diverge (i.e. execute forever). This condition ensures that the abstract events can still occur. Since the concrete events operate on the state variables of the refined model, they must implicitly refine the abstract event *skip*.

3   VDM Composites

A composite type consists of a name followed by a list of component (field) names, each of which is accompanied by its type. In general, this looks like:

$$type\_name :: component\_name_1 : component\_type_1$$

$$\vdots$$

$$component\_name_n : component\_type_n$$

One can see that this resembles record declarations in many programming languages. However, it is possible to constrain the type of a composite further by including an invariant for the values of the components. Note that the nature of invariants in VDM is different from invariants in Event-B: invariants in Event-B have to be proven, whilst in VDM they are enforced. State in VDM is declared as a special kind of record whose components are the state variables which can be accessed and modified via *operations* (functions having side effects on the state).

Even though we have focused on VDM composite types specifically, record-like structures are also present in other formal notations (for example, composite data types in Z schemas [12], or signatures in Alloy [2]).

4   A Set-Based Approach in Event-B

This approach attempts to mimic the record type definitions of VDM by using the **SETS**, **CONSTANTS** and **PROPERTIES** clauses of an Event-B context. One of the motivations of this work is to enable a stepwise development of complex record structures (in the spirit of refinement) by introducing additional

CONTEXT *Func*
SETS R ; A ; B
CONSTANTS $r1$, $r2$
PROPERTIES
$\quad r1 \in R \to A \wedge$
$\quad r2 \in R \to B \wedge$
$\quad r1 \otimes r2 \in R \twoheadrightarrow A \times B$
END

Fig. 1. A simple record type

fields as and when they become necessary. This is also comparable to inheritance in object-oriented programming in which classes are *restricted* or *specialised* by introducing additional attributes.

Consider the following VDM composite type declaration R

$$R :: r1 : A$$
$$r2 : B$$

That is, R is a record with two fields, named $r1$ and $r2$, of type A and B respectively. In B, we can model this by declaring three deferred sets R, A and B in the **SETS** clause. This is shown in Figure 1 in a context named *Func*. The sets A and B correspond to the types A and B in the declaration and, as such, these could be replaced by specific B types (such as *NAT*), or could themselves be other record types. Note that recursive record types are not part of this proposal, although we are investigating this for future work.

The set R represents the record type that we are trying to specify. We can think of this set as representing all of the potential models of the record type. Since we are unaware of the appropriate model for the record, because we may want to refine it during later stages, this set remains deferred until we are sure that we do not want to refine it any further. Instead, we can specify properties of the set within the **PROPERTIES** clause.

Two *accessor* functions are declared in the **CONSTANTS** clause to retrieve the fields of an R record instance: $r1$ retrieves the value of the field of type A, and $r2$ retrieves the value of the field of type B. The properties of these functions are given in the **PROPERTIES** clause. In particular, note that for every pair of values from A and B there is a record instance (i.e. a member of R) whose fields have these values. This is expressed succinctly using Event-B's direct product operator $\otimes$ and the surjective mapping $\twoheadrightarrow$, where

$$r1 \otimes r2 = \{ (x, (y, z)) \mid (x, y) \in r1 \wedge (x, z) \in r2 \}$$

This approach to modelling composites is quite verbose for a two-field record. Instead, we propose some syntactic sugar. Within the **SETS** clause, we propose composite-like declarations for records. Hence, for this example, we would allow an equivalent context as shown in Figure 2. We choose to put such definitions in the **SETS** clause because this clause is most closely associated with type definitions.

CONTEXT *Func*
SETS
$\quad R :: r1 : A,$
$\quad\quad\quad r2 : B$
END

Fig. 2. Syntactic sugar for record types

A machine that **SEES** this context may contain state variables of type R. Such variables hold an instance of the record, and events can be defined to update the values of their fields using the accessor functions. The structure of these events follows a definite pattern: non-deterministically choose an instance of the record type such that its fields have certain values. For example, consider the event in Figure 3 that changes the $r1$ field of a variable r of type R with a value x. The new value y is chosen so that its $r1$ value is equal to x, and its $r2$ value remains unchanged. It is important to state explicitly which fields do not change, otherwise they will be assigned non-deterministically.

Update_r1_of_r $(x) \mathrel{\widehat{=}}$
$\quad$ **ANY** y **WHERE**
$\quad\quad y \in R \wedge$
$\quad\quad r1 (y) = x \wedge$
$\quad\quad r2 (y) = r2 (r)$
$\quad$ **THEN**
$\quad\quad r := y$
$\quad$ **END**

Fig. 3. A record update operation

Before we proceed to consider refinement, it is worth mentioning an alternative approach which, under suitable conditions, individual state variables are used to model the fields of a record directly. The approach in [4] uses the structuring mechanisms of classical B (in particular, the **INCLUDES** mechanism) and naming conventions to model the record structure. Their approach resulted from an attempt to construct a translation from VDM to B. A shortcoming of their approach is that it would be impossible to perform parallel updates of 'fields' that reside in the same machine (a constraint imposed by **INCLUDES**). Although renaming can be employed to re-use such definitions, we feel that our approach (with its syntactic sugar) gives a representation that is more suitable at an abstract level; and it is also amenable to parallel updates. More fundamentally, however, renaming and machine inclusion are not available in Event-B.

It would be possible to use variables instead of constants to model accessor functions. In some way this would simplify the approach as updates to a field could be specified more succinctly. For example, if $r1$ and $r2$ were specified as variables, then the update in Figure 3 could be specified as

Update_r1_of_r$(x) \mathrel{\widehat{=}} r1(r) := x$

The variable $r2$ is not modified by this assignment. The problem with using variables rather than constants for accessor functions is that it does not work in a distributed setting. In a distributed development we wish to avoid designs in which variables are globally available since maintaining a consistent global view of variables is too much effort. Constants, on the other hand, can easily be globally agreed since they never change. Using constants as accessor functions means we specify a fixed way of accessing fields of a record that is globally agreed.

5   Refining Record Types

We now investigate the effect of refining the record type R defined in Section 4 by introducing a new accessor function. There are two ways of doing this: we can either 'extend' R by adding the accessor function directly, or we can declare a new subtype of R (which we call Q), on which the accessor function is declared. Since the latter refinement will add further constraints to R, Q's set of potential models will be a subset of R's. In this example, both kinds of refinement have an additional field $r3$ of type C. For a simple record extension, we propose a syntax as follows:

$$\textbf{EXTEND } R \textbf{ WITH } r3 : C$$

For subtyping, we propose the following syntax:

$$Q \textbf{ SUBTYPES } R \textbf{ WITH } r3 : C$$

Their verbose definitions are shown in Figures 4 and 5 respectively. The proposed syntax means that the developer does not have to interact with the verbose definitions directly. Notice that these definitions are both refinements of the context machine given in Figure 1. Hence, the properties declared in the refinement are in addition to those of the original machine. The final property in Figure 4 states that all possible field combinations are still available in R, and the corresponding property in Figure 5 states that all possible field combinations are available in Q (without adding any further constraints to R).

Subtyping of this kind can be seen in programming languages such as Niklaus Wirth's Oberon [11], and specification languages such as Alloy [2]. The accessors $r1$ and $r2$ can still be applied to objects of type Q in Figure 5, but $r3$ can *only* be applied to objects of type Q (and any of its subtypes).

> **CONTEXT** *FuncR*
> **REFINES** *Func*
> **SETS** C
> **CONSTANTS** $r3$
> **PROPERTIES**
> $r3 \in R \rightarrow C \wedge$
> $(r1 \otimes r2 \otimes r3) \in R \twoheadrightarrow A \times B \times C$
> **END**

Fig. 4. An extended record type

CONTEXT *FuncR*
REFINES *Func*
SETS *C*
CONSTANTS Q , *r3*
PROPERTIES
$\quad Q \subseteq R \wedge$
$\quad r3 \in Q \rightarrow C \wedge$
$\quad (r1 \otimes r2 \otimes r3) \in Q \twoheadrightarrow A \times B \times C$
END

Fig. 5. A record subtype

Depending on whether extension or subtyping is used, a certain amount of care is required when refining the events associated with the records. The event **Update_r1_of_r** shown in Figure 3 is still applicable in the refined context of Figure 4, even though it would assign r's new $r3$ field non-deterministically. Refinement could then be used to assign something meaningful to this field. However, using the refined context of Figure 5, if the model is refined so that r is defined to be of type Q then this event is no longer applicable without modification because the quantified variable y ranges over Q's superset R. The **ANY** clause would need to be strengthened so that it chooses an element of Q (rather than R). Note that the surjectivity constraints of a record extension are consistent with the constraints of the original record definition. Indeed, the original constraints follow from those of the extension, i.e.:

$$(r1 \otimes r2 \otimes r3) \in R \twoheadrightarrow A \times B \times C \;\Rightarrow\; (r1 \otimes r2) \in R \twoheadrightarrow A \times B$$

5.1   Other Possible Refinement Combinations

In addition to a single chain of record refinements, which is most easily achieved by record extension, the subtyping of record types presented above permits other, less restrictive, kinds of development.

The diagrams shown in Figure 6 give two possible extension hierarchies. Each of these is meaningful, and we would like them to be available in Event-B. Hence, records should not constrain the structuring of context machines.

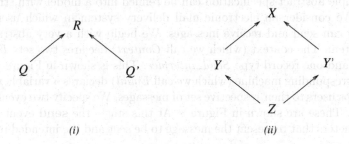

Fig. 6. Possible Record Hierarchies

In Figure 6(i), two different sets, Q and Q', subtype the same record type R. That is, Q and Q' have the common ancestor R, and both are defined to be subsets of R. (The relationship between Q and Q' in this case is left unspecified, but we can impose an extra property to ensure they are disjoint if necessary.) In (ii), the record type Z combines the record subtypes Y and Y'. In this situation, the model for Z must be a model for both Y and Y', and the accessor functions of both Y and Y' can be applied to objects of type Z. The least constrained set of models that fulfils this relationship is the intersection of Y and Y'. Hence, they should not be disjoint. Syntactically, the fields belonging to a record of type Z (prior to any extensions to Z) are the union of the fields of Y and Y' [3].

6   One-Field Variables

In section 5, we have seen how existing record types can be refined to give new record types with more complex structure. At the most abstract level, the specifier might be unaware that a simple (non-record) state variable requires a record structure at a later stage in the development. For example, we may declare a variable v to be of type $VALUE$, but then decide that for every value we need to associate some other characteristic (say, a format). We would then need to define a record type

$$FVALUE :: val : VALUE,$$
$$format : FORMAT$$

and declare a concrete variable fv of type $FVALUE$. In order to link the variables v and fv in a refinement, the gluing invariant must link the val component of fv with v. In this case, we have

$$v = val(fv)$$

Hence, at the most abstract level, we are not expected to identify all record types. These can be introduced during the refinement stages.

7   Extension Example

In order to motivate the use of record types, we present an example to show how a very simple abstract specification can be refined into a model with structured objects. We consider an electronic mail delivery system in which users (with identities) can send and receive messages. We begin with a very abstract view of the system. The context (which we call $Context$) declares two sets $User$ and $Message$, and one record type $Send\_interface$. This is shown in Figure 7.

The corresponding machine (which we call $Email$) declares a variable $mailbox$, which maps users to their respective set of messages. We specify two events: **send** and **read**. These are shown in Figure 8. At this stage, the **send** event requires two parameters that represent the message to be sent and the intended recipient.

---

[3] We assume there are no name clashes between the accessors of Y and Y'.

```
CONTEXT Context
SETS
    User ; Message ;
    Send_interface :: dest : User,
                      mess : Message
END
```

Fig. 7. The Abstract Context

However, during the refinement stages **send** will require additional parameters. Interface extension is not possible in the current B tools, but by using record types instead we can extend the interface of **send** via record extension. The record type *Send_interface* is declared for this purpose. Note that this is a very abstract representation of the system because the **send** operation magically deposits the message in the appropriate user's mailbox. Subsequent refinements will model how this is actually achieved. The **read** event non-deterministically retrieves a message from the input user's mailbox and returns it as an output.

As a first refinement we begin to introduce more detail in the form of a more realistic architecture. This is depicted in Figure 9. Each user is associated with a mail server that is responsible for forwarding mail and retrieving mail from the middleware. As part of this refinement, we introduce a record type to structure the data passing from senders to receivers via the communications medium. The record type called *Package* is declared using our proposed syntax in the context

```
MACHINE Email
SEES Context
VARIABLES mailbox
INVARIANT mailbox ∈ User → ℙ ( Message )
INITIALISATION mailbox := User × { ∅ }

OPERATIONS
    send ( ii ) ≙
    PRE   ii ∈ Send_interface THEN
        mailbox ( dest ( ii ) ) := mailbox ( dest ( ii ) ) ∪ { mess ( ii ) }
    END ;

    mm ⟵ read ( uu ) ≙
      PRE  uu ∈ User THEN
        ANY  xx WHERE
            xx ∈ Message ∧ xx ∈ mailbox ( uu )
        THEN
            mm := xx
        END
      END
END
```

Fig. 8. The Abstract Machine

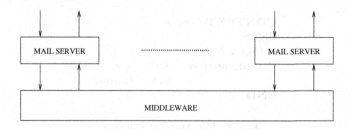

Fig. 9. Architecture for the e-mail system

CONTEXT *Context2*
REFINES *Context*
SETS
    Server **;**
    Package :: *destination* : *Server* ,
                recipient : *User* ,
                contents : *Message* **;**
    EXTEND *Send_interface* **WITH** *source* : *User*
CONSTANTS
    address
PROPERTIES
    address $\in$ *User* $\rightarrow$ *Server*
END

Fig. 10. First refined context

refinement named *Context2*. This is shown in Figure 10. Note that in addition to *Package* we declare a new set *Server* which represents the different mail servers, and we declare a function *address* that returns the (unique) server hosting a particular user. We also extend *Send_interface* by adding a new field *source* that contains the identities of the senders.

The refined state comprises new variables *sendbuf*, *receivebuf* and *middleware*. The variable *middleware* holds the packages on the communications medium, and each mail server has separate buffers for messages waiting to be sent and messages waiting to be read (i.e. mappings from *Server* to $\mathbb{P}$ (*Package*)). The refined event **send** constructs packages and adds them to the server associated with the sender. The event **read** selects packages from a user's server and output's their contents. These are shown in Figure 11.

As part of this Event B refinement, we introduce two new events **forward** (which passes packages from servers to the middleware) and **deliver** (which takes packages from the middleware and adds them to the appropriate server's receive buffer). Note that these events (also shown in Figure 11) will not collectively diverge because only a finite number of packages will be waiting to be transferred.

The gluing invariant that links the refined state with the abstract state is dictated by the need to preserve outputs. Since we are refining from simple messages to packages, we use the technique given in Section 6. In the abstract model,

$$\mathbf{send} \ (\ ii \ ) \ \hat{=}$$
$$\mathbf{PRE} \quad ii \in Send\_interface \ \mathbf{THEN}$$
$$\mathbf{ANY} \ ss \ , \ pp \ \mathbf{WHERE}$$
$$ss \in Server \land pp \in Package \land$$
$$ss = address \ (\ source \ (\ ii \ ) \ ) \land$$
$$destination \ (\ pp \ ) = address \ (\ dest \ (\ ii \ ) \ ) \land$$
$$recipient \ (\ pp \ ) = dest \ (\ ii \ ) \land$$
$$contents \ (\ pp \ ) = mess \ (\ ii \ )$$
$$\mathbf{THEN}$$
$$sendbuf \ (\ ss \ ) := sendbuf \ (\ ss \ ) \cup \{ \ pp \ \}$$
$$\mathbf{END}$$
$$\mathbf{END} \ ;$$

$$mm \longleftarrow \mathbf{read} \ (\ uu \ ) \ \hat{=}$$
$$\mathbf{PRE} \quad uu \in User \ \mathbf{THEN}$$
$$\mathbf{ANY} \ ss \ , \ pp \ \mathbf{WHERE}$$
$$ss \in Server \land pp \in Package \land$$
$$ss = address \ (\ uu \ )$$
$$pp \in receivebuf \ (\ ss \ ) \land$$
$$recipient \ (\ pp \ ) = uu$$
$$\mathbf{THEN}$$
$$mm := contents \ (\ pp \ )$$
$$\mathbf{END}$$
$$\mathbf{END} \ ;$$

$$\mathbf{forward} \ \hat{=}$$
$$\mathbf{ANY} \ ss \ , \ pp \ \mathbf{WHERE}$$
$$ss \in Server \land pp \in Package \land$$
$$pp \in sendbuf \ (\ ss \ )$$
$$\mathbf{THEN}$$
$$sendbuf \ (\ ss \ ) := sendbuf \ (\ ss \ ) - \{ \ pp \ \} \ \|$$
$$middleware := middleware \cup \{ \ pp \ \}$$
$$\mathbf{END} \ ;$$

$$\mathbf{deliver} \ \hat{=}$$
$$\mathbf{ANY} \ ss \ , \ pp \ \mathbf{WHERE}$$
$$ss \in Server \land pp \in Package \land$$
$$pp \in middleware \land$$
$$destination \ (\ pp \ ) = ss$$
$$\mathbf{THEN}$$
$$middleware := middleware - \{ \ pp \ \} \ \|$$
$$receivebuf \ (\ ss \ ) := receivebuf \ (\ ss \ ) \cup \{ \ pp \ \}$$
$$\mathbf{END}$$

Fig. 11. First refinement events

the output from **read** is obtained from the input user's mailbox, whereas it is retrieved from *receivebuf* in the refined model. We link the *contents* field of the packages in *receivebuf* with *mailbox*. Hence, we introduce the following invariant

$$\forall s, u, p.(s \in Server \ \wedge \ u \in User \ \wedge \ p \in Package \ \Rightarrow$$
$$p \in receivebuf(s) \ \wedge \ recipient(p) = u \ \Rightarrow \ contents(p) \in mailbox(u))$$

This fulfils the proof obligation derived from the output of **read** but, since the event **deliver** adds packages to *receivebuf*, we must strengthen the invariant as follows

$$\forall u, p.(u \in User \ \wedge \ p \in Package \ \Rightarrow$$
$$p \in middleware \ \wedge \ recipient(p) = u \ \Rightarrow \ contents(p) \in mailbox(u))$$

That is, in addition to the contents of the packages in *receivebuf*, the contents of the packages on the medium must also be elements of *mailbox*. By attempting to discharge the proof obligations once more, we discover that we have to strengthen the invariant further

$$\forall s, u, p.(s \in Server \ \wedge \ u \in User \ \wedge \ p \in Package \ \Rightarrow$$
$$p \in sendbuf(s) \ \wedge \ recipient(p) = u \ \Rightarrow \ contents(p) \in mailbox(u))$$

This is sufficient to discharge all of the proof obligations. Hence, we have shown that the contents of *any* package in transit must be an element of the corresponding abstract mailbox. Of course, it would be possible to strengthen the invariant further by stating other properties of the system, but this is not pursued here.

As a second refinement, we extend *Package* with a priority field. In addition, we extend *Send_interface* with a field *pri*. These refinements are shown (using our proposed notation) in Figure 12.

> **CONTEXT** *Context3*
> **REFINES** *Context2*
> **SETS**
>   **EXTEND** *Package* **WITH** *priority* : *BOOL* ;
>   **EXTEND** *Send_interface* **WITH** *pri* : *BOOL*
> **END**

Fig. 12. The second context refinement

This refinement specifically affects the order in which packages are moved onto the middleware: packages with priority *TRUE* take precedence over packages with priority *FALSE*. In order to model this, we refine the events **send** and **forward** (as shown in Figure 13). The **send** event is refined because we have extended its interface to incorporate a priority field (named *pri*). Using this extension to *Send_interface*, we can assign priorities to the refined packages. The refinement of **forward** is an example of the refinement of a single event into two events. The first refined event (also called **forward**) only selects packages with high priority (i.e. those packages whose priority field is *TRUE*). The second event, called **forward2** selects low priority packages, but only if there are no high priority packages at the same server. Hence, high priority packages are forwarded before low priority packages. Since this refinement does not introduce any new variables, no gluing invariant is required.

send (ii) $\hat{=}$
  PRE $ii \in Send\_interface$ **THEN**
    ANY ss , pp **WHERE**
      $ss \in Server \wedge pp \in Package$
      $ss = address (source (ii)) \wedge$
      $destination (pp) = address (dest (ii)) \wedge$
      $recipient (pp) = dest (ii) \wedge$
      $contents (pp) = mess (ii) \wedge$
      $priority (pp) = pri (ii)$
    THEN
      $sendbuf (ss) := sendbuf (ss) \cup \{ pp \}$
    END
  END ;

forward $\hat{=}$
  ANY ss , pp **WHERE**
    $ss \in Server \wedge$
    $pp \in Package \wedge$
    $pp \in sendbuf (ss) \wedge$
    $priority (pp) = TRUE$
  THEN
    $sendbuf (ss) := sendbuf (ss) - \{ pp \}$ ‖
    $middleware := middleware \cup \{ pp \}$
  END ;

forward2 $\hat{=}$
  ANY ss , pp **WHERE**
    $ss \in Server \wedge$
    $pp \in Package \wedge$
    $pp \in sendbuf (ss) \wedge$
    $\forall qq . (qq \in sendbuf (ss) \Rightarrow priority (qq) = FALSE)$
  THEN
    $sendbuf (ss) := sendbuf (ss) - \{ pp \}$ ‖
    $middleware := middleware \cup \{ pp \}$
  END

Fig. 13. The second refinement

8 Subtyping Refinement

The example could be refined further by specialising *Package* using subtyping. Using this technique, it is possible to refine *Package* in more than one way (see Figure 6(i)) so that different kinds of packages are dealt with in different ways. For example, consider the following subtype declarations

    AirportPackage **SUBTYPES** *Package* **WITH** ...
    RunwayPackage **SUBTYPES** *Package* **WITH** ...

It would then be possible to specialise the servers to meet the needs of the different kinds of package. On the other hand, we would be able to continue to use the middleware unaltered because it would simply treat both subtypes uniformly (i.e. as objects of type *Package*). In the CDIS case study, this technique is being used to model VDM union types in Event-B.

9   Wider Issues

Although we have not set out with the aim of addressing object oriented modelling or programming approaches, there is a link between our work and various formal approaches to object oriented modelling and programming. Directly relevant to our work is the UML-B approach of Snook and Butler [10] which defines a mapping from a UML profile to B. In UML-B, class attributes and associations are modelled in B as accessor functions on object instance identifiers, i.e., if a is an attribute of type A of class C, then a is modelled in the B notation as a function $a \in C \rightarrow A$. UML-B effectively combines our form of subtyping with extension to represent class inheritance. In our approach accessor functions are represented as constants whereas in UML-B attributes and associations can be declared as either constant or variable and the corresponding accessor functions are in turn either constants or variables.

Naumann's work [8] is a good example of a relevant formal framework for reasoning about object oriented programs. This uses records and record subtyping to represent objects in an object oriented programming language. There are two significant differences from our work. Firstly, Naumann allows record fields to be methods thus modelling method overriding and dynamic dispatch of method calls, an important feature of object oriented programming. We do not address overriding of events rather we focus on refinement. Secondly, Naumann uses record constructors and a rich notion of subtyping for record types as is commonly found in formal approaches to object oriented programming. Our notion of subtyping is simply subsetting of the deferred B type used to model records and is independent of any subtyping of the fields. This means we avoid having to address the issue of covariance versus contravariance of method arguments [6]. Naumann's language is influenced by Oberon [11] which provides inheritance through record extension.

10   Conclusion

Without changing its semantics, we have proposed a method of introducing record types in Event-B that is amenable to refinement. Our experience in the redevelopment of CDIS has identified the benefits of such an approach. In particular, it allows us to start with a very abstract model and defer the introduction of airport-specific information until later in the development.

Our example has demonstrated how it is possible to specify an abstract view of a system with a very abstract representation of the data that it handles. In addition to the existing refinement techniques of Event-B, our refinements show how it is possible to introduce structured data in a stepwise manner in order to progress towards the formal design and implementation of the system.

During the implementation phase of a B development, it may be necessary to describe how records are to be implemented. Since a record is defined as a deferred set, a decision must be made to give an explicit representation of the set. In addition, fields of such records are declared as constant functions whose algorithmic behaviour must be given as part of the implementation.

Of course, it is not the case that the records within a B development will necessarily be implemented as records in program code - for example, a record could be used to model structured data such as XML messages. However, there is provision for the implementation of record-like structures using existing B technology: **SYSTEM** definitions of **BASE** machines are macros for the implementation (using B libraries) of database style structures. (See [9] for a detailed description of **BASE** machines and the common B libraries.) The similarities between our proposed syntax and the syntax of **BASE** machines suggest that they provide a natural progression from the specification and refinement of records to their implementation, although this has yet to be investigated.

Acknowledgements

The authors thank Jean-Raymond Abrial and Cliff Jones for many valuable discussions, and are also grateful to Helen Treharne for useful advice and suggestions.

References

1. Abrial J. R.: *The B Book: Assigning Programs to Meanings*, Cambridge University Press (1996).
2. The Alloy Analyzer, http://alloy.mit.edu.
3. Atelier B, http://www.atelierb.societe.com.
4. Bicarregui J. C.,Matthews B. M., Ritchie B., Agerholm S.: *Investigating the integration of two formal methods*, Proceedings of the 3rd ERCIM Workshop on Formal Methods for Industrial Critical Systems (1998).
5. B Core (U.K.) Ltd, http://www.b-core.com.
6. Castagna G.: *Covariance and Contravariance: Conflict without a Cause.*, in ACM Trans. Program. Lang. Syst., volume 17, number 3, pages 431-447 (1995).
7. Métayer C., Abrial J. R., Voisin L.: *Event-B Language*, RODIN deliverable 3.2, http://rodin.cs.ncl.ac.uk (2005).
8. Naumann D. A.: *Predicate transformer semantics of a higher-order imperative language with record subtyping*, in Sci. Comput. Program., volume 41, number 1, pages 1-51 (2001).
9. Schneider S.: *The B Method: An Introduction*, Palgrave (2001).
10. Snook C., Butler M. J.: *UML-B: Formal modelling and design aided by UML.*, in ACM Trans. Software Engineering and Methodology, to appear (2006).
11. Wirth N. : *The Programming Language Oberon*, in Softw., Pract. Exper., volume 18, number 7, pages 671-690 (1988).
12. Woodcock J. C. P., Davies J.: *Using Z: Specification, Refinement, and Proof*, Prentice Hall (1996).

Pointfree Factorization of Operation Refinement

José N. Oliveira and César J. Rodrigues

Dep. Informática, Universidade do Minho, 4700-320 Braga, Portugal
{jno, cjr}@di.uminho.pt

Abstract. The standard operation refinement ordering is a kind of "meet of opposites": non-determinism reduction suggests "smaller" behaviour while increase of definition suggests "larger" behaviour. Groves' factorization of this ordering into two simpler relations, one per refinement concern, makes it more mathematically tractable but is far from fully exploited in the literature. We present a *pointfree* theory for this factorization which is more agile and calculational than the standard set-theoretic approach. In particular, we show that factorization leads to a simple proof of structural refinement for arbitrary parametric types and exploit factor instantiation across different subclasses of (relational) operation. The prospect of generalizing the factorization to *coalgebraic* refinement is discussed.

Keywords: Theoretical foundations, refinement, calculation, reusable theories.

1 Introduction

Suppose a component s of some piece of hardware fails and needs to be replaced. Should no exact match be found off the shelf, the maintenance team will have to look around for *compatible* alternatives. What does *compatibility* mean in this context?

Let r be a candidate replacement for s and let the behaviour of both s and r be described by state-transition diagrams indicating, for each state a, the set of states reachable from a. So both s and r can be regarded as set-valued functions such that, for instance, component s may step from state a to state b iff $b \in (s\,a)$, failing (or behaving unexpectedly) wherever $s\,a$ is the empty set.

The intuition behind r being a safe replacement for s — written $s \vdash r$ — is that not only r should not fail where s does not,

$$\langle \forall a \,:\, \emptyset \subset (s\,a) \,:\, \emptyset \subset (r\,a) \rangle$$

but also that it should behave *"as s does"*. Wherever $(s\,a)$ is nonempty, there is some freedom for r to behave within such a set of choices: r is allowed be more deterministic than s. Altogether, one writes

$$s \vdash r \stackrel{\text{def}}{=} \langle \forall a \,:\, \emptyset \subset (s\,a) \,:\, \emptyset \subset (r\,a) \subseteq (s\,a) \rangle \qquad (1)$$

This definition of machine compatibility is nothing but a simplified version of that of *operation refinement* [22], the simplification being that one is not spelling out inputs and outputs and that, in general, the two machines s and r above need not share the same state space. This refinement ordering is standard in the discipline of *programming*

J. Misra, T. Nipkow, and E. Sekerinski (Eds.): FM 2006, LNCS 4085, pp. 236–251, 2006.
© Springer-Verlag Berlin Heidelberg 2006

from specifications [17] and can be found in various guises in the literature — see eg. references [22,6,23,10] among many others. Reference [6] should be singled out for its detailed discussion of the lattice-theoretical properties of the ⊢ ordering.

Despite its wide adoption, this definition of ⊢ is not free from difficulties. It is a kind of "meet of opposites": non-determinism reduction suggests "smaller" behaviours while increase of definition suggests "larger" behaviours. This "anomaly" makes this standard notion of refinement less mathematically tractable than one would expect. For instance, Groves [10] points out that the principal operators in the Z schema calculus [23] are not monotonic with respect to ⊢-refinement [1]. As a way of (partly) overcoming this problem, he puts forward an alternative characterisation of refinement based on the decomposition of ⊢ into two simpler relations,

$$s \vdash r \equiv \langle \exists t :: s \vdash_{pre} t \wedge t \vdash_{post} r \rangle \tag{2}$$

one per refinement concern: $\vdash_{pre}$ caters for increasing definition while $\vdash_{post}$ deals with decreasing non-determinism.

The same partition of the refinement relation is addressed in [14], where previous work by Frappier [9] on the $\vdash_{pre}$ ordering is referred to [2]. One of the aims of the current paper is to extend and consolidate the work scattered in [6,10,14], where some results are presented without proof and others are supported by either sketchy or convoluted arguments. The idea is to address the subject by reasoning in the pointfree relational calculus which is at the core of the *algebra of programming* [5,3]. It should be noted that both [6,10] already use some form of relational notation, somewhat mixed with the Z notation in the case of [10] or interpreted in terms of set-valued functions in [6]. The reasoning, however, is carried out at point-level, either involving predicate logic [10] or set-theory [6].

We follow [14] in resorting to the pointfree relational calculus (which we will refer to as the *pointfree (PF) transform*, see Section 2) all the way through, benefiting from not only its notation economy but also from its elegant reasoning style. It turns out that the theory becomes more general and simpler. Elegant expressions replace lengthy formulæ and easy-to-follow calculations replace pointwise proofs based on case analyses and natural language explanations.

Groves' factorization (2) — which is stated in [14] at PF-level simply by writing

$$\vdash_{pre} \cdot \vdash_{post} = \vdash = \vdash_{post} \cdot \vdash_{pre} \tag{3}$$

— is central to our approach. Thanks to this factorization — which we calculate and justify in a way simpler than in [10] [3] — we are able to justify facts which are stated

---

[1] According to [10,8], the literature is scarce in formally approaching this failure of monotonicity, which seems to be well-known among the Z community since the 1980s. See [8] for recent work in the area.

[2] The $\vdash_{pre}/\vdash_{post}$ factorization was suggested around the same time by one of the authors of the current paper [20], but the underlying theory was left unexplored.

[3] No proofs support the factorization in [14], where it is stated in two steps, under the headings: *reduction of nondeterminism commutes with domain extension* and *combination of domain extension and reduction of nondeterminism is refinement*.

but not proved in [6]. Among these, we present a detailed analysis, across the binary relation taxonomy, of the *lattice of specifications* proposed by [6].

As will be explained in the conclusions, this research is part of a broader research initiative aiming at developing a PF-theory for coalgebraic refinement integrating earlier efforts already reported in [16,4].

Paper Structure. This paper is laid out as follows. Concerning background, Section 2 provides some motivation on the PF-transform and Section 3 presents an overview of (pointfree) relation algebra. The PF-transformation of (1) is addressed in Section 4. Groves factorization (3) is calculated in sections 5 and 6. Benefits from such a factorization and a proof of structural refinement based on it are presented in Section 7. The paper closes by drawing conclusions which lead to plans for future work.

2   On the PF-Transform

The main purpose of formal modelling is to identify properties of real-world situations which, once expressed by mathematical formulæ, become abstract models which can be queried and reasoned about. This often raises a kind of *notation* conflict between *descriptiveness* (ie., adequacy to describe domain-specific objects and properties, inc. diagrams or other graphical objects) and *compactness* (as required by algebraic reasoning and solution calculation).

Classical *pointwise* notation in logics involves operators as well as variable symbols, logical connectives, quantifiers, etc. in a way which is hard to scale-up to complex models. This is not, however, the first time this kind of notational conflict arises in mathematics. Elsewhere in physics and engineering, people have learned to overcome it by changing the "mathematical space", for instance by moving (temporarily) from the time-space to the s-space in the *Laplace transformation*. Quoting [15], p.242:

> The Laplace transformation is a method for solving differential equations (...) The process of solution consists of three main steps:
>
> **1st step.** The given "hard" problem is transformed into a "simple" equation (subsidiary equation).
>
> **2nd step.** The subsidiary equation is solved by **purely algebraic** manipulations.
>
> **3rd step.** The solution of the subsidiary equation is transformed back to obtain the solution of the given problem.
>
> In this way the Laplace transformation reduces the problem of solving a differential equation to an **algebraic problem**.

The *pointfree (PF) transform* adopted in this paper is at the heels of this old reasoning technique. Standard set-theory-formulated refinement concepts — such as eg. (1) — are regarded as "hard" problems to be transformed into "simple", *subsidiary equations* dispensing with points and involving only binary relation concepts. As in the Laplace transformation, these are solved by *purely algebraic* manipulations and the outcome is mapped back to the original (descriptive) mathematical space wherever required.

Note the advantages of this two-tiered approach: intuitive, domain-specific descriptive formulæ are used wherever the model is to be "felt" by people. Such formulæ are transformed into a more *elegant*, simple and compact — but also more cryptic — algebraic notation whose single purpose is easy manipulation.

3 Overview of the Relational Calculus

Relations. Let $B \xleftarrow{\quad R \quad} A$ denote a binary relation on datatypes A (source) and B (target). We write bRa to mean that pair (b, a) is in R. The underlying partial order on relations will be written $R \subseteq S$, meaning that S is either more defined or less deterministic than R, that is, $R \subseteq S \equiv bRa \Rightarrow bSa$ for all a, b. $R \cup S$ denotes the union of two relations and $\top$ is the largest relation of its type. Its dual is $\bot$, the smallest such relation. Equality on relations can be established by $\subseteq$-antisymmetry: $R = S \equiv R \subseteq S \wedge S \subseteq R$, or indirect equality: $R = S \equiv \langle \forall X :: X \subseteq R \equiv X \subseteq S \rangle$.

Relations can be combined by three basic operators: composition $(R \cdot S)$, converse (R°) and meet $(R \cap S)$. R° is such that $a(R^\circ)b$ iff bRa holds. Meet corresponds to set-theoretical intersection and composition is defined in the usual way: $b(R \cdot S)c$ holds wherever there exists some mediating $a \in A$ such that $bRa \wedge aSc$. Everywhere $T = R \cdot S$ holds, the replacement of T by $R \cdot S$ will be referred to as a "factorization" and that of $R \cdot S$ by T as "fusion". (Equation (3) is thus an example of a factorization.) Every relation $B \xleftarrow{\quad R \quad} A$ admits two trivial factorizations, $R = R \cdot id_A$ and $R = id_B \cdot R$ where, for every X, id_X is the identity relation mapping every element of X onto itself.

Coreflexives and Orders. Some standard terminology arises from the id relation: a (endo) relation $A \xleftarrow{\quad R \quad} A$ (often called an *order*) will be referred to as *reflexive* iff $id_A \subseteq R$ holds and as *coreflexive* iff $R \subseteq id_A$ holds. As a rule, subscripts are dropped wherever types are implicit or easy to infer.

Coreflexive relations are fragments of the identity relation which model predicates or sets. The meaning of a *predicate* p is the coreflexive $[\![p]\!]$ such that $b[\![p]\!]a \equiv (b = a) \wedge (p\, a)$, that is, the relation that maps every a which satisfies p (and only such a) onto itself. The meaning of a *set* $S \subseteq A$ is $[\![\lambda a.a \in S]\!]$, that is, $b[\![S]\!]a \equiv (b = a) \wedge a \in S$. Wherever clear from the context, we will omit the $[\![\ ]\!]$ brackets.

Preorders are reflexive, transitive relations, where R is transitive iff $R \cdot R \subseteq R$. Partial orders are anti-symmetric preorders, where R being anti-symmetric means $R \cap R^\circ \subseteq id$. A preorder R is an *equivalence* if it is symmetric, that is, if $R = R^\circ$.

Taxonomy. Converse is of paramount importance in establishing a wider taxonomy of binary relations. Let us first define the *kernel* of a relation, $\ker R = R^\circ \cdot R$ and its dual, $\mathsf{img}\, R = \ker(R^\circ)$, called the *image* of R. Since converse commutes with composition, $(R \cdot S)^\circ = S^\circ \cdot R^\circ$ and is involutive, $(R^\circ)^\circ = R$, one has $\mathsf{img}\, R = R \cdot R^\circ$.

Kernel and image lead to the following terminology: a relation R is said to be *entire* (or total) iff its kernel is reflexive; or *simple* (or functional) iff its image is coreflexive. Dually, R is *surjective* iff R° is entire, and R is *injective* iff R° is simple. This terminology is recorded in the following summary table:

		Reflexive	*Coreflexive*
$\ker R$		entire R	injective R
$\mathsf{img}\, R$		surjective R	simple R

(4)

A relation is a *function* iff it is both simple and entire. Functions will be denoted by lowercase letters (f, g, etc.) and are such that bfa means $b = f\,a$. Function converses enjoy a number of properties of which the following is singled out because of its rôle in pointwise-pointfree conversion [2] :

$$b(f^\circ \cdot R \cdot g)a \equiv (f\,b)R(g\,a) \tag{5}$$

The pointwise definition of kernel of a function f, $b(\ker f)a \equiv f\,b = f\,a$, stems from (5), whereby it is easy to see that $\top$ is the kernel of every constant function, $1 \xleftarrow{\;!\;} A$ included (! is the unique function of its type, where 1 denotes the singleton type).

Isomorphisms are functions which are surjective and injective at the same time. A particular isomorphism is the identity function id, which also is the smallest equivalence relation on a particular data domain. So, $b\,id\,a$ means the same as $b = a$.

Functions and Relations. The interplay between functions and relations is a rich part of the binary relation calculus. In particular, given two preorders $\le$ and $\sqsubseteq$, one may relate arguments and results of pairs of functions f and g in, essentially, two ways:

$$f \cdot {\sqsubseteq} \subseteq {\le} \cdot g \tag{6}$$
$$f^\circ \cdot {\sqsubseteq} = {\le} \cdot g \tag{7}$$

As we shall see shortly, (6) is equivalent to ${\sqsubseteq} \subseteq f^\circ \cdot {\le} \cdot g$. For $f = g$, this establishes $\sqsubseteq$ to $\le$ monotonicity, thanks to (5). Both f, g in the other case (7) are monotone and said to be *Galois connected*, f (resp. g) being referred to as the *lower* (resp. *upper*) adjoint of the connection. By introducing variables in both sides of (6) via (5), we obtain

$$(f\,b) \sqsubseteq a \equiv b \le (g\,a) \tag{8}$$

For further details on the rich theory of Galois connections and examples of application see [1,2]. Galois connections in which the two preorders are relation inclusion ($\le, \sqsubseteq := \subseteq, \subseteq$) are particularly interesting because the two adjoints are relational combinators and the connection itself is their universal property. The following table lists connections which are relevant for this paper:

$(f\,X) \subseteq Y \equiv X \subseteq (g\,Y)$			
Description	f	g	**Obs.**
Converse	$(\_)^\circ$	$(\_)^\circ$	
Shunting rule	$(f\cdot)$	$(f^\circ\cdot)$	NB: f is a function
"Converse" *shunting* rule	$(\cdot f^\circ)$	$(\cdot f)$	NB: f is a function
Left-division	$(R\cdot)$	$(R\setminus\;)$	read "R under ..."
Right-division	$(\cdot R)$	$(\;/\;R)$	read "... over R"
range	ρ	$(\cdot\top)$	lower $\subseteq$ restricted to coreflexives
domain	δ	$(\top\cdot)$	lower $\subseteq$ restricted to coreflexives

$$\tag{9}$$

The connection associated with the *domain* operator will be particularly useful later on, whereby we infer that it is monotonic and commutes with join

$$\delta(R \cup S) = (\delta\,R) \cup (\delta\,S) \tag{10}$$

(as all lower-adjoints do [4]) and can be switched to so-called *conditions* [12]

$$\delta R \subseteq \delta S \equiv ! \cdot R \subseteq ! \cdot S \qquad (11)$$

wherever required, since $\top = \mathsf{ker}\,!$.

Left-division is another relational combinator relevant for this paper, from whose connection in (9) not only the following pointwise definition can be inferred [3],

$$b\,(R \setminus Y)\,a \equiv \langle \forall c\,:\, c\,R\,b :\, c\,Y\,a \rangle \qquad (12)$$

but also the following properties which will be useful in the sequel, for Φ coreflexive:

$$(R \cup T) \setminus S = (R \setminus S) \cap (T \setminus S) \qquad (13)$$
$$(R \cdot \Phi \setminus S) \cap \Phi = (R \setminus S) \cap \Phi \qquad (14)$$

4   Warming Up

According to the PF-transformation strategy announced in Section 2, our first task will be to PF-transform (1). We first concentrate on transforming the test for non-failure states, which occurs twice in the formula, $(s\,a) \supset \emptyset$ and $(r\,a) \supset \emptyset$. A set is nonempty iff it contains at least one element. Therefore,

$$(s\,a) \supset \emptyset \equiv \langle \exists x\,::\, x \in (s\,a) \rangle$$

$$\equiv \quad \{ \text{ idempotence of } \wedge \}$$

$$\langle \exists x\,::\, x \in (s\,a) \wedge x \in (s\,a) \rangle$$

$$\equiv \quad \{ \text{ (5) twice and converse } \}$$

$$\langle \exists x\,::\, a(\in \cdot s)^{\circ} x \wedge x(\in \cdot s)a \rangle$$

$$\equiv \quad \{ \text{ introduce } b = a \,; \text{ composition } \}$$

$$b = a \wedge b((\in \cdot s)^{\circ} \cdot (\in \cdot s))a$$

$$\equiv \quad \{ \text{ introduce kernel } \}$$

$$b = a \wedge b(\mathsf{ker}\,(\in \cdot s))a$$

Then we address the whole formula:

$$s \vdash r$$

$$\equiv \quad \{ \text{ (1) } \}$$

$$\langle \forall a\,:\, (s\,a) \supset \emptyset :\, \emptyset \subset (r\,a) \subseteq (s\,a) \rangle$$

---

[4] All f and g are monotonic by definition, as Galois adjoints. Moreover, the fs commute with join and the gs with meet. Thus we obtain monotonicity and (10) for free, whose proof as law 3.2 in [10] is unnecessary. It should be mentioned that some rules in table (9) appear in the literature under different guises and usually not identified as Galois connections. For instance, the *shunting* rule is called *cancellation law* in [23].

$\equiv \quad \{$ expand $\emptyset \subset (r\,a) \subseteq (s\,a)$ $\}$

$\langle \forall\, a \;:\; (s\,a) \supset \emptyset :\; \emptyset \subset (r\,a) \;\wedge\; (r\,a) \subseteq (s\,a) \rangle$

$\equiv \quad \{$ expand tests for non-failure state and replace $(r\,a)$ by $(r\,b)$, cf. $b = a$ $\}$

$\langle \forall\, a, b \;:\; b = a \;\wedge\; b(\mathsf{ker}\,(\in \cdot s))a :\; b = a \;\wedge\; b(\mathsf{ker}\,(\in \cdot r))a \;\wedge\; (r\,b) \subseteq (s\,a) \rangle$

$\equiv \quad \{$ $\delta\,R = \mathsf{ker}\,R \cap id$ is a closed formula for the domain operator [5,3] $\}$

$\langle \forall\, a, b \;:\; b(\delta\,(\in \cdot s))a :\; b(\delta\,(\in \cdot r))a \;\wedge\; (r\,b) \subseteq (s\,a) \rangle$

$\equiv \quad \{$ expand set-theoretic inclusion $\}$

$\langle \forall\, a, b \;:\; b(\delta\,(\in \cdot s))a :\; b(\delta\,(\in \cdot r))a \;\wedge\; \langle \forall\, c \;:\; c \in (r\,b) :\; c \in (s\,b) \rangle \rangle$

$\equiv \quad \{$ (5) twice ; then introduce left-division (12) $\}$

$\langle \forall\, a, b \;:\; b(\delta\,(\in \cdot s))a :\; b(\delta\,(\in \cdot r))a \;\wedge\; b((\in \cdot r) \setminus (\in \cdot s))a \rangle$

$\equiv \quad \{$ remove points ; relational inclusion and meet $\}$

$\delta\,(\in \cdot s) \subseteq \delta\,(\in \cdot r) \cap ((\in \cdot r) \setminus (\in \cdot s))$

$\equiv \quad \{$ remove membership by defining $R = \in \cdot r$ and $S = \in \cdot S$ $\}$

$\delta\,S \subseteq \delta\,R \cap (R \setminus S)$

Function s (resp. r) can be identified with the *power-transpose* [5,19] of binary relation S (resp. R). Since transposition is an isomorphism, we can safely lift our original ordering on set-valued state-transition functions to state-transition relations and establish the relational PF-transform of (1) as follows:

$$S \vdash R \;\equiv\; \delta\,S \subseteq (R \setminus S) \cap \delta\,R \tag{15}$$

which converts to

$$S \vdash R \;\equiv\; (\delta\,S \subseteq \delta\,R) \;\wedge\; (R \cdot \delta\,S \subseteq S) \tag{16}$$

once Galois connections of meet and left-division (9) are taken into account.

Most definitions of the refinement ordering in the literature — eg. [22,6,23,10] — are pointwise variants of (16). The calculations above show these to be equivalent to our starting version (1), which instantiates a "coalgebraic pattern" favoured in automata theory and coalgebraic refinement [16].

It is easy to see that the target types of both S, R in (16) need not be the same:

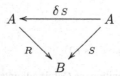

So, PF-transformed $S \vdash R$ covers other refinement situations, namely that of an *implicit specification* [13] S being refined by some function f,

$$S \vdash f \;\equiv\; \delta\,S \subseteq f^\circ \cdot S$$

whereby — back to points and thanks to (5) — we obtain, in classical "VDM-speak"

$$\forall a.\ \text{pre-}S(a) \Rightarrow \text{post-}S(f\,a, a)$$

which is nothing but the *implicit function specification* proof-rule given by [13].

It is in this (wider) context that the $\vdash$ ordering is presented in [6], where it is called the *less-defined* relation on specifications and is shown to be a semi-lattice universally lower-bounded by the empty specification $\perp$. The proof that it is a partial order is telegram-like in the paper. By contrast, the existence of a greatest lower bound (*glb*) is the subject of a proposition proved in typical *invent & verify* style — a *glb* definition is guessed first, which is then shown to be a lower bound and finally proved to be maximal among all lower bounds.

To illustrate the shift from *verification* to *calculation* brought forth by the PF-transform, we will *calculate* the *glb* of $\vdash$ (denoted $\sqcap$) as the (unique) solution to universal property

$$X \vdash R \sqcap S \equiv X \vdash R \wedge X \vdash S \tag{17}$$

Let us solve this equation for unknown $\sqcap$:

$$X \vdash R \sqcap S$$

$\equiv$ $\qquad \{\ (17)\ \}$

$$X \vdash R \wedge X \vdash S$$

$\equiv$ $\qquad \{\ (15)\ \text{twice; composition of coreflexives is intersection}\ \}$

$$\delta X \subseteq ((R \setminus X \cap S \setminus X)) \cap \delta R \cdot \delta S$$

$\equiv$ $\qquad \{\ (13)\ \}$

$$\delta X \subseteq (R \cup S) \setminus X \cap \delta R \cdot \delta S$$

$\equiv$ $\qquad \{\ (14)\ \text{for}\ R, S, \Phi := R \cup S, X, \delta R \cdot \delta S\ \}$

$$\delta X \subseteq (((R \cup S) \cdot \delta R \cdot \delta S) \setminus X) \cap (\delta R \cdot \delta S)$$

$\equiv$ $\qquad \{\ \delta((R \cup S) \cdot \delta R \cdot \delta S) = \delta R \cdot \delta S\ \text{(coreflexives)}\ ;\ (15)\ \}$

$$X \vdash ((R \cup S) \cdot \delta R \cdot \delta S)$$

$::$ $\qquad \{\ \text{indirect equality (Section 3) on partial order}\ \vdash\ [1,3]\ \}$

$$R \sqcap S = (R \cup S) \cdot \delta R \cdot \delta S$$

Thus we have deduced

$$R \sqcap S = (R \cup S) \cdot \delta R \cdot \delta S \tag{18}$$

which, back to points (1), will look like

$$(r \sqcap s)a \ \equiv \ if\ (r\,a) = \emptyset \vee (s\,a) = \emptyset\ then\ \emptyset\ else\ (r\,a) \cup (s\,a) \tag{19}$$

where r (resp. s) is the power-transpose of R (resp. S). (The reader is invited to calculate (19) as solution to (17) by directly resorting to pointwise $\vdash$ (1) instead of (15).)

5   Refinement Sub-relations

Recall the two conjuncts of (16), $\delta S \subseteq \delta R$ and $R \cdot \delta S \subseteq S$. Groves [10] freezes the former in defining a sub-relation $\vdash_{post}$ of $\vdash$,

$$S \vdash_{post} R \equiv S \vdash R \wedge \delta R \subseteq \delta S \qquad (20)$$

where extra clause $\delta R \subseteq \delta S$ prevents definition increase (by antisymmetry). Similarly, he puts forward another sub-relation $\vdash_{pre}$ of $\vdash$,

$$S \vdash_{pre} R \equiv S \vdash R \wedge S \subseteq R \cdot \delta S \qquad (21)$$

where extra clause $S \subseteq R \cdot \delta S$ prevents from increasing determinacy.

How useful are these sub-orderings? We will devote the remainder of the paper to exploiting the underlying theory and showing them to be useful beyond their original context of definition [10]. First of all, facts

$$\vdash_{pre} \subseteq \vdash , \vdash_{post} \subseteq \vdash \qquad (22)$$

follow immediately from the definitions (20,21) above. That both $\vdash_{pre}$ and $\vdash_{post}$ can be expressed independently of $\vdash$ is simple to calculate, first for $\vdash_{pre}$,

$\qquad S \vdash_{pre} R$

$\equiv \qquad \{$ (21) and (16) ; antisymmetry $\}$

$\qquad R \cdot \delta S = S \wedge \delta S \subseteq \delta R$

$\equiv \qquad \{$ switch to conditions (11) $\}$

$\qquad R \cdot \delta S = S \wedge ! \cdot S \subseteq ! \cdot R$

$\equiv \qquad \{$ substitution of S by $R \cdot \delta S \}$

$\qquad R \cdot \delta S = S \wedge ! \cdot R \cdot \delta S \subseteq ! \cdot R$

$\equiv \qquad \{$ δS is coreflexive ($\delta S \subseteq id$) ; monotonicity of composition $\}$

$\qquad R \cdot \delta S = S \wedge \text{TRUE}$

$\equiv \qquad \{$ trivia $\}$

$\qquad R \cdot \delta S = S$

and then for $\vdash_{post}$:

$\qquad\qquad S \vdash_{post} R$

$\qquad \equiv \qquad \{$ (20) and (16) $\}$

$\qquad\qquad R \cdot \delta S \subseteq S \wedge \delta R = \delta S$

$\qquad \equiv \qquad \{$ substitution of δS by $\delta R \}$

$\qquad\qquad R \cdot \delta R \subseteq S \wedge \delta R = \delta S$

$\qquad \equiv \qquad \{$ $R \cdot \delta R = R \}$

$\qquad\qquad R \subseteq S \wedge \delta R = \delta S$

Let us record these results, which are the PF-counterparts to laws 4.3 and 4.4 in [10], respectively,

$$S \vdash_{pre} R \ \equiv \ R \cdot \delta\, S = S \tag{23}$$
$$S \vdash_{post} R \ \equiv \ R \subseteq S \wedge \delta\, R = \delta\, S \tag{24}$$

noting that (24) can be written in less symbols as PF-equality

$$\vdash_{post} \ = \ \subseteq^\circ \cap \ker \delta \tag{25}$$

Thus, by definition, $\vdash_{post}$ is a partial order, since the meet of a partial order ($\subseteq^\circ$) with an equivalence ($\ker \delta$) is a partial order. (The proof that $\vdash_{pre}$ is also a partial order is elementary, see eg. [21].)

What does it mean to impose $\vdash_{pre}$ and $\vdash_{post}$ at the same time? We calculate:

$$S \vdash_{pre} R \wedge S \vdash_{post} R$$

$$\equiv \quad \{\ (23), (24)\ \}$$

$$R \cdot \delta\, S = S \wedge \delta\, S = \delta\, R \wedge R \subseteq S$$

$$\equiv \quad \{\ \text{substitution of } \delta\, S \text{ by } \delta\, R\ \}$$

$$R \cdot \delta\, R = S \wedge \delta\, R = \delta\, R \wedge R \subseteq S$$

$$\equiv \quad \{\ \text{property } R = R \cdot \delta\, R\ \}$$

$$R = S \wedge R \subseteq S$$

$$\equiv \quad \{\ R = S \Rightarrow R \subseteq S\ \}$$

$$R = S$$

This result (law 4.7 in [10]) PF-transforms to $\vdash_{pre} \cap \vdash_{post} = id$, whose "antisymmetric pattern" captures the opposition between the components $\vdash_{pre}$ and $\vdash_{post}$ of $\vdash$: to increase determinism only *and* definition only at the same time is contradictory. This relative antisymmetry between $\vdash_{pre}$ and $\vdash_{post}$ can also be inferred from facts

$$S \vdash_{post} R \Rightarrow R \subseteq S \tag{26}$$
$$S \vdash_{pre} R \Rightarrow S \subseteq R \tag{27}$$

the former arising immediately from (24) and the latter holding by transitivity: $S \vdash_{pre} R$ implies $S \subseteq R \cdot \delta\, S$ and $R \cdot \delta\, S \subseteq R$ holds.

6   Factorization of the Refinement Relation

We proceed to showing that the sequential composition of subrelations $\vdash_{pre}$ and $\vdash_{post}$ is — in any order — the refinement relation $\vdash$ itself. As we shall briefly see, this is where our calculational style differs more substantially from that of [10].

That $\vdash_{pre}$ and $\vdash_{post}$ are *factors* of $\vdash$ — that is, $\vdash_{post} \cdot \vdash_{pre} \subseteq \vdash$ and $\vdash_{pre} \cdot \vdash_{post} \subseteq \vdash$ — is obvious, recall (22) and composition monotonicity. So we are left with facts

$$\vdash \subseteq \vdash_{pre} \cdot \vdash_{post} \tag{28}$$

$$\vdash \subseteq \vdash_{post} \cdot \vdash_{pre} \tag{29}$$

to prove. As earlier on, instead of postulating the decompositions and then proving them, we will calculate (deduce) them. Two auxiliary results will be required:

$$S \vdash_{post} S \cap R \;\equiv\; \delta S = \delta(R \cap S) \tag{30}$$

$$S \vdash_{pre} S \cup R \;\equiv\; R \cdot \delta S \subseteq S \tag{31}$$

The proof of (30) immediate from the definition of $\vdash_{post}$ (24). That of (31) follows:

$$S \vdash_{pre} S \cup R$$

$\equiv$ $\{$ definition of $\vdash_{pre}$ $\}$

$$(S \cup R) \cdot \delta S = S$$

$\equiv$ $\{$ $(\cdot \delta S)$ is a lower adjoint (9) $\}$

$$(S \cdot \delta S) \cup (R \cdot \delta S) = S$$

$\equiv$ $\{$ $S \cdot \delta S = S$ $\}$

$$S \cup R \cdot \delta S = S$$

$\equiv$ $\{$ $A \cup B = B \equiv A \subseteq B$ $\}$

$$R \cdot \delta S \subseteq S$$

We are now ready to calculate (28):

$$S \vdash R$$

$\equiv$ $\{$ (16) $\}$

$$R \cdot \delta S \subseteq S \,\wedge\, \delta S \subseteq \delta R$$

$\equiv$ $\{$ $A \cup B = B \equiv A \subseteq B$ $\}$

$$R \cdot \delta S \subseteq S \,\wedge\, (\delta S) \cup (\delta R) = \delta R$$

$\equiv$ $\{$ (10) $\}$

$$R \cdot \delta S \subseteq S \,\wedge\, \delta(S \cup R) = \delta R$$

$\equiv$ $\{$ (30), since $R = R \cap (S \cup R)$ $\}$

$$R \cdot \delta S \subseteq S \,\wedge\, (S \cup R) \vdash_{post} R \cap (S \cup R)$$

$\equiv$ $\{$ (31) and $R = R \cap (S \cup R)$ $\}$

$$(S \vdash_{pre} S \cup R) \,\wedge\, (S \cup R) \vdash_{post} R$$

$\Rightarrow$ $\{$ logic $\}$

$$\langle \exists\, T \,::\, S \vdash_{pre} T \,\wedge\, T \vdash_{post} R \rangle$$

$$\equiv \quad \{ \text{ composition } \}$$

$$S(\vdash_{pre} \cdot \vdash_{post})R$$

Concerning (29):

$$S \vdash R$$

$$\Rightarrow \quad \{ \text{ since } S \vdash R \Rightarrow \delta S = \delta(S \cap R) \text{ [21]; (16) } \}$$

$$\delta S = \delta(S \cap R) \,\wedge\, R \cdot \delta S \subseteq S$$

$$\equiv \quad \{ \cap\text{-universal and } \delta S \text{ is coreflexive } \}$$

$$\delta S = \delta(S \cap R) \,\wedge\, R \cdot \delta S \subseteq S \cap R$$

$$\equiv \quad \{ \text{ substitution } \}$$

$$\delta S = \delta(S \cap R) \,\wedge\, R \cdot \delta(S \cap R) \subseteq S \cap R$$

$$\equiv \quad \{ \text{ (31) } \}$$

$$\delta S = \delta(S \cap R) \,\wedge\, (S \cap R) \vdash_{pre} (S \cap R) \cup R$$

$$\equiv \quad \{ \text{ (30) and } S \cap R \subseteq R \}$$

$$(S \vdash_{post} S \cap R) \,\wedge\, (S \cap R) \vdash_{pre} R$$

$$\Rightarrow \quad \{ \text{ logic } \}$$

$$\langle \exists\, T \,::\, S \vdash_{post} T \,\wedge\, T \vdash_{pre} R \rangle$$

$$\equiv \quad \{ \text{ composition } \}$$

$$S(\vdash_{post} \cdot \vdash_{pre})R$$

In summary, we have the two alternative ways to factor the refinement relation announced in (3). This embodies laws 4.8 and 4.9 of [10], where they are proved in first-order logic requiring negation and consistency [5]. These requirements, which have no counterpart in our calculations above, should be regarded as spurious.

7   Taking Advantage of the Factorization

Factorizations such as that given by (3) are very useful in mathematics in general. For our purposes, the rôle of (3) is three-fold. On the one hand, properties of the composition — eg. transitivity, reflexivity — can be easily inferred from similar properties of factors $\vdash_{pre}$ and $\vdash_{post}$ [21]. On the other hand, one can look for results with hold for the individual factors $\vdash_{pre}$ and/or $\vdash_{post}$ and do not hold (in general) for $\vdash$. For instance, meet $(R \cap S)$ is $\vdash_{pre}$-monotonic but not $\vdash$-monotonic (law 5.1 in [10]). This aspect of

---

[5] In [10,6], two relations R and S are regarded as *consistent* iff $\delta(R \cap S) = (\delta R) \cap (\delta S)$ holds.

the factorization is of practical value and in fact the main motivation in [10]: complex refinement steps can be factored in *less big a gap* ones involving only one factor $\vdash_{pre}$ (resp. $\vdash_{post}$) and $\vdash_{pre}$ (resp. $\vdash_{post}$) monotonic operators.

Space restraints prevent us from presenting our calculation of monotonicity laws 5.1 and 5.4 of [10], respectively

$$S \vdash_{pre} R \,\wedge\, T \vdash_{pre} U \;\Rightarrow\; S \cap T \vdash_{pre} R \cap U \tag{32}$$

$$S \vdash_{post} R \,\wedge\, T \vdash_{post} U \;\Rightarrow\; S \cup T \vdash_{post} R \cup U \tag{33}$$

which the interested reader will find in [21]. We anticipate that, unlike [10], pointfree calculation doesn't require negation.

Last but not least, there is another practical outcome of factorization (3) which was left unexploited in [10]: the fact that it makes it easy to analyse the (semi-)lattice of operations ordered by $\vdash$ [6], in particular concerning the behaviour of factors $\vdash_{pre}$ and $\vdash_{post}$ for some of the relation subclasses studied in Section 3. For instance, if by construction one knows that the operation under refinement is *simple* (vulg. a partial function), one can safely replace $\vdash$ by the appropriate factors tabulated in

Binary relation sub-class	$\vdash_{post}$	$\vdash_{pre}$	$\vdash$	
Entire relations	$\subseteq^\circ$	id	$\subseteq^\circ$	(a)
Simple relations	id	$\subseteq$	$\subseteq$	(b)
Functions	id	id	id	(c)

$$\tag{34}$$

Let us justify (34): $\vdash_{pre} = id$ in case (34a) follows directly from (23), in which case equation (3) yields $\vdash = \vdash_{post}$. Moreover, $\vdash_{post} = \subseteq^\circ$ holds since domain (δ) is a constant function within the class of *entire* relations and thus $\ker \delta = \top$ in (25). The proof of (34b) is immediate in the case of $\vdash_{post} = id$, since (24) restricted to simple relations establishes equality at once. Concerning $\vdash_{pre} = \subseteq$, our calculation to follow will rely on relaxing function f to a simple relation S in the *shunting* rules in (9), leading to rules [18]

$$S \cdot R \subseteq T \;\equiv\; (\delta S) \cdot R \subseteq S^\circ \cdot T \tag{35}$$

$$R \cdot S^\circ \subseteq T \;\equiv\; R \cdot \delta S \subseteq T \cdot S \tag{36}$$

which, however, are not Galois connections. We reason:

$$S \vdash_{pre} R$$

$\equiv$ { (23) ; anti-symmetry }

$$R \cdot \delta S \subseteq S \,\wedge\, S \subseteq R \cdot \delta S$$

$\equiv$ { shunt on simple R (35) and S (36) ; $S = S \cdot \delta S$ }

$$\delta R \cdot S^\circ \subseteq R^\circ \,\wedge\, S \cdot \delta S \subseteq R \cdot \delta S$$

$\equiv$ { converses }

$$S \cdot \delta R \subseteq R \,\wedge\, S \cdot \delta S \subseteq R \cdot \delta S$$

$\equiv$ { $\delta S \subseteq \delta R$, cf. (27) and monotonicity of δ }

$$S \subseteq R \wedge S \cdot \delta S \subseteq R \cdot \delta S$$

$\equiv$ $\qquad$ { first conjunct implies the second (monotonicity) }

$$S \subseteq R$$

Finally, (34c) follows from functions being entire and simple at the same time.

A comment on the *glb* of $\vdash_{pre}$ restricted to simple relations, ie. deterministic but possibly failing operations (partial functions): pointfree calculation yields $R \sqcap S = R \cap S$ in this case, which agrees with $\subseteq$ in (34b) but contrasts to factor $R \cup S$ in (18). It can be easily calculated that simplicity of $R \sqcap S$ (18) is equivalent to both R, S being simple and $R \cdot S^\circ \subseteq id$, which is equivalent, thanks to (36), to $R \cdot \delta S \subseteq S$, itself equivalent to $S \cdot \delta R \subseteq R$. From these we calculate $(R \cup S) \cdot \delta R \cdot \delta S \subseteq R \cap S$. Since $R \cap S \subseteq (R \cup S) \cdot \delta R \cdot \delta S$, we obtain $\sqcap = \cap$ for simple relations.

Structural Refinement. We close the technical part of the paper by presenting a law which is particularly useful in modular (structural) refinement and whose proof relies heavily on factorization (3):

$$S \vdash R \;\Rightarrow\; \mathsf{F}\,S \vdash \mathsf{F}\,R \tag{37}$$

This law expresses $\vdash$-monotonicity of an arbitrary parametric type F. Technically, the parametricity of F is captured by regarding it as a *relator* [1,5], a concept which extends *functors* to relations: F A describes a parametric type while F R is a relation from F A to F B provided R is a relation from A to B. Relators are monotonic and commute with composition, converse and the identity.

Fact (37) is another example of a property of operation refinement whose proof uses the strategy of promoting $\vdash_{post}/\vdash_{pre}$ properties to $\vdash$. We need the auxiliary result that every relator F is both $\vdash_{pre}/\vdash_{post}$-monotonic:

$$\mathsf{F} \cdot \vdash_{post} \;\subseteq\; \vdash_{post} \cdot \mathsf{F} \tag{38}$$
$$\mathsf{F} \cdot \vdash_{pre} \;\subseteq\; \vdash_{pre} \cdot \mathsf{F} \tag{39}$$

The PF-calculations which support (38,39) are omitted for space economy and can be found in [21]. Then the calculation of (37) is an easy task:

TRUE

$\equiv$ $\qquad$ { (38) }

$\mathsf{F} \cdot \vdash_{post} \;\subseteq\; \vdash_{post} \cdot \mathsf{F}$

$\Rightarrow$ $\qquad$ { monotonicity of composition }

$\mathsf{F} \cdot \vdash_{post} \cdot \vdash_{pre} \;\subseteq\; \vdash_{post} \cdot \mathsf{F} \cdot \vdash_{pre}$

$\Rightarrow$ $\qquad$ { (39) and $\subseteq$-transitivity }

$\mathsf{F} \cdot \vdash_{post} \cdot \vdash_{pre} \;\subseteq\; \vdash_{post} \cdot \vdash_{pre} \cdot \mathsf{F}$

$\equiv$ $\qquad$ { (3) }

$$\mathsf{F} \cdot \vdash \; \subseteq \; \vdash \cdot \mathsf{F}$$

$$\equiv \quad \{ \text{ shunt over F (9) and then go pointwise on } S \text{ and } R \; \}$$

$$R \vdash S \Rightarrow \mathsf{F} \, R \vdash \mathsf{F} \, S$$

8   Conclusions and Future Work

Refinement is among the most studied topics in software design theory. An extensive treatment of the subject can be found in [7]. It is, however, far from being an easy-to-use body of knowledge, a remark which is mirrored on terminology — cf. *downward*, *upward* refinement [11], *forwards*, *backwards* refinement [11,23,16], *S,SP,SC*-refinement [8] and so on.

Boudriga *et al* [6] refer prosaically to the refinement ordering (denoted $\vdash$ in the current paper) as the *less defined ordering* on pre/post-specifications. "Less defined" has a double meaning in this context: smaller domain-wise and vaguer range-wise. But such a linguistic consensus is not found in the underlying mathematics: $\vdash$ merges two opposite orderings, one pushing towards "smaller" specs and another to "larger" ones.

With the purpose to better understand this opposition, we decided to take advantage of a factorization of the refinement ordering which we found in [10,14] but does not seem to have attracted much attention henceforth. Our approach to this result, which is calculational and *pointfree*-relational, contrasts with the hybrid models usually found in the literature, which typically use relational combinators to express definitions and properties but perform most reasoning steps at point-level, eg. using set-valued functions. A similar concern for pointfree relational reasoning can be found in [14], which we would like to study more in depth concerning the *demonic* calculus of relations.

The work reported in this paper should be regarded as a step towards a broader research aim: that of developing a clear-cut PF-theory of *coalgebraic* refinement. The intuition is provided by formula (1) once again, whose set-valued functions can be regarded *both* as power-transposes of binary relations [19] and coalgebras of the powerset functor. Instead of favouring the former view as in the current paper, we want to exploit the latter and follow the approach of [16], who study refinement of software components modelled by coalgebras of functor $\mathsf{F}X = (O \times (\mathsf{B}X))^I$, where I and O model inputs and outputs and B is a monad describing the component's behaviour pattern.

The approach has already been treated generically in the pointfree style [4], whereby set inclusion in (1) is generalized to a sub-preorder of F-membership-based inclusion. There is, however, no coalgebraic counterpart to the $\vdash_{pre}/\vdash_{post}$ factorization studied in the current paper. Such a generalization is a prompt topic for future research.

Acknowledgments

We thank Lindsay Groves for pointing us to reference [14] and the anonymous referees for helpful comments on the original submission. This research was carried out in the context of the PURE Project *(Program Understanding and Re-engineering: Calculi and Applications)* funded by FCT contract POSI/ICHS/44304/2002.

References

1. C. Aarts, R. Backhouse, P. Hoogendijk, E. Voermans, and J. van der Woude. A relational theory of datatypes, Dec. 1992. Available from www.cs.nott.ac.uk/~rcb/papers.
2. K. Backhouse and R.C. Backhouse. Safety of abstract interpretations for free, via logical relations and Galois connections. *Sci. of Comp. Programming*, 15(1–2):153–196, 2004.
3. R.C. Backhouse. *Mathematics of Program Construction*. Univ. of Nottingham, 2004. Draft of book in preparation. 608 pages.
4. L.S. Barbosa and J.N. Oliveira. Transposing partial components — an exercise on coalgebraic refinement. Technical report, DI/UM, Sep. 2005. (Submitted).
5. R. Bird and O. de Moor. *Algebra of Programming*. C.A.R. Hoare editor, Series in Computer Science. Prentice-Hall Int., 1997.
6. N. Boudriga, F. Elloumi, and A. Mili. On the lattice of specifications: Applications to a specification methodology. *Formal Asp. Comput.*, 4(6):544–571, 1992.
7. W.-P. de Roever, K. Engelhardt with the assistance of J. Coenen, K.-H. Buth, P. Gardiner, Y. Lakhnech, and F. Stomp. *Data Refinement Model-Oriented Proof methods and their Comparison*. Cambridge University Press, 1999. ISBN 0521641705.
8. M. Deutsch, M. Henson, and S. Reeves. Modular reasoning in Z: scrutinising monotonicity and refinement, 2006. Under consideration for publication in *Formal Asp. Comput.*.
9. M. Frappier. *A Relational Basis for Program Construction by Parts*. PhD thesis, University of Ottawa, 1995.
10. L. Groves. Refinement and the Z schema calculus. *ENTCS*, 70(3), 2002. Extended version available as Vict. Univ. of Wellington, CS Tech. Report CS-TR-02-31.
11. Jifeng He, C.A.R. Hoare, and J.W. Sanders. Data refinement refined. In B. Robinet and R. Wilhelm, editors, *ESOP'86*, Springer LNCS (213), pages 187–196, 1986.
12. P. Hoogendijk. *A Generic Theory of Data Types*. PhD thesis, Univ. Eindhoven, NL, 1997.
13. C.B. Jones. *Software Development — A Rigorous Approach*. C.A.R. Hoare editor, Series in Computer Science. Prentice-Hall Int., 1980.
14. W. Kahl. Refinement and development of programs from relational specifications. *ENTCS*, 44(3):4.1–4.43, 2003.
15. E. Kreyszig. *Advanced Engineering Mathematics*. John Wiley & Sons, Inc., 6th ed., 1988.
16. Sun Meng and L.S. Barbosa. On refinement of generic state-based software components. In C. Rettray, S. Maharaj, and C. Shankland, editors, *10th Int. Conf. Algebraic Methods and Software Technology (AMAST'04)*, pages 506–520. Springer LNCS (3116). 2004.
17. C. Morgan. *Programming from Specification*. C.A.R. Hoare editor, Series in Computer Science. Prentice-Hall Int., 3rd edition, 1998.
18. S.C. Mu and R.S. Bird. Inverting functions as folds. In E. Boiten and B. Möller, editors, *6th Int. Conf. on Math. of Program Construction*, Springer LNCS (2386), pages 209–232. 2002.
19. J.N. Oliveira and C.J. Rodrigues. Transposing relations: from *Maybe* functions to hash tables. In *MPC'04 : 7th Int. Conf. on Math. of Program Construction*, Springer LNCS (3125), pages 334–356. 2004.
20. C.J. Rodrigues. Reificação e cálculos de reificação. Technical report, Universidade do Minho, April 1995. (In Portuguese).
21. C.J. Rodrigues. *Software Refinement by Calculation*. PhD thesis, Departamento de Informática, Universidade do Minho, 2006. (Forthcoming.).
22. J.M. Spivey. *The Z Notation — A Reference Manual*. C.A.R. Hoare editor, Series in Computer Science. Prentice-Hall Int., 1989.
23. J. Woodcock and J. Davies. *Using Z: Specification, Refinement, and Proof*. Prentice-Hall, Inc., Upper Saddle River, NJ, USA, 1996.

A Formal Template Language Enabling Metaproof

Nuno Amálio, Susan Stepney, and Fiona Polack

Department of Computer Science, University of York, York, YO10 5DD, UK
{namalio, susan, fiona}@cs.york.ac.uk

Abstract. Design patterns are usually described in terms of instances. Templates describe sentences of some language with a particular form, generate sentences upon instantiation, and can be used to describe those commonly occurring structures that make a pattern. This paper presents FTL, a language to express templates, and an approach to proof with templates. This enables reuse at the level of formal modelling and verification: patterns of models are captured once and their structure is explored for proof, so that patterns instances can be generated mechanically and proved results related with the pattern can be reused in any context. The paper uses templates to capture the Z promotion pattern and metaproof to prove properties of Z promotion. The proved properties are applicable directly to Z promotions built by template instantiation.

Keywords: patterns, templates, proof, Z, formal development.

1 Introduction

Design patterns [1] have had an impact in software engineering. There is also a growing interest in patterns for formal development (e.g. [2,3,4,5]). Patterns, however, are usually described in terms of instances, making their mechanical adaption to a context impossible. We faced this problem while using and building patterns for Z [4,6,7,8], and so we resorted to *templates* to describe structural patterns. Templates capture the form (or shape) of sentences of some language, generate, upon instantiation, sentences whose form is as prescribed by the template, and can be used to describe those commonly occurring structures that make a pattern. This paper presents the formal template language (FTL), a language to express templates, a calculus for the instantiation of FTL templates, and an approach to proof with FTL templates of formal models.

Templates of some form appear often in the computer science literature. For example, a popular Z book [9, p. 150] introduces the Z schema with a template:

$Name == [\ declaration \mid predicates\ ]$

This is an *informal template*, it says that a schema has a name, a set of declarations and a set of predicates. Intuitively, we guess that the names of the template are to be substituted by values, which is confirmed by a template instance:

J. Misra, T. Nipkow, and E. Sekerinski (Eds.): FM 2006, LNCS 4085, pp. 252–267, 2006.
© Springer-Verlag Berlin Heidelberg 2006

$$Bank == [accs : \mathbb{P} \; ACCID; \; accSt : ACCID \nrightarrow Account \mid \text{dom} \; accSt = accs]$$

The problem with informal templates is that it is difficult to distinguish the template from the instance, and is difficult to know what instantiations are valid, making it impossible to reason rigorously with them. FTL can represent templates of any formal language precisely; it is used here with Z. The informal template given above in FTL is:

$$<Name> == [\; [\![\; <declaration> \;]\!] \mid [\![\; <predicate> \;]\!] \;]$$

A variable within <> denotes a *placeholder*, which is substituted by a value when the template is instantiated; a term within $[\![\;]\!]$ denotes a list, which is replaced by many occurrences of the term in the instantiation.

1.1 Metaproof

The form of Z sentences can be represented as FTL templates. It is also possible to explore templates of Z for reasoning (or proof). This has practical value: template developers can establish *metatheorems* for templates that are applicable to all instantiations of the templates involved. This is motivated with an example.

In Z, the introduction of a state space definition of an abstract data type (ADT), such as *Bank* above, into a specification, entails a demonstration that the description is consistent: at least one state satisfying the description should exist. This normally involves defining the initial state of the ADT (the initialisation) and proving that the initial state does exist (the initialisation theorem). The *Bank* is initialised assuming that in the initial state there are no accounts:

$$BankInit == [\; Bank \; ' \mid accs' = \varnothing \land accSt' = \varnothing \;]$$

The consistency of *Bank* is demonstrated by proving the Z conjecture, $\vdash? \; \exists \, BankInit \bullet \text{true}$. A proof-sketch of this conjecture is (see appendix A for the Z inference rules used):

$\vdash \exists \; BankInit \bullet \text{true}$

$\equiv$ [By $\exists \; Sc$ (twice)]

$\vdash \exists \; accs' : \mathbb{P} \, ACCID; \; accSt' : ACCID \nrightarrow Account \bullet accs' = \varnothing \land accSt' = \varnothing$

$\equiv$ [By one-point]

$\vdash \text{dom} \, \varnothing = \varnothing \land \varnothing \in \mathbb{P} \; ACCID \land \varnothing \in ACCID \nrightarrow Account$

$\equiv$ [By set theory and propositional calculus]

true

This is proved automatically in the Z/Eves [10] theorem prover.

The *Bank* schema is an instance of a common structure of Z specifications: the state of a *promoted* ADT [9,4]. The theorem proved above applies to the *Bank* ADT, but does it apply also to all promoted ADTs that are similar in form to *Bank*? If it does, can this result be proved once and for all?

Bank was generated from a template, but that template is too general and not useful for the kind of investigation that we want to do. Instead, we use a more restricted template representing a promoted Z ADT, of which *Bank* is an instance. A promoted ADT comprises a set of identifiers, a function mapping identifiers to state, a predicate restricting the mapping function, and a predicate representing an optional state invariant:

$$<P> == [\ <ids> : \mathbb{P}\ <ID>;\ <st> : <ID> \nrightarrow <S>\ |$$
$$\mathrm{dom}\ <st> = <ids> \wedge <I>\ ]$$

(Promoted ADT's without the optional invariant, such as *Bank* above, are instantiated from this template by instantiating $<I>$ with the value *true*.)

Likewise, we represent as templates the empty initialisation of a promoted ADT, and the initialisation conjecture:

$$<P>Init == [\ <P>\ '\ |\ <ids>' = \varnothing \wedge <st>' = \varnothing\ ]$$
$$\vdash?\ \exists\ <P>Init \bullet \mathrm{true}$$

We can reason with these templates by analysing their *welformed* instantiations. In those cases, P, *id* and *st* hold names, *ID* and *S* are sets, and *I* is a predicate. By expanding the template schemas using the laws of the schema calculus, and apply the one-point rule (see proof above), we get the formula,

$$\vdash \mathrm{dom}\ \varnothing = \varnothing \wedge \varnothing \in \mathbb{P}<ID> \wedge \varnothing \in <ID> \nrightarrow <S>$$
$$\wedge <I>'[<ids>' := \varnothing, <st>' := \varnothing]$$

which reduces to, $<I>'[<ids>' := \varnothing, <st>' := \varnothing]$. If $<I>$ is instantiated with *true*, then the formula reduces to *true*. This establishes two metatheorems, where the latter is a specialisation (or a corollary) of the former, that are applicable to all promoted ADTs instantiated from these templates. The specialised metatheorem gives the nice property of *true by construction*: whenever these templates are instantiated, such that $<I>$ is instantiated with *true*, then the initialisation conjecture is simply *true*. Even when $<I>$ is not instantiated with *true*, the formula to prove is simpler than the initial one.

The argument outlined above is rigorous and valid, but it is not formal. To work towards formal metaproof, so that tool support is possible, a formal semantics for the template language is required.

In the following, FTL is given a brief introduction followed by an overview of its formal definition. Then, the instantiation calculus of FTL, a calculus for the partial instantiation of templates, is presented. Finally, a metaproof approach for Z based on FTL is developed and illustrated for the rigorous proof above.

2   A Short Introduction to FTL

FTL expresses templates that can be instantiated to yield sentences of some language (the target language). FTL is general in the sense that it can capture the form (or shape) of sentences of any formal language, and although designed with Z in mind, it is not tied to Z or to any other language.

FTL's abstraction mechanism is based on *variables*, which allow the representation of variation points in structures. Variables have, in FTL, their usual mathematical meaning: they denote some value in a scope. Template instantiation is, essentially, substitution of variables by values.

As FTL is general, it is possible to instantiate a template so that the resulting sentence is meaningless. FTL templates assist the author; they do not remove the obligation to check that what the author writes is sensible.

The following illustrates the main constructs of FTL.

Text. A template may contain text of the target language, which is present in every instance. For example, the trivial template, *true*, always yields, *true*, when instantiated. Usually, templates comprise text combined with other constructs.

Placeholder. A placeholder is represented by enclosing one variable within <>. Placeholders, when not within lists, denote one variable occurrence, and they are substituted by the value assigned to the variable when the template is instantiated. The template, $<x> : <t>; <y> : <t>$, includes four placeholders and three variables, x, t and y; this can be instantiated with the substitution set, $\{x \mapsto \text{“}a\text{”}, t \mapsto \text{“}\mathbb{N}\text{”}, y \mapsto \text{“}b\text{”}\}$, to yield: $a : \mathbb{N}; \ b : \mathbb{N}$.

List. A list comprises one list term, a list separator (the separator of the instantiated list terms) and a string representing the empty instantiation of the list, and it is represented by enclosing the list term within ⟦ ⟧. The list term is a combination of text, parameters and possibly other lists. Often, the abbreviated form of lists, without separator and empty instantiation, is used.

A placeholder within a list denotes an *indexed set* of variable occurrences. This means that $<x>$ and ⟦ $<x>$ ⟧ actually denote different variable occurrences; $<x>$ denotes an occurrence of the variable x, but ⟦ $<x>$ ⟧ denotes the occurrence of the indexed set of variables, $\{x_1, \ldots, x_n\}$.

The template, ⟦ $<x> : <t>$ ⟧$_{(\text{“;”},\text{“}\{\}\text{”})}$, can be instantiated with the sequence of substitution sets, $\langle\{x \mapsto \text{“}a\text{”}, t \mapsto \text{“}\mathbb{N}\text{”}\}, \{x \mapsto \text{“}b\text{”}, t \mapsto \text{“}\mathbb{P} \ \mathbb{N}\text{”}\}\rangle$. This yields: $a : \mathbb{N}; \ b : \mathbb{P}\mathbb{N}$. Lists can be instantiated with an empty instantiation, $\langle \ \rangle$; here this gives $\{\}$, the list's empty instantiation.

Choice. The FTL choice construct expresses *choice* of template expressions. That is, only one of the choices is present in the instantiation. There are two kinds of choice: optional and multiple. In optional, the single expression may be present in the instantiation or not. In multiple, one of the choices must be present in the instantiation. Choices are instantiated with a choice-selection, a natural number, indicating the selected choice; non-selection takes the value zero.

The template ⟨ $<x> : <t>$ ⟩$^?$ can be instantiated with $(1, \{x \mapsto \text{“}a\text{”}, t \mapsto \text{“}\mathbb{N}\text{”}\})$, to yield: $a : \mathbb{N}$. To avoid the presence of the expression in the instantiation, the template can be instantiated with $(0, \{\})$, which simply yields the empty string. In the multiple-choice template,

$$(<x> : <t> \; [\; <x> : <t_1> \twoheadrightarrow <t_2>)$$

the first choice is instantiated with $(1, \{x \mapsto \text{``}a\text{''}, t \mapsto \text{``}\mathbb{N}\text{''}\})$ to yield: $a : \mathbb{N}$; the second with $(2, \{x \mapsto \text{``}f\text{''}, t_1 \mapsto \text{``}\mathbb{N}\text{''}, t_2 \mapsto \text{``}\mathbb{N}\text{''}\})$ to yield: $f : \mathbb{N} \twoheadrightarrow \mathbb{N}$.

3   The Formal Definition of FTL

FTL has a denotational semantics [11] based on its abstract syntax. The instantiation of an FTL template should give sentences in some target language, and this is naturally represented in the domain of strings (the semantic domain).

FTL is fully specified in Z elsewhere [12]. Here, we present its definitions in a form that is easier to read, which combines Z sets and operators, the BNF (Backus-Naur form) notation and an equational style.

3.1   Syntax

This section defines the syntactic sets of the language. The set of all identifiers (I) gives variables to construct placeholders. The set of all text symbols $(SYMB)$ is used to construct the set of all strings, which are sequences of text symbols:

$$[I, SYMB] \qquad\qquad Str == \text{seq}\, SYMB$$

The remaining syntactic sets are defined by structural induction, using the BNF notation. The set of template expressions comprises objects that are either an atom (A), a choice (C), or either of these followed by another expression:

$$E ::= A \mid C \mid A\,E \mid C\,E$$

The set of choices comprises optional and multiple choice; optional is formed by one expression, and multiple by a sequence of expressions (set CL):

$$C ::= (E)^? \mid (CL) \qquad\qquad CL ::= E_1 \; [\; E_2 \mid E \; [\; CL$$

The set of atoms, A, comprises placeholders, text (T), and lists (L); a placeholder is formed by an identifier, the name of a variable:

$$A ::= <I> \mid T \mid L$$

The set of lists, L, comprises two forms of list: normal and abbreviated. A normal list comprises a list term (set LT, a sequence of atoms), a list separator (SEP) and the empty instantiation of the list (EI); the abbreviated form just includes the list term:

$$L ::= [LT]_{(SEP,EI)} \mid [LT] \qquad\qquad LT ::= A \mid A\,LT$$

List separators, list empty instantiations and text are just strings:

$$SEP ::= Str \qquad\qquad EI ::= Str \qquad\qquad T ::= Str$$

3.2   Semantics

Templates   **Str**

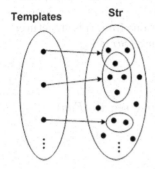

Fig. 1. Templates and the sets of strings they denote (all possible instances)

A template denotes a set of strings, corresponding to all its possible instances (Fig. 1).[1] The semantics of FTL could be specified by calculating all possible instances of a template. That is, given the set of template expressions (E) defined above, the meaning of a template would be given by the function:

$$\mathcal{M} : E \rightarrow \mathbb{P}\,Str$$

But this does not explain *instantiation*, that is, how users generate sentences from templates.

The same meaning of templates as denoting a set of strings, can be achieved by considering instantiation, which consists of substitutions for the template's variables and selections for the template's choices. A template has a set of all possible instantiations; by instantiating a template with these instantiations we get the set of all strings denoted by the template.

So, instead, the semantics is defined by an instantiation function, which calculates the string (sentence) generated by instantiating a template with an instantiation. That is:

$$\mathcal{M} : E \rightarrow TInst \nrightarrow Str$$

The semantic functions are defined by structural induction on the syntax of FTL. The following presents the semantics for atoms and expressions; the complete definitions are given in [12].

Semantics of Atoms. Atoms are instantiated with substitutions for the variables that occur within placeholders, which may stand-alone or be within lists.

The environment structure (Env), defined as a partial function from identifiers (variables) to strings (values), represents a set of variable substitutions:

$$Env == I \nrightarrow Str$$

This allows the instantiation of placeholders that are not within lists. For example, the template `<x> : <t>` is instantiated with, $\{x \mapsto a, t \mapsto \mathbb{N}\}$, an instance of Env, to yield $x : \mathbb{N}$. As a placeholder within a list denotes an indexed set of variable occurrences, it seems natural to instantiate these variables with a sequence of substitution sets (seq Env), but this does not work with nested lists. So, a recursive structure is required, the environment tree:

$$TreeEnv ::= \mathsf{tree}\,\langle\!\langle Env \times \mathrm{seq}\ TreeEnv \rangle\!\rangle$$

---

[1] But only a subset of these strings has a meaning in the target language.

TreeEnv comprises one environment, to instantiate the placeholders that stand alone in the current scope, and a sequence of *TreeEnv* to instantiate the placeholders that are within the lists of the current scope. See [12] for further details.

The semantic function extracts the required substitutions from this structure; it takes an atom (A) and a *TreeEnv*, and returns a string (Str):

$$\mathcal{M}_{\mathcal{A}} : A \rightarrow TreeEnv \nrightarrow Str$$

This is defined by the equations (where $e \in Env$ and $ste \in$ seq $TreeEnv$):

$$\mathcal{M}_{\mathcal{A}}(\ T\ )(\text{tree}(e, ste)) = T$$

$$\mathcal{M}_{\mathcal{A}}(\ <I>\ )(\text{tree}(e, ste)) = \begin{cases} e(I) & \text{if } I \in \text{dom } e \\ undefined & \text{otherwise} \end{cases}$$

$$\mathcal{M}_{\mathcal{A}}(\ L\ )(\text{tree}(e, ste)) = \mathcal{M}_{\mathcal{L}}(\ L\ )\ ste$$

If the atom is a piece of text (a string), then the text is returned. If the atom is a placeholder, then either there is a substitution for the placeholder's variable in the current environment (e) and the substitution is returned, or otherwise and the function is undefined. If the atom is a list, then the list instantiation function is called in the current sequence of environment trees (ste).

Semantics of Expressions. The global environment ($GEnv$) structure, which represents a total template instantiation, builds on the *TreeEnv* structure; ; it comprises a sequence of natural numbers, the selections of the template's choices, and a *TreeEnv* structure, the substitutions of the template's variables:

$$GEnv == \text{seq } \mathbb{N} \times TreeEnv$$

The semantic function for template expressions takes an expression (E) and a $GEnv$ and returns a string:

$$\mathcal{M}_{\mathcal{E}} : E \rightarrow GEnv \nrightarrow Str$$

The equation definitions for expressions made up of atoms (see [12] for choice) is (where $chs \in$ seq $\mathbb{N}$ and $te \in TreeEnv$):[2]

$$\mathcal{M}_{\mathcal{E}}(\ A\ )(chs, te) = \mathcal{M}_{\mathcal{A}}(\ A\ )\ te$$

$$\mathcal{M}_{\mathcal{E}}(\ A\ E\ )(chs, te) = \mathcal{M}_{\mathcal{A}}(\ A\ )\ te \mathbin{+\!\!+} \mathcal{M}_{\mathcal{E}}(\ E\ )(chs, te)$$

If the expression is an atom, then the atom is instantiated in the environment tree (call to $\mathcal{M}_{\mathcal{A}}$ with te). If the expression is an atom followed by another expression, then the instantiation of the atom (call to $\mathcal{M}_{\mathcal{A}}$ with te) is concatenated with the instantiation of the rest of the expression (recursive call to $\mathcal{M}_{\mathcal{E}}$).

---

[2] The operator $\mathbin{+\!\!+}$ denotes string concatenation (defined as sequence concatenation).

3.3   Illustration: Instantiating Templates Using the Semantics

The language definition can be used to instantiate templates. This is illustrated here for the template of the promoted Z ADT:

$$TPADT == \langle P \rangle == [\ \langle ids \rangle : \mathbb{P}\langle ID \rangle; \ \langle st \rangle : \langle ID \rangle \nrightarrow \langle S \rangle \ |$$
$$\text{dom } \langle st \rangle = \langle ids \rangle \land \langle I \rangle]$$

First, the substitution set for the template is specified in the environment e:

$$e == \{ P \mapsto \text{``}Bank\text{''}, ids \mapsto \text{``}accs\text{''}, st \mapsto \text{``}accst\text{''}, ID \mapsto \text{``}ACCID\text{''},$$
$$S \mapsto \text{``}Account\text{''}, I \mapsto \text{``}true\text{''} \}$$

The environment tree and the global environment build upon e. As there are no lists or choices, the sequences of trees and choice selections are empty:

$$t == \mathsf{tree}(e, \langle \rangle) \qquad\qquad g == (\langle \rangle, t)$$

The template is now instantiated by applying the semantic functions:

$\mathcal{M_E}(TPADT)(g)$

$\equiv$ [By defs of $TPADT$, $\mathcal{M_E}$ and g]
$\mathcal{M_A}(\langle P \rangle)(t) + \mathcal{M_E}(== [\ \langle ids \rangle : \mathbb{P} \ \langle ID \rangle; \ \langle st \rangle : \langle ID \rangle \nrightarrow \langle S \rangle \ |$
  $\text{dom } \langle st \rangle = \langle ids \rangle \land \langle I \rangle \ ])(g)$

$\equiv$ [by defs of $\mathcal{M_A}$ and $\mathcal{M_E}$]
$e(P) + \mathcal{M_A}(\text{`` } == [\text{ ''}})(t) + \mathcal{M_E}(\langle ids \rangle : \mathbb{P} \ \langle ID \rangle;$
  $\langle st \rangle : \langle ID \rangle \nrightarrow \langle S \rangle \ | \ \text{dom } \langle st \rangle = \langle ids \rangle \land \langle I \rangle \ ])(g)$

$\equiv$ [by defs of e, $+$, $\mathcal{M_A}$, $\mathcal{M_E}$]
$\text{``}Bank == [\text{ ''} + \mathcal{M_A}(\langle ids \rangle)(t) + \mathcal{M_E}(: \mathbb{P}\langle ID \rangle;$
  $\langle st \rangle : \langle ID \rangle \nrightarrow \langle S \rangle \ | \ \text{dom } \langle st \rangle = \langle ids \rangle \land \langle I \rangle \ ])(g)$

By applying the semantic functions in this way, we obtain:

$\text{``}Bank == [\ accs : \mathbb{P} \ ACCID; \ accSt : ACCID \nrightarrow Account \ |$
  $\text{dom } accSt = accs \land true]\text{''}$

3.4   Testing

FTL's semantics has been tested using the Z/Eves theorem prover, based on its Z definition. The proved theorems demonstrate that the semantic functions when applied to sample templates and instantiations yield the expected Z sentence. Test conjectures were chosen to give a good coverage of all FTL constructs and all possible instances of templates containing those constructs (see [12] for details).
  The derivation presented above is demonstrated by proving the conjecture:

$\vdash? \ \mathcal{M_E}(TPADT)(g)$
  $= \text{``}Bank == [\ accs : \mathbb{P} \ ACCID; \ accSt : ACCID \nrightarrow Account \ |$
    $\text{dom } accSt = accs \land true]\text{''}$

And this conjecture is proved automatically in the Z/Eves prover.

4   The Instantiation Calculus

The semantics of FTL is defined by calculating the string (sentence) that is
generated from a template given an instantiation. The instantiations of the semantics are *total*, that is, there must be substitutions for all the template's
variables and selections for all the template's choices. Sometimes, however, we
may be interested in *partially* instantiating a template, for example, substituting
just one variable in a template and leaving the rest of the template unchanged.

The *instantiation calculus* (IC) of FTL is an approach to transform templates
by taking instantiation decisions on a step-by-step basis. In this setting, a template has been fully instantiated when there no placeholders, choices or lists left;
all instantiation decisions have been resolved.

To have a better idea of the calculus, consider a transformation of the promoted ADT template where the variable P is substituted with "*Bank*":

$$Bank == [\ <ids> : \mathbb{P}\ <ID>;\ <st> : <ID> \nrightarrow <S> |$$
$$\text{dom}\ <st> = <ids> \wedge <I>]$$

This is a more refined template, one in which the decision of substituting the
variable P has been taken. By applying a similar sequence of transformations,
the *Bank* schema would be reached.

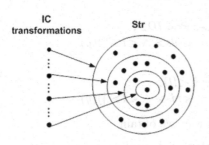

Fig. 2. Templates transformed with
the instantiation calculus and the
sets of strings they denote

The calculus is defined by instantiation
functions, which take a template expression
(E) and a partial instantiation, and return
the template resulting from the partial instantiation of the given template:

$$I : E \rightarrow PInst \rightarrow E$$

Templates refined with the IC are just
like any other FTL template: they denote a
set of strings. As templates are refined with
the calculus, the sets of strings they denote
become smaller and smaller, until they cannot be refined any further and just denote
a singleton set of strings (Fig. 2).

The IC is divided into placeholders, lists and choice. The IC functions, like
in the semantics, are defined by structural induction on the syntax of FTL. The
complete definitions are given elsewhere [12]. The IC was tested, in a similar
fashion to the semantics (see above), by using its Z definition and the Z/Eves
prover. The following presents part of the definition of the IC for placeholders.

4.1   Placeholders

The IC function simply replaces placeholders by a substitution of their variables,
provided that a substitution has been provided. To represent a set of variable
substitutions, the *Env* structure (see above) is reused.

The instantiation function for atoms takes an atom (A) and an environment, and returns another atom:

$$\mathcal{IP}_{\mathcal{A}} : A \to Env \to A$$

This is defined by the equations (where $e \in Env$):

$$\mathcal{IP}_{\mathcal{A}}(T) \; e = T$$

$$\mathcal{IP}_{\mathcal{A}}(\texttt{<}I\texttt{>}) \; e = \begin{cases} e(I) & \text{If } I \in \text{ dom } e \\ \texttt{<}I\texttt{>} & \text{otherwise} \end{cases}$$

$$\mathcal{IP}_{\mathcal{A}}(L) \; e = L$$

If the atom is text then the text is returned. If the atom is a placeholder, then either there is a substitution for the variable in the environment (e) and instantiation takes place, or otherwise and the placeholder is returned uninstantiated. If the atom is a list then the list is returned; lists have their own function.

The instantiation function for expressions takes an expression (E) and an environment, and returns an expression:

$$\mathcal{IP}_{\mathcal{E}} : E \to Env \to E$$

The equations for expressions made up of atoms are:

$$\mathcal{IP}_{\mathcal{E}}(A) \; e = \mathcal{IP}_{\mathcal{A}} \; (A) \; e$$

$$\mathcal{IP}_{\mathcal{E}}(A \; E)e = (\mathcal{IP}_{\mathcal{A}} \; (A) \; e) \; (\mathcal{IP}_{\mathcal{E}} \; (E) \; e)$$

Essentially, the atoms that make the template expression are instantiated recursively for the given set of substitutions (e).

5   Metaproof

The formal definition of FTL and the IC can be used to support metaproof. The approach presented here is developed for Z, but it is more general; the same ideas can be applied to any language with a proof logic.

Metaproof with Z is a proof on a generalisation of a commonly occurring Z conjecture. First, the setting for metaproof with Z is presented, by discussing the link between FTL and Z for metaproof, and by considering generalisation and the concept of characteristic instantiation. Then, the approach is illustrated for the initialisation conjecture of promoted ADTs.

5.1   Linking FTL with Z

FTL is a general language: it captures the form of sentences and makes no assumptions in terms of meaning from the target language. Metaproof, however, requires FTL to be linked with the target language, so that reasoning with template representations makes sense. So, metaproof with Z considers only those templates that yield Z sentences and instances that are *welformed*. In Z, *welformed* means that the sentence is type-correct.

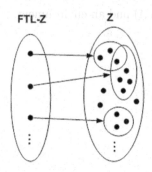

Fig. 3. FTL-Z templates denote sets of Z specifications

Formally, given the syntactic and semantic definitions above, the set of all possible instances of a template is given by the function:

$$S == (\lambda\, t : E \bullet \{gi : GEnv \bullet \mathcal{M}_{\mathcal{E}}(t)\ gi\})$$

The function $\mathcal{ZTC}$ tells whether the given string is a type-correct Z specification:

$$\mathcal{ZTC}_- : \mathbb{P}\, Str$$
$$\mathcal{ZTC}\ s \Leftrightarrow s\ is\ type\ correct$$

Then, the set of all welformed Z instances of a template, a subset of all possible instances, is given by:

$$WFS == (\lambda\, t : E \bullet \{s : S(t)\ |\ \mathcal{ZTC}\ s\})$$

Essentially, this is how FTL is linked with Z for metaproof: through the welformed instances of Z templates. A Z template denotes a set of Z specifications (Fig. 3), the set of all possible type-correct instances.

5.2   Characteristic Instantiation and the Rule of Generalisation

In the process of reasoning with Z templates, there is a point where a switch from the world of templates into the world of Z occurs: a general template formula becomes an instance. This involves a *characteristic* instantiation. For example, in the template formula, $\varnothing \in \mathbb{P}{<}ID{>}$, it is clear that ID must hold a name referring to a set; the sentence would not be type-correct otherwise. So, here, a characteristic instantiation is required: let X be an arbitrary set, instantiate ID with X to give, $\varnothing \in \mathbb{P}\, X$, which is trivially true. The set X is a characteristic instantiation of that formula. In this simple case, only one characteristic instantiation needs to be considered. Other cases require induction (for lists) or case analysis (for choice).

But, when is it safe to conclude the truth of the template statement from the proof of its instance? In formal logic there is a similar problem. Suppose a set A and a predicate P, the truth of the predicate logic statement, $\forall\, x : A \bullet P$, implies that it is true for every value in A. But how can such a statement be proved? We could prove that it is true for each value in A, but this is not practical because it may involve a large or even infinite number of proofs. This is solved by proving that P holds for an *arbitrary* member of A: if no assumptions about which member of A is chosen in order to prove P, then the proof generalises to all members. This is, in fact, a known inference rule of predicate logic called *generalisation* (or *universal introduction*) [9]:

$$\frac{\Gamma \vdash \forall x : A \bullet P}{\Gamma;\ x \in A \vdash P}\ [\forall\text{-I}]\quad [x \notin FV(\Gamma)]$$

The is the principle behind *characteristic* instantiation. An arbitrary instantiation of a template formula is introduced so that the proof of the instance generalises to the proof of the template.

5.3 A Logic for Template-Z

If we just use characteristic instantiation, all we can do with templates in proofs is instantiation. Only when everything has been instantiated can other inference rules be applied in proofs (see [12] for examples of this).

A better approach is to build a logic (a set of inference rules) for proof with template formulas, which extends the logic of the target language. These inference rules are proved in the logic of the target language. [12] defines a draft logic for proof with Z templates.

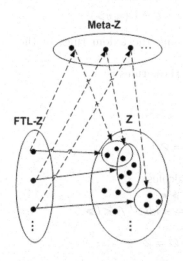

In the template-Z logic, the inference rules of characteristic instantiation are, for now, axioms (unproved), which could be proved by considering a meta-world of Z (Fig. 4), where its objects represent FTL templates of Z and denote sets of Z specifications. For example, the formula, $\varnothing \in \mathbb{P}{<}ID{>}$, can be proved in meta-Z; suppose that in meta-Z there is a universal set, $\mathbb{U}$, of which all sets in a Z specification are a subset of.[3] That formula is interpreted in meta-Z as:

$$\vdash \forall ID : \mathbb{P}\,\mathbb{U} \bullet \varnothing \in \mathbb{P}\ ID$$

Now, by the law of universal introduction,

$$ID \in \mathbb{P}\,\mathbb{U} \vdash \varnothing \in \mathbb{P}\ ID$$

which is trivially true.

The following illustrates metaproof with the template-Z logic, using the initialisation conjecture of the promoted ADT.

Fig. 4. A Z template denotes one meta-Z object and a set of Z specifications. A meta-Z object denotes a set of Z specifications

5.4 Proof with the Template-Z Logic

We now go back to the proof of the initialisation of the promoted ADT to illustrate proof with the template-Z logic.

First, there is an inference rule for characteristic instantiation, which allows a variable to be replaced with a name referring to a set. This transformation uses the IC to replace all occurrences of a variable in a template formula with its substitution. For now, it is an axiom (unproved) of the template-Z logic:

---

[3] In fact, this is precisely the case in the ISO standard semantics of Z [13].

$$\frac{\Gamma \vdash E_1 <S> E_2}{S \in \mathbb{U};\ (\mathcal{IP}_\mathcal{E}(\Gamma \vdash E_1 <S> E_2)\{S \mapsto \text{``}S\text{''}\})\ [S \notin FV(\Gamma)]} \quad \text{[I-S]}$$

An inference rule for Z templates for the schema calculus inference rule $\exists\ Sc$ (appendix A), is also required; given a template representation of a Z schema,

$$<Sc> == [\ <ScD> \mid <ScP>\ ]$$

then the template inference rule is:[4]

$$\frac{\Gamma;\ <Sc> == [\ <ScD> \mid <ScP>\ ] \vdash \exists\ <Sc> \bullet <P>}{\Gamma;\ <Sc> == [\ <ScD> \mid <ScP>\ ] \vdash \exists<ScD> \bullet <P> \wedge <ScP>} \quad \text{[T } \exists\ Sc]$$

We also need the one-point rule (appendix A) for templates:

$$\frac{\Gamma \vdash \exists\ <x> : <t> \bullet <P> \wedge <x> = <v>}{\Gamma \vdash <P>[\ <x> := <v>\ ] \wedge <v> \in <t>\ [<x> \notin FV(<v>)]} \quad \text{[T one-point]}$$

These two inference rules are easily proved by using the axiom rules of the template-Z logic and the logic of Z (see [12]).

The metaproof of, $\vdash?\ \exists\ <P>Init \bullet true$, using these rules is:

$\equiv [\text{by } T\ \exists\ Sc]$
$<P> == [\ <ids> : \mathbb{P}<ID>;\ <st> : <ID> \nrightarrow <S> \mid$
$\quad \text{dom}<st> = <ids> \wedge <I>\ ];$
$<P>Init == [\ <P>\ ' \mid <ids>' = \varnothing \wedge <st>' = \varnothing\ ]$
$\vdash \exists\ <P>\ ' \bullet <ids>' = \varnothing \wedge <st>' = \varnothing \wedge true$
$\equiv [\text{by } T\ \exists\ Sc;\ \text{sequent calculus; propositional calculus}]$
$\vdash \exists\ <ids>' : \mathbb{P}\ <ID>;\ <st>' : <ID> \nrightarrow <S> \bullet$
$\quad <ids>' = \varnothing \wedge <st>' = \varnothing \wedge \text{dom}\ <st>' = <ids>' \wedge <I>$
$\equiv [\text{by } T\ one - point]$
$\vdash \varnothing \in \mathbb{P}\ <ID> \wedge \varnothing \in <ID> \nrightarrow <S> \wedge \text{dom}\ \varnothing = \varnothing$
$\quad \wedge <I>'[<ids>' := \varnothing, <st>' := \varnothing]$
$\equiv [\text{by I-S twice and set theory}]$
$ID \in \mathbb{U};\ S \in \mathbb{U}$
$\vdash \varnothing \in \mathbb{P}\ ID \wedge \varnothing \in ID \nrightarrow S \wedge <I>'[<ids>' := \varnothing, <st>' := \varnothing]$
$\equiv [\text{by set theory and propositional calculus}]$
$<I>'[<ids>' := \varnothing, <st>' := \varnothing]$

And if I is instantiated with *true*, then the formula reduces to true.

6   Discussion

The Z language supports generic structures, but these are not a substitute for templates. Z generics only allow parameterisation with sets. This makes it impossible, for instance, to represent the templates presented here with Z generics.

---

[4] Template inference rules are preceeded by T.

FTL was defined formally with the aim of mechanical metaproof. However, the language became much clearer, we gained a better understanding of what templates are, what can be done with them, and of metaproof, and it also makes the construction of an FTL tool a simple extension of our work so far.

Testing the FTL semantics and IC with the Z/Eves prover helped to uncover many errors. Placeholders are simple and easy to get right, but more complex constructs (such as lists) required a lot more testing to get their definitions right. The consistency between the calculus and the semantics was tested, and a full proof of consistency was not yet done at this stage. In fact, both the IC and the actual semantics give the semantics of FTL: the actual semantics does it in terms of total instantiations, whereas the IC does it in terms of partial instantiations.

As said above, inference rules related with *characteristic instantiation* are, for now, axioms (unproved) of the template-Z logic, which would have to be proved for the logic to be claimed sound. We believe that this is proved by applications of the generalisation rule in a proper meta-world of Z (as discussed in sec. 5). metatheorems capture our experience in proving theorems with instances of some structure; they formalise something done and perceived in practice.

As the example shows, templates may need to be constrained so that useful results can be extracted. So, template design needs to consider what is to be described, and the results to be proved. The most attractive aspect of metaproof is the property *true by construction*. Often, however, metaproof gives a simplification of the original conjecture, which, in many cases, is sufficient to allow the prover to discharge the remaining formula automatically.

Metaproof has been applied to proofs that are more complex than the one presented here. For example, metatheorems for our object-oriented (OO) style for Z [6], such as, initialisation of the whole system (built as composition of components), promoted operations, and composite system operations [12].

The approach presented here was used to build a catalogue of templates and metatheorems for a framework to construct UML-based models [12,14]. Templates capture the form of OO Z models [6], metatheorems capture model-consistency results, so that UML models are represented in Z by instantiating templates, and required consistency conjectures simplified with metatheorems.

7 Related Work

Catalysis [15] proposes templates and hints at variable substitution for instantiation, but this is defined informally. Moreover, its template notation has fewer features than FTL (Catalysis has only placeholders; FTL has lists and choice).

Patterns have been used in the setting of temporal logic [2,3]. These works use *schematic* representations of patterns (similar to logical inference rules); instantiation is variable substituion. However, this has less abstraction contructs than FTL (placeholders only), and mechanisation is not addressed.

The approach behind FTL and the IC is akin to term-rewriting systems [16], which are methods for replacing subterms of a formula with other terms based on rewriting rules. In our approach, the FTL semantics and IC define rules for the substitution of placeholders, lists and choice. Term-rewriting is used to capture the form of objects; *L-Systems* [17], for instance, is a string rewriting system designed to capture the form of plant growth, which has many application in computer graphics. FTL captures the form of formal language sentences.

The term *template* is sometimes used to refer to generics (e.g. C++ templates), which allow parameterisation based on types, and may involve subtyping and polymorphism. Generics are more restricted than FTL templates.

8   Conclusions and Future Work

This paper presents FTL, a language to express templates, a calculus of instantiations for FTL templates and an approach that explores templates of formal models for proof. FTL allows the representation of structural patterns of modelling and proof and their mechanical instantiation. This enables reuse in formal development, which contributes to reduce the effort involved in formal modelling and verification. In our experience, the use of modelling patterns allow us to concentrate more on the problem and less on formalisation issues, and metaproof helps to reduce the proof overhead associated with formal development.

Our approach tries to address several requirements. We want to capture the form of sentences of any language, trying to separate form from content, and use templates for reasoning. So, FTL has a very general semantics, and requires further work to be integrated with some target language for reasoning. There is a separation of concerns: on one side the language to describe form, on the other the approach to reason with those representations. This constitutes a pragmatic and non-intrusive approach, rather than extending a language to support templates, we designed a general language to capture form.

Formal development requires expertise in the use of proof tools. Our approach allows experts to build templates and prove metatheorems (perhaps assisted by proof tools), so that software developers who are not experts in formal-methods can still build formal models that are proved consistent.

Future work will look at completing the proof logic for template-Z, by proving the inference rules that are now laid as axioms of the logic. We also want to add more features to FTL, such as, naming of templates and conditional instantiation. It would be interesting to apply FTL to another formal-method, and then plug a template-logic to enable formal metaproof.

This work lays the ground for tool support for FTL and metaproof. So that users can automatically generate models by instantiating templates of a catalogue, and to simplify conjectures by instantiating metatheorems. It would also be interesting to define a theory for template-Z logic in a prover, such as Proofpower [18], to enable mechanical theorem proving with template-Z.

Acknowledgements. We would like to thank Jim Woodcock for his interesting comments. This research was supported for Amálio by the Portuguese Foundation for Science and Technology under grant 6904/2001.

References

1. Gamma, E., Helm, R., Johnson, R., Vlissides, J. *Design Patterns: Elements of Reusable Object-Oriented Software*. Professional Computing. Addison-Wesley (1995)
2. Darimont, R., van Lamsweerde, A. Formal refinement patterns for goal-driven requirements elaboration. In *SIGSOFT '96*, pp. 179–190. ACM Press (1996)
3. Dwyer, M. B., Avrunin, G. S., Corbett, J. C. Patterns in property specifications for finite-state verification. In *ICSE '99*, pp. 411–420. IEEE (1999)
4. Stepney, S., Polack, F., Toyn, I. Patterns to guide practical refactoring: examples targetting promotion in Z. In Bert, D., et al., eds., *ZB 2003, Turku, Finland*, vol. 2651 of *LNCS*, pp. 20–39. Springer (2003)
5. Abrial, J.-R. Using design patterns in formal developments. In *RefineNet, Workshop of ICFEM 2005* (2005)
6. Amálio, N., Polack, F., Stepney, S. An object-oriented structuring for Z based on views. In Treharne et al. [19], pp. 262–278
7. Amálio, N., Polack, F., Stepney, S. *Software Specification Methods: an overview using a case study*, chapter UML+Z: UML augmented with Z. Hermes Science (2006)
8. Amálio, N., Stepney, S., Polack, F. Formal proof from UML models. In Davies, J., et al., eds., *ICFEM 2004*, vol. 3308 of *LNCS*, pp. 418–433. Springer (2004)
9. Woodcock, J., Davies, J. *Using Z: Specification, Refinement, and Proof*. Prentice-Hall (1996)
10. Saaltink, M. The Z/EVES system. In *ZUM'97*, vol. 1212 of *LNCS*. Springer (1997)
11. Tennent, R. D. The denotational semantics of programming languages. *Commun. ACM*, 19(8):437–453 (1976)
12. Amálio, N. *Rigorous model-driven development with frameworks and templates*. Ph.D. thesis, Dept of Computer Science, Univ of York (2006)
13. ISO. Information technology—Z formal specification notation—syntax, type system and semantics (2002). ISO/IEC 13568:2002, International Standard
14. Amálio, N. Frameworks based on templates for rigorous model-driven development. In Romijn, J., et al., eds., *IFM 2005, Doctoral symposium*, pp. 62–68 (2005). Technical report, University of Eindhoven, CS-05-29
15. D'Sousa, D., Wills, A. C. *Object Components and Frameworks with UML: the Catalysis approach*. Addison-Wesley (1998)
16. Bezem, M., et al. *Term Rewriting Systems*. Cambridge University Press (2003)
17. Prusinkiewicz, P., Lindenmayer, A. *The algorithmic beauty of plants*. Springer (1990)
18. Arthan, R. ProofPower. http://www.lemma-one.com/ProofPower/index/index.html
19. Treharne, H., et al., eds. *ZB 2005*, vol. 3455 of *LNCS*. Springer (2005)

A   Z Inference Rules [9]

$$\frac{\Gamma \vdash \exists\, Sc \bullet P}{\Gamma \vdash \exists\, ScD \bullet P \wedge ScP} \; [\exists\ Sc] \qquad\qquad \frac{\Gamma \vdash \exists\, x : A \bullet P \wedge x = v}{\Gamma \vdash P[x := v] \wedge v \in A} \; [\text{one-point}] \; [x \notin FV(v)]$$

Sc is any schema; ScD is its declarations and ScP its predicate. P is any predicate.

Dynamic Frames: Support for Framing, Dependencies and Sharing Without Restrictions

Ioannis T. Kassios

Dept. of Computer Science, University of Toronto
BA5212, 40 St.George St. Toronto ON M5S 2E4 Canada
ykass@cs.toronto.edu

Abstract. This paper addresses the frame problem for programming theories that support both sharing and encapsulation through specification variables. The concept of dynamic frames is introduced. It is shown how a programming theory with dynamic frames supports both features, without the use of alias control or any other kind of restriction. In contrast, other approaches introduce a number of restrictions to the programs to ensure soundness.

Keywords: framing, object orientation.

1   Introduction

When specifying a piece of computation, we should also specify its *frame*, i.e. the part of the state that it operates upon. Without framing, our specification language is not very useful. For example, suppose that we want to specify that a computation C increments program variable x by 1. In a relational setting like [9], the specification would be

$$x' = x + 1 \tag{1}$$

where the primed identifier x' represents the final value of program variable x and the plain identifier x its initial value. The specification (1) says how C changes x but it says nothing about the effect of C on other program variables. A client which uses more program variables will have trouble using C.

In a non-modular setting like [9], we know all the program variables. We can use this knowledge to add framing requirements to (1). For example, if x, y, z are all the program variables, then the specification becomes

$$x' = x + 1 \ \wedge \ y' = y \ \wedge \ z' = z \tag{2}$$

Modular programming makes it impossible to write such assertions: we do not know all the variables of the program at the time that we specify a computation. In modular programming theories, it is standard to separate the framing specification from the functional specification like that:

$$\textbf{ensures } x' = x + 1 \quad \textbf{modifies } x \tag{3}$$

J. Misra, T. Nipkow, and E. Sekerinski (Eds.): FM 2006, LNCS 4085, pp. 268–283, 2006.
© Springer-Verlag Berlin Heidelberg 2006

The above specification says that the value of x is increased by 1 and that the computation only modifies the program variable x. Its translation into a relational specification depends on the client. For example, if a client introduces variables y, z then (3) is translated to (2) for that client.

Now, let us add encapsulation to the picture: we want modules to support private program variables. We also want them to support public *specification variables*. Specification variables are abstract representations of the encapsulated state that are visible to the client. Their exact relation with the private program variables is known only to the implementer of the module.

One standard example of using specification variables is the specification and implementation of a module that formalizes sets of integers. The module provides an operation that inserts elements into the set and an operation that queries whether an element is in the set. The specification of the module uses a public specification variable S to represent the value of the set. This is the specification of the module as the client sees it:

> **module** *ASpec*
> **spec var** $S \subseteq \mathbb{Z}$
>
> $insert(x \in \mathbb{Z})$ **ensures** $S' = S \cup \{x\}$
> $find(x \in \mathbb{Z})$ **ensures** $S' = S \ \wedge \ return' = (x \in S)$
> **end module**

The client knows nothing about the internal representation of S and how it relates to its private variables.

The implementer's job is to refine the module *ASpec* using concrete program variables and concrete programs. A possibility is to use a private array L to hold all the elements of S. The exact representation of S is given in terms of the private program variable L. The refinement looks like this[1]:

> **module** *AImpl*
> **prog var** $L \in \mathbb{Z}^*$
> **spec var** $S = \{x \in \mathbb{Z} \cdot \ \exists i \in \mathbb{N} \cdot \ x = L\,i\}$
>
> $insert(x \in \mathbb{Z})$ **ensures** $L' = [x]^\frown L$
> $find(x \in \mathbb{Z})$ **ensures** $L' = L \ \wedge \ return' = (\exists i \in \mathbb{N} \cdot \ L\,i = x)$
> **end module**

Framing specifications in this new setting cannot mention the private program variables, which are unknown to the client. They must instead mention public specification variables, like S. For example, the framing specification of the method *insert* should be

> **modifies** S $\hfill$ (4)

---

[1] Of course, this is not yet an implementation, because the operations are not implemented. Further refinements will give an implementation, but this is not the point of this example.

which means that the computation is allowed to change S *and all specification and program variables on which S depends*. In our example, this means that the computation changes S and L. As in the case without specification variables, if a client introduces specification or program variables y, z, the specification (4) is translated to:

$$y' = y \land z' = z \tag{5}$$

since S is not known to depend on y, z. Thus the reasoning on the level of specifications expects that a computation that satisfies (4) preserves y, z.

Unfortunately, in the presence of pointers, the translation may be unsound. This is because, the representation of y may actually share heap locations with the representation of S. For example, y could be given by the following representation:

prog var $p \in pointerTo\ (\mathbb{Z}^*)$
$y = (contentOf\ p)0$

and the pointer p might happen to point to the private array L of module $AImpl$. When that happens, changes to L may change the value of y, contrary to what is predicted by the theory. In our example, our implementation of *insert* will change the value of y, unless the parameter x is equal to the initial value of y. This situation is called *abstract aliasing* [18].

To avoid the problem, existing solutions [18, 20, 16] impose a series of programming restrictions, which guarantee absence of abstract aliasing: if two variables are not known to be dependent then they can be assumed independent. Unfortunately, these solutions come at a price. One problem is formal complication: the theories either introduce new formalisms (universes in [20], packing and unpacking in [16] or a big collection of ad hoc rules [18]). Another problem is inflexibility: the restrictions imposed rule out several useful implementation patterns. These patterns have to do with objects that cross encapsulation boundaries and with sharing.

The contribution of this paper is a formal theory that supports specification variables and pointers without any programming restriction. The basic idea is to make the specification language strong enough to express the property "at the present state the values of x and y are independent", i.e. absence of abstract aliasing. Because this property is expressible as a state predicate, it can be asserted and assumed by the user of the theory at any point where it is needed. This means that it is not necessary for the programming theory to ensure that it is always true and thus to impose any restriction whatsoever. Furthermore, our approach is very simple in that it does not introduce any new formal concept: dynamic frames are a special case of specification variables and they are handled in exactly the same way by the user of the theory.

2   Theory of Dynamic Frames

2.1   Notation

Here we introduce some of the notation to be used in the rest of the paper.

Equality. The operator $==$ has the same semantics as $=$ but lowest precedence. It is used to reduce the number of parentheses in expressions.

Sets and Set Notation. The set of booleans $\{\top, \bot\}$ is denoted $\mathbb{B}$. Set comprehension is denoted $\{x \in D \cdot P\}$ where D is a set and P is a boolean expression with free occurrences of variable x.

If i, j are integers, then the sets $\{i, ..j\}$ and $\{i, .., j\}$ are defined as follows:

$$\begin{aligned} \{i, ..j\} &= \{x \in \mathbb{Z} \cdot i \leq x < j\} \\ \{i, .., j\} &= \{x \in \mathbb{Z} \cdot i \leq x \leq j\} \end{aligned}$$

Functions. Functions are introduced using syntax $\lambda x \in D \cdot B$ where D is the domain and B is the body of the function. Operator Dom extracts the domain of a function. Function application is denoted by juxtaposition. The domain restriction operator $\triangleright$ and the one-point update $\mapsto \mid$ operator are defined by:

$$\begin{aligned} f \triangleright D &= \lambda x \in D \cap \text{Dom } f \cdot f\, x \\ y \mapsto z \mid f &= \lambda x \in \{y\} \cup \text{Dom } f \cdot \textbf{if } x = y \textbf{ then } z \textbf{ else } f\, x \end{aligned}$$

Lists. A *list* L is a function whose domain is $\{0, ..i\}$ for some natural number i called the *length* of L and denoted $\#L$. We can use syntax $[x; y; ...]$ to construct lists. The concatenation of lists L and M is denoted $L^\frown M$. Notation $L[i; ..j]$ extracts the part of the list between indices i (incl.) and j (excl.). The predicate *disjoint* takes a list of sets L and asserts that the sets in L are mutually disjoint. Formally:

$$disjoint\ L \ = \ \forall i \in \{0, ..\#L\} \cdot \forall j \in \{0, ..\#L\} \cdot\ i = j\ \lor\ L\,i \cap L\,j = \emptyset$$

Open Expressions. In this paper, some identifiers *stand for* expressions that may contain free variables. We may say e.g. that E is an *expression* on variables $x, y, ...$ We call such identifiers "open expressions". Although use of open expressions is practiced in some influential formal theories, like for example [10, 1, 9], some people are not comfortable with them. Readers who do not like open expressions, may consider the occurrence of an expression E on variables $x, y, ...$ as a purely syntactical abbreviation of $\overline{E}\ x\ y\ ...$ where $\overline{E}$ is a function.

Let E, t be expressions and x a variable. Then $E(t/x)$ denotes expression E with all free occurrences of x substituted by t.

2.2   Basic Definitions

State and Variables. There is an infinite set of *locations* Loc. Any subset of Loc is called a *region*. A *state* σ is a finite mapping from locations to values. A location in Dom σ is *used* or *allocated* in σ. The *set of all states* is denoted Σ.

A *specification variable* is an expression that depends on the state (i.e. with free occurrences of variable $\sigma \in \Sigma$). Two important specification variables are the set of all allocated locations Used and the set of all unallocated locations Unused, defined as follows:

$$\text{Used} = \text{Dom } \sigma \qquad\qquad \text{Unused} = Loc \setminus \text{Used}$$

For any specification variable v, the expression v' is defined by:

$$v' = v(\sigma'/\sigma)$$

The expression v' is called the *final value of* v.

A *program variable* x is a special case of specification variable whose value is the content of the state at a constant location $addr\_x$, called the *address* of x:

$$x = \sigma(addr\_x)$$

Imperative Specifications. An *imperative specification* is a boolean expression on the state-valued variables $\sigma \in \Sigma$ and $\sigma' \in \Sigma$. The state σ is called the *pre-state* and the state σ' is called the *post-state*. Programming constructs are defined as imperative specifications. The program *ok* leaves the state unchanged:

$$ok \;=\; \sigma' = \sigma$$

If x is a program variable and E is an expression on σ, then the program $x := E$, called *concrete assignment*, is defined by:

$$x := E \;=\; \sigma' = addr\_x \mapsto E \mid \sigma$$

If l is a location-valued expression on σ and E is an expression on σ, then the program $*l := E$, called *pointer assignment*, is defined by:

$$*l := E \;=\; \sigma' = l \mapsto E \mid \sigma$$

If P and Q are imperative specifications, then the specification $P;Q$, called the *sequential composition* of P and Q is defined by:

$$P;Q \;=\; \exists \sigma'' \cdot P(\sigma''/\sigma') \wedge Q(\sigma''/\sigma)$$

If P is an imperative specification, then the specification **var** $x \cdot P$, called *local program variable introduction*, is defined by:

$$\mathbf{var}\ x \cdot P \;=\; \exists addr\_x \in \text{Unused} \cdot P$$

In P, occurrences of the identifier x are abbreviations of expression $\sigma(addr\_x)$. More programming constructs can be introduced; here we present only those used in this paper.

Modules. A *module* is a collection of name declarations and axioms. We introduce a module using syntax **module** N, where N is the name of the module and we conclude its definition using syntax **end module** . Keywords **spec var** and **prog var** declare specification variables and program variables respectively. Syntax **import** M is used to import all names and axioms of module M into the module in which it appears. A module M *refines* (or *implements*) a module N if its axioms imply the axioms of N.

2.3   Dynamic Frames and Framing Specifications

A *dynamic frame* f is a specification variable whose value is a set of allocated locations, i.e. $f \subseteq$ Used. For any dynamic frame f, we define three new imperative specifications. The *preservation* Ξf is satisfied by every computation that does not touch region f. The *modification* Δf is satisfied by every computation that only touches region f or at most allocates new memory. Finally, the *swinging pivots requirement* Λf does not allow f to increase in any way other than allocation of new memory. The formal definitions are:

$$\Xi f = \sigma' \triangleright f = \sigma \triangleright f \qquad \Delta f = \Xi(\text{Used} \setminus f) \qquad \Lambda f = f' \subseteq f \cup \text{Unused}$$

Let f be a dynamic frame. Let v be a specification variable. The state condition f **frames** v is defined as follows:

$$f \text{ frames } v \;=\; \forall \sigma' \cdot \Xi f \;\Rightarrow\; v' = v$$

In a state σ in which this condition is true, we say that f *frames* v or that f *is a frame for* v. When that happens, v depends only on locations in f, i.e. leaving those locations untouched preserves the value of v. There can be more than one variable to the right of **frames** :

$$f \text{ frames } (x, y, ...) \;=\; f \text{ frames } x \;\wedge\; f \text{ frames } y \;\wedge\; ...$$

Framing properties are usually introduced as axioms in a module. The implementer of the module is then obliged to provide a definition for the specification variables and their frames such that the framing property is always true. For example, in the following definitions, Module *CImpl* refines Module *C*.

module C	module *CImpl*
spec var $x \in \mathbb{Z}$, $f \subseteq$ Used	**prog var** $y \in \mathbb{Z}$, $z \in \mathbb{Z}$
f **frames** x	**spec var** $x = y + z$, $f = \{ addr\_y, addr\_z \}$
end module	**end module**

Independence of two variables (absence of abstract aliasing) is expressible as disjointness of dynamic frames. In particular, if f is the frame of x and g is the frame of y and the f, g are disjoint, then the specification variables x and y are independent. If we want to change only variable x, then we frame on f, which guarantees preservation of y (and all other known and unknown specification variables that are independent of x):

$$f \text{ frames } x \;\wedge\; g \text{ frames } y \;\wedge\; disjoint[f; g] \;\wedge\; \Delta f \;\Rightarrow\; y' = y$$

Disjointness of frames is an important property and therefore one we want to preserve. To do that, dynamic frames need to be framed too. We usually axiomatize a dynamic frame to frame itself, i.e. f **frames** $(f, x, ...)$. Given self-framing dynamic frames, a way to preserve disjointness is the conjunction of framing on f with the *swinging pivots requirement* on f. Suppose that g is a self-framing frame disjoint from f. Then $\Delta f \wedge \Lambda f$ preserves the disjointness:

$$disjoint[f; g] \;\wedge\; \Delta f \;\wedge\; \Lambda f \;\Rightarrow\; disjoint[f'; g'] \tag{6}$$

Intuitively, the reason is that Δf preserves g while Λf ensures that f only grows with previously unallocated locations, i.e. with locations that are not in g. The formal proof is found in [14]. Notice that the implementer of $\Delta f \wedge \Lambda f$ does not even have to know g, which makes the property (6) very useful for modular reasoning.

The combination of Δ and Λ is very useful. It is a good idea to give it its own notation. Suppose that:

f **frames** $(f, x, y, z, ...)$

is given as an axiom. Then, we define *abstract assignment* to specification variable x (and similarly for the other specification variables $y, z, ...$) as follows:

$$x := E \;\; = \;\; \Delta f \wedge \Lambda f \wedge x' = E \wedge y' = y \wedge z' = z \wedge \; ...$$

2.4   Objects

Basics. The theory of dynamic frames has already been exposed and it is orthogonal to object oriented programming. However, the examples that we use are based on object orientation so we need some formal support for objects. This section is by no means a complete formalization of object orientation.

There is a set $\mathcal{O}$. The elements of $\mathcal{O}$ are called *object references*. The special value *null* denotes the null reference. It is not included in $\mathcal{O}$.

A *specification attribute* is an expression with free occurrences of the identifiers $\sigma \in \Sigma$ and *self* $\in \mathcal{O}$. A *program attribute* x is a special case of specification attribute such that

$$x = \sigma(addr\_x)$$

for some location $addr\_x$ that depends on *self* but not on σ. The location $addr\_x$ is called the *address* of x. The keyword **spec attr** introduces specification attributes. The keyword **prog attr** introduces program attributes. The definitions for concrete assignment and abstract assignment are valid for program and specification attributes as well

The following abbreviation is introduced to facilitate the access of attributes of object references other than *self*:

$$p.E \;\; = \;\; E(p/self)$$

for object reference p and any expression E that depends on *self*. The notation (.) can be generalized to apply many times: (for any $k \in \mathbb{N}$)

$$[E]^0 = self \qquad\qquad [E]^{k+1} = [E]^k.E$$

We use three specification attributes, the initialization constraint *init*, the invariant *inv* and the representation region *rep*. These specification attributes obey the following axioms for all object references and states:

$$init \in \mathbb{B} \qquad inv \in \mathbb{B} \qquad init \Rightarrow inv \qquad inv \Rightarrow rep \subseteq \text{Used} \qquad (7)$$

For our convenience we specify that the representation region of the null reference is empty:

$$null.rep = \emptyset$$

If o is an object reference, l is an identifier and $x, y, ...$ are values, then $o.l(x; y; ...)$ is an imperative specification called *method invocation* of l on o with parameters $x; y; ....$

Class Specifications. A *class* is a set of object references. The specification of class C is a collection of axioms that begins with **class** C and ends with keyword **end class** . In each axiom, the identifier *self* is implicitly universally quantified over C, and the identifiers σ, σ' are implicitly universally quantified over Σ. Within the specification of C, the identifier *self* represents the *current* object reference. There are usually two kinds of axioms in a class specification: the *attribute specifications* and the *method specifications*.

Attribute Specifications. The attribute specifications axiomatize the specification and program attributes of a class. In a class implementation, the attribute specifications have the form $a = E$, where a is a specification attribute and E is an expression.

Framing properties are attribute specifications. Frequently we assert that the representation region frames itself, the invariant and other specification attributes, i.e.:

$$inv \; \Rightarrow \; rep \; \textbf{frames} \; (rep \, , \; inv \, , ...)$$

There are cases, like *IteratorSpec* of Sect. 3.3, where we do not use such framing.

Method Specifications. Method specifications have the form:

$$\forall x \cdot \forall y \cdot \; ... \; self.l(x; y; ...) \; \Rightarrow \; S \tag{8}$$

where l is an identifier, $x, y, ...$ are data-valued identifiers and S is an imperative specification, called the *body of method* l. The expression (8) is abbreviated by

method $l(x; y; ...) \cdot S$

In a class implementation, S must be a program.

Object Creation. To create a new object of class C, we allocate fresh memory for its representation region and we ensure that its initialization condition is met. This is all done by the specification $x := \textbf{new} \; C$ defined as follows:

$$x := \textbf{new} \; C$$
$$= \Delta\{addr\_x\} \; \wedge \; x' \in C \; \wedge \; (x.init)' \; \wedge \; (x.rep)' \subseteq \text{Unused} \setminus \{addr\_x\}$$

where x is a program variable.

3   Examples

In this section, we present some examples of specification and implementation in our theory. Proofs of correctness are omitted for lack of space; the reader is instead referred to [13] and [14]. Also, for the sake of brevity, we have omitted all queries from the class specifications, because they add nothing to the examples.

3.1   Lists

This example concerns the specification and implementation of a class *List* that formalizes lists of integers. The specification comes in a module named *ListSpec*. It introduces the class *List* and a specification attribute L whose value is the represented list. The frame *rep* frames itself, the invariant and L. The initial value of L is the empty list.

> **module** *ListSpec*
> **class** *List*
> **spec attr** L
> $inv \Rightarrow L \in \mathbb{Z}^* \wedge rep$ **frames** (rep, inv, L)
> $init \Rightarrow L = []$

The method *insert* inserts an item at the beginning of the list:

$$\textbf{method } insert(x) \cdot \; inv \; \wedge \; x \in \mathbb{Z} \; \Rightarrow \; (L := [x]^\frown L)$$

The method *cut* takes two parameters, an address l and an integer *pos*. It breaks the list in two (at the point where *pos* is pointing). The first part of the old list is returned as a result (the address l serves as returning address). The second part is the new value of the current list. The specification of *cut* allows this method to be implemented by pointer operations: in particular, it allows the representation region of the returned list to contain memory that used to belong to the representation region of *self*. The final representation regions of the two lists are disjoint:

$$\begin{aligned} \textbf{method } cut(l; pos) \cdot \\ inv \; \wedge \; l \in Loc \setminus rep \; \wedge \; pos \in \{0, .., \#L\} \\ \Rightarrow \quad \Delta(\{l\} \cup rep) \; \wedge \; L' = L[pos; ..\#L] \; \wedge \; inv' \; \wedge \; \Lambda rep \\ \wedge \; \sigma'l \in List \; \wedge \; (\sigma l.L)' = L[0; ..pos] \; \wedge \; (\sigma l.inv)' \\ \wedge \; (\sigma l.rep)' \subseteq rep \cup \text{Unused} \; \wedge \; disjoint[rep \; ; \; \sigma l.rep \; ; \; \{l\}] \end{aligned}$$

Finally, the method *paste* concatenates a list to the beginning of the current list. The initial representation regions of the two lists must be disjoint. The specification says that the representation region of the parameter may be "swallowed" by the representation region of the current list object. This allows implementation with pointer operations:

method $paste(p)$·
$\quad inv \ \wedge \ p \in List \ \wedge \ p.inv \ \wedge \ rep \cap p.rep = \emptyset$
$\Rightarrow \quad \Delta(rep \cup p.rep) \ \wedge \ L' = p.L \frown L \ \wedge \ inv'$
$\quad\quad \wedge \ rep' \subseteq rep \cup \text{Unused} \cup p.rep$
end class
end module

To implement *ListSpec*, we define a new module *ListImpl*. We use a standard linked list implementation. The nodes are object references with program attributes *val* and *next*, where *val* stores a list item and *next* refers to the next node in list (or is equal to *null* if there is no next node). The list object has a reference *head* to the first node.

module *ListImpl*
  class *Node*
    prog attr *val* , *next*
    $init \ = \ next = null \ \wedge \ val \in \mathbb{Z}$
    $rep = \{ addr\_val, addr\_next \}$
  end class

  class *List*
  prog attr *head*

The specification attributes and the methods for linked lists are implemented as follows:

  spec attr $len \ = \ min\{ i \in \mathbb{N} \cdot \ head.[next]^i = null \}$
  spec attr $L = \lambda i \in \{0, .. len\} \cdot head.[next]^i.val$
  $rep \ = \ \{ addr\_head \} \cup \bigcup i \in \{0, .. len\} \cdot head.[next]^i.rep$
  $inv \ = \quad (\forall i \in \{0, .. len\} \cdot head.[next]^i.val \in \mathbb{Z})$
           $\wedge \ disjoint(\ [\{ addr\_head \}]$
                        $\frown \lambda i \in \{0, .. len\} \cdot head.[next]^i.rep \ )$
  $init \ = \ head = null$

  method $insert(x)$ · **var** n·
    $n := $ **new** $Node$; $n.val := x$; $n.next := head$; $head := n$
  method $cut(l; pos)$·
    $*l := $ **new** $List$
    ; **if** $pos = 0$ **then** ok
    else (**var** $q \cdot \quad \circ l.head := head$; $q := head.[next]^{pos-1}$
                 ; $head := q.next$; $q.next := null \ )$
  method $paste(p)$·
    if $p.head = null$ **then** ok
    else (**var** q·
        $q := p.head.[next]^{p.len-1}$; $q.next := head$; $head := p.head \ )$
  end class
end module

3.2   Sets

This example presents the specification *SetSpec* of a class *Set* that formalizes sets of integers. The class supports an insertion method *insert* and a method *paste* that performs the union of the current set to its parameter. Like its *List* counterpart, the method *paste* allows the current set object to "swallow" part of the representation region of the parameter:

> **module** *SetSpec*
>   **class** *Set*
>   **spec attr** S
> $inv \Rightarrow S \subseteq \mathbb{Z} \wedge rep$ **frames** (S, rep, inv)
> $init \Rightarrow S = \emptyset$
>
>   **method** $insert(x) \cdot inv \wedge x \in \mathbb{Z} \Rightarrow (S := S \cup \{x\})$
>   **method** $paste(p) \cdot$
> $inv \wedge p \in Set \wedge p.inv \wedge rep \cap p.rep = \emptyset$
> $\Rightarrow \Delta(rep \cup p.rep) \wedge S' = p.S \cup S \wedge inv'$
> $\wedge rep' \subseteq rep \cup \text{Unused} \cup p.rep$
>   **end class**
> **end module**

We can implement the class by using an internal list object:

> **module** *SetImpl*
>   **import** *ListSpec*
>
>   **class** *Set*
>   **spec attr** S
>   **prog attr** *contents*
> $inv = contents \in List \wedge contents.inv$
> $\wedge addr\_contents \notin contents.rep$
> $init = inv \wedge contents.init$
> $rep = \{addr\_contents\} \cup contents.rep$
> $S = \{x \in \mathbb{Z} \cdot \exists i \in \{0, ..\#(contents.L)\} \cdot contents.L\ i = x\}$
>
>   **method** $insert(x) \cdot contents.insert(x)$
>   **method** $paste(p) \cdot contents.paste(p.contents)$
>   **end class**
> **end module**

3.3   Iterators

This example shows how the theory handles sharing and friend classes. We specify iterators in a module *IteratorSpec* which imports the *ListSpec* module. An iterator has a list attached to it, given by the value of the program attribute *attl*. It also points to an item in the list, or perhaps to the end of the list. The index of the pointed item is given by the value of the specification attribute *pos*. The representation region of an iterator is disjoint from that of the attached list.

> **module** *IteratorSpec*
> **import** *ListSpec*
>
> **class** *Iterator*
> **prog attr** *attl*
> **spec attr** *pos*
>   *inv*
> $\Rightarrow$ ($attl = null$ $\vee$ ($attl \in List$ $\wedge$ $attl.inv$))
> $\wedge$ $disjoint[rep; attl.rep]$ $\wedge$ rep **frames** ($attl, rep$)
> $\wedge$ ($rep \cup attl.rep$) **frames** inv
>
> inv $\wedge$ $attl \neq null$
> $\Rightarrow pos \in \{0, .., attl.(\#L)\}$ $\wedge$ ($rep \cup attl.rep$) **frames** pos
>
>   *init* $\Rightarrow$ $attl = null$

The class of iterators supports methods for attachment and traversal:

> **method** *attach*(*l*)·
> inv $\wedge$ $l \in List$ $\wedge$ $l.inv$
> $\Rightarrow \Delta rep$ $\wedge$ inv' $\wedge$ $pos' = 0$ $\wedge$ $attl' = l$ $\wedge$ Λrep
> **method** *next*()·
> inv $\wedge$ $pos < attl.(\#L)$
> $\Rightarrow \Delta rep$ $\wedge$ inv' $\wedge$ $pos' = pos + 1$ $\wedge$ $attl' = attl$ $\wedge$ Λrep
> **end class**
> **end module**

The implementation of iterators imports *ListImpl*. This means that the implementer of the *Iterator* class has access to the implementation of the *List* class. This makes *Iterator* a *friend* of *List*. Compare that to the implementation of the *Set* class which imports *ListSpec* and therefore does not have access to the implementation of *List*: the class *Set* is not a friend of *List*. Iterators are implemented as pointers to list nodes:

> **module** *IteratorImpl*
> **import** *ListImpl*
>
> **class** *Iterator*
> **prog attr** *attl* , *currentNode*
> **spec attr** *pos*
>
> inv = ($attl = null$ $\vee$ ($attl \in List$ $\wedge$ $attl.inv$))
> $\wedge$ ($attl \neq null$ $\Rightarrow$ $pos \in \{0, .., attl.(\#L)\}$) $\wedge$ $rep \subseteq$ Used
> $\wedge$ $disjoint[rep ; attl.rep]$
> pos = $min\{i \in \mathbb{N} \cdot attl.head.[next]^i = currentNode\}$

$$rep = \{ addr\_attl , \ addr\_currentNode \}$$
$$init \ = \ attl = currentNode = null$$

method $attach(l) \cdot \ attl := l \ ; \ currentNode := l.head$
method $next() \cdot \ currentNode := currentNode.next$
   end class
 end module

4 Discussion

The theory of Dynamic Frames is part of the more general theory of object oriented refinement that appears in [14]. It is an application of the design principles of *decoupling* and *unification* as advertised in [11, 12]: it decouples the feature of alias control from other formal constructs, like the class, the module or even the object and it unifies frame specifications with functional specifications.

The two important merits of the theory are simplicity and generality. It is formally simple because it solves the problem without introducing any new concept, formalism or axiomatization (dynamic frames are a special case of specification variables). It is general because, unlike competing theories, to guarantee its soundness we do not need to enforce any programming restrictions.

One objection to the theory of Dynamic Frames is that specifications in it may become too verbose. This is always a danger when designing a more flexible system: the extra generality provides more options to the user; thus more things to say. However, there are good ways to deal with this problem. For example, common specification cases may be given their own notation and reasoning laws. Such specifications include the swinging pivots requirement and the abstract assignment. Further notational and reasoning conveniences are found in [14].

4.1 Related Work

Older Approaches. Leino and Nelson's work [18] is a big collection of rules that deal with some of the most frequent cases of the problem. The approach has considerable complexity and it does not address all cases uniformly. Its most drastic restriction is that it forces each method to obey the swinging pivots requirement. This, even in its less restrictive version [5], rules out the implementation for *paste* in Sect. 3.1. In a variant [19], the authors use *data groups* [15] instead of variables in frame specifications. However, absence of abstract aliasing is still not expressible in the specification language and thus the swinging pivots requirement together with other restrictions similar to those in [18] are enforced.

The *Universes* type system [20] is a much simpler and more uniform approach to the problem, also adopted by the JML language [21, 6]. It too imposes restrictions that have to do with objects travelling through encapsulation boundaries. Our implementation for *List* is possible in [20], although somewhat awkwardly, by declaring the node objects "peers" to their containing list object. Our implementation of the *paste* method for *Set* is impossible, because for the peer solution to work, *Set* and *List* should be declared in the same module.

Boogie. A less restrictive variant of Universes is the Boogie methodology [2, 16, 4, 17] used in Spec# [3]. Its most important improvement over Universes is that it allows objects to cross encapsulation boundaries. However, the Boogie methodology has the same visibility restriction concerning "peer" objects as the Universes type system: a class of shareable objects must be aware of all its sharing clients. This causes a modularity problem: the creation of a new sharing client of a class C means that the specification of C must be revised. Moreover, if C happens to be a library class whose specification and implementation cannot be modified, the creation of new sharing clients is not even possible [16].

The Dynamic Frames theory imposes no such restriction and therefore it is more flexible than Boogie. The Iterator example of Sect. 3.3 shows an example of sharing. In this particular example, the class *Iterator* happens to be a friend of the class *List*. This is a coincidence. An example of sharing without friendship appears in the treatment of the Observer pattern in [14].

Separation Logic. The development of separation logic [7, 23] attacks the framing problem from a different more low-level perspective. The idea is to extend the condition language of Hoare logic with a *separating conjunction* operator $\star$, with the following intuitive semantics: condition $P \star Q$ is true if and only if P and Q hold for disjoint parts of the heap. Framing is handled by the following *frame rule*:

$$\frac{\{P\}C\{Q\}}{\{P \star R\}C\{Q \star R\}}$$

where R is a condition that has none of the variables modified by C. The idea is that the implementer of a program C proves the local property $P\{C\}Q$ and the client uses the frame rule to prove the wider property $\{P \star R\}C\{Q \star R\}$ that the client needs. Separation logic handles well many intricate low-level examples with pointers, even with pointer arithmetic, but until recently it has not been considered in the presence of information hiding.

O'Hearn et al.'s work [8] is a first attempt to deal with information hiding in separation logic. The solution does not scale to dynamic modularity, i.e. it deals only with single instances of a hidden data structure [22]. Thus, it is not suitable for the dynamic modularity of object orientation in which the solution must usually be applied to arbitrarily many objects.

Parkinson and Bierman [22] provide a much more complete treatment based on their introduction of *abstract predicates* (very similar to our notion of invariant). However, this work is heavily based on the Frame Rule, which insists on complete heap-separation of the client predicate R from the implementer's predicates P, Q. This is inappropriate in the case of sharing, like the example of Sect. 3.3. A client of the *IteratorSpec* module may hold two iterators attached to the same list object. The representation of their *pos* specification attribute depends on their representation regions as well as the representation region of the shared list object. Thus, the representations of these two specification attributes are not heap-separated. The dynamic frames theory can show that invoking *next* on one of them preserves the value of the other. It is unclear how to do that using the frame rule of separation logic.

5 Conclusion

This paper has introduced *Dynamic Frames*, a simple and flexible solution to the frame problem for programming theories that support both specification variables and pointers. The solution is simple in that it uses the already existing and well-understood formalism of specification variables. It is more flexible than other approaches because it does not introduce any methodological restrictions for the programmer. *Dynamic Frames* is part of the object oriented theory of [14]. The reader is referred to [14] for further notational and methodological conventions, metatheorems and examples.

Acknowledgments. I would like to thank Eric Hehner, Gary Leavens, Rustan Leino, and Peter Müller, the members of the IFIP WG2.3 and the members of the Formal Methods Group of the University of Toronto for valuable feedback concerning the theory, the presentation and the related work.

References

[1] R. Back and J. vonWright. *Refinement Calculus. A Systematic Introduction.* Graduate Texts in Computer Science. Springer-Verlag, 1998.

[2] M. Barnett, R. DeLine, M. Fahndrich, K. R. M. Leino, and W. Schulte. Verification of object-oriented programs with invariants. *Journal of Object Technology,* 2004.

[3] M. Barnett, K. R. M. Leino, and W. Schulte. The Spec# specification language: an overview. In G. Barthe, L. Burdy, M. Huisman, J.-L. Lanet, and T. Muntean, editors, *Construction and Analysis of Safe, Secure, and Interoperable Smart Devices,* volume 3362 of *Lecture Notes in Computer Science,* pages 49–69. Springer-Verlag, 2004.

[4] M. Barnett and D. Naumann. Friends need a bit more: maintaining invariants over shared state. In D. Kozen, editor, *Proceedings of MPC'04: Mathematics of Program Construction,* volume 3125 of *Lecture Notes in Computer Science,* pages 54–84. Springer-Verlag, 2004.

[5] D. L. Detlefs, K. R. M. Leino, and G. Nelson. Wrestling with rep-exposure. Technical Report 156, DEC-SRC, 1998.

[6] W. Dietl and P. Müller. Universes: Lightweight ownership for JML. *Journal of Object Technology,* 2005. To appear. Available on-line at http://sct.inf.ethz.-ch/publications/index.html .

[7] P. O' Hearn, J. Reynolds, and H. Yang. Local reasoning about programs that alter data structures. In *Proceedings of CSL'01: Computer Science Logic,* volume 2142 of *Lecture Notes in Computer Science,* pages 1–19. Springer-Verlag, 2001.

[8] P. O' Hearn, H. Yang, and J. Reynolds. Separation and information hiding. In *Proceedings of POPL'04: Principles of Programming Languages,* pages 268–280, 2004.

[9] E. C. R. Hehner. *A Practical Theory of Programming.* Current edition, 2004. Available on-line: http://www.cs.toronto.edu/~hehner/aPToP/ First edition was published by Springer-Verlag in 1993.

[10] C. A. R. Hoare and J. He. *Unifying Theories of Programming.* Prentice Hall Series in Computer Science. Prentice Hall, 1998.

[11] I. T. Kassios. Object orientation in predicative programming, unification and decoupling in object orientation. Technical Report 500, Computer Systems Research Group, University of Toronto, 2004. Available on-line: http://www.cs.-toronto.edu/~ykass/work/oopp.ps.gz.

[12] I. T. Kassios. Decoupling in object orientation. In *FM'05 World Congress on Formal Methods*, Lecture Notes in Computer Science, pages 43–58, 2005.

[13] I. T. Kassios. Dynamic frames: Support for framing, dependencies and sharing without restrictions. Technical Report 528, Computer Systems Research Group, University of Toronto, 2005. Current version available on-line: http://www.cs.-toronto.edu/~ykass/work/DFcv.ps.

[14] I. T. Kassios. *A theory of object oriented refinement.* PhD thesis, Dept. of Computer Science, University of Toronto, 2006.

[15] K. R. M. Leino. Data groups: Specifying the modification of extended state. In *OOPSLA'98 Conference on Object Oriented Programming Systems Languages and Applications*, pages 144–153. ACM, 1998.

[16] K. R. M. Leino and P. Müller. Object invariants in dynamic contexts. In M. Odersky, editor, *Proceedings of ECOOP'04: European Conference on Object-Oriented Programming*, volume 3086 of *Lecture Notes in Computer Science*, pages 491–516. Springer-Verlag, 2004.

[17] K. R. M. Leino and P. Müller. A verification methodology for model fields. In P. Sestoft, editor, *Proceedings of ESOP'06: European Symposium on Programming*, volume 3924 of *Lecture Notes in Computer Science*, pages 115–130. Springer-Verlag, 2006.

[18] K. R. M. Leino and G. Nelson. Data abstraction and information hiding. *TOPLAS*, 24(5), 2002.

[19] K. R. M. Leino, A. Poetzsch-Heffter, and Y. Zhou. Using data groups to specify and check side effects. In *Proceedings of the ACM SIGPLAN 2002 Conference on Programming Language Design and Implementation (PLDI'02)*, volume 37, 5 of *SIGPLAN*, pages 246–257. ACM Press, 2002.

[20] P. Müller. *Modular Specification and Verification of Object-Oriented Programs.* Lecture Notes in Computer Science. Springer-Verlag, 2002.

[21] P. Müller, A. Poetzsch-Heffter, and G. T. Leavens. Modular specification of frame properties in JML. *Concurrency Computation Practice and Experience*, 15:117–154, 2003.

[22] Matthew Parkinson and Gavin Bierman. Separation logic and abstraction. In *Proceedings of POPL'05: Principles of Programming Languages*, pages 247–258, 2005.

[23] J. Reynolds. Separation logic: A logic for shared mutable data structures. In *LICS'02: Proceedings of the 17th Annual IEEE Symposium on Logic in Computer Science*, pages 55–74. IEEE Computer Society, 2002.

Type-Safe Two-Level Data Transformation

Alcino Cunha, José Nuno Oliveira, and Joost Visser

Departamento de Informática, Universidade do Minho
Campus de Gualtar, 4710-057 Braga, Portugal

Abstract. A *two-level data transformation* consists of a type-level transformation of a data format coupled with value-level transformations of data instances corresponding to that format. Examples of two-level data transformations include XML schema evolution coupled with document migration, and data mappings used for interoperability and persistence.

We provide a formal treatment of two-level data transformations that is *type-safe* in the sense that the well-formedness of the value-level transformations with respect to the type-level transformation is guarded by a strong type system. We rely on various techniques for generic functional programming to implement the formalization in Haskell.

The formalization addresses various two-level transformation scenarios, covering fully automated as well as user-driven transformations, and allowing transformations that are information-preserving or not. In each case, two-level transformations are disciplined by one-step transformation rules and type-level transformations induce value-level transformations. We demonstrate an example hierarchical-relational mapping and subsequent migration of relational data induced by hierarchical format evolution.

Keywords: Two-level transformation, Program calculation, Refinement calculus, Strategic term rewriting, Generalized abstract datatypes, Generic programming, Coupled transformation, Format evolution, Data mappings.

1 Introduction

Changes in data types call for corresponding changes in data values. For instance, when a database schema is adapted in the context of system maintenance, the persistent data residing in the system's database needs to be migrated to conform to the adapted schema. Or, when the grammar of a programming language is modified, the source code of existing applications and libraries written in that language must be upgraded to the new language version. These scenarios are examples of *format evolution* [12] where a data structure and corresponding data instances are transformed in small, infrequent, steps, interactively driven during system maintenance.

Similar coupled transformation of data types and corresponding data instances are involved in *data mappings* [13]. Such mappings generally occur on the boundaries between programming paradigms, where for example object models, relational schemas, and XML schemas need to be mapped onto each other for purposes of interoperability or persistence. Data mappings tend not to be evolutionary, but rather involve fully automatic translation of entire data structures, carried out during system operation.

J. Misra, T. Nipkow, and E. Sekerinski (Eds.): FM 2006, LNCS 4085, pp. 284–299, 2006.
© Springer-Verlag Berlin Heidelberg 2006

Both format evolution and data mappings are instances of what we call *two-level* transformations, where a type-level transformation (of the data type) determines or constrains value-level transformations (of the data instances).

When developing a two-level data transformation system, a challenge arises regarding the degree of type-safety that can be achieved. Two approaches to deal with this challenge are common: (i) define a universal representation in which any data can be encoded, or (ii) merge the input, output, and intermediate types into a single union type. Transformation steps can then be implemented as type-preserving transformations on either the universal representation or the union type. The first approach is simple, but practically abandons all typing. The second approach maintains a certain degree of typing at the cost of the effort of defining the union type. In either case, defensive programming and extensive testing are required to ensure that the transformation is well-behaved.

In this paper, we show how two-level data transformation systems can be developed in a type-safe manner. In this approach, value-level transformations are statically checked to be well-typed with respect to the type-level transformations to which they are associated, and well-typed composition of type-level transformation steps induces well-typed compositions of value-level transformation steps. Unlike the mentioned approaches, our solution does not compromise precise typing of intermediate values.

In Section 2 we present a formalization of two-level transformations based on a theory of data refinement. Apart from some general laws for any transformation system, we present two groups of laws that cater for data mapping and format evolution scenarios, respectively. In Section 3, we implement our formalization in the functional programming language Haskell. We rely on various techniques for data-generic functional programming with strong mathematical foundations. In Section 4 we return to the data mapping and format evolution scenarios and demonstrate them by example. Section 5 discusses related work, and Section 6 discusses future extensions and applications.

2   Data Refinement Calculus

The theory which underlies our approach to two-level transformations finds its roots in a data refinement calculus which originated in [17,19,20]. This calculus has been applied to relational database design [21] reverse engineering of legacy databases [18].

Abstraction and Representation. Two-level transformation steps are modeled by inequations between datatypes and accompanying functions of the following form:

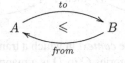

Here, the inequation $A \leqslant B$ models a type-level transformation where datatype A gets transformed into datatype B, and abbreviates the fact that there is an injective, total relation *to* (the *representation relation*) and a surjective, possibly partial function *from* (the *abstraction relation*) such that $from \cdot to = id_A$, where id_A is the identity function on datatype A. Though in general to can be a relation, it is usually a function as well, and functions to and $from$ model the value-level transformations that accompany the type-level transformation.

Since the equality of two relations is a bi-inclusion we have two readings of the above equation: $id_A \subseteq from \cdot to$, which ensures that every inhabitant of datatype A has a representation in datatype B; and $from \cdot to \subseteq id_A$, which prevents "confusion" in the transformation process, in the sense that only one inhabitant of the datatype A will be transformed to a given representative in datatype B.

In a situation where the abstraction is also a representation and vice-versa we have an isomorphism $A \cong B$, a special case of $\leqslant$-law which works in both directions.

Thus, type-level transformations are not arbitrary. They arise from the existence of value-level transformations whose properties preclude data mixup. When applied left-to-right, an inequation $A \leqslant B$ will preserve or enrich information content, while applied in the right-to-left direction it will preserve or restrict information content.

Below we will present a series of general laws for composition of two-level transformations that form a framework for any two-level transformation system. This framework can be instantiated with sets of problem-specific two-level transformations steps to obtain a two-level transformation system for a specific purpose. We will show sets of rules for data mapping and for format evolution.

Sequential and Structural Composition Laws. Individual two-level transformation steps can be chained by sequentially composing abstractions and representations:

$$\text{if } A \underset{from}{\overset{to}{\leqslant}} B \text{ and } B \underset{from'}{\overset{to'}{\leqslant}} C \text{ then } A \underset{from \cdot from'}{\overset{to' \cdot to}{\leqslant}} C$$

Such transitivity, together with the fact that any datatype can be transformed to itself (reflexivity), witnessed by identity value-level transformations ($from = to = id$), means that $\leqslant$ is a preorder.

Two-level transformation steps can be applied, not only at the top-level of a datatype, but also at deeper levels. Such transformations on locally nested datatypes must then be propagated to the global datatype in which they are embedded. For example, a transformation on a local XML element must induce a transformation on the level of a complete XML document. The following law captures such upward propagation:

$$\text{if } A \underset{from}{\overset{to}{\leqslant}} B \text{ then } \mathsf{F} A \underset{\mathsf{F} from}{\overset{\mathsf{F} to}{\leqslant}} \mathsf{F} B \tag{1}$$

Here F is a *functor* that models the *context* in which a transformation step is performed. Recall that a functor F from categories C to D is a mapping that (i) associates to each object X in C an object $\mathsf{F}X$ in D, and (ii) associates to each morphism $f : X \to Y$ in C a morphism $\mathsf{F}f : \mathsf{F}X \to \mathsf{F}Y$ in D such that identity morphisms and composition of morphisms are preserved. When modeling two-level transformations, the objects X and Y are data types, and the morphism f and g are value-level transformations.

Thus, a functor F captures (i) the embedding of local datatypes A or B inside global datatypes, and (ii) the lifting of value-level transformations *to* and *from* on the local datatypes to value-level transformations on the global datatypes, in a way such that the preorder (transitivity and reflexivity) on local datatypes is preserved on the global datatypes. Generally, a functor that mediates between a global datatype and a local datatype is constructed from primitive functors, such as products $A \times B$, sums $A + B$, finite maps $A \rightharpoonup B$, sequences $A^\star$, sets 2^A, etc. By modeling the context of a local datatype by a composition of such functors, the propagation of two-level transformations from local to global datatype can be derived.

Rules for Data Mapping and Format Evolution. In [1] we presented a set of two-level transformation rules that can be combined with the general laws presented above into a calculator that automatically converts a hierarchic, possibly recursive data structure to a flat, relational representation. These rules are summarized in Figure 1. They are designed for step-wise elimination of sums, sets, optionals, lists, recursion, and such, in favor of finite maps and products. When applied according to an appropriate strategy, they will lead to a normal form that consists of a product of basic types and maps, which is readily translatable to a relational database schema in SQL. There are rules for elimination and distribution, and a particularly challenging rule for recursion elimination, which introduces pointers in the locations of recursive occurrences.

While data mappings rely on a automatic and fully systematic strategy for applying individual transformation rules, format evolution assumes more surgical and adhoc modifications. For instance, new requirements might call for the introduction of a new data field, or for the possible omission of a previously mandatory field. Figure 2 shows a set of two-level transformation rules that cater for these scenarios. These rules formalize co-evolution of XML documents and their DTDs as discussed by Lämmel *et al* [12]. Note that the rule for adding a field assumes that a new value x for that field is somehow supplied. This may be done through a generic default for type B, through interaction with a user or some other oracle, or by querying another part of the data.

3   Two-Level Transformations in Haskell

Our solution to modeling two-level data transformations in Haskell consists of four components. Firstly, we will define a *datatype* to represent the types that are subject to rewriting. Secondly, we will extend that datatype with a *view* constructor that can encapsulate the result of a type-level rewrite step together with the corresponding value-level functions. Such encapsulation will allow type-changing rewrite steps to masquerade as type-preserving ones. Thirdly, we define combinators that allow us to fuse local, single-step transformations into a single global transformation. Finally, we provide functions to release these transformations out of their type-preserving shell, thus obtaining the corresponding type-changing, bi-directional data migration functions.

We will illustrate the Haskell encoding with this example transformation sequence:

$$(A + B)^\star \quad \leqslant \quad \mathbb{N} \rightharpoonup (A + B) \quad \leqslant \quad (\mathbb{N} \rightharpoonup A) \times (\mathbb{N} \rightharpoonup B)$$

This is a valid sequence according to rules (2) and (5) presented in Figure 1.

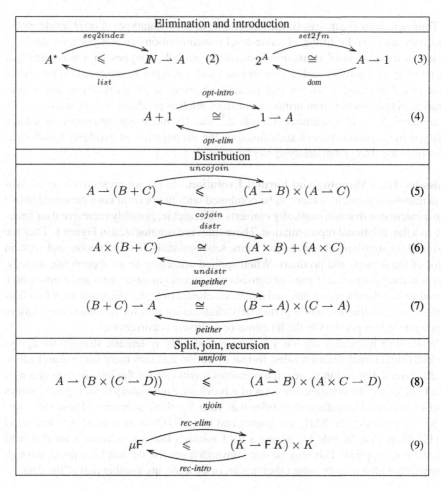

Fig. 1. One-step rules for a two-level transformation system that maps hierarchic, recursive data structures to flat relational mappings. Only the names of type-level functions are given. More details can be found elsewhere [20,21,1].

Representation of Types. Assume that $I\!N$ will be represented by Haskell type *Int*, $A \rightharpoonup B$ by the data type *Map a b* (finite maps from standard library module *Data. Map*), and $A+B$ by **data** *Either a b* = *Left a* | *Right b*. We would like now to define a rewriting strategy that converts type [*Either a b*] to type (*Map Int a, Map Int b*), building at the same time a function of type [*Either a b*] $\rightarrow$ (*Map Int a, Map Int b*) to perform the data migration.

Both type-level and value-level components of this transformation will be performed on the Haskell term-level, and to this end we need to represent types by terms. Rather than resorting to an untyped universal representation of types, we define the following *type-safe* representation, adapted from [8]:

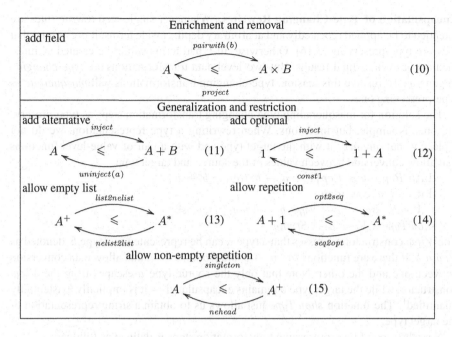

Fig. 2. One-step rules for a two-level transformation system for format evolution. These rules formalize the discussion of XML format evolution of Lämmel *et al* [12].

data *Type a* **where**
  Int :: *Type Int*
  String :: *Type String*
  One :: *Type* ()
  List :: *Type a* → *Type* [*a*]
  Set :: *Type a* → *Type* (*Set a*)
  Map :: *Type a* → *Type b* → *Type* (*Map a b*)
  Either :: *Type a* → *Type b* → *Type* (*Either a b*)
  Prod :: *Type a* → *Type b* → *Type* (*a, b*)
  Tag :: *String* → *Type a* → *Type a*

This definition ensures that *Type a* can only be inhabited by representations of type *a*. For example, the pre-defined type *Int* of integers is represented by the data constructor *Int* of type *Type Int*, and the type [*Int*] of lists of integers is represented by the value *List Int* of type *Type* [*Int*]. The *Tag* constructor allows us to tag types with names.

The datatype *Type* is an example of a *generalized algebraic data type* (GADT) [22], a recent Haskell extension that allows to assign more precise types to data constructors by restricting the variables of the datatype in the constructors' result types. Note also that the argument *a* of the *Type* datatype is a so-called phantom type [7], since no value of type *a* needs to be provided when building a value of type *Type a*. Using a phantom type we can represent a type at the term level without building any term of that type.

Going back to our example, our intended transformation must convert type representation *List* (*Either a b*) into *Prod* (*Map Int a*) (*Map Int b*).

Encapsulation of Type-Changing Rewrites. Whenever single-step rewrite rules are intended to be applied repeatedly and at arbitrary depths inside terms, it is essential that they are type-preserving [3,16]. Otherwise, ill-typed terms would be created as intermediate or even as final results. But two-level data transformations are *type-changing* in general. To resolve this tension, type-changing transformations will *masquerade* as type-preserving ones.

The solution for masquerading type-changing transformation steps as type-preserving ones is simple, but ingenious. When rewriting a type representation, we do not replace it, but *augment* it with the target type and with a pair of value-level functions that allow conversion between values of the source and target type.

> **data** $Rep\ a\ b = Rep\{to :: a \rightarrow b, from :: b \rightarrow a\}$
> **data** $View\ a$ **where**
> $View :: Rep\ a\ b \rightarrow Type\ b \rightarrow View\ (Type\ a)$
> $showType :: View\ a \rightarrow String$

The $View$ constructor expresses that a type a can be represented as a type b, denoted as $Rep\ a\ b$, if there are functions $to :: a \rightarrow b$ and $from :: b \rightarrow a$ that allow data conversion between one and the other. Note that only the source type a escapes from the $View$ constructor, while the target type b remains encapsulated — it is implicitly existentially quantified[1]. The function $showType$ just allows us to obtain a string representation of the target type.

Now the type of type-preserving transformation steps is defined as follows[2]:

> **type** $Rule = \forall a.\ Type\ a \rightarrow Maybe\ (View\ (Type\ a))$

Note that the explicit quantification of the type variable a will allow us to apply the same rewrite step of type $Rule$ to various different subterms of a given type representation, e.g. to both Int and $String$ in $Prod\ Int\ String$. Thus, when rewriting a type representation we will not change its type, but just signal that it can also be *viewed* as a different type.

We can now start encoding some transformation rules of our data refinement calculus. For instance, given value-level functions (see Figure 1):

> $list :: Map\ Int\ a \rightarrow [a]$
> $seq2index :: [a] \rightarrow Map\ Int\ a$
> $uncojoin :: Map\ a\ (Either\ b\ c) \rightarrow (Map\ a\ b, Map\ a\ c)$
> $cojoin :: (Map\ a\ b, Map\ a\ c) \rightarrow Map\ a\ (Either\ b\ c)$

the rule (2) that convert a list into a map, and the rule (5) that converts a map of sums into a pair of maps can be defined as follows:

> $listmap :: Rule$
> $listmap\ (List\ a) = Just\ (View\ rep\ (Map\ Int\ a))$
>   **where** $rep = Rep\{to = seq2index, from = list\}$
> $listmap\ \_ = Nothing$
>
> $mapsum :: Rule$
> $mapsum(Map\ a(Either\ b\ c)) = Just\ (View\ rep\ (Prod\ (Map\ a\ b)\ (Map\ a\ c)))$

---

[1] $View$ is somewhat similar to the folklore **data** $Dynamic = \forall a.Dyn\ a\ (Type\ a)$, which pairs a *value* of an existentially quantified type with its representation.

[2] We model partiality with **data** $Maybe\ a = Nothing\ |\ Just\ a$.

where $rep = Rep\{\,to = uncojoin, from = cojoin\,\}$
$mapsum\;\_ = Nothing$

The remaining rules of Figure 1 can be implemented in a similar way.

The only rule that poses a significant technical challenge is rule (9) for recursion elimination. We will only present an outline of our solution (more details in [5]), which uses the Haskell class mechanism and monadic programming. Firstly, we represent the fixpoint operator μ as follows:

newtype $Mu\ f = In\{\,out :: f\ (Mu\ f)\,\}$
data $Type\ a$ **where**
   ...
$Mu :: Dist\ f \Rightarrow (\forall a.\,Type\ a \to Type\ (f\ a)) \to Type\ (Mu\ f)$

Here f is a functor[3], and the class constraint $Dist\ f$ expresses that we require functors to commute with monads. Rule (9) can now be implemented:

type $Table\ f = (Map\ Int\ (f\ Int),\ Int)$

$fixastable :: Rule$
$fixastable\ (Mu\ f) = Just\ (View\ rep\ (Prod\ (Map\ Int\ (f\ Int))\ Int))$
   where $rep = Rep\{\,to = recelim, from = recintro\,\}$
$fixastable\;\_ = Nothing$

$recelim :: Dist\ f \Rightarrow Mu\ f \to Table\ f$
$recintro :: Functor\ f \Rightarrow Table\ f \to Mu\ f$

Internally, *recelim* incrementally builds a table while traversing over a recursive data instance. It uses monadic code to thread the growing table through the recursion pattern.

Strategy Combinators for Two-Level Transformation. To build a full two-level transformation system, we must be able to apply two-level transformation steps sequentially, alternatively, repetitively, and at arbitrary levels inside type representations. For this we introduce strategy combinators for two-level term rewriting. They are similar to strategy combinators for ordinary single-level term rewriting [16], except that they simultaneously fuse the type-level steps and the value-level steps. As we will see, the joint effect of two-level strategy combinators is to combine the view introduced locally by individual steps into a single view around the root of the representation of the target type.

Let us begin by supplying combinators for identity, sequential composition, and structural composition of pairs of value-level functions:

$idrep :: Rep\ a\ a$
$idrep = Rep\{\,to = id, from = id\,\}$

$comprep :: Rep\ a\ b \to Rep\ b\ c \to Rep\ a\ c$
$comprep\ f\ g = Rep\{\,from = (from\ f).(from\ g), to = (to\ g).(to\ f)\,\}$

$maprep :: Functor\ f \Rightarrow Rep\ a\ b \to Rep\ (f\ a)\ (f\ b)$
$maprep\ r = Rep\{\,to = fmap\ (to\ r), from = fmap\ (from\ r)\,\}$

Using these combinators for pairs of value-level functions, we can define the two-level combinators. Sequential composition is defined as follows[4]:

---

[3] Functors are instances of: **class** $Functor\ f$ **where** $fmap :: (a \to b) \to f\ a \to f\ b$.

[4] For composing partial functions we use the monadic **do**-notation, exploiting the fact that $Maybe$ is an instance of a Monad [23].

$(\triangleright) :: Rule \rightarrow Rule \rightarrow Rule$
$(f \triangleright g)\ a = \mathbf{do}\ View\ r\ b \leftarrow f\ a$
$\qquad\qquad\qquad View\ s\ c \leftarrow g\ b$
$\qquad\qquad\qquad return\ (View\ (comprep\ r\ s)\ c)$

We further define combinators for left-biased choice ($f \oslash g$ tries f, and if it fails, tries g instead), a "do nothing" combinator, and repetitive application of a rule until it fails[5]:

$(\oslash) :: Rule \rightarrow Rule \rightarrow Rule$
$(f \oslash g)\ x = f\ x\ `mplus`\ g\ x$

$nop :: Rule$
$nop\ x = Just\ (View\ idrep\ x)$

$many :: Rule \rightarrow Rule$
$many\ r = (r \triangleright many\ r) \oslash nop$

These combinators suffice for combining transformations at a single level inside a term.

Two-level combinators that descend into terms are more challenging to define. They rely on the functorial structure of type representations and use $maprep$ defined above to push pairs of value-level functions up through functors. An example is the $once$ combinator that applies a given rule exactly once somewhere inside a type representation:

$once :: Rule \rightarrow Rule$
$once\ r\ Int = r\ Int$
$once\ r\ (List\ a) = r\ (List\ a)\ `mplus`$
$\qquad\qquad\qquad (\mathbf{do}\ View\ s\ b \leftarrow once\ r\ a$
$\qquad\qquad\qquad\qquad return\ (View\ (maprep\ s)\ (List\ b)))$
$\ldots$

Note that $once$ performs a pre-order which stops as soon as its argument rule is applied successfully. Other strategy combinators can be defined similarly.

It is now possible to combine individual two-level transformation rules into the following rewrite system:

$flatten :: Rule$
$flatten = many\ (once\ (listmap \oslash mapsum \oslash \ldots))$

which can be successfully applied to our running example, as the following interaction with the Haskell interpreter shows:

$>\ flatten\ (List\ (Either\ Int\ Bool))$
$Just\ (View\ (Rep\ <to>\ <from>)\ (Prod\ (Map\ Int\ Int)\ (Map\ Int\ Bool)))$

Note that the result shown by the interpreter is a $String$ representation of a value of type $Maybe\ (View\ (Type\ (List\ (Either\ Int\ Bool))))$. Placeholders $<to>$ and $<from>$ are shown in place of function objects, which are not printable. Thus, the existentially quantified result type of the transformation is *not* available statically, though its string representation is available dynamically.

Unleashing Composed Data Migration Functions. So far, we have developed techniques to implement rewrite strategies on types, building at the same time functions for data migration between the original and the resulting type. Unfortunately, it is still not possible to use such functions with the machinery developed so far. The problem

---

[5] $mplus :: Maybe\ a \rightarrow Maybe\ a \rightarrow Maybe\ a$ returns the first argument if it is constructed with $Just$ or the second argument otherwise.

is that the target type is encapsulated as an existentially quantified type variable inside the *View* constructor. This was necessary to make the type-changing transformation masquerade as a type-preserving one.

We can access the hidden data migration functions in two ways. If we happen to know what the target type is, we can simply take them out as follows:

> *forth* :: *View* (*Type a*) → *Type b* → *a* → *Maybe b*
> *forth* (*View rep tb'*) *tb a* = **do** { *Eq* ← *teq tb tb'*; *return* (*to rep a*) }
>
> *back* :: *View* (*Type a*) → *Type b* → *b* → *Maybe a*
> *back* (*View rep tb'*) *tb b* = **do** { *Eq* ← *teq tb tb'*; *return* (*from rep b*) }

Again, GADTs are of great help in defining a data type that provides evidence to the type-checker that two types are equal (*cf* [22]):

> **data** *Equal a b* **where**
>   *Eq* :: *Equal a a*

Notice that a value *Eq* of type *Equal a b* is a witness that types *a* and *b* are indeed equal. A function that provides such a witness based on the structural equality of type representations is then fairly easy to implement.

> *teq* :: *Type a* → *Type b* → *Maybe* (*Equal a b*)
> *teq Int Int* = *return Eq*
> *teq* (*List a*) (*List b*) = **do** { *Eq* ← *teq a b*; *return Eq* }
>   ...

In the format evolution scenario, where a transformation is specified manually at system design or maintenance time, the static availability of the target type is realistic.

But in general, and in particular in the data mapping scenario, we should expect the target type to be statically unknown, and only available dynamically. In that case we can access the result type via a *staged* approach. In the first stage, we apply the transformation to obtain its result type dynamically, using *showType*, in the form of its string representation. In the second stage, that string representation is incorporated in our source code, and gets parsed and compiled and becomes statically available after all. Below, we will use such staging in Haskell interpreter sessions.

4 Application Scenarios

We demonstrate two-level transformations with two small, but representative examples.

Evolution of a Music Album Format. Suppose rudimentary music album information is kept in XML files that conform to the following XML Schema fragment:

```
<element name="Album" type="AlbumType"/>
<complexType name="AlbumType">
  <attribute name="ASIN" type="string"/>
  <attribute name="Title" type="string"/>
  <attribute name="Artist" type="string"/>
  <attribute name="Format"><simpleType base="string">
    <enumeration value="LP"/><enumeration value="CD"/>
  </simpleType></attribute>
</complexType>
```

In a first evolution step, we want to allow an additional media type beyond CDs and LPs, namely DVDs. In a second step, we want to add a list of track names to the format.

We can represent the album schema and an example album document as follows:

$albumFormat = Tag$ "Album" (
    $Prod$ (Tag "ASIN" $String$) (
    $Prod$ (Tag "Title" $String$) (
    $Prod$ (Tag "Artist" $String$)
      (Tag "Format" ($Either$ (Tag "LP" One) (Tag "CD" One))))))
$lp = ($"B000002UB2",("Abbey Road",("The Beatles",$Left$ ()))))

With a generic show function $gshow :: Type\ a \rightarrow a \rightarrow String$, taking the format as first argument, we can print the album with tag information included:

> $putStrLn$ \$ $gshow\ albumFormat\ lp$
$Album = (ASIN = $"B000002UB2"$,(\ Title = $"Abbey Road"$,($
        $Artist = $"The Beatles"$, Format = Left\ (LP = ()))))$

This function also ensures us that lp is actually well-typed with respect to $album$ $Format$.

To enable evolution, we define the following additional combinators for adding alternatives, adding fields, and triggering rules inside tagged types:

$addalt :: Type\ b \rightarrow Rule$
$addalt\ b\ a = Just\ (View\ rep\ (Either\ a\ b))$
   where $rep = Rep\{ to = Left, from = \lambda(Left\ x) \rightarrow x \}$

type $Query\ b = \forall a.\ Type\ a \rightarrow a \rightarrow b$
$addfield :: Type\ b \rightarrow Query\ b \rightarrow Rule$
$addfield\ b\ f\ a = Just\ (View\ rep\ (Prod\ a\ b))$
   where $rep = Rep\{ to = \lambda y \rightarrow (y, f\ a\ y), from = fst \}$

$inside :: String \rightarrow Rule \rightarrow Rule$
$inside\ n\ r\ (Tag\ m\ a)$
   $|\ n \equiv m = $ **do** $\{ View\ r\ b \leftarrow r\ a;\ return\ (View\ r\ (Tag\ m\ b)) \}$
$inside\ \_\ \_\ \_ = Nothing$

Note that the $addalt$ combinator inserts and removes $Left$ constructors on the data level. The $addfield$ combinator takes as additional argument a query that gets applied to the argument of to to come up with a value of type b, which gets inserted into the new field.

With these combinators in place, we can specify the desired evolution steps:

$addDvd = once\ (inside\ $"Format"$\ (addalt\ (Tag\ $"DVD"$\ One)))$

$addTracks = once(inside\ $"Album"$(addfield(List(Tag\ $"Title"$String))\ q))$
   where $q :: Query\ [String]$
        $q\ (Prod\ (Tag\ $"ASIN"$\ String)\ _)\ (asin, _) = ...$
        $q\ \_\ \_ = []$

The query q uses the album identifier to lookup from another data source, e.g. via a query over the internet[6]. Subsequently, we can run the type-level transformation, and print the result type:

> **let** $(Just\ vw) = (addTracks \triangleright addDvd)\ albumFormat$
> $showType\ vw$

---

[6] For such a side effect, an impure function is needed.

Tag "Album" (*Prod* (*Prod* (
  Tag "ASIN" *String*) (*Prod* (
  Tag "Title" *String*)(*Prod* (
  Tag "Artist" *String*)(
  Tag "Format" (*Either* (*Either* (
    Tag "LP" *One*)(*Tag* "CD" *One*)) (*Tag* "DVD" *One*))))) (
  List (*Tag* "Title" *String*))))

The value-level transformation is executed in forward direction as follows:

  > **let** *targetFormat* = *Tag* "Album" (*Prod* (*Prod* (...
  > **let** (*Just targetAlbum*) = *forth vw targetFormat lp*
  > *putStrLn* $ *gshow targetFormat targetAlbum*
  Album = ((*ASIN* = "B000002UB2",(*Title* = "Abbey Road",(
        Artist = "The Beatles",*Format* = *Left* (*Left* (*LP* = ()))))),
        [*Title* = "Come Together",...]))

In backward direction, we can recover the original LP:

  > **let** (*Just originalAlbum*) = *back vw targetFormat targetAlbum*
  > *lp* ≡ *originalAlbum*
  True

Any attempt to execute the backward value-level transformation on a DVD, i.e. on an album that uses a newly added alternative, will fail.

Mapping Album Data to Relational Tables. We pursue our music album example to demonstrate data mappings. In this case, we are interested in mapping the hierarchical album format, which models the XML schema, onto a flat schema, which could be stored in a relational database. This data mapping is performed by the *flatten* transformation defined above, but before applying it, we need to prepare the format in two respects. Firstly, we want the enumeration type for formats to be stored as integers. Secondly, we need to remove the tags from our datatype, since the *flatten* transformation assumes their absence. For brevity we omit the definitions of *enum2int* and *removetags*; they are easy to define.

Our relational mapping for music albums is now defined and applied to both our original and our evolved formats as follows:

  > **let** *toRDB* = *once enum2int* ▷ *removetags* ▷ *flatten*
  > **let** (*Just vw0*) = *toRDB* (*List albumFormat*)
  > *showType vw0*
  Map Int (*Prod* (*Prod* (*Prod String String*) *String*) *Int*)
  > **let** (*Just vw1*) = *toRDB* (*List targetFormat*)
  > *showType vw1*
  Prod (*Map Int* (*Prod* (*Prod* (*Prod String String*) *String*) *Int*)) (
    Map (*Prod Int Int*) *String*)

Note that we apply the transformations to the type of *lists* of albums – we want to store a collection of them. The original format is mapped to a single table, which maps album numbers to 4-tuples of ASIN, title, name, and an integer that represents the format. The target format is mapped to *two* tables, where the extra table maps compound keys of album and track numbers to track names.

Let's store our first two albums in relational form:

> let $dbs0 = Map\ Int\ (Prod\ (Prod\ (Prod\ String\ String)\ String)\ Int)$
> let $(Just\ db) = forth\ vw0\ dbs0\ [lp, cd]$
> db
{0 := ((("B000002UB2", "Abbey Road"), "The Beatles"), 0),
  1 := ((("B000002HCO", "Debut"), "Bjork"), 1)}

As expected, two records are produced with different keys. The last 1 indicates that the second album is a CD.

The reverse value-level transformation restores flattened data to hierarchical form. By composing the value-level transformations induced by data mappings with those induced by format evolution, we can migrate from and old database to a new one[7]:

> let $(Just\ lvw) = (addTracks \triangleright addDvd)\ (List\ albumFormat)$
> let $dbs1 = Prod\ (Map\ ...)\ (Map\ (Prod\ Int\ Int)\ String)$
> let $(Just\ x) = back\ vw0\ dbs0\ db$
> let $(Just\ y) = forth\ lvw\ (List\ targetFormat)\ x$
> let $(Just\ z) = forth\ vw1\ dbs1\ y$
> z
({0 := ((("B000002UB2", "Abbey Road"), "The Beatles"), 0),
  1 := ((("B000002HCO", "Debut"), "Bjork"), 1)},
  {(0, 0) := "Come Together", ...})

In this simple example, the migration amounts to adding a single table with track names retrieved from another data source, but in general, the induced value-level data transformations can augment, reorganize, and discard relational data in customizable ways.

5   Related Work

Software Transformation. Lämmel *et al* [12] propose a systematic approach to evolution of XML-based formats, where DTDs are transformed in a well-defined, stepwise fashion, and migration of corresponding documents can largely be induced from the DTD-level transformations. They discuss properties of transformations and identify categories of transformation steps, such as renaming, introduction and elimination, folding and unfolding, generalization and restriction, enrichment and removal, taking into account many XML-specific issues, but they stop short of formalization and implementation of two-level transformations. In fact, they identify the following 'challenge':

> "We have examined typeful functional XML transformation languages, term rewriting systems, combinator libraries, and logic programming. However, the coupled treatment of DTD transformations and induced XML transformations in a typeful and generic manner, poses a challenge for formal reasoning, type systems, and language design."

We have taken up this challenge by showing that formalization and implementation are feasible. A fully worked out application of our approach in the XML domain can now be attempted.

---

[7] Such compositions of *to* and *from* of different refinements are *representation changers* [9].

Lämmel *et al* [13] have identified data mappings as a challenging problem that permeates software engineering practice, and data-processing application development in particular. An overview is provided over examples of data mappings and of existing approaches in various paradigms and domains. Some key ingredients are described for an emerging conceptual framework for mapping approaches, and 'cross-paradigm impedance mismatches' are identified as important mapping challenges. According to the authors, better understanding and mastery of mappings is crucial, and they identify the need for "general and scalable *foundations*" for mappings. Our formalization of two-level data transformation provides such foundations.

Generic Functional Programming. Type-safe combinators for strategic rewriting were introduced by Lämmel *et al* in [16], after which several simplified and generalized approaches were proposed [15,14,8]. These approaches cover type-preserving transformations (input and output types are the same), and type-unifying ones (all input types mapped to a single output type), but not *type-changing* ones.

Atanassow *et al* show how canonical isomorphisms (corresponding to laws for zeros, units, and associativity) between types can induce the value-level conversion functions [2]. They provide an encoding in the polytypic programming language Generic Haskell involving a universal representation of types, and demonstrate how it can be applied to mappings between XML Schema and Haskell datatypes. Recursive datatypes are not addressed. Beyond canonical isomorphisms, a few limited forms of refinement are also addressed, but these induce single-directional conversion functions only. A fixed strategy for normalization of types is used to discover isomorphisms and generate their corresponding conversion functions. By contrast, our type-changing two-level transformations encompass a larger class of isomorphism and refinements, and their compositions are not fixed, but definable with two-level strategy combinators. This allows us to address more scenarios such as format evolution, data cleansing, hierarchical-relational mappings, and database re-engineering. We stay within Haskell rather than resorting to Generic Haskell, and avoid the use of a universal representation.

Bi-directional Programming. Foster *et al* tackle the *view-update problem* for databases with *lenses*: combinators for bi-directional programming [6]. Each lens connects a concrete representation C with an abstract view A on it by means of two functions *get* : $C{\rightarrow}A$ and *put* : $A{\times}C{\rightarrow}C$. Thus, *get* and *put* are similar to our *from* and *to*, except for *put*'s additional argument of type C. Also, an additional law on these functions guarantees that *put* can be used to reconstruct an updated C from an updated A.

On the level of problem statement, a basic difference exists between lenses and two-level transformations (or data refinements). In refinement, a (previously unknown) concrete representation is intended to be derived by calculation from an abstract one, while lenses start from a concrete representation on which one or more abstract views are then explicitly defined. This explains why some ingredients of our solution, such as representation of types at the value level, statically unkown types, and combinators for strategic rewriting, are absent in bi-directional programming.

6 Future Work

We have provided a type-safe formalization of two-level data transformations, and we have shown its implementation in Haskell, using various generic programming techniques. We discuss some current limitations and future efforts to remove them.

Co-transformation. Cleve *et al* use the term 'co-transformation' for the process of re-engineering three kinds of artifacts simultaneously: a database schema, database contents, and application programs linked to the database [4]. Currently, our approach formalizes the use of *wrappers* for this purpose, where the application program gets pre- and post-fixed by induced value-level data migration functions. We intend to extend our approach to formalize induction of actual application program transformations, without resorting to wrappers.

Coupled Transformations. Lämmel [11,10] identifies *coupled transformation*, where 'nets' of software artifacts are transformed simultaneously, as an important research challenge. Format evolution, data-mapping, and co-transformations are instances where two or three transformations are coupled. We believe that our formalization provides an important step towards a better grasp of this challenge.

Bi-directional Programming. Among the outstanding problems in bi-directional programming are decidable type checking and type inference, automatic optimization of bi-directional programs, lens inference from given abstract and concrete formats, and support for proving lens properties. We aim to leverage the techniques we used for two-level transformations for these purposes.

Front-Ends. Work is underway to develop front-ends that convert between our type-representations and formats such as XML Schemas, SQL database schemas, and nominal user-defined Haskell types.

Acknowledgments. Thanks to Bruno Oliveira for inspiring discussions on GADTs. The work reported in this paper was supported by *Fundação para a Ciência e a Tecnologia*, grant number POSI/ICHS/44304/2002.

References

1. T.L. Alves, P.F. Silva, J. Visser, and J.N. Oliveira. Strategic term rewriting and its application to a VDM-SL to SQL conversion. In J. Fitzgerald, IJ. Hayes, and A. Tarlecki, editors, *Proc. Int. Symposium of Formal Methods Europe*, volume 3582 of *LNCS*, pages 399–414. Springer, 2005.
2. F. Atanassow and J. Jeuring. Inferring type isomorphisms generically. In D. Kozen, editor, *Proc. 7th Int. Conference on Mathematics of Program Construction*, volume 3125 of *LNCS*, pages 32–53. Springer, 2004.
3. M.v.d Brand, P. Klint, and J. Vinju. Term rewriting with type-safe traversal functions. *ENTCS*, 70(6), 2002.
4. A. Cleve, J. Henrard, and J.-L. Hainaut. Co-transformations in information system reengineering. *ENTCS*, 137(3):5–15, 2005.

5. A. Cunha, J.N. Oliveira, and J.Visser. Type-safe two-level data transformation – with dere-cursivation and dynamic typing. Technical Report DI-PURe-06.03.01, Univ. Minho, 2006.
6. J.N. Foster et al. Combinators for bi-directional tree transformations: a linguistic approach to the view update problem. In *Proc. 32nd ACM SIGPLAN-SIGACT Symposium on Principles of Programming Languages*, pages 233–246. ACM Press, 2005.
7. R. Hinze. Fun with phantom types. In J. Gibbons and O. de Moor, editors, *The Fun of Programming*, pages 245–262. Palgrave, 2003.
8. R. Hinze, A. Löh, and B. Oliveira. "Scrap your boilerplate" reloaded. In *Proc. 8th Int. Symposium on Functional and Logic Programming*, volume 3945 of *LNCS*, pages 13–29. Springer, 2006.
9. G. Hutton and E. Meijer. Back to Basics: Deriving Representation Changers Functionally. *Journal of Functional Programming*, 6(1):181–188, January 1996.
10. R. Lämmel. Coupled Software Transformations (Extended Abstract). In *First International Workshop on Software Evolution Transformations*, November 2004.
11. R. Lämmel. Transformations everywhere. *Sci. Comput. Program.*, 52:1–8, 2004. Guest editor's introduction to special issue on program transformation.
12. R. Lämmel and W. Lohmann. Format Evolution. In *Proc. 7th Int. Conf. on Reverse Engineering for Information Systems*, volume 155 of *books@ocg.at*, pages 113–134. OCG, 2001.
13. R. Lämmel and E. Meijer. Mappings make data processing go 'round. In R. Lämmel, J. Saraiva, and J. Visser, editors, *Proc. Int. Summer School on Generative and Transformational Techniques in Software Engineering, Braga, Portugal, July 4–8, 2005*, LNCS. Springer, 2006. To appear.
14. R. Lämmel and S. Peyton Jones. Scrap your boilerplate: a practical design pattern for generic programming. In *Proc. ACM SIGPLAN Workshop on Types in Language Design and Implementation*, pages 26–37. ACM Press, March 2003.
15. R. Lämmel and J. Visser. Strategic polymorphism requires just two combinators! Technical Report cs.PL/0212048, arXiv, December 2002. An early version was published in the informal preproceedings IFL 2002.
16. R. Lämmel and J. Visser. Typed combinators for generic traversal. In *Proc. Practical Aspects of Declarative Programming*, volume 2257 of *LNCS*, pages 137–154. Springer, January 2002.
17. C. Morgan and P.H. B. Gardiner. Data refinement by calculation. *Acta Informatica*, 27:481–503, 1990.
18. F.L. Neves, J.C. Silva, and J.N. Oliveira. Converting Informal Meta-data to VDM-SL: A Reverse Calculation Approach . In *VDM in Practice! A Workshop co-located with FM'99: The World Congress on Formal Methods, Toulouse, France*, September 1999.
19. J.N. Oliveira. A reification calculus for model-oriented software specification. *Formal Aspects of Computing*, 2(1):1–23, April 1990.
20. J.N. Oliveira. Software reification using the SETS calculus. In T. Denvir, C.B. Jones, and R.C. Shaw, editors, *Proc. of the BCS FACS 5th Refinement Workshop, Theory and Practice of Formal Software Development*, pages 140–171. Springer, 1992.
21. J.N. Oliveira. Calculate databases with 'simplicity', September 2004. Presentation at the IFIP WG 2.1 #59 Meeting, Nottingham, UK.
22. S. Peyton Jones, G. Washburn, and S. Weirich. Wobbly types: type inference for generalised algebraic data types. Technical Report MS-CIS-05-26, Univ. of Pennsylvania, July 2004.
23. P. Wadler. The essence of functional programming. In *Proc. 19th ACM SIGPLAN-SIGACT Symposium on Principles of Programming Languages*, pages 1–14. ACM Press, 1992.

Feature Algebra

Peter Höfner[1,*], Ridha Khedri[2,**], and Bernhard Möller[1]

[1] Institut für Informatik, Universität Augsburg
D-86135 Augsburg, Germany
{hoefner, moeller}@informatik.uni-augsburg.de
[2] Department of Computing and Software, McMaster University
Canada L8S 4L7, Hamilton, Ontario
khedri@mcmaster.ca

Abstract. Based on experience from the hardware industry, *product families* have entered the software development process as well, since software developers often prefer not to build a single product but rather a family of similar products that share at least one common functionality while having well-identified variabilities. Such shared commonalities, also called *features*, reach from common hardware parts to software artefacts such as requirements, architectural properties, components, middleware, or code. We use idempotent semirings as the basis for a *feature algebra* that allows a formal treatment of the above notions as well as calculations with them. In particular models of feature algebra the elements are sets of products, i.e. product families. We extend the algebra to cover product lines, refinement, product development and product classification. Finally we briefly describe a prototype implementation of one particular model.

1   Introduction

Software development models relate, in general, to the development of single software systems from the requirements stage to the maintenance one. This classical method of developing software is described in [13] as *sequential completion*. There, a particular system is developed completely to the delivery stage; only after that similar systems are developed by keeping large parts of the working system and changing relatively small parts of it. Contrarily, in [13], Parnas introduces the notion of *program family* and defines it as follows:

> "We consider a set of programs to constitute a *family*, whenever it is worthwhile to study programs from the set by *first* studying the common properties of the set and *then* determining the special properties of the individual family members."

---

* This research was supported by DFG (German Research Foundation).
** This research was supported by Natural Sciences and Engineering Research Council of Canada.

J. Misra, T. Nipkow, and E. Sekerinski (Eds.): FM 2006, LNCS 4085, pp. 300–315, 2006.
© Springer-Verlag Berlin Heidelberg 2006

Parnas also proposes a design process for the concurrent development of the members of a program family. Since his paper [13], the notion of product family has gained a lot of attention and has found its way into the software development process in industry [14]. Indeed, software developers that are pressured by the increase in the speed of time-to-market and the necessity of launching new products do not build a single product but a family of similar products that share at least one common functionality and have well identified variabilities [5]. Their goal is to target many market segments or domains. Also, in the competitive market of today, they cannot afford to decline a request from a client who wants a special variant that is slightly different from the company's other products. In this situation, the company would have advantage in gathering the requirements for and designing families of software systems instead of single software systems. For example, in embedded system development, software depends on hardware and the developer needs to change software specifications frequently because of hardware specification changes. Hence, the developer ends up with many variations of the intended system that need to be managed. Prioritising development tasks and planning them become very challenging. A model that helps to capture the variabilities and commonalities of the members of a system family would be very helpful in dealing with these difficulties.

The concept of software product family comes from the hardware industry. There, hardware product lines allow manufacturing several variants of products, which leads to a significant reduction of operational costs. The paradigm of *product line* has been transferred to the software embedded in the products. To cope with a large number of software variants needed by an industrial product line, the software industry has been organising its software assets in software product families [14]. Hence, plainly, a *product family* can be defined as a set of products that share common hardware or software artefacts such as requirements, architectural properties, components, middleware, or code. In the remainder, we denote by *feature* any of these artefacts. We note that, according to [15], a feature is a conceptual characteristic that is visible to stakeholders (e.g., users, customers, developers, managers, etc.). A subfamily of a family F is a subset whose elements share more features than are shared by all the members of F. Sometimes, for practical reasons, a specific software subfamily is called a *product line*. For instance, in a context of software development based on the family approach, a subfamily is called a *product line* when its members have a common managed set of features that satisfy the specific needs of a particular market segment or mission and that are developed from a common set of a core assets in a prescribed way [5,15]. Therefore, factors other than the structure of the members of a family are involved in defining a product line.

The family-oriented software development is based on the assumption that it is possible to predict the changes that are likely to be performed on a system. This assumption is true in most of the cases. For instance, the manufacturers of robots (and their embedded software) know from the start that customers will want to have robots with several basic means of locomotion, such as treads, wheels, or legs and with several navigation systems which are more or less sophisticated.

The aim of the present paper is to underpin these ideas with a formalism that allows a mathematically precise description of product families as well as calculations with them. To this end we propose an algebra that we use to describe and analyse the commonalities and variabilities of a system family.

Since systems are characterised by their features, we call our approach *feature algebra*. We will present models where elements of feature algebras are sets of products, i.e. product families. Starting from idempotent semirings, we will define feature algebra in Section 4, extend it to cover product lines, refinements, product development and product classification. This approach allows compact and precise algebraic manipulations and calculations on these structures.

2   Literature Review

In the literature, we find several feature-driven processes for the development of software system families that propose models to describe the commonalities and variabilities of a system family. For brevity, we focus on the key processes relevant to the family description technique that we propose: Feature-Oriented Domain Analysis (FODA) [10], Feature-Oriented Reuse Method (FORM) [11], Featured Reuse-Driven Software Engineering Business (FeatuRSEB) [8] and Generative Programming (GP) [6]. The reader can find other feature modelling techniques in [2].

FODA uses feature models which are the means to give the mandatory, optional and alternative concepts within a domain [10,15]. For example, in a car, we have a transmission system as a mandatory feature, and an air conditioning as an optional feature. However, the transmission system can either be manual or automatic. These two feature-options (manual and automatic) are said to be alternative features. The part of the FODA feature model most related to our work is the *feature diagram*. It constitutes a tree of features and captures the above relationships (i.e., mandatory, optional, and alternative) among features.

In [15], the authors propose the use of feature diagrams which are trees. Each feature may be annotated with a weight giving a kind of priority assigned to it. Then, they use basic concepts of fuzzy set theory to model variability in software product lines.

FORM starts with an analysis of commonalities among applications in a particular domain in terms of services, operating environments, domain technologies and implementation techniques. Then a model called *feature model* is constructed to capture commonalities as an AND/OR graph [12, pages 40-41& 99-100]. The AND nodes in this graph indicate mandatory features and OR nodes indicate alternative features selectable for different applications. The model is then used to derive parameterised reference architectures and appropriate reusable components instantiable during application development [11].

In FeatuRSEB, the feature model is represented by a graph (not necessary a tree) of features. The edges are mainly UML dependence relationships: *composed_of*, *optional_feature* and *alternative_relationship*. The graph enables to specify the *requires* and *mutual exclusion* constraints. The feature model in FeatuRSEB can be seen as an improvement of the model of FODA.

GP is a software engineering paradigm based on modelling of software system families. Its feature modelling aims to capture commonalities and variation points within the family. A feature model is represented by a hierarchically arranged diagram where a parent feature is composed of a combination of some or all of its children. A vertex parent feature and its children in this diagram can have one of the following relationships [6]:

- And: indicates that all children must be considered in the composition of the parent feature;
- Alternative: indicates that only one child forms the parent feature;
- Or: indicates that one or more children features can be involved in the composition of the parent feature (a cardinality (n, m) can be added where n gives a minimum number of features and m gives the maximum number of features that can compose the parent);
- Mandatory: indicates that children features are required;
- Optional: indicates that children features are optional.

3 Example of a Simple Product Family

The following example is adapted from a case study given in [4]. An electronic company might have a family of three product lines: mp3 Players, DVD Players and Hard Disk Recorders. Table 1 presents the commonalities and the variability of this family. All its members share the list of features given in the *Commonalities* column. A member can have some mandatory features and might have some optional features that another member of the same product line lacks. For instance, we can have a *DVD Player* that is able to play music CDs while another does not have this feature. However, all the DVD players of the *DVD Player* product line must have the *Play DVD* feature. Also, it is possible to have a DVD player that is able to play several DVDs simultaneously.

Table 1. Commonalities and variability of a set of product lines

Product line	Mandatory	Optional	Commonalities
mp3 Player	– Play mp3 files	– Record mp3 files	– Audio equaliser – Video algorithms for DVD players and hard disk recorders – Dolby surround (advanced audio features)
DVD Player	– Play DVD	– Play music CD – View pictures from picture CD – Burn CD – Play n additional DVDs at the same time	
Hard Disk Recorder		– mp3 player – organise mp3 files	

We see that there are at least two different models of DVD players described. But how many different models are described in Table 1? And what are the properties/features of these products? Later on we will give the answer to these two questions. If we had a model which gives us all combinations of features we would be able to build new products. Vice versa, such a model would allow us to calculate commonalities of a given set of products.

4   Algebraic Structure and Basic Properties

In this section we introduce the algebraic structure of feature algebra. Since it is based on semirings we will first present these. Afterwards, we will define product families, feature algebra, a refinement relation on feature algebra and, in a set based model, features and products. In Section 6 the latter two are defined in general.

Definition 4.1. A *semiring* is a quintuple $(S, +, 0, \cdot, 1)$ such that $(S, +, 0)$ is a commutative monoid and $(S, \cdot, 1)$ is a monoid such that $\cdot$ distributes over $+$ and 0 is an annihilator, i.e., $0 \cdot a = 0 = a \cdot 0$. The semiring is *commutative* if $\cdot$ is commutative and it is *idempotent* if $+$ is idempotent, i.e., $a + a = a$. In the latter case the relation $a \le b \Leftrightarrow_{df} a + b = b$ is a partial order, i.e., a reflexive, antisymmetric and transitive relation, called the *natural order* on S. It has 0 as its least element. Moreover, $+$ and $\cdot$ are isotone with respect to $\le$.

In our current context, $+$ can be interpreted as a choice between optionalities of products and features and $\cdot$ as their composition or mandatory presence. An important example of an idempotent (but not commutative) semiring is REL, the algebra of binary relations over a set under relational composition. More details about (idempotent) semirings and examples of their relevance to computer science can be found,e.g., in [7].

For abbreviation and to handle the given case studies, we call an idempotent commutative semiring a *feature algebra*. Its elements are termed *product families* and can be considered as abstractly representing sets of products each of which is composed of a number of features. On every feature algebra we can define a relation that expresses that one product family refines another in a certain sense.

Example 4.2. Let $\mathbb{F}$ be a set of arbitrary elements that we call *features*. Often, features can be seen as basic properties of products. Therefore we call a collection (set) of features a *product*. The set of all possible products is $\mathbb{P} =_{df} \mathcal{P}(\mathbb{F})$, the power set or set of all subsets of $\mathbb{F}$. A collection of products (an element of $\mathcal{P}(\mathbb{P})$) is called *product family*. Note that according to this general definition the members of a product family need not have common features. Commonalities will be discussed in Section 6.

For example, looking at the DVD example of Table 1, an mp3 player is a product with the features 'play mp3 files', 'record mp3 files', 'audio visualiser' and so on.

We use the following abbreviations:

Abbreviations:	
p_mp3	Play mp3 files
r_mp3	Record mp3 files
c_1	Audio equaliser
c_2	Video algorithms
c_3	Dolby surround

Now we can describe the mp3 players algebraically as

$$mp3\_player = p\_mp3 \cdot (r\_mp3 + 1) \cdot c_1 \cdot c_2 \cdot c_3 \,.$$

Here $1 = \{\emptyset\}$ denotes the family consisting just of the empty product that has no features, so that $(r\_mp3 + 1)$ expresses optionality of r_mp3. For clarity the algebraic notation omits the set brackets.

We now formally define the operation $\cdot$ which is a composition or a merging operator for all features:

$$\cdot : \mathcal{P}(\mathbb{P}) \times \mathcal{P}(\mathbb{P}) \to \mathcal{P}(\mathbb{P})$$
$$P \cdot Q = \{p \cup q : p \in P, q \in Q\} \,.$$

The second operation $+$ offers a choice between products of different product families:

$$+ : \mathcal{P}(\mathbb{P}) \times \mathcal{P}(\mathbb{P}) \to \mathcal{P}(\mathbb{P})$$
$$P + Q = P \cup Q \,,$$

With these definitions the structure

$$\mathbb{PFS} =_{df} (\mathcal{P}(\mathbb{P}), +, \emptyset, \cdot, \{\emptyset\})$$

forms a feature algebra called *product family algebra*. The set-based model does not allow multiple occurrences of the same feature in a product. If this is desired, one can use an analogous model that employs multisets (also called bags) of features. This bag-based model is denoted by $\mathbb{PFB}$.   □

Using feature algebra offers abstraction from set-theory. On the one hand it provides a common structure that subsumes $\mathbb{PFB}$ and $\mathbb{PFS}$ and on the other hand it avoids many set-theoretic notations, like accumulations of braces, and emphasises the relevant aspects like commonalities.

The *refinement relation* $\sqsubseteq$ on a feature algebra is defined as

$$a \sqsubseteq b \Leftrightarrow_{df} \exists\, c : a \le b \cdot c \,.$$

As an example we use again the DVD product line. A standard mp3-player that can only play mp3 files is refined by a mp3-recorder that can play and record mp3 files. In the algebraic setting this behaviour is expressed by

$$p\_mp3 \cdot r\_mp3 \cdot c_1 \cdot c_2 \cdot c_3 \sqsubseteq p\_mp3 \cdot c_1 \cdot c_2 \cdot c_3 \,.$$

It is easy to see that the refinement relation is a preorder, i.e., a reflexive and transitive relation. Informally, $a \sqsubseteq b$ means that every product in a has at least all the features of some product in b, but possibly additional ones.

Further examples for feature algebras are all lattices with join as $+$ and meet as $\cdot$ operation. In this case the refinement relation is the same as the natural order (which coincides with the lattice order).

Until now we have not made use of the commutativity of multiplication. Most of the following basic properties hold only if $\cdot$ is commutative. In the context of our case studies and the corresponding algebras IPFS and IPFB the commutativity is significant, since products and product families should not depend on the ordering of features.

Lemma 4.3. *Let a, b, c be elements of a feature algebra, then we have*

$$a \leq b \Rightarrow a \sqsubseteq b , \tag{1}$$

$$a \cdot b \sqsubseteq b , \tag{2}$$

$$a \sqsubseteq a + b , \tag{3}$$

$$a \sqsubseteq b \Rightarrow a + c \sqsubseteq b + c , \tag{4}$$

$$a \sqsubseteq b \Rightarrow a \cdot c \sqsubseteq b \cdot c , \tag{5}$$

$$a \sqsubseteq 0 \Leftrightarrow a \leq 0 , \tag{6}$$

$$0 \sqsubseteq a \sqsubseteq 1 . \tag{7}$$

Proof. (1) Set $c = 1$ in the definition of $\sqsubseteq$.

(2) $a \cdot b \sqsubseteq b \Leftrightarrow \exists c : a \cdot b \leq b \cdot c \Leftarrow a \cdot b \leq b \cdot a \Leftrightarrow$ true .

The last step only holds if $\cdot$ is commutative.

(3) Immediate from $a \leq a + b$ and (1).

(4) Suppose $a \sqsubseteq b$, say $a \leq b \cdot d$. Then by isotony

$$a + c \leq b \cdot d + c \leq b \cdot d + c + c \cdot d + b = (b + c) \cdot (d + 1) ,$$

i.e., $a + c \sqsubseteq b + c$.

(5) By definition, isotony w.r.t. $\leq$ and commutativity we get

$a \sqsubseteq b \Leftrightarrow \exists d : a \leq b \cdot d \Rightarrow \exists d : a \cdot c \leq b \cdot c \cdot d \Leftrightarrow a \cdot c \sqsubseteq b \cdot c.$

(6) By annihilation, $a \sqsubseteq 0 \Leftrightarrow \exists c : a \leq 0 \cdot c \Leftrightarrow a \leq 0$.

(7) Set $a = 0$ and $b = 1$, resp., in (2). □

In IPFS and IPFB, (2) describes the situation that adding features (multiplying by an element in our algebra) refines products. (3) offers an alternative product on the right hand side. So we have a choice. But this does not affect that a refines itself ($a \sqsubseteq a$). (4) and (5) are standard isotony laws. (7) says that the empty set of products 0 refines all families — all its products indeed have at least as many features as some product in a. Moreover, (7) reflects that the product without any features (which is represented by 1) is refined by any family.

Lemma 4.4. *If a feature algebra contains a $\leq$-greatest element $\top$, we have*

$$a \sqsubseteq b \Leftrightarrow a \leq b \cdot \top \Leftrightarrow a \cdot \top \leq b \cdot \top .$$

Proof. First we show $a \sqsubseteq b \Leftrightarrow a \leq b \cdot \top$.

$(\Rightarrow)$ $a \sqsubseteq b \Leftrightarrow \exists\, c : a \leq b \cdot c \Rightarrow a \leq b \cdot \top$.
$(\Leftarrow)$ Set $c = \top$.

Now, we show $a \leq b \cdot \top \Leftrightarrow a \cdot \top \leq b \cdot \top$.

$(\Leftarrow)$ By isotony and $a \leq a \cdot \top$.
$(\Rightarrow)$ By isotony and $\top \cdot \top = \top$ (which follows by $\top \cdot \top \leq \top$). $\qquad\square$

E.g., in IPFS the greatest element is $\mathcal{P}(\mathbb{P})$, whereas in IPFB there is no greatest element.

As already mentioned, $\sqsubseteq$ is a preorder. We now show that $\sqsubseteq$ forms a partial order only in a very special case.

Lemma 4.5. $\sqsubseteq$ *is antisymmetric if and only if it is the identity relation, i.e.,* *iff* $a \sqsubseteq b \Rightarrow a = b$.

Proof. First, the identity relation clearly is antisymmetric.

Now suppose that $\sqsubseteq$ is antisymmetric and assume $a \sqsubseteq b$. Then by isotony (4) and idempotence of $+$ we get $a + b \sqsubseteq b$. By (3) we also have $b \sqsubseteq a + b$. Now antisymmetry shows $a = b$. $\qquad\square$

As the last property of $\sqsubseteq$, we show that the choice operator can be split w.r.t. $\sqsubseteq$ or, in other words, that $+$ produces a supremum w.r.t. $\sqsubseteq$ as well.

Lemma 4.6
$$a + b \sqsubseteq c \Leftrightarrow a \sqsubseteq c \wedge b \sqsubseteq c.$$

Proof

$(\Rightarrow)$ By the definition of $\sqsubseteq$, lattice algebra and the definition again
$a + b \sqsubseteq c \Leftrightarrow \exists\, d : a + b \leq c \cdot d \Leftrightarrow \exists\, d : a \leq c \cdot d \wedge b \leq c \cdot d \Rightarrow a \sqsubseteq c \wedge b \sqsubseteq c$.
$(\Leftarrow)$ By isotony and distributivity
$a \leq c \cdot d \wedge b \leq c \cdot e \Rightarrow a + b \leq c \cdot d + c \cdot e = c \cdot (d + e)$.
Hence, $a \sqsubseteq c \wedge b \sqsubseteq c \Rightarrow a + b \sqsubseteq c$. $\qquad\square$

5 Example of a More Complex Product Family

Our next case study is borrowed from [16] where it is used to illustrate a set-theoretic approach to reasoning about domains of what is called *n-dimensional and hierarchical* product families. It consists of a product family of mobile robots that reflect different hardware platforms and several different behaviours. The robot family is constructed using two hardware platforms: a *Pioneer* platform and a *logo-bot* platform. The behaviour of the robots ranges from a random exploration of an area to a more or less sophisticated navigation inside an area that is cluttered with obstacles. More details about the case study can be found in Thompson et al. [17], where the platforms are thoroughly described, and in [9], where two tables give an overview over the robots' behaviours. One table describes the robot family from a hardware perspective and the other from a behaviour perspective.

We briefly explain the main parts of the robots' behaviours. The robot family includes three product lines: Basic Platform, Enhanced Obstacle Detection and Environmental Vision. All the members of the Basic Platform product line share the following features:

- basic means of locomotion that could be *treads*, *wheels*, or *legs*;
- ability to turn an angle α from the initial heading;
- ability to move forward;
- ability to move backward;
- ability to stay inactive.

The variability among the members of a product line is due in part to the use of a variety of hardware. For instance, if we take the robotic collision sensors that protect robots from being damaged when they approach an obstruction or contact, then we obtain members with different sensing technologies. In our case, there are three main methods to sense contact with an obstruction: pneumatic, mechanical and a combination of mechanical and pneumatic. A member of the Basic Platform can have more than one collision sensor. The sensors could be of different types. The optional features of the members of *Basic Platform* product line concern their locomotion abilities as well as their locomotion means (treads, wheels or legs).

The DVD example of Section 3 was chosen for its simplicity to illustrate basic notions. The present example illustrates a family of products that exposes a more sophisticated structure of its subfamilies. It emphasises the fact that products can be defined from more than one perspective. Within a given perspective, subfamilies are defined based on other subfamilies. For instance, in the robot example the subfamily *Enhanced Obstacle Detection* is constructed on top of *basic platform* subfamily. For more details we refer the reader to [17,9]. The specification of the robot family using our formalism can be found in [9].

6   Further Notions and Properties

In the literature, terms like product family and subfamily are used without any exact definition. Therefore, we want to make these terms formally precise. Already in Section 4 we have defined some notions like feature and product in the special models of IPFS and IPFB, however, in terms of these particular models and not in general algebraic terms. In the remainder let $F = (S, +, 0, \cdot, 1)$ be a feature algebra.

Definition 6.1. An element a is said to be a *product*, if $a \neq 0$ and

$$\forall\, b : b \leq a \;\Rightarrow\; b = 0 \vee b = a \;\wedge\; \forall\, b, c : a \leq b + c \;\Rightarrow\; (a \leq b \vee a \leq c)\,. \quad (8)$$

The set of all products is denoted by IP.

Intuitively, this means that a product cannot be split using the choice operator $+$. In IPFS and IPFB an element is a product iff it contains only one element, i.e., it is a singleton set.

In Example 4.2 we have also given a definition of features for the concrete case. Again we want to give an abstract algebraic counterpart. Analogously to Definition 6.1, we ask for indecomposability, but this time w.r.t. multiplication rather than addition.

Definition 6.2. An element a is called *feature* if it is a product and

$$\forall\, b : b \mid a \Rightarrow b = 0 \lor b = a \quad \land \quad \forall\, b, c : a \mid b + c \Rightarrow (a \mid b \lor a \mid c) \,, \qquad (9)$$

where the divisibility relation $\mid$ is given by $x \mid y \Leftrightarrow_{df} \exists\, z : x = y \cdot z$. The set of all features is denoted by $\mathbb{F}$.

From the mathematical point of view, the characteristics of products (8) and features (9) are similar and well known. We give a uniform treatment of both notions in the Appendix of [9], where we also discuss the order-theoretic background.

As a special kind of products we have the *generated products* (for short g$\mathbb{P}$), i.e., those products that are obtained by multiplication of features:

$$g\mathbb{P} =_{df} \mathbb{P} \cap \mathbb{F}^*,$$

where $\mathbb{F}^* =_{df} \left\{ \prod_{i=1}^{n} x_i : n \in \mathbb{N}, x_i \in \mathbb{F} \right\}$ is the set of all elements that arise by multiplying an arbitrary finite number of features. Over a finite set $\mathbb{F}$ of features, in IPFS as well as in IPFB the set of generated products is equal to the set of all products, i.e., g$\mathbb{P} = \mathbb{P}$.

Definition 6.3. A *product family* or *family* (IPFam) is a set of generated products that have at least one common feature, i.e,

$$a \in \mathbb{P}\text{Fam} \Leftrightarrow \exists\, f \in \mathbb{F} : \exists\, I \subseteq g\mathbb{P} : a = f \cdot \sum_{x_i \in I} x_i \,.$$

We call b a *subfamily* of a iff $b \leq a$.

Of course, the family a may have more common features than just f; they could be extracted from the sum by distributivity. But in our definition we wanted to emphasise that there is *at least one*. It is obvious that each subfamily of a forms a family again, since it has f as a common feature.

Sometimes, for practical reasons, a specific subfamily is called a *product line*. For instance, in a context of software development based on the family approach, a subfamily that needs to be developed in the same production site or by the same development team is called a product line. Therefore, factors other than the structure of its members can be involved in defining a product line.

To get a measure for *similarity* we give the following definitions:

Definition 6.4. Let $k \in \mathbb{N}$. The family f_1 is said to be k-*near* the family f_2, if

$$\exists \, g \neq 0 : \exists x, y \in \mathbb{F}^{\leq k} : x \neq y \wedge f_1 = x \cdot g \wedge f_2 = y \cdot g,$$

where $\mathbb{F}^{\leq k} =_{df} \left\{ \prod_{i=1}^{n} x_i : k \in \mathbb{N}, n \leq k, x_i \in \mathbb{F} \right\}$.

Since every product is also a product family (which has only one member), we also have a notion for measure similarity of products. In particular, each product of a family is at least 1-near any other element of the same family (they have the common feature f).

Finally, we discuss the case of a finite set of features $\mathbb{F}$. Then we have an additional special element in $\mathbb{PFS}$, which is characterised by

$$\Pi =_{df} \left\{ \left\{ \prod_{x_i \in \mathbb{F}} x_i \right\} \right\}.$$

This element contains only one product, namely the product that has all possible features. In this case we have $a \cdot \Pi = \Pi$ if $a \neq 0$. Then, by setting $c = \Pi$ in the definition of the refinement relation $\sqsubseteq$ Section 4)

$$\Pi \sqsubseteq a \, .$$

In general, we call an element $p \neq 0$ satisfying, for all $a \in S \backslash \{0\}$, $a \cdot p = p$ ($= p \cdot a$ by commutativity) a *weak zero*, since it annihilates *almost* all elements.

Lemma 6.5. *(i) A weak zero is unique if it exists.*
(ii) A weak zero p refines everything except 0, i.e., $p \sqsubseteq a \Leftrightarrow a \neq 0$.
(iii) If p is a weak zero then $a \sqsubseteq p \Leftrightarrow a \leq p$.

Proof.   (i) Assume p and q to be weak zeros. Then, by definition, $p = p \cdot q = q$.
  (ii)($\Rightarrow$) Assume $a = 0$. Then by definition of weak zero and annihilation $p = 0$,
      which contradicts the definition of p.
    ($\Leftarrow$) By definition $p \leq p \cdot a$ if $a \neq 0$ and hence, $p \sqsubseteq a$.
  (iii) By definition of $\sqsubseteq$ and weak zero,
      $a \sqsubseteq p \Leftrightarrow \exists \, c : a \leq p \cdot c \Leftrightarrow a \leq 0 \vee a \leq p \Leftrightarrow a \leq p.$ □

Note that in $\mathbb{PFB}$ there is no weak zero, since multiple occurrences of features are allowed.

7   Building Product Families and Generating Product Lines

In this section we present some useful properties of feature algebras concerning finding common features, building up product families, finding new products and excluding special feature combinations.

We first address the issue of finding the commonalities of a given set of products. This is a very relevant issue since the identification of common artifacts within systems (e.g. chips, software modules, etc.) enhances hardware/software reuse. If we look at feature algebras like IPFS and IPFB we can formalise this problem as finding "the greatest common divisor" or to factor out the features common to all given products. This relation to "classical" algorithms again shows an advantage of using an algebraic approach. Solving gcd (greatest common divisor) is well known and easy, whereas finding commonalities using diagrams (e.g., FODA) or trees (e.g., FORM) is more complex.

Example 7.1. Resuming the product line of Section 3 and Example 4.2, we give an explicit example. Assume two different products: An mp3-player defined as

$$p\_mp3 \cdot c_1 \cdot c_2 \cdot c_3$$

and an mp3-recorder given by

$$p\_mp3 \cdot r\_mp3 \cdot c_1 \cdot c_2 \ .$$

To find all common parts we look at the sum of the two products, i.e., we create a set of products, and by simple calculations using distributivity we get

$$p\_mp3 \cdot c_1 \cdot c_2 \cdot (c_3 + r\_mp3) \ .$$

Thus the common parts are p_mp3, c_1 and c_2. □

Such calculations can easily done by a program; we will briefly describe a prototype in the next section. Of course one can calculate the common parts of any set of products. If there is at least one common feature, all the products form a product family. After factoring out the common parts, we can iterate this procedure for a subset of the given products and find again common parts. In this way we can form *subproduct families* if necessary. Hence, using the algebraic rules in different directions, we can both structure and generate product families and product lines.

Starting with a set of features, we can create new products just by combining these features in all possible ways. This can easily be automated. For example, using our prototype which is described in Section 8, we calculate that the *Basic Platform* subfamily consists of 13635 products.

However, there are products with combinations of features that are impossible or undesirable. For example, it is unreasonable to have a robot that has both wheels and legs as basic means of locomotion. This requirement can be coded in feature algebra by postulating the additional equation

$$wheels \cdot legs = 0 \ .$$

This exclusion property is also implemented in our prototype. For the robot example we also exclude combinations of impossible or undesirable features (see next section) from the *Basic Platform* subfamily and are left with 1539 products.

There are many other properties like:

"If a product has feature f_1 it also needs to have feature f_2".

Most of these requirements can easily be modelled and implemented using our algebra.

8 A Prototype Implementation in Haskell

To check the adequacy of our definitions we have written a prototype implementation of the IPFB model[1] in the functional programming language *Haskell*. Features are simply encoded as strings. Bags are represented as ordered lists and · as bag union by merging. Sets of bags are implemented as repetition-free ordered lists and + as repetition-removing merge.

This prototype can normalise algebraic expressions over features into a sum-of-products-form. A small pretty-printing facility allows us to display the results as the sequence of all products described by such an expression.

As an example we give the code corresponding to Table 1 of Section 3.

```
-- basic features:
p_mp3 = bf "play mp3-files"
r_mp3 = bf "record mp3-files"
o_mp3 = bf "organise mp3-files"
p_dvd = bf "play DVD"
p_cd  = bf "play CD"
v_cd  = bf "view picture CD"
b_cd  = bf "burn CD"
a_cd  = bf "play additional CD"
c1    = bf "audio equaliser"
c2    = bf "video algorithms"
c3    = bf "dolby surround"

-- composed features
mp3_player = p_mp3 .*. (opt [r_mp3])
dvd_player = p_dvd .*. (opt [p_cd , v_cd , b_cd , a_cd])
hd = opt [mp3_player, o_mp3]

--whole product line
p_line = c1 .*. c2 .*. c3 .*. (mp3_player .+. dvd_player .+. hd)
```

The product line contains 22 products, printed out as follows:

```
========================================================================
                    Common Parts
------------------------------------------------------------------------
```

---

[1] The program and a short description can be found at: http://www.informatik.uni-augsburg.de/lehrstuehle/dbis/pmi/publications/all_pmi_tech-reports

```
audio equaliser
dolby surround
video algorithms
-----------------------------------------------------------------
=================================================================
              Variabilities
-----------------------------------------------------------------
burn CD
play CD
play DVD
play additional CD
-----------------------------------------------------------------
burn CD
play CD
play DVD
play additional CD
view picture CD
-----------------------------------------------------------------
burn CD
...
```

Feature exclusion as discussed in the previous section, can be also encoded using an algebraic expression. For instance, all the required exclusion properties of the robot example are given by

```
excludes =      treads .*. wheels
         .+. treads .*.  legs
         .+. wheels .*. legs
         .+. limited_spd   .*. extended_spd
         .+. basic_ctrl    .*. digital_ctrl
         .+. small_pltfrm  .*. large_pltfrm
         .+. medium_pltfrm .*. large_pltfrm
         .+. small_pltfrm  .*. c_sensor .^. 4
         .+. medium_pltfrm .*. c_sensor .^. 5
         .+. large_pltfrm  .*. c_sensor .^. 6
```

Here ^ is the exponentiation operator. Due to the fact that 0 is an annihilator for ·, the last line excludes large platforms with more than 5 collision sensors.

9   Conclusion and Outlook

The adoption of the product family paradigm in software development aims at recognising a reality in software development industry noticed decades ago [13]: economical constraints impose a concurrent approach to software development replacing the early sequential one. The research work about software product families aims at studying the commonalities/variability occurring among the products in order to have a better management of software production. However, a review of the literature reveals a wide set of notions and terms used without formal definitions. A clear and simple mathematical setting for the usage of this paradigm arises as a necessity.

In this paper we have introduced feature algebra as an idempotent commutative semiring. We have given a set-based and a bag-based model of the proposed algebra. To compare elements of our algebra, besides the natural order defined on an idempotent semiring we use a refinement relation and have established some of its basic properties. Then we have given formal definitions of common terms that are intuitively used in the literature such as product, feature, and family. We introduced as well new notions such as that of a weak zero, and a measure for similarity among products and families.

The proposed algebra not only allows us to express the basic notions used by the product family paradigm community, but also enables algebraic manipulations of families of specifications, which enhances the generation of new knowledge about them. The notions and relationships introduced in FODA [10], FORM [11], FeatuRSEB [8] and GP [6] and expressed with graphical notations can easily be stated within our algebra. For instance, the alternative is expressed using the $+$ operator, and we write $f = b \cdot (1 + a) \cdot c$ (where b, and c are families) to express that a feature a is optional in a family f.

In contrast to other product family specification formalisms, like FODA and FORM, there exists a large body of theoretical results for idempotent commutative semiring and for algebraic techniques in general with strong impact for research related to problems of consistency, correctness, compatibility and reusability.

Many items found in the literature support the potential scalability of algebraic approaches in specifying industrial-scale software product families [1,3]. However, we think that empirical substantiation of the scalability of our approach is needed.

This work opens new questions and brings in new research horizons. One of the questions is how to generate the specification of individual members of a given family from the specifications of features and the feature-algebraic specification of a family. One can envisage that the specifications of all the features are stored in a specification depository and the specification of a product is generated on the fly. There is no need to have rigid specifications of products that are members of a family. This flexibility in generating specifications on the fly eases coping with the changes that frequently affect specifications of features. The proposed feature algebra provides a solid base on which to build for answering these questions.

As illustrated in [16], a product family might need to be specified from several perspectives. For example, in embedded systems, a product family needs to be specified from hardware and software perspectives. We conjecture that these perspectives are somehow interdependent. When this interdependence is known, how can we model the global specification of a family (involves all the perspectives) within a super-structure (such as a product structure) of feature algebras? The aim of further work in this area is to tackle these questions.

References

1. D. Batory. The road to utopia: A future for generative programming. Keynote presentation at the Dagstuhl Seminar for Domain Specific Program Generation, March 2003.
2. D. Batory. Feature models, grammars, and propositional formulas. In *Proceedings of the 9th International Software Product Line Conference (SPLC-EUROPE 2005)*, 26-29 September 2005.
3. D. Batory, R. Lopez-Herrejon, and J.-P. Martin. Generating product-lines of product-families. In *Conference on Automated-Software Engineering*, September 2002.
4. S. Bühne, K. Lauenroth, and K. Pohl. Modelling requirements variability across product lines. In *13th IEEE International Requirements Engineering Conference*, pages 41–50. IEEE Computer Society, August 29–September 2 2005.
5. P. Clements, L. M. Northrop, and L. M. Northrop. *Software Product Lines: Practices and Patterns*. Addison Wesley Professional, 2002.
6. K. Czarnecki and U. Eisenecker. *Generative Programming, Methods, Tools and Applications*. Addison-Wesley, 2000.
7. J. Desharnais, B. Möller, and G. Struth. Modal Kleene Algebra and Applications – A Survey. *Journal on Relational Methods in Computer Science*, (1):93–131, 2004. http://www.cosc.brocku.ca/Faculty/Winter/JoRMiCS/.
8. M. L. Griss, J. Favaro, and M. d'Alessandro. Integrating feature modeling with the RSEB. In P. Devanbu and J. Poulin, editors, *Proceedings of the 5th International Conference on Software Reuse*, pages 76–85. IEEE Computer Society, 1998.
9. P. Höfner, R. Khedri, and B. Möller. Feature algebra. Technical Report 2006-04, Institut für Informatik, Universität Augsburg, February 2006.
10. K. Kang, S. Cohen, J. Hess, W. Novak, and A. Peterson. Feature-oriented domain analysis (foda) feasibility study. Technical Report CMU/SEI-90-TR-021, Carnegie Mellon Software Engineering Institute, Carnegie Mellon University, 1990.
11. K. C. Kang, S. Kim, J. Lee, K. Kim, E. Shin, and M. Huh. FORM: A feature-oriented reuse method with domain-specific reference architectures. *Annals of Software Engineering*, 5(1):143–168, 1998.
12. N. J. Nilsson. *Principles of Artificial Intelligence*. Tioga Publishing Co., 1980.
13. D. L. Parnas. On the design and development of program families. *IEEE Transactions on Software Engineering*, SE2(1):1–9, March 1976.
14. C. Riva and C. D. Rosso. Experiences with software product family evolution. In *Sixth International Workshop on Principles of Software Evolution (IWPSE'03)*, pages 161–169. IEEE Computer Society, 2003.
15. S. Roback and A. Pieczynski. Employing fuzzy logic in feature diagrams to model variability in software product-lines. In *10th IEEE International Conference and Workshop on the Engineering of Computer-Based Systems (ECBS'03)*, pages 305–311. IEEE Computer Society, 2003.
16. J. M. Thompson and M. P. Heimdahl. Structuring product family requirements for n-dimensional and hierarchical product lines. *Requirements Engineering Journal*, 2002.
17. J. M. Thompson, M. P. Heimdahl, and D. M. Erickson. Structuring formal control systems specifications for reuse: Surviving hardware changes. Technical Report TR 00-004, Department of Computer Science and Engineering, University of Minnesota, February 2000.

Using Domain-Independent Problems for Introducing Formal Methods

Raymond Boute

INTEC, Universiteit Gent, Belgium
Raymond.Boute@intec.UGent.be

Abstract. The key to the integration of formal methods into engineering practice is education. In teaching, domain-independent problems — i.e., not requiring prior engineering background— offer many advantages.

Such problems are widely available, but this paper adds two dimensions that are lacking in typical solutions yet are crucial to formal methods: (i) the translation of informal statements into formal expressions; (ii) the role of formal calculation (including proofs) in exposing risks or misunderstandings and in discovering pathways to solutions.

A few example problems illustrate this: (a) a small logical one showing the importance of fully capturing informal statements; (b) a combinatorial one showing how, in going from "real-world" formulations to mathematical ones, formal methods can cover more aspects than classical mathematics, and a half-page formal program semantics suitable for beginners is presented as a support; (c) a larger one showing how a single problem can contain enough elements to serve as a Leitmotiv for all notational and reasoning issues in a complete introductory course.

An important final observation is that, in teaching formal methods, no approach can be a substitute for an open mind, as extreme mathphobia appears resistant to any motivation.

Index Terms: Domain-independent problems, Formal methods, Functional Predicate Calculus, Funmath, Generic functionals, Teaching, Specification, Word problems.

1 Introduction: Motivation and Overview

A Gap in Engineering Professionalism. One often hears the complaint that the use of formal methods into everyday software engineering practice is taking a long time in becoming commonplace (except for critical and some embedded systems) and that, as a result, professionalism in software design is generally low.

Yet, the published literature reports many projects for which formal methods were essential or at least the key to success. Why, then, is the software industry at large so slow in exploiting the advantages?

Many explanations have been conjectured by diverse people, but the following one seems inescapable as "Occam's razor": universities are providing far from sufficient education in formal methods to generate the massive injection of qualified people necessary for enabling industry to integrate formal methods into

J. Misra, T. Nipkow, and E. Sekerinski (Eds.): FM 2006, LNCS 4085, pp. 316–331, 2006.
© Springer-Verlag Berlin Heidelberg 2006

their everyday software design practice. The success stories remain restricted to companies that are either consultants specialized in the area of formal methods or users of ad hoc support for specific projects from consultants and universities.

The contrast with classical engineering disciplines, in particular electrical engineering, is significant. Mathematical modelling has not only proven indispensable for todays communications technology, but has been accepted de facto since centuries as an essential part of engineering education. It is commonplace in industry, and no university engineer would dare confessing to his project leader that he doesn't know enough elementary calculus or algebra to cope with this.

Yet, some universities still turn out software "engineers" whose grasp of logic is not better than high school level, and whose highest abstraction "tool" for specifying systems is some program-like code which they are unable to model and analyze mathematically. Complaints from industry are not surprising [19]. A serious educational obstacle pointed out by one of the reviewers is that logic is much harder than differential calculus, as also indicated by other studies [1].

On Using Tools. A similar gap exists in the ability to use software tools judiciously. High school education provides sufficient mathematics for starting to use tools for classical mathematics like Mathematica, Maple, Matlab, Mathcad with ease, and a good calculus or analysis course at the freshman and junior level prepares for more advanced use by providing a solid basis and insight (not a luxury, given the many "bugs" reported in the literature). Mathematicians and engineers 150 years ago would have no difficulty in using today's tools without a "tutorial".

By contrast, for software tools supporting CS-oriented formal methods, classical mathematics offers no preparation, and too many computing curricula do not even start filling this gap. Using the tools themselves in an introductory course as a vehicle for introducing (or, worse, as a surrogate for) the relevant mathematics is highly inappropriate[1] since such tools are still very design-specific[2] and hence induce a narrow and misleading view in beginners, turning them into sorcerer's apprentices. Of course, tools can be very useful as an illustration, especially for the shortcomings in and the differences between them. In fact, in the same vein some of the best analysis texts provide exercises with tools precisely to show the pitfalls [21], and always keep the mathematics and "thinking" central.

In brief: the best preparation for using tools is solid mathematics education.

Curriculum Design. Providing the relevant mathematics early creates the opportunity for other computer-oriented courses (HW and SW) to start using serious mathematical modeling, rather than remaining stuck at the old descriptive level with some elementary programming exercises as the highest intellectual activity. For classical mathematics, preparation usually starts in high school but, as universities have no control at this level, the earliest opportunity to teach the basic

---

[1] This observation assumes today's state of the art; only vast progress can alter it.
[2] Unlike software tools for classical mathematics, which support mature notational and formal calculation conventions, current tools in the formal methods area are still based on overly specific logics and too reflective of various implementation decisions.

mathematics for computing science and engineering is the freshman level. A typical embedding in a traditional curriculum is achieved by thoroughly changing the content of an existing discrete mathematics course for this purpose, as exemplified in the textbook by Gries and Schneider [11] and the BESEME (BEtter Software Engineering through Mathematics Education) project [15].

To summarize, an early start paves the way for "weaving formal methods into the undergraduate curriculum" as advocated by Wing [23]. The extent to which other courses catch this opportunity depends on the quality of the staff, and determines the ability of the students to use formal methods.

The Role of Domain-Independent Problems. Providing the mathematical basis for CS early in the curriculum is facilitated by assuming no prior technical or engineering background, as is also customary in calculus courses. An independent reason is the principle of separation of concerns: not overburdening the student by combining new mathematical with new (or recent) engineering concepts.

Any basic course needs illustrations and, more importantly, problems to enhance insight in the concepts and to learn using them in problem solving.

Domain-independent problems combine all the above requirements. They can be understood by anyone, and are fun to solve. Furthermore, they are widely available in both educational [2,11] and recreational literature [9,17]. Finally, courses and textbooks on this basis can reach more easily over boundaries between disciplines. One might ask how this pertains to CS-oriented mathematics, given its specialistic reputation. Actually, this reputation is undeserved, given the rapidly growing evidence that the insights and reasoning styles fostered by CS have wide applicability in mathematics [8], in science and in engineering [5].

New Dimensions in Solving Domain-Independent Problems. Concerns arising from the application of formal methods add new dimensions to problem solving that are also best illustrated by domain-independent problems.

Indeed, solutions to such problems, especially "puzzles", are traditionally often presented with a "look how clever" undertone of impressing the audience. Unfortunately, this effect often comes at the expense of hiding steps in the calculation or in the conversion from the informal statement to mathematical formulas. Sometimes this is forgivable, e.g., when common notation falls short.

When using formal methods in practice, avoiding or exposing hidden steps and assumptions is part of the task. Hence, in the introduction of formal methods, domain-independent problems can help emphasizing the following two important issues: (i) the translation of informal statements into formal expressions; (ii) the role of formal calculation (including proofs) in exposing misunderstandings or possible risks and in discovering pathways to solutions.

Scope of This Paper and Approach. We will show that even small domain-independent problems can have sufficiently rich ramifications for illustrating central issues in formal methods, and that medium ones can contain enough elements to serve as the Leitmotiv for illustrating all notational and reasoning issues in a complete introductory course on basic mathematics for CS.

For notation and reasoning we use *Funmath* (Functional Mathematics) [3,5], a very general formalism unifying mathematics for classical engineering and CS.

The language [3] uses just four constructs, yet suffices to synthesize familiar notations (minus the defects) as well as new ones. It supports formal calculation rules convenient for hand calculation and amenable to automation.

The reasoning framework has two main elements. First, concrete generic functionals [4] support smooth transition between pointwise and point-free formulations, facilitating calculation with functionals and exploiting formal commonalities between various engineering mathematics. Second, a functional predicate calculus [5] makes formal logic practical for engineers, allowing them to calculate with predicates and quantifiers as fluently as with derivatives and integrals.

Here we use the language mostly in its "conservative mode", restricted to expressions with the same look and feel as common mathematical conventions. We only lift this restriction when common notation cannot express what is needed.

As a result, most of this paper requires neither prior knowledge of nor introduction to Funmath, and we can refer to [5] for details or for exploring deeper.

Overview. We consider some selected issues only; any attempt at completeness would rapidly grow into a textbook. Section 2 uses a very small word problem (at the level of propositional logic) to highlight some psychological and educational issues and to demonstrate the importance of completeness when capturing informal statements. Section 3 shows via a small combinatorial problem how steps in the transition from "real-world" formulations to mathematical ones are missed in traditional solutions, yet can be captured by formal methods. A half-page formal program semantics suitable for beginners is presented as a support. Section 4 shows how a single problem can give rise to enough topics for a complete introductory course on formal methods. Section 5 presents some conclusions and observes that, in teaching formal methods, no approach can be a substitute for an open mind, as extreme mathphobia appears resistant to any motivation.

2 On Logic and Properly Formalizing Informal Statements

Most people would attribute to themselves a basic "natural" understanding of logic. Yet, studies by Johnson-Laird [13] about logic reasoning by humans expose serious flaws. Table 1 describes two typical experiments and their outcomes.

One step further: most engineers and mathematicians would consider themselves fairly fluent in logic by profession[3]. We have no data on how this group as a whole would perform on the test, but experience with the subgroup in computer science/engineering —where logic is vital— gives reason for concern.

Indeed, we found that even CS students who previously had a full semester course on formal logic elsewhere generally did poorly on this test.

---

[3] Introductions to logic that are too elementary (as in traditional discrete math courses) only strengthen this feeling, since they offer little more than a semi-formal notation or even syncopation [20] for expressing something they were already doing informally in mathematics before and will continue doing informally afterwards.

Table 1. Two experiments as reported by Johnson-Laird

(a) One of the following assertions is true about a particular hand of cards,
and one of them is false about the same hand of cards:
    If there is a king in the hand, then there is an ace in the hand
    If there isn't a king in the hand, then there is an ace in the hand.
Q: What follows?
Subjects overwhelmingly infer that there is an ace in the hand.

(b) Only one of the following assertions is true about a particular hand of cards:
    There is a king in the hand, or an ace, or both.
    There is a queen in the hand, or an ace, or both.
    There is a jack in the hand, or a ten, or both.
Q: Is it possible that there is an ace in the hand?
Nearly every participant in our experiment responded: 'yes'.

Analysis of the answers suggests that here some other effect is responsible
than the one Johnson-Laird observes in people without logic background. Indeed,
the most common error for problem (a) was taking the conjunction of the two
assertions listed. The errors for problem (b) were more diverse. However, the
answers indicated that often the "preamble" (the part of the problem statement
before the list of assertions) was simply ignored. Even students who attempted
formalizing the problem statement left the preamble out of this process.

In general there seems to be a strong tendency to skip parts of the problem statement (which are perhaps perceived as mere padding) and, as a result,
"jumping to conclusions". It is safe assuming that the same effect occurs with
more complex specifications stated as many pages of text. Recently, Vaandrager
mentioned that IEEE specifications of complex protocols are typically stated in
words, with at best an appendix where fragments are formalized [22].

We suggest the following discipline to eliminate, or at least reduce, this effect:
start by formalizing every sentence separately as accurately as the formalism
used permits, and simplify or combine only afterwards. . In particular, discard
seemingly irrelevant parts only if due consideration justifies doing so.

For instance, in solving (a), do not directly formalize the problem statement
in one step as $(k \Rightarrow a) \oplus (\neg k \Rightarrow a) \equiv 1$ (the identifier conventions are obvious).
Instead, in a first version, maintain one-to-one correspondence with the text, as
illustrated in the following set of equations, and simplify afterwards.

$$\alpha \oplus \beta \equiv 1$$
$$\alpha \equiv k \Rightarrow a$$
$$\beta \equiv \neg k \Rightarrow a$$

As an aside: in programming, one discourages writing if b = true then ...
since if b then ... is better style. In logic, it is often better style to give
equations the shape of equations; so we wrote $\alpha \oplus \beta \equiv 1$ rather than just $\alpha \oplus \beta$.

More importantly, in view of faithfully formalizing informal statements, one
might argue that using $\oplus$ in the first equation already skips ahead of things,

since the preamble is a conjunction of two sentences. The shortcut reflects the fact that proposition logic is insufficiently expressive to formalize this.

Indeed, the sentences in the preamble imply counting the number of true and false assertions. For many reasons not discussed here, Funmath views Booleans as numbers, subject to common arithmetic, which turns out advantageous for this kind of problems as well. We first make "one of the following assertions" more precise as "at least one of the following assertions", since interpretation with "exactly one" would make the second conjunct redundant, albeit this is clear only in the total context and gives the same end result (but that is hindsight).

A faithful translation of the preamble then proceeds as follows. The sentence "[at least] one assertion is true (false)" is in natural language shorthand for "the number of assertions that are true (false) is [at least] one". So, for the preamble,

$$\sum (\alpha, \beta) \geq 1 \quad \wedge \quad \sum (\neg\alpha, \neg\beta) \geq 1 \ . \tag{1}$$

Equivalence with $\alpha \oplus \beta \equiv 1$ for Boolean α and β can be shown in many ways, e.g., the following head calculation in 3 steps using the formal rules of Funmath.

Generally, a family of sentences (such as α, β in problem (a) or α, β, γ in problem (b)) is a predicate, say P, and expressions like $\sum P \geq n$ or $\sum P = n$ as appropriate reflect the counting. The case $\sum P \geq 1$ is equivalent to $\exists P$, which is the formal rule for rewriting (1) in one step as $\exists (\alpha, \beta) \wedge \exists (\neg\alpha, \neg\beta)$. A second step using $\exists (p, q) \equiv p \vee q$ yields $(\alpha \vee \beta) \wedge (\neg\alpha \vee \neg\beta)$, which equals $\alpha \oplus \beta$.

The reader may wish to try this approach on problem (b) and then on some of the word problems in [11] or in the mathematical puzzles literature [9,17].

From the classical "cleverness-oriented" problem solving point of view, faithful translation may seem overkill, but in the context of formal methods and textual specifications it can reduce errors. In view of the expressiveness and rich collection of formal rules in Funmath, the extra work need not be prohibitive.

3   Intermediate Phases in Formalizing Informal Statements

The preceding example already illustrated how to handle certain intermediate phases, but the problem statement itself was "static" and already logic-oriented. Some interesting additional issues arise in the following problem from [7].

A school has 1000 students and 1000 lockers, all in a row. They all start out closed. The first student walks down the line and opens each one. The second student closes the even numbered lockers. The third student approaches every third locker and changes its state. If it was open he closes it; if it was closed he opens it. The fourth student does the same to every fourth locker, and so on through 1000 students. To illustrate, the tenth locker is opened by the first student, closed by the second, reopened by the fifth, and then closed by the tenth. All the other students pass by the tenth locker, so it winds up being closed. How many lockers are open?

Here is the solution offered in [7].

The nth locker is opened or closed by student number k precisely when k divides n. So if student k changes locker n, so does student n/k. They cancel each other out. This always holds unless students k and n/k are precisely the same person. That is, $k = n/k$. The lockers that are exact squares will remain open. These are lockers 1, 4, 9, 16, 25, etc. How many of these are there in a row of 1000? You can go all the way up to $31 \times 31 = 961$, hence there are 31 lockers open.

In formalizing the problem statement, a first step is tightening the wording and removing examples. Here is the result.

A school has 1000 students and 1000 lockers in a row, all initially closed. All students walk successively along the row, and the kth student inverts the state of every k^{th} locker, that is: opens the locker if it was closed and vice versa. How many lockers are open in the end?

The formal equations reflecting the informal reasoning in the proposed solution, parametrized by the number of lockers N and the number of students K, are

$Answer = |\{n : 1 .. N \mid Open\,n\}|$ $\qquad$ Legend: $|S| = $ size of set S

$Open\,n \equiv \mathsf{Odd}\,|\{k : 1 .. K \mid k \text{ divides } n\}|$ $\quad$ Legend: $\mathsf{Odd}\,m \equiv$ number m is odd

Elaborating yields a "nicer" expression for the answer, but this is not the issue.

The problem statement describes a procedure, the equations only the result. Classical mathematics cannot express the intermediate steps, but a procedural language can, and formal semantics allows deriving the equations formally.

A more faithful rendering of the procedure in the problem statement is

```
for k in 1..K do
    (for n in 1..N do if (k divides n) then inv (L n) fi od) od   .
```

Here `inv (L n)` (for "invert the state of locker `L n`") can be refined in many ways, for instance `L n := L n` $\oplus$ `1` if `Ln` is defined as taking values in $0 .. 1$. Program semantics allows calculating the final value of L (given that initially L is zero everywhere) and hence the answer $\sum L$. The calculation is facilitated by observing that the loops are interchangeable (even parallelization is possible).

In an introductory course, a scaled-down formal semantics can be used, kept simple by some restrictions on generality, as exemplified next.

Intermezzo: Microsemantics, a Scaled-Down Formal Semantics. We show one of many forms for a simple program semantics presentable early in an introductory course when handling problems of this kind. It is assumed that one of the starting lessons was about substitution and instantiation, as in Gries and Schneider [11]. Substituting expression d for variable v in expression e is written $e\,[v := d]$, compacted as $e[^v_d$ (written e^v_d in [11]). As in [11], v and d may be tuples. The operator $[^v_d$ affects expressions only, the counterpart for commands is $\langle^v_d$.

In this example of a scaled-down semantics, the state s is the tuple of variables, in simple problems the one variable that is changed. A command c is a function from states to states (*direct functional semantics*) defined recursively by axioms of the form $c\,s = e$ (instantiated $c\,d = e[^s_d]$). Here are axioms for the *basic* commands assignment ($v := e$), composition ($c\ ;\ c'$) and selection.

$$(v := e)\,s = s[^v_e] \quad \text{or, as a nice pun,} \quad (v := e)\,s = s\,[v := e]$$
$$(c\ ;\ c')\,s = c'\,(c\,s)$$
$$(\texttt{if }b\texttt{ then }c\texttt{ else }c'\texttt{ fi})\,s = b\,?\,c\,s \mid c'\,s$$

The last right hand side is a *conditional expression* with axiom $(b\,?\,e_1 \mid e_0) = e_b$. The following *derived* commands are expressed in terms of the basic ones.

$$\texttt{skip} = v := v$$
$$\texttt{if }b\texttt{ then }c\texttt{ fi} = \texttt{if }b\texttt{ then }c\texttt{ else skip fi}$$
$$\texttt{while }b\texttt{ do }c\texttt{ od} = \texttt{if }b\texttt{ then }(c\ ;\ \texttt{while }b\texttt{ do }c\texttt{ od})\texttt{ fi}$$
$$\texttt{for }i\texttt{ in }e\,..\,e'\texttt{ do }c\texttt{ od} = i, i' := e, e'\ ;\ \texttt{while }i \leq i'\texttt{ do }c\ ;\ i := i{+}1\texttt{ od}$$

Finally, for arrays, $A\,i := e$ is by definition shorthand for $A := (i \mapsto e) \otimes A$. In Funmath, $d \mapsto e$ is a *maplet* as in Z [18], and $(f \otimes g)\,x = (x \in \mathcal{D}\,f)\,?\,f\,x \mid g\,x$.

With these preliminaries, calculating the final value for L (after loop interchange) is left as an exercise for the reader. As this kind of approach is meant for an introductory course, elaboration should be done carefully and in detail (at least the first time) and at a pace that all students can follow.

Variants and Ramifications. An interesting item is the `k divides n` test, which is an indirect interpretation of "every k^{th} locker" in the problem statement. A more direct interpretation is that the kth student always proceeds directly to the kth following locker. This is reflected by the inner loop in the procedure below.

```
for k in 1..K do (n := k; while n ≤ N do inv (L n); n := n + k od) od
```

Some might find (`n := 0; while n + k ≤ N do n := n + k; inv (L n) od`) more stylish (I do). Anyway, now the loops are not interchangeable any more. Clearly the interplay between faithfulness of translation and simplicity of derivation provides enough sustenance for an entire course on specification and transformation.

As an aside, observe that this problem illustrates the reverse of program design, which starts from an abstract specification and results in a procedure. Here we start with a procedure and derive mathematical equations. In terms of axiomatic semantics, the solution involves calculating strongest postconditions, which also play an important role in the theory of reverse software engineering.

In the literature, the theoretical basis for postconditions is somewhat neglected as compared to preconditions (or anteconditions as we prefer to call them) and often presented as a footnote or afterthought. This is why we provide a more symmetric treatment in [6], where furthermore axiomatic semantics is not formulated via postulates but derived calculationally from *program equations*.

Again from the "cleverness-oriented" viewpoint, the procedural description and its analysis may seem superfluous, yet it shows how formal methods can attach "handles" to intermediate steps not expressible in standard mathematics. A wealth of examples on *algorithmic problem solving* can be found in [2].

4   Using Wide-Scope Domain-Independent Problems

Finally, we show that domain-independent problems can have a sufficiently wide scope to serve as a running example for all notational and reasoning issues in a complete introductory course on a mathematical basis for formal methods.

The chosen puzzle is designed as a brain-teaser and hence may appear somewhat artificial, but this is compensated by the fact that it was not designed at all for our purpose: it was proposed by Propp [16] in *Mathematical Horizons*. Moreover, its self-referential character is a good preparation for CS students.

Problem Statement. Table 2 is the test from [16]; we only renumbered the questions to range from 0 to 19. The author of the test further comments:

> The solution to [this] puzzle is unique; in some cases the knowledge that the solution is unique may actually give you a short-cut to finding the answer to a particular question, but it's possible to find the unique solution even without making use of the fact that the solution is unique. (Thanks to Andy Latto for bringing this subtlety to my attention.)
> I should mention that if you don't agree with me about the answer to #19, you will get a different solution to the puzzle than the one I had in mind. But I should also mention that if you don't agree with me about the answer to #19, you are just plain wrong. :-)

Formalization in Funmath. Table 3 is the translation of Table 2 into mathematical equations. We directly encode the letters $A..E$ for the answers by $0..4$ to avoid the unnecessary clutter of explicit conversion mappings, so the answer to the test is a string $a : \square\, 20 \to \square\, 5$ satisfying this system of equations.

Most operators are basic Funmath [4,5] and, as said, need little explanation. We just mention $m..n = \{k : \mathbb{Z} \mid m \le k \le n\}$ and $\square\, n = 0..n-1$. A property of $\bigwedge$ is that $m = \bigwedge (n : S \mid P\,n) \equiv P\,m \wedge \forall n : S\,.\,P\,n \Rightarrow m \le n$ for any subset S of $\mathbb{N}$ and predicate P on $\mathbb{N}$ with $\exists n : S\,.\,P\,n$. The choice operator $[\!]$ has axiom $[\!]\, f \in \mathcal{R}\, f$, and f^{-} is the generalized inverse of f, yielding inverse images iff they are unique [4]. Also, $n\,\$\,a = \sum i : \mathcal{D}\,a\,.\,a\,i = n$ counts occurrences of n in a.

A few ad hoc operators: abs is the absolute value operator, and Evn etc. are appropriate predicates on $\mathbb{N}$ (i.e., their type is $\mathbb{N} \to \mathbb{B}$).

Note: we provide some extra information by stating here that no equation contains out-of-domain applications (e.g., a right-hand side outside $\square\, 5$). This is ensured by the designer of the test and captured in the formalization.

Calculating the Solution(s). We shall use very few words; justifications are written between $\langle\ \rangle$, equation references between $[\ ]$, using [20] for the "extra eqn.". Heuristic: we scan the list various times; first looking for equations yielding an answer by themselves, then extracting the maximum of information out of single equations, then in combination etc.. The numbering indicates how many answers are still left. Obviously, at the side we keep a running inventory of all answers found thus far, and occasionally we will show it.

Table 2. Self-referential Aptitude Test

---

0. The first question whose answer is B is question
    (A) 0 (B) 1 (C) 2 (D) 3 (E) 4
1. The only two consecutive questions with identical answers are questions
    (A) 5 and 6 (B) 6 and 7 (C) 7 and 8 (D) 8 and 9 (E) 9 and 10
2. The number of questions with the answer E is
    (A) 0 (B) 1 (C) 2 (D) 3 (E) 4
3. The number of questions with the answer A is
    (A) 4 (B) 5 (C) 6 (D) 7 (E) 8
4. The answer to this question is the same as the answer to question
    (A) 0 (B) 1 (C) 2 (D) 3 (E) 4
5. The answer to question 16 is
    (A) C (B) D (C) E (D) none of the above (E) all of the above
6. Alphabetically, the answer to this question and the answer to the following one are
    (A) 4 apart (B) 3 apart (C) 2 apart (D) 1 apart (E) the same
7. The number of questions whose answers are vowels is
    (A) 4 (B) 5 (C) 6 (D) 7 (E)
8. The next question with the same answer as this one is question
    (A) 9 (B) 10 (C) 11 (D) 12 (E) 13
9. The answer to question 15 is
    (A) D (B) A (C) E (D) B (E) C
10. The number of questions preceding this one with the answer B is
    (A) 0 (B) 1 (C) 2 (D) 3 (E) 4
11. The number of questions whose answer is a consonant is
    (A) even (B) odd (C) a perfect square (D) a prime (E) divisible by 5
12. The only even-numbered problem with answer A is
    (A) 8 (B) 10 (C) 12 (D) 14 (E) 16
13. The number of questions with answer D is
    (A) 6 (B) 7 (C) 8 (D) 9 (E) 10
14. The answer to question 11 is
    (A) A (B) B (C) C (D) D (E) E
15. The answer to question 9 is
    (A) D (B) C (C) B (D) A (E) E
16. The answer to question 5 is
    (A) C (B) D (C) E (D) none of the above (E) all of the above
17. The number of questions with answer A equals the number of questions with answer
    (A) B (B) C (C) D (D) E (E) none of the above
18. The answer to this question is:
    (A) A (B) B (C) C (D) D (E) E
19. Standardized test is to intelligence as barometer is to
    (A) temperature (B) wind-velocity (C) latitude (D) longitude (E) all of the above

---

With the numbering conventions as explained, here are the calculations.

20. [19] $a\,19 = 4$

19. [4] $a\,4 = (a_{<5})^- (a\,4)$
    $\equiv \langle \text{Note} \rangle\ a\,4 = (a_{<5})^- (a\,4) \wedge a\,4 \in \mathcal{D}\,(a_{<5})^-$
    $\equiv \langle \text{Lemma }^- \rangle\ \boldsymbol{a\,4 = 4} \wedge \forall i : \square 5\,.\,i \neq 4 \Rightarrow a\,i \neq a\,4$
    Lemma: $f\,j \in \mathcal{D}\,f^- \equiv j \in \mathcal{D}\,f \wedge \forall i : \mathcal{D}\,f\,.\,i \neq j \Rightarrow f\,i \neq f\,j$ (exercise)

Table 3. Equations formalizing Table 2

$a\ 0\ =\ \bigwedge i:\square 5\mid ai=1$

$a\ 1\ =\ [\![\,i:\square 5\mid a\,(i+5)=a\,(i+6)\quad$ Extra (uniqueness): $\exists!\,i:\square 18\,.\,ai=a\,(i+1)$

$a\ 2\ =\ 4\,\$\,a$

$a\ 3\ =\ 0\,\$\,a-4$

$a\ 4\ =\ (a_{<5})^{-}\,(a\,4)$

$a\ 5\ =\ (3,3,0,1,2)\,(a\,16)$

$a\ 6\ =\ 4-\mathsf{abs}\,(a\,7-a\,6)$

$a\ 7\ =\ (0\,\$\,a+4\,\$\,a)-4$

$a\ 8\ =\ \bigwedge i:\square 5\mid a\,(i+9)=a\,8$

$a\ 9\ =\ (3,0,4,1,2)^{-}\,(a\,15)$

$a\,10\ =\ 1\,\$\,a_{<10}$

$a\,11\ =\ ((\mathsf{Evn},\mathsf{Odd},\mathsf{Sqr},\mathsf{Prm},\mathsf{Mof})^{\mathsf{T}}\,(1\,\$\,a+2\,\$\,a+3\,\$\,a))^{-}\,1$

$a\,12\ =\ ((a_{\mathsf{Evn}})^{-}\,0-8)/2$

$a\,13\ =\ 3\,\$\,a-6$

$a\,14\ =\ a\,11$

$a\,15\ =\ (3,2,1,0,4)^{-}\,(a\,9)$

$a\,16\ =\ (3,3,0,1,2)\,(a\,5)$

$a\,17\ =\ \forall\,(i:1\,..\,4\,.\,0\,\$\,a\neq i\,\$\,a)\,?\,4\mid((\$\,a)\,]\,(1\,..\,4))^{-}\,(0\,\$\,a)-1$

$a\,18\ =\ a\,18$

$a\,19\ =\ 4\qquad$ Question 19 is not mathematical, but asks an opinion.

---

18. $[0]\ a\,0=\bigwedge i:\square 5\mid ai=1$

$\equiv\ \langle\text{Prop. }\textstyle\bigwedge\rangle\ \ a\,(a\,0)=1$ $\hspace{3cm}[\alpha]$

$\wedge\ \ \forall i:\square 5\,.\,ai=1\Rightarrow a\,0\leq i$ $\hspace{2cm}[\beta]$

$[\alpha]\ \Rightarrow\ \langle\text{Leibniz}\rangle\ a\,0=0\Rightarrow a\,0=1$

$\Rightarrow\ \langle\text{Leibniz}\rangle\ a\,0=0\Rightarrow 0=1$

$\equiv\ \langle p\Rightarrow 0\equiv\neg p\rangle\ a\,0\neq 0$ $\hspace{3cm}[\alpha']$

$[\beta]\ \Rightarrow\ \langle\text{Instantiate }i:=0\rangle\ a\,0=1\Rightarrow a\,0\leq 0$

$\Rightarrow\ \langle\text{Leibniz}\rangle\ a\,0=1\Rightarrow 1\leq 0$

$\equiv\ \langle p\Rightarrow 0\equiv\neg p\rangle\ a\,0\neq 1$ $\hspace{3cm}[\beta']$

$[\alpha]\ \Rightarrow\ \langle\text{Leibniz}\rangle\ a\,0=2\Rightarrow a\,2=1$

$\equiv\ \langle[2]\rangle\ a\,0=0\Rightarrow a\,2=1\wedge a\,2=4\,\$\,a$

$\Rightarrow\ \langle a\,4=4\wedge a\,19=4\rangle\ a\,0=2\Rightarrow a\,2=1\wedge a\,2\geq 2$

$\equiv\ \langle p\Rightarrow 0\equiv\neg p\rangle\ a\,0\neq 2$ $\hspace{3cm}[\gamma']$

$[4]\ \Rightarrow\ \langle\text{From step 19, Leibniz}\rangle\ \forall i:\square 4\,.\,ai\neq 4$

$\Rightarrow\ \langle\text{Instantiate }i:=0\rangle\ a\,0\neq 4$

$\Rightarrow\ \langle[\alpha',\beta',\gamma'],a\,0\in\square 5\rangle\ \mathbf{a\,0=3}$

17. $[\alpha]\ \Rightarrow\ \langle a\,0=3\rangle\ \mathbf{a\,3=1}\ \Rightarrow\ \langle[3]\rangle\ 0\,\$\,a=5$

16. $[9]\ a\,9=\text{`30412'}^{-}\,(a\,15)$

$\equiv\ \langle\text{Note}\rangle\ a\,9=\text{`30412'}^{-}\,(a\,15)\ \wedge\ a\,15\in\mathcal{D}\,\text{`30412'}^{-}$

$\Rightarrow\ \langle y\in\mathcal{D}\,f^{-}\Rightarrow x=f^{-}y\Rightarrow y=f\,x\rangle\ a\,15=\text{`30412'}\,(a\,9)\ \ [\delta]$

$[15]\ a\,15=\text{`32104'}^{-}\,(a\,9),$ hence:

$a\,9\ =\ \langle\text{Similarly}\rangle\ \text{`32104'}\,(a\,15)$

$=\ \langle[\delta]\rangle\ \text{`32104'}\,(\text{`30412'}\,(a\,9))$

$=\ \langle\text{Def. }\circ\rangle\ (\text{`32104'}\circ\text{`30412'})\,(a\,9)$

$=\ \langle\text{Calcul. }\circ\rangle\ \text{`03421'}\,(a\,9)$

The equation $x = \text{`03421'}\,x$ has just one solution, $x = 0$, so $\boldsymbol{a\,9 = 0}$.

15. $a\,15\ =\ \langle[\delta], a\,9 = 0\rangle\ 3$ Hence $\boldsymbol{a\,15 = 3}$

14. [16] $a\,16 = \text{`33012'}\,(a\ 5)$

$\Rightarrow\ \langle[5]\rangle\ a\,16 = \text{`33012'}^{2}\,(a\,16)$

$\Rightarrow\ \langle\text{Calcul. }\circ\rangle\ a\,16 = \text{`11330'}\,(a\,16)$

$\Rightarrow\ \langle\text{Solutions}\rangle\ a\,16 = 1 \vee a\,16 = 3$

[1] $a\,1 = [\!] \, i : \square\,5 \mid a\,(i+5) = a\,(i+6)$

$\Rightarrow\ \langle e = [\!]\,(x : \mathcal{D}\,P \mid P\,x) \Rightarrow \exists\,P\rangle\ \exists\,i : \square\,5\,.\,a\,(i+5) = a\,(i+6)$

$\equiv\ \langle\text{Ch. var.}\rangle\ \exists\,i : 5\,..\,9\,.\,a\,i = a\,(i+1)$

$\Rightarrow\ \langle[20], \text{lemma}\rangle\ \forall\,i : 0\,..\,18\,.\,i \notin 5\,..\,9 \Rightarrow a\,i \neq a\,(i+1)$

$\Rightarrow\ \langle\text{Instantiate } i := 15\rangle\ a\,15 \neq a\,16$

$\Rightarrow\ \langle\text{Leibniz}, a\,15 = 3\rangle\ a\,16 \neq 3$

$\Rightarrow\ \langle a\,16 = 1 \vee a\,16 = 3\rangle\ \boldsymbol{a\,16 = 1}$

Lemma: $\exists!\,P \Rightarrow X \subseteq \mathcal{D}\,P \Rightarrow \exists\,(P \upharpoonright X) \Rightarrow \forall\,x : \mathcal{D}\,P\,.\,x \notin X \Rightarrow \neg P\,x$

13. $a\,5\ =\ \langle[5], a\,16 = 1\rangle\ 3$ Hence $\boldsymbol{a\,5 = 3}$

12. [6] $a\,6 = 4 - \mathsf{abs}\,(a\,7 - a\,6)$

$\Rightarrow\ \langle\text{Arithmetic}\rangle\ a\,6 = 4 - (a\,7 - a\,6)$

$\vee\ a\,6 = 4 - (a\,6 - a\,7)$

$\Rightarrow\ \langle\text{Arithmetic}\rangle\ a\,7 = 4$

$\vee\ a\,7 = 2 \cdot (a\,6 - 2)$

$\Rightarrow\ \langle\text{Weaken}\rangle\ \mathsf{Evn}\,(a\,7)$

[7] $a\,7 = (0\,\$\,a + 4\,\$\,a) - 4$

$\Rightarrow\ \langle[2, 3], a\,3 = 1\rangle\ a\,7 = a\,2 + 1$ $[\sigma]$

$\Rightarrow\ \langle[\gamma'']\,a\,2 \geq 2\rangle\ a\,7 \geq 3$

$\Rightarrow\ \langle\mathsf{Evn}\,(a\,7)\rangle\ \boldsymbol{a\,7 = 4}$

11. $[\sigma]\ \Rightarrow\ \langle a\,7 = 4\rangle\ \boldsymbol{a\,2 = 3}$

We show the inventory thus far. Note: no more answers can be 4 (all used up).

i	0	1	2	3	4	5	6	7	8	9	10	11	12	13	14	15	16	17	18	19
$a\,i$	3		3	1	4	3		4		0						3	1			4

10. [12] $a\,12 = ((a_{\mathsf{Evn}})^{-}\,0 - 8)/2$

$a\,12 = 0\ \equiv\ \langle\text{Def. }^{-}\rangle\ (a_{\mathsf{Evn}})^{-}\,0 = 12$

$\equiv\ \langle\text{Eq. 12}\rangle\ a\,12 = 2$

$a\,12 = 1\ \equiv\ \langle\text{Eq. 12}\rangle\ (a_{\mathsf{Evn}})^{-}\,0 = 10$

$\equiv\ \langle\text{Def. }^{-}\rangle\ a\,10 = 0$

$\equiv\ \langle[10], a\,3 = 1\rangle\ 0$

So $a\,12 \notin \{0, 1, 2\}$, hence $\boldsymbol{a\,12 = 3}$

9. [12] $a\,12 = ((a_{\mathsf{Evn}})^{-}\,0 - 8)/2$

$\equiv\ \langle a\,12 = 3\rangle\ 3 = ((a_{\mathsf{Evn}})^{-}\,0 - 8)/2$

$\equiv\ \langle\text{Arithmetic}\rangle\ (a_{\mathsf{Evn}})^{-}\,0 = 14$

$\Rightarrow\ \langle\text{Def. }^{-}\rangle\ \boldsymbol{a\,14 = 0}$

8. [14] $a\,14 = a\,11$
   $\Rightarrow \langle a\,14 = 0\rangle\ \boldsymbol{a\,11 = 0}$

7. [1] $\Rightarrow \langle\text{Step 14.}\rangle\ \exists i:5\mathrel{..}9\mathrel{.} a\,i = a\,(i+1)$
   $\equiv \langle\text{Expand}\rangle\ a\,5 = a\,6 \vee a\,6 = a\,7 \vee a\,7 = a\,8 \vee a\,8 = a\,9 \vee a\,9 = a\,10$
   $\equiv \langle\text{Known}\rangle\ 3 = a\,6 \vee a\,6 = 4 \vee 4 = a\,8 \vee a\,8 = 0 \vee 0 = a\,10$
   $\equiv \langle\text{No more 4}\rangle\ 3 = a\,6 \vee a\,8 = 0 \vee 0 = a\,10$
   $\equiv \langle(a_{\mathsf{Evn}})^{-}\,0 = 14\rangle\ \boldsymbol{a\,6 = 3}$

6. [1] $a\,1 = [\!]\,i:\square 5 \mid a\,(i+5) = a\,(i+6)$
   $\Rightarrow \langle\text{Lemma } a\,5 = a\,6\rangle\ \boldsymbol{a\,1 = 0}$
   Lemma: $X \subseteq \mathcal{D}\,P \;\Rightarrow\; \exists!\,P \wedge e = [\!]\,(x:X \mid P\,x) \;\Rightarrow\; e \in X$

5. [8] $a\,8 = \bigwedge i:\square 5 \mid a\,(i+9) = a\,8$
   $\Rightarrow \langle\text{Prop. } \bigwedge\rangle\ a\,(a\,8+9) = a\,8$ $[\kappa]$
   $a\,8 = 0 \;\Rightarrow\; \langle[12], a\,12 \neq 0\rangle\ 0$
   $a\,8 = 1 \;\Rightarrow\; \langle[\kappa, 10]\rangle\ a\,10 = 1 \wedge a\,10 = 2$
   $a\,8 = 2 \;\Rightarrow\; \langle[\kappa], 8.\rangle\ a\,11 = 2 \wedge a\,11 = 0$
   So $a\,8 \notin \{0,1,2\}$, hence $\boldsymbol{a\,8 = 3}$

4. [10] $a\,10 = 1\,\$\,a_{<10}$
   $\Rightarrow \langle a_{<10} = \text{'3031433430'}\rangle\ \boldsymbol{a\,10 = 1}$
   We show once more the running inventory.

i	0	1	2	3	4	5	6	7	8	9	10	11	12	13	14	15	16	17	18	19
$a\,i$	3	0	3	1	4	3	3	4	3	0	1	0	3		0	3	1			4

3. Letting $b := a_{\notin\{13,17,18\}}$, earlier answers yield

i	0	1	2	3	4
$i\,\$\,b$	4	3	0	7	3

   From step 17, $0\,\$\,a = 5$, so calculation (not shown) yields $0\,\$\,a_{\in\{13,17,18\}} = 1$.
   [17] $\Rightarrow \langle a\,17 \neq 4, 0\,\$\,a = 5\rangle\ a\,17 = ((\$\,a)\!\upharpoonright(1\mathrel{..}4))^{-}\,5 - 1$ $[\mu]$
   $\Rightarrow \langle\text{Note, prop.}^{-}\rangle\ \exists!\,i:1\mathrel{..}4\mathrel{.} i\,\$\,a = 5$
   $\Rightarrow \langle\text{Arith.}\rangle\ 1\,\$\,a = 5$
   $\Rightarrow \langle[\mu], 1\,\$\,b = 3\rangle\ \boldsymbol{a\,17 = 0 \wedge a\,13 = a\,18 = 1}$

0. Result: $a = \text{'30314334301031031014'}$.

This was a first version, still needing some restyling, but instructive as a first attempt. Although detailed, the formal derivation is not much larger than the informal statement. Deep mathematical problems like Fermat's "last theorem" will cause more expansion, "real-life" problems usually less.

As before, the point is *not* solving problems that cannot be solved without formal methods: the web contains informal solutions for this example. Even more: for a beginner, solving any but the smallest problem formally is harder, since it forces concentrating on solving the problem and learning the formalism.

The point is that the statement of this problem can be understood by any student without background in computing or other fields of engineering, yet the formalization provides the opportunity for illustrating all notational issues relevant in modeling engineering systems and most formal rules needed to reason calculationally about them. Therefore, problems of this kind are ideal as running examples for any introductory course or textbook on formal methods.

5   Final Remarks

An Important Observation. Popular belief holds that formal methods are of little use in deriving formulas from informal statements, almost by definition. Yet, formal methods are especially valuable for this translation in the following way.

Precisely because informal statements are subject to interpretation, translation into formulas will generally yield different results — in fact, almost certainly if done from different viewpoints or, ideally, by different people. Formal calculation can then elucidate the relationship between the formalizations: equivalence, refinement, contradiction, hidden hypotheses etc., as the case may be.

Again, the problem in Section 4 can illustrate this: a literal translation of the statements in Table 2 will, for most of them, yield precursors of the equations in Table 3 rather than the equations themselves. Even more: problem solvers cited on the website mentioned in [16] have observed that some questions can be interpreted in emtirely different ways.

On Language Expressiveness. Faithful translation requires a very expressive language, otherwise steps have to be skipped or even the link between the informal specification and the formulas is not easy to see. Since, with the current state of the art, automated tools still reflect to a large degree the restrictions imposed by the implementation or even some peculiar logic, they cause gaps.

An example of a tool-supported specification language that suffers less from this drawback than its peers is Lamport's TLA$^+$ [14], as it was designed with mathematical expression in mind. Therefore I particularly enjoy using this language and support tool (TLC) for the laboratory exercises in one of my courses.

Yet, a fully-fledged declarative language, designed with a preference for expressiveness over implementability, still offers advantages. Here is an example.

Informal specification: given a sequence of symbols, replace successive appearances of the same symbol (aptly called *stuttering* in the context of [14]) by a single appearance of that symbol. Sequences are defined as functions on natural numbers, e.g., of type $\mathbb{N} \rightarrow S$ for infinite sequences of elements of S.

Before continuing, the reader should express this in his/her preferred formalism. Even more interesting is letting students do this as a homework assignment.

Lamport's formal specification is the following. For any infinite sequences σ,

$$\natural\sigma \; \overset{\Delta}{=} \; \text{LET } f[n \in Nat] \; \overset{\Delta}{=} \; \text{IF } n = 0 \text{ THEN } 0$$
$$\text{ELSE }\ \text{IF } \sigma[n] = \sigma[n-1]$$
$$\text{THEN } f[n-1]$$
$$\text{ELSE } f[n-1]+1$$
$$S \; \overset{\Delta}{=} \; \{f[n] : n \in Nat\}$$
$$\text{IN}\quad [n \in S \mapsto \sigma[\text{CHOOSE } i \in Nat : f[i] = n]]$$

I wanted to derive a formula from the informal specification that reflects the intuitive simplicity of the mapping. An essential feature that emerges from the statement is that the elements the sequence remain intact and in order; only the corresponding domain points are changed. This is exploited as follows.

Let us first provide some background. In Funmath, any function f satisfies $f = x : \mathcal{D} f . f x$ for new variable x (like $N = \lambda x . N x$ for lambda terms), but also $f = \bigcup x : \mathcal{D} f . x \mapsto f x$, a merge of maplets. The effect of *merge* ($\bigcup$) for simple cases can be inferred from its use here, but its generic definition in [4] is more subtle and yields extra properties that make it extremely flexible, as illustrated by $f^{-} = \bigcup x : \mathcal{D} f . f x \mapsto x$ for *any* (not necessarily injective) function.

With this background, any sequence β can be written $\bigcup n : \mathcal{D} \beta . n \mapsto \beta n$. To transform this according to the specification, it suffices replacing the the domain point n to the left of $\mapsto$ by the number of times that a new "stutter" started before, which is $\sum k : \Box n . \beta (k + 1) \neq \beta k$. This yields the Funmath definition

$$\natural \beta = \bigcup n : \mathcal{D} \beta . \sum (k : \Box n . \beta (k + 1) \neq \beta k) \mapsto \beta n \qquad (2)$$

for finite as well as infinite sequences. In a complete Funmath definition, equation (2) would be preceded by **def** $\natural : S^{\omega} \to S^{\omega}$ **with**, specifying the types.

Note that equation (2) is as succinct as the informal specification and easy to relate to the informal specification: immediately for those familiar with the formalism, and with the above derivation otherwise. Proving equivalence of equation (2) with Lamport's specification for infinite sequences, or with the semantics of a recursive Haskell program having the stated effect on finite sequences is a typical exam problem (subdivided into subproblems with helpful hints).

Educational Issues. In an ideal world, separation of concerns would be well-served by domain-independent problems making things easier on students. Yet, this does not guarantee a positive reception by all concerned. In courses, we found that some students react adversely, and a small minority (about 2 in 25) 'strongly asserts' (!) not being interested in puzzles or even in analogies with more tangible phenomena, but only wanting to do "real" applications and programming.

Taking such comments at face value is misleading. Indeed, when offered the choice between a 'theoretical' and an 'application' problem in a test, students mostly choose the former. In class exercises, they do less well on practical problems, and the mistakes or breaks in the answers show difficulties with combined concerns. Deeper probing via separate questionnaires strongly suggests that stating a preference for "real" problems is often only a pose, and that a dislike of mathematics is the real problem. Many prefer programming because of the immediate feedback from the computer and the chance to tinker until it works.

We conjecture that the growing supply of CS courses with just programming assignments on seemingly 'practical' but intellectually insignificant problems [19] degrades the ability to cope with the delay in gratification when doing math.

Yet, not taking the aforesaid comments for granted is also risky, because colleagues responsible for interpreting the questionnaires may well take them literally, especially if they are adverse to formal methods. In that case, the teacher faces the choice between serving the students or serving the administrators.

References

1. Vicki L. Almstrum, "Investigating Student Difficulties With Mathematical Logic", in: C. Neville Dean, Michael G. Hinchey, eds, *Teaching and Learning Formal Methods*, pp. 131–160. Academic Press (1996)
2. Roland Backhouse, *Algorithmic Problem Solving*. Lecture Notes, University of Nottingham (2005). On the web: http://www.cs.nott.ac.uk/~rcb/G5AAPS/aps.ps
3. Raymond T. Boute, *Funmath illustrated: a declarative formalism and application examples*. Declarative Systems Series No. 1, Computing Science Institute, University of Nijmegen (1993)
4. R. Boute, "Concrete Generic Functionals: Principles, Design and Applications", in: Jeremy Gibbons and Johan Jeuring, eds., *Generic Programming*, pp. 89–119, Kluwer (2003)
5. Raymond Boute, "Functional declarative language design and predicate calculus: a practical approach", *ACM TOPLAS, Vol. 27*, No. 5, pp. 988–1047 (Sep. 2005)
6. Raymond Boute, "Calculational semantics: deriving programming theories from equations by functional predicate calculus", to appear in *ACM TOPLAS* (2006)
7. Karl Dahlke, "Fun and Challenging Math Problems for the Young, and Young At Heart " http://www.eklhad.net/funmath.html
8. Edsger W. Dijkstra, "How Computing Science created a new mathematical style", *EWD 1073* (1990) http://www.cs.utexas.edu/users/EWD/ewd10xx/EWD1073.PDF
9. Martin Gardner, *My Best Mathematical and Logic Puzzles*. Dover (1994)
10. David Gries, *The Science of Programming*. Springer (1981, 5th printing 1989)
11. David Gries and Fred Schneider, *A Logical Approach to Discrete Math*. Springer (1993)
12. David Gries, "The need for education in useful formal logic", *IEEE Computer 29*, 4, pp. 29–30 (Apr. 1996)
13. Philip N. Johnson-Laird, (example problems in the psychological study of human reasoning), http://www.princeton.edu/~psych/PsychSite/fac_phil.html
14. Leslie Lamport, *Specifying Systems: The TLA+ Language and Tools for Hardware and Software Engineers*. Addison-Wesley (2002)
15. Rex Page, *BESEME: Better Software Engineering through Mathematics Education*, project presentation http://www.cs.ou.edu/~beseme/besemePres.pdf
16. Jim Propp, "Self-Referential Aptitude Test", *Math Horizons, Vol. 12*, Feb. 2005, p. 35 (Feb. 2005) http://www.maa.org/mathhorizons/volume/volume12.html
17. Raymond Smullyan, *The Lady or the Tiger*. Random House (1992)
18. J. Mike Spivey, *The Z notation: A Reference Manual*. Prentice-Hall (1989).
19. Joel Spolsky, "The Perils of JavaSchools", in: *Joel on Software* (Dec. 29, 2005) http://www.joelonsoftware.com/articles/ThePerilsofJavaSchools.html
20. Paul Taylor, *Practical Foundations of Mathematics* (second printing), No. 59 in *Cambridge Studies in Advanced Mathematics*, Cambridge University Press (2000); quotation from comment on chapter 1 in http://www.dcs.qmul.ac.uk/~pt/Practical_Foundations/html/s10.html
21. George B. Thomas, Maurice D. Weir, Joel Hass, Frank R. Giordano, *Thomas's Calculus* (11th. ed.). Addison Wesley (2004)
22. Frits Vaandrager, private communication (Feb. 2006)
23. Jeannette M. Wing, "Weaving Formal Methods into the Undergraduate Curriculum", *Proceedings of the 8th International Conference on Algebraic Methodology and Software Technology (AMAST)* pp. 2–7 (May 2000) http://www-2.cs.cmu.edu/afs/cs.cmu.edu/project/calder/www/amast00.html

Compositional Binding in Network Domains

Pamela Zave

AT&T Laboratories—Research, Florham Park, New Jersey USA
`pamela@research.att.com`

Abstract. This paper considers network services that bind identifiers in the course of delivering messages, and also persistent, point-to-point connections made in the context of such bindings. Five patterns represent the different ways that identifier binding can be accomplished. A formal model incorporating these patterns is used to compare the properties of the patterns, to define desirable network properties related to identifier binding, and to establish sufficient conditions for guaranteeing them. The results provide new insights into connections between mobile endpoints.

1 Introduction

1.1 The Problem

The most complex aspect of network design and operation is routing. Although network routing has been studied intensively, almost all investigations are focused on the goals of performance and reliability. This paper is also about routing, but its focus is on services: How should network services be built and deployed? How can network architecture best support the needs of services?

Of all the possible purposes and behaviors of network services, this paper concerns two: (1) Delivering a message that requires binding of an identifier. In other words, the sender of the message knows the intended receiver of the message by one identifier, and the network knows that receiver by another identifier. To deliver the message, it is necessary to bind the first identifier to the second. (2) Providing a persistent, point-to-point connection in the presence of identifier binding. In other words, one or both of the connection endpoints knows each other by an identifier that requires binding.

The specific goal of the paper with respect to these services is to classify all the ways that they can be performed, and to elucidate the properties of each. The potential benefit to service builders is that they can make informed design decisions. The potential benefit to network architects is that they can determine whether an architecture provides good support for services.

There are many reasons why a service might maintain two distinct identifiers I_1 and I_2 with the same meaning, in the sense that both identify the desired receiver of a message. Four of the most common reasons are:

- I_1 represents an abstraction such as a group of equivalent endpoints, and I_2 represents a concrete instance of the abstraction such as a member of the group.

J. Misra, T. Nipkow, and E. Sekerinski (Eds.): FM 2006, LNCS 4085, pp. 332–347, 2006.
© Springer-Verlag Berlin Heidelberg 2006

- I_1 is a long-lasting identifier such as the published address of a mobile end-point, and I_2 is a short-lived identifier such as the current network address of the mobile endpoint.
- I_1 is a public identifier and I_2 is a private one.
- I_1 belongs to the address space of the subnetwork to which the sender is attached, while I_2 belongs to the address space of the subnetwork to which the destination is attached. In this situation the sender cannot send the message with address I_2 because it is either illegal or has a different meaning in the sender's locality.

These bindings have interesting properties and interactions from a service perspective [10].

1.2   Approach to a Solution

It is widely accepted in the network literature that naming and routing are related (Balakrishnan et al. have assembled an excellent bibliography on the subject [1]), but it is difficult to say exactly how they are related. What we find in the literature is a bewildering variety of examples, particularly because the explosive growth of the Internet has been accompanied by an explosion in the ways its structures are used and the purposes they are used for.

The first contribution of this paper is a formal model that gives a precise answer to the question of how identifier binding can be accomplished in the course of message delivery (Sections 2 and 3). The scope of the formal model is a network *domain*, which corresponds loosely to the use of one protocol within one network layer. Three "patterns" identify the three major variations on the theme of identifier binding.

The model is compositional in the sense that message delivery can involve a composition of any number of bindings. It is used to define the domain properties of reachability, determinism, and nonlooping, and to state some simple theorems concerning them.

The formal model appears to apply equally well to all network layers and protocols. Most interestingly, application of the model to the "link" and "network" (IP) layers shows that IP routing is simply a special case of identifier binding. This adds a fifth reason for binding to the list above, the new reason being to get the message closer to its destination.

The second contribution of this paper concerns the structure necessary to implement persistent connections in the presence of identifier binding. For this to work, an endpoint must be able to send messages that respond to a message it has received, and these messages must be delivered to the sender of the original message. Two ways to do this are presented as patterns that can be combined with the patterns for message delivery (Sections 4 and 5).

Returnability is the domain property ensuring correct connections (Section 4). For a domain to have returnability, its various bindings must interact correctly. Section 6 proposes a set of constraints for ensuring returnability in a domain, and gives evidence of their sufficiency. Section 7 shows how the results apply to the problem of sustaining connections between mobile endpoints.

The model is written in Alloy [3]. The formal reasoning is performed by the Alloy Analyzer, which checks all possible instantiations of a model up to a specified size. The size limits used were not arbitrary, but rather based on reasoning about the model itself. Nevertheless, the claimed results should still be confirmed by proof. For reasons of space this paper shows only fragments of the model; the full model, including information about analysis bounds, is available on the author's Web site.

2 Domains

A *domain* exists to provide network communication among a set of agents known as *endpoints*. Typically a domain is associated with the protocol that the endpoints use to communicate with each other, so there is an IP domain in the network layer of the Internet, and TCP and UDP domains in the transport layer of the Internet. In the application layer there are many domains associated with protocols; for example, the SIP domain is associated with the SIP protocol for for voice-over-IP and other media services [8].

The address *space* of a domain is the set of strings that the routing infrastructure of the domain can interpret. This infrastructure is represented by a relation *routing* from the address space to the endpoints. For example, in the IP domain, IP routing maps IP addresses to hosts.

Although *routing* is not constrained by the formal model, it is best to think of it, at least initially, as an immutable function. More flexible mappings to endpoints, such as mappings defined on abstract identifiers, one-to-many mappings, and transient mappings, are all provided by the bindings that are the subject of this paper.

A *path* packages together agent attributes *generator* and *absorber* and address attributes *source* and *dest*. If a domain *supports* a path, then it is consistent with the domain model for the path's generator to send a message in the domain with those source and destination addresses, and for that message to be received by the absorber. For a given *generator, source,* and *dest* a domain might support more than one path, which means that it can route nondeterministically to any one of a set of absorbers. In Alloy, the signature of domains and paths, and the definition of support, are:

```
sig Domain {                            sig Path {
   endpoints: set Agent,                   source: Address,
   space: set Address,                     dest: Address,
-- Arrow is Cartesian product.             generator: Agent,
   routing: space -> endpoints }           absorber: Agent      }


pred DomainSupportsPath (d: Domain, p: Path) { {
-- Source address routes to generator (dot is relational join).
   p.source in (d.routing).(p.generator)
-- The destination address routes to the absorber.
   p.absorber in (p.dest).(d.routing)                           } }
```

Often a domain is partitioned by subnetworks, each of which may have its own administration, address space, and routing function. Although interoperation of subnetworks requires binding [11], this example of binding is not necessary for exploring binding issues, so subnetworks are ignored in this paper.

3   Bindings and Reachability

Endpoints are not the only agents participating in domains. There are also *handlers*, which (among many other activities) absorb messages or forward them on their way to their destinations. In the SIP domain, the handlers are SIP application servers. In the IP domain, the handlers include firewalls, gateways, and Mobile IP home agents [7]. In a lower-layer domain implementing IP, the handlers are IP routers.

If a path from one endpoint to another includes handlers, it is divided into *hops* as shown in Figure 1. One of the reasons for having handlers in paths is to bind identifiers. The figure shows three patterns for delivering a message when binding of an identifier I_1 to an identifier I_2 is required. Of the three patterns, two entail the use of handlers in the message path.

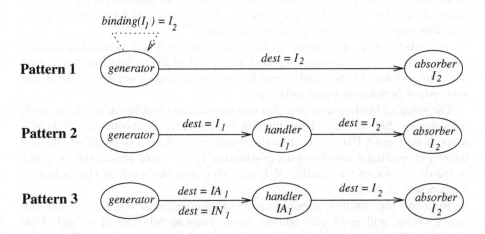

Fig. 1. Three patterns for delivering a message with binding

In Pattern 1, the initiator does its own lookup of the binding of I_1, and then sends a message whose destination is the resulting identifier I_2. An example of Pattern 1 is the binding of DNS names to IP addresses in the IP domain.

In Pattern 2, the initiator sends the message with destination I_1, which is mapped by *routing* to a handler. The handler handles the message by looking up the binding of I_1 to I_2, changing the message destination to I_2, and forwarding it. Most messages in the SIP domain employ Pattern 2. The domain has its own address space, in which all addresses begin with the prefix sip. If a message is sent with destination sip:I1, and if sip:I1 is associated with a server, the message goes to the server. The server looks up the binding and changes the destination to sip:I2 before forwarding the message.

In Pattern 3, I_1 has two parts. The initiator sends the message with destination IA_1, which is the address part of the identifier. IN_1 is the name part of the identifier, which is encapsulated in the message as a secondary destination. IA_1 is routed to a handler, just as I_1 in Pattern 2 is. The handler has access to the binding of (IA_1, IN_1), and handles the message by changing the destination to the resulting identifier I_2 and forwarding it. A good example of Pattern 3 is a single-address Network Address Translator (NAT). In this case, IA_1 is the IP address of the NAT. IN_1 is a port number, which is used to identify different hosts behind the NAT.

The primary distinction between the three patterns is the type of identifier that they can bind. Pattern 2 can only bind addresses in the address space of the domain, because the message is sent with destination I_1, and the destination field of a message must be in the address space of the domain. For the same reason, Pattern 3 can only bind pairs whose first components are addresses, although their second components are unrestricted. We refer to unrestricted identifiers as *names*. Pattern 1 can bind unrestricted *names*.

Another important distinction between the patterns lies in the distribution of binding data. In Patterns 2 and 3, the binding of an identifier need be accessible only to the handler for that identifier. In Pattern 1, the binding for every identifier must be accessible to every endpoint.

Other distinctions arise from the fact that Patterns 2 and 3 employ a handler in the path of every message destined for the identifier, while Pattern 1 does not. The presence of the handler can be used to increase security [1], yet it can also reduce performance and reliability.

The result of binding any identifier can be another identifier of any type, itself requiring further binding. Thus binding is inherently compositional. If I_2 is a name bound using Pattern 1, then the descriptions above are modified slightly: instead of sending a message with destination I_2, as stated above, the endpoint or handler looks up the binding of I_2 and then uses the result of the lookup as appropriate to its type.

To create the simplest possible model of compositional binding, we can abstract names, addresses, and address/name pairs as subtypes of a single type *identifier*. Then domains and paths can be extended as shown below. The union of all bindings that apply to message destinations in a domain is *dstBinding*.

```
sig Domain {                              sig Path {
  ...                                       ...
  dstBinding: Identifier -> Identifier      origDst: Identifier
}                                         }

pred DomainSupportsPath (d: Domain, p: Path) { {
  ...
-- Starting from origDst, dest is in the reflexive transitive
-- closure of binding.
```

```
   p.dest in (p.origDst).(*(d.dstBinding))
-- No further binding applies to dest.
   p.dest !in (d.dstBinding).Identifier                     } }

pred ReachableInDomain (d: Domain, i: Identifier, g: Agent) {
   some a: Address | a in i.(*(d.dstBinding)) &&
                     a !in (d.dstBinding).Identifier &&
                     g in a.(d.routing)                           }
```

Paths are extended with an *origDst* attribute holding the identifier originally given as a destination. Binding transforms it to *dest*, which must (as shown above) be in the closure of the binding relation but not in its domain. Thus the transformation from *origDst* to *dest* models a path of hops and handlers extending as far as possible before the last hop is routed to the absorbing endpoint.

An endpoint is *reachable* in a domain, from an identifier, if there could be a path in that domain with that identifier as *origDst* and that endpoint as *absorber*.

It is now possible to define some useful domain properties. A domain is *non-looping* if chains of hops and handlers cannot be infinitely extended, or

```
pred NonloopingDomain (d: Domain) {no ( ^(d.dstBinding) & iden )}
```

This says that there is no intersection between the irreflexive transitive closure of *dstBinding* and the identity relation. A domain is *deterministic* if an identifier reaches at most one endpoint, or

```
pred DeterministicDomain (d: Domain) {
   all i: Identifier | lone g: Agent | ReachableInDomain(d,i,g) }
```

Adding a new binding to a domain is performed by an operation whose signature is:

```
pred AddBinding ( d, d': Domain,
                  newBinding: Identifier -> Identifier )
```

A precondition ensures that if a newly bound identifier (member of *newBinding.Identifier*) is an address or address/name pair, then its address part belongs to the address space of the domain. The operation simply puts the *newBinding* tuples into *dstBinding*.

The domain properties of reachability, nonlooping, and determinism are preserved by adding a binding, provided that some unsurprising preconditions on the arguments are added. A particularly important group of preconditions ensures that the newly bound identifiers are unused in the old domain. The preconditions are packaged in this definition:

```
pred IdentifiersUnused (d: Domain, new: Identifier ) { {
   no ((d.routing).Agent & new)
   no ((d.dstBinding).Identifier & new)
   no (Identifier.(d.dstBinding) & new)                   } }
```

The three conditions say that the identifiers in the argument set *new* are not in the domain of *routing*, are not in the domain of the old *dstBinding*, and are not in the range of the old *dstBinding*, respectively. To ensure that reachability in the new domain is a superset of reachability in the old domain, it is sufficient to have *IdentifiersUnused(d,newBinding.Identifier)*. To preserve determinism, it is sufficient to have unused identifiers and a precondition that *newBinding* is itself deterministic. To preserve nonlooping, it is sufficient to have unused identifiers and a precondition that *newBinding* is itself nonlooping.

4   Connections and Returnability

From the perspective of binding, the most interesting use of message delivery is to create persistent network connections between endpoints. Figure 2 illustrates the setup of a connection.

The *request* message from the generator (now *initiator* of the connection) is delivered to the absorber (now *acceptor* of the connection) as described in Section 3. Because the source address can be altered in the course of the path, the figure shows a new path attribute *finSrc*, which is the final source identifier delivered to the acceptor.

To complete setup of the connection, the acceptor must send a response message, and the response message must be delivered to the initiator. The remainder of the paper concerns how the acceptor sends the response message, how we can be sure that it is delivered to the initiator, and related matters.

In the terminology of this model, to *return* a message is to send a message related to a previously received message, with the intention that the message will go to the generator of the previous message. The returning agent must do this in a fixed way, which is to invert the *source* and *dest* identifiers it received in the message being returned. The necessary relationship between the path *p1* being returned and the return path *p2* is as follows:

```
pred ReturnPath (p1, p2: Path) {
   p1.absorber = p2.generator &&
   p2.source = p1.dest && p2.origDst = p1.finSrc  }
```

As shown in Figure 2, the acceptor of the connection responds to the request message by *returning* it. Once the connection is set up, either endpoint should send messages within the connection by *returning* the last message they received within the connection. This is also shown in Figure 2, where the initiator sends its next message to the acceptor by *returning* the response message it has received.

The requirement on agents to *return* messages within a connection is an architectural constraint. It is being imposed for the purpose of ensuring that the return message goes to the generator of the message being returned, thus maintaining a healthy connection. As explained in the next section, both the *finSrc* and *dest* fields of a received message are related to bindings in the domain. The

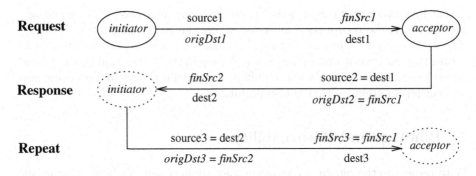

Fig. 2. The anatomy of a connection. Path attributes in Roman type are addresses, while path attributes in Italic type are identifiers.

returner of the message must use *dest* as source and *finSrc* as destination to invoke the bindings as intended. For example, in the figure *finSrc2* may not be the same as *origDst1*, and the repeat message must use the more recent *finSrc2* as its *origDst*.

Rather than being an onerous constraint, this requirement is easy to satisfy and beneficial for other reasons. The source address of any message should be an address that routes to the generating endpoint in the current state of the network (see Section 2). This constraint provides a measure of security, and is enforced in the Internet today by IP firewalls that perform ingress filtering. *Returning* messages is an easy way to get this security.

A domain in which every return message is delivered to the generator of the message being returned has the desirable property of *returnability*. This property of a domain is defined as follows:

```
pred ReturnableDomain (d: Domain) {
-- If there is a terminating attempt to return a path, it must
-- go to the generator of the message being returned.
(   all p1, p2: Path |
    DomainSupportsPath(d,p1) && DomainSupportsPath(d,p2) &&
    ReturnPath(p1,p2)
=> p2.absorber = p1.generator
) &&
-- If there is an attempt to return a path, it must terminate.
NonloopingDomain(d) &&
(   all p1: Path | DomainSupportsPath(d,p1) =>
    (all a: Address |
        a in (p1.finSrc).(*(d.dstBinding)) &&
        a !in (d.dstBinding).Identifier
    => a in (d.routing).Agent )
)
                                                                }
```

The first major conjunct says that if a domain supports two paths, one returning the other, the return path must end where the path being returned began. The second major conjunct says that if a domain supports a path, an attempt to return that path must always terminate. A loop in the destination binding could prevent termination, so that is prohibited. An undefined *dest* address could also prevent termination, so that is also prohibited.

5   Bindings and Returnability

With respect to the return of a message whose delivery entails binding by means of a handler, there are two patterns, as shown in Figure 3. A handler is inserted in the path from initiator to acceptor, just to remind us of its presence.

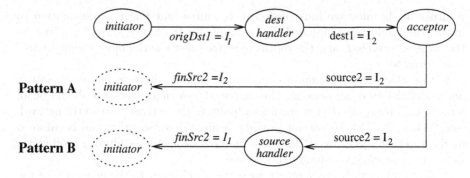

Fig. 3. Two patterns for returning a message with binding. If the original message follows Pattern 3 and the return message follows Pattern B, then *finSrc2* has both address and name parts.

In Pattern A, address I_2 is the final source of the return message as delivered to the initiator. In Pattern B, the return message goes through a handler *because it has source I_2*, not because of its destination. The handler inverts the binding, so that the final source of the return message is I_1.

Most domains do not have a built-in mechanism for routing a message to a handler on the basis of its source address. However, DFC [2,4] and SIP domains have it, and it can be simulated by various mechanisms.

The two patterns lead to fundamentally different network behaviors. With Pattern A only the first message of a connection goes through a handler, which evaluates the binding exactly once for the connection. With Pattern B, every message of a connection goes through a handler: each message from the acceptor to the initiator goes through a handler that hides I_2, and each message from the initiator to the acceptor goes through a handler that re-evaluates the binding of I_1.

As a result of these differences, the two patterns are good for different purposes. Pattern A is good for one-to-many bindings, for example bindings that distribute requests across a pool of equivalent endpoints. For a particular request, the destination handler chooses a particular endpoint and its address I_2. All subsequent messages of the connection go directly between the requestor and the chosen endpoint. The destination handler is free to choose a different endpoint and address for the next request.

Pattern B is good for long-lasting connections to identifiers whose binding changes over time, for example mobile bindings. Every message of the connection goes through the destination handler, so these messages will continue to be delivered to the same endpoint even as its network address changes.

Pattern B is far more expensive than Pattern A. Nevertheless, Pattern B appears to be the only well-structured way to achieve true mobility. The meagre deployment of Mobile IP, as described by Perkins [7], can be explained by the absence of a mechanism functioning as the source handler in Pattern B. Without it, the only way to get connection messages through the destination handler (so the binding can change over time without disrupting the connection) is to have $source2 = I_1$. Such messages, however, are often blocked by ingress filtering because I_1 appears unrelated to the current address of the mobile endpoint.

Because every message of a connection using Pattern B goes through at least one handler, the pattern provides extra opportunities for security and privacy, which should be included as benefits to balance its costs. For example, Pattern B conceals I_2 from the initiator of the connection, thus maintaining privacy for the acceptor.

Referring back to Figure 2, this section so far has described the binding of *origDst1* to *dest1*, and how the choice of Pattern A or B determines whether *finSrc2* is the same as *dest1* (Pattern A) or *origDst1* (Pattern B). In other words, it concerns how the initiator reaches the acceptor.

The patterns apply equally to how the acceptor reaches the initiator. In this direction, the identifier by which the initiator is known to the acceptor is *finSrc1*. In this direction Pattern A is vacuous, as *source1* will be the same as *finSrc1*. With Pattern B, however, a handler invoked when the source address is *source1* changes it to a different *finSrc1*, and every message from the acceptor to the initiator goes through a destination handler for *finSrc1*.

The A/B distinction does not apply to Pattern 1 because there the initiator knows address I_2 from the beginning. In effect, all Pattern 1 bindings are also Pattern A bindings.

6   Structured Bindings

To add Patterns A and B to our model of composable bindings, it is necessary to extend domains and paths as follows:

```
sig Domain {                              sig Path {
   ...                                       ...
   srcBinding: Identifier -> Identifier,     finSrc: Identifier
   AdstBinding: Identifier -> Identifier,  }
```

```
    BdstBinding: Identifier -> Identifier
} {
    dstBinding = AdstBinding + BdstBinding
}

pred DomainSupportsPath (d: Domain, p: Path)  {
    ...
    p.finSrc in (p.source).(*(d.srcBinding)) &&
    p.finSrc !in (d.srcBinding).Identifier        }
```

The generalization *dstBinding* is now the union of two destination bindings, one following Pattern A and one following Pattern B. There is also a *srcBinding* that transforms a *source* address to a *finSrc* identifier exactly as *dstBinding* transforms an *origDst* identifier to a *dest* address.

Note that, in this simple model, source and destination bindings are applied independently to each message. In a more complex model, the handlers might do more than just bind, and their order might be significant. Routing to all source handlers before any destination handlers has proven to be a very successful rule for this situation [4].

The easiest way to ensure returnability in a domain with many bindings is to impose structure on them. The following definition of a structured domain is stronger than it needs to be for many real situations, where sufficient conditions can be defined more locally. The point here is not to find the narrowest constraints, but rather to understand why certain domain properties are important in general, and how they contribute to returnability.

```
pred StructuredDomain (d: Domain) {
    let ADom = (d.AdstBinding).Identifier,
        BDom = (d.BdstBinding).Identifier,
        RDom = (d.routing).Agent,
        BRan = Identifier.(d.BdstBinding)  | {
    NonloopingDomain(d)
-- The two bindings and routing operate on different identifiers.
    no (ADom & BDom)
    no (ADom & RDom)
    no (BDom & RDom)
-- Except for AdstBinding, delivering a message is deterministic.
    (all i: Identifier | lone i.(d.BdstBinding) )
    (all i: Identifier | lone i.(d.routing) )
-- B bindings are invertible, are inverted by srcBinding.
    all i: Identifier | lone (d.BdstBinding).i
    d.srcBinding = ~(d.BdstBinding)
-- Pattern A bindings precede Pattern B bindings.
    no ( BRan & ADom )                              } }
```

The *let* clauses establish *ADom*, *BDom*, and *RDom* as the mapping domains of A binding, B binding, and routing, respectively. These sets are constrained to be disjoint because it is too difficult to write constraints if one identifier can be treated, nondeterministically, in two different ways.

Routing and B binding must be deterministic because (for instance) they are repeatedly applied to the messages of a connection. If these operations could have multiple legal outcomes, there would be no assurance that all the messages belonging to one connection would go to the same endpoint. Note that A bindings can be nondeterministic (one-to-many), because an A binding is only evaluated once per connection.

B bindings must also be invertible, because they must be (and are) inverted by source binding. Seeing this constraint, one might wonder why routing does not have to be invertible. What if a B binding maps identifier I to address A_1, and both A_1 and A_2 route to the same endpoint? The answer to the question lies in the definition of returning a message, which requires that if the message being returned came to the endpoint by means of I and A_1, the source field of the return message is A_1 and not A_2. This is important because A_2 is not in the range of *BdstBinding*, and therefore not in the domain of *srcBinding*.

Finally, there is no intersection between the range of B binding and the domain of A binding, which means that in any composition of bindings, all A bindings must precede all B bindings. The reason for this constraint is illustrated by Figure 4, in which a B binding precedes an A binding in a compositional chain. The return message has *source* $= I_3$. This address is unknown to *srcBinding*, because it was produced by an A binding. Consequently the B binding is not inverted, and the return message is handled as if both bindings were A bindings. If A bindings precede B bindings, on the other hand, the return works properly, and the *finSrc* received by the initiator is the last result of A binding and the first input to B binding.

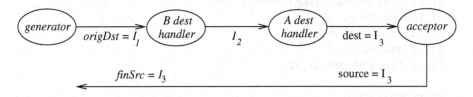

Fig. 4. An A binding following a B binding nullifies the B binding

Fortunately the most natural uses of A and B bindings obey this rule. For example, in the IP domain, DNS lookups (A bindings) precede all other bindings. The rule is most likely to be broken by accident, when a binding of either type is acceptable, and a binding of the wrong type is chosen because of lack of awareness of the consequences.

The *AddBinding* operation is extended in two ways to add A and B bindings, respectively. The preconditions on the extended operations are sufficient to preserve the structure of a domain.

Analysis with the Alloy Analyzer establishes that structure guarantees return ability—a structured domain is a returnable domain as defined in Section 4. A finite counterexample to the assertion could not have more than 2 paths, 3 agents, and 10 identifiers, even if both paths entail the application of two bindings in either direction. The Alloy Analyzer found no counterexamples to the assertion, checking all possible instances with up to 2 paths, 3 agents, and 10 identifiers. The possibility of an infinite counterexample is precluded because a structured domain is nonlooping.

7   Mobility

The most interesting example of a B binding is one used to reach a mobile agent. When a mobile agent moves its network attachment, the domain changes, or, in logical terms, becomes a different domain. The following operation is an example of the effect a move might have on a domain. In domain *d1*, endpoint *g* is attached to the network at address *a1*. In domain *d2*, it is attached to the network at address *a2*. The operation updates *BdstBinding* to track the change, and *srcBinding* to preserve the structure of the domain. Analysis establishes that if *d1* is structured, *d2* is also structured.

```
pred MobileAgentMove (g: Agent, a1, a2: Address, d1, d2: Domain)
{ {
-- Preconditions:
-- a1 is the result of a B binding.
   a1 in Identifier.(d1.BdstBinding)
-- a1 is not in the domain of a B binding.
   a1 !in (d1.BdstBinding).Identifier
-- a1 routes to g.
   a1.(d1.routing) = g
-- a2 is unused.
   IdentifiersUnused(d1,a2)

-- Postconditions:
-- Update the domain.
   (let a3 = (d1.BdstBinding).a1 |
        d2.routing = d1.routing + (a2->g) - (a1->g) &&
        d2.BdstBinding = d1.BdstBinding + (a3->a2) - (a3->a1) &&
        d2.srcBinding = d1.srcBinding + (a2->a3) - (a1->a3)
   )
-- Frame conditions on domain parts that don't change:
   d2.endpoints = d1.endpoints
   d2.space = d1.space
   d2.AdstBinding = d1.AdstBinding                                } }
```

To check that a mobile move preserves returnability, we need a new definition of returnability with a temporal dimension, because a message can be delivered

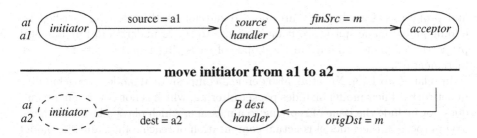

Fig. 5. How a connection is maintained to a mobile endpoint

in one domain and returned in another. This situation is illustrated by Figure 5. In this figure, a request message is delivered, then the initiator (a mobile agent) moves, and the response message is delivered in the new domain. The mobile address m of the initiator is bound using a B binding.

The new definition of *ReturnableDomainPair* is very similar to the definition of *ReturnableDomain* in Section 4. The only differences are that there are two domains $d1$ and $d2$, it is $d1$ that must support the path being returned, and it is $d2$ that must support the return path or attempted return path. Alloy analysis establishes that the following assertion is true for all instantiations with up to 2 paths, 3 agents, and 8 identifiers. A finite counterexample to the assertion could not have more than 2 paths, 3 agents, and 8 identifiers, even if if acceptor's identifier of the initiator has two bindings and the initiator's identifier of the acceptor has one binding.

```
assert StructureSufficientForPairReturnability   {
    all g: Agent, a1, a2: Address, d1, d2: Domain |
        StructuredDomain(d1) &&
        MobileAgentMove(g,a1,a2,d1,d2)
    => ReturnableDomainPair(d1,d2)                }
```

The form of this assertion emphasizes that we are making a major simplification: we are assuming that message delivery and moving a mobile agent are serializable with respect to each other.

8   Related Work, Limitations, and Future Work

The current Internet architecture has two global name spaces, DNS (domain) names and IP addresses. Various researchers have proposed that additional global name spaces should be added to the Internet architecture. For example, the Name Space Research Group has explored the possibility of adding one name space [5], O'Donnell proposes adding one name space [6], and Balakrishnan et al. have considered the addition of two [1].

The problem with the "global" approach is illustrated clearly by the fact that no two of these four proposed global name spaces are exactly alike in their goals and properties. Clearly there are more requirements than can be satisfied by adding global name spaces, so it makes sense to try to understand fundamental properties of name binding, in the hopes of satisfying requirements in a more incremental way.

In related work [9], Xie et al. also define a compositional model of reachability in networks. Their model includes packet filtering, which is not covered here, and does not include the issue of replying to a message, which plays a large role here. The purpose of their model is actual computation of reachability, and the model is not related to general network properties.

A study of interoperating subnetworks [11] is related to the present work in its approach and concerns. The present work improves on the previous study in three ways: (1) It covers bindings created for all reasons, not just interoperation. For example, of all the binding situations mentioned above, only one is related to interoperation. The present work gives special prominence to bindings supporting mobility, which requires a model having a temporal dimension not present in [11]. (2) Here, the sufficient conditions for returnability do not require that routing be completely deterministic. This is an important relaxation of demands. (3) Here, the sufficient conditions for desirable properties are simpler and easier to understand.

The model in this paper does not preserve the actual history of handlers or bindings that contribute to a path. This is a limitation, as many interesting capabilities and properties rely on this history.

Figure 6 illustrates this limitation. Alice has an identifier *anon* that she publishes in certain contexts, giving address *alice* only to trusted associates. If *anon* is bound with a B binding as modeled in this paper, every return message from Alice will have *finSrc = anon*, regardless of whether the connection was requested by a friend or by a stranger. If *anon* is bound with an A binding the problem is even worse, as a stranger will receive return messages with *finSrc = alice*.

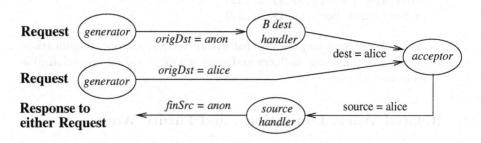

Fig. 6. These bindings do not support privacy well

This limitation can only be removed by adding a mechanism that remembers more about the request message. The issue is not adding history to the formal model—which is straightforward—but rather understanding all the possible mechanisms, their properties, and their architectural implications.

Another limitation, made obvious by Section 7, is that delivering a message through a domain and modifying the domain are assumed to be serializable with respect to each other. This assumption is far from reality, and insights into realistic network behavior based on rigorous reasoning would be an important contribution.

Another limitation of this work is that the rules for managing bindings are global with respect to the domain, and therefore difficult to apply. A more pragmatic approach might be to introduce the concept of hierarchical name spaces, which are widely used for scalability, to convert the rules into a form that is local and easy to apply.

By extending this work in the directions mentioned above, we would very quickly be studying problems at the very heart of Internet routing, security, and scalability. The prospect is equally exciting and daunting. By working top-down from abstract models and extending them carefully, however, we have a chance of making valuable discoveries that the usual bottom-up approach to networking will never reach.

References

1. H. Balakrishnan, K. Lakshminarayanan, S. Ratnasamy, S. Shenker, I. Stoica, and M. Walfish. A layered naming architecture for the Internet. In *Proceedings of SIGCOMM '04*. ACM, August 2004.
2. G. W. Bond, E. Cheung, K. H. Purdy, P. Zave, and J. C. Ramming. An open architecture for next-generation telecommunication services. *ACM Transactions on Internet Technology*, 4(1):83–123, February 2004.
3. D. Jackson. *Software Abstractions: Logic, Language, and Analysis*. MIT Press, 2006.
4. M. Jackson and P. Zave. Distributed Feature Composition: A virtual architecture for telecommunications services. *IEEE Transactions on Software Engineering*, 24(10):831–847, October 1998.
5. E. Lear and R. Droms. What's in a name: Thoughts from the NSRG. IETF Name Space Research Group, work in progress, 2003.
6. M. J. O'Donnell. Separate handles from names on the Internet. *Communications of the ACM*, 48(12):79–83, December 2005.
7. C. E. Perkins. Mobile IP. *IEEE Communications*, May 1997.
8. J. Rosenberg, H. Schulzrinne, G. Camarillo, A. Johnston, J. Peterson, R. Sparks, M. Handley, and E. Schooler. SIP: Session Initiation Protocol. IETF Network Working Group Request for Comments 3261, 2002.
9. G. Xie, J. Zhan, D. A. Maltz, H. Zhang, A. Greenberg, G. Hjalmtysson, and J. Rexford. On static reachability analysis of IP networks. In *Proceedings of IEEE Infocom*. IEEE, March 2005.
10. P. Zave. Address translation in telecommunication features. *ACM Transactions on Software Engineering and Methodology*, 13(1):1–36, January 2004.
11. P. Zave. A formal model of addressing for interoperating networks. In *Proceedings of the Thirteenth International Symposium of Formal Methods Europe*, pages 318–333. Springer-Verlag LNCS 3582, 2005.

Formal Modeling of Communication Protocols by Graph Transformation

Zarrin Langari and Richard Trefler[*]

David R. Cheriton School of Computer Science
University of Waterloo, Canada
{zlangari, trefler}@cs.uwaterloo.ca

Abstract. Formal modeling is a crucial first step in the analysis of safety critical communication protocols such as IP Telephony. These protocols are notoriously resistant to formal modeling due to their sheer size and complexity. We propose using graph transformation, a straight forward, visual approach to do this. In experiments with Distributed Feature Composition (DFC) protocol and its implementation in BoxOs, we find that graph transformation offers several key advantages over naive methods in modeling the dynamic evolution of a reactive communication protocol. The generated model closely follows the way in which communication protocols are typically separated into three levels: the first describing local features or components, the second characterizing interactions among components, and the third showing the evolution of the component set. The graph transformation semantics described here follows this scheme, enabling a clean separation of concerns when describing a protocol. Using DFC semantics one can easily focus on individual telephones, features, and communication structures without reference to components not directly of interest. This separation is a key to being able to deal with even modestly sized communication protocols. Graph transformation is also a powerful formalism, allowing for very expressive and accurate modeling of the systems under study. Finally, the relative ease of using this semantics is demonstrated, and likely avenues for further use are outlined.

1   Introduction

Currently, there is intense pressure to rapidly migrate complex communication protocols to the Internet. In this context, systems are particularly vulnerable to problems, and an accurate yet usable formal method of describing and analyzing these systems is vitally important [8]. We propose using visual semantics [11] to describe the behavior of distributed communication protocols as a first step toward such a formal analysis. We show that *graph transformation* provides a natural and expressive formalism for describing such semantics and we illustrate its use by giving a visual, graph based semantics to an Internet based communication protocol.

---

[*] The authors research is supported in part by grants from NSERC of Canada and Nortel Networks.

J. Misra, T. Nipkow, and E. Sekerinski (Eds.): FM 2006, LNCS 4085, pp. 348–363, 2006.
© Springer-Verlag Berlin Heidelberg 2006

1.1 Objectives

Our objective is to describe the behavior of a distributed communication protocol using graph transformation [25], a visual and intuitive formalism. As a
motivating example, we have focused on the semantics of the Distributed Feature Composition (DFC) architecture of Jackson and Zave [15]. DFC has been
used at AT&T as the basis for BoxOs [7], its next generation IP communication
protocol. Our graphical description of the semantics has several important features, most notably, the ability to cleanly separate out those system features of
current interest. This separation of concerns is a necessity for formal analysis of
system behavior (cf [1,17]).

1.2 Contribution and Approach

To the best of our knowledge there is no extant formal model for DFC. Although
DFC semantics can be extracted by naively building a single giant finite state
machine (FSM) together with queues as communication channels, this results in
the state explosion problem and does not give a dynamic approach to describe
different functionalities of the system.

   We propose an approach that allows the designer to formalize the behavior of
each designated component individually. The approach uncouples those components of interest from those that are not currently interacting with them. Our
model is well-suited for describing the behavior of individual features, perfect
communication channels amongst the features, and dynamic feature creation
and elimination.

   To model the dynamic behavior of a communication system as it changes over
time, we utilize a graph transition or a graph transformation system (GTS), in
which nodes represent states of the system at a particular point in time and
transitions show how the system evolves from one state to the next. System
evolution, or computation, is thus expressed as sequences of transitions beginning
from a source or initial state. Each state of the system is modeled as a graph
and by using the graph transformation system we describe how a system changes
from one state to another. We use an attributed graph and a set of rules to show
dynamic changes in the system.

   GTS allows us to generate an individual communication *usage* for analysis
and verification purposes without considering other processes participating in
the protocol. In the DFC example, a usage describes the dynamics of a telephone
call between two or more parties. A usage grows over time with the addition of
components. Therefore at each stage of the connection we have a partial usage.
The connection between two components of the system, which may be either an
end party or a feature box, is a point-to-point connection with a bi-directional
signaling channel called an *internal call*. In our proposed model a (partial) usage is presented visually as a graph, according to DFC semantics, with boxes
representing features, and arrows representing internal calls. This behavior is
one of the advantages of using GTS to describe communication protocols. Its

other advantage is to describe computations of communication protocols at an appropriately abstract level.

To show these advantages, we propose an operational semantics to describe the DFC behavior, as an example, using a 3-level hierarchical graph model. At the first level, the functionality of a feature is shown as a finite state machine graph, with each machine describing the behavior of an individual telephony feature. One typical example feature is the basic telephone; another, *call-forwarding*, operates from one local machine but both receives messages from, and sends messages to non-local machines. A feature may be composed by several modules. This modularity may result in decomposition into additional components, but for the sake of clarity and our interest in component interaction we consider each feature as a single component. The second level shows a composition of features and telephones (as end processes) communicating through channels via internal calls. This composition is shown as a higher level graph. This level represents a Communicating Finite State Machine (CFSM) architecture [20] (see Figure 1). DFC assumes the existence of essentially perfect and unbounded channels over which features communicate. The third level shows changes to the global state of the system. The global state of the system may be modified due to a local change of state in any of the features or via a topological change. Topology changes show how a feature or telephone may be added to a usage or how a feature may depart from a usage.

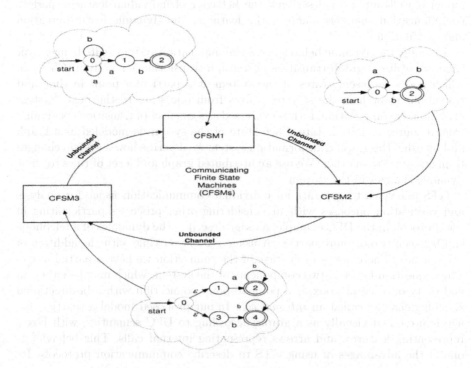

Fig. 1. Graph of Communicating Finite State Machines

The basis of our model is treating states of the system as graphs and computations of the system as transformations of these graphs. Similar to the description of a system based on formal language grammars, our graph transformation system presents a visual notation that is based on *graph grammar* rules. Fundamental elements of our visual notation are graph alphabets and rewriting rules. In the work presented here we model both topology changes and global state changes that are due to local state changes of components. A local state change happens when the content of a channel is changed and a message is sent or received by the component. Consequently each local state change implies the global state of the model to be changed. A global state of the protocol is the set of components local states and contents of the channels. The idea is to use single-pushout production rules to formally define the communication protocol's dynamic transformations.

1.3   Related Work

To our knowledge, this is the first work to use graph transformation machinery to model details of the dynamic behavior of a distributed communication protocol. In fact, Heckel [13] and Taentzer [26] have both explicitly noted the omission of reactive protocols from the GTS literature. While DFC is a rich architecture, due to space limitations, we have been restricted to discussing just a few of its representative features.

Among other works that detail system semantics we note the "Abstract State Machines (ASM)," or "Evolving Algebras," of Gurevich [12]. ASM's present states of a system as algebras and transitions from one state to another one as evolution of the algebras. ASM's are powerful enough to represent step-by-step system semantics. AsmL is an associated programming language for building ASM models. The work presented here uses a visual ASM style to capture the semantics of distributed reactive protocols.

Other works, such as [18,14], illustrate how graph transformation is applied to define dynamic semantics of systems by UML state machines. These systems present an operational semantics for local systems, but do not treat the communicating state machines. Grammar rules of these models are context-free and local, with the restriction of accessing one component and its neighborhood in a production rule. Furthermore, context-free grammars may well define the evolution of the system when components are added, but when components are deleted and the graph is shrinking we need to replace a subgraph with a smaller subgraph. In contrast, our proposed model uses context-sensitive graph transformation rules to cover distributed systems semantics; we note that the added power of context-sensitivity seems to be a requirement to deal with models as rich as DFC.

Interesting works by Ribeiro [23,24] and Baldan, Corradini, and König [3] consider an unfolding semantics and recent work by Baldan, König and Rensink [5] uses an abstraction approach for verification of graph grammars using Petri graphs. Finally, we note the extensive literature on graph transformation as a formalism for describing Petri net behavior, but again, Petri nets are a less powerful formalism. Among these works we mention that of [9,4].

Structure of the Paper. In Section 2, graphs that describe the communicating automata levels are defined. Then, graph morphism and a graph transition system to be used for modeling the third level are explained. We then describe the single-pushout (SPO) approach to define transformation rules. In Section 3 we give an informal description of DFC semantics, and in Section 4 our model is presented and DFC graph transformation rules are defined. We then show how a production rule is applied to a graph, producing the resulting transformed graph. Section 5 outlines conclusions and directions for future research.

2 Graph Transformation System

2.1 Definitions

In this section we review some definitions and approaches from the graph transformation context. Later we describe the DFC production rules, and transformations based on these definitions.

Definition 1 (Graph). *A graph is a set of nodes connected by edges. Formally it is defined as $G = (N, E, S, T, L)$, where N, E are, respectively sets of nodes and edges, and S, T, L are functions. S, T, respectively, source and target, map an edge to a node, $S, T : E \rightarrow N$. The labeling function, L, maps an edge or a node to a label, $L : E, N \rightarrow lab$, where lab belongs to a set of labels [2].*

Definition 2 (Graph Morphism). *A graph morphism $f : G \rightarrow H$ maps nodes (V) and edges (E) of graph G to nodes and edges of graph H. $f_v : V_G \rightarrow V_H$ and $f_e : E_G \rightarrow E_H$ are structure-preserving. This is defined as: for all edges $e \in E_G$, $f_v(S_G(e)) = S_H(f_e(e))$, $f_v(T_G(e)) = T_H(f_e(e))$, and $L_H(f_e(e)) = L_G(e)$. If $f_v : domain(V_G) \rightarrow V_H$ and $f_e : domain(E_G) \rightarrow E_H$ where $domain(V_G)$ and $domain(E_G)$ are the set of all nodes and edges of graph G respectively, then we have a total morphism. On the other hand f_v and f_e are partial iff $domain(V_G)$ and $domain(E_G)$ are not the whole source graph nodes and edges[22].*

Note that in a structure-preserving mapping the shape and the edge labeling of the original graph is preserved.

Definition 3 (Graph Transition System). *A transition system is generally defined as: $\mathcal{G} = (N, E, P, S_0)$. N is a set of states (nodes), where each state has a graph, G, structure, defined in Definition 1. P is a set of production rules, and S_0 is an initial state. E is a set of transitions based on graph morphism: $E \subseteq N \times P \times N$. A transition T is defined as $T : G \xrightarrow{P_1} H$ where $P_1 \in P$. The production rule P_1 has three components, left-hand side (L), right-hand side (R), and depending on the type of grammar used, a constraint (C) which can be a propositional logic formula. P_1 appears in the form: $L \rightarrow R$. The application of a rule P_1 to a graph S, is based on a total morphism between L and graph S. We write $s_1 \xrightarrow{P_1} s_2$ to show the system will be reconfigured from the state s_1 to s_2 by the application of rule P_1 [2].*

By a graph transition or a *graph transformation* system we apply a set of rules to an initial graph and replace one part of it with another graph. The initial state of a system is changed over time by a series of local computations or by addition/deletion of components to/from the system. The concept of graph transformation is equivalent to the concept of graph grammar, where we start from an initial graph and go through all derivable graphs and end up with a derivation tree.

Different ways of rule application introduce variations of graph grammars [25,10]. Among those we mention node replacement and hyperedge replacement grammars that are context-free. Context-free graph grammars are not powerful enough to describe the dynamic behavior of the telephony system we are studying. Hence, what we are proposing here is a set of context-sensitive [19] rules that allows us to describe the transformation of a telephony system.

2.2   The Algebraic Approach to Production Rules

In the algebraic approach, graphs are considered as algebras and embedding is defined by an algebraic construction (pushout). There are two popular algebraic approaches, *Double-Pushout*(DPO) and *Single-Pushout*(SPO). In the SPO approach, production rules are presented as $P : L \rightarrow R$, illustrated in Figure 2. In

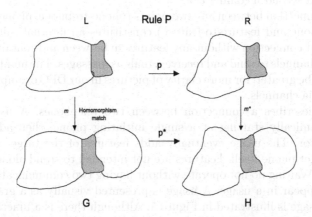

Fig. 2. Applying rule P to graph G and deriving H from G in SPO

SPO, the production rule P may be a partial morphism, and it is applied in one gluing step. First, a total match, m, between the subgraph in the left-side of a production and a subgraph in G is made, then the subgraph of G is deleted and replaced by the right-side subgraph R, resulting in H. Therefore everything in L but not in R will be *deleted*, everything in R which is not in L will be *created*, and everything that is in both sides will be *preserved* [10].

The shaded area in Figure 2 shows the common subgraph in both sides that is going to be preserved by the rule application. In Figure 2 it can easily be observed that the morphism m is a total mapping from the L subgraph to its image in G, but the morphism m^* is a partial mapping from R to the image of R in H since deletion has priority over preservation. In other words there might be elements in R that do not have an image on H.

On the other hand, DPO is a method in which a derivation step or a production rule, P, is applied in two gluing constructions or pushouts. Readers may refer to details of this approach in [10]. Although DPO has some restrictions due to explicit gluing conditions, but in our model both approaches can be used. However we adopted SPO, since it uses one gluing step and therefore is easier in applying to graphs.

3 Basic Semantics of DFC Architecture

The goal of DFC is to increase feature modularity and to structure the way in which features interact. In the most straightforward situation the DFC protocol should provide stand-alone functionalities such as basic phone service. Features are used to add incremental functionalities to existing services, as illustrated in Figure 5. Examples of features include Call-Forwarding-on-No-Answer, which allows incoming calls to be redirected to another address based on a trigger from the callee, and Call-Waiting, which provides a subscriber with the ability to switch to a second incoming call.

A basic connection between any two points (phone-to-phone, phone-to-feature, feature-to-phone and feature-to-feature) constitutes an internal call which is a point-to-point connection without any features in between and contains two communication channels to send and receive signals as messages. The number of media channels can be greater; for more clarity of pictures in our DFC examples we avoid showing media channels.

A usage describes a connection between two telephones. A usage grows/ shrinks dynamically starting at a single initiating phone, then adds features of the initiator. The usage eventually adds features of the target phone, and then the target phone itself. Features are not intended to stand alone (i.e. Voice Mail or Call-Waiting do not operate without having two communicating phones) when they appear in a usage. A usage is presented visually as a graph. An example of a usage is illustrated in Figure 5. Although there is a function for each feature, during a connection a feature may act transparently; that is, as if it does not exist. In this case a feature receives a signal message on a receiving channel, and sends the message on through a sending channel. When a feature is in a service mode it can generate, absorb, send or reverse a signal. Features also receive and transmit media through their media channels. The interaction of features is enabled via their signal channels. Although features interact, it is expected that feature operation is independent of the specific network condition; hence features can easily be added/deleted to/from the system configuration.

This communication service behaves as a network with a DFC *router* controlling the reception and transmission of signals through a routing algorithm. To make a simple phone call with one telephone at each end and no features in between, the router may need to make several internal calls. The party initiating a connection (*caller*) and the party accepting the connection (*callee*) may both subscribe to several features. Figure 3 shows that a caller initiates a call by sending a setup signal to the router through the *box_out* channel. Following that, the router sends the setup signal to the other features. If all features agree to setup they acknowledge that by sending back the *upack* signal to the caller. The caller communicates its signal messages with the other features downstream through the signal channel *ch*.

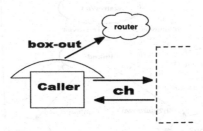

Fig. 3. Caller is communicating via the channel **ch** to a component at its right, sending its setup signal to the router through **box-out** channel

The FSM at the Figure 4 describes part of the caller box process [16]. After sending the setup caller waits for the reception of *upack* (acknowledgement signal that the setup has been received by downstream boxes) and then *avail* or *unavail* signals through the *ch* channel. The communication holds and the line links until a *teardown* is demanded from either parties. In a connection those features subscribed to by the caller lie in the *source zone* and those subscribed by the callee are located in the *target zone*; see Figure 5.

In general, there are several types of features. *Source* features are those features that are activated when the telephone is initiating the call, for example the Teen-Line feature which restricts outgoing calls at certain times of the day. These features act transparently if the subscriber is the recipient of the call. *Source/target* features are activated when the subscriber is both a caller and a callee. These features allow the subscriber to be involved in multiple calls simultaneously. An example is Call-Waiting. For *Target* features activation happens when they are subscribed to a telephone which is accepting calls, like Call-Forwarding-on-No-Answer.

Another characteristic of a feature is its boundedness. A feature is *free* if new instances of that feature are created whenever the feature appears in a usage. When a telephone is involved in a usage and instances of its features have been created for that usage, if a second usage requires that telephone, then new instances of the telephone's free features will be created. In contrast, a *bound* feature has only one instantiation, and other calls involving the subscriber telephone route through this instance. Bound features must be of type source/target.

Although the router controls the network behavior, it is not specific to DFC and therefore not described here. Since all the computation steps of features

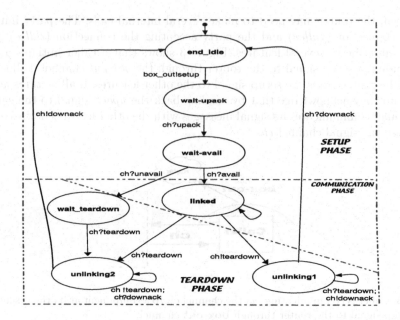

Fig. 4. Caller Process Finite State Machine. !: signal transmission, ?: signal reception.

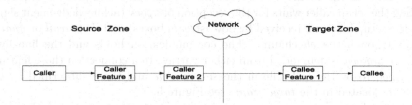

Fig. 5. A simple DFC service with 3 feature boxes

are triggered by signals (internal calls), feature interaction and composition of features are very important in DFC architecture. In the next section, semantics of DFC is presented as a graph transformation system showing the evolution of its computation due to transmission and reception of signals.

4   DFC Semantics Using GTS

4.1   Three Level Semantics

The graph model at the first level simply uses the standard notation for an FSM graph. A state of an FSM is a node and state transitions are directed edges with suitable labeling for both states and transitions. In the literature [25,6] several types of graphs have been defined that are suitable for different system structures and models. Among them we use both hierarchical graphs,

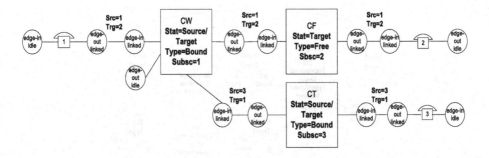

Fig. 6. A DFC example representing the second level of computation

where a node may contain a subgraph, and attributed graphs, where nodes and/or edges are labelled with attributes. The notion of hierarchical graphs is especially suitable to show that our local rules include nodes that are FSM graphs themselves. An example of a caller FSM graph has been illustrated in Figure 4.

The graph model at the second level uses three notations for nodes: a phone symbol, a feature box and a circle to be used as the connection point between two components (see Figure 6). Each telephone or feature box can be connected to other components via several input or output connection points. Edges or transitions are drawn as undirected arrows, to show bidirectional connections. Each feature node is labelled with a set of attributes such as name of the feature, and the status (Stat) of a feature with values: {source, target, source/target}. In building a usage graph, we insert all the subscribed features of an end party in the order of source, source/target, and target features, cf. [15]. Then there is a Type attribute that accepts the values bound and free, and the attribute Subsc which accepts the subscriber's telephone identification as its value. A connection point node (a circle) has two attributes. The first one explains whether that connection edge is an input edge (edge-in), or an output edge (edge-out). The second describes if it is linked to another connection point or if it is idle and can be used later.

A component potentially has many points of input and output connections, and all of them are idle before locating in a usage. For the sake of clarity we simply show some of the idle input and output nodes and all the linked ones in the second level graph of usage, illustrated in Figure 6. Those edges that show a link between connection points of two components are labelled with the direction of call to represent the source and target of the call.

This example shows a usage for the call from end party 1 with a Call-Waiting (CW) feature to end party 2 with a Call-Forwarding (CF) feature. The example also includes another partial call from the end party 3, with the Call-Transfer (CT) feature, to the end party 1. Since CW is a bound box, the second call also joins this feature. Therefore we see several linked connection points for CW. Components in this example may have more idle edge-in and edge-out connection points, but for clarity sake we do not show them here. The connection edges show

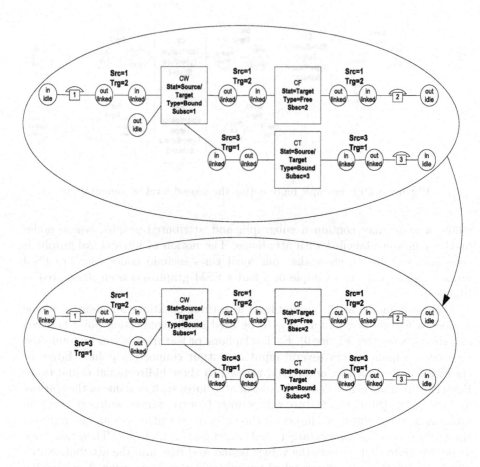

Fig. 7. A Graph derivation step representing the third level of computation by the application of production rule *JoinCallee*

the direction of each individual call, e.g. from 1 to 2 or from 3 to 1, although in reality there is only one outgoing port switching between calls in CW.

The third level is a transition graph presenting how the global state of a telephony system changes over time. There are two possible reasons for this change. The first is when a usage adds new participating features or end processes. A good example of this is when one of the end parties has subscribed to a Call-Waiting feature and during the usage a third party joins the call. This results in change of the graph structure. The example in Figure 7 shows two nodes of the transition graph at the third level. This is one computation step developed by the application of rule *JoinCallee* depicted in Figure 8, joining the CW feature to the end party 1 (callee) due to a call from the end party 3 (caller) to 1. The partial call from end party 3 toward 1 has been evolved during several steps until we get the graph at the first node of Figure 7. We omitted these steps but the last one due to the space limitation. The last evolution step depicted in this figure results in the joining of end party 1 to the call from 3 and makes the usage complete. From the picture we see the status of two connection edges (one attached to party 1 and the other to CW) have changed from idle to linked. The second type of change is a local change in a single process (or feature) and its associated channels. This occurs when the local process changes its state and either sends or receives a message. To distinguish the difference between these two cases we define two sets of rules: *global rules* and *local rules* [21].

4.2   DFC Production Rules

The rules presented in Figure 8 are SPO production rules as defined in Definition 2.2. They show the transformation of an FSM graph (local rule) and the transformation of the global architecture (global rules). The local rule shows a computation step in a process of one component (a Call-Forwarding feature), where the topology is unchanged.

Rule AppendFeature describes the addition of feature F2 to an already existing feature F1. We would like to keep the same direction of call for new features that are attached to the usage. To satisfy this requirement we keep the same feature's connection edge label of the left-hand side on the right-hand side. To apply the AppendFeature rule, the left side of this rule shows that a mapping for the idle connection point, edge-out of feature F1, should be found and it will be transformed to a linked state after being connected to the newly created component F2. The edge-in connection point of F2 is also linked, while its edge-out connection point is idle to provide the possibility of connecting another component in the future. Note that all the components in these rules have more than one idle connection point and they may have more than one linked connection point as well, but to have a clear picture we show only one of them. A constraint on this rule expresses either the non-existence of F2 or freeness of F2. Recall from Section 3 that only free features can have multiple instances in the usage graph associated with a particular telephone. The other parts of the constraint control the ordering of features based on the picture at the top of Figure 8.

Reverse application of these rules allow the shrinkage of our graph model in the second level. Partial morphism in SPO can specifically be seen in reverse rules, e.g. the reverse application of first rule in Figure 8 ends up in an empty graph. In this rule domain of nodes and edges from the left side graph that are mapped to the right side elements are not the whole source graph nodes and edges. Therefore the telephone, edges and connection nodes map to nothing in the right. In the other words, no element from the left side graph is preserved on the right side. Application of global rules and their reverses results in our third level graph model as pictured in Figure 7. While this picture shows a two-node graph, our third level graph may become very large with many transformation nodes. Many processes may exist in a distributed IP-based telephony protocol, but each node of this graph is a partial usage that can be analyzed and verified separately, without dealing with the processes not directly involved in the same usage.

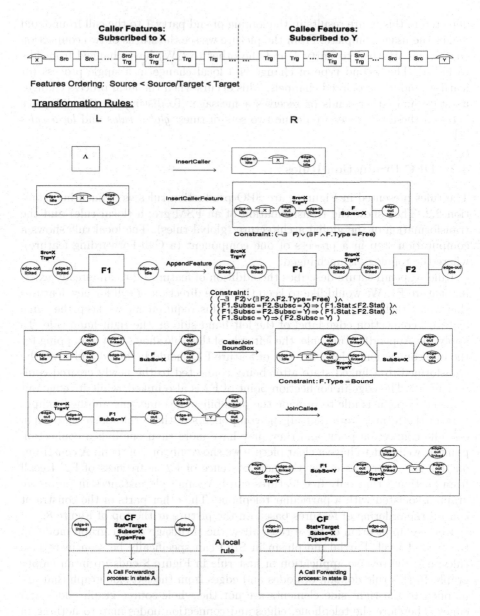

Fig. 8. Several DFC Architecture Rules

5   Conclusion and Future Work

Graph grammars have primarily been used in areas like pattern recognition, compiler construction, and data type specification. More recently, their areas of application have been broadened to include concurrent system modeling, software specification and development, database and VLSI.

In the present work, graph grammar rules together with graph transformations have been used to explain the dynamic behavior of a distributed communication protocol. Our work produces a visualization of behavior in three different levels. We explicate the three-level semantics of our model on an IP-based telephony system called Distributed Feature Composition (DFC) using graph transformations. A description of DFC semantics has been presented by a graph transformation system with a hierarchical, attributed graph model and an SPO approach for the production rules.

The first level of our model describes the semantics of a telephone or a feature process as an FSM graph, and the second level details a graph model of communicating FSM's. The third level describes dynamic evolution of the telephony system via a graph transformation system. At this level we generate a transformation graph with nodes representing the second level graphs and edges representing transformations of the second level graphs. At each transformation, the third level graph provides the ability to focus on a partial connection, a usage in DFC, without inclusion of other distributed processes that are not involved in the call. Therefore each partial usage can be analyzed and verified separately. This is a key advantage over other models because of its visual presentation, and ease of use. Another advantage of our model is that it cleanly addresses typical communication protocol layers with the ability to focus on dynamic evolution of these systems.

Our future work includes elaboration on formalizing composition of FSM's and explication on the bridge between the first and the second level graphs of our model. Later, we would also like to analyze usages against their properties. Usages in DFC can be viewed as scenarios, and our graph model as a way of expressing scenarios. We will also investigate whether the temporal logic properties of features hold over particular scenarios.

Acknowledgement

We are grateful to Pamela Zave for her many insights into this area of study.

References

1. Amla, N., Emerson, E. A., Namjoshi, K., Trefler, R.: Abstract Patterns of Compositional Reasoning. In Proc. CONCUR, 14th International Conference on Concurrency Theory, Marseille, France, September (2003) 423-438
2. Andries, M., Engles, G., Habel, A., Hoffmann, B., Kreowski, H.-J., Kuske, S., Plump, D., Schürr, A., Taentzer, G.: Graph Transformation for Specification and Programming. Science of Computer Programming. Vol. 34 , Issue 1. Elsevier North-Holland (1999) 1-54
3. Baldan P., Corradini, A., König, B.: Verifying Finite-State Graph Grammars: an Unfolding-Based Approach. CONCUR'04 Conference Proceedings, In P. Gardner and N. Yoshida (eds.): Lecture Notes in Computer Science, Vol. 3170. Springer-Verlag (2004) 83-98

4. Baldan, P., Corradini, A., Montanari, U., Rossi, F., Ehrig, H., Löwe, M.: Concurrent Semantics of Algebraic Graph Transformations. In: Rozenberg (ed.): Handbook of Graph Grammars and Computing by Graph Transformation, Vol. 3: Concurrency, Parallelism, and Distribution. World Scientific (1999) 107-185
5. Baldan, P., König, B., Rensink, A.: Summary 2: Graph Grammar Verification through Abstraction. In B. König, U. Montanari and P. Gardner (eds.): Graph Transformations and Process Algebras for Modeling Distributed and Mobile Systems, number 04241 in Dagstuhl Seminar Proceedings. Internationales Begegnungs- und Forschungszentrum (IBFI), Schloss Dagstuhl, Germany (2005)
6. Baresi, L., Heckel, R.: Tutorial Introduction to Graph Transformation: A Software Engineering Perspective. In: Corradini, A., et al. (eds.): ICGT 2002, Lecture Notes in Computer Science, Vol. **2505**. Springer-Verlag (2002) 402-429
7. Bond, G., Cheung, E., Purdy, K. H., Zave, P., Ramming, J. C.: An Open Architecture For Next-Generation Telecommunication Services. ACM Transactions on Internet Technology **IV(1)**: (2004) 83-123
8. Bousquet, L., Gaudoin, O.: Telephony Feature Validation against Eventuality Properties and Interaction Detection based on Statistical Analysis of the Time to Service. ICFI'05, Eight International Conference on Feature Interactions in Telecommunications and Software Systems, Leicester, UK, (2005)
9. Corradini, A., Heckel, R., Montanari, U.: Graphical Operational Semantics. In: Rolim, J.D.P. et al. (eds.): ICALP 2000. Workshop on Graph Transformation and Visual Modeling Techniques, Geneva, Switzerland, Carleton Scientific (2000)
10. Ehrig, H., Heckel, R., Korff, M., Löwe, M., Ribeiro, L., Wagner, A., Corradini, A.: Algebraic Approaches to Graph Transformation Part II: Single Pushout Approach and Comparison with Double Pushout. In: Rozenberg (ed.): Handbook of Graph Grammars and Computing by Graph Transformation, Vol. 1: Foundations. World Scientific (1997) 247-312
11. Engels, G., Heckel, R.: From Trees to Graphs: Defining The Semantics of Diagram Languages with Graph Transformation. In: Rolim, J.D.P. et al. (eds.): ICALP 2000. Workshop on Graph Transformation and Visual Modeling Techniques, Geneva, Switzerland, Carleton Scientific (2000) 373-382
12. Gurevich, Y.: Abstract State Machines: An Overview of The Project in Foundations of Information and Knowledge Systems. In: Seipel, D., Turull-Torres, J. M. (eds.): Lecture Notes in Computer Science, Vol. **2942**. Springer-Verlag (2004) 6-13
13. Heckel, R.: Compositional Verification of Reactive Systems Specified by Graph Transformation. In: Astesiano, E. (ed.): FASE'98, LNCS **1382**. Springer-Verlag (1998) 138-153
14. Hoffman, B., Minas, M.: A Generic Model for Diagram Syntax and Semantics. In Proc. ICALP 2000 Workshop on Graph Transformation and Visul Modeling Techniques, Geneva, Switzerland. Carleton Scientific (2000)
15. Jackson, M., Zave, P.: Distributed Feature Composition: A Virtual Architecture for Telecommunications Services. IEEE Transactions on Software Engineering **XXIV(10)**: October (1998) 831-847
16. Juarez D., A. L.: Verification of DFC Call Protocol Correctness Criteria. MMath thesis, University of Waterloo, Waterloo, Canada, May (2005)
17. Ghafari N., Trefler R.: Piecewise FIFO Channels are Analyzable. Seventh International Conference on Verification, Model Checking, and Abstract Interpretation (VMCAI 06), Charleston, SC, LNCS **3855**, (2006) 252 - 266
18. Kuske, S.: A Formal Semantics of UML State Machines Based on Structured Graph Transformation. In: Gogolla and Kobryn (eds.): UML 2001, LNCS **2185**. Springer-Verlag (2001) 241-256

19. Morvan, C., Stirling, C.: Rational Graphs Trace Context-Sensitive Languages. In A. Pultr, J. Sgall, and P. Kolman (eds.): MFCS'2001, LNCS **2136**, Marianske Lazne (2001)
20. Pachl, J.: Reachability Problems for Communicating Finite State Machines. University of Waterloo, Department of Computer Science Research Report (1982)
21. Padberg, J.: Basic Ideas for Transformations of Specification Architectures. Electronic Notes in Theoretical Computer Science, Vol. **72**, Number 4, Elseveir Sciences (2003)
22. Rensink, A.: Towards Model Checking Graph Grammars. In Leuschel, Grumer and Lo Presti (eds.): 3rd Workshop on Automated Verification of Critical Systems (2003)
23. Ribeiro, L.: Parallel Composition and Unfolding Semantics of Graph Grammars. Ph.D. Thesis, TU Berlin (1996)
24. Ribeiro, L.: Parallel Composition of Graph Grammars. In Journal of Applied Categorical Structures. Vol **7** (1999) 405-430
25. Rozenberg, G. (ed.): Handbook of Graph Grammars and Computing by Graph Transformation, Vol. 1: Foundations. World Scientific (1997)
26. Taentzer, G.: Distributed Graph Transformation with Application to Visual Design of Distributed Systems. In: Rozenberg (ed.): Handbook of Graph Grammars and Computing by Graph Transformation, Vol. 3: Concurrency, Parallelism, and Distribution. World Scientific (1999) 269-340

Feature Specification and Static Analysis for Interaction Resolution

Marc Aiguier[1], Karim Berkani[2], and Pascale Le Gall[1,*]

[1] Université d'Évry, LaMI CNRS UMR 8042,
523 pl. des Terrasses F-91000 Évry
{aiguier, legall}@lami.univ-evry.fr
[2] Laboratoire Heudiasyc, UMR CNRS 6599
BP 20529 60205 Compiègne Cedex
kberkani@hds.utc.fr

Abstract. While designing a service-oriented system, deciding whether a service interaction is desired or harmful is a subjective choice which depends on the requirements expressed by the user with respect to the service integration. In this paper, we define both a formalism and a methodology which, respectively, allow us to automatically analyse interactions based on specification consistency. For the latter (i.e. the methodology), we take advantage of both specifier expertise and formal methods.

Keywords: pre-post formalism, specification consistency, static analysis, feature integration, feature interaction resolution.

1 Introduction

The work presented in this paper was performed within the French project ValiServ[1] in collaboration with the French telecommunication company FranceTelecom and the LSR team of the university J. Fourier of Grenoble [8]. This project was devoted to service (feature) design for telecommunication purposes. The aim of this project was to better answer both feature system specification and the underlying problems: *feature integration* and *feature interactions*. Indeed, software telecommunication systems are composed of a kernel providing the basic expected functionalities and a set of satellite entities, called features[2]. Each of them aims to modify the set of functionalities characterising the rest of the system (possibly including other already existing features). This project also aimed to develop an assistant tool for integrating new phone services. The interest was to provide support for rapid service-oriented development which is an important issue, especially for telecommunication operators. Indeed, the primary motivation to offer numerous features to users is that the set of offered features differentiates providers, and then becomes a significant source of income. However, if some

---

* This work was partially supported by the RNRT French project ValiServ and by the European Commission under WGs Fireworks (23531).

[1] The acronym of which means "Validation de Services".

[2] In the following, we will indifferently use the two words feature and service although we are aware of that services also represent more particularly the notion of components such as web services.

J. Misra, T. Nipkow, and E. Sekerinski (Eds.): FM 2006, LNCS 4085, pp. 364–379, 2006.
© Springer-Verlag Berlin Heidelberg 2006

behaviours of a telecommunication system do not conform to some feature descriptions offered to customers, this may have calamitous effects on the public image of the concerned provider.

The paper is the continuation of the works developed in [3,4] by giving the theoretical basis of the methodology and the tool presented respectively in [4] and in [3]. This will be briefly recalled in Section 4. Our purpose is then to formally define an integration methodology allowing to solve interactions resulting from an inconsistent integration of a feature in a system specification, according to expert's point of view. The theoretical foundations will be based on algorithms the correctness of which will be stated (see Theorem 2 and Theorem 3). These algorithms deal with specification consistency. More precisely, interactions are properties which are violated. They may be qualified as desirable or not by an expert who can modify both the considered property, and integration choices to make service integration conform to its judgement. Thus, interaction resolution takes care of interactions which may be introduced during the integration process. To ease the service design, we define an axiomatic formalism (i.e. system behaviour is specified by logical properties) which will be used for detection and resolution. This formalism aims to specify telecommunication systems viewed along phone services at which customers can subscribe. Now, both formalism and methodology can be obviously extended and applied to specify and automatically analyse interaction in systems viewed along services (not necessarily phone services) at which objects can subscribe (e.g. lifts equipped with different services such as the basic service and the service which indicates a priority floor).

The methodology presented in this paper will then take advantage of designer's expertise with an interactive integration activity assisted by static analysis of specification consistency. This static analysis will be based on symbolic techniques dealing with phone variables to deduce the appropriate subscription configuration. Hence, the formalism defined in this paper will manipulate state transition rules (str), invariants and inequations between phone variables. The formalism developed in the paper is then a simple restriction of classic pre -post logical language. The interest of such a language is twofold:

1. it allows to automatically detect inconsistencies after integrating a new feature in a system specification. This is precisely the main goal of the present paper.
2. its syntax is very simple up to some syntactical sugar[3]. Hence, specifications are made readable for the expert what will ease his(her) choices to circumvent inconsistencies. Besides, this has been experimented in the ValiServ project with some experts of our partner France Telecom.

The paper is structured as follows. Section 2 presents the formalism and the notion of specification consistency on which our interactions are based on. Specifications are provided in the form of invariant properties and state transition rules, very much as in [20]. Examples are also provided. For lack of space, we present a simple and pedagogical example which only integrates three features on a basic system. More generally, our method can deal with all services which can be expressed within our specification

---

[3] Which will not be presented in the paper in order not to make heavy the presentation. The interested readers can find them in [3,10].

formalism and integrated on the intelligent network (see [2] and [14] for more than 20 examples of such service specifications). Section 3 details the algorithms used to check specification consistency in the integration process. Section 4 presents the methodology and our results on usual services using the tool [3] developed in the ValiServ project. Finally, related works are addressed in Section 5.

By lack of space, most of the proofs of propositions and theorems are not given in this paper. However, they can be found in the preliminary version of this paper [1]. Only the proof of Theorem 1 is given because the algorithms described in this paper are based on it.

2   Service Specification

Here, we define a formalism dedicated to service (so-called feature) telecommunication systems. Services will be specified along two types of predicates, *subscription* and *status*. By the former, we will specify what and how customers subscribe to a service. For instance[4], $TCS(x, y)$ will mean that x has subscribed to TCS and any call from y to x is forbidden. By the latter, we will specify communication situations such as to be busy, idle, etc... Moreover, telecommunication systems are dynamic systems. Therefore, in order to automatically analyse interactions, the formalism under definition will manipulate sentences of the form $(pre, event, post)$ where pre and $post$ will be finite sets of atoms denoting respectively pre and post-conditions and $event$ will be an event triggering side-effect. Moreover, some invariants roughly defined by free-quantifier first-order formulas (i.e. state-evolution independent) will be stated.

2.1   Syntax

The formalism is devoted to specify features in telecommunication systems. Its syntax is closely related to the one developed in [10]. Vocabularies (so-called signatures) over which pre and post-conditions and invariants will be built on, will then contain two types of predicates: status and subscription predicates.

Definition 1 (Signature). *A signature Σ is a triple (St, Sb, E) where St and Sb are two sets of predicates names, and E is a set of events names. Each element in $St \cup Sb \cup E$ are equipped with an arity $n \in \mathbb{N}$. St, Sb and E are disjoint sets.*
A signature is said finite *when both St, Sb and E are finite sets. An element $p \in St \cup Sb \cup E$ equipped with the arity n is noted p^n.*
St and Sb contain respectively, status *and* subscription *predicates.*

Note, by the definition of signatures, that variables are the only allowed arguments for the predicates and the events. Hence, variables will necessarily denote terminals.

Systems will be specified by means of two kinds of formulas: State transition rules (str) and Invariants. Moreover, as we are interested by automatically analysing interactions (which will be defined by properties), manipulated formulas will be constrained on their form.

Notation 2. *Let $\Sigma = (St, Sb, E)$ be a signature. Let X be a set of variables. Note $At_\Sigma(X)$ and $\overline{At}_\Sigma(X)$ the two sets defined by:*

---

[4] TCS is an usual acronym for the Terminating Call Screening.

1. $At_\Sigma(X) = \{p(x_1, \ldots, x_n) \mid p^n \in St \cup Sb, x_i \in X, 1 \le i \le n\}$
2. $\overline{At}_\Sigma(X) = \{\neg p(x_1, \ldots, x_n) \mid p^n \in St \cup Sb, x_i \in X, 1 \le i \le n\}$

Note $Sb_\Sigma(X)$ and $\overline{Sb}_\Sigma(X)$ (resp. $St_\Sigma(X)$ and $\overline{St}_\Sigma(X)$) the two subsets of $At_\Sigma(X)$ and $\overline{At}_\Sigma(X)$ restricted to predicates in Sb (resp. in St).

Definition 3 (Formulas). *Let $\Sigma = (St, Sb, E)$ be a signature. Let X be a set of variables.*

1. *A str-formula over Σ is a sentence of the form $< ctr|subs : pre \xrightarrow{e(x_1, \ldots, x_n)} post >$ where:*
   - *ctr is a set of inequations $x \ne y$ with $x, y \in X$,*
   - *$subs \subseteq Sb_\Sigma(X) \cup \overline{Sb}_\Sigma(X)$,*
   - *$pre, post \subseteq St_\Sigma(X) \cup \overline{St}_\Sigma(X)$ are two finite sets, and*
   - *$e^n \in E$ and $x_i \in X$ for $1 \le i \le n$.*
2. *An invariant over Σ is a sentence of the form $< ctr|\varphi >$ where ctr is defined as above, and φ is a quantifier-free first-order formula over $St \cup Sb$.*

In the sequel, quantifier-free first-order formulas will be simply called formulas. We will note $Var(x)$ the set of variables occurring in $x \in \{ctr, subs, pre, post, \varphi\}$.

We have chosen to separate in str-formulas, subscription atoms from pre and post-conditions because events do not modify subscriptions. Hence, subscriptions are necessarily preserved along transitions.

Definition 4 (Service specification). *A service specification $\mathcal{F}$ is a 2-tuple (Σ, Ax) where Σ is a signature and Ax is a set of str-formulas and invariants over Σ. $\mathcal{F}$ is said finite if both Σ and Ax are a finite signature and finite set of axioms, respectively. In the sequel Ax will be also noted $STR \coprod I$. STR and I will then contain all the str-formulas and invariants, respectively, of Ax.*

2.2 Examples

We now provide examples: the specifications of the basic telecommunication system, classically called POTS, and of three common services destined to be plugged on it. The different components of the specifications will be indexed by the specification name. Moreover, elements of the underlying system POTS are implicitly present for the specification of the three services.

Example 1: POTS, the Plain Old Telephone Service
St_{POTS} contains $idle(x)$ ("x is idle"), $dialwait(x)$ ("x is in dial waiting state"), $caller(x, y)$ (resp. $callee(x, y)$) ("x is in communication with y as the caller (resp. callee) part"), $ringing(x, y)$ ("x is ringing from the caller y"), $hearing(x, y)$ ("x is hearing the tone of the call to y"), $busytone(x)$ ("x is hearing the busy tone"). By convention, Sb_{POTS} is empty since by default all phones are supposed to subscribe to the basic service POTS. E_{POTS} contains $offhook(x)$ meaning that x hooks off, $onhook(x)$ (x hooks on), $dial(x, y)$ (x dials y). STR_{POTS} contains:

$\phi_1 : \quad < \mid idle(A) \xrightarrow{offhook(A)} dialwait(A) >$

$\phi_2 : \quad < A \ne B \mid dialwait(A), idle(B) \xrightarrow{dial(A,B)} hearing(A, B), ringing(B, A) >$

$\phi_3: \ < \ | \ dialwait(A), \overline{idle(B)} \ \overset{dial(A,B)}{\longrightarrow} \ busytone(A) >$

$\phi_4: \ < A \neq B \ | \ hearing(A,B), ringing(B,A) \ \overset{offhook(B)}{\longrightarrow} \ caller(A,B), callee(B,A) >$

$\phi_5: \ < A \neq B \ | \ caller(A,B), callee(B,A) \ \overset{onhook(A)}{\longrightarrow} \ idle(A), busytone(B) >$

$\phi_6: \ < A \neq B \ | \ caller(A,B), callee(B,A) \ \overset{onhook(B)}{\longrightarrow} \ idle(B), busytone(A) >$

$\phi_7: \ < A \neq B \ | \ hearing(A,B), ringing(B,A) \ \overset{onhook(A)}{\longrightarrow} \ idle(A), idle(B) >$

$\phi_8: \ < \ | \ busytone(A) \ \overset{onhook(A)}{\longrightarrow} \ idle(A) >$

$\phi_9: \ < \ | \ dialwait(A) \ \overset{onhook(A)}{\longrightarrow} \ idle(A) >$

I_{POTS} contains several invariants expressing that status predicates are mutually exclusive when they concern the same variables. For example, it contains:

$< B \neq C \ | \ \neg(talking(A,B) \wedge talking(A,C)) >$
$< \ | \ \neg(idle(A) \wedge talking(A,B)) >$

For lack of space, we do not give all such invariants. However, they can be found in [2].

POTS characterises the behaviour of a terminal which has just subscribed to the basic telephone service, when communicating with another terminal with the same subscription. For example, ϕ_5 says that if the call initiator hangs up during a communication, then his party gets a busy tone.

Example 2: *TCS*, Terminating Call Screening (this service screens out incoming calls from terminals belonging to the *TCS* subscriber's black list).
Sb_{TCS} contains $Tcs(y,x)$: calls from x to y are forbidden by y. I_{TCS} contains

$\psi_1: \ < A \neq B \ | \ Tcs(A,B) \Rightarrow \neg hearing(B,A) >$

while STR_{TCS} contains

$\psi_2: \ < \ | \ Tcs(B,A), dialwait(A), idle(B) \ \overset{dial(A,B)}{\longrightarrow} \ busytone(A) >$

Example 3: *CFB*, Call Forward on Busy (this service allows a subscriber to forward all incoming calls to a designated terminal, when the subscriber's terminal is busy).
Sb_{CFB} contains $Cfb(x,y)$: when x is not idle, forward incoming calls to y. I_{CFB} contains

$\chi_1: \ < \ | \ \neg Cfb(A,A) >$

$\chi_2: \ < B \neq C \ | \ Cfb(A,B) \Rightarrow \neg Cfb(A,C) >$

and STR_{CFB} contains

$\chi_3: \ < B \neq C \ | \ Cfb(B,C), dialwait(A), \overline{idle(B)}, idle(C) \ \overset{dial(A,B)}{\longrightarrow}$
$hearing(A,C), ringing(C,A) >$

$\chi_4: \ < B \neq C \ | \ Cfb(B,C), dialwait(A), \overline{idle(B)}, \overline{idle(C)} \ \overset{dial(A,B)}{\longrightarrow} \ busytone(A) >$

Example 4: *INTL*, IN Teen Line (this service allows a user to restrict outgoing calls during a specified daily period. The restriction can be over-ridden by entering a pin. If the given pin is the right one, then a normal call can be initiated, else the user is requested to abort his call.)

S_{INTL} contains S_{POTS} and specific predicates: $time(x)$ characterises the time slot where a pin is required from the user x to perform outgoing calls, $waitpin(x)$ means that the user x should now dial its personal pin, and $invalid(x)$ means that the dialled pin is not valid. Sb_{INTL} contains $Intl(x)$: x is subscribing for the *INTL* service.

E_{INTL} contains two new events related to the pin dialling: $dialgoodpin(x)$ for "x is dialling the expected correct pin", and $dialbadpin(x)$ for "x is dialling a wrong pin". I_{INTL} contains new invariants expressing that the status *invalid* and *waitpin* are exclusive with the POTS status *idle*, *dialing*, …and are also mutually exclusive. STR_{INTL} contains:

$$\kappa_1 : \quad < \mid Intl(A), time(A), idle(A) \xrightarrow{offhook(A)} waitpin(A), time(A) >$$
$$\kappa_2 : \quad < \mid waitpin(A) \xrightarrow{dialgoodpin(A)} dialwait(A) >$$
$$\kappa_3 : \quad < \mid waitpin(A) \xrightarrow{dialbadpin(A)} invalid(A) >$$
$$\kappa_4 : \quad < \mid invalid(A) \xrightarrow{onhook(A)} idle(A) >$$
$$\kappa_5 : \quad < \mid waitpin(A) \xrightarrow{onhook(A)} idle(A) >$$

Specifications are restricted to service specificities. They implicitly refer to the underlying system. For example, the TCS specification contains a service invariant characterising a newly prohibited situation (the subscriber terminal cannot be put in communication with a terminal from its screening list) and a limited behavioural description (what happens when a forbidden terminal attempts to call the subscribing terminal).

2.3   Semantics

Definition 5 (Models). *Let $\Sigma = (St, Sb, E)$ be a signature.*

A Σ-model $\mathcal{A} = (U, S, (e^{\mathcal{A}})_{e \in E})$ is a set U (terminals) and a set $S \subseteq \mathcal{P}(At_{\Sigma}(U))$ (states) equipped for every $e^n \in E$ and every $(u_1, \ldots, u_n) \in \underbrace{U \times \ldots \times U}_{n \ times}$ with a binary relation[5] $e^{\mathcal{A}}(u_1, \ldots, u_n) \subseteq S \times S$.
$\mathcal{A}$ is deterministic if and only if for every $e^n \in E$ and every $(u_1, \ldots, u_n) \in \underbrace{U \times \ldots \times U}_{n \ times}$, $e^{\mathcal{A}}(u_1, \ldots, u_n)$ is a partial function.

Definition 6 (Formula satisfaction). *Let $\Sigma = (St, Sb, E)$ be a signature. Let $\mathcal{A}$ be a Σ-model. A state $s \in S$ and an interpretation $\iota : X \to U$ satisfy a formula φ, noted $(\iota, s) \models \varphi$, if and only if:*

- *$(\iota, s) \models p(x_1, \ldots, x_n) \iff p(\iota(x_1), \ldots, \iota(x_n)) \in s$*
- *propositional connectives are handled as usual.*

$\mathcal{A}$ satisfies a formula φ, noted $\mathcal{A} \models \varphi$, if and only if for every $s \in S$ and every $\iota : X \to U$, $(\iota, s) \models \varphi$.

Definition 7 (Transition satisfaction). *A Σ-model $\mathcal{A}$ satisfies for $s \in S$ and $\iota : X \to U$ a str-formula φ of the form $< ctr \mid subs : pre \xrightarrow{e(x_1, \ldots, x_n)} post >$, noted $\mathcal{A} \models_{\iota, s} \varphi$, if and only if, if for every $x \neq y \in ctr$, $\iota(x) \neq \iota(y)$ then:*

---

[5] We note $s\ e^{\mathcal{A}}(u_1, \ldots, u_n)\ s'$ to mean that $(s, s') \in e^{\mathcal{A}}(u_1, \ldots, u_n)$.

$$if\,(\iota,s) \models \bigwedge_{\alpha \in subs \cup pre} \alpha \; then \; \forall s' \in S, s\, e^{\mathcal{A}}(\iota(x_1),\ldots,\iota(x_n))\, s' \Rightarrow (\iota,s') \models \bigwedge_{\alpha \in post} \alpha)$$

Definition 8 (Invariant satisfaction). *A Σ-model $\mathcal{A}$ satisfies for $s \in S$ and $\iota : X \to U$ an invariant $< ctr|\varphi >$, noted $\mathcal{A} \models_{\iota,s} < ctr|\varphi >$, if and only if, if for every $x \neq y \in ctr, \iota(x) \neq \iota(y)$ then $(\iota,s) \models \varphi$.*

Definition 9 (Specification satisfaction). *A Σ-model $\mathcal{A}$ satisfies a service specification $\mathcal{F} = (\Sigma, STR \coprod I)$ if and only if it satisfies for every $s \in S$ and every $\iota : X \to U$ each formula of $A\mathcal{x}$.*
A service specification is said consistent *if and only if there exists a non-empty Σ-model $\mathcal{A}$ which satisfies it and such that the cardinality of its set U of terminals satisfies:*

$$|U| \geq max\{Var(ctr)|\exists < ctr|subs : pre \xrightarrow{e} post >\in STR \vee \exists < ctr|\varphi >\in I\}$$

The last condition on the carrier cardinality of Σ-models prevents trivial Σ-models. A trivial Σ-model is such that the number of terminals in U is not sufficient to satisfy each inequation occurring in the ctr part of each formula in STR and I.

2.4   Fundamental Results

We first define a Σ-model which will be useful to us in the next section. Let $\Sigma = (St, Sb, E)$ be a signature. Let U and $S \subseteq \mathcal{P}(St_\Sigma(U))$ be two sets of terminals and states, respectively. Let STR be a set of str-formulas over Σ. Therefore, define the Σ-model $\mathcal{G}(U, S) = (U, S', (e^{\mathcal{G}(U,S)})_{e \in E})$ as follows:

- S' is the set inductively defined by $S' = \bigcup_{i < \omega} S_i$ with:

  - $S_0 = S$

  - $s' \in S_n \iff \begin{cases} \exists < ctr|subs : pre \xrightarrow{e(x_1,\ldots,x_n)} post >\in STR, \exists \iota : X \to U, \\ \exists s \in S_{n-1}, (\forall x \neq y \in ctr, \iota(x) \neq \iota(y)) \wedge \\ (\iota,s) \models \bigwedge_{\alpha \in subs \cup pre} \alpha \wedge \\ s' = (s \setminus \{p(\iota(y_1),\ldots,\iota(y_m))|\neg p(y_1,\ldots,y_m) \in post\}) \\ \qquad \cup \\ \{p(\iota(y_1),\ldots,\iota(y_m))|p(y_1,\ldots,y_m) \in post\} \end{cases}$

- For every $e^n \in E$ and every $(u_1,\ldots,u_n) \in \underbrace{U \times \ldots \times U}_{n\ times}, e^{\mathcal{G}(U,S)}(u_1,\ldots,u_n)$ is

  defined: $s\, e^{\mathcal{G}(U,S)}(u_1,\ldots,u_n)\, s' \iff$

  $$\begin{cases} \exists < ctr|subs : pre \xrightarrow{e(x_1,\ldots,x_n)} post >\in STR, \exists \iota : X \to U, \\ (\forall 1 \leq j \leq n, \iota(x_j) = u_j) \wedge \\ (\forall x \neq y \in ctr, \iota(x) \neq \iota(y)) \wedge \\ (\iota,s) \models \bigwedge_{\alpha \in subs \cup pre} \alpha \wedge \\ s' = (s \setminus \{p(\iota(y_1),\ldots,\iota(y_m))|\neg p(y_1,\ldots,y_m) \in post\} \\ \qquad \cup \\ \{p(\iota(y_1),\ldots,\iota(y_m))|p(y_1,\ldots,y_m) \in post\}) \end{cases}$$

Let us point out that when X, U, S and STR are finite sets, then $\mathcal{G}(U, S)$ is computable. Let us consider Σ a signature, X a set of variables over Σ and I a set of invariants. Define

$$E_\Sigma(X) = \{s \subseteq At_\Sigma(X)| \; \forall \iota : X \to X, \forall < ctr|\varphi >\in I,$$
$$(\forall x \neq y \in ctr, \iota(x) \neq \iota(y)) \Rightarrow (s, \iota) \models \varphi\}$$

then define $I_\Sigma(X) = \{s \in E_\Sigma(X)| \; \nexists s' \in E_\Sigma(X), s' \subseteq s\}$.

Proposition 1. *When Σ is a finite signature and X and I are finite sets, then $E_\Sigma(X)$ and $I_\Sigma(X)$ are computable.*

Theorem 1. *Let $\mathcal{F} = (\Sigma, STR \coprod I)$ be a service specification. $\mathcal{F}$ is consistent if and only if $\mathcal{G}(X, I_\Sigma(X))$ satisfies all the axioms of $\mathcal{F}$.*

Proof. The *if part* is obvious.

The only if part. Suppose that $\mathcal{F}$ is consistent but $\mathcal{G}(X, I_\Sigma(X))$ does not satisfy it.

Obviously, the consistency of $\mathcal{F}$ means the consistency of STR and of I. By construction, the consistency of I implies that $I_\Sigma(X)$ is not empty. In the following, the question of (the verification of) the consistency of I will be simply denoted by **InvCons**.

Therefore, if $\mathcal{G}(X, I_\Sigma(X))$ does not satisfy $\mathcal{F}$ then by construction of $\mathcal{G}(X, I_\Sigma(X))$ which relies on str-formulas, either two str-formulas with the same event lead to two incompatible states or a str-formula leads to a state violating the invariants. These two cases are denoted by respectively **NonDet** for non-deterministic str-formulas and **ViolInv** for the non preservation of the invariants by str-formulas. Then, let us prove that both **NonDet** and **ViolInv** lead to a contradiction.

1. **NonDet** there exists[6] $\psi =< ctr|subs : pre \xrightarrow{e(x_1,...,x_n)} post >\in STR$, $s \in S'$ and $\iota : X \to X$ such that for every $x \neq y \in ctr$, $\iota(x) \neq \iota(y)$, $(s, \iota) \models \bigwedge\limits_{\alpha \in subs \cup pre} \alpha$, but there exists s' and[7] $p(y_1, \ldots, y_m) \in post$ such that $s \; e^{\mathcal{G}(X,I_\Sigma(X))}$ $(\iota(x_1), \ldots, \iota(x_n)) \; s'$ and $p(\iota(y_1), \ldots, \iota(y_m)) \notin s'$. By definition, this means that there exists $\psi' =< ctr'|subs' : pre' \xrightarrow{e(z_1,...,z_n)} post' >\in STR$ and $\iota' : X \to X$ such that for every $x' \neq y' \in ctr'$, $\iota'(x') \neq \iota'(y')$, $(s, \iota') \models \bigwedge\limits_{\alpha \in subs' \cup pre'} \alpha$, $\neg p(w_1, \ldots, w_m) \in post'$ and $\iota(y_i) = \iota'(w_i)$ $(1 \leq i \leq m)$. As $\mathcal{F}$ is consistent, there exists a Σ-model $\mathcal{A}$ which satisfies it. Let $\iota'' : X \to U$ be an interpretation in $\mathcal{A}$ such that for every $x \neq y \in ctr$ and $x' \neq y' \in ctr'$, $\iota''(x) \neq \iota''(y)$ and $\iota''(x') \neq \iota''(y')$, and $\iota''(x_i) = \iota''(w_i)$ $1 \leq i \leq n$. By the property on the carrier cardinality of Σ-models, ι'' exists.

   By construction of $\mathcal{G}(X, I_\Sigma(X))$, there exists a state s'' in $\mathcal{A}$ such that $\iota''(s) \subseteq s''$. We then have for every $\alpha \in subs \cup subs' \cup pre \cup pre'$ that $(s'', \iota'') \models \alpha$. Therefore, there exists s^3 in $\mathcal{A}$ such that $s'' \; e^{\mathcal{G}(X,I_\Sigma(X))}(\iota''(x_1), \ldots, \iota''(x_n)) \; s^3$. But, we have both $p(\iota''(y_1), \ldots \iota''(y_m)) \in s^3$ and $p(\iota''(y_1), \ldots \iota''(y_m)) \notin s^3$ what is impossible.

---

[6] S' is the set of state of $\mathcal{G}(X, I_\Sigma(X))$.

[7] Without any loss of generality, we only consider the case of a positive literal $p(y_1, \ldots, y_m)$ in *post*. The case of a negative literal $\neg p(y_1, \ldots, y_m)$ can be handled in a similar way.

2. **ViolInv** there exists $s' \in S' \setminus I_\Sigma(X)$ [8], an invariant $< ctr|\varphi >$ and an interpretation $\iota : X \to X$ such that for every $x \neq y \in ctr\ \iota(x) \neq \iota(y)$ but $(s', \iota) \not\models \varphi$.

By definition, this means that there exists $s \in I_\Sigma(X)$, n str-formulas $< ctr_i|$

$$subs_i : pre_i \xrightarrow{e_i(x_1^i, \ldots, x_{n_i}^i)} post_i > \text{ in STR}, n \text{ interpretations } \iota_i : X \to X \text{ and } n+1$$

states s_i with $s_1 = s$ and $s_{n+1} = s'$, such that for every $1 \leq i \leq n$ and every $x \neq y \in ctr_i\ \iota_i(x) \neq \iota_i(y), (s_i, \iota_i) \models \bigwedge_{\alpha \in subs_i \cup pre_i} \alpha, s_i\ e_i^{\mathcal{G}(X, I_\Sigma(X))}(\iota_i(x_1^i), \ldots, \iota_i(x_{n_i}^i))$

s_{i+1} and $(s_{i+1}, \iota_i) \models \bigwedge_{\alpha \in post_i} \alpha$. By construction of $\mathcal{G}(X, I_\Sigma(X))$, this then means there exists for every $1 \leq i \leq n$, $p_i(y_1^i, \ldots, y_{m_i}^i) \in At_\Sigma(X)$ such that $\iota(y_j^i) = \iota_i(y_j^i)$ for every $1 \leq j \leq m_i$, and $p_i(\iota(y_1^i), \ldots, \iota(y_{m_i}^i)) \in s$ but $p_i(\iota(y_1^i), \ldots, \iota(y_{m_i}^i)) \notin s'$.

As $\mathcal{F}$ is consistent, there exists a Σ-model $\mathcal{A}$ which satisfies it. Let $\iota' : X \to U$ be an interpretation in $\mathcal{A}$ such that for every $x \neq y \in ctr \cup \bigcup_{1 \leq i \leq n} ctr_i, \iota'(x) \neq \iota'(y)$.

By the property on the carrier cardinality of Σ-models, ι' exists. By construction of $\mathcal{G}(X, I_\Sigma(X))$, for every $1 \leq i \leq n+1$, there exists in $\mathcal{A}$ a state s_i' such that $\iota'(s_i) \subseteq s_i'$. Moreover, for every $1 \leq i \leq n$, $s_i'\ e_i^{\mathcal{A}}(\iota'(x_1^i), \ldots, \iota'(x_{n_i}^i))\ s_{i+1}'$. We the have for every $1 \leq i \leq n$ and every $\alpha \in subs_i \cup pre_i$ that $(s_i', \iota') \models \alpha$, and then $(s_{i+1}', \iota') \models \bigwedge_{\alpha \in post_i} \alpha$. Whence we deduce that for every $1 \leq i \leq n$, $p_i(\iota'(y_1^i), \ldots, \iota'(y_{m_i}^i)) \in s_{n+1}'$ and $p_i(\iota'(y_1^i), \ldots, \iota'(y_{m_i}^i)) \notin s_{n+1}'$ what is impossible.

Let us note that the proof of Theorem 1 highlights the 3 questions to solve in order to show specification consistency. They have been noted **InvCons**, **NonDet** and **ViolInv**. The two last ones will be solved by the two algorithms given in Section 3. The first question will be tackled in Section 4.2.

Let us remark that str-formula determinism is sufficient to ensure specification consistency but in no case it is necessary.

2.5 Service Integration

The key question now is how to define service integration provided with an adequate semantic counterpart. A first answer might be to consider the union of axioms issued from different service specifications. However, this is not a good solution. Indeed, recall that a service is defined as possibly modifying the behaviour of the existing system on which it will be plugged on. Hence, any system obtained by the union of axioms of its different services would be lucky enough to be inconsistent. Therefore, in order to avoid to introduce inconsistencies during integration steps, choices are needed about which axioms are preserved, lost, modified and added. Hence, the integration of two services will be parameterised by choices. In this paper, we propose an interactive methodology based on algorithms introduced in Section 3 to determine these choices. These

---

[8] S' is the set of state of $\mathcal{G}(X, I_\Sigma(X))$.

algorithms will automatically check consistency of service specifications. When inconsistencies (i.e. interactions) are detected, they are presented to an expert who makes integration choices (see Section 4 for more explanations on how this methodology is worked up).

3   Interactions

We have seen in the proof of Theorem 1 that the inconsistency of a service specification may be the result of: the inconsistency of invariants **InvCons**, or the non-determinism of some events such as specified in the service specification **NonDet**, or because some str-formulas question some invariants **ViolInv**.

The first step, that is the question of invariant consistency **InvCons**, boils down to a classical boolean satisfiability problem[9]. The way we reduce **InvCons** to the boolean satisfiability problem will be handled in Section 4.2. Below, we detail the algorithms which solve the two last questions **NonDet** and **ViolInv**.

3.1   Non-determinism

Input A finite specification $\mathcal{F} = (\Sigma, I \coprod STR)$ such that I is consistent. A finite set
of variables X. Two str-formulas in STR, $< ctr_1|subs_1 : pre_1 \xrightarrow{e(x_1,...,x_n)} post_1 >$
and $< ctr_2|subs_2 : pre_2 \xrightarrow{e(y_1,...,y_n)} post_2 >$

Initialisation Compute $I_\Sigma(X)$ and $\mathcal{G}(X, I_\Sigma(X))$. Note S' the set of states of $\mathcal{G}(X, I_\Sigma(X))$ and X^X the whole set of endofunctions from X to X. $Tmp := S'$ and $answer :=$ $true$.

Loop while $Tmp \neq \emptyset$ and $answer = false$ do:
1) choose s in Tmp and $Tmp := Tmp \setminus \{s\}$;
2) $Tmp' := X^X$;
3) **Loop** while $Tmp' \neq \emptyset$ and $answer = false$ do:
   3.1) choose ι in Tmp' s.t. $\iota(x_i) = \iota(y_i)$ ($1 \leq i \leq n$), and $Tmp' := Tmp' \setminus \{\iota\}$;
   3.2) if $\forall x \neq y \in \bigcup_{j=1,2} ctr_j, \iota(x) = \iota(y)$ then if $\forall \alpha \in \bigcup_{j=1,2} subs_j \cup pre_j, (\iota, s) \models \alpha$
   then $answer := true$;
   end of loop
end of loop
Output $return(answer)$

Theorem 2. *Let* $\mathcal{F} = (\Sigma, I \coprod STR)$ *be a specification where* Σ *is a finite signature, and* I *and* STR *are finite sets. Let* X *be a finite set of variables which contains all variables occurring in* $I \coprod STR$. *Then,* $\mathcal{G}(X, I_\Sigma(X))$ *is deterministic if and only if for every pair of str-formulas in* STR, $< ctr_1|subs_1 : pre_1 \xrightarrow{e(x_1,...,x_n)} post_1 >$ *and* $< ctr_2|subs_2 : pre_2 \xrightarrow{e(y_1,...,y_n)} post_2 >$, *the above algorithm terminates and answers false.*

---

[9] The boolean satisfiability problem is solved by SAT solvers, e.g. GRASP [18] and Chaff [19].

3.2 Invariant Preserving

Let $\mathcal{F} = (\Sigma, STR \coprod I)$ be a specification. Let X be a set of variables which contains all variables occurring in $\mathcal{F}$. By definition, we have:

$$\forall \Psi \in I, \forall s \in I_\Sigma(X), \forall \iota : X \to X, \mathcal{G}(X, I_\Sigma(X)) \models_{\iota,s} \Psi$$

The question **ViolInv** is equivalent to the following one: *are invariants preserved for states in $S' \setminus I_\Sigma(X)$?* where S' is the set of states of $\mathcal{G}(X, I_\Sigma(X))$.

When STR, I and X are finite sets, the above problem is computable as expressed by the following algorithm:

Input A finite specification $\mathcal{F} = (\Sigma, I \coprod STR)$. A finite set of variables X which contains all the variables that occur in axioms of $\mathcal{F}$. An invariant $< ctr|\varphi >$ in I.

Initialisation Compute $I_\Sigma(X)$ and $\mathcal{G}(X, I_\Sigma(X))$. Let us note S' the set of states of $\mathcal{G}(X, I_\Sigma(X))$ and X^X the whole set of endofunction from X to X. $Tmp :=$ $S' \setminus I_\Sigma(X)$ and $answer := false$.

Loop while $Tmp \neq \emptyset$ and $answer = false$ do:

   1) choose s in Tmp and $Tmp := Tmp \setminus \{s\}$;
   2) $Tmp' := X^X$;
   3) **Loop** while $Tmp' \neq \emptyset$ and $answer = false$ do:
      3.1) choose ι in Tmp' and $Tmp' := Tmp' \setminus \{\iota\}$;
      3.2) if $\forall x \neq y \in ctr, \iota(x) \neq \iota(y)$
            then $answer := not((\iota, s) \models \varphi)$
      end of loop
   end of loop
Output $return(answer)$

Theorem 3. $\mathcal{G}(X, I_\Sigma(X))$ *satisfies I if and only if for every invariant in I, the above algorithm terminates and answers false.*

4 Methodology and Experiments

When integrating a new feature, we enter upon the problem of how to apply the algorithms and in which order, to ensure the consistency of the resulting specification.

4.1 The Design Phase Process

We have seen in Section 2.5 that to avoid introducing inconsistency during integration, choices are needed about which formulas are preserved, lost, modified or added. We propose an interactive approach based on the algorithms introduced before. Interactions are detected and presented to an expert who makes integration choices.

A service specification $\mathcal{F}$ provides modifications with respect to an implicit system. From a formal point of view, the integration of $\mathcal{F}$ on a system Sys is a composition which is parameterised by the required choices, i.e., it is abstractly denoted by $Sys +_{choices} \mathcal{F}$. It generally leads to some modifications of Sys; thus, we do not easily get the addition of two services together to a system $(Sys +_c \{\mathcal{F}_1, \mathcal{F}_2\})$ from the addition of each of them, $SYS +_{c1} \mathcal{F}_1$ and $SYS +_{c2} \mathcal{F}_2$. Indeed, it would suppose not only to confront the specifications $\mathcal{F}_1$ and $\mathcal{F}_2$, but also to re-examine c_1 and c_2 because c_1 was thought on Sys and not on Sys modified by c_2, and conversely. Thus our approach is to integrate services one by one. Therefore, given $POTS$ and services $\mathcal{F}_1, \ldots, \mathcal{F}_n$, we build an integration $(\ldots (POTS +_{c_1} \mathcal{F}_{i_1}) +_{c_2} \cdots +_{c_n} \mathcal{F}_{i_n})$, where the order $i_1, \cdots, i_n$ is significant with respect to the choices $c_1, \cdots, c_n$.

Note $Sys_{j-1} = (\Sigma_{j-1}, STR_{j-1} \coprod I_{j-1})$ the system specification resulting from $(\ldots (POTS +_{c_1} \mathcal{F}_{i_1}) +_{c_2} \cdots +_{c_{j_1}} \mathcal{F}_{i_{j-1}})$ and $\mathcal{F}_{i_j} = (\Sigma_{i_j}, STR_{i_j} \coprod I_{i_j})$. In order to determine the next choice $+_{c_{i_j}}$ for integrating $\mathcal{F}_{i_j}$, the following process is applied:

1. (a) Checking the invariant consistency of $I_{j-1} \cup I_{i_j}$ using the algorithm **ConsInv** by considering one by one the invariants of I_{i_j}
   (b) Solving inconsistency as soon as it occurs by modifying one of the involved invariants and starting again Point 1.a after each encountered inconsistency.
   This first step generates a consistent set $I_{\Sigma_{j-1} \cup \Sigma_{i_j}}$, or more simply I, of invariants which will be used in the reference specification for the next two following points.
2. (a) Performing the algorithm **NonDet** on every pair (ψ_1, ψ_2) where $\psi_1 \in STR_{j-1}$ and $\psi_2 \in STR_{i_j}$ such that ψ_1 and ψ_2 satisfy the condition of the input part of the algorithm (i.e. the event which occurs in ψ_1 and ψ_2 is the same).
   (b) Solving non-determinism conflicts as soon as they occur, and starting again Point 2.(a) after each one of them. This gives rise to a new set of str-formulas STR.
3. (a) Performing the algorithm **ViolInv** on every invariant in I with respect to the $\Sigma_{j-1} \cup \Sigma_{i_j}$-model $\mathcal{G}(X, I_{\Sigma_{j-1} \cup \Sigma_{i_j}}(X))$ computed from I and the set STR resulting from Point 2. above.
   (b) Solving inconsistency conflicts as soon as they occur.
4. Point 3. possibly modifies both sets STR and I, and then gives rise to two new sets STR' and I'. If this is the case, then starting again the above process for I' and STR'. Otherwise, the process is terminating.

To ensure termination of the above process, a strategy is to impose that:

1. for every pair (ψ_1, ψ_2) where ψ_1 and ψ_2 are two str-formulas satisfying conditions of Point 2.(a), if all non-determinism conflicts for ψ_1 with all str-formulas of STR_{j-1} have been already handled (i.e. ψ_2 is a str-formula which has been added or modified during some previous steps of the first algorithm) then the choice of the expert to solve the non-determinism conflict between ψ_1 and ψ_2 (when it exists) necessarily rests on ψ_2.
2. when a consistency conflict occurs on invariants by the algorithm **ViolInv**, the choice of the expert necessarily rests on invariants (i.e. str-formulas of STR are preserved).

4.2 Implementation

In the ValiServ project framework, the process presented in the previous section has been implemented. We have then defined a prototype to help the expert for specifying and validating service-oriented telecommunication systems. To produce more efficient implementations of algorithms, a first step of the above process has been to restrict the cardinality of the set of variables X occurring in axioms of the specification under consideration. This has allowed to reduce the invariant consistency **InvCons** to a propositional satisfiability problem of reasonable size and to decrease the complexity of the step **3)** in both algorithms **NonDet** and **ViolInv** in Section 3. The point is to translate a set of invariants into an equivalent single invariant. To achieve this purpose we first transform any axiom into its Skolem form. To simplify, let us consider an invariant of the form $< ctr|\phi >$ where X is its vector of variables occurring in ctr and ϕ. Obviously, such a formula can be written under its equivalent Skolem form: $\forall X, \bigwedge_{x_i \neq y_i \in ctr} x_i \neq y_i \Rightarrow \phi$. If we consider two such formulas ψ_i of the form $< ctr_i|\phi_i >$ for $i = 1, 2$ with X_i their respective variable set and provided that $X_1 \cap X_2 = \emptyset$, a naive approach consists on putting $\forall X_1 \cup X_2$ as a global universal variable vector quantifier. But such a solution has the main drawback of building formulas with too many variables. Under the hypothesis that the size of X_1 is less or equal to the one of X_2, in order to minimise the number of variables, we search for substitutions $\iota : X_1 \rightarrow X_1 \cup X_2$ such that every inequality on two variables of X_1 is preserved by ι in $X_1 \cup X_2$. There necessarily exist such substitutions (e.g. the identity). In fact, we are looking for such substitutions which minimise for the size of the set $\iota(X_1) \cup X_2$. When such a substitution is found, then $\iota(X_1) \cup X_2$ will become the variable vector used to universally quantify the resulting Skolem formula $\forall \iota(X_1) \cup X_2, \bigwedge_{x_i \neq y_i \in \iota(ctr_1) \cup ctr_2} x_i \neq y_i \Rightarrow \phi$. The computation of an optimal substitution is done by means of systematic study of all substitutions compatible with the inequality constraints. By iterating such a variable factorisation between all invariants, we can control the whole number of variables to be considered. The boolean satisfiability problem corresponding to a formula $\forall X, \bigwedge_{x_i \neq y_i \in ctr} x_i \neq y_i \Rightarrow \phi$ is then simply given by the propositional formula $\bigvee_{\sigma:X \rightarrow X, \forall x_i \neq y_i \in ctr, \sigma(x_i) \neq \sigma(y_i)} \sigma(\phi)$ where the atoms $p(x_1, \ldots, x_n)$ occurring in $\sigma(\phi)$ are viewed as simple propositional variables.

4.3 Case Study

The above methodology has been applied on many telecommunication examples. Among other, it has been applied on the example presented in Section 2. Here, we give the report of this case study. Its interest is it is significant enough but short enough to be presented in this paper. We incrementally integrate several services yielding the system $(((POTS +_{c_1} TCS) +_{c_2} CFB) +_{c_3} INTL)$. The main steps have been the following:

- $POTS +_{c_1} TCS$: a non-determinism has been detected between ϕ_2 and ψ_1. We have modified ϕ_2, intuitively giving the priority to TCS on $POTS$.
- $((POTS +_{c_1} TCS) +_{c_2} CFB)$: a non-determinism has been detected between ϕ_3 and χ_3. We have modified ϕ_3. We have then detected that χ_3 violates the TCS invariant ψ_1. We have corrected it by adding $\neg Tcs(C, A)$ to the subscription set of χ_3. Then, we add the following str-formula for the case we have $Tcs(C, A)$:

$$\chi'_3 : \ < B \neq C \mid \mathit{Cfb}(B,C), \mathit{Tcs}(C,A), \mathit{dialwait}(A), \overline{\mathit{idle}(B)}, \mathit{idle}(C) \xrightarrow{\mathit{dial}(A,B)}$$
$$\mathit{busytone}(C), \mathit{idle}(C) >$$

Thus, *TCS* has the priority on *CFB* and *CFB* has the priority on *POTS*.

- $(((POTS+_{c_1}TCS)+_{c_2}CFB)+_{c_3}INTL)$: a non-determinism has been detected between ϕ_1 and κ_1. We have modified ϕ_1, intuitively giving the priority to *INTL* on *POTS*, *TCS* and *CFB*.

The specification of *POTS*, *TCS*, *CFB* and *INTL* together contains twenty formulas. During the integration process, we have modified four of them and introduced a new one. The ValiServ tool automatically detects current interactions, presents the detected interactions to the expert under a detailed form and allows the expert to modify the related specification part so that the considered interaction is suppressed according to its judgment. Such an approach allows to manage the intrinsic complexity of service-oriented systems since the expert only intervenes to solve interactions according to their subjective status. Thus, our service integration method may be viewed as a sequence of expert choices in a set of resolution options, each of these expert choices coming from an automatic feature interaction detection.

5   Related Work

Several previous works have been interested by feature integration and interaction detection issues from a high level of abstraction. In particular, new architectures have been designed for telecommunications systems in order to facilitate the addition of a new service. [5] or [13] present such approaches, useful for designing and implementing new services but not to found rigorous interaction detection methods. [23] gives a general framework to systematically combine services together. Only consistent combinations of services are considered. When an inconsistency is detected for a given combination of services, this means that there exists an interaction between combined features. However, the paper is not concerned by the need of providing theoretical and methodological help in order to combine service in presence of interactions. Some other works, like [9], are also based on the use of model-checking tools in order to detect interactions. This allows to consider general temporal properties. The main drawback of all these approaches is that they require to instantiate *a priori* different configurations to build all the interesting subscription patterns among a small number of fixed phones.

We claim that the use of symbolic techniques for dealing with phone variables is the key to deduce interactions built over an appropriate number of phones equipped with their subscriptions. Some other works manipulate generic variables to represent phones, without restricting the number of phones to be considered. In particular, several approaches rely on STR-like specifications. [10] precisely explains the interest of using STR formulas, invariants and inequality preconditions. The authors were already concerned with providing guidelines to integrate a service on the basic call system and hints on how to perform non-determinism checks. Unfortunately, the described detections are mainly guided by hand-waving and thus, there was no study of how to systematically support this process. Our framework which is largely inspired by their process, addresses this weakness. [20,24] have proposed specialised techniques for interaction detection based on STR-like specifications. From a given initial state, they analyse properties of reachability graphs in terms of non-determinism or deadlock or contradictions raised by the simultaneous application of two STR sentences ... Works introduced in [26,25] discuss the advantage of dealing with static methods, without building any intermediate graph. They introduce techniques for finding interactions from non-determinism criteria or from elicitation knowledge between two services. They compute a lot of interactions, but as they do not look for service integration, they do not exploit their presence to compose services in an adequate way. Moreover, as they do not use invariants, they cannot help the specifier in designing STR specifications. Let us remark that we handle the preservation of invariants as in [6]. However, the underlying proof-based techniques require too much expertise to our point of view. [22,7,11] introduce systematic mechanisms of service composition avoiding a lot of interactions. Roughly speaking, all of these works are based on some precedence relations between services: the last integrated feature seems to have the highest priority level. However, if undesirable interactions subsist, then it is not possible to review the integrated system, except if a new design process is managed from the beginning.

6   Conclusion and Perspectives

We presented a methodology for service-oriented development that takes interaction and integration issues into account. We introduced a dedicated formalism taking into account subscriptions. and manipulating two kinds of formulas, state invariants and state transition rules. We gave algorithms allowing the specifier to check the consistency of the specification under consideration. The service integration results from the incremental insertion of formulas preserving at each step the consistency of the target specification. Each detected consistency problem represents an interaction and requires an expert decision to modify, and to replace the formula(s) causing inconsistency. The whole methodology has been validating by the industrial partner France Telecom of the project ValiServ.

This work can be pursued in several ways. We want to study state reachability issues to ensure that each detected non-determinism case corresponds to a real interaction case. We also want to study how it is possible to introduce different types on variables to capture different rôles (users, phone numbers or IP addresses) in order to apply our algorithms and methodology to application domains such as voice over IP [15]. From a methodological point of view, we aim to strengthen expert assistance by minimising choices and backtrack at design step. Such improvement should rely not only on theoretical consideration but also on expertise about the telecommunication domain.

References

1. M. Aiguier, K. Berkani, and P. Le Gall. Feature specification and static analysis for interaction resolution. Technical report, University of Evry, 2005. available at www.lami.univ-evry.fr/~aiguier.
2. K. Berkani. Un cadre méthodologique pour l'intégration de services par évitement des interactions. Phd thesis, France, October 2003.
3. K. Berkani, R. Cave, S. Coudert, F. Klay, P. Le Gall, F. Ouabdesselam, and J.-L. Richier. An Environment for Interaction Service Specification. [17], 2003.

4. K. Berkani, P. Le Gall, and F. Klay. An Incremental Method for the Design of Feature-oriented Systems. In *[12]*, pages 45–64. Springer, 2000.

5. J. Bredereke. Maintening telephone switching software requirements. *IEEE Communications Magazine*, Nov, 2002.

6. D. Cansell and D. Méry. Abstraction and Refinement of Features. In *[12]*, pages 65–84. Springer, 2000.

7. D.P. Guelev, M.D. Ryan, and P.Y. Schobbens. Feature Integration as Substitution. [17], 2003.

8. L. du Bousquet, F. Ouabdesselam, J.-L. Richier, and N. Zuanon. Feature Interaction Detection using Synchronous Approach and Testing. *Computer Networks and ISDN Systems*, 11(4):419–446, 2000.

9. A. Felty and K. Namjoshi. Feature specification and automated conflict detection. *ACM Transactions on Software Engineering and Methodology*, 12(1):3–27, 2003.

10. A. Gammelgaard and J.E. Kristensen. Interaction Detection, a Logical Approach. In *Feature Interactions in Telecommunications Systems II*, pages 178–196. IOS Press, 1994.

11. C. Gaston, M. Aiguier, and P. Le Gall. Algebraic Treatment of Feature-oriented Systems. In *[12]*, pages 105–124. Springer, 2000.

12. S. Gilmore and M. Ryan, editors. *Langage Constructs for Describing Features*. Springer-Verlag, 2000.

13. M. Jackson and P. Zave. Distributed feature composition: A virtual architecture for telecommunications services. *IEEE Transactions on Software Engineering*, 24(10):831–847, 1998.

14. H. Jouve. *Caractérisation et détection automatique d'interactions de services à partir de spécifications graphiques*. Phd thesis, France, October 2003.

15. H. Jouve, P. Le Gall, and S. Coudert. An Automatic Off-Line Feature Interaction Detection Method by Static Analysis of Specifications. [21], 2005.

16. K. Kimbler and L.G. Bouma, editors. *Feature Interactions in Telecommunications and Software Systems (FIW'98)*. IOS Press, 1998.

17. L. Logrippo and D. Amyot, editors. *Feature Interactions in Telecommunications and Software Systems (FIW'03)*. IOS Press, 2003.

18. J. P. Marques-Silva and K. A. Sakallah. GRASP: A search algorithm for propositional satisfiability. *IEEE Transactions on Computers*, 1999.

19. M. W. Moskewicz, C. F. Madigan, Y. Zhao, and S. Malik. Chaff : Engineering an efficient SAT solver. In *Proceedings of the 38th Design Automation Conference (DAC'01)*, 2001.

20. M. Nakamura. *Design and Evaluation of Efficient Algorithms for Feature Interaction Detection in Telecommunication Services*. Phd thesis, Japan, June 1999.

21. S. Reiff-Marganiec and M.D. Ryan, editors. *Feature Interactions in Telecommunications and Software Systems (FIW'05)*. IOS Press, 2005.

22. D. Samborski. Stack Service Model. In *[12]*, pages 177–196. Springer, 2000.

23. B. Schätz and C. Salzmamm. Service-based systems engineering : Consistent combination of services. In LNCS Springer, editor, *ICFEM 2003,Fifth International Conference on Formal Engineering Methods*, volume 2885, 2003.

24. K. Tatekuwa and T. Ohta. Automatic deleting specification errors which cause miss-detection of feature interactions. In *[21]*, pages 320–326, 2005.

25. T. Yoneda, S. Kawauchi, J. Yoshida, and T. Ohta. Formal approaches for detecting feature interactions, their experimental results, and application to voip. [17], 2003.

26. T. Yoneda and T. Ohta. A Formal Approach for Definition and Detection of Feature Interaction. In *[16]*, pages 202–216. IOS Press, 1998.

A Fully General Operational Semantics for UML 2.0 Sequence Diagrams with Potential and Mandatory Choice*

Mass Soldal Lund[1,2] and Ketil Stølen[1,2]

[1] University of Oslo, Norway
[2] SINTEF Information and Communication Technology, Norway
{msl, kst}@sintef.no

Abstract. UML sequence diagrams is a specification language that has proved itself to be of great value in system development. When put to applications such as simulation, testing and other kinds of automated analysis there is a need for formal semantics. Such methods of automated analysis are by nature operational, and this motivates formalizing an operational semantics. In this paper we present an operational semantics for UML 2.0 sequence diagrams that we believe gives a solid starting point for developing methods for automated analysis. The operational semantics has been proved to be sound and complete with respect to a denotational semantics for the same language. It handles negative behavior as well as potential and mandatory choice. We are not aware of any other operational semantics for sequence diagrams of this strength.

1 Introduction

Unified Modeling Language (UML) sequence diagrams [1] and their predecessor Message Sequence Charts (MSC) [2] are specification languages that have proved themselves to be of great practical value in system development. When sequence diagrams are used to get a better understanding of the system through modeling, as system documentation or as means of communication between stakeholders of the system, it is important that the precise meaning of the diagrams is understood; in other words, there is need for a well-defined semantics. Sequence diagrams may also be put to further applications, such as simulation, testing and other kinds of automated analysis. This further increases the need for a formalized semantics; not only must the people who make and read diagrams have a common understanding of their meaning, but also the makers of methods and tools for analyzing the diagrams must share this understanding.

Methods of analysis like simulation and testing are in their nature operational; they are used for investigating what will happen when a system is executing.

---

* The work of this paper was conducted within and funded by the Basic ICT Research project SARDAS (15295/431) under the Research Council of Norway. We would like to thank Rolv Bræk, Manfred Broy, Kathrin Greiner, Øystein Haugen, Birger Møller-Pedersen, Atle Refsdal, Ragnhild Kobro Runde, Ina Schieferdecker and Thomas Weigert for useful comments on this work.

J. Misra, T. Nipkow, and E. Sekerinski (Eds.): FM 2006, LNCS 4085, pp. 380–395, 2006.
© Springer-Verlag Berlin Heidelberg 2006

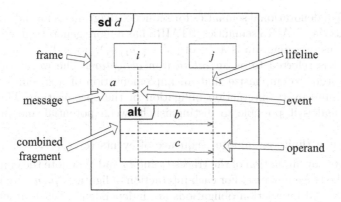

Fig. 1. Sequence diagram

When developing techniques for such analysis, not only do we need to understand the precise meaning of a specification, we also need to understand precisely the executions that are specified. This motivates formalization of semantics in an operational style. In this paper we present an operational semantics for UML sequence diagrams that we believe gives a solid starting point for developing such methods of analysis.

Sequence diagrams is a graphical specification language defined in the UML 2.0 standard [1]. The standard defines the graphical notation, but also an abstract syntax for the diagrams. Further the UML standard provides an informal semantics of the diagrams. Figure 1 shows a sequence diagram d in the graphical notation. A sequence diagram consists of a *frame*, representing the environment of the specified system, and one or more *lifelines*, representing components of the system. Arrows represent *messages* sent between lifelines or between a lifeline and the environment, and if the beginning or end of an arrow is at a lifeline this represents an *event*. *Combined fragments* are operators, like the choice operator alt, and each combined fragment has one or more *operands*.

The semantics of UML 2.0 sequence diagrams is trace based. The standard states that the semantics of a sequence diagram is a pair of traces (p, n) such that p is interpreted as valid (positive) traces and n is interpreted as invalid (negative) traces. Further, the union of p and n need not exhaust the trace universe.

Several properties of sequence diagrams prevent us from adopting a simple automata or process algebra approach to defining the formal semantics. First of all, sequence diagrams are partial specifications, and invalid behavior is specified explicitily by an operator neg. This means we cannot treat valid and invalid behavior as complementary sets. Further, communication between lifelines is asynchronous and lifelines are non-synchronizing, but choices, like the alt operator, are global. This means that sequence diagrams have a semi-global nature. Finally, the choice operator alt is ambiguous, and may be interpreted as either potential choice or mandatory choice. In our approach, this ambiguity is resolved by interpreting alt as potential choice and introducing a new operator xalt to do the job as mandatory choice.

In [3,4,5] a denotational semantics for sequence diagrams is formalized. We refer to this as the STAIRS semantics. STAIRS has a more general semantic model; the semantics of a diagram is a set of pairs $\{(p_1, n_1), (p_2, n_2), \ldots, (p_m, n_m)\}$. A pair (p_i, n_i) is referred to as an *interaction obligation*. The word "obligation" is used in order to emphasize that an implementation of a specification is required to fulfill every interaction obligation of the specification. This semantic model makes it possible to distinguish between potential and mandatory choice.

A trace is a (finite or infinite) sequence of events $\langle e_1, e_2, \ldots, e_i, \ldots \rangle$. We let $t_1 \frown t_2$ denote concatenation of the traces t_1 and t_2 and $\langle \rangle$ denote the empty trace. Let $\mathcal{H}$ be the trace universe. For each interaction obligation (p_i, n_i) we have that $p_i \cup n_i \subseteq \mathcal{H}$. All interaction obligations are independent of each other, and an interaction obligation is allowed to be inconsistent (i.e., we allow $p_i \cap n_i \neq \emptyset$).

The contribution of this paper is an operational semantics for UML 2.0 sequence diagrams. Obviously, choices must be made where the UML standard is ambiguous, but as far as possible the semantics is faithful to the standard. The semantics is easy to extend and modify. This allows us to give a "default" or "standard" interpretation, but also to experiment with the semantics and make variations on points unspecified by the standard. Specifically it has a formalized meta-level which allows definition of different execution strategies. It is not based on transformations to other formalisms, which makes it easy to work with. Further it has been proved to be sound and complete with respect to the STAIRS semantics.

The structure of this paper is as follows: In Sect. 2 we present the syntax over which the semantics is defined and in Sect. 3 the operational semantics. Soundness and completeness is treated in Sect. 4. In Sect. 5 we present related work and, finally, in Sect. 6 conclusions are provided. A short presentation of the denotational semantics of STAIRS is provided in Appendix A.

2   Syntax

The graphical notation of sequence diagrams is not suited as a basis for defining semantics, and the abstract syntax of the UML standard contains more information than we need for the task. Our operational semantics is defined over a simpler abstract syntax defined in [4, 5]. This is an event centric syntax in which the weak sequential operator seq is employed as the basic construct for combining diagram fragments.

The atom of a sequence diagram is the *event*. An event consists of a *message* and a *kind* where the kind decides whether it is the *transmit* or the *receive* event of the message. A message is a *signal*, which represents the contents of the message, together with the addresses of the transmitter and the receiver. Formally a signal is a label, and we let $\mathcal{S}$ denote the set of all signals. The transmitters and receivers are lifelines. Let $\mathcal{L}$ denote the set of all lifelines. A message m is defined as a triple $(s, t, r) \in \mathcal{S} \times \mathcal{L} \times \mathcal{L}$ with signal s, transmitter

t and receiver r. $\mathcal{M}$ denotes the set of all messages. On messages we define a transmitter function $tr._{-} \in \mathcal{M} \to \mathcal{L}$ and a receiver function $re._{-} \in \mathcal{M} \to \mathcal{L}$:

$$tr.(s, t, r) \overset{\text{def}}{=} t \qquad re.(s, t, r) \overset{\text{def}}{=} r$$

We let $\mathcal{K} = \{!, ?\}$ be the set of kinds, where ! represents transmit and ? represents receive. An event e is then a pair of a kind and a message: $(k, m) \in \mathcal{K} \times \mathcal{M}$. $\mathcal{E}$ denotes the set of all events. On events we define a kind function $k._{-} \in \mathcal{E} \to \mathcal{K}$ and a message function $m._{-} \in \mathcal{E} \to \mathcal{M}$:

$$k.(k, m) \overset{\text{def}}{=} k \qquad m.(k, m) \overset{\text{def}}{=} m$$

We let the transmitter and receiver functions also range over events, $tr._{-}, re._{-} \in \mathcal{E} \to \mathcal{L}$, and define a lifeline function $l._{-} \in \mathcal{E} \to \mathcal{L}$ that returns the lifeline of an event:

$$tr.(k, m) \overset{\text{def}}{=} tr.m \qquad re.(k, m) \overset{\text{def}}{=} re.m \qquad l.e \overset{\text{def}}{=} \begin{cases} tr.e \textbf{ if } k.e = ! \\ re.e \textbf{ if } k.e = ? \end{cases}$$

A sequence diagram is built out of events, the binary operators seq, par, alt and xalt, and the unary operators neg and loop. Related to the graphical syntax, the operators represent combined fragments and their arguments the operands. In addition we let skip represent the empty sequence diagram. Let $\mathcal{D}$ be the set of all syntactically correct sequence diagrams. $\mathcal{D}$ is defined recursively as follows:

$$\text{skip} \in \mathcal{D}$$
$$e \in \mathcal{E} \qquad \Rightarrow e \in \mathcal{D}$$
$$d_1, d_2 \in \mathcal{D} \qquad \Rightarrow d_1 \text{ seq } d_2 \in \mathcal{D} \wedge d_1 \text{ par } d_2 \in \mathcal{D} \wedge$$
$$d_1 \text{ alt } d_2 \in \mathcal{D} \wedge d_1 \text{ xalt } d_2 \in \mathcal{D}$$
$$d \in \mathcal{D} \qquad \Rightarrow \text{neg } d \in \mathcal{D}$$
$$d \in \mathcal{D} \wedge I \subseteq \mathbb{N}_\infty \Rightarrow \text{loop } I \; d \in \mathcal{D}$$
$$d \in \mathcal{D} \wedge n \in \mathbb{N}_\infty \Rightarrow \text{loop}\langle n \rangle \; d \in \mathcal{D}$$

In the definitions of the two loops we have $\mathbb{N}_\infty \overset{\text{def}}{=} \mathbb{N} \cup \{\infty\}$, where ∞ is a number greater than all other numbers and has the property $\infty - 1 = \infty$. The intention behind loop I d is that d should be looped any number $n \in I$ times. The UML standard describes two loops $\text{loop}(n)$ and $\text{loop}(n, m)$, where n is the minimum number and m the maximum number of iterations. We may define these as:

$$\text{loop}(n) \; d \overset{\text{def}}{=} \text{loop } [n..\infty] \; d \qquad \text{loop}(n, m) \; d \overset{\text{def}}{=} \text{loop } [n..m] \; d$$

As can be expected, we have associativity of seq, par, alt and xalt. We also have commutativity of par, alt and xalt. Furthermore the empty sequence diagram skip is the identity element of seq and par. The combination of skip and loop is discussed in Sect. 3.2.

In this abstract syntax the diagram of Fig. 1 is expressed as:[1]

$$d = (?, (a, env, i)) \text{ seq } ((!, (b, i, j)) \text{ seq } (?, (b, i, j)) \text{ alt } (!, (c, i, j)) \text{ seq } (?, (c, i, j)))$$

---

[1] Here we let env denote the environment of the diagram. Formally this is a gate, but gates are outside the scope of this paper. Also note that seq binds stronger than alt.

3   Operational Semantics

An operational semantics of a language defines an interpreter for the language. In our case the input to the interpreter is a sequence diagram represented in the abstract syntax defined above. The output of the interpreter is a trace of events representing an execution. It is defined as the combination of two transition systems, which we refer to as the *execution system* and the *projection system*. The execution system is a transition system over

$$[\_,\_] \in \mathcal{B} \times \mathcal{D}$$

where $\mathcal{B}$ represents the set of all states of the communication medium and $\mathcal{D}$ the set of all syntactically correct sequence diagrams. The projection system is a transition system over

$$\Pi(\_,\_,\_) \in \mathbb{P}(\mathcal{L}) \times \mathcal{B} \times \mathcal{D}$$

where $\mathbb{P}(\mathcal{L})$ is the powerset of the set of all lifelines. The projection system is used for finding enabled events at each stage of the execution and is defined recursively.

These two systems work together in such a way that for each step in the execution, the execution system updates the projection system by passing on the current state of the communication medium, and the projection system updates the execution system by selecting the event to execute and returning the state of the diagram after the execution of the event.

We also formalize a meta-level that encloses the execution system. At this meta-level we may define several meta-strategies that guide the execution and that are used for formalizing our notions of negative, potential and mandatory behavior.

3.1   The Execution System

The execution system has two rules. The first rule represents the execution of a single event and uses the projection system to find an enabled event to execute. It is defined as

$$[\beta,d] \xrightarrow{e} [update(\beta,e),d'] \text{ if } \Pi(ll.d,\beta,d) \xrightarrow{e} \Pi(ll.d,\beta,d') \wedge e \in \mathcal{E} \quad (1)$$

where e is an event and $ll.d$ is a function returning the set of lifelines in d.

In general we assume the structure of the communication medium, i.e. the means of communication, to be underspecified. The only requirement is that the following functions are defined:

- $add \in \mathcal{B} \times \mathcal{M} \to \mathcal{B}$: Adds a message.
- $rm \in \mathcal{B} \times \mathcal{M} \to \mathcal{B}$: Removes a message.
- $ready \in \mathcal{B} \times \mathcal{M} \to \mathbb{B}$: Returns **true** if the communication medium is in a state where it can deliver the message and **false** otherwise.

The function $update \in \mathcal{B} \times \mathcal{E} \to \mathcal{B}$ is defined as:

$$update(\beta, e) \stackrel{\text{def}}{=} \begin{cases} add(\beta, m.e) & \text{if } k.e = ! \\ rm(\beta, m.e) & \text{if } k.e = ? \end{cases}$$

Since receiver information is embedded into the messages, these functions are sufficient. In this paper we assume the most general communication model, i.e.: no ordering on the messages. This means that, e.g., message overtaking is possible. Formally then, $\mathcal{B}$ may be defined as the set of all multisets over $\mathcal{M}$, add as multiset union, rm as multiset minus and $ready$ as multiset containment.

The second rule of the execution system executes silent events. The rules of the projection system handle the sequence diagram operators alt, xalt, neg and loop. Resolving these operators, such as choosing the branch of an alt are considered silent events. We define the set of silent events to be

$$\mathcal{T} = \{\tau_{alt}, \tau_{xalt}, \tau_{neg}, \tau_{pos}, \tau_{loop}\}$$

with $\mathcal{E} \cap \mathcal{T} = \emptyset$. The reason for introducing all these different silent events is that they give high flexibility in defining execution strategies by making the silent events and their kinds available at the meta-level. The rule is simple:

$$[\beta, d] \stackrel{\tau}{\longrightarrow} [\beta, d'] \text{ if } \Pi(ll.d, \beta, d) \stackrel{\tau}{\longrightarrow} \Pi(ll.d, \beta, d') \wedge \tau \in \mathcal{T} \tag{2}$$

The empty diagram skip cannot be rewritten, but we assert that it produces the empty trace, i.e.:

$$[\beta, \text{skip}] \stackrel{\langle\rangle}{\longrightarrow} [\beta, \text{skip}] \tag{3}$$

This also means that execution terminates when skip is reached.

3.2 The Projection System

The Empty Diagram. It is not possible to rewrite $\Pi(L, \beta, \text{skip})$. skip being the identity element of seq and par, skip seq d, d seq skip, skip par d and d par skip are treated as identical to d.

loop$\langle\infty\rangle$ skip is more problematic. Seen as a program this construct is similar to the java fragment while(true) { }, i.e., a program that produces nothing and never terminates. When related to the denotational semantics, however, the semantics of loop$\langle\infty\rangle$ skip should be the empty trace $\langle\rangle$, since the denotational semantics characterize observation after infinite time. A simple solution would be to syntactically disallow the construct all together. Because we do not want to make too many syntactic constraints, and because we want to stay close to the denotational semantics we choose to let loop$\langle\infty\rangle$ skip reduce to skip, even though this may be seen as counter-intuitive from an operational point of view.

Event. The simplest case is the diagram consisting of only one event e. In this case the system delivers the event if the event is enabled given the set of lifelines and the state of the communication medium. This means firstly that the event must belong to one of the lifelines, and secondly that either the event must be a transmit event or its message must be available in the communication medium. The need for L will be evident in the definition of rules for seq below.

$$\Pi(L, \beta, e) \xrightarrow{e} \Pi(L, \beta, \text{skip}) \text{ if } l.e \in L \wedge (k.e = ! \vee ready(\beta, m.e)) \qquad (4)$$

Weak Sequencing. The weak sequencing operator seq defines a partial order on the events in a diagram; the ordering of events on each lifeline and between the transmit and receive of a message is preserved, but all other ordering of events is arbitrary. Because of this, there may be enabled events in both the left and the right argument of a seq if there are lifelines represented in the right argument of the operator that are not represented in the left argument. This leads to two rules for the seq operator.

If there is an overlap between the given set of lifelines and the lifelines of the left hand side of the seq, this means that the lifelines in this intersection may have enabled events on the left hand side only. Hence, with respect to these lifelines, the system must look for enabled events in the left operand.

$$\Pi(L, \beta, d_1 \text{ seq } d_2) \xrightarrow{e} \Pi(L, \beta, d_1' \text{ seq } d_2)$$
$$\text{if } ll.d_1 \cap L \neq \emptyset \wedge \Pi(ll.d_1 \cap L, \beta, d_1) \xrightarrow{e} \Pi(ll.d_1 \cap L, \beta, d_1') \qquad (5)$$

If the lifelines of the left hand side do not exhaust the given set of lifelines, this means there are lifelines only represented on the right hand side, and that there may be enabled events on the right hand side of the operator. This means the system may look for enabled events at the right hand side of the seq, but only with respect to the lifelines not represented on the left hand side.

$$\Pi(L, \beta, d_1 \text{ seq } d_2) \xrightarrow{e} \Pi(L, \beta, d_1 \text{ seq } d_2')$$
$$\text{if } L \setminus ll.d_1 \neq \emptyset \wedge \Pi(L \setminus ll.d_1, \beta, d_2) \xrightarrow{e} \Pi(L \setminus ll.d_1, \beta, d_2') \qquad (6)$$

Note that the two conditions $ll.d_1 \cap L \neq \emptyset$ and $ll.d_1 \setminus L \neq \emptyset$ are not mutually exclusive. If both these condition are true at the same time there may be enabled events at both sides of the seq operator. These events are then interleaved arbitrarily. In such a case the rules may be applied in arbitrary order.

Because the transitions of the system are used as conditions in the recursion of these rules, the rules will not be applied unless an enabled event is found deeper in the recursion. Because of this the system will always be able to return an enabled event if enabled events exist.

Interleaving. The parallel operator par specifies interleaving of the events from each of its arguments; in other words parallel merge of the executions of each of the arguments. The rules of par are similar to the rules of seq, but simpler since we do not have to preserve any order between the two operands. One of the operands is chosen arbitrarily. As with the seq rules, the use of transitions as the conditions of the rules ensures that an enabled event is found if enabled events exist.

$$\Pi(L, \beta, d_1 \text{ par } d_2) \xrightarrow{e} \Pi(L, \beta, d_1' \text{ par } d_2)$$
$$\text{if } \Pi(ll.d_1 \cap L, \beta, d_1) \xrightarrow{e} \Pi(ll.d_1 \cap L, \beta, d_1') \qquad (7)$$

$$\Pi(L, \beta, d_1 \text{ par } d_2) \xrightarrow{e} \Pi(L, \beta, d_1 \text{ par } d_2')$$
$$\text{if } \Pi(ll.d_2 \cap L, \beta, d_2) \xrightarrow{e} \Pi(ll.d_2 \cap L, \beta, d_2') \tag{8}$$

Choice. The rules for choices end the recursion; the choice is resolved and a silent event is produced. By resolving the choice instead of looking for events deeper down, we ensure that the same choice is made for all the lifelines covered by the choice operator.

$$\Pi(L, \beta, d_1 \text{ alt } d_2) \xrightarrow{\tau_{alt}} \Pi(L, \beta, d_k), \text{ for } k \in \{1, 2\} \tag{9}$$

$$\Pi(L, \beta, d_1 \text{ xalt } d_2) \xrightarrow{\tau_{xalt}} \Pi(L, \beta, d_k), \text{ for } k \in \{1, 2\} \tag{10}$$

The rules for alt and xalt are identical except for the kind of event they produce. This reflects the fact that the operators are indistinguishable at the execution level, but since they produce different events, the kind of the choice is available at the meta-level and this will be used in the definition of meta-strategies. Because we have that $ll.(d_1 \text{ alt } d_2) \cap L \neq \emptyset$ and $ll.(d_1 \text{ xalt } d_2) \cap L \neq \emptyset$ no conditions or restrictions on L are needed.

Negative. The operator neg is treated as a choice with one negative branch and one empty branch. Silent events are used to flag which branch is chosen, and hence the choice is made available at the meta-level.

$$\Pi(L, \beta, \text{neg } d) \xrightarrow{\tau_{pos}} \Pi(L, \beta, \text{skip}) \tag{11}$$

$$\Pi(L, \beta, \text{neg } d) \xrightarrow{\tau_{neg}} \Pi(L, \beta, d) \tag{12}$$

Similar to the choice rules, we have that $ll.(\text{neg } d) \cap L = ll.d \cap L \neq \emptyset$.

Iteration. Informally, in loop I d there is a non-deterministic choice between the numbers of I. If $n \in I$ is picked, d should be iterated n times. This is formalized by a rule that chooses which number to use:

$$\Pi(L, \beta, \text{loop } I \, d) \xrightarrow{\tau_{alt}} \Pi(L, \beta, \text{loop}\langle n \rangle \, d) \text{ if } n \in I \tag{13}$$

loop$\langle n \rangle$ d is a loop with a counter. In the rule the counter is decreased by one for each iteration. We also produce a silent event to represent the iteration of a loop. Even though iteration of a loop in itself is not the most relevant information at the meta-level, it may be useful for defining execution strategies, for example if we want to give iteration of the loop low priority.

$$\Pi(L, \beta, \text{loop}\langle n \rangle \, d) \xrightarrow{\tau_{loop}} \Pi(L, \beta, d \text{ seq loop}\langle n - 1 \rangle \, d) \tag{14}$$

Also here we have the property that $ll.(\text{loop}\langle n \rangle \, d) \cap L = ll.d \cap L \neq \emptyset$. Since we have that $\infty - 1 = \infty$, loop$\langle \infty \rangle$ d specifies an infinite loop. Further we assert that loop$\langle 0 \rangle$ d is equal to skip, i.e., loop$\langle 0 \rangle$ $d \stackrel{\text{def}}{=}$ skip, so we do not need a special rule for this situation.

3.3   Meta-strategies

There are several strategies we may choose when executing a sequence diagram and generating the histories of its possible executions. Examples of this may be generating one or a specific number of random traces, all traces, all prefixes of a certain length, etc. We wish to have the possibility of varying the execution strategy. The way to do this is to define different meta-strategies for executing the diagrams with the operational semantics. Two examples are given below. In both we make use of a meta-system over

$$\{\!\!\{ -, - \}\!\!\} \in \mathcal{H} \times \mathcal{EX}$$

where $\mathcal{H}$ is the set of all traces and $\mathcal{EX}$ denotes the set of states of the execution system. The first place of this pair is a "container" for a trace and the second place is the current state of the execution system.

One Random Trace. The strategy may be defined by the means of two rules, one rule for normal events and one rule for silent events:

$$\{\!\!\{ t, V \}\!\!\} \longrightarrow \{\!\!\{ t^\frown \langle e \rangle, V' \}\!\!\} \text{ if } V \xrightarrow{e} V' \wedge e \in \mathcal{E} \tag{15}$$

$$\{\!\!\{ t, V \}\!\!\} \longrightarrow \{\!\!\{ t, V' \}\!\!\} \text{ if } V \xrightarrow{\tau} V' \wedge \tau \in \mathcal{T} \tag{16}$$

The initial state for execution of a sequence diagram d is:

$$\{\!\!\{ \langle \rangle, [\emptyset, d] \}\!\!\}$$

All Traces. With this strategy we want to generate all possible traces of a diagram d and place them in the correct semantic structure of STAIRS. As explained in Sect. 1, the semantic model of STAIRS is a set of interaction obligations $\{(p_1, n_1), \ldots, (p_m, n_m)\}$. For each interaction obligation (p_i, n_i), p_i is a set of positive traces and n_i is a set of negative traces.

Instead of sets of traces we will use "interaction obligations" of sets of positive and negative executions, i.e. meta-system states. Initially we have a set consisting of a single interaction obligation with the initial state of d as the only positive element and no negative elements:

$$\{(\{\!\!\{ \langle \rangle, [\emptyset, d] \}\!\!\}, \emptyset)\}$$

In the following we define rules that for each execution state deduce the next steps to be made, and in executing these steps rewrite the whole structure. To make the rules more readable, we only show as much of the context, the surrounding structure, as is needed for defining the rules.

If we want all traces, we need to make a branch in the execution every time there is a possibility of more than one event occurring first. The rule for executing events asserts that for a given state, the generation must branch for every enabled event:

$$T \cup \{\!\!\{ t, V \}\!\!\} \longrightarrow T \cup \{\!\!\{ t^\frown \langle e \rangle, V' \}\!\!\} \mid V \xrightarrow{e} V' \wedge e \in \mathcal{E}\} \tag{17}$$

The rule for resolving an alt is similar. For each branch of the alt, the execution must branch:

$$T \cup \{\{\!| t, V |\!\}\} \longrightarrow T \cup \{\{\!| t, V' |\!\} \mid V \xrightarrow{T_{alt}} V'\} \tag{18}$$

The rule for iteration of loop is defined in the same fashion:

$$T \cup \{\{\!| t, V |\!\}\} \longrightarrow T \cup \{\{\!| t, V' |\!\} \mid V \xrightarrow{T_{loop}} V'\} \tag{19}$$

The rules for resolving a neg are more complicated since they concern an interaction obligation and not only one of the sets in an interaction obligation. Let P, P', N, N' be sets. The rule for resolving a neg in a valid execution is then:

$$(P \cup \{\{\!| t, V |\!\}\}, N) \longrightarrow (P', N') \tag{20}$$

where

$$P' = P \cup \{\{\!| t, V' |\!\} \mid V \xrightarrow{T_{pos}} V'\}$$
$$N' = N \cup \{\{\!| t, V' |\!\} \mid V \xrightarrow{T_{neg}} V'\}$$

In an already invalid execution, there is no difference between choosing the positive or negative branch:

$$(P, N \cup \{\{\!| t, V |\!\}\}) \longrightarrow (P, N') \tag{21}$$

where

$$N' = N \cup \{\{\!| t, V' |\!\} \mid V \xrightarrow{T_{pos}} V' \vee V \xrightarrow{T_{neg}} V'\}$$

Resolving an xalt involves splitting an interaction obligation, and hence, the rules for xalt need even more context:

$$O \cup \{(P \cup \{\{\!| t, V |\!\}\}, N)\} \longrightarrow O \cup \{(P \cup \{\{\!| t, V' |\!\}\}, N) \mid V \xrightarrow{T_{xalt}} V'\} \tag{22}$$

$$O \cup \{(P, N \cup \{\{\!| t, V |\!\}\})\} \longrightarrow O \cup \{(P, N \cup \{\{\!| t, V' |\!\}\}) \mid V \xrightarrow{T_{xalt}} V'\} \tag{23}$$

Using these rules will in some cases give a result that differs from the denotational semantics. For example, consider the diagram

$$d = (e_1 \text{ alt } e_2) \text{ seq } (e_3 \text{ xalt } e_4)$$

where (for simplicity) the events e_1, e_2, e_3, e_4 are all on the same lifeline. The denotation of d is:

$$[\![d]\!] = \{(\{\langle e_1, e_3 \rangle, \langle e_2, e_3 \rangle\}, \emptyset), (\{\langle e_1, e_4 \rangle, \langle e_2, e_4 \rangle\}, \emptyset)\}$$

The operational semantics gives us executions:

$$[\beta_0, (e_1 \text{ alt } e_2) \text{ seq } (e_3 \text{ xalt } e_4)] \xrightarrow{T_{alt}} [\beta_0, e_i \text{ seq } (e_3 \text{ xalt } e_4)]$$
$$\xrightarrow{e_i} [\beta_1, e_3 \text{ xalt } e_4] \xrightarrow{T_{xalt}} [\beta_1, e_j] \xrightarrow{e_j} [\beta_2, \text{skip}]$$

with $i \in \{1,2\}$ and $j \in \{3,4\}$. With the above strategy the execution first branches because of the alt, and then the xalt splits the interaction obligation for each of these executions. Because of this we get four interaction obligations:

$$\{(\{\langle e_1, e_3\rangle, \langle e_2, e_3\rangle\}, \emptyset), (\{\langle e_1, e_4\rangle, \langle e_2, e_4\rangle\}, \emptyset),$$
$$(\{\langle e_1, e_3\rangle, \langle e_2, e_4\rangle\}, \emptyset), (\{\langle e_1, e_4\rangle, \langle e_2, e_3\rangle\}, \emptyset)\}$$

To deal with this we need to give priority resolving xalts over resolving the other kinds of choices. We define a special rule allowing xalts on the right hand side of a seq being resolved regardless of the lifeline constraints:

$$\Pi(L, \beta, d_1 \text{ seq } d_2) \xrightarrow{\tau_{xalt}} \Pi(L, \beta, d_1 \text{ seq } d_2') \text{ if } \Pi(L, \beta, d_2) \xrightarrow{\tau_{xalt}} \Pi(L, \beta, d_2') \quad (24)$$

In addition (22) and (23) are given priority over (18)-(21). The execution strategy then gives the same interaction obligations as the denotational semantics.

4   Soundness and Completeness

The operational semantics is sound and complete with respect to the denotational semantics presented in [3,4,5]. Informally, the *soundness* property means that if the operational semantics produces a trace from a given diagram, this trace should be included in the denotational semantics of that diagram. By *completeness* we mean that all traces in the denotational semantics of a diagram should be producible applying the operational semantics on that diagram. In this section we state our soundness and completeness results and provide sketches of the proofs. The full proofs are found in [6].

Let $\mathcal{O}$ be the set of all interaction obligations. $[\![d]\!] \in \mathbb{P}(\mathcal{O})$ is the denotation of d (the formal definition is found in Appendix A). We write $t \in [\![d]\!]$ for $t \in \bigcup_{(p,n) \in [\![d]\!]} (p \cup n)$. $E \circledS t$ denotes the trace t with all events not in E filtered away. $env^!_\mathcal{M}.d$ is the multiset of messages m such that the receive event but not the transmit event of m is present in d.

Theorem 1 (Termination). *Given a diagram $d \in \mathcal{D}$ without infinite loop. Then execution of $[env^!_\mathcal{M}.d, d]$ will terminate.*

Proof. Define a function $w \in \mathcal{D} \to \mathbb{N}$ such that $w(\text{skip}) \overset{\text{def}}{=} 0$, $w(e) \overset{\text{def}}{=} 1$, $w(d_1 \text{ seq } d_2) = w(d_1 \text{ par } d_2) \overset{\text{def}}{=} w(d_1) + w(d_2) + 1$, $w(d_1 \text{ alt } d_2) = w(d_1 \text{ xalt } d_2) \overset{\text{def}}{=} \max(w(d_1), w(d_2)) + 1$, $w(\text{neg } d) \overset{\text{def}}{=} w(d) + 1$, $w(\text{loop}\langle n\rangle \ d) \overset{\text{def}}{=} n(w(d) + 2)$ and $w(\text{loop } I \ d) \overset{\text{def}}{=} \max(I)(w(d) + 2) + 1$. It is easy to see that for all $d \in \mathcal{D}$, $w(d) \geq 0$, and that for every execution step $[\beta, d] \xrightarrow{e} [\beta', d']$ or $[\beta, d] \xrightarrow{\tau} [\beta, d']$, $w(d) > w(d')$. Thus, execution of $[env^!_\mathcal{M}.d, d]$ must terminate. $\quad\square$

Theorem 2 (Soundness). *Given a diagram $d \in \mathcal{D}$ without infinite loop. For all $t \in (\mathcal{E} \cup \mathcal{T})^*$, if there exists $\beta \in \mathcal{B}$ such that $[env^!_\mathcal{M}.d, d] \xrightarrow{t} [\beta, \text{skip}]$ then $\mathcal{E} \circledS t \in [\![d]\!]$.*

Proof. We show this by induction on the structure of d. The induction start $d = \mathsf{skip}$ or $d = e$ is trivial. As induction hypothesis, we assume that the theorem holds for d_1 and d_2. There are seven cases to consider. We start with $d = d_1 \mathsf{\ seq\ } d_2$. Assume that $[env^!_{\mathcal{M}}.d, d_1 \mathsf{\ seq\ } d_2] \xrightarrow{t} [\beta, \mathsf{skip}]$, then by (1), (2), (5), (6), t is obtained by executing d_1 and d_2 in an alternate fashion. This means we have $[env^!_{\mathcal{M}}.d_k, d_k] \xrightarrow{t_k} [\beta_k, \mathsf{skip}]$ such that t is a merge of t_1 and t_2. By the induction hypothesis $\mathcal{E} \circledS t_k \in [\![d_k]\!]$ so we must show that the merge preserves the causality of messages and ordering of events on each lifeline. The first is assured by (1) and (4), and the second by (5) and (6). The proof for $d = d_1 \mathsf{\ par\ } d_2$ is similar except we do not have to think about preserving the ordering along lifelines. For $d = d_1 \mathsf{\ alt\ } d_2$ we must show that $\mathcal{E} \circledS t \in [\![d_k]\!]$ for $k = 1$ or $k = 2$. We observe that, by (2) and (9), $[env^!_{\mathcal{M}}.d, d] \xrightarrow{\tau_{alt}} [env^!_{\mathcal{M}}.d, d_k] \xrightarrow{t} [\beta, \mathsf{skip}]$, so by induction hypothesis $\mathcal{E} \circledS t \in [\![d_k]\!]$. Because $\tau_{alt} \notin \mathcal{E}$ it is sufficient simply to choose the right k. The case of $d = d_1 \mathsf{\ xalt\ } d_2$ is identical. So is $d = \mathsf{neg\ } d_1$ by observing that this is a choice between d_1 and skip. $d = \mathsf{loop\ } I \mathsf{\ } d_1$ is treated in the same way as alt, and $d = \mathsf{loop}\langle n \rangle \mathsf{\ } d_1$ as n consecutive seqs. $\qquad\square$

Theorem 3 (Completeness). *Given a diagram $d \in \mathcal{D}$ without infinite loop. For all $t \in \mathcal{E}^*$, if $t \in [\![d]\!]$ then there exist trace $t' \in (\mathcal{E} \cup \mathcal{T})^*$ and $\beta \in \mathcal{B}$ such that $[env^!_{\mathcal{M}}.d, d] \xrightarrow{t'} [\beta, \mathsf{skip}]$ and $\mathcal{E} \circledS t' = t$.*

Proof. By induction on the structure of d. The induction start $d = \mathsf{skip}$ or $d = e$ is trivial. We assume that the theorem holds for d_1 and d_2 as the induction hypothesis. There are seven cases to consider. Assume $t \in [\![d_1 \mathsf{\ seq\ } d_2]\!]$. Then $t_k \in [\![d_k]\!]$ must exist such that t is a merge of t_1 and t_2, but in such a way that (a) the causality of messages is preserved and (b) for all lifelines l, the events on lifeline l in t_1 precede the events on lifeline l in t_2. By the induction hypothesis $[env^!_{\mathcal{M}}.d_k, d_k] \xrightarrow{t'_k} [\beta_k, \mathsf{skip}]$ and $\mathcal{E} \circledS t'_k = t_k$. This means we may obtain t' such that $t' = \mathcal{E} \circledS t$ by executing d_1 and d_2 in an alternating fashion. (a) ensures that this execution never is blocked by (4) and (b) ensures that execution is never blocked by (6). The case for $d = d_1 \mathsf{\ par\ } d_2$ is similar, but we do not have to take (b) into consideration. For $t \in [\![d_1 \mathsf{\ alt\ } d_2]\!]$ we must have that $t \in [\![d_k]\!]$ for $k = 1$ or $k = 2$. By the induction hypothesis we have t'' such that $[env^!_{\mathcal{M}}.d_k, d_k] \xrightarrow{t''} [\beta_k, \mathsf{skip}]$ and $\mathcal{E} \circledS t'' = t$. By choosing the appropriate k, and letting $t' = \langle \tau_{alt} \rangle {}^\frown t''$ we easily see that $[env^!_{\mathcal{M}}.d, d] \xrightarrow{t'} [\beta, \mathsf{skip}]$ (by (2) and (9)) and $\mathcal{E} \circledS t' = t$ (because $\tau_{alt} \notin \mathcal{E}$). As above, xalt, neg and $\mathsf{loop\ } I$ are treated in the same way as alt, and $\mathsf{loop}\langle n \rangle$ is treated as n consecutive seqs. $\qquad\square$

With respect to diagrams that contain infinite loop, we must assume weak fairness between diagram fragments for the operational semantics to be sound. This means that an arbitrary diagram fragment may not be reachable by the projection system for infinitely many consecutive execution steps without being executed. With this assumption we avoid situations where some part of a diagram only is executed finitely often even though it is inside an infinite loop.

5   Related Work

Several approaches to defining operational semantics for UML sequence diagrams and MSC have been made. The MSC semantics presented in [7] is similar to our execution system, but lacks the formal meta-level. In [8] semantics for the MSC variant Live Sequence Charts (LSC) is defined. This semantics has a meta-level, formalized by pseudo-code, which is used for assigning meaning to invalid executions. In both [9] and [10] LSC semantics is applied to UML sequence diagrams, but none of them conform to the intended UML semantics. In [11] safety and liveness properties are used for distinguishing valid from invalid behavior, but the approach is based on a large amount of transformation and diagrams are not composed by weak sequencing. The MSC semantics presented in [12] has some of the same variability and extendibility that we are aiming at in our semantics, but is heavily based on synchronization of lifelines. The UML semantics of [13] is similar to ours in that it is defined by rewrite rules operating directly on a syntactical representation of sequence diagrams, but treats invalid behavior as the complement of valid behavior.

On inspection of these and other approaches to operational semantics for sequence diagrams and MSCs, like [14, 15, 16, 17, 18, 19, 20], we find that they differ from our semantics in one or more of the following:

- Non-conformance with the intended semantics of UML.
- No notion of explicit negative behavior and no distinction between negative behavior and unspecified behavior
- No distinction between potential and mandatory choice.
- Lack of a proper meta-level that may be used for assigning meaning to negative and potential/mandatory behavior.
- Lack of possibility and freedom in defining and formalizing a meta-level.
- Lack of modifiability and extensibility, e.g., with respect to the communication model.
- Requiring transformations from the textual syntax into the formalism of the approach.

Our aim has been to stay close to the UML standard in both syntax and semantics. Further we have aimed to facilitate ease of extension and modification when adapting the semantics to different interpretations and applications of sequence diagrams.

6   Conclusions

In this paper we have presented an operational semantics for UML 2.0 sequence diagrams. We are not aware of any other operational semantics for UML 2.0 sequence diagrams or MSCs with the same strength and generality as ours. Several approaches have been made, but all with significant shortcomings.

Our operational semantics for UML 2.0 sequence diagrams is simple and is defined with extensibility and variation in mind. It does not involve any translation or transformation of the diagrams into other formalisms, which makes it easy to use and understand. It is sound and complete with respect to a reasonable denotational formalization of the UML standard.

The operational semantics have a formalized meta-level for defining execution strategies. This meta-level is used for distinguishing valid from invalid traces, and for distinguishing between traces of different interaction obligations. Further it may be used for defining different meta-strategies that guide the execution. We have shown two examples: generating a single trace and generating all traces with a white box view of the diagram. Other examples may be to generate a specific number of traces or prefixes of a specific length. It is also possible to define strategies that take a black box view of the diagram.

The semantics is implemented in the term rewriting language Maude [21], and forms the basis of a tool for analysis of sequence diagrams currently under development. Recent work includes test generation from sequence diagrams; see [22] for more details.

References

1. Object Management Group: Unified Modeling Language: Superstructure, version 2.0. (2005) OMG Document: formal/2005-07-04.
2. International Telecommunication Union: Message Sequence Chart (MSC), ITU-T Recommendation Z.120. (1999)
3. Haugen, Ø., Husa, K.E., Runde, R.K., Stølen, K.: STAIRS towards formal design with sequence diagrams. Software and Systems Modeling 4 (2005) 355–367
4. Haugen, Ø., Husa, K.E., Runde, R.K., Stølen, K.: Why timed sequence diagrams require three-event semantics. In: Scenarios: Models, transformations and tools. International Workshop, Dagstuhl Castle, Germany, September 2003. Revised selected papers. Number 3466 in LNCS. Springer (2005) 1–25
5. Haugen, Ø., Husa, K.E., Runde, R.K., Stølen, K.: Why timed sequence diagrams require three-event semantics. Research report 309, Department of Informatics, University of Oslo (2004) Revised June 2005.
6. Lund, M.S., Stølen, K.: A fully general operational semantics for UML sequence diagrams with potential and mandatory choice. Research report 330, Department of Informatics, University of Oslo (2006)
7. Jonsson, B., Padilla, G.: An execution semantics for MSC-2000. In: 10th International SDL Forum: Meeting UML (SDL'01). Number 2078 in LNCS, Springer (2001) 365–378
8. Harel, D., Marelly, R.: Come, let's play: Scenario-based programming using LSCs and the Play-Engine. Springer (2003)
9. Cavarra, A., Küster-Filipe, J.: Formalizing liveness-enriched sequence diagrams using ASMs. In: 11th International Workshop on Abstract State Machines 2004, Advances in Theory and Practice (ASM'04). Number 3052 in LNCS, Springer (2004) 67–77
10. Harel, D., Maoz, S.: Assert and negate revisited: Modal semantics for UML sequence diagrams. In: 5th International Workshop on Scenarios and State Machines: Models, Algorithms, and Tools (SCESM'06), ACM Press (2006) 13–19
11. Grosu, R., Smolka, S.A.: Safety-liveness semantics for UML 2.0 sequence diagrams. In: 5th International Conference on Application of Concurrency to System Design (ACSD'05), IEEE Computer Society (2005) 6–14

12. Letichevsky, A., Kapitonova, J., Kotlyarov, V., Volkov, V., Letichevsky, A., Weigert, T.: Semantics of Message Sequence Charts. In: 12th International SDL Forum: Model Driven Systems Design (SDL'05). Number 3530 in LNCS, Springer (2005) 117–132
13. Cengarle, M.V., Knapp, A.: Operational semantics of UML 2.0 interactions. Technical report TUM-I0505, Technische Universität München (2005)
14. Alur, R., Etessami, K., Yannakakis, M.: Inference of Message Sequence Charts. IEEE Transactions on Software Engineering **29** (2003) 623–633
15. Alur, R., Etessami, K., Yannakakis, M.: Realizability and verification of MSC graphs. Theoretical Computer Science **331** (2005) 97–114
16. Mauw, S., Reniers, M.A.: Operational semantics for MSC'96. Computer Networks **31** (1999) 1785–1799
17. Mauw, S., Reniers, M.A.: High-level Message Sequence Charts. In: 8th International SDL Forum: Time for Testing, SDL, MSC and Trends (SDL'97), Elsevier (1997) 291–306
18. International Telecommunication Union: Message Sequence Chart (MSC), ITU-T Recommendation Z.120, Annex B: Formal semantics of Message Sequence Charts. (1998)
19. Uchitel, S., Kramer, J., Magee, J.: Incremental elaboration of scenario-based specification and behavior models using implied scenarios. ACM Transactions on Software Engineering and Methodology **13** (2004) 37–85
20. Kosiuczenko, P., Wirsing, M.: Towards an integration of Message Sequence Charts and Timed Maude. Journal of Integrated Design & Process Science **5** (2001) 23–44
21. Clavel, M., Durán, F., Eker, S., Lincoln, P., Martí-Oliet, N., Meseguer, J., Talcott, C.: Maude Manual (Version 2.2). SRI International, Menlo Park. (2005)
22. Lund, M.S., Stølen, K.: Deriving tests from UML 2.0 sequence diagrams with neg and assert. In: 1st International Workshop on Automation of Software Test (AST'06), ACM Press (2006) 22–28

A   Denotational Semantics

On diagrams we have the constraints that a given message should syntactically occur only once, and if both the transmitter and the receiver lifelines of the message are present in the diagram, then both the transmit event and receive event of that message must be in the diagram. In each trace, a transmit event should always be ordered before the corresponding receive event. We let $\mathcal{H}$ denote the set of all traces that complies with this requirement.

$\mathcal{O}$ is the set of interaction obligations. The semantics of a diagram is defined by a function $[\![\_]\!] \in \mathcal{D} \to \mathbb{P}(\mathcal{O})$. For the empty diagram and the diagram consisting of a single event, the semantics is given by:

$$[\![\mathsf{skip}]\!] \overset{\text{def}}{=} \{(\{\langle\rangle\}, \emptyset)\} \qquad\qquad [\![e]\!] \overset{\text{def}}{=} \{(\{\langle e\rangle\}, \emptyset)\}$$

We define weak sequencing of trace sets:

$$s_1 \succsim s_2 \overset{\text{def}}{=} \{h \in \mathcal{H} \mid \exists h_1 \in s_1, h_2 \in s_2 : \forall l \in \mathcal{L} : e.l\text{\textcircled{s}}h = e.l\text{\textcircled{s}}h_1 \frown e.l\text{\textcircled{s}}h_2\}$$

where $e.l$ denotes the set of events that may take place on the lifeline l. The seq construct is defined as:

$$\llbracket d_1 \text{ seq } d_2 \rrbracket \stackrel{\text{def}}{=} \{o_1 \succeq o_2 \mid o_1 \in \llbracket d_1 \rrbracket \wedge o_2 \in \llbracket d_2 \rrbracket\}$$

where weak sequencing of interaction obligations is defined as:

$$(p_1, n_1) \succeq (p_2, n_2) \stackrel{\text{def}}{=} (p_1 \succeq p_2, (n_1 \succeq p_2) \cup (n_1 \succeq n_2) \cup (p_1 \succeq n_2))$$

In order to define par, we first define parallel execution on trace sets:

$$s_1 \parallel s_2 \stackrel{\text{def}}{=} \{h \in \mathcal{H} \mid \exists p \in \{1,2\}^\infty : \pi_2((\{1\} \times \mathcal{E}) \textcircled{\tiny T}(p, h)) \in s_1 \wedge \pi_2((\{2\} \times \mathcal{E}) \textcircled{\tiny T}(p, h)) \in s_2\}$$

In this definition, the oracle p resolves the non-determinism in the interleaving. π_2 is a projection operator returning the second element of a pair, and $\textcircled{\tiny T}$ is an operator for filtering pairs of traces (see [6] for formal definitions). The par construct itself is defined as:

$$\llbracket d_1 \text{ par } d_2 \rrbracket \stackrel{\text{def}}{=} \{o_1 \parallel o_2 \mid o_1 \in \llbracket d_1 \rrbracket \wedge o_2 \in \llbracket d_2 \rrbracket\}$$

where parallel execution of interaction obligations is defined as:

$$(p_1, n_1) \parallel (p_2, n_2) \stackrel{\text{def}}{=} (p_1 \parallel p_2, (n_1 \parallel p_2) \cup (n_1 \parallel n_2) \cup (p_1 \parallel n_2))$$

The semantics of alt is the inner union of the interaction obligations:

$$\llbracket d_1 \text{ alt } d_2 \rrbracket \stackrel{\text{def}}{=} \{(p_1 \cup p_2, n_1 \cup n_2) \mid (p_1, n_1) \in \llbracket d_1 \rrbracket \wedge (p_2, n_2) \in \llbracket d_2 \rrbracket\}$$

The xalt is defined as the union of interaction obligations:

$$\llbracket d_1 \text{ xalt } d_2 \rrbracket \stackrel{\text{def}}{=} \llbracket d_1 \rrbracket \cup \llbracket d_2 \rrbracket$$

The neg construct defines negative traces:

$$\llbracket \text{neg } d \rrbracket \stackrel{\text{def}}{=} \{(\{\langle\rangle\}, p \cup n) \mid (p, n) \in \llbracket d \rrbracket\}$$

The semantics of loop is defined by a semantic loop construct μ_n, where n is the number of times the loop should be iterated. Let $\uplus$ be a generalization of potential choice (inner union of interaction obligation). loop is then defined as:

$$\llbracket \text{loop } I \ d \rrbracket \stackrel{\text{def}}{=} \biguplus_{i \in I} \mu_i \ \llbracket d \rrbracket$$

For $n \in \mathbb{N}$ (finite loop), μ_n is defined as

$$\mu_0 \ O \stackrel{\text{def}}{=} \{(\{\langle\rangle\}, \emptyset)\} \qquad \mu_n \ O \stackrel{\text{def}}{=} O \succeq \mu_{n-1} \ O \quad \text{if } n > 0$$

For a treatment of infinite loop, see [5] or [6].

Towards Automatic Exception Safety Verification

Xin Li, H. James Hoover, and Piotr Rudnicki

Department of Computing Science
University of Alberta
Edmonton, Alberta, Canada T6G 2E8
{xinli, hoover, piotr}@cs.ualberta.ca

Abstract. Many programming languages provide exceptions as a structured way for detecting and recovering from abnormal conditions. However, using exceptions properly is non-trivial. Programmers are often careless when handling exceptions, and exception related mistakes are common in software products. We present a technique for verifying that exceptions are used in a safe way. This technique integrates static analysis with model checking to visit all possible exception-raising execution paths. To demonstrate the potential utility of our approach, we applied it to two open source Java applications.

Keywords: static analysis, model checking, verification, exceptions.

1 Introduction

Exception handling is used in programming languages as a structured way to detect and recover from abnormal conditions such as data corruption, precondition violation or environmental errors. Exceptions help the programmer to simplify program structure by eliminating the clutter associated with inspecting and acting on return codes. They also ensure that errors are handled at relatively well-defined points in the program. However, exceptions complicate the potential control flow paths in a program and make it difficult for the programmer to reason about the program behavior under interacting error situations. It has been reported that up to two thirds of system crashes and fifty percent of system security vulnerabilities are caused by mishandled exceptions [13].

Despite the importance of exception handling, programmers are often careless when using exceptions. Exception related mistakes like "swallow exceptions and do nothing" or "forget about the clean-up actions when handling exceptions" are very common in software products. We are interested in techniques which can verify that a program is "exception reliable" and "exception safe" — terms that we will elaborate on shortly.

In this paper, we present a verification framework which combines static analysis and model checking techniques to do exhaustive checking of a program's exceptional behaviors. The program is instrumented with support for exploring

J. Misra, T. Nipkow, and E. Sekerinski (Eds.): FM 2006, LNCS 4085, pp. 396–411, 2006.
© Springer-Verlag Berlin Heidelberg 2006

all exceptional flows of control so that the back-end model checker is able to inspect all possible exceptions. To avoid the state explosion problem, we propose some program slicing criteria which attempt to preserve the control flow in the face of environmental and data diversity.

In Section 2, we describe general exception handling issues and introduce exception reliability and safety. In section 3, we discuss our framework for exceptional program behavior verification. Section 4 discusses implementation details about the framework. Section 5 presents two small case studies supporting the efficacy of our method. Section 6 concludes with the next steps in this effort.

2   Exception Handling Issues

2.1   Exception Classification

Leino et al. [12] classify exceptions into *client failure* and *provider failure*. Client failure occurs when a precondition of an operation is violated. For instance, the operation is expecting a number but got a string instead. Provider failure occurs when an operation finds it is unable to satisfy its post-conditions. For example, a socket read operation does not satisfy its postcondition when it encounters a broken connection during the read of a record. Furthermore, provider failures can be divided into two subclasses, *observed program error* and *admissible failure*. Observed program error refers to an intrinsic program error such as array index out of bounds, or program out of memory. On the other hand, *admissible failure* refers to an exception where one can recover from the failure state. For instance, an operation is intended to read bits from a network channel but the received bits contain too many parity errors, so a retry is initiated. In Java terminology, a *checked exception* is an admissible failure. An *unchecked exception* is a client failure or observed program error.

Several exception handling patterns are identified by Goodwin et al. in [8]. In general, two exception handling philosophies are used:

1. **Catch what you can handle:** For a client failure and an admissible failure, the callee must be given enough information about the failure so that it can attempt to fix the problem. If the callee is unable to fix the problem itself, it should be permitted to report the problem to the caller or simply terminate the whole program. Detailed information about the failure and the current execution stack should be preserved.
2. **Let exceptions propagate:** In general, it is impossible to correct an observed program error. The general approach is to release any resources acquired in the current control context, add additional diagnostic information to the caught exception, and then re-throw and propagate the exception. In some situations one might consider terminating the program and reporting the details about the exception and current execution stack.

2.2   Exception Reliability and Safety

Exception reliability is a fundamental requirement for a robust program. In general, we call a program *exception handling reliable* when the following two conditions are satisfied:

1. All raised exceptions are handled.
2. Every handler is reachable by some exception.

The second condition is supposed to capture the idea that every handler is intended to catch some particular exceptions, and if it does not catch any, then it is likely that some other handler is inadvertently do an earlier catch. An example of unreachable exception handler is a handler for `IOException` right after a handler for `Exception`.

Based on Stroustrup's [16] definition, we define *exception safety* in terms of the following four guarantees of increasing quality:

1. *No-leak guarantee:* The program is exception reliable and no resource leaks.
2. *Basic guarantee:* In addition to the no-leak guarantee, the basic invariants of classes are maintained.
3. *Strong guarantee:* In addition to the basic guarantee, every operation either succeeds or has no effect.
4. *No-throw guarantee:* In addition to the basic guarantee, no exception is thrown.

In this paper we focus on automatically verifying the no-leak guarantee. Of course, robust software should at a minimum provide basic exception safety. This is a future goal.

2.3   Related Work

There are several static analysis tools and techniques proposed to tackle the exception handling analysis problem.

Robillard and Murphy [15] developed the Jex tool, which gathers exception-related information for a Java program. Based on a class-hierarchy analysis, Jex can conservatively determine the control-flow graph of the program and then trace exception propagation. Jex can also handle unchecked exceptions.

Jo et al. [10] proposed an inter-procedural exception analysis based on a set-constraints framework. Compared to conventional analysis methods based on the control-flow graph, it can more precisely determine the type of exceptions that can be propagated by each method. But this analysis doesn't include unchecked exceptions.

Both techniques can be used to solve the exception reliability problem but not the exception safety problem. Weimer and Necula [18] present a static analysis tool for finding run-time error-handling mistakes. Our eventual goal is to handle both the exception reliability problem and the exception safety problem.

3   A Model Checking Framework for Exceptional Program Behavior Verification

To be useful, any verification processes must be efficient in both human and machine resources. Efficient static analysis techniques only inspect the code at compile time; they are imprecise as they only approximate the inter-procedural control-flow. Using model checking [9] we can explore some possible run-time behavior of the simplified program and thus more accurately analyze control-flow.

Model checking addresses the behavior of finite-state *closed systems* whose future behavior is completely determined by the current state of the system. To deal with *open systems* that interact with their environment the model checker must also model the environment. This is typically done by modelling all possible sequences of events and inputs that can come from the environment. The state space of a typical program is too large to be explored, so model checking is done in the context of an abstraction function that limits the number of explored variables and their associated ranges, thus keeping the size of the state space manageable.

Since exceptions are typically the result of unusual circumstances, the possible exceptional flows of control raised by rarely encountered data or environmental errors should be explored by the model checker if we want to assure proper exception handling. Therefore, choosing the appropriate abstraction function is a challenge.

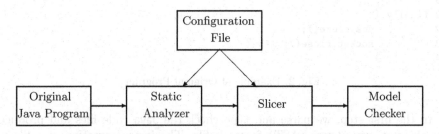

Fig. 1. Verification Process

In our framework, the verification process is iterative, with each cycle divided into three steps (Figure 1).

1. With support from a static analyzer, the program is instrumented such that all possible exceptions can be easily raised.
2. The instrumented program is fed into a slicer to remove all irrelevant program constructs.
3. The sliced program is fed into a model checker to detect exception specification violations.

Since the model checker typically finds only one problem at a time, each iteration corrects a single problem and the process is repeated.

To illustrate the process, Figure 2 presents a sample Java program. This program first tries to acquire two resources: socket and dataOutputStream, then performs some operations. When leaving the try, it attempts to release these two resources. At the first glance, it should work properly since all the close() operations are inside a finally block. But the code is flawed. First, failure to close dos object (Figure 2 line 12) will raise an exception and lead to line 13 socket.close() being bypassed. Therefore, resource socket leaks. Second, if operation serverSocket.accept() on line 4 or new DataOutputStream() on line 5 fails, variable socket or dos will be null on line 12 or 13. Then a null pointer dereferencing error will happen. While these errors can't be discovered by static analysis tools like ESC/Java [7], our tool can. Note that we do not detect the typical error of acquiring a resource (like DataOutputStream) a second time without closing the previous instance since this is not an error that results in an exception.

```
01 Socket socket = null;
02 DataOutputStream dos = null;
03 try {
04      socket = serverSocket.accept();
05      dos = new DataOutputStream(socket.getOutputStream());
06      // other operations
07      }
08 catch (IOException e) {
09      // handling exceptions here
10      }
11 finally {
12          dos.close();
13          socket.close();
14          }
```

Fig. 2. Example of Original Program

In the first step, we parse and type check the Java code files and produce an abstract syntax tree (AST) for each file. The instrumentation of a file is accomplished by traversing the AST. For each statement, the analyzer instruments possible exceptions according to the Java language specification [3]. For example, a statement attempting a division might raise ArithmeticException and therefore need to be instrumented. For each method call, the analyzer first determines if the method source code is available. If available, the analyzer instruments the method directly. If not, the analyzer instruments the exception interface extracted from the byte code of that method.

The result of the first step of static analysis and instrumentation is shown in Figure 3. Notice how lines 5, 7, 15, 17 in Figure 3 are added to represent possible exceptions raised by lines 4, 6, 14, 16. (We are assuming that the method source code is unavailable.) The instrumentation call Verify.getBoolean() models

```
01 Socket socket = null;
02 DataOutputStream dos = null;
03 try {
04      socket = serverSocket.accept();
05      if (Verify.getBoolean()) throw new java.io.IOException();
06      dos = new DataOutputStream(socket.getOutputStream());
07      if (Verify.getBoolean()) throw new java.io.IOException();
08      // other operations
09      }
10 catch (IOException e) {
11      // handling exceptions here
12      }
13 finally {
14    dos.close();
15    if (Verify.getBoolean()) throw new java.io.IOException();
16    socket.close();
17    if (Verify.getBoolean()) throw new java.io.IOException();
18 }
```

Fig. 3. Example of Instrumented Program

the environment by nondeterministically returning a Boolean value. This ensures that future model checking explores all exception-triggered execution paths in the original program.

The second step of our process applies a program slicer to remove all program constructs that are irrelevant for checking exception safety. The sliced program contains nothing but the execution flow constructs and all resource or exception related information. A configuration file specifies the abstraction function that informs the slicer about what kind of objects should be considered as a resource in this verification process. The slicer replaces each of these objects with a generic representation Resource.

Figure 4 shows the generic resource representation. This Resource class is extendible to support additional resource related operations. Figure 5 presents the sliced program based on Figure 3. In Figure 5, lines 1–3 and lines 24–28 are the resource leak specification part as generated by the slicer. Lines 6–23 correspond the same lines in Figure 3. Since all the statements are relevant to resources or exceptions, they are preserved by the slicer, although the type of object socket and dataOutputStream have been changed to a unified type Resource. The resource allocation operation is simulated nondeterministically, that is, the resource allocation operation either succeeds or fails. If it fails, null is returned.

The third step of our analysis feeds the sliced program into the software model checker, Java Pathfinder, JPF, [17]. Based on the given program and associated environment abstraction, JPF systematically exhausts all possible execution paths. It checks if there is any uncaught exception or assertion violations in the sliced program. If so, JPF dumps out an execution path leading to the violation. The execution path can help the programmer to fix the problem. This verification process is iterated until no further violation is reported.

```
public class Resource { ... ...
    public boolean inuse = true;

    public void open() {
        inuse = true;
    }

    public void close() {
        inuse = false;
    }
... ... }
```

Fig. 4. Resource Class Example

The current version of JPF works directly on Java byte code and can handle all Java features including commonly used libraries. The environment is modelled by nondeterministic choice expressed as method calls to a special class Verify. For example, the method getBoolean() from class Verify returns a boolean value nondeterministically.

We selected JPF as our model checker for a number of reasons: Compared to other model checkers like Bandera [4] or Bogor [14], JPF can handle more Java features. As an explicit state model checker, JPF adopts several efficient state reduction techniques like heap symmetry reduction and partial order reduction. JPF provides nondeterministic constructs for modelling environment-driven choices. JPF is an open source project.

4   Implementation Issues

4.1   Program Instrumenting

Our verification framework takes a set of Java source files and a configuration file as input. The configuration file is used to provide application related information. Figure 6 gives out an example of a configuration file. The <exception> item is used to identify these exceptions which are ignored by the static analyzer. By default our analyzer instruments every possible exception, but the user can choose to skip some kinds of exceptions. <import> specifies the Java packages to be verified. <resource> item identifies these objects which are considered as a resource. In this example, all instances from Socket, FileInputStream or BufferedReader are considered as resources.

Our static analysis is built on top of KJC, the Kopi open source Java compiler [2], and the Jex tool [15] for exception analysis. Jex is implemented as an extension to the KJC project. Jex first produces an abstract syntax tree (AST) for each file. While traversing the AST, Jex computes the type and origins of exceptions that could be thrown by each statement according to the Java Language Specification[3]. For each method call, Jex first uses conservative class hierarchy analysis to determine all possible dynamic bindings for the call and then calculates the exceptions which might be propagated by the method call.

```
01  Resource socket= null;
02  Resource dos= null;
03  try {
04    socket = null;
05    dos = null;
06      try {
07            if (Verify.getBoolean()) socket = new Resource();
08                else socket = null;
09            if (Verify.getBoolean()) throw new java.io.IOException();
10            if (Verify.getBoolean()) dos = new  Resource();
11                  else dos = null;
12            if (Verify.getBoolean()) throw new java.io.IOException();
13            // other operations
14            }
15      catch (java.io.IOException e) {
16                // handling exceptions here
17            }
18      finally {
19                dos.close();
20                if (Verify.getBoolean()) throw new java.io.IOException();
21                socket.close();
22                if (Verify.getBoolean()) throw new java.io.IOException();
23            }
24      }
25  finally {
26  assert socket == null || socket.inuse == false;
27  assert dos == null || dos.inuse == false;
28  }
```

Fig. 5. Example of Sliced Program

This process may iterate several times until a global fixed point is reached for all methods in the system.

Our static analyzer is built on the Jex tool with several modifications.

1. We do not need inter-procedural analysis to determine the control flow graph since this is effectively achieved in the model checking phase. Our analysis procedure is much simpler, and we only have to traverse the AST once.
2. Since Jex generates only the type and the origins of exceptions, our analyzer needs to record the exact place where that exception might be thrown, such that we can instrument the code with a statement like

```
if (Verify.getBoolean()) throw new ExceptionType();
```

In most cases, this statement is inserted immediately after the statement that can throw the exception. But in some cases, it is added somewhere else. For example, if a **return** statement may throw exceptions, these exceptions should be instrumented before that **return** statement.
3. Jex is designed to address all exceptions that can be raised in a Java program, so it supports both checked and unchecked exceptions. By default,

```
.. ... <exception> java.lang.OutOfMemoryError
... ...
<exception>javalang.ArrayStoreException
<exception> java.lang.ClassCastException
<dir>    /Users/xinli/examples
<import> jnfs
<import> jnfs.security
<import> jnfs.security.acl
<resource> java.net.Socket
<resource> java.io.FileInputStream
<resource> java.io.BufferedReader
... ...
```

Fig. 6. Example of Configuration File

we consider all possible exceptions flagged by Jex (although not all possible exceptions are reported by the tool) but also can specify which exceptions to ignore. For example, the unchecked exception, OutOfMemoryError could be raised after every new operation and method call. The user might want to turn off the instrumentation of this exception until the more common modes of failure have been addressed.

4.2   Program Slicing

Directly applying model checking to a full program quickly leads to state explosion. It is necessary to reduce the size of the program state as much as possible, while still preserving properties of interest. Program slicing [19] is a technique to reduce the program size while keeping all the interesting program constructs. Our program slicing rules are described below

For brevity, we consider a subset of Java with almost all language features [5] Its abstract syntax is in Figure 7. In this figure, RType represents those types which are defined as resource types of interest to the user. LType represents those types that come from the Java library, or from third party application whose source code is not available.

The following rules give our slicing criteria in the form of program transformation rules based on the abstract syntax from Figure 7. A rule of the form

$$[\,A\,]\,B \quad \frac{C}{D}$$

means that when visiting program construct A, and while condition B is true, program fragment C (one of the variants of A) is be transformed to D. In these rules, we frequently use the following two operations

- type(*expr*) returns the type of parameter *expr*.
- eval(*expr*) returns true iff *expr* is not resource related.

$$
\begin{array}{lll}
Prog & ::= & Class^* \\
Class & ::= & \textbf{class } \text{CId } \textbf{extends } \text{CName} \\
& & \{ CMember^* \} \\
CMember & ::= & Field \mid Method \\
Field & ::= & VarType \text{ VarId;} \\
Method & ::= & MHeader\ MBody \\
MHeader & ::= & (\textbf{void} \mid VarType)\ \text{MId } ((VarType\ PId)^*)\ \textbf{throws } CName^* \\
MBody & ::= & \{ Stmts\ [\textbf{return } Expr] \} \\
Stmts & ::= & (stmt;)^* \\
Stmt & ::= & \textbf{if } Expr\ \textbf{then } Stmts\ \textbf{else } Stmts \\
& \mid & Var = Expr \mid Expr.\text{MName}(Expr^*) \\
& \mid & \textbf{throw } Expr \\
& \mid & \textbf{while } Expr\ Stmts \\
& \mid & \textbf{try } Stmts\ (\textbf{catch } \text{CName Id } Stmts)^*\ \textbf{finally } Stmts \\
& \mid & \textbf{try } Stmts\ (\textbf{catch } \text{CName Id } Stmts)^+ \\
Expr & ::= & Value \mid \text{Var} \mid Expr.MName(Expr^*) \\
& \mid & \textbf{new } \text{CName}() \mid \textbf{this} \\
Var & ::= & \text{Name} \mid Expr.VarName \mid Expr[Expr] \\
Value & ::= & PrimValue \mid RefValue \\
RefValue & ::= & \text{null} \mid .. \\
PrimValue & ::= & intValue \mid charValue \mid boolValue \mid ... \\
VarType & ::= & PrimType \mid \text{CName} \mid \text{RType} \mid \text{LType} \\
PrimType & ::= & \textbf{bool} \mid \textbf{char} \mid \textbf{int} \mid ...
\end{array}
$$

Fig. 7. Abstract Syntax of Core Java

In conditional statements, if the guard expression does not involve resources (that is `eval(`*expr*`)` returns true), we use `Verify.getBoolean()` to replace the *expr* to ensure that model checking examines all possible paths.

$$
[Field]\ VarType \notin \text{RType} \quad \frac{VarType\ \text{VarId}}{[\ ]} \tag{1}
$$

The above rule concerns class fields: every class field that is not a resource type is removed.

$$
[MBody]\ \text{type}(Expr) \notin PrimType \cup \text{RType} \quad \frac{\{ Stmts\ [\textbf{return } Expr] \}}{\{ Stmts\ [\textbf{return null}] \}} \tag{2}
$$

This rule concerns return statements: if the type of *Expr* is not a primary type or a resource type, we return `null` instead.

$$
[MBody]\ \text{type}(Expr) \in PrimType \quad \frac{\{ Stmts\ [\textbf{return } Expr] \}}{\{ Stmts\ [\textbf{return } PrimValue] \}} \tag{3}
$$

When the type of the return expression is primitive, then a predefined value of the corresponding primitive type (see below) is returned.

$$
[Stmt]\ \text{eval}(Expr) \quad \frac{\textbf{if } Expr \cdots}{\textbf{if } \texttt{Verify.getBoolean()} \cdots} \tag{4}
$$

If the guard expression *Expr* is not resource relevant, it is replaced by
`Verify.getBoolean()`.

$$[Stmt] \; \mathbf{eval}(Expr) \quad \frac{\mathbf{while} \; Expr \; Stmts}{\mathbf{if} \; \mathtt{Verify.getBoolean()} \; Stmts} \tag{5}$$

For while loops, if the guard expression *Expr* is not resource relevant, it is replaced by `Verify.getBoolean()`. Therefore, the loop body is executed once
or not at all. Please note that this slicing is incapable of handling arrays of
resources.

$$[PrimValue] \quad \frac{int\,Value \mid bool\,Value \mid \cdots}{3 \mid \mathtt{true} \mid \cdots} \tag{6}$$

Every primitive value is replaced by a predefined value. For instance, we use 3
to replace any **int** value.

$$[Stmt] \; \mathbf{type}(Expr) \in PrimType \cup \mathrm{LType} \quad \frac{Var = Expr}{[\,]} \tag{7}$$

All assignment statements of primitive types or library type objects are removed.

$$[Stmt] \; \mathbf{type}(Expr) \in \mathrm{LType} \quad \frac{Expr.MName(Expr^*)}{[\,]} \tag{8}$$

Each library call is removed (as its exceptions have been already instrumented).

$$[Stmt] \; \mathbf{type}(Expr_1) \notin \mathrm{LType} \; \& \; \mathbf{type}(expr) \notin PrimType \cup \mathrm{RType}$$

$$\frac{Expr_1.MName(expr, \; Expr^*)}{Expr_1.MName(\mathtt{null}, Expr^*)} \tag{9}$$

If we invoke a method not from a library, and the parameter is not of primitive
type or resource type, we use `null` to replace that parameter.

In addition to the above, other **Java** program constructs not included in
Figure 7 are handled as follows:

1. Abstract classes and interfaces are sliced like a standard class
2. Array types are sliced in the same way as the basic type of the array
3. All thread related program constructs are preserved since they are essential
   for program execution. This can be seen as treating them like RType in their
   slicing rules.

Since we relax the guards of all program control statements, there is a possibility that we generate false alarms, that is, we generate an assertion violation
execution path which never happens in the original program. It requires substantial human effort to inspect the output of the model checker in order to dismiss
a false alarm. Reducing the frequency of false alarms is one of our future goals.
Surprisingly, we have not met such situations in our experiments, see Section 5.

4.3   Generating Specifications for Resource Leaks

Since JPF can automatically detect all unhandled exceptions and report them as
a program error, no specification is needed for exception reliability verification.
In order to do the resource leak verification, some specification annotations are
inserted as assertions into the sliced Java program. Some of these specifications
are inserted automatically. JPF then examines all the execution paths, and if
along any path there is an assertion violation, we have a resource leak.

Program resources may be declared at two levels: method and class. At the
method level, resources are declared as local objects that should be released
before termination of the method. (Note: this only works for the situation that
the return type is not a resource type.) Our slicer automatically inserts a new
try-finally block. The new try block embeds all of the original method body
while assertions that all resources have been released are inserted into the new
finally block. In that way, JPF can check if there is any assertion violation at the
end of method execution.

```
01 public String RETR( String name ) throws Exception
02 {
03   // ... ...
04   Socket dConnection = buildDataConnection(name,getDataType(),obj.size());
05   OutputStream out = dConnection.getOutputStream();
06   obj.read( out, dataMode, restartOffset );
07   restartOffset = 0;
08   dConnection.close();
09   return "226 " + getDataType() + " transfer complete.";
10 }
```

Fig. 8. Example: Assertions for Resource leak (Original Program)

In order to observe scope issues, all method level resource objects should be
predefined before the new try-finally block. Figure 9 contains a sliced example
of the original program in Figure 8.

In Figure 9, line 2 declares resource object dConnection. Lines 3–15 are the
newly formed try block. Lines 4–14 are the original method body sliced and
instrumented. Lines 16–18 form the newly added finally block. Line 17 asserts
that resource dConnection is released.

At the class level, it is usually difficult to decide the exact point where a
resource should be released. Additional information about the interactions between classes is required, and users may need to insert additional specifications.
However, for transaction style applications (such as web applications), the objects that handle a transaction have a well defined life cycle. When a class is
a descendant of Thread or Runnable, all related external resources should be
released before the run method terminates. Therefore, in this particular case,
we can add assertions to the run method just as for ordinary method.

```
01 public java.lang.String RETR(String name) Exception {
02   Resource dConnection = null;
03   try {
04   {
05     //... ...
06     dConnection = buildDataConnection(null, null, 0);
07     if (Verify.getBoolean()) throw new java.io.IOException();
08     if (Verify.getBoolean()) throw new kmy.net.ftpd.FTPDException();
09     if (Verify.getBoolean()) throw new java.lang.InterruptedException();
10     obj.read((java.io.OutputStream)null, 2, 0);
11     dConnection.close();
12     if (Verify.getBoolean()) throw new java.io.IOException();
13     return (java.lang.String)null;
14   }
15   }
16   finally {
17       assert dConnection == null || dConnection.inuse == false;
18   }
19 }
```

Fig. 9. Example: Assertions for Resource Leak (Sliced Program)

5   Experimental Results

We present experimental results[1] obtained by using our tool on two Java web applications. Table 1 shows the running time and state space size of these experiments. As resources we have considered Socket from java.net and from java.io: FileInputStream, DataOutputStream, and BufferedReader.

Table 1. Running time and state space size for the experiments

	NanoHTTP	FizmezWebServer
Time	57.6 s	75.3 s
Visited States	15905	38875

5.1   NanoHTTPD

Project NanoHTTPD [6] is a simple embeddable HTTP server application written in Java. After instrumentation and slicing, model checking discovered an uncaught NumberFormatException. Examining the execution path that triggered the exception we found that in the main function, there is a call to the library function Integer.parseInt(). The fact that this may raise an exception was

[1] All experiments were performed on a PowerBook with PowerPC G4, 1.67 GHz, 2.0 GB RAM, running Mac OS X 10.4.6, Sun Java SDK build 1.5.0_06-112 and Java Pathfinder Version 3.1.2.

totally neglected by the programmer. After fixing this problem, the application has been verified as exception reliable code.

Next we explored potential resource leaks. First, the object mySocket of type java.net.Socket is defined as a field in class NanoHTTPD. It is initialized when an HTTPSession is created and should be closed before this HTTP session is terminated, that is before the corresponding run method ends. The program does call mySocket.close() by the end of the run() procedure, but this call may be not executed as it is not enclosed in a finally block. JPF shows us an execution path which under high load causes an exception prior to the socket closure, and leads to the mySocket leak. Thus the application can fail under a very high number of requests.

We also found two other resource leak problems. A BufferedReader type object in is declared in method run() in class HTTPSession and a FileInput Stream type object fis is declared in method serveFile() in class NanoHTTPD. The author closes these resources at the end of the corresponding try block but again not in a finally section. As a result, when exceptions are thrown these resources are never closed and thus may leak.

5.2   FizmezWebServer

Project FizmezWebServer [1] is an open source Web server application implemented in Java. Applying our tool to this application detected several errors. First, the application has a potential unhandled exception. In method getServerSocket(), the socket port number is provided in string format, and therefore needs to be transformed into integer format. The transformation process might throw NumberFormatException and is neglected by the programmer. This puts the application into an exception unreliable situation.

There are several resource leak problems in this application. Inside method getConfig(), although the programmer comments the bufferedReader.close() saying that "close the mime file so others can use it!" there is still a resource leak problem with the object bufferedReader because it is not protected by a finally block. The same problem happens again in method getMimeTypes(), leading to another BufferedReader type of object execBufferedReader not being properly closed.

At the class level, a java.net.Socket type of object socket is defined as a field in class WebServer. The author intends to close it by the end of the try block in run method. But since there are many operations which might throw exceptions inside the try prior to the close operation, we find yet another leak.

We also find an interesting program error. After fixing all the above problems, JPF reported that there was an uncaught NullPointerException where the close() method is being called on a null object. After inspecting the execution path JPF provided, we discovered that although the object dataOutputStream is closed in a finally block, there is a possibility that some exceptions are raised before initializing dataOutputStream. The control flow then jumps to the exception handler and executes the close operation on dataOutputStream in `finally` block. Since the pointer is not guarded with a test for null, a `NullPointerException` is thrown and the application crashes.

6   Conclusion

In this paper, we describe an approach to exception safety verification that combines static analysis and model checking. Model checking gives increased confidence in the run-time handling of exceptions, and our initial case studies indicate that it can catch problems that elude static analysis.

A basic guarantee of exception safety requires that there be no resource leaks and preservation of program invariants. How much of this can be done with JPF as the model checker? Basic class invariants can be annotated using Java Modeling Language (JML) [11], a behavioral specification language which is widely used to specify the behavior of Java modules. It should be possible to extend the program slicer to translate these class invariants into JPF assertions and insert them into the sliced code.

Another future direction is to extend the existing exception safety framework to other interesting properties beyond the model checking capabilities of JPF. With a proper back-end model checker, we can verify resource usage properties (stated in temporal logic) like "all resources are acquired before any attempting manipulations." A target is a framework to model check Java programs annotated with full JML features.

Acknowledgments

The authors would like to thank the anonymous reviewers for their helpful suggestions. We also thank the creators of Jex [15], KJC [2] and JPF [17] for making their tools available. Without them, this work would be much more difficult.

References

1. The fizmez web server. see `http://fizmez.com/`.
2. Kopi Java open source compiler. see `http://www.dms.at/kopi`.
3. Ken Arnold, James Gosling, and David Holmes. *The Java Programming Language*. Addison-Wesley Longman Publishing Co., Inc., Boston, MA, USA, 2000.
4. James C. Corbett, Matthew B. Dwyer, John Hatcliff, Shawn Laubach, Corina S. Păsăreanu, Robby, and Hongjun Zheng. Bandera: extracting finite-state models from Java source code. In *International Conference on Software Engineering*, pages 439–448, 2000.
5. S. Drossopoulou, T. Valkevych, and S. Eisenbach. Java type soundness revisited. Technical report, Imperial College, 2000.
6. Jarno Elonen. The nanohttpd http server. see `elonen.iki.fi/code/nanohttpd`.
7. Cormac Flanagan, K. Rustan M. Leino, Mark Lillibridge, Greg Nelson, James B. Saxe, and Raymie Stata. Extended static checking for java. In *PLDI*, pages 234–245, 2002.

8. Phil Goodwin. Exception patterns. see www.c2.com/cgi/wiki?ExceptionPatterns.
9. Michael Huth and Mark Ryan. *Logic in Computer Science: Modelling and Reasoning about Systems, 2nd Ed.* Cambridge, 2004.
10. Jang-Wu Jo, Byeong-Mo Chang, Kwangkeun Yi, and Kwang-Moo Choe. An uncaught exception analysis for Java. *Journal of Systems and Software*, 72(1):59–69, 2004.
11. Gary T. Leavens, Albert L. Baker, and Clyde Ruby. JML: A notation for detailed design. In Haim Kilov, Bernhard Rumpe, and Ian Simmonds, editors, *Behavioral Specifications of Businesses and Systems*, pages 175–188. Kluwer Academic Publishers, 1999.
12. K. Rustan M. Leino and Wolfram Schulte. Exception safety for C#. In *SEFM*, pages 218–227, 2004.
13. R.A. Maxion and R.T. Olszewski. Improving software robustness with dependability cases. In *Digest of Papers. Twenty-Eighth Annual International Symposium on Fault-Tolerant Computing*, pages 346–55, 1998.
14. Robby, Matthew B. Dwyer, and John Hatcliff. Bogor: an extensible and highly-modular software model checking framework. In *ESEC / SIGSOFT FSE*, pages 267–276, 2003.
15. Martin P. Robillard and Gail C. Murphy. Static analysis to support the evolution of exception structure in object-oriented systems. *ACM Trans. Softw. Eng. Methodol.*, 12(2):191–221, 2003.
16. Bjarne Stroustrup. *The C++ Programming Language*. Addison-Wesley, 1997.
17. Willem Visser, Klaus Havelund, Guillaume Brat, and SeungJoon Park. Model checking programs. In *ASE '00: Proceedings of the The Fifteenth IEEE International Conference on Automated Software Engineering (ASE'00)*, page 3, Washington, DC, USA, 2000. IEEE Computer Society.
18. Westley Weimer and George C. Necula. Finding and preventing run-time error handling mistakes. In *OOPSLA*, pages 419–431, 2004.
19. Mark Weiser. Program slicing. *IEEE Trans. Software Eng.*, 10(4):352–357, 1984.

Enforcer – Efficient Failure Injection

Cyrille Artho[1], Armin Biere[2], and Shinichi Honiden[1]

[1] National Institute of Informatics, Tokyo, Japan
[2] Johannes Kepler University, Linz, Austria

Abstract. Non-determinism of the thread schedule is a well-known problem in concurrent programming. However, other sources of non-determinism exist which cannot be controlled by an application, such as network availability. Testing a program with its communication resources being unavailable is difficult, as it requires a change on the host system, which has to be coordinated with the test suite. Essentially, each interaction of the application with the environment can result in a failure. Only some of these failures can be tested. Our work identifies such potential failures and develops a strategy for testing all relevant outcomes of such actions. Our tool, Enforcer, combines the structure of unit tests, coverage information, and fault injection. By taking advantage of a unit test infrastructure, performance can be improved by orders of magnitude compared to previous approaches. Our tool has been tested on several real-world programs, where it found faults without requiring extra test code.

1 Introduction

Testing is a scalable, economic, and effective way to uncover faults in software [19,21]. Even though it is limited to a finite set of example scenarios, it is very flexible and by far the most widespread quality assurance method today. Testing is often carried out without formal rigor. However, coverage measurement tools provide a quantitative measure of the quality of a test suite [7,21]. Uncovered (and thus untested) code may still contain faults.

In practice, the most severe limitation of testing is non-determinism, given by both the thread schedule and the actions of the environment. It may cause a program to produce different results under different schedules, even with the same input. Non-determinism has been used in model checking to model choices that have several possible outcomes [25]. Usually, three kinds of non-determinism are distinguished [20]: non-determinism arising from different thread schedules, from choices made by the environment, and from abstractions within an application. The latter is an artifact of abstraction in static analysis and not of concern here. Non-determinism arising from different thread schedules has been tackled by previous work in run-time verification and is subject to ongoing study [1,23]. This paper focuses on non-determinism arising from unexpected failures by the environment, such as system library calls.

For system calls, there are usually two basic outcomes: success or failure. Typically the successful case is easy to test, while the failure case can be nearly impossible to trigger. For instance, simulating network outage is non-trivial. If a mechanism exists, though, testing both outcomes will be very efficient, only requiring a duplication of a

J. Misra, T. Nipkow, and E. Sekerinski (Eds.): FM 2006, LNCS 4085, pp. 412–427, 2006.
© Springer-Verlag Berlin Heidelberg 2006

particular test case. Existing ad-hoc approaches include factoring out small blocks of code in order to manually test error handlers, or adding extra flags to conditionals that could trigger outcomes that are normally not reachable by modeling test data alone. Figure 1 illustrates this. In the first example, any exception handling is performed by a special method, which can be tested separately, but does not have access to local variables used by the caller. In the second example, which has inspired our work, the unit test has to set a special flag which causes the error handling code to run artificially.

```
                                    try {
try {                                   if (testShouldFail) {
    socket = new ServerSocket();            throw new IOException();
} catch (IOException e) {                }
    handleIOException();                socket = new ServerSocket();
    // error handling code          } catch (IOException e) {
}                                       // error handling code
                                    }
```

Factoring out error handling.   Extra conditional for testing.

Fig. 1. Two manual approaches for exception handler coverage

The Java programming language uses exceptions to signal failure of a library or system call [12]. The ideas in this paper are applicable to any other programming language supporting exceptions, such as C++ [24], Eiffel [17], or C# [18]. When an exception is thrown, the current stack frame is cleared, and its content replaced with a single instance of type `Exception`. This mechanism helps our goal in two ways:

– Detection of potentially failed system calls is reduced to the analysis of exceptions.
– No special context data is needed except for information contained in the method signature and the exception.

Our tool is built on these observations. It systematically analyzes a program for untested exceptional outcomes of library method calls by using fault injection [13]. Automatically instrumented code measures coverage of unit tests w.r.t. exceptions, utilizing the Java reflection API to extract information about the current test case. After execution of the test suite, a number of tests is re-executed with fault injection enabled, triggering previously untested exceptions. Our tool wraps invocation of repeated tests automatically, i.e., only one launch of the test suite is required by the user.

Similar tools have analyzed exception handling in Java code and improved coverage by fault injection [4,11]. Previous tools have not been able to connect information about unit tests with exception coverage. Our tool gathers method signature information statically and the remaining data at run-time. Being integrated with unit testing, it avoids re-executing the entire program many times, and therefore can scale to test suites of large programs. It also supports tuples of failures when analyzing test outcomes at run-time. Our tool is fully automated and can test the outcome of significant failure scenarios in real software. By doing so, it finds faults in previously untested code, without requiring a single extra line in the test setup or test code.

The contribution of our work is as follows:

- We present a fully automated, high-performance approach at gathering specialized coverage information which is integrated with JUnit.
- Fault injection is based on a combined static and dynamic analysis.
- Tuples of faults are supported based on dynamically gathered data.

Section 2 gives the necessary background about sources of failures considered here, and possible implementation approaches. Section 3 describes our implementation used for experiments, of which the results are given in Section 4. Section 5 describes related work. Section 6 concludes and outlines future work.

2   Background

An *exception* as commonly used in many programming languages [12,17,18,24] indicates an extraordinary condition in the program, such as the unavailability of a resource. Exceptions are used instead of error codes to return information about the reason why a method call failed. Java also supports *errors,* which indicate "serious problems that a reasonable application should not try to catch" [12]. A method call that fails may "throw" an exception by constructing a new instance of java.lang.Exception or a subtype thereof, and using a throw statement to "return" this exception to the caller. At the call site, the exception will override normal control flow. The caller may install an exception *handler* by using the try/catch statement. A try block includes a sequence of operations that may fail. Upon failure, remaining instructions of the try block are skipped, the current method stack frame is replaced by a stack frame containing only the new exception, and control is transferred to the exception handler, indicated in Java by the corresponding catch block. This process will also be referred to as *error handling.*

The usage and semantics of exceptions covers a wide range of behaviors. In Java, exceptions are used to signal the unavailability of a resource (e.g., when a file is not found or cannot be written), failure of a communication (e.g., when a socket connection is closed), when data does not have the expected format, or simply for programming errors such as accessing an array at an illegal index. Two fundamentally different types of exceptions can be distinguished: *Unchecked* exceptions and *checked* exceptions. Unchecked exceptions are of type RuntimeException and do not have to be declared in a method. They typically concern programming errors, such as array bounds overflows, and can be tested through conventional means. On the other hand, checked exceptions have to be declared by a method which may throw them. Failure of external operations results in such checked exceptions [4,10]. This work therefore focuses on checked exceptions. For the remainder of this paper, a *checked method call* refers to a call to a method which declared checked exceptions.

Code instrumentation consists of injecting additional code into an application, in order to augment its behavior while not affecting the original behavior, or only changing it in a very limited way. It corresponds to a generic form of aspect-oriented programming [14], which organizes code instrumentation into a finite set of operations. A *unit test* is a procedure to verify individual modules of code. A *test harness* executes unit tests. *Test suites* combine multiple unit tests into a single set. Execution of a single unit test is defined as *test execution,* running all unit tests as *test suite execution.* In this paper, a *repeated test suite* denotes an automatically generated test suite that will re-execute certain unit tests, which will be referred to as repeated tests.

Program steering [15] allows overriding normal execution flow. Program steering typically refers to altering program behavior using application-specific properties [15], or as schedule perturbation [23], which covers non-determinism in thread schedules. Fault injection [13] refers to influencing program behavior by simulations failures in hardware or software.

Coverage information describes whether a certain piece of code has been executed or not. In this paper, only coverage of checked method calls is relevant. The goal of our work was to test program behavior at each location where exceptions are handled, for each possible occurrence of an exception. This corresponds to the *all-e-deacts* criterion [22]. Treating each checked method call individually allows distinction between error handling before and after a resource, or several resources, have been allocated.

The first source of potential failures considered here are input/output (I/O) failures, particularly on networks. The problem is that a test environment is typically set up to test the normal behavior of a program. While it is possible to temporarily disable the required resources by software, such as shell scripts, such actions often affect the entire system running, not just the current application. Furthermore, it is difficult and error-prone to coordinate such system-wide changes with a test harness. The same applies to certain other types of I/O failures, such as running out of disk space, packet loss on a UDP connection, or communication timeout. While the presence of key actions such as resource deallocations can be checked statically [6,26], static analysis is imprecise in the presence of complex data structures. Testing can analyze the exact behavior.

The second goal is to cover potential failures of external programs. It is always possible that a system call fails due to insufficient resources or for other reasons. Testing such failures when interacting with a program through inter-process communication such as pipes is difficult and results in much testing-specific code.

Our tool, Enforcer, is written in Java and geared towards failures which are signaled by Java exceptions. There exist other hard-to-test operations that are not available in Java: In C programs, pointer arithmetic can be used. The exact address returned by memory allocation cannot be predicted by the application, causing portability and testing problems for low-level operations such as sorting data by their physical address. Other low-level operations such as floating point calculations may also have different outcomes on different platforms.

The idea of using program steering to simulate rare outcomes may even be expanded further. Previous work has made initial steps towards verifying the contract required by hashing and comparison functions, which states that equal data must result in equal hash codes, but equal hash codes do not necessarily imply data equality [2,12]. The latter case is known as a hash code collision, where two objects containing different data have the same hash code. This case cannot be tested effectively since hash keys may vary on different platforms and test cases to provoke such a collision are hard to write for non-trivial hash functions, and practically impossible for hash functions that are cryptographically secure. Other mathematical algorithms have similar properties, and are subject of future work.

3   Implementation

Java-based applications using JUnit [16] for unit testing have been chosen as the target for this study. Java bytecode is easy to understand and well-documented. JUnit is widely used for unit testing. In terms of programming constructs, the target consists of any unthrown exceptions, i.e., checked method calls where a corresponding `catch` statement exists and that `catch` statement was not reached from an exception originating from said method call. Only checked exceptions were considered because other exceptions can be triggered through conventional testing [4,10]. Artificially generated exceptions are initialized with a special string denoting that this exception was triggered by Enforcer.

A key goal of the tool is not to have to re-execute the entire test suite after coverage measurement. Therefore the project executes in three stages:

1. Code instrumentation, at compile time or at class load time. This includes injecting code for coverage measurement and for execution of the repeated test suite.
2. Execution of unit tests. Coverage information is now gathered.
3. Re-execution of certain tests, forcing execution to take new paths. This has to be taken into account by coverage measurement code, in order to require only a single instrumentation step.

As a consequence of treating each checked method call rather than just each unit test individually, a more fine-grained behavior is achieved. Each unit test may execute several checked method calls. Our approach allows for re-executing individual unit tests several times within the repeated test suite, injecting a different exception each time. This achieves better control of application behavior, as the remaining execution path after an exception is thrown likely no longer coincides with the original test execution. Furthermore, it simplifies debugging, since the behavior of the application is generally changed in only one location for each repeated test execution. Unit tests themselves are excluded from coverage measurement and fault injection, as exception handlers within unit tests serve for diagnostics and are not part of the actual application. We did not consider random fault injection [8], as our goal is to achieve high coverage in a reliable way, and to take advantage of the structure of unit tests for making fault injection scalable. Simply injecting exceptions at random would require re-running the entire test suite, and does not necessarily guarantee high coverage.

The intent behind the creation of the Enforcer tool is to use technologies that can be combined with other approaches, such that the system under test (SUT) can be tested in a way that is as close to the original test setup as possible, while still allowing for full automation of the process. Code instrumentation fulfills this requirement perfectly, since the code generated can be executed on the same platform as the original SUT. Instrumentation is performed directly on Java bytecode [27]. This has the advantage that the source code of libraries is not required.

3.1   Re-execution of Test Cases

After execution of the original test suite, coverage information is evaluated. For each exception that was not thrown, the test case that covered the corresponding checked method call is added to the repeated test suite. Execution of the repeated test suite follows directly after coverage evaluation. Instrumented code handling test execution re-executes the repeated test suite as long as uncovered exceptions exist, and progress is being made w.r.t. coverage (for nested try/catch blocks, see below). Each time, a new repeated test suite is constructed on the fly by the Enforcer run-time library, and then executed.

3.2 Injecting Exceptions

The final change to the application by instrumentation will force tests to go through a different path when re-executing. Two points have to be taken into consideration: Where the exception should be thrown, and how.

In our implementation, exceptions are triggered just before checked method calls. A try block may include several checked method calls. By generating an exception before each corresponding checked method call, steering simulates actions that were successful up to the last critical operation. If the program is deterministic, it can be assumed that the try block will not fail before that point in repeated test execution, as all inputs leading up to that point are equal.

```
try {

        curr_id = __ID__; /* to register exception coverage */
        /* fault injection code */
        if (enforcer.rt.Eval.reRunID == __ID__) { // __ID__ = static
            throw new ...Exception();
            // Exception type depends on catch block argument.
        }

        /* checked method call in the original code */
        call_method_that_declares_checked_exceptions();

        /* coverage code */
        enforcer.rt.Coverage.recordMethodCoverage(__ID__);

        // same instrumentation for each checked method call

    } catch(...Exception e) {
        enforcer.rt.Coverage.recordCatchCoverage[curr_id] = true;
        // one instrumentation for each catch block

        /* original catch block follows */
}
```

Fig. 2. Instrumented code in try/finally blocks

Generating exceptions when running the repeated test suite is achieved by inserting code before and after checked method calls. It is possible that the same test case calls several such methods, but only a single exception should be artificially triggered for each test execution. Achieving this is difficult because the checked method call ID is not known by the test suite or the test case at run time. Due to this, a test wrapper is used to wrap each test and set the necessary steering information prior to each individual test execution. Figure 2 shows the resulting code to be added to each try/catch block, which records coverage in the initial test execution and applies program steering when executing the repeated test suite. At each checked method call, code is inserted before and after that method call. Note that the value of __ID__ is determined statically and replaced by a unique constant each time when instrumentation takes place.

The inserted code before each checked method call injects faults. It compares its static ID to the index of the exception to be generated. This index, reRunID, is set by the test wrapper. Due to the uniqueness of the ID, it is therefore possible to instrument many checked method calls, but still only inject a fault in a single such method call. If the IDs match, an exception of the appropriate type is constructed and thrown. A number of possible constructors for exception instances are supported, covering all commonly used exception constructors where reasonable default arguments can be applied. Sometimes the signature of a called method cannot be determined at compile time. In such cases it is conservatively assumed that the method may throw an exception of the type declared in the catch clause.[1]

3.3   Coverage Measurement

Coverage of exceptions thrown is recorded by instrumented code inside each try block, and at the beginning of each catch block. Coverage within try blocks is recorded as follows: Whenever a checked method call that may throw an exception returned successfully, the test case further up in the calling chain is recorded, such that this test case can be re-run later. This is performed by a call to the Enforcer run-time library with the static ID of the checked method call as argument (see Figure 2). The run-time library evaluates the stack trace in order to find the class and method name of the current unit test.

Coverage information about executed exception handlers is recorded by inserting code at the beginning of each catch block. Before each checked method call, the ID of that method is stored in local variable curr_id. This allows the coverage measurement code within the exception handler to know which checked method caused an exception. A try block may contain several checked method calls, each one requiring instrumentation; the corresponding catch block, however, only requires a single instrumentation, because the usage of curr_id allows for registering coverage of several checked method calls.

3.4   Extension to Nested Exception Handlers

Nested exceptions can be responsible for program behavior that only occurs in extremely rare circumstances, such as when both a disk and a network failure are present. A graceful recovery from such failures is difficult to implement, and therefore we found it very important to support combined failures by injection of tuples of faults.

Nested try statements cause no additional problems for the algorithm described above. Figure 3 shows an example with two nested try blocks. There are three possible final values for i in this program: 2, when no exception occurs; 3, when the inner

---

[1] This assumption has to be made if the type of the method cannot be determined due to incompleteness of alias analysis, or usage of dynamic class loading. It may introduce false positives.

exception e_2 occurs; and 4, if the outer exception e_1 is thrown. Both try statements are reachable when exceptions are absent. Therefore, if either e_1 or e_2 are not covered by the normal test suite, our algorithm either forces e_1 after i has been set to 1, or e_2 when i equals 2.

```
int i = 0;
try {                                        // try 1
    call_method_throwing_exceptions();
    i = 1;
    try {                                    // try 2
        call_method_throwing_exceptions();
        i = 2;
    } catch (Exception e2) { // catch 2
        i = 3;
    }
} catch (Exception e1) {       // catch 1
    i = 4;
}
```

Fig. 3. Nested try statements

However, the design described so far is limited to try blocks which do not occur inside other exception handlers. Fortunately, even this case of nesting can be covered quite elegantly. In nested try blocks, execution of the inner try block may depend on the outer catch block being executed. Suppose the outer catch block is not executed by initial tests, but only by the repeated test suite. The repeated test suite may again not cover the inner catch block. Figure 4 illustrates such difficulties arising with nested try/catch statements. The compiler generates two exception handlers for this code.

```
int i = 0;
try {                                        // try 1
    call_method_throwing_exceptions();
    i = 1;
} catch (Exception e1) {       // catch 1
    try {                                    // try 2
        call_method_throwing_exceptions();
        i = 2;
    } catch (Exception e2) { // catch 2
        i = 3;
    }
}
```

Fig. 4. A try block inside an exception handler

When no exceptions occur in this example, the final value of i equals 1. Let us call that scenario run 0, the default test execution without steering. Subsequent re-runs of this test will try to force execution through each catch block. The outer catch blocks can be triggered with the algorithm described so far. Repeated test execution 1 thus forces corresponding catch clause 1 to be executed, setting i to 2. Furthermore, coverage measurement will now register the repeated test as a candidate for covering catch block 2. This will constitute the new repeated test suite containing run 2, which has the goal of forcing catch block 2 to be reached. However, injecting exception e_2 requires reaching catch block 1. This is only the case in run 1; run 2 therefore would never reach the fault injection code if only e_2 was injected. In order to solve this problem, one has to inject *sets* of faults, not just single faults. In the example of Figure 4, e_1 has to be injected for both runs 1 and 2. Coverage measurement in run 1 registers that run 1 has executed try block 2; therefore both e_1 and e_2 are injected in run 2. In our implementation, we restricted the nesting depth of exception handlers to one, as this does not require nested dynamic data structures for the run-time library. In practice, a nesting depth greater than two is rare, and can be supported by using vectors of sets.

Because of such initially uncovered try blocks, coverage of nested exceptions may require the construction of several repeated test suites. The first one includes a unit test for each uncovered checked method call. Execution of this repeated test suite may cover other previously unreached try blocks, which are target of the next iteration. The iteration of repeated test suites terminates when no progress is made for coverage. Hence, certain unit tests may be executed several times within the same iteration (for different exceptions) and across iterations.

3.5 Complexity

The complexity incurred by our approach can be divided into two parts: Coverage measurement, and construction and execution of repeated test suites. Coverage is measured for each checked method call. The code which updates run-time data structures runs in constant time. This overhead is of coverage measurement is proportional to the number checked method calls executed at run-time.

Execution of repeated test suites may incur a larger overhead. For each uncovered exception, a unit test has to be re-executed. However, each uncovered exception incurs at most one repeated test. Nested exceptions may require multiple injected faults for a repeated test. The key to a good performance is that only one unit test, which is known to execute the checked method call in question, is repeated. Large projects contain hundreds or thousands of unit tests; previous approaches [4,10,11] would re-execute them all for each possible failure, while our tool only re-executes one unit test for each failure. This improves performance by several orders of magnitude and allows our tool to scale up to large test suites. Moreover, the situation is even more favorable when comparing repeated tests with an ideal test suite featuring full coverage of exceptions in checked method calls. Automatic repeated execution of test cases does not require significantly more time than such an ideal test suite, because the only minor overhead that could be eliminated lies in the instrumented code. Compared to manual approaches, our approach finds faults without incurring a significant overhead, with the additional capability of covering outcomes that are not directly testable.

4   Experiments

To ensure solid quality of the implementation, 30 test classes were written to test different aspects and problem cases for code instrumentation, coverage measurement, and test execution. Due to rigorous testing, the tool is mature enough to be applicable to large and complex programs. Therefore, several real-world applications and libraries were used to demonstrate the usefulness of the approach. Unfortunately, realistic Java programs using both network I/O and JUnit-based test suites are hard to come by. A web search for Java applications and JUnit returns tools and libraries enhancing JUnit, but not applications using it. Therefore a different approach was chosen: Based on the listing of all Java program on freshmeat.net [9], 1647 direct links to downloadable archives could be extracted. These resulted in 926 successful automatic downloads, where no registration or manual redirection was used. Out of these applications, 100 used JUnit test suites and also employed at least some networking functionality. Further criteria, such as the use of multiple threads and the absence of a GUI, were used to narrow down the selection to 29 applications. Out of these, nine could be compiled and run on Java 1.5 with no or minor modifications, and no installations of third-party libraries or tools that were not shipped with the original archives.

Table 1. Applications of which the unit tests were used in the experiments

Application or library	Description	# classes	Size [LOC]	# test classes	Test code size [LOC]
Echomine	Communication services API	144	14331	46	3550
Informa	News channel API	150	20682	48	6855
jConfig	Configuration library	77	9611	39	2974
jZonic-cache	Caching library	26	2142	14	737
SFUtils	Sourceforge utilities	21	6222	9	1041
SixBS	Java beans persistency	34	4666	9	1072
Slimdog	Web application testing framework	30	1959	11	616
STUN	Extensible programming system	27	1706	3	229
XTC	Napster search tool	455	77114	57	8070

The main reason for this low number is the fact that the entire pool of applications included many projects that have been abandoned or not yet been completed. Table 1 shows an overview of the applications used. The first two columns briefly describe each application, while the other columns give an indication of the size of each project, showing the number of classes and the lines of code used for them. This information is shown separately for unit test code. The presence of helper classes was responsible for a rather large number of test classes in some cases.

Enforcer was then used on these example applications. Table 2 gives an overview of the test results. Tests were executed on a dual-processor 2.7 GHz PowerPC G5 with 8 GB of RAM and 512 KB of L2 cache per CPU running Mac OS 10.4.5. The table is divided into three parts. The first part shows the test results when running the given test suite. A test failure in JUnit corresponds to an incorrect value of a property, while uncaught exceptions are shown as errors. Note that failures or errors can either be caused due to incorrect code or missing components in the installation. Although it was attempted to fix any installation-related errors, not all cases could be covered.

Part two of the table shows the overhead of the instrumentation code for measuring test coverage. Original and instrumented execution time of the normal test suite are

Table 2. Results of unit tests and injected exception coverage

Application or library	# tests	# fail.	# err.	Time [s]	Time, inst. [s]	Time, re-ex. [s]	# instr. calls	# exec. calls	# unex. catch	Cov. (orig.)	# unr. catch	Cov. (inst.)
Echomine	170	2	0	6.3	6.3	1.7	165	61	54	8 %	0	100 %
Informa	119	15	32	33.2	34.4	132.2	306	139	136	2 %	28	80 %
jConfig	97	3	0	2.3	4.7	n/a	299	169	162	3 %	65	61 %
jZonic-c.	16	2	0	0.4	0.7	0.02	22	8	6	25 %	0	100 %
SFUtils	11	1	3	76.3	81.6	0.001	112	6	2	67 %	0	100 %
SixBS	30	0	0	34.6	55.6	38.7	56	31	28	10 %	2	94 %
Slimdog	10	4	0	228.6	233.6	n/a	41	15	14	7 %	n/a	n/a
STUN	14	0	0	0.06	0.7	0	2	0	0	0 %	0	0 %
XTC	294	0	0	28.8	30.6	4.9	168	112	112	0 %	9	92 %

shown first.[2] The final execution time measurement shows the time needed to execute repeated test suites. This figure depends much on the coverage of the test suite and the nature of exception handlers, and is given for completeness; it cannot be used to draw conclusions about the quality of the test suite or the Enforcer tool. A better measure is actual coverage of exceptions in checked method calls, as shown by part three of Table 2.

Part three shows details about code instrumentation and coverage. The number of instrumented checked method calls is given first, followed by the number of checked method calls executed by unit tests. Usually a large number of checked method calls never triggered an exception, as shown by the next column, "unexec. catch". The following column indicates the percentage of executed checked method calls that did generate an exception. As can be seen, that percentage is typically very low. These untested exception cases may each cause previously undiscovered failures and were targeted by the Enforcer tool. In most cases, Enforcer could successfully force inject exceptions; in some cases, deeply nested exceptions or the lack of a fully deterministic test setup prevented full coverage. The rightmost two columns show the number of such uncovered checked method calls, and the final exception coverage after Enforcer was used. As can be easily seen, Enforcer could often change a nearly nonexistent coverage to a nearly full coverage. However, it depends on a test suite that is able to execute checked method calls in the first place. This criterion is fulfilled if full statement coverage is achieved, which is often the case for larger projects [1] but was not the case for the given programs.

In some cases, injected exceptions affected background threads that were assumed to be running throughout multiple test cases. When these threads failed to terminate properly, or to restart, the test suite would wait indefinitely for them. This was the case for applications jConfig and Slimdog. In jConfig, such problems prevented higher coverage. For Slimdog, two tests had to be disabled even when running without instrumentation, because the multi-threaded test code was too fragile to execute reliably. In test setup, the background thread may allocate a port but then fail to complete initialization, throwing an exception. JUnit does not release any resources allocated in such

---

[2] The time required for code instrumentation itself was negligible.

a failed setup. This problem has been discussed in the mailing list and is going to be addressed in the future. Stopping and restarting the background thread before each test run is expected to fix this problem, at the cost of slowing down test execution.

The overhead caused by coverage measurement was usually negligible, as can be seen by comparing columns one and two of part two of Table 2. SixBS is an exception, where coverage measurement caused a resulting overhead of factor two. The reason for this is that instrumentation significantly increased the run time of the thread controlling the XML parser. This thread contains several exception handlers but relatively little other code, hence amplifying the usual effect of instrumentation on run-time. Reducing the overhead is going to entail the use of additional data structures in order to avoid expensive calls to the Java reflection API at run time.

Our tool generated a total number of 352 exceptions for checked method calls in all applications. The majority of these exceptions (200 instances) concerned I/O, either on a network or a file. 56 exceptions were generated as parse exceptions, while 69 exceptions were of generic type `java.lang.Exception` and could not be classified more closely. Finally, 27 exceptions were of other types, such as `IllegalAccessException`. Exceptions that do not concern I/O were not originally the target of our tool. Nonetheless, the fact that these were also triggered frequently shows that our tool may partially replace test case generation when no tests exist for certain exceptional scenarios.

In most of the 352 cases where an exception was injected, the application ultimately rethrows the exception in question, usually in a slightly different form. It was not possible for us to tell whether this simple behavior was adequate. Because these exceptions were encountered within unit tests, it is possible that the main application front end performs some kind of cleanup before shutting down. However, in general, a call to a low-level library should take exceptions into account. Otherwise, an I/O exception can lead to the termination of the entire thread, and usually the entire program. If untested parts of the application catch such exceptions where unit tests do not, then the unit tests are incomplete since they do not reflect the behavior of the application, failing to account for exceptional behavior. However, considering the fact that some benchmark programs were libraries to be used by an application, rethrowing exceptions may be acceptable in some cases. Therefore we did not analyze these 352 cases in detail. Many of them were redundant, as triggering the same exception handlers from different places in the same `try` block often produces equivalent results. Some cases were false positives arising from incomplete type information at instrumentation time.

Much more interesting than rethrown exceptions were exceptions that were triggered by failed error handling. These exceptions were not just rethrown, but caused by another part of the program that tried to deal with the initial exceptions.[3] A few of these cases resulted in rethrown exceptions, which were not counted for the reasons stated above. Table 3 shows the failures resulting from incorrect error handlers. Each unique program location was only counted once. We found 12 faults in the nine given applications this way. As can be seen, the lack of testing in error handlers caused typical programming errors to appear (null pointers, illegal arguments, failed class casts). In applications jConfig and Slimdog, the error handling code tried to re-open a socket

---

[3] Distinguishing these "secondary" exceptions was trivial as the injected exceptions were all marked as such by having a special message string.

that was already in use, which resulted in termination of the entire test suite. That defect therefore masked other potential failures. Informa contained various problems in its fallback code concerning I/O (file not found, generic I/O exception, feed manager failure). These problems could perhaps be solved by a different configuration; we used the configuration that came with the default installation. Certainly, it is clear that for some of the given applications, our tool did not only significantly improve coverage of exceptions, but also found several defects in the code.

Table 3. Failures resulting from incorrect error handling

App./lib.	FileNotFound	NullPointer	IO	FeedManager	IllegalArgument	Bind	ClassCast	Total
Echomine		1					1	2
Informa	1	4	2	1	1			9
jConfig						1		1
Slimdog							1	1
Total	1	5	2	1	1	1	1	12

To summarize, our tool was very successful in improving the exception coverage of realistic test suites in a variety of projects. Coverage measurement usually only caused a minor overhead. Without writing any additional code, extra faults were found, where error handlers for exceptions contained defects. With the exception of certain multi-threading problems, normal operation of the application tests was not affected by steering. Some of the triggered exceptions should be tested by conventional means. It can be expected that a higher-quality test suite will not have any such uncovered exceptions left, so our tool would likely produce even better results for thoroughly tested code.

5 Related Work

Test cases are typically written as additional program code for the system under test. White-box testing tries to execute as much program code as possible [19]. In traditional software testing, *coverage* metrics such as statement coverage [7,21] have been used to determine the effectiveness of a test suite. The key problem with software testing is that it cannot guarantee execution of parts of the system where the outcome of a decision is non-deterministic. In multi-threading, the thread schedule affects determinism. For external operations, the small possibility of failure makes testing that case extremely difficult. Traditional testing and test case generation methods are ineffective to solve this problem.

Static analysis investigates properties "at compile time", without executing the actual program. Non-deterministic decisions are explored exhaustively by verifying all possible outcomes. For analyzing whether resources allocated are deallocated correctly, there exist static analysis tools which consider each possible exception location [26]. However, static analysis can only cover a part of the program behavior, such as resource handling. For a more detailed analysis of program behavior, code execution (by testing) is often unavoidable.

Model Checking explores the entire behavior of a system by investigating each reachable state. Model checkers treat non-determinism exhaustively. Results of system-level operations have been successfully modeled this way to detect failures in applications [5] and device drivers [3]. However, model checking suffers from the state space explosion problem: The size of the state space is exponential in the size of the system.

Therefore approaches that directly tackle testing are very promising, as potential failures of library calls are independent of non-deterministic thread scheduling. Such failures can be simulated by fault injection [13]. Random fault injection is a black-box technique and useful on an application level [8]. Our goal was to achieve a high test coverage, and therefore we target white-box testing techniques.

Java is a popular target for measuring and improving error handling, as error handling locations are relatively well defined [4,10,11]. Our approach of measuring exception handler coverage corresponds to the *all-e-deacts* criterion [22]. The static analysis used to determine whether checked method calls may generate exceptions have some similarity with a previous implementation of such a coverage metric [11]. However, our implementation does not aim at a precise instrumentation for the coverage metric. We only target checked exceptions, within the method where they occur. As the generated exceptions are created at the caller site, not in the library method, an interprocedural analysis is not required. Unreachable statements will be reported as instrumented, but uncovered checked method calls. Such uncovered calls never incur an unnecessary test run and are therefore benign, but hint at poor coverage of the test suite. Furthermore, unlike some previous work [11], our tool has a run-time component that registers which unit test may cause an exception. This allows us to re-execute only a particular unit test, which is orders of magnitude more efficient than running the entire test suite for each exception site. Furthermore, our tool can dynamically discover the need for combined occurrences of failures when error handling code should be reached. Such a dynamic analysis is comparable to another fault injection approach [4], but the aim of that project is totally different: It analyzes failure dependencies, while our project targets code execution and improves coverage of error handling code.

Similar code injection techniques are involved in program steering [15], which allows overriding the normal execution flow. However, such steering is usually very problematic because correct execution of certain basic blocks depends on a semantically consistent program state. Thus program steering has so far only been applied using application-specific properties [15], or as schedule perturbation [23], which only covers non-determinism in thread schedules. Our work is application-independent and targeted to fault injection.

6   Conclusions and Future Work

In software, non-deterministic decisions are not only taken by the thread scheduler, but also by the environment. Calls to system libraries may fail. Such failures can be nearly impossible to test. Our work uses fault injection to achieve coverage of such untestable properties. During test execution, coverage information is gathered. This information is used in a repeated test execution to execute previously untested exception handlers. The process can be fully automated and still leads to meaningful execution of exception handlers. Unlike previous approaches, we take advantage of the structure of unit tests in order to avoid re-execution an entire application. This makes our approach orders of magnitude faster for large test suites. The Enforcer tool which implements this approach has been successfully applied to several complex Java applications. It has executed previously untested error handlers and uncovered several faults. Furthermore, our approach may even partially replace test case generation.

The area of such generic program steering likely has further applications that have not yet been covered. Future work includes elimination of false positives by including run-time information for method calls whose signature is unknown. Another improvement is analysis of test case execution time, in order to select the fastest test case for re-execution. The treatment of difficult-to-test outcomes can be expanded to other properties mentioned in this paper. Finally, we are very interested in applying our Enforcer tool to high-quality commercial test suites. It can be expected that exception coverage will be incomplete but already quite high, unlike in cases tested so far. This will make evaluation of test results more interesting.

References

1. C. Artho. *Combining Static and Dynamic Analysis to Find Multi-threading Faults Beyond Data Races*. PhD thesis, ETH Zürich, 2005.
2. C. Artho and A. Biere. Applying static analysis to large-scale, multithreaded Java programs. In *Proc. 13th Australian Software Engineering Conference (ASWEC 2001)*, pages 68–75, Canberra, Australia, 2001. IEEE Computer Society Press.
3. T. Ball, A. Podelski, and S. Rajamani. Boolean and Cartesian Abstractions for Model Checking C Programs. In *Proc. 7th Intl. Conf. on Tools and Algorithms for the Construction and Analysis of Systems (TACAS 2001)*, volume 2031 of *LNCS*, pages 268–285, Genova, Italy, 2001. Springer.
4. G. Candea, M. Delgado, M. Chen, and A. Fox. Automatic failure-path inference: A generic introspection technique for Internet applications. In *Proc. 3rd IEEE Workshop on Internet Applications (WIAPP 2003)*, page 132, Washington, USA, 2003. IEEE Computer Society.
5. C. Colby, P. Godefroid, and L. Jagadeesan. Automatically closing open reactive programs. In *Proc. SIGPLAN Conf. on Programming Language Design and Implementation (PLDI 1998)*, pages 345–357, Montreal, Canada, 1998.
6. D. Engler and M. Musuvathi. Static analysis versus software model checking for bug finding. In *Proc. 5th Intl. Conf. on Verification, Model Checking and Abstract Interpretation (VMCAI 2004)*, volume 2937 of *LNCS*, pages 191–210, Venice, Italy, 2004. Springer.
7. N. Fenton and S. Pfleeger. *Software metrics (2nd Ed.): a rigorous and practical approach*. PWS Publishing Co., Boston, USA, 1997.
8. Justin E. Forrester and Barton P. Miller. An empirical study of the robustness of windows NT applications using random testing. In *4th USENIX Windows System Symposium*, pages 59–68, Seattle, USA, 2000.
9. Freshmeat, 2005. http://freshmeat.net/.
10. C. Fu, R. Martin, K. Nagaraja, T. Nguyen, B. Ryder, and D. Wonnacott. Compiler-directed program-fault coverage for highly available Java internet services. In *Proc. 2003 Intl. Conf. on Dependable Systems and Networks (DSN 2003)*, pages 595–604, San Francisco, USA, 2003.
11. C. Fu, B. Ryder, A. Milanova, and D. Wonnacott. Testing of Java web services for robustness. In *Proc. ACM/SIGSOFT Intl. Symposium on Software Testing and Analysis (ISSTA 2004)*, pages 23–34, Boston, USA, 2004.

12. J. Gosling, B. Joy, G. Steele, and G. Bracha. *The Java Language Specification, Second Edition*. Addison-Wesley, 2000.
13. M. Hsueh, T. Tsai, and R. Iyer. Fault injection techniques and tools. *IEEE Computer*, 30(4):75–82, 1997.
14. G. Kiczales, E. Hilsdale, J. Hugunin, M. Kersten, J. Palm, and W. Griswold. An overview of AspectJ. *LNCS*, 2072:327–355, 2001.
15. M. Kim, I. Lee, U. Sammapun, J. Shin, and O. Sokolsky. Monitoring, checking, and steering of real-time systems. In *Proc. 2nd Intl. Workshop on Run-time Verification (RV 2002)*, volume 70 of *ENTCS*. Elsevier, 2002.
16. J. Link and P. Fröhlich. *Unit Testing in Java: How Tests Drive the Code*. Morgan Kaufmann Publishers, Inc., 2003.
17. B. Meyer. *Eiffel: the language*. Prentice-Hall, Inc., Upper Saddle River, USA, 1992.
18. Microsoft Corporation. *Microsoft Visual C# .NET Language Reference*. Microsoft Press, Redmond, USA, 2002.
19. G. Myers. *Art of Software Testing*. John Wiley & Sons, Inc., 1979.
20. C. Pasareanu, M. Dwyer, and W. Visser. Finding feasible abstract counter-examples. *Intl. Journal on Software Tools for Technology Transfer (STTT)*, 5(1):34–48, 2003.
21. D. Peled. *Software Reliability Methods*. Springer, 2001.
22. S. Sinha and M. Harrold. Criteria for testing exception-handling constructs in Java programs. In *Proc. IEEE Intl. Conf. on Software Maintenance (ICSM 1999)*, page 265, Washington, USA, 1999. IEEE Computer Society.
23. S. Stoller. Testing concurrent Java programs using randomized scheduling. In *Proc. 2nd Intl. Workshop on Run-time Verification (RV 2002)*, volume 70(4) of *ENTCS*, pages 143–158, Copenhagen, Denmark, 2002. Elsevier.
24. B. Stroustrup. *The C++ Programming Language, Third Edition*. Addison-Wesley Longman Publishing Co., Inc., Boston, USA, 1997.
25. W. Visser, K. Havelund, G. Brat, S. Park, and F. Lerda. Model checking programs. *Automated Software Engineering Journal*, 10(2):203–232, 2003.
26. W. Weimer and G. Necula. Finding and preventing run-time error handling mistakes. In *Proc. 19th ACM SIGPLAN Conf. on Object-Oriented Programming Systems, Languages & Applications (OOPSLA 2004)*, pages 419–431, Vancouver, Canada, 2004. ACM Press.
27. A. White. SERP, an Open Source framework for manipulating Java bytecode, 2002. http://serp.sourceforge.net/.

Automated Boundary Test Generation from JML Specifications*

Fabrice Bouquet, Frédéric Dadeau, and Bruno Legeard

Laboratoire d'Informatique (LIFC)
Université de Franche-Comté, CNRS - INRIA
16, route de Gray - 25030 Besançon cedex, France
{bouquet, dadeau, legeard}@lifc.univ-fcomte.fr

Abstract. We present an original approach for the automated computation of model-based test cases from specifications written in Java
Modeling Language (JML). We aim at activating all the behaviors from
the JML method specifications. Therefore, we extract each behavior and
we compute the pertinent test data for the input parameters; we select
the boundary values of the ordered domains, and we consider specific
features for the objects, involving inheritance and aliasing. Finally, a
preamble for each test case is computed by symbolic animation of the
JML specification using constraint logic programming techniques. Thus,
we are able to automatically generate executable Java test sequences to
be run on the system under test. Moreover, this process requires the less
possible intervention from a validation engineer.

Keywords: Test generation, model-based, Java Modeling Language, automated, boundary values.

1 Introduction

Model-based testing (MBT) [21] has become an efficient way for validating an
implementation. While the program is being developed, based on informal requirements, the formal model is written, validated and verified. Tests are then
derived from the model and run on the system under test (SUT). Different kinds
of testing can be performed. In particular, *conformance testing* aims at observing
the responses of the SUT w.r.t. a specification-compliant use of this latter. If the
program is correct, then the test should succeed. On the other hand, *robustness
testing* consists in observing the responses of the SUT w.r.t. an incorrect use of
the system. These non-nominal cases also have to be specified in the model.

The Java Modeling Language (JML) [12,13] is an assertion language for Java,
that can be used either to design a formal model or to strengthen the code with
assertions. The main advantage of JML is that it makes it possible to provide
both model and code in the same file, sharing the same class attributes and
methods. This is a very interesting point since one important problem in MBT

---

* This work has been realized within the GECCOO project of program "ACI Sécurité
Informatique" supported by the French Ministry of Research and New Technologies.

J. Misra, T. Nipkow, and E. Sekerinski (Eds.): FM 2006, LNCS 4085, pp. 428–443, 2006.
© Springer-Verlag Berlin Heidelberg 2006

is to "connect" the variables of the specification with the variables of the SUT. In object-oriented testing, a key issue is to compute the oracle, which is the expected result of the test case. Thanks to its assertions JML provides a natural oracle for the Java programs. Indeed, the JML Run-Time Assertion Checker [7] compiles JML-annotated source to a Java byte-code containing on-the-fly checking of the JML assertions.

A previous work [3] has presented a way to express an interesting subset of the JML specifications within a set-theoretic framework, so that we were able to perform a symbolic animation of the JML specification. Using underlying constraints solvers, we represent object system states as constraints systems. From there, we simulate the invocation of methods by solving a constraint satisfaction problem involving the state before, the before-after predicates that describes the behavior of the method, and the state after. We present in this paper the direct application of this work, which is the generation of boundary test cases applied both to conformance and robustness testing. This approach has been applied on model-based test generation from B machines within the BZ-Testing-Tools project [1]. The symbolic representation of the system is employed to compute the test data, and the symbolic animation engine is employed to compute the preamble of the test cases.

The main contributions of the paper are the following. We introduce an approach to model-based testing for Java based on the JML specifications. We use model coverage for selecting our tests involving structural coverage of the specification and data coverage using a boundary analysis for numerical data. This is, to our knowledge, a novelty for Java/JML. This approach is fully model-based, and aims at generating automatically functional test cases, i.e., black-box test cases, by using the specification both as an oracle, and as a support for computing the test data.

The paper is organized as follows. Section 2 introduces the Java Modeling Language, and presents an example to illustrate its principles, it also describes the symbolic representation of a JML-specified system, introducing the notion of underlying constraint stores. Section 3 presents the test selection we apply to JML, decomposed into two parts: the structural coverage of the JML specifications, detailed in Section 4, and the test data computation, explained in Section 5. Section 6 details the generation of the test cases, by computing the preamble. The implementation of our approach and an experimental result on a case study is given in Section 7. Section 8 presents the related work on model-based test generation for Java and states on the originality of our approach. Finally, Section 9 concludes and announces the future work.

2   Java Modeling Language

This section presents the Java Modeling Language [13] and introduces an example that will be used throughout the remainder of the paper to illustrate our approach. Then, we describe the symbolic representation of an object-oriented system using underlying constraint solvers. This representation will later on be used for the computation of the tests.

2.1   Overview of JML

The Java Modeling Language is the specification language dedicated to the Java programming language. The model is expressed by assertions embedded within the Java code. These assertions describe the specification associated to the class, in terms of static or dynamic properties. The static properties are the invariant (`invariant` clause), and the history constraints (`constraints` clause), which are applied to the entire class. On the contrary, the dynamic properties are applied to the methods, through method specifications, and they describe the behavior of the method using a pre- and post-condition semantics. The method specification may contain several clauses, such as the preconditions (`requires` clause), the frame condition (`assignable` clauses), the normal post-condition (`ensures` clause) and the exceptional post-conditions (`signals` clauses). Since JML is based on the Design By Contract principles [17], the pre-condition represents the contract that the system has to fulfill for the method to be executed. In this case, the normal post-condition describes a property that is established when the method terminates normally, i.e., without throwing an exception. The exceptional post-conditions state the properties that are established when the method terminates by throwing a specified exception. Apart from that, the frame condition indicates which fields are modified during by the execution of the method. Method clauses are gathered within method behaviors, separated by `also`.

The syntax of the JML predicates is similar to the Java syntax, enriched with special keywords, beginning with a \, such as `\result` which represents the return value of a method, or `\not_modified(X)` whose meaning is obvious. The JML clauses are written using these first-order logic predicates. The history constraints and the postconditions are written using before-after predicates in which it is possible to refer to the before value of an expression `expr` by surrounding it by `\old(expr)`.

Figure 1 illustrates the use of JML through an example. The specification describes an electronic purse (`Purse` class), that is extended by a limitation (`LimitedPurse` class) which requires the `balance` of the purse to be limited by a given value `max`. It is possible to add money to the purse (`credit(short)` method) or to remove money from it (`debit(short)` method). Moreover, it is possible to transfer the content of a purse (`transfer(Purse)` method) by copying its `balance`.

2.2   Symbolic Representation of Object-Oriented Systems

Our symbolic representation of object-oriented and especially Java/JML systems, involves the use of underlying constraint solvers. They manage a constraint store, involving symbolic variables that are used to designate different elements of the system, such as the instances, the value of the attributes, etc. Thus, this representation relies on an solver on finite domain integers, CLP(FD), and a set-theoretic solver, named CLPS-BZ [4], and part of the BZ-Testing-Tools project [1]. This latter is able to manage constraints on sets, functions and relations. This section summarizes our previous work presented in [3].

```
class Purse {

    //@ invariant balance >= 0;
    protected short balance;

    /*@ normal_behavior
      @   requires b >= 0;
      @   assignable balance;
      @   ensures balance == b;    */
    public Purse(short b) {...}

    /*@ behavior
      @     requires a >= 0 && balance >= a;
      @     assignable balance;
      @     ensures balance ==
      @             (short) \old(balance) - a;
      @ also
      @     requires a > balance;
      @     assignable balance;
      @     signals (NoCreditException e)
      @             balance == \old(balance); */
    public void debit(short a)
                throws NoCreditException {...}

    /*@ normal_behavior
      @   p != null;
      @   assignable balance;
      @   ensures this.equals(p);  */
    public void transfer(Purse p) {...}

    /*@ normal_behavior
      @   assignable \nothing;
      @   ensures \result <==>
      @           (this.balance == p.balance)  */
    /*@ pure */ boolean equals(Purse p) {...}
```

```
    /*@ behavior
      @   requires a > 0;
      @   assignable balance;
      @   ensures balance ==
      @           (short) \old(balance) + a; */
    public void credit(short a) {...}
}

class LimitedPurse extends Purse {

    //@ invariant max == 10000 && balance <= max;
    //@ constraint \not_modified(max);
    static short max = 10000;

    /*@ normal_behavior
      @   requires b >= 0 && b <= max;
      @   assignable balance;
      @   ensures balance == b;
      @*/
    public LimitedPurse(short b) {...}

    /*@ normal_behavior
      @   requires a >= 0 && balance+a <= max;
      @   assignable balance;
      @   ensures balance == \old(balance)+a;
      @ also
      @   requires a < 0 || balance+a > max;
      @   assignable balance;
      @   ensures balance == \old(balance);
      @*/
    public void credit(short a) {...}
}
```

Fig. 1. Example of a JML specification

In our approach, an object-oriented system state is defined by: (i) a set of existing instances, whose dynamic types are classes, and (ii) each instance possesses attributes, whose values are either a built-in type value (such as integers, characters, etc.), or an object-typed value (i.e., another instance).

Definition 1 (Symbolic States). *We represent a symbolic states as a pair composed of an environment and an associated constraint system $C_s(V)$, that manages constraints on the environment's variables. An environment is defined by a set of specification variables identified by a module name M and a data name N, mapped to a kind K (*input, output, constant, variable, prime*), a type T, and a set of variables V that occurs in $C_s(V)$.*

$$\langle C_s(V), M \times N \to V \times K \times T \rangle \tag{1}$$

We define a special module, named model that describes the heap, and stores the dynamic type of the different instances. The heap is a set of atoms, containing memory addresses represented as atoms null, addr0, addr1,..., addr$N$ where N is a user-defined number. The set of addresses that is used is stored in set variable, named instances, constrained to be a subset of the heap. The dynamic type of the instances is known by a function that maps the created instance to a corresponding class name. Each class is considered as a module. Each module has a variable named `instances` that represents the set of created instances of this class. Each class attribute is a module variable. If this attribute is not static, its value depends on the considered instance and so, it is represented as a total function –a set of pairs– mapping the instance to its value. If the attribute is static, its value is directly given.

Example 1 (Symbolic representation of the system states). Consider the classes presented in the example in Fig. 1. The symbolic state representing all the possible configurations of the system is defined by:

$$\langle \{A = \{\texttt{null}, \texttt{addr0}, \dots, \texttt{addrN}\}, B \subseteq A, \texttt{null} \notin B, C \subseteq B, D \in B \rightarrow \{\texttt{Purse}, \texttt{Limited-}$$
$$\texttt{Purse}\}, E \subseteq C, F \in E \rightarrow -32768..32767, G \subseteq E, H \in -32768..32767\},$$
$$\{(\texttt{model}, \texttt{heap}) \mapsto (A, \texttt{constant}, \texttt{set(atom)}), (\texttt{model}, \texttt{instances}) \mapsto (B, \texttt{variable},$$
$$\texttt{set(atom)}), (\texttt{model}, \texttt{accessible}) \mapsto (C, \texttt{variable}, \texttt{set(atom)}), (\texttt{model}, \texttt{typeof}) \mapsto$$
$$(D, \texttt{variable}, \texttt{set(atom)}), (\texttt{Purse}, \texttt{instances}) \mapsto (E, \texttt{variable}, \texttt{set(atom)}), (\texttt{Purse},$$
$$\texttt{balance}) \mapsto (F, \texttt{variable}, \texttt{set(pair(atom,int))}), (\texttt{LimitedPurse}, \texttt{instances}) \mapsto$$
$$(G, \texttt{variable}, \texttt{set(atom)}), (\texttt{LimitedPurse}, \texttt{max}) \mapsto (H, \texttt{variable}, \texttt{int})\}\rangle$$

where A, B, C, D, E, F, G and H are environment variables on which constraints are applied within the store.

From this representation, we are able to perform the symbolic animation of the JML specification, by considering the predicates extracted from the method specifications and translated in our internal representation's syntax. Thus, executing a method for animating the specification is equivalent to solving a constraint satisfaction problem between two symbolic states. More details about it can be found in [3].

3   Test Selection Criteria for JML

The test selection criteria defines what motivates the way we build our test cases. It can be either a test case specification provided by a validation engineer, such as in TOBIAS [14] or STG [8], a stochastic/probabilistic approach as in Jartege [19], or a *model coverage* criteria, which is our choice for the JML specifications.

This criteria focuses on producing the tests by exploiting the informations contained in the specification at two levels. The first level is the *structural coverage*, composed by the transition coverage, and the data coverage. The transition coverage aims at activating the behaviors of the system, and the decision coverage aims at covering the decisions within the predicates describing the behaviors. The second level is the *data coverage*, achieved, in our case, by performing the boundary analysis of the data w.r.t. the behaviors.

Figure 2 summarizes the process of our approach. A JML model is analyzed and partitioned w.r.t. model coverage criteria, selected by the validation engineer and automatically applied on the specification. This produces test targets, which will be used to generate the executable Java test cases.

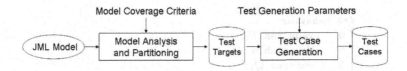

Fig. 2. Summary of our approach

Definition 2 (Test Target). *A test target is defined by the activation of a behavior B within a specific context defined by:*

$$Inv \wedge B \wedge P_{spe} \tag{2}$$

where Inv is the system invariant, B designates the behavior expressed as a before-after predicate and P_{spe} designates a specialization predicate that specifies additional constraints.

The specialization predicate can be specified by the validation engineer; by default, it is set to *true*. P_{spe} is then enriched during the computation of the test data, in order to require a particular parameter or attribute to be set at a particular value, e.g. an extremum of its domain, as explained in section 5. Before that, the next section explains the structural coverage applied to the JML specification.

4 Structural Coverage of the JML Specification

This section firstly focuses on the extraction of the behaviors from the JML method specifications. Secondly, we present the different rewritings to apply on the decisions nested in the predicates of the considered behavior. These rewritings have to be selected by the validation engineer.

4.1 Extraction of the Behaviors from the Method Specifications

The partitioning of the JML method specifications into behaviors is illustrated by Fig. 3. In this figure, $P_k (k \in 1..N)$ are the precondition predicates, A gives the frame condition, $Q_k (k \in 1..N)$ are the normal postconditions, $S_p (p \in 1..M)$ are the exceptional postconditions related to the exceptions E_p. The terminations are distinguished by T, which might be either *no_exception* indicating a normal behavior, or any of the declared exceptions E_p. We call a *behavior* a branch of this graph. Each behavior represents a particular transition of the system according to the different possible terminations. We require the terminations to be exclusive between the normal termination and the exceptional terminations.

From this before-after predicate expressed in the Java/JML logic, we apply user-defined decision coverage criteria as defined hereafter. Notice that the inconsistent behaviors are filtered.

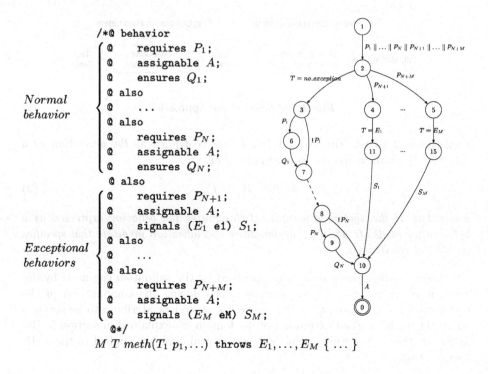

```
     /*@ behavior
       @       requires P₁;
       @       assignable A;
       @       ensures Q₁;
Normal @ also
behavior @      ...
       @ also
       @       requires Pₙ;
       @       assignable A;
       @       ensures Qₙ;
       @ also
       @       requires Pₙ₊₁;
       @       assignable A;
       @       signals (E₁ e1) S₁;
Exceptional @ also
behaviors @      ...
       @ also
       @       requires Pₙ₊ₘ;
       @       assignable A;
       @       signals (Eₘ eM) Sₘ;
     @*/
     M T meth(T₁ p₁,...) throws E₁,...,Eₘ { ... }
```

Fig. 3. Extraction of the behaviors from a JML method specification

4.2   Application of the Decision Coverage Criteria

In order to exploit the specification, we perform a flow-graph coverage, based on the rewriting of the disjunctions contained in the first-order logic predicates composing the behaviors. We distinguish 4 possible rewritings, presented in Fig. 4, each one of them corresponding to a different decision coverage criteria. They create an additional deployment of the original method specification, adding more granularity to the test targets. In the figure, we denote by [] (read "choice") the choice-point between predicates.

Rewriting 1 consists in leaving the disjunction unmodified. Thus, the first branch that succeeds at being evaluated is enough. This rewriting satisfies the Decision Coverage (DC). As an extension, it also satisfies the Statement

Id	Rewriting of $P_1 \vee P_2$	Decision Coverage
1	$P_1 \vee P_2$	DC and SC
2	$P_1 \, [] \, P_2$	D/CC
3	$(P_1 \wedge \neg P_2) \, [] \, (\neg P_1 \wedge P_2)$	FPC
4	$(P_1 \wedge P_2) \, [] \, (P_1 \wedge \neg P_2) \, [] \, (\neg P_1 \wedge P_2)$	MCC

Fig. 4. Definition of the rewritings of the disjunctive predicates

Coverage criteria (SC). Rewriting 2 consists in creating a choice between the two predicates. Thus, the first branch and the second branch independently have to succeed when being evaluated. This rewriting satisfies the decision/condition coverage criteria (D/CC) since it satisfies the DC and the Condition Coverage (CC) criteria. Rewriting 3 consists in creating an exclusive choice between the two predicates. Only one of the sub-predicates of the disjunction is checked at one time. This rewriting satisfies the full predicate coverage (FPC) [18] criteria. Rewriting 4 consists in testing all the possible values for the two sub-predicates to satisfy the disjunction. This rewriting satisfies the multiple condition coverage criteria (MCC).

Example 2. Consider the method `credit` from class `LimitedPurse` given in the example presented in Fig. 1. The application of rewriting 4 on the behavior from the method specification gives the following deployment.

Behavior predicates
`a >= 0 && balance + a <= max && balance == \old(balance) + a`   (1)
`a <  0 && balance + a >  max && balance == \old(balance)`   (2)
`a <  0 && balance + a <= max && balance == \old(balance)`   (3)
`a >= 0 && balance + a >  max && balance == \old(balance)`   (4)

Notice that the behavior (2) is inconsistent w.r.t. the `LimitedPurse` class invariant `balance >= 0 && balance <= max`, and thus will not be considered for the test target computation.

Once the structural coverage is defined, we need to set up the test data that will be inputted in terms of method parameters. Therefore, we use the specialization predicate of the test target to define additional constraints on the test data, such as selecting their boundary values.

5   Test Data Computation

For each behavior that we want to activate, we generate specific test data, according to the type of the data. Our approach is based on selecting the boundary values, which is known as a good strategy for finding errors [20]. This section presents the computation of the boundary values for data whose domains are ordered (e.g. integers, characters, etc.), and the computation of the boundary values for objects, which consists in selecting a boundary value to one of the object's attribute. Whereas the first part provides numerical input values that have no relation with the rest of the environment, the second one provides either a context-independent object value (`this` or `null`), or a symbolic value for an object instance, depending on the context which provides boundary values.

   The definition of the boundary goal computation is done in two steps. We consider D_i as the set of object attributes and input parameters that occur in the behavior B_i targeted by the test. These data are determined through a static analysis of the behavior. We decompose D_i into two subsets D_{ord}, representing data whose domain are ordered (e.g. integers, characters, etc.), and D_{obj}, representing object data (i.e., without order relation on their domain), so that $D_i = D_{ord} \cup D_{obj}$.

5.1   Built-In Typed Data

If the data type is a built-in type (integer, character, etc., that can be considered as an integer value), it has an ordered domain, and we select the values at the bounds of this domain. These bounds are computed based on the range of values for the considered type, whose domain is reduced by the constraints from the class invariant, and the behavior we want to test. As a consequence, the data value conforms to the specification and no irrelevant tests values will be produced.

Definition 3 (Built-in Typed Data Coverage). *Let D_{ord} be the ordered-domain data occurring in a behavior B_i extracted from the method under test, let Inv be the system invariant, and let f be an optimization function, so that $f(X) = \sum_{x \in X}(x)$. The test data are defined by the boundary values of D_{ord}, computed using the functions:*

$$BV_i^{min}(B_i) = minimize(f(D_{ord}), Inv \wedge B_i) \tag{3}$$
$$BV_i^{max}(B_i) = maximize(f(D_{ord}), Inv \wedge B_i) \tag{4}$$

where minimize (resp. maximize) is the labeling function that computes the minimal (resp. maximal) value of its parameter, by selecting the lower (resp. upper) bound of its domain.

Additional constraints are thus added to the specialization predicate P_{spe} defining the test target in order to force the considered variables to meet their boundary values. Thus, we call the test target a *boundary goal*.

5.2   Object Typed Data

If the data is an object, a special mechanism is applied, based on object concepts of inheritance and aliasing. Contrary to built-in types, we are not looking for a direct value for the test data, but for a symbolic value, that will represent an object in the environment that has been created and which possesses particular properties. These properties will be required in the test target through the specialization predicate P_{spe}.

Definition 4 (Object Typed Data Coverage). *Let $D_{obj} = \{\langle T_1, o_1 \rangle, \langle T_2, o_2 \rangle, \ldots\}$ be the set of object data (composed by a couple $\langle static\ type, variable \rangle$) of the behavior B_i extracted from method under test. We call ID_{obj} the set of input data ($ID_{obj} \subseteq D_{obj}$). The test data is defined for each $\langle T_i, o_i \rangle \in D_{obj}$ by:*

1. o_i == null
2. o_i == this
3. o_i != null && o_i != this && \typeof(o_i) == \type(T_i)

4. o_i != null && o_i != this && \typeof(o_i) <: \type(T_i)
5. o_i != null && o_i != this && o_i == o_j *where* $o_j \in ID_{obj}$

These predicates, expressed in the JML syntax, can lead to inconsistencies, depending on the context in which they are employed. In this case, the value is filtered, and thus not selected.

We now explain informally these predicates. (1) We assign a null reference to the object o_i, if this particular value is not forbidden by the specification. (2) If the type is compliant, we assign to o_i the reference of the object under test, this. (3) We try to assign any object whose dynamic type (\typeof(o_i)) is the static type of the object (\type(T_i)). This object will have to be created during the preamble of the test case. (4) In order to check inheritance compliance, and according to Liskov's Substitution Principle –*"Whenever an instance of a class is expected, one can always substitute an instance of any of its subclasses"*– we assign to the object an instance of each of its direct subclasses, i.e., whose dynamic type is a subtype (operator <:) of the static type. (5) In order to check aliasing, and if the type is compliant, we assign the same object for two different parameters.

Example 3 (Test Data Computation). Consider the method transfer from class Purse, inherited by an object of dynamic type (LimitedPurse). This method has only one behavior, which does not contain any disjunction. After a static analysis, this behavior involves two attributes this.balance and p.balance nested behind the this.equals(p) pure method call. These two attributes are of type short, and thus we will select the bounds of their domains to build a pertinent context. Moreover, we also apply the mechanism on the parameter p of the transfer method. The test targets extracted for the activation of the only behavior of the method specifications are given by:

$$\text{balance} >= 0 \text{ \&\& balance} <= \text{max \&\& p} != \text{null \&\& } P_{spe}$$

where P_{spe} is given in the table below. In this table, we have removed the P_{spe} producing an inconsistent context. R_{ord} (resp. R_{obj}) designates the computation rule that applies on ordered-domains (resp. objects) data.

	Specialization predicate P_{spe}	R_{ord}	R_{obj}
(a)	this.balance == 0 && p == this	minimize	(1)
(b)	this.balance == 10000 && p == this	maximize	(1)
(c)	this.balance == 0 && p != null && p != this && \typeof(p) == \type(Purse) && p.balance == 0	minimize	(3)
(d)	this.balance == 10000 && p != null && p != this && \typeof(p) == \type(Purse) && p.balance == 32767	maximize	(3)
(e)	this.balance == 0 && p != null && p != this && \typeof(p) == \type(LimitedPurse) && p.balance == 0	minimize	(4)
(f)	this.balance == 10000 && p != null && p != this && \typeof(p) == \type(LimitedPurse) && p.balance == 10000	maximize	(4)

The context defined in equation (2), and illustrated by the previous example, provides both constraints on the environment and values for the input parameters. By adding these constraints to the symbolic representation of the system, we build a boundary goal. For example, adding the constraints of the specialization predicate (d) leads to the following boundary goal:

⟨{A = {null, addr0, ..., addrN}, B ⊆ A, C ⊆ B, D ∈ B → {Purse, LimitedPurse},
   null ∉ B, E ⊆ C, F ∈ E → −32768..32767, G ⊆ E, H = 10000, I ∈ G, I ∈ E,
   J ∈ E, J ∈ C, (I ↦ LimitedPurse) ∈ D, (I ↦ 10000) ∈ F, J ≠ null, J ≠ I,
   (J ↦ Purse) ∈ D, (J ↦ 32767) ∈ F},
   {(model, heap) ↦ ..., (LimitedPurse, this) ↦ (I, input(transfer), atom),
   (LimitedPurse, p) ↦ (J, input(transfer), atom), }⟩

6   Preamble Computation

Once a boundary goal is identified, we need to compute the preamble that will,
from the initial state, build the method sequence that will lead to the boundary
state from which the test itself, i.e., the activation of the considered behavior,
will be performed.

6.1   Computation of the Preamble Using Symbolic Animation

As we have seen in the previous section, a boundary state is defined w.r.t. the
inputs and the attributes of objects that occur within the considered behavior.
Thus, the preamble is driven by two objectives. (*i*) Activating the considered
behavior: this requires to create the considered object which will invoke the
method under test, but this may also require that its attributes have a specific
value given by the behavior. (*ii*) Creating the objects to provide method parameters and setting their attributes to a specific value. Both of these objectives are
expressed within a symbolic state, associated to a constraint system. The symbolic animation of the model is then performed using a "best-first" algorithm
guided by specific heuristics (see [9] for more details). Once a satisfying state is
reached all the remaining method parameters that are still constrained are instantiated so that a specific execution sequence can be produced. This execution
sequence is then reified into an executable Java test case. Since the reachability
problem can not be decided, we parameterize the boundary goal research by a
user-defined depth.

Example 4. Consider the test target computed in example 3. The corresponding
Java test cases for targets and their results at when performed using the JML
Run-Time Assertion Checking are the given in Fig. 5. In this figure, a1 and
a2 are automatically generated variables names. We notice that the failed test
case reveals a conceptual error since method transfer has not been redefined in
the LimitedPurse subclass, and allows any value of the parameter Purse to be
transferred, especially objects whose attribute is greater than the limitation max.

6.2   Reachability of the Boundary State

As the experienced reader may have noticed, the constraints defining the boundary state may be too strong to be easily reachable automatically, especially to
assign a boundary value to a given attribute. Indeed, in object programming,
the class attributes are rarely visible as public, and thus their value can not be
accessed and modified directly. This leads to considering two options that may
solve this potential problem.

Target	Java Test case	Verdict
(a)	`LimitedPurse a1 = new LimitedPurse(0);` `a1.transfer(a1);`	Success
(b)	`LimitedPurse a1 = new LimitedPurse(10000);` `a1.transfer(a1);`	Success

(c)	`LimitedPurse a1 = new LimitedPurse(0);`
	`Purse a2 = new Purse(0);`
	`a1.transfer(a2);`
		Success

(d)	`LimitedPurse a1 = new LimitedPurse(10000);`
	`Purse a2 = new Purse(32767);`
	`a1.transfer(a2);`
		Failure → JMLInvariantException

(e)	`LimitedPurse a1 = new LimitedPurse(0);`
	`LimitedPurse a2 = new LimitedPurse(0);`
	`a1.transfer(a2);`
		Success

(f)	`LimitedPurse a1 = new LimitedPurse(10000);`
	`LimitedPurse a2 = new LimitedPurse(10000);`
	`a1.transfer(a2);`
		Success

Fig. 5. Resulting test cases for the `transfer` method from the example

The first solution is that the modeler provides specific methods, in the different classes, that are in charge of assigning a given value to a non-public field of the class. We have noticed that it is a good programming practice, and thus, this restriction should not be a problem. Moreover, the properties that can never be reached (such as an attribute that may never be `null`) have to be stated in the class invariant, so that the unreachable values for the test data are filtered and removed from the test target.

The second solution is to weaken the constraints of the boundary state, considering the test data computation, only once the context allowing the activation of the behavior is reached, with P_{spe} reduced to *true*. The boundary values are then computed w.r.t. the resulting configurations. If this solution increases the reachability of the test targets, the resulting test data might be less pertinent that with the original approach. For example, the bug found in the global boundary approach would not have been found.

7   Experimentations with JML-Testing-Tools

This approach has been implemented in a tool-set, named JML-TESTING-TOOLS– JML-TT– which proposes both an animation tool [2] and a test generation tool, and experimented on a case study.

7.1   JML-Testing-Tools

The architecture of JML-TT is depicted hereby. The Java/JML source file is translated into an intermediate format file from which the animation and the test generation are performed.

The animation uses three Prolog modules (named Executer, Reducer and Solvers). The test generation modules are used to extract the test targets, compute the test data, and build the test cases.

JML-TT takes as an input a JML-annotated Java class description, and gathers all the additional classes (exceptions, attributes types, etc.) that are required to performed the animation, and to build a context for the test generation data. The user chooses (i) the methods to test, (ii) the specification coverage criteria, using disjunction rewritings, (iii) the data coverage criteria applied on the method parameters and the object attributes, and (iv) the maximal preamble depth.

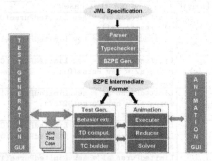

The test generation tool computes the test suite, composed by a sequence of object creations and method invocations, ended by the invocation of the method under test. It produces a Java test file, that can be run on the RAC-compiled classes to perform the test. A screen-shot of the tool is given in Fig. 6.

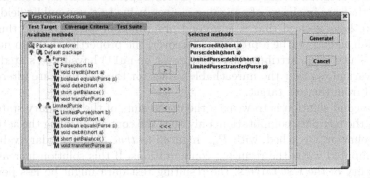

Fig. 6. Screen-shot of JML-TESTING-TOOLS test criteria selection

7.2   Experimental Results

We have applied our approach on a case study: a JML specification of the Demoney Java Card applet [16]. It is composed of 35 classes (of which 19 exceptions). The main class contains 12 methods to test, decomposed into 14 normal behaviors and 17 exceptional behaviors. This specification has first been validated on the JML-TESTING-TOOLS symbolic animator to check its conformance w.r.t. the initial informal requirements. The results of the test generation are given in Fig. 7 in terms of behaviors and test cases for each possible rewriting. The results are very promising since all behaviors have been covered twice (one by minimization, one by maximization of numerical attributes).

8   Related Work

Many work has been done on producing test cases from Java programs, using a structural, or white-box, approach. This section only focuses on the JML-related

Criteria	RW 1	RW 2	RW 3	RW 4
Nb of behaviors	31	33	33	35
Nb of test targets	62	66	66	70
Nb of test cases	62 (100%)	66 (100%)	66 (100%)	70 (100%)

Fig. 7. Results of the test generation for the case study

test generation work. The first obvious reference is the JMLUnit approach developed by Leavens and Cheon [6]. This approach uses the JUnit framework to write the test cases and the JML Run-Time Assertion Checker as an oracle for the tests. This combination is enriched by the automatic building of JUnit test frameworks, for automatically generating systematic test data (e.g. for integers: 0, 1, −1, Integer.MIN_VALUE, Integer.MAX_VALUE, and a random value between 0 and each of the integer's extrema). This approaches produces many irrelevant test cases that are filtered at run-time. On the same principle, Jartege [19] aims at generating random test cases for Java. If the process is fully automated, and well-known for being efficient at finding bugs, it faces the problem of building irrelevant test cases w.r.t. the specification, compensated by the number of generated test cases. In our approach, the tests are based on the specification and is guided by the activation of a specific behavior, described in the specification.

The TOBIAS tool [14] produces combinatorial test cases from a given user-defined pattern. The tests are then filtered using the JML annotations to eliminate the irrelevant test cases. The major advantage of this tool is that it is an efficient way to produce a huge number of test cases, and to potentially find numerous bugs. Nevertheless, this approach requires a lot of experience from the validation engineer, since he has to provide the test pattern and the test data. On the contrary, our point of view is to automate the test generation the most possible.

TestEra [11] and Korat [5], from Khurshid et al., have also interesting arguments. These tools are able to build all the possible input data, for a given finite structure size, that satisfy a given Java predicate. Our approach is quite similar since we also consider a context, given by the precondition and a boundary value analysis, in which the methods can be invoked. But, our originality is (i) the use of boundary values to select the possible input data, and (ii) the automated computation of a preamble using the symbolic animation of the model in order to reach this context.

9   Conclusion and Future Work

We have presented an original approach to the test generation for Java programs, based on the Java Modeling Language, to be used not only as an oracle, but especially as a reference for functional test generation. This approach is based on the symbolic representation of object states, and the symbolic animation of the JML specifications, that make it possible to respectively compute the test data to generate, and to build the preamble for the test cases. Boundary testing is a pertinent way to find bugs within an implementation. The combination of boundary testing for numerical data, and object-oriented features appears to be interesting, and not targeted before. Moreover, our technique is fully automated and requires a minimal user intervention.

Experimentations have shown interesting results on realistic examples, in both test data generation and preamble computation. Nevertheless, there is a trade-off between full automation and efficiency of the approach. If the preamble can not be computed, we plan to ask the user to intervene, in order to provide a satisfying method sequence.

The computation of boundary test data, to produce test data given one particular context, is efficiently performed using our technology. Thus, we plan, for the future, to reinvest this capability to serve other test selection criteria, such as combinatorial or randomized/probabilistic test generation. This will make it possible to compare these approaches on a relevant case study. We would also like to extend the subset of JML that we can deal with, in order to take floats into account, by integrating a floating point data solver. Finally, we notice that our approach may also be adapted to other object-oriented modeling languages, so we will consider adapting it to Spec# [15], which is close to JML.

References

1. F. Ambert, F. Bouquet, S. Chemin, S. Guenaud, B. Legeard, F. Peureux, N. Vacelet, and M. Utting. BZ-TT: A Tool-Set for Test Generation from Z and B using Contraint Logic Programming. In Robert Hierons and Thierry Jeron, editors, *Formal Approaches to Testing of Software, FATES 2002 workshop of CONCUR'02*, pages 105–120. INRIA Report, August 2002.
2. F. Bouquet, F. Dadeau, B. Legeard, and M. Utting. JML-Testing-Tools: a Symbolic Animator for JML Specifications using CLP. In Nicolas Halbwachs and Lenore Zuck, editors, *Proceedings of 11th Int. Conf. on Tools and Algorithms for the Construction and Analysis of Systems, Tool session (TACAS'05)*, volume 3440 of *LNCS*, pages 551–556, Edinburgh, United Kingdom, April 2005. Springer-Verlag.
3. F. Bouquet, F. Dadeau, B. Legeard, and M. Utting. Symbolic animation of JML specifications. In J.S. Fitzgerald, I.J. Hayes, and A. Tarlecki, editors, *Proceedings of the International Conference on Formal Methods (FM'2005)*, volume 3582 of *LNCS*, pages 75–90, Newcastle Upon Tyne, UK, July 2005. Springer-Verlag.
4. F. Bouquet, B. Legeard, and F. Peureux. CLPS-B – A constraint solver for B. In *Proceedings of the ETAPS'02 International Conference on Tools and Algorithms for the Construction and Analysis of Systems (TACAS'02)*, volume 2280 of *LNCS*, pages 188–204, Grenoble, France, April 2002. Springer-Verlag.
5. C. Boyapati, S. Khurshid, and D. Marinov. Korat: automated testing based on java predicates. In *ISSTA'02: Proceedings of the ACM SIGSOFT international symposium on Software testing and analysis*, pages 123–133, New York, NY, USA, 2002. ACM Press.
6. Y. Cheon and G.T. Leavens. A simple and practical approach to unit testing: The JML and JUnit way. Technical Report 01-12, Department of Computer Science, Iowa State University, November 2001. Available from archives.cs.iastate.edu.

7. Y. Cheon and G.T. Leavens. A Runtime Assertion Checker for the Java Modeling Language (JML). In Hamid R. Arabnia and Youngsong Mun, editors, *Proceedings of the International Conference on Software Engineering Research and Practice (SERP '02), Las Vegas, Nevada, USA, June 24-27, 2002*, pages 322–328. CSREA Press, June 2002.

8. D. Clarke, T. Jéron, V. Rusu, and E. Zinovieva. Stg: a tool for generating symbolic test programs and oracles from operational specifications. In *ESEC/FSE-9: Proceedings of the 8th European software engineering conference held jointly with 9th ACM SIGSOFT international symposium on Foundations of software engineering*, pages 301–302, New York, NY, USA, 2001. ACM Press.

9. S. Colin, B. Legeard, and F. Peureux. Preamble Computation in Automated Test Case Generation using Constraint Logic Programming. *The Journal of Software Testing, Verification and Reliability*, 14(3):213–235, 2004.

10. Daniel Jackson. Alloy: a lightweight object modelling notation. *ACM Trans. Softw. Eng. Methodol.*, 11(2):256–290, 2002.

11. S. Khurshid and D. Marinov. Testera: Specification-based testing of java programs using sat. *Automated Software Engineering*, 11(4):403–434, 2004.

12. G.T. Leavens, A.L. Baker, and C. Ruby. JML: a Java Modeling Language. In *Formal Underpinnings of Java Workshop (at OOPSLA '98)*, October 1998.

13. G.T. Leavens, A.L. Baker, and C Ruby. JML: A notation for detailed design. In Haim Kilov, Bernhard Rumpe, and Ian Simmonds, editors, *Behavioral Specifications of Businesses and Systems*, pages 175–188. Kluwer Academic Publishers, Boston, 1999.

14. Y. Ledru, L. du Bousquet, O. Maury, and P. Bontron. Filtering tobias combinatorial test suites. In Michel Wermelinger and Tiziana Margaria, editors, *Fundamental Approaches to Software Engineering, 7th International Conference, FASE 2004*, volume 2984 of *LNCS*, pages 281–294, Barcelona, Spain, 2004. Springer-Verlag.

15. K.R.M. Leino M. Barnett and W. Schulte. The Spec# Programming System: An Overview. In *Proceedings of the International Workshop on Construction and Analysis of Safe, Secure and Interoperable Smart devices (CASSIS'04)*, volume 3362 of *LNCS*, pages 49–69, Marseille, France, March 2004. Springer-Verlag.

16. R. Marlet and C. Mesnil. Demoney: A demonstrative electronic purse - card specification.

17. Bertrand Meyer. *Object-Oriented Software Construction*. Prentice Hall, 2 edition, 1997.

18. A. Jefferson Offutt, Y. Xiong, and S. Liu. Criteria for generating specification-based tests. In *5th International Conference on Engineering of Complex Computer Systems (ICECCS '99)*, pages 119–, Las Vegas, NV, USA, Oct 1999. IEEE Computer Society.

19. Catherine Oriat. Jartege: A tool for random generation of unit tests for java classes. In *Proceedings of the Second International Workshop on Software Quality, SOQUA 2005*, volume 3712 of *LNCS*, pages 242–256, Erfurt, Germany, September 2005. Springer-Verlag.

20. Amit Paradkar. Case studies on fault detection effectiveness of model based test generation techniques. *SIGSOFT Softw. Eng. Notes*, 30(4):1–7, 2005.

21. Alexander Pretschner. Model-based testing. In *ICSE '05: Proceedings of the 27th international conference on Software engineering*, pages 722–723, New York, NY, USA, 2005. ACM Press.

Formal Reasoning About Non-atomic Java Card Methods in Dynamic Logic

Wojciech Mostowski

Department of Computing Science, Radboud University Nijmegen
P.O. Box 9010, 6500 GL Nijmegen, The Netherlands
W.Mostowski@cs.ru.nl

Abstract. We present an extension to Java Card Dynamic Logic, a program logic for reasoning about Java Card programs, to handle Java Card's so-called non-atomic methods. Although Java Card DL already supports the atomic transaction mechanism of Java Card, non-atomic methods present an additional challenge: state updates triggered by such a non-atomic method are not subjected to any transaction that may possibly be in progress. The semantics of a non-atomic method itself seems to be simple and straightforward to formalise, however experimental studies showed that non-atomic methods affect the whole semantics of the Java Card transaction mechanism in a subtle way, in particular, it affects the notion of a transaction roll-back. In this paper we show how to adapt Java Card DL to accommodate this newly discovered complex transaction behaviour. The extension completes the formalisation of *all* of Java Card in Dynamic Logic.

1 Introduction

Overview. The work we present in this paper can be seen as a final step to complete formalisation of Java Card in Dynamic Logic [2]. Java Card Dynamic Logic (Java Card DL) is a program logic specifically designed to reason about sequential Java programs and, in particular, programs written in Java Card, a Java dialect used to program smart cards. Java Card DL is implemented in the KeY system [1], an integrated design and verification system for object-oriented programs. In an earlier paper we presented an extension to Java Card DL to handle the Java Card's transaction mechanism [3]. The transaction mechanism is a feature specific to Java Card technology. In the context of the persistent data stored in smart card's memory, it allows to ensure that a given program block is executed atomically (to completion or not at all), even when loss of power occurs. The transaction mechanism is deeply embedded in the language specification, i.e. transaction triggering methods in Java Card are native, their implementation cannot be expressed in terms of pure Java code. The support for handling transactions in Java Card DL is important for two reasons: to be able to formally verify atomicity properties in the event of unexpected/premature program termination, and to properly model program state updates caused by transaction roll-back (i.e. *undoing* updates). Indeed, the extended logic allowed

J. Misra, T. Nipkow, and E. Sekerinski (Eds.): FM 2006, LNCS 4085, pp. 444–459, 2006.
© Springer-Verlag Berlin Heidelberg 2006

us to prove many interesting properties about real JAVA CARD programs with the KeY system [7,15]. Although we have treated the transaction mechanism thoroughly in our extension to JAVA CARD DL, one particular detail was omitted, namely, two specific *non-atomic* native methods provided by the JAVA CARD API. The intuitive semantics of non-atomic methods seems to be straightforward—a non-atomic method simply excludes the updates it performs from any transaction that might be in progress. However, recent experimental studies [10] show that the intended semantics of JAVA CARD transactions, in particular transaction roll-back, and non-atomic methods is more complex than described in the official JAVA CARD platform documentation [18]. In this paper we present further extensions to JAVA CARD DL to accommodate the extended semantics of the transaction mechanism.

Non-atomic methods are rarely used in JAVA CARD programming, but certain security requirements actually necessitate the use of these methods. An often quoted example concerns PIN try counters. Such a counter is decremented each time a PIN code provided by the user is verified against the code stored on the smart card and the card "shuts down" if too many incorrect guesses are done. By calling the PIN verification routine inside a transaction and deliberately aborting that transaction, the update to the try counter would be rolled back together with all the other updates performed within the transaction. This would be a major security breach, giving a malicious user an infinite number of tries to check PIN validity (the try counter would never be decremented). To avoid such situation a non-atomic method is used to exclude the try counter decrement from the transaction mechanism. Thus, it is really important to be able to reason about non-atomic JAVA CARD methods so that similar security properties can be formally verified. We briefly discuss verification of such a property in Sect. 7.

Related Work. There exist numerous tools and formal systems to reason about JAVA programs on the source code level. Just to name the most important ones: ESC/JAVA2 [6] performs extended static checking of JAVA programs, the LOOP tool [12] employs a Hoare-like logic encoded in higher-order logic (PVS) [11], higher-order logic is also used to formalise a JAVA fragment in Isabelle [19] and in the KRAKATOA tool [13]. The Jive system [14] is based on an extended Hoare style calculus, Jack [4] on weakest precondition calculus, and KIV on yet another version of Dynamic Logic for JAVA CARD [17]. Despite the multiplicity of formal systems designed for JAVA CARD and other "small" JAVA dialects, it seems that (so far) only our framework can truly deal with all of JAVA CARD, including the intricate details of the transaction mechanism. The only other work that investigated JAVA CARD transactions is [9], however the proposed formalism has not been implemented in a tool. The same authors performed experimental studies of the JAVA CARD transaction mechanism [10] that we refer to in this paper.

Structure of the Paper. Sect. 2 and 3 give an overview of the KeY system and JAVA CARD DL, in Sect. 4 we describe the JAVA CARD transaction mechanism and non-atomic JAVA CARD methods. Sect. 5 gives a high-level description of how transactions are treated in JAVA CARD DL, then in Sect. 6 we extend this description to cover non-atomic methods with a sample of actual calculus rules. Finally, Sect. 7 discusses verification examples and Sect. 8 summarises the paper.

2   The KeY System

JAVA CARD DL has been designed to be the logical infrastructure of the KeY prover. The KeY prover is the core verification component of the KeY system[1] [1]—a tool that enhances a commercial software engineering tool with functionality for formal specification and deductive verification of object oriented programs to be used in real-world software development. Accordingly, the design principles for the software verification component of the KeY system are:

- The specification language should be usable by people who do not have years of training in formal methods. The Object Constraint Language (OCL), which is incorporated into current version of the Unified Modelling Language (UML), is one specification language that can be used for formal specification. The other language is JAVA Modelling Language (JML), which has recently become very popular among *formal* JAVA programmers.
- The programs that are verified should be written in a real object-oriented programming language. The KeY system supports most of sequential JAVA, and in particular the whole JAVA CARD standard. Since smart card applications are often safety and security critical, JAVA CARD seems to be a perfect target for formal verification.

Our recent research shows that the KeY system performs its job very well— verification of advanced security properties for industrial JAVA CARD applets of non-trivial size is highly feasible and time-wise very efficient [7,15]. In the KeY verification process the OCL or JML specifications are automatically translated into JAVA CARD DL proof obligations, whose validity can then be (in most part automatically) established with the KeY prover. Apart from OCL and JML, JAVA CARD DL can be used explicitly for writing specifications. In the following we briefly describe JAVA CARD DL.

3   JAVA CARD Dynamic Logic

Dynamic Logic [8] can be seen as an extension of Hoare logic. It is a first-order modal logic with modalities $[p]$ and $\langle p \rangle$ for every program p (p can be any sequence of JAVA CARD statements). In the semantics of these modalities a state w is accessible from the current state, if the program p terminates in w when started in the current state. The formula $[p]\phi$ expresses that ϕ holds in *all* final states of p, and $\langle p \rangle \phi$ expresses that ϕ holds in *some* final state of p. In versions of DL with a non-deterministic programming language there can be several such final states. Here, since JAVA CARD programs are deterministic, there is exactly one such state (if p terminates) or there is no such state (if p does not terminate).

---

[1] http://www.key-project.org

The formula $\phi \rightarrow \langle p \rangle \psi$ is valid if, for every state s satisfying precondition ϕ, a run of the program p starting in s terminates, and in the terminating state the postcondition ψ holds (total correctness). The formula $\phi \rightarrow [p]\psi$ expresses the same, except that termination of p is not required, i.e. ψ must only hold *if* p terminates (partial correctness).

Syntax of JAVA CARD DL. As said above, a dynamic logic is constructed by extending some non-dynamic logic with modal operators $\langle \cdot \rangle$ and $[\cdot]$. The non-dynamic base logic of our DL is a typed first-order predicate logic. We do not describe in detail what the types of our logic are (basically they are identical with the JAVA types) nor how exactly terms and formulae are built. The definitions can be found in [2]. Note that terms (which we often call "logical terms" in the following) are different from JAVA expressions—they never have side effects.

In order to reduce the complexity of the programs occurring in DL formulae, we introduce the notion of a *program context*. The context consists of API and any additional classes/interfaces used in the program. Syntax and semantics of DL formulae are then defined w.r.t. a given context; the programs in DL formulae are simply blocks of executable JAVA code (method bodies). Programs occurring in DL formulae can also contain special constructs not available in plain JAVA CARD, whose purpose is, among other things, the handling of method calls and the transaction mechanism. For transactions, e.g. JAVA CARD DL recognises special "low-level" transaction statements bT, cT, and aT, which are triggered by the "high-level" API transaction methods `beginTransaction`, etc.

Semantics of JAVA CARD DL. The semantics of a program p is a state transition, i.e. it assigns to each state s the set of all states that can be reached by running p starting in s. Since JAVA CARD is deterministic, that set either contains exactly one state (if p terminates normally) or is empty (if p does not terminate or terminates abruptly). For formulae ϕ that do not contain programs, the notion of ϕ being satisfied by a state is defined as usual in first-order logic. A formula $\langle p \rangle \phi$ is satisfied by a state s if the program p, when started in s, terminates normally in a state s' in which ϕ is satisfied.

As mentioned above, we consider programs that terminate abruptly to be non-terminating. Thus, e.g. $\langle \texttt{throw x;} \rangle \phi$ is unsatisfiable for all ϕ. Nevertheless, it is possible to express and (if true) prove that a program p terminates abruptly by a simple program transformation. For example, the formula

$$\texttt{exc = null} \rightarrow \langle \texttt{try\{}p\texttt{\}catch(Exception e)\{exc = e;\}} \rangle (\neg(\texttt{exc = null}) \wedge \phi)$$

is true in a state s if and only if the program p, when started in s, terminates abruptly by throwing an exception and condition ϕ is satisfied. The `try-catch` block around program p ensures that the program fragment inside the modality always terminates in a non-abrupt fashion. The postcondition requires p to throw an exception (as otherwise no object is bound to `exc`) and formula ϕ can be established in the abrupt termination state (in fact, this is how JML `signals` clauses are represented in JAVA CARD DL).

Sequents are notated following the scheme $\phi_1, \ldots, \phi_m \vdash \psi_1, \ldots, \psi_n$ which has the same semantics as the formula $(\phi_1 \wedge \ldots \wedge \phi_m) \rightarrow (\psi_1 \vee \ldots \vee \psi_n)$.

Strong Invariants. On top of the notion of total (resp. partial) correctness stipulated by the $\langle \cdot \rangle$ (resp. $[\cdot]$) modality, JAVA CARD DL also allows expressing strong invariant properties. A strong invariant specifies that a certain property should be maintained *throughout* the execution of the program (in all the intermediate computation states), which in JAVA CARD DL is expressed with the throughout modality $[\![\cdot]\!]$. This allows one to prove that a given property is preserved even when a premature termination (e.g. card *tear*) of the program occurs. Such properties were the motivation to include support for the transaction mechanism in JAVA CARD DL in the first place [3]. The semantics of the $[\![\cdot]\!]$ modality relies heavily on the notion of atomicity in JAVA CARD, which is affected by non-atomic methods. Because of this, small subtleties are introduced to the formal semantics of $[\![\cdot]\!]$ and a few extra calculus rules are needed. However, in principle, the formalisation for the $[\![\cdot]\!]$ (as well as $[\cdot]$) modality in the context of non-atomic methods does not differ substantially from the formalisation of $\langle \cdot \rangle$, thus, we are not going to discuss the rules for $[\![\cdot]\!]$. We stress though, that we did implement necessary rules for $[\![\cdot]\!]$ and tested them on relevant examples.

State Updates. We allow *updates* of the form $\{x := t\}$ resp. $\{o.a := t\}$ to be attached to terms and formulae, where x is a program variable, o is a term denoting an object with attribute a, and t is a term. The intuitive meaning of an update is that the term or formula that it is attached to is to be evaluated after changing the state accordingly, i.e. $\{x := t\}\phi$ has the same semantics as $\langle \mathtt{x = t;} \rangle \phi$.

Rules of the Sequent Calculus. Here we present two sample rules to give the reader intuition of how the JAVA CARD DL sequent calculus works.

Notation. The rules of our calculus operate on the first *active* statement p of a program $\pi\,p\,\omega$. The non-active prefix π consists of, e.g. an arbitrary sequence of opening braces "{", labels, beginnings "try{" of try-catch blocks. The prefix is needed to keep track of the blocks that the (first) active command is part of, such that the abruptly terminating statements **throw**, **return**, **break**, and **continue** can be handled appropriately.[2] The postfix ω denotes the "rest" of the program, i.e. everything except the non-active prefix and the part of the program the rule operates on. For example, if a rule is applied to the following JAVA block operating on its first active command i=0; then the non-active prefix π and the "rest" ω are the marked parts of the block:

$$\underbrace{\mathtt{l:\{try\{}}_{\pi} \mathtt{\ i=0;}\ \underbrace{\mathtt{j=0;\ \}catch(Exception\ e)\{\ k=0;\ \}\}}}_{\omega}$$

---

[2] In DL versions for simple artificial programming languages, where no prefixes are needed, any formula of the form $\langle pq \rangle \phi$ can be replaced by $\langle p \rangle \langle q \rangle \phi$ with a sequential composition rule. In our calculus, splitting of $\langle \pi pq\omega \rangle \phi$ into $\langle \pi p \rangle \langle q\omega \rangle \phi$ is not possible (unless the prefix π is empty) because πp is not a valid program; and the formula $\langle \pi p\omega \rangle \langle \pi q\omega \rangle \phi$ cannot be used either because its semantics is in general different from that of $\langle \pi pq\omega \rangle \phi$.

In the following rule schemata, $\mathcal{U}$ stands for an arbitrary list of updates, $\mathcal{U}\{u\}$ for an update u appended to $\mathcal{U}$, and $\mathcal{U}\phi$ for ϕ evaluated by applying updates in $\mathcal{U}$.

The Rule for if. As the first simple example, we present the rule for the if statement:

$$\frac{\Gamma,\ \mathcal{U}(b = \mathsf{TRUE})\ \vdash\ \mathcal{U}\langle\pi\,p\,\omega\rangle\phi \qquad \Gamma,\ \mathcal{U}(b = \mathsf{FALSE})\ \vdash\ \mathcal{U}\langle\pi\,q\,\omega\rangle\phi}{\Gamma\ \vdash\ \mathcal{U}\langle\pi\,\mathtt{if(b)}\,p\,\mathtt{else}\,q\,\omega\rangle\phi} \qquad (\mathrm{R}1)$$

The rule has two premises, which correspond to the two cases of the if statement. The semantics of this rule is that, if the two premises hold in a state, then the conclusion is true in that state. In particular, if the two premises are valid, then the conclusion is valid. In practice, rules are applied from bottom to top: from the old proof obligation new proof obligations are derived. As the if rule demonstrates, applying a rule from bottom to top corresponds to a symbolic execution of the program to be verified. For every JAVA programming construct there is such a symbolic execution rule, later we explain how transactions are handled rather in terms of symbolic execution, than by discussing all of the relevant calculus rules.

The Assignment Rule and Handling State Updates. The assignment rule:

$$\frac{\Gamma\ \vdash\ \mathcal{U}\{\mathtt{loc} := \mathtt{expr}\}\langle\pi\,\omega\rangle\phi}{\Gamma\ \vdash\ \mathcal{U}\langle\pi\,\mathtt{loc}\ \mathtt{=}\ \mathtt{expr;}\,\omega\rangle\phi} \qquad (\mathrm{R}2)$$

adds the assignment to the list of updates $\mathcal{U}$. Of course, this does not solve the problem of computing the effect of an assignment, which is particularly complicated in JAVA because of aliasing. This problem is postponed and solved by rules for simplifying updates that are attached to formulae whenever possible (without branching the proof). The assignment rule can only be used if the expression `expr` is a logical term. Otherwise, other rules have to be applied first to evaluate `expr` (as that evaluation may have side effects). For example, these rules replace the formula $\langle\mathtt{x}\ \mathtt{=}\ \mathtt{i++;}\rangle\phi$ with $\langle\mathtt{x}\ \mathtt{=}\ \mathtt{i;}\ \mathtt{i}\ \mathtt{=}\ \mathtt{i}\ \mathtt{+}\ \mathtt{1;}\rangle\phi$.

4   JAVA CARD Transaction Mechanism

The memory model of JAVA CARD [5,18] differs slightly from JAVA's model. In smart cards there are two kinds of writable memory: persistent memory (EEP-ROM), which holds its contents between card sessions, and transient memory (RAM), whose contents disappear when power loss occurs, in particular, when the card is removed from the card reader (card *tear*). Thus every memory element in JAVA CARD (variable or object field) is either persistent or transient. Based on the JAVA CARD language specification the following rules can be given:

 - All objects (including the reference to the currently running applet, this, and arrays) are created in persistent memory. Thus, in JAVA CARD all assignments like `o.attr = 2`, `this.a = 3`, and `arr[i] = 4` have permanent character, i.e. the assigned values will be kept after the card loses power.

- A programmer can create an array with transient elements by calling a certain method from the JAVA CARD API (e.g. JCSystem.makeTransientByte-Array), but currently there is no possibility to make objects (fields) other than array elements transient.
- All local variables are transient.

The distinction between persistent and transient objects is very important since these two types of objects are treated in a different way by JAVA CARD's transaction mechanism. The following are the JAVA CARD API calls for transactions:

- JCSystem.beginTransaction() begins an atomic transaction. From this point on, all assignments to fields of persistent objects are executed conditionally, while assignments to transient variables or transient array elements are executed unconditionally.[3]
- JCSystem.commitTransaction() commits the transaction. All conditional assignments are committed (in one atomic step).
- JCSystem.abortTransaction() aborts the transaction. All the conditional assignments are rolled back to the state in which the transaction started (at least that is what [18] suggests, we explain what really happens shortly). Assignments to transient data remain unchanged (as if there had not been a transaction in progress).

Considering the persistent objects, the whole program block inside the transaction is seen by the outside world as if it were executed in one atomic step, completely (upon commit), or nor at all (upon abort). A transaction can be aborted explicitly by the programmer, but also implicitly by the JAVA CARD Runtime Environment, when a transaction cannot be completed due to lack of resources or other unexpected program termination (e.g. card *tear*). In the first case, the JAVA CARD program continues its execution with the assignments performed inside the transaction rolled back, in the second case the program is terminated immediately and updates are rolled back during transaction recovery process next time the JAVA CARD applet is initialised. The possibility of an explicit transaction abort has important consequences for the design of the logic to handle transactions; in the logic aborting a transaction can be seen as *undoing assignment* and needs appropriate handling.

Transactions do not have to be nested properly with other program constructs, e.g. a transaction can be started within one method and committed within another method. However, transactions must be nested properly with each other. In the current version of JAVA CARD (2.2.2) the nesting depth of transactions is restricted to 1—only one transaction can be active at a time.

On top of that, JAVA CARD API provides the programmer with two native *non-atomic* methods: arrayCopyNonAtomic and arrayFillNonAtomic from the

---

[3] Terms "conditional and unconditional assignments" that are used in the official JAVA CARD documentation may be a little bit misleading in the context of this work. For our purposes, unconditional assignment should be interpreted as "irreversible" or "immediately permanent", while conditional assignments should be interpreted as "assignments made on copies", so that they can be reverted.

Util class. In [10], based on extensive experiments performed with JAVA CARD devices, the behaviour of the two methods is thoroughly analysed. Here we only present the highlights that motivated our work.

Methods arrayCopyNonAtomic and arrayFillNonAtomic copy resp. reset an array, bypassing any transaction that might be in progress, i.e. any changes made to the array will not be rolled-back. We have already motivated the need for exclusion of certain persistent memory locations from the transaction mechanism with the PIN try counter example in the introduction.[4] In the current version, JAVA CARD only allows such non-atomic updates for elements of byte arrays, and hence there are only two API methods to take care of non-atomic updates. The consequence for our logic is the following. Apart from committing or aborting, a transaction can also be *suspended* to perform unconditional updates to persistent array elements and later *resumed* to continue updating persistent data conditionally, following the rules of the transaction mechanism again. With the notion of transaction suspension it is also possible to incorporate other non-atomic methods that may appear in future versions of JAVA CARD.

This, however, is not all. The experiments in [10] show that the notion of transaction roll-back is under-specified in the official JAVA CARD documentation [18].[5] Consider two short pieces of JAVA CARD code in Fig. 1. Persistent array a stores elements of type byte and the arrayFillNonAtomic method has the following signature:

```
/** Fill elements off..off+len-1 of bArray with value */
public static void native arrayFillNonAtomic(
  byte[] bArray, short off, short len, byte value);
```

Thus, the call to arrayFillNonAtomic in the two examples is equivalent to a[0] = 2, with the difference that it bypasses the transaction mechanism. The main difference in the two programs is the value of a[0] after the transaction abort. In the program on the left, a[0] is rolled-back to 0, the value it was assigned before the transaction was started. In the program on the right, a[0] is rolled back to 2, the most recent value it was assigned before the first conditional update happened. To put it in a simpler form, the value to be restored in case of an abort is recorded just before the first conditional update happens, and not when the transaction is started. This is not what the official JAVA CARD documentation would make us believe, it would suggests that the value of a[0]

---

[4] Another reason for introducing native, non-atomic methods for array operations is efficiency, which in the context of this work is not relevant.

[5] Actually, parts of this *under-specification* are deliberate to account for nondeterministic behaviour of some JAVA CARD devices w.r.t. non-atomic methods [10]. Despite this liberal approach there still exist JAVA CARD devices that do not implement non-atomic methods in a correct way—they still go beyond the level of nondeterminism allowed by the official JAVA CARD specification [10]. In our formal model we assume that cards are well behaved (deterministic). Although we present one fixed approach in this paper, the underlying principles of our extension allow us to easily formalise other variants of the transaction model, including a nondeterministic (random) behaviour allowed by the official specification.

```
a[0] = 0;                          a[0] = 0;
beginTransaction();                beginTransaction();
  a[0] = 1;                          arrayFillNonAtomic(a,0,1,2);
  arrayFillNonAtomic(a,0,1,2);       a[0] = 1;
abortTransaction();                abortTransaction();
```

Fig. 1. Two transaction roll-back examples

should be 0 in both cases. To properly handle the transaction mechanism, our extended logic should distinguish the two situations described above.

5 Symbolic Execution of the Transaction Mechanism

Before we describe how non-atomic methods are handled in JAVA CARD DL, we explain how the basic transaction mechanism is modelled [3]. The main idea is to partly imitate what is actually happening in the JAVA CARD Virtual Machine (or, what we *imagine* is happening); generally, when a transaction is in progress, instead of modifying the original data (unconditional update), the updates are performed on the backup copies of that data (conditional update).

When a call to `beginTransaction` is encountered during the symbolic execution, program analysis (i.e. the proof) is split into two branches. In the first branch the program is analysed with the assumption that the transaction will commit, in the second branch it is assumed that the transaction will be aborted. Later, when an `abortTransaction` statement is encountered on the commit branch, the branch is simply discarded—the symbolic execution is focused on the abort branch. The same exact thing happens in the opposite situation, i.e. when a `commitTransaction` is encountered on the abort branch. On the calculus level, a rule for `beginTransaction` splits the proof into two branches, and each branch (more precisely, the modality containing the program) is marked with an appropriate tag (TRC: or TRA:) saying what kind of transaction finish is expected. Depending on the tag different rules for assignments are applied. Making the distinction between the commit and abort case is very helpful in handling the assignments inside the transaction. On the first branch, since we assume that the transaction is going to commit, we do not have to worry about keeping the backup copies of the modified data, we can commit all the changes as we encounter them. Conversely, on the abort branch, we know that the assignments eventually (upon encountering `abortTransaction`) will have to be rolled back, so we can choose not to perform them in the first place.[6] Here, however, we encounter a complication: in JAVA CARD only the assignments to the persistent data are rolled back, the assignments to transient data are always performed unconditionally. Moreover, conditionally updated persistent values may be used to update transient variables. Thus, we cannot simply ignore the assignments inside the transactions. Instead, we operate on backup (also called shadow) copies

---

[6] The two branches correspond to resp. *optimistic* or *pessimistic* approach usually taken in implementing a transaction mechanism.

of the persistent data, keeping the original persistent data unmodified, while the updates to transient objects are always performed on the original data.

`this.a = v1;`	`this.a = v1;`
`this.ar[0] = v2;`	`this.ar[0] = v2;`
`int i = 0;`	`i = 0;`
`beginTransaction();`	*The symbolic execution splits into two branches, here we ignore the 'commit' branch, which upon encountering* `abort` *will be discarded. The fact that a transaction was started is recorded.*
`this.a++;`	*First assignment to* `this.a` *inside transaction, create a new backup copy of* `this.a`: `this.a' = this.a' + 1;` $\rightarrow$ `this.a' = this.a + 1;` $\rightarrow$ `this.a' = v1 + 1;`

`this.ar[0]++;`	`if(this.ar.<transient>)` *// false*
	 `this.ar[0] = this.ar[0] + 1;` `else`
	 `this.ar[0]' = this.ar[0]' + 1;` $\rightarrow$
	 Here, `this.ar[0]'` *also not initialised, use* `this.ar[0]` *on the RHS:*
	 `this.ar[0]' = v2 + 1;`

`i = this.a +` `    this.ar[0];`	*i is local (transient), update unconditionally, on the RHS use already initialised backup copies of* `this.a` *and* `this.ar[0]`: `i = this.a' + this.ar[0]';` $\rightarrow$ `i = v1 + v2 + 2;`
`abortTransaction();`	*Transaction aborted, back to non-transaction mode.*

Fig. 2. Symbolic execution of a Java Card transaction

Let us illustrate this idea with an example in Fig. 2. On the left we give an actual Java Card program, on the right we explain how the symbolic execution (i.e. how the program is interpreted in Java Card DL) of the code on the left proceeds. The prime symbol ' in combination with the attribute (resp. array element) access operator . denotes accessing backup copy of a given attribute (resp. array element) instead of the original value. The arrow $\rightarrow$ represents subsequent steps in the symbolic execution. If a backup value is required during the evaluation but is not known (has not yet been assigned) the original value is used. The `<transient>` field is assigned to every array object in the Java Card DL model and indicates whether a given array is transient or persistent. Depending on this, the elements of such an array are updated conditionally or unconditionally, following the specification of Java Card transactions. Here we assume that the fact that `this.ar` is persistent (`this.ar.<transient>` is false) is already present in the program analysis. At the end of this symbolic execution it can be established that i = v1 + v2 + 2, but the persistent data, `this.a` and `this.ar[0]`, is not affected, the values are equal to v1 and v2, respectively. By performing the assignments on the backup copies, the effect of a transaction roll-back is achieved in the Java Card DL execution model. To sum up, inside a transaction that is assumed to abort, assignments involving persistent data are performed on copies of that data, so that the original values, used again after the abort, remain unchanged. Such specific assignment handling is taken care of specialised JAVA CARD DL calculus rules, which are applied on the (specially tagged for this purpose) abort branch of the proof. The actual rules are described in detail in [3]. In the next section we give a representative sample of these rules updated to accommodate the behaviour of non-atomic methods.

6   Non-atomic Methods in JAVA CARD DL

Assuming the transaction model just presented we now have to incorporate the semantics of the non-atomic JAVA CARD methods. What `arrayCopyNonAtomic` or `arrayFillNonAtomic` basically do is updating given array elements unconditionally, despite the fact there might be a transaction in progress—the transaction is *suspended* for the time of execution of a non-atomic method. Note, that we cannot assume that the transaction is simply finalised when a non-atomic method is executed, and then a new transaction is started—while the non-atomic method is executed all the conditional assignments executed before the non-atomic method was started are still in effect. When a non-atomic method is finished, the transaction is continued with all the conditional assignments recorded previously. Thus, we introduce the notion of transaction *suspending* and *resuming* to our JAVA CARD DL model.

The symbolic execution model of transactions is affected in the following way. In the commit branch non-atomic methods are not treated in any special way; since we assume that the transaction will commit, it means that all the assignments inside a transaction, including the ones performed by non-atomic methods, will be committed. In the abort branch however, the assignments performed by non-atomic methods should be committed (despite aborted transaction) and all the other assignments should be committed or aborted following the regular JAVA CARD transaction rules. Thus, for the time of execution of a non-atomic method we have to inform the symbolic execution mechanism that the transaction is suspended. The corresponding JAVA CARD DL rule is the following:

$$\frac{\Gamma \vdash \mathcal{U}\langle \mathsf{TRSUSP}{:}\pi\,\omega\rangle\phi}{\Gamma \vdash \mathcal{U}\langle \mathsf{TRA}{:}\pi\,\texttt{suspendTransaction;}\,\omega\rangle\phi} \tag{R3}$$

The meaning of the rule is this: on the abort (TRA: tag) proof branch upon encountering the suspend transaction statement (this statement is only present in the logic, it is triggered by a call to non-atomic method) mark the branch (modality) with a tag indicating that the transaction is suspended, so that corresponding "non-atomic" assignment rules can be applied. When a non-atomic method is finished, transaction resume statement is triggered and normal transaction processing is again in effect:

$$\frac{\Gamma \vdash \mathcal{U}\langle \mathsf{TRA}{:}\pi\,\omega\rangle\phi}{\Gamma \vdash \mathcal{U}\langle \mathsf{TRSUSP}{:}\pi\,\texttt{resumeTransaction;}\,\omega\rangle\phi} \tag{R4}$$

The idea of symbolic execution of a non-atomic method based on the notion of transaction suspension is illustrated with an example in Fig. 3. As with the

previous example, it can be established that after the execution of the program
i = v1 + v2 + 2 and this.a = v1 (here the update was rolled-back), but the
value of this.ar[0] is v2 + 1—it has been unconditionally updated inside a
transaction through transaction suspension that took effect for the time of symbolic execution of arrayFillNonAtomic.

this.a = v1;	this.a = v1;
this.ar[0] = v2;	this.ar[0] = v2;
int i = 0;	i = 0;
beginTransaction();	*Transaction started, transaction mode for assignments.*
this.a++;	this.a' = this.a' + 1; → this.a' = this.a + 1; → this.a' = v1 + 1;
arrayFillNonAtomic(this.ar, 0, 1, this.ar[0]+1);	*Transaction is suspended, the code executed by arrayFill-NonAtomic is interpreted as follows. On the LHS update the original (unconditional assignment), on the RHS use backup copies where possible:* this.ar[0] = this.ar[0]' + 1; this.ar[0] = this.ar[0] + 1; → this.ar[0] = v2 + 1;
i = this.a + this.ar[0];	*Non-atomic call is finished, resume transaction mode. Here* this.ar[0]' *still not initialised, use* this.ar[0]: i = this.a' + this.ar[0]'; i = this.a' + this.ar[0]; → i = v1 + v2 + 2;
abortTransaction();	*Transaction aborted, back to non-transaction mode.*

Fig. 3. Symbolic execution of a non-atomic method

6.1 Transaction Roll-Back

Finally we have to adapt our model to properly handle transaction roll-back. In
Sect. 4 we have already discussed how the values of persistent data are rolled
back based on recording values just before the first conditional assignment is
executed. Hence, our symbolic execution needs to take care of two more things:

- When an assignment to an array element is done inside a transaction, but
  not inside a non-atomic method, then we need to record the fact that an
  array element has been conditionally assigned. In our model, this information is kept in a boolean array <trinit> associated with each array (similarly to the <transient> attribute that indicates the persistency type of
  an array). Unless explicitly initialised, a.<trinit>[x] always defaults to
  false (the update simplification rules of the JAVA CARD DL take care of
  this).
- When transaction is suspended, before we make an assignment to an array
  element, we first have to check whether it has been conditionally updated,
  and depending on the result do a conditional or unconditional assignment.

The corresponding JAVA CARD DL rules are the following. First the rule for
the abort branch that records the fact that a given array element has been
conditionally assigned and does the actual assignment:

$$\Gamma, \; \mathcal{U}(\texttt{arr.<transient>} = \textsf{TRUE}) \; \vdash \; \mathcal{U}\{\texttt{arr[e]} := \texttt{expr}'\}\langle \textsf{TRA}{:}\pi\,\omega\rangle\phi$$

$$\frac{\Gamma, \; \mathcal{U}(\texttt{arr.<transient>} = \textsf{FALSE}) \; \vdash}{\mathcal{U}\{\texttt{arr.<trinit>[e]} := \textsf{TRUE}, \texttt{arr[e]}' := \texttt{expr}'\}\langle \textsf{TRA}{:}\pi\,\omega\rangle\phi}{\Gamma \; \vdash \; \mathcal{U}\langle \textsf{TRA}{:}\pi\,\texttt{arr[e]} = \texttt{expr}; \omega\rangle\phi} \qquad \text{(R5)}$$

For transient arrays, the assignment of the array element is always unconditional (first premise), for persistent arrays (`arr.<transient>` = FALSE), record the information that the given array element has been initialised (`arr.<trinit>[e]` := TRUE) and perform a conditional assignment to that array element (`arr[e]'` := `expr'`). As with the regular assignment rule (R2), `expr` has to be free of side effects. The prime operator applied to `expr` makes sure that the backup copies are used for all relevant subexpressions occurring in `expr`.

When a transaction is suspended, the rule that takes care of assigning a value to an array element conditionally or unconditionally depending on whether the array element has been already initialised takes the following form:

$$\Gamma, \; \mathcal{U}(\texttt{arr.<trinit>[e]} = \textsf{FALSE}) \; \vdash \; \mathcal{U}\{\texttt{arr[e]} := \texttt{expr}'\}\langle \textsf{TRSUSP}{:}\pi\,\omega\rangle\phi$$

$$\frac{\Gamma, \; \mathcal{U}(\texttt{arr.<trinit>[e]} = \textsf{TRUE}) \; \vdash \; \mathcal{U}\{\texttt{arr[e]}' := \texttt{expr}'\}\langle \textsf{TRSUSP}{:}\pi\,\omega\rangle\phi}{\Gamma \; \vdash \; \mathcal{U}\langle \textsf{TRSUSP}{:}\pi\,\texttt{arr[e]} = \texttt{expr}; \omega\rangle\phi}$$

$$\text{(R6)}$$

The interpretation of the rule is this: inside a suspended transaction, if an array element has not yet been conditionally assigned (`arr.<trinit>[e]` = FALSE), update it unconditionally (`arr[e]` := `expr'`), if it has been already conditionally assigned (`arr.<trinit>[e]` = TRUE), keep the assignments conditional (`arr[e]'` := `expr'`).

These two rules follow the informal description of transactions and non-atomic methods given in Sect. 4. To clarify this, Fig. 4 explains the symbolic execution of the two programs in Fig. 1. Finally, we should note that only the rules for transaction triggering statements and assignments inside a transaction are specific in the context of non-atomic methods, the rules for other programming

a[0] = 0;	a[0] = 0;
Transaction started, conditional updates.	*Transaction started, conditional updates.*

a[0]' = 1;
a.<trinit>[0] = true;
	Transaction suspended, the execution of ***arrayFillNonAtomic*** *unfolds to:*
	  if(a.<trinit>[0]) // *false*
	  a[0]'=2; else a[0]=2; → a[0]=2;
	Transaction resumed.

Transaction suspended, the execution of ***arrayFillNonAtomic*** *unfolds to:*
  if(a.<trinit>[0]) // *true*
  a[0]'=2; else a[0]=2; → a[0]'=2;
Transaction resumed.
	a[0]' = 1;
	a.<trinit>[0] = true;

Transaction aborted, a[0] is 0.	*Transaction aborted, a[0] is 2.*

Fig. 4. Symbolic execution for the transaction roll-back

constructs (e.g. the `if` statement) are the same as in the basic JAVA CARD DL calculus.

7 Examples

All the rules for the extended JAVA CARD DL to handle non-atomic methods have been implemented in the KeY prover. For the test, we verified the reference implementation of the `check` method from the `OwnerPIN` API class. The prop-

```
JCSystem.transactionDepth = 0 ∧ ¬(pin = null) ∧ ¬(pin._triesLeft = null) ∧
... rest of the OwnerPIN basic class specification (class invariant)
_triesLeft@pre = pin._triesLeft[0] ∧ result = −1 →
  ⟨ try {
      JCSystem.beginTransaction();
        if(pin.check(pin,offset,length)) result = 1; else result = 0;
        if(b) JCSystem.abortTransaction();
        else  JCSystem.commitTransaction();
    }catch(Exception ex) {}⟩(
      (_triesLeft@pre = 0 → result = 0 ∧ pin._triesLeft[0] = 0) ∧
      (_triesLeft@pre > 0 → (result = 0 →
          pin._triesLeft[0] = _triesLeft@pre − 1)))
```

Fig. 5. JAVA CARD DL specification of the `check` method

```
¬(a = null) ∧ a.<transient> = FALSE →       ¬(a = null) ∧ a.<transient> = FALSE →
  ⟨a[0] = 0;                                   ⟨a[0] = 0;
  beginTransaction();                          beginTransaction();
    a[0] = 1;                                    arrayFillNonAtomic(a,0,1,2);
    arrayFillNonAtomic(a,0,1,2);                 a[0] = 1;
  abortTransaction();⟩(a[0] = 0)             abortTransaction();⟩(a[0] = 2)
```

Fig. 6. JAVA CARD DL specifications for the two transaction roll-back examples

erty under consideration is the one we mentioned in the introduction: the `check` method should always decrement the try counter (given of course the PIN is not correct and the try counter is not already 0) regardless of any transaction (one about to commit or abort) that might be in progress or any exception that may occur. The JAVA CARD DL formula specifying this is presented in Fig. 5. Since the value of the variable b in the program inside the modality is not specified, both possibilities (the transaction will commit or abort) have to be checked, thus we establish the desired property. This formula is proved automatically by the KeY prover in a matter of seconds on a regular Linux desktop computer. Of course, the smaller examples that we have discussed in the paper are also verifiable with the KeY prover. Recall the two programs from Fig. 1. The corresponding JAVA CARD DL formulae (abbreviated) describing their behaviour are presented in Fig. 6—both are quickly discharged by the KeY prover.

8 Summary

We have presented an extension to JAVA CARD Dynamic Logic to handle JAVA CARD non-atomic methods—methods that allow the programmer to exclude updates to persistent data from the transaction mechanism. Although there are only two such methods in the JAVA CARD API, they are of critical importance when certain security issues for smart card applications are considered, as we argued based on the PIN try counter example. Although many people have focused on program verification for JAVA CARD as interesting, small but real, language [12,9,13,14,4,17], JAVA CARD DL with the extension we have presented here is the first complete program logic for all of JAVA CARD. Due to space restrictions we only discussed a small, but representative sample of the actual JAVA CARD DL calculus rules, however the whole set of rules to deal with non-atomic methods will soon be available in [16]. All the rules have been implemented in the KeY prover and we showed examples of programs that can be verified (automatically) using the extended logic.

Acknowledgements. This research is supported by the research program Sentinels (http://www.sentinels.nl). Sentinels is financed by the Technology Foundation STW, the Netherlands, Organisation for Scientific Research (NWO), and the Dutch Ministry of Economic Affairs. We would also like to thank anonymous reviewers and Erik Poll for their helpful comments.

References

1. W. Ahrendt, T. Baar, B. Beckert, R. Bubel, M. Giese, R. Hähnle, W. Menzel, W. Mostowski, A. Roth, S. Schlager, and P. H. Schmitt. The KeY tool. *Software and Systems Modeling*, 4(1):32–54, February 2005.
2. B. Beckert. A dynamic logic for the formal verification of JAVA CARD programs. In I. Attali and T. Jensen, editors, *JAVA on Smart Cards: Programming and Security. Revised Papers, JAVA CARD 2000, International Workshop, Cannes, France*, volume 2041 of *LNCS*, pages 6–24. Springer, 2001.
3. B. Beckert and W. Mostowski. A program logic for handling JAVA CARD's transaction mechanism. In M. Pezzè, editor, *Proceedings, Fundamental Approaches to Software Engineering (FASE) Conference 2003, Warsaw, Poland*, volume 2621 of *LNCS*, pages 246–260. Springer, April 2003.
4. L. Burdy, A. Requet, and J.-L. Lanet. JAVA applet correctness: A developer-oriented approach. In *Proceedings, Formal Methods Europe 2003*, volume 2805 of *LNCS*, pages 422–439. Springer, 2003.
5. Z. Chen. *JAVA CARD Technology for Smart Cards: Architecture and Programmer's Guide*. JAVA Series. Addison-Wesley, June 2000.
6. C. Flanagan, K. R. M. Leino, M. Lillibridge, G. Nelson, J. B. Saxe, and R. Stata. Extended static checking for JAVA. In *Proceedings, ACM SIGPLAN 2002 Conference on Programming Language Design and Implementation, Berlin*, pages 234–245. ACM Press, 2002.

7. R. Hähnle and W. Mostowski. Verification of safety properties in the presence of transactions. In G. Barthe and M. Huisman, editors, *Proceedings, Construction and Analysis of Safe, Secure and Interoperable Smart devices (CASSIS'04) Workshop*, volume 3362 of *LNCS*, pages 151–171. Springer, 2005.

8. D. Harel, D. Kozen, and J. Tiuryn. *Dynamic Logic*. MIT Press, 2000.

9. E. Hubbers and E. Poll. Reasoning about card tears and transactions in JAVA CARD. In *Fundamental Approaches to Software Engineering (FASE'2004)*, Barcelona, Spain, volume 2984 of *LNCS*, pages 114–128. Springer, 2004.

10. E. Hubbers and E. Poll. Transactions and non-atomic API calls in JAVA CARD: Specification ambiguity and strange implementation behaviours. Deptartment of Computer Science NIII-R0438, Radboud University Nijmegen, 2004.

11. M. Huisman and B. Jacobs. JAVA program verification via a Hoare logic with abrupt termination. In *Proceedings, Fundamental Approaches to Software Engineering (FASE 2000)*, volume 1783 of *LNCS*, pages 284–303. Springer, 2000.

12. B. Jacobs and E. Poll. JAVA program verification at Nijmegen: Developments and perspective. In *Software Security – Theories and Systems: Second Mext-NSF-JSPS International Symposium, ISSS 2003, Tokyo, Japan, November 4–6, 2003. Revised Papers*, volume 3233 of *LNCS*, pages 134–153. Springer, 2003.

13. C. Marché, C. Paulin-Mohring, and X. Urbain. The KRAKATOA tool for certification of JAVA/JAVA CARD programs annotated in JML. *Journal of Logic and Algebraic Programming*, 58(1–2):89–106, 2004.

14. J. Meyer and A. Poetzsch-Heffter. An architecture for interactive program provers. In S. Graf and M. Schwartzbach, editors, *Tools and Algorithms for the Construction and Analysis of Systems: 6th International Conference, TACAS 2000, Berlin, Germany*, volume 1785 of *LNCS*, pages 63–77. Springer, April 2000.

15. W. Mostowski. Formalisation and verification of JAVA CARD security properties in Dynamic Logic. In M. Cerioli, editor, *Proceedings, Fundamental Approaches to Software Engineering (FASE) Conference 2005, Edinburgh, Scotland*, volume 3442 of *LNCS*, pages 357–371. Springer, April 2005.

16. W. Mostowski. *The KeY Book*, chapter 9. From Sequential JAVA to JAVA CARD. Springer, 2006. To appear.

17. K. Stenzel. A formally verified calculus for full JAVA CARD. In C. Rattray, S. Maharaj, and C. Shankland, editors, *Proceedings, Algebraic Methodology and Software Technology 2004, Stirling, Scotland*, volume 3116 of *LNCS*. Springer, July 2004.

18. Sun Microsystems, Inc., Santa Clara, California, USA. *JAVA CARD 2.2.1 Runtime Environment Specification*, Oct. 2003.

19. D. von Oheimb. *Analyzing JAVA in Isabelle/HOL*. PhD thesis, Institut für Informatik, Technische Universität München, January 2001.

Formal Verification of a C Compiler Front-End

Sandrine Blazy, Zaynah Dargaye, and Xavier Leroy

INRIA Rocquencourt, 78153 Le Chesnay, France
{Sandrine.Blazy, Zaynah.Dargaye, Xavier.Leroy}@inria.fr

Abstract. This paper presents the formal verification of a compiler front-end that translates a subset of the C language into the Cminor intermediate language. The semantics of the source and target languages as well as the translation between them have been written in the specification language of the Coq proof assistant. The proof of observational semantic equivalence between the source and generated code has been machine-checked using Coq. An executable compiler was obtained by automatic extraction of executable Caml code from the Coq specification of the translator, combined with a certified compiler back-end generating PowerPC assembly code from Cminor, described in previous work.

1   Introduction

Formal methods in general and program proof in particular are increasingly being applied to safety-critical software. These applications create a strong need for on-machine formalization and verification of programming language semantics and tools such as compilers, type-checkers and static analyzers. In particular, formal operational semantics are required to validate the logic of programs (e.g. axiomatic semantics) used to reason about programs. As for tools, the formal certification of compilers—that is, a proof that the generated executable code behaves as prescribed by the semantics of the source program—is needed to ensure that the guarantees obtained by formal verification of the source program carry over to the executable code.

For high-level programming languages such as Java and functional languages, there exists a considerable body of on-machine formalizations and verifications of operational semantics and programming tools such as compilers and bytecode verifiers. Despite being more popular for writing critical embedded software, lower-level languages such as C have attracted less interest: several formal semantics for various subsets of C have been published, but few have been carried on machine. (See section 5 for a review.)

The work presented in this paper is part of an ongoing project that aims at developing a realistic compiler for the C language and formally verifying that it preserves the semantics of the programs being compiled. A previous paper [8] describes the verification, using the Coq proof assistant, of the back-end of this compiler, which generates moderately optimized PowerPC assembly code from a low-level, imperative intermediate language called Cminor. The present paper reports on the development and proof of semantic preservation in Coq of a C

J. Misra, T. Nipkow, and E. Sekerinski (Eds.): FM 2006, LNCS 4085, pp. 460–475, 2006.
© Springer-Verlag Berlin Heidelberg 2006

front-end for this compiler: a translator from Clight, a subset of the C language, to Cminor. To conduct the verification, a precise operational semantics of Clight was formalized in Coq. Clight features all C arithmetic types and operators, as well as arrays, pointers, pointers to functions, and all C control structures except `goto` and `switch`.

From a formal methods standpoint, this work is interesting in two respects. First, compilers are complex programs that perform sophisticated symbolic computations. Their formal verification is challenging, requiring difficult proofs by induction that are beyond the reach of many program provers. Second, proving the correctness of a compiler provides an indirect but original way to validate the semantics of the source language. It is relatively easy to formalize an operational semantics, but much harder to make sure that this semantics is correct and captures the intended meaning of programs. Typically, extensive testing and manual reviews of the semantics are needed. In our experience, proving the correctness of a translator to a simpler, lower-level language detects many small errors in the semantics of the source and target languages, and therefore generates additional confidence in both.

The remainder of this paper is organized as follows. Section 2 describes the Clight language and gives an overview of its operational semantics. Section 3 presents the translation from Clight to Cminor. Section 4 outlines the proof of correctness of this translation. Related work is discussed in section 5, followed by conclusions in section 6.

2   The Clight Language and Its Semantics

2.1   Abstract Syntax

The abstract syntax of Clight is given in figure 1. In the Coq formalization, this abstract syntax is presented as inductive data types, therefore achieving a deep embedding of Clight into Coq.

At the level of types, Clight features all the integral types of C, along with array, pointer and function types; `struct`, `union` and `typedef` types are currently omitted. The integral types fully specify the bit size of integers and floats, unlike the semi-specified C types `int`, `long`, etc.

Within expressions, all C operators are supported except those related to structs and unions. Expressions may have side-effects. All expressions and their sub-expressions are annotated by their static types. We write a^τ for the expression a carrying type τ. These types are necessary to determine the semantics of type-dependent operators such as the overloaded arithmetic operators. Similarly, combined arithmetic-assignment operators such as `+=` carry an additional type σ (as in $(a_1 +=^\sigma a_2)^\tau$) representing the result type of the arithmetic operation, which can differ from the type τ of the whole expression.

At the level of statements, all structured control statements of C (conditional, loops, `break`, `continue` and `return`) are supported, but not unstructured statements (`goto`, `switch`, `longjmp`). Two kinds of variables are allowed: global variables and local `auto` variables declared at the beginning of a function.

Types:

$$
\begin{aligned}
signedness &::= \textsf{Signed} \mid \textsf{Unsigned} \\
intsize &::= \textsf{I8} \mid \textsf{I16} \mid \textsf{I32} \\
floatsize &::= \textsf{F32} \mid \textsf{F64} \\
\tau &::= \textsf{Tint}(intsize, signedness) \mid \textsf{Tfloat}(floatsize) \\
&\quad \mid \textsf{Tarray}(\tau, n) \mid \textsf{Tpointer}(\tau) \mid \textsf{Tvoid} \mid \textsf{Tfunction}(\tau^*, \tau)
\end{aligned}
$$

Expressions annotated with types:

$$a ::= b^\tau$$

Unannotated expressions:

b	$::= id$	variable identifier
	$\mid n \mid f$	integer or float constant
	$\mid \textsf{sizeof}(\tau)$	size of a type
	$\mid op_u\, a$	unary arithmetic operation
	$\mid a_1\, op_b\, a_2 \mid a_1\, op_r\, a_2$	binary arithmetic operation
	$\mid *a$	dereferencing
	$\mid a_1[a_2]$	array indexing
	$\mid \&a$	address of
	$\mid \text{++}a \mid \text{--}a \mid a\text{++} \mid a\text{--}$	pre/post increment/decrement
	$\mid (\tau)a$	cast
	$\mid a_1 = a_2$	assignment
	$\mid a_1\, op_b =^\tau a_2$	arithmetic with assignment
	$\mid a_1\ \&\&\ a_2 \mid a_1\ \mid\mid\ a_2$	sequential boolean operations
	$\mid a_1, a_2$	sequence of expressions
	$\mid a(a^*)$	function call
	$\mid a_1\ ?\ a_2\ :\ a_3$	conditional expression
op_b	$::= + \mid - \mid * \mid / \mid \%$	arithmetic operators
	$\mid << \mid >> \mid \& \mid \mid \mid \hat{}\ $	bitwise operators
op_r	$::= < \mid <= \mid > \mid >= \mid == \mid\ !=$	relational operators
op_u	$::= - \mid\ \tilde{}\ \mid\ !$	unary operators

Statements:

s	$::= \textsf{skip}$	empty statement
	$\mid a;$	expression evaluation
	$\mid s_1; s_2$	sequence
	$\mid \textsf{if}(a)\ s_1\ \textsf{else}\ s_2$	conditional
	$\mid \textsf{while}(a)\ s$	"while" loop
	$\mid \textsf{do}\ s\ \textsf{while}(a)$	"do" loop
	$\mid \textsf{for}(a_1^?, a_2^?, a_3^?)\ s$	"for" loop
	$\mid \textsf{break}$	exit from the current loop
	$\mid \textsf{continue}$	next iteration of the current loop
	$\mid \textsf{return}\ a^?$	return from current function

Functions:

fn	$::= (\ldots id_i : \tau_i \ldots) : \tau$	declaration of type and parameters
	$\{\ \ldots \tau_j\ id_j; \ldots$	declaration of local variables
	$s\ \}$	function body

Fig. 1. Abstract syntax of Clight. a^* denotes 0, 1 or several occurrences of syntactic category a. $a^?$ denotes an optional occurrence of category a.

Block-scoped local variables and `static` variables are omitted, but can be emulated by pulling their declarations to function scope or global scope, respectively. Consequently, there is no block statement in Clight.

A Clight program consists of a list of function definitions, a list of global variable declarations, and an identifier naming the entry point of the program (the `main` function in C).

2.2 Dynamic Semantics

The dynamic semantics of Clight is specified using natural semantics, also known as big-step operational semantics. While the semantics of C is not deterministic (the evaluation order for expressions is not completely specified and compilers are free to choose between several orders), the semantics of Clight is completely deterministic and imposes a left-to-right evaluation order, consistent with the order implemented by our compiler. This choice simplifies greatly the semantics compared with, for instance, Norrish's semantics for C [10], which captures the non-determinism allowed by the ISO C specification. Our semantics can therefore be viewed as a refinement of (a subset of) the ISO C semantics, or of that of Norrish.

The semantics is defined by 7 judgements (relations):

$$
\begin{array}{ll}
G, E \vdash a, M \stackrel{l}{\Rightarrow} loc, M' & \text{(expressions in l-value position)} \\
G, E \vdash a, M \Rightarrow v, M' & \text{(expressions in r-value position)} \\
G, E \vdash a^?, M \Rightarrow v, M' & \text{(optional expressions)} \\
G, E \vdash a^*, M \Rightarrow v^*, M' & \text{(list of expressions)} \\
G, E \vdash s, M \Rightarrow out, M' & \text{(statements)} \\
G \vdash f(v^*), M \Rightarrow v, M' & \text{(function invocations)} \\
\vdash p \Rightarrow v & \text{(programs)}
\end{array}
$$

Each judgement relates a syntactic element (expression, statement, etc) and an initial memory state to the result of executing this syntactic element, as well as the final memory state at the end of execution. The various kinds of results, as well as the evaluation environments, are defined in figure 2.

For instance, executing an expression a in l-value position results in a memory location loc (a memory block reference and an offset within that block), while executing an expression a in r-value position results in the value v of the expression. Values range over 32-bit integers, 64-bit floats, memory locations (pointers), and an undefined value that represents for instance the value of uninitialized variables. The result associated with the execution of a statement s is an "outcome" out indicating how the execution terminated: either normally by running to completion or prematurely via a `break`, `continue` or `return` statement. The invocation of a function f yields its return value v, and so does the execution of a program p.

Two evaluation environments, defined in figure 2, appear as parameters to the judgements. The local environment E maps local variables to references of memory blocks containing the values of these variables. These blocks are allocated

Values:

$$loc ::= (b, n) \qquad \text{location (byte offset } n \text{ in block referenced by } b)$$
$$v \;\; ::= \texttt{Vint}(n) \qquad \text{integer value}$$
$$| \;\texttt{Vfloat}(f) \qquad \text{floating-point value}$$
$$| \;\texttt{Vptr}(loc) \qquad \text{pointer value}$$
$$| \;\texttt{Vundef} \qquad \text{undefined value}$$

Statement outcomes:

$$out ::= \texttt{Out\_normal} \qquad \text{go to the next statement}$$
$$| \;\texttt{Out\_continue} \qquad \text{go to the next iteration of the current loop}$$
$$| \;\texttt{Out\_break} \qquad \text{exit from the current loop}$$
$$| \;\texttt{Out\_return} \qquad \text{function exit}$$
$$| \;\texttt{Out\_return}(v, \tau) \qquad \text{function exit, returning the value } v \text{ of type } \tau$$

Global environments:

$$G \;\; ::= (id \mapsto b) \qquad \text{map from global variables to block references}$$
$$\times (b \mapsto fn) \qquad \text{and map from references to function definitions}$$

Local environments:

$$E \;\; ::= id \mapsto b \qquad \text{map from local variables to block references}$$

Fig. 2. Values, outcomes, and evaluation environments

at function entry and freed at function return. The global environment G maps global variables and function names to memory references. It also maps some references (those corresponding to function pointers) to function definitions.

In the Coq specification, the 7 judgements of the dynamic semantics are encoded as mutually-inductive predicates. Each defining case of each predicate corresponds exactly to an inference rule in the conventional, on-paper presentation of natural semantics. We have one inference rule for each kind of expression and statement described in figure 1. We do not list all the inference rules by lack of space, but show some representative examples in figure 3.

The first two rules of figure 3 illustrate the evaluation of an expression in l-value position. A variable x evaluates to the location $(E(x), 0)$. If an expression a evaluates to a pointer value $\texttt{Vptr}(loc)$, then the location of the dereferencing expression $(*a)^\tau$ is loc.

Rule 3 evaluates an application of a binary operator op to expressions a_1 and a_2. Both sub-expressions are evaluated in sequence, and their values are combined with the `eval_binary_operation` function, which takes as additional arguments the types τ_1 and τ_2 of the arguments, in order to resolve overloaded and type-dependent operators. This is a partial function: it can be undefined if the types and the shapes of argument values are incompatible (e.g. a floating-point addition of two pointer values). In the Coq specification, `eval_binary_operation` is a total function returning optional values: either None in case of failure, or $\texttt{Some}(v)$, abbreviated as $\lfloor v \rfloor$, in case of success.

Rule 4 rule shows the evaluation of an l-value expression in a r-value context. The expression is evaluated to its location loc, with final memory state M'. The value at location loc in M' is fetched using the `loadval` function (see section 2.3) and returned.

Expressions in l-value position:

$$\frac{E(x) = b}{G, E \vdash x^\tau, M \overset{l}{\Rightarrow} (b, 0), M} \quad (1) \qquad \frac{G, E \vdash a, M \Rightarrow \mathtt{Vptr}(loc), M'}{G, E \vdash (\ast a)^\tau, M \overset{l}{\Rightarrow} loc, M'} \quad (2)$$

Expressions in r-value position:

$$\frac{G, E \vdash a_1^{\tau_1}, M \Rightarrow v_1, M_1 \quad G, E \vdash a_2^{\tau_2}, M_1 \Rightarrow v_2, M_2 \quad \mathtt{eval\_binary\_operation}(op, v_1, \tau_1, v_2, \tau_2) = \lfloor v \rfloor}{G, E \vdash (a_1^{\tau_1} \; op \; a_2^{\tau_2})^\tau, M \Rightarrow v, M_2} \quad (3)$$

$$\frac{G, E \vdash a^\tau, M \overset{l}{\Rightarrow} loc, M' \quad \mathtt{loadval}(\tau, M', loc) = \lfloor v \rfloor}{G, E \vdash a^\tau, M \Rightarrow v, M'} \quad (4)$$

$$\frac{G, E \vdash a^\tau, M \overset{l}{\Rightarrow} loc, M_1 \quad G, E \vdash b^\sigma, M_1 \Rightarrow v_1, M_2 \quad \mathtt{cast}(v_1, \sigma, \tau) = \lfloor v \rfloor \quad \mathtt{storeval}(\tau, M_2, loc, v) = \lfloor M_3 \rfloor}{G, E \vdash (a^\tau \; = \; b^\sigma)^\tau, M \Rightarrow v, M_3} \quad (5)$$

Statements:

$$G, E \vdash \mathtt{break}, M \Rightarrow \mathtt{Out\_break}, M \quad (6)$$

$$\frac{G, E \vdash s_1, M \Rightarrow \mathtt{Out\_normal}, M_1 \quad G, E \vdash s_2, M_1 \Rightarrow out, M_2}{G, E \vdash (s_1; s_2), M \Rightarrow out, M_2} \quad (7)$$

$$\frac{G, E \vdash s_1, M \Rightarrow out, M' \quad out \neq \mathtt{Out\_normal}}{G, E \vdash (s_1; s_2), M \Rightarrow out, M'} \quad (8)$$

$$\frac{G, E \vdash a, M \Rightarrow v, M' \quad \mathtt{is\_false}(v)}{G, E \vdash (\mathtt{while}(a) \; s), M \Rightarrow \mathtt{Out\_normal}, M'} \quad (9)$$

$$\frac{G, E \vdash a, M \Rightarrow v, M_1 \quad \mathtt{is\_true}(v) \quad G, E \vdash s, M_1 \Rightarrow \mathtt{Out\_break}, M_2}{G, E \vdash (\mathtt{while}(a) \; s), M \Rightarrow \mathtt{Out\_normal}, M_2} \quad (10)$$

$$\frac{G, E \vdash a, M \Rightarrow v, M_1 \quad \mathtt{is\_true}(v) \quad G, E \vdash s, M_1 \Rightarrow out, M_2 \quad out \in \{\mathtt{Out\_normal}, \mathtt{Out\_continue}\} \quad G, E \vdash (\mathtt{while}(a) \; s), M_2 \Rightarrow out', M_3}{G, E \vdash (\mathtt{while}(a) \; s), M \Rightarrow out', M_3} \quad (11)$$

Fig. 3. Selected rules of the dynamic semantics of Clight

Rule 5 evaluates an assignment expression. An assignment expression $a^\tau = b^\sigma$ evaluates the l-value a to a location loc, then the r-value b to a value v_1. This value is cast from its natural type σ to the expected type τ using the partial function $\mathtt{cast}$. This function performs appropriate conversions, truncations and sign-extensions over integers and floats, and may fail for undefined casts. The result v of the cast is then stored in memory at location loc, resulting in the final memory state M_3, and returned as the value of the assignment expression.

The bottom group of rules in figure 3 are examples of statement executions. The execution of a break statement yields an Out_break outcome (rule 6). The execution of a sequence of two statements starts with the execution of the first statement, yielding an outcome that determines if the second statement must be executed or not (rules 7 and 8). Finally, rules 9–11 describe the execution of a while loop. Once the condition of a while loop is evaluated to a value v, the execution of the loop terminates normally if v is false. If v is true, the loop body is executed, yielding an outcome out. If out is Out_break, the loop terminates normally. If out is Out_normal or Out_continue, the whole loop is reexecuted in the memory state modified by the execution of the body.

2.3   The Memory Model of the Semantics

The memory model used in the dynamic semantics is described in [1]. It is a compromise between a low-level view of memory as an array of bytes and a high-level view as a mapping from abstract references to contents. In our model, the memory is arranged in independent blocks, identified by block references b. A memory state M maps references b to block contents, which are themselves mappings from byte offsets to values. Each block has a low bound $L(M, b)$ and a high bound $H(M, b)$, determined at allocation time and representing the interval of valid byte offsets within this block. This memory model guarantees separation properties between two distinct blocks, yet enables pointer arithmetic within a given block, as prescribed by the ISO C specification. The same memory model is common to the semantics of all intermediate languages of our certified compiler.

The memory model provides 4 basic operations:

$alloc(M, lo, hi) = (M', b)$
   Allocate a fresh block of bounds $[lo, hi)$. Returns extended memory M' and reference b to fresh block.
$free(M, b) = M'$
   Free (invalidate) the block b.
$load(\kappa, M, b, n) = \lfloor v \rfloor$
   Read one or several consecutive bytes (as determined by κ) at block b, offset n in memory state M. If successful return the contents of these bytes as value v.
$store(\kappa, M, b, n, v) = \lfloor M' \rfloor$
   Store the value v into one or several consecutive bytes (as determined by κ) at offset n in block b of memory state M. If successful, return an updated memory state M'.

The memory chunks κ appearing in load and store operations describe concisely the size, type and signedness of the memory quantities involved:

$$\kappa ::= \text{Mint8signed} \mid \text{Mint8unsigned}$$
$$\mid \text{Mint16signed} \mid \text{Mint16unsigned} \quad \text{small integers}$$
$$\mid \text{Mint32} \qquad\qquad\qquad\qquad\qquad \text{integers and pointers}$$
$$\mid \text{Mfloat32} \mid \text{Mfloat64} \qquad\qquad \text{floats}$$

In the semantics of C, those quantities are determined by the C types of the datum being addressed. The following $\mathcal{A}$ ("access mode") function mediates between C types and the corresponding memory chunks:

$$\mathcal{A}(\text{Tint}(\text{I8}, \text{Signed})) = \text{By\_value}(\text{Mint8signed})$$
$$\mathcal{A}(\text{Tint}(\text{I8}, \text{Unsigned})) = \text{By\_value}(\text{Mint8unsigned})$$
$$\mathcal{A}(\text{Tint}(\text{I16}, \text{Signed})) = \text{By\_value}(\text{Mint16signed})$$
$$\mathcal{A}(\text{Tint}(\text{I16}, \text{Unsigned})) = \text{By\_value}(\text{Mint16unsigned})$$
$$\mathcal{A}(\text{Tint}(\text{I32}, \_)) = \mathcal{A}(\text{Tpointer}(\_)) = \text{By\_value}(\text{Mint32})$$
$$\mathcal{A}(\text{Tarray}(\_, \_)) = \mathcal{A}(\text{Tfunction}(\_, \_)) = \text{By\_reference}$$
$$\mathcal{A}(\text{Tvoid}) = \text{By\_nothing}$$

Integer, float and pointer types involve an actual memory load when accessed, as captured by the By_value cases. However, accesses to arrays and functions return the location of the array or function, without any load; this is indicated by the By_reference access mode. Finally, expressions of type void cannot be accessed at all. This is reflected in the definitions of the loadval and storeval functions used in the dynamic semantics:

$$
\begin{aligned}
\text{loadval}(\tau, M, (b, n)) &= \text{load}(\kappa, M, b, n) & &\text{if } \mathcal{A}(\tau) = \text{By\_value}(\kappa) \\
\text{loadval}(\tau, M, (b, n)) &= \lfloor b, n \rfloor & &\text{if } \mathcal{A}(\tau) = \text{By\_reference} \\
\text{loadval}(\tau, M, (b, n)) &= \text{None} & &\text{if } \mathcal{A}(\tau) = \text{By\_nothing} \\
\text{storeval}(\tau, M, (b, n), v) &= \text{store}(\kappa, M, b, n, v) & &\text{if } \mathcal{A}(\tau) = \text{By\_value}(\kappa) \\
\text{storeval}(\tau, M, (b, n), v) &= \text{None} & &\text{otherwise}
\end{aligned}
$$

2.4   Static Semantics (Typing Rules)

We have also formalized in Coq typing rules and a type checking algorithm for Clight. The algorithm is presented as a function from abstract syntax trees without type annotations to the abstract syntax trees with type annotations over expressions given in figure 1. We omit the typing rules by lack of space. Note that the dynamic semantics are defined for arbitrarily annotated expressions, not just well-typed expressions; however, the semantics can get stuck or produce results that disagree with ISO C when given an incorrectly-annotated expression. The translation scheme presented in section 3 demands well-typed programs and may fail to preserve semantics otherwise.

3   Translation from Clight to Cminor

3.1   Overview of Cminor

The Cminor language is the target language of our front-end compiler for C and the input language for our certified back-end. We now give a short overview of Cminor; see [8] for a more detailed description, and [7] for a complete formal specification.

Cminor is a low-level imperative language, structured like our subset of C into expressions, statements, and functions. We summarize the main differences with Clight. First, arithmetic operators are not overloaded and their behavior is independent of the static types of their operands. Distinct operators are provided for integer arithmetic and floating-point arithmetic. Conversions between integers and floats are explicit. Arithmetic is always performed over 32-bit integers and 64-bit floats; explicit truncation and sign-extension operators are provided to implement smaller integral types. Finally, the combined arithmetic-with-assignment operators of C (+=, ++, etc) are not provided. For instance, the C expression i += f where i is of type int and f of type double is expressed as i = intoffloat(floatofint(i) +$_f$ f).

Address computations are explicit, as well as individual load and store operations. For instance, the C expression a[i] where a is a pointer to int is expressed as load(int32, a +$_i$ i *$_i$ 4), making explicit the memory chunk being addressed (int32) as well as the computation of the address.

At the level of statements, Cminor has only 4 control structures: if-then-else conditionals, infinite loops, block-exit, and early return. The exit n statement terminates the $(n + 1)$ enclosing block statements. These structures are lower-level than those of C, but suffice to implement all reducible flow graphs.

Within Cminor functions, local variables can only hold scalar values (integers, pointers, floats) and they do not reside in memory, making it impossible to take a pointer to a local variable like the C operator & does. Instead, each Cminor function declares the size of a stack-allocated block, allocated in memory at function entry and automatically freed at function return. The expression addrstack(n) returns a pointer within that block at constant offset n. The Cminor producer can use this block to store local arrays as well as local scalar variables whose addresses need to be taken.[1]

The semantics of Cminor is defined in big-step operational style and resembles that of Clight. The following evaluation judgements are defined in [7]:

$$G, sp, L \vdash a, E, M \to v, E', M' \qquad \text{(expressions)}$$
$$G, sp, L \vdash a^*, E, M \to v^*, E', M' \qquad \text{(expression lists)}$$
$$G, sp \vdash s, E, M \to out, E', M' \qquad \text{(statements)}$$
$$G \vdash fn(v^*), M \to v, M' \qquad \text{(function calls)}$$
$$\vdash prog \to v \qquad \text{(whole programs)}$$

The main difference with the semantics of Clight is that the local evaluation environment E maps local variables to their values, instead of their memory addresses; consequently, E is modified during evaluation of expressions and statements. Additional parameters are sp, the reference to the stack block for the current function, and L, the environment giving values to variables let-bound within expressions.

---

[1] While suboptimal in terms of performance of generated code, this systematic stack allocation of local variables whose addresses are taken is common practice for moderately optimizing C compilers such as gcc versions 2 and 3.

3.2   Overview of the Translation

The translation from our subset of Clight to Cminor performs three basic tasks:

- Resolution of operator overloading and explication of all type-dependent behaviors. Based on the types that annotate Clight expressions, the appropriate flavors (integer or float) of arithmetic operators are chosen; conversions between ints and floats, truncations and sign-extensions are introduced to reflect casts, both explicit in the source and implicit in the semantics of Clight; address computations are generated based on the types of array elements and pointer targets; and appropriate memory chunks are selected for every memory access.
- Translation of while, do...while and for loops into infinite loops with blocks and early exits. The statements break and continue are translated as appropriate exit constructs, as shown in figure 4.
- Placement of Clight variables, either as Cminor local variables (for local scalar variables whose address is never taken), sub-areas of the Cminor stack block for the current function (for local non-scalar variables or local scalar variables whose address is taken), or globally allocated memory areas (for global variables).[2]

The translation is specified as Coq functions from Clight abstract syntax to Cminor abstract syntax, defined by structural recursion. From these Coq functions, executable Caml code can be mechanically generated using the Coq extraction facility, making the specification directly executable. Several translation functions are defined: $\mathcal{L}$ and $\mathcal{R}$ for expressions in l-value and r-value position, respectively; $\mathcal{S}$ for statements; and $\mathcal{F}$ for functions. Some representative cases of the definitions of these functions are shown in figure 4, giving the general flavor of the translation.

The translation can fail when given invalid Clight source code, e.g. containing an assignment between arrays. To enable error reporting, the translation functions return option types: either None denoting an error, or $\lfloor x \rfloor$ denoting successful translation with result x. Systematic propagation of errors is achieved using a monadic programming style (the bind combinator of the error monad), as customary in purely functional programming. This monadic "plumbing" is omitted in figure 4 for simplicity.

Most translation functions are parameterized by a translation environment γ reflecting the placement of Clight variables. It maps every variable x to either Local (denoting the Cminor local variable named x), Stack(δ) (denoting a sub-area of the Cminor stack block at offset δ), or Global (denoting the address of the Cminor global symbol named x). This environment is constructed at the beginning of the translation of a Clight function. The function body is

---

[2] It would be semantically correct to stack-allocate all local variables, like the C0 verified compiler does [6,12]. However, keeping scalar local variables in Cminor local variables as much as possible enables the back-end to generate much more efficient machine code.

Casts ($C_\tau^\sigma(e)$ casts e from type τ to type σ):
$$C_\tau^\sigma(e) = C_2(C_1(e, \tau, \sigma), \sigma)$$

$$C_1(e, \tau, \sigma) = \begin{cases} \texttt{floatofint}(e), & \text{if } \tau = \texttt{Tint}(\_, \texttt{Signed}) \text{ and } \sigma = \texttt{Tfloat}(\_); \\ \texttt{floatofintu}(e), & \text{if } \tau = \texttt{Tint}(\_, \texttt{Unsigned}) \text{ and } \sigma = \texttt{Tfloat}(\_); \\ \texttt{intoffloat}(e), & \text{if } \tau = \texttt{Tfloat}(\_) \text{ and } \sigma = \texttt{Tint}(\_, \_); \\ e & \text{otherwise} \end{cases}$$

$$C_2(e, \sigma) = \begin{cases} \texttt{cast8signed}(e), & \text{if } \sigma = \texttt{Tint}(\texttt{I8}, \texttt{Signed}); \\ \texttt{cast8unsigned}(e), & \text{if } \sigma = \texttt{Tint}(\texttt{I8}, \texttt{Unsigned}); \\ \texttt{cast16signed}(e), & \text{if } \sigma = \texttt{Tint}(\texttt{I16}, \texttt{Signed}); \\ \texttt{cast16unsigned}(e), & \text{if } \sigma = \texttt{Tint}(\texttt{I16}, \texttt{Unsigned}); \\ \texttt{singleoffloat}(e), & \text{if } \sigma = \texttt{Tfloat}(\texttt{F32}); \\ e & \text{otherwise} \end{cases}$$

Expressions in l-value position:
$$\mathcal{L}_\gamma(x) = \texttt{addrstack}(\delta) \quad \text{if } \gamma(x) = \texttt{Stack}(\delta)$$
$$\mathcal{L}_\gamma(x) = \texttt{addrglobal}(x) \quad \text{if } \gamma(x) = \texttt{Global}$$
$$\mathcal{L}_\gamma(*e) = \mathcal{R}_\gamma(e)$$
$$\mathcal{L}_\gamma(e_1[e_2]) = \mathcal{R}_\gamma(e_1 + e_2)$$

Expressions in r-value position:
$$\mathcal{R}_\gamma(x) = x \quad \text{if } \gamma(x) = \texttt{Local}$$
$$\mathcal{R}_\gamma(e^\tau) = \texttt{load}(\kappa, \mathcal{L}_\gamma(e^\tau)) \quad \text{if } \mathcal{L}_\gamma(e) \text{ is defined and } \mathcal{A}(\tau) = \texttt{By\_value}(\kappa)$$
$$\mathcal{R}_\gamma(e^\tau) = \mathcal{L}_\gamma(e^\tau) \quad \text{if } \mathcal{L}_\gamma(e) \text{ is defined and } \mathcal{A}(\tau) = \texttt{By\_reference}$$
$$\mathcal{R}_\gamma(x^\tau = e^\sigma) = x = C_\sigma^\tau(\mathcal{R}(e^\sigma)) \quad \text{if } \gamma(x) = \texttt{Local}$$
$$\mathcal{R}_\gamma(e_1^\tau = e_2^\sigma) = \texttt{store}(\kappa, \mathcal{L}_\gamma(e_1^\tau), C_\sigma^\tau(\mathcal{R}(e_2^\sigma))) \quad \text{if } \mathcal{A}(\tau) = \texttt{By\_value}(\kappa)$$
$$\mathcal{R}_\gamma(\&e) = \mathcal{L}_\gamma(e)$$
$$\mathcal{R}_\gamma(e_1^\tau + e_2^\sigma) = \mathcal{R}_\gamma(e_1^\tau) +_i \mathcal{R}_\gamma(e_2^\sigma) \quad \text{if } \tau \text{ and } \sigma \text{ are integer types}$$
$$\mathcal{R}_\gamma(e_1^\tau + e_2^\sigma) = C_\tau^{\texttt{double}}(\mathcal{R}_\gamma(e_1^\tau)) +_f C_\sigma^{\texttt{double}}(\mathcal{R}_\gamma(e_2^\sigma)) \quad \text{if } \tau \text{ or } \sigma \text{ are float types}$$
$$\mathcal{R}_\gamma(e_1^\tau + e_2^\sigma) = \mathcal{R}_\gamma(e_1^\tau) +_i \mathcal{R}_\gamma(e_2^\sigma) *_i \texttt{sizeof}(\rho) \quad \text{if } \tau \text{ is a pointer or array of } \rho$$

Statements:
$$\mathcal{S}_\gamma(\texttt{while}(e)\ s) = \texttt{block}\{\ \texttt{loop}\{\ \texttt{if } (!\mathcal{R}_\gamma(e))\ \texttt{exit } 0;\ \texttt{block}\{\ \mathcal{S}_\gamma(s)\ \}\}\}$$
$$\mathcal{S}_\gamma(\texttt{do } s \texttt{ while}(e)) = \texttt{block}\{\ \texttt{loop}\{\ \texttt{block}\{\ \mathcal{S}_\gamma(s)\ \};\ \texttt{if } (!\mathcal{R}_\gamma(e))\ \texttt{exit } 0\ \}\}$$
$$\mathcal{S}_\gamma(\texttt{for}(e_1; e_2; e_3)\ s) = \mathcal{R}_\gamma(e_1);$$
$$\texttt{block}\{\ \texttt{loop}\{\ \texttt{if } (!\mathcal{R}_\gamma(e_2))\ \texttt{exit } 0;\ \texttt{block}\{\ \mathcal{S}_\gamma(s)\ \};\ \mathcal{R}_\gamma(e_3)\ \}\}$$
$$\mathcal{S}_\gamma(\texttt{break}) = \texttt{exit } 1$$
$$\mathcal{S}_\gamma(\texttt{continue}) = \texttt{exit } 0$$

Fig. 4. Selected translation rules

scanned for occurrences of `&x` (taking the address of a variable). Local variables that are not scalar or whose address is taken are assigned $\texttt{Stack}(\delta)$ locations, with δ chosen so that distinct variables map to non-overlapping areas of the stack block. Other local variables are set to $\texttt{Local}$, and global variables to $\texttt{Global}$.

4   Proof of Correctness of the Translation

4.1   Relating Memory States

To prove the correctness of the translation, the major difficulty is to relate the memory states occurring during the execution of the Clight source code and that of the generated Cminor code. The semantics of Clight allocates a distinct block for every local variable at function entry. Some of those blocks (those for scalar variables whose address is not taken) have no correspondence in the Cminor memory state; others become sub-block of the Cminor stack block for the function.

To account for these differences in allocation patterns between the source and target code, we introduce the notion of *memory injections*. A memory injection α is a function from Clight block references b to either None, meaning that this block has no counterpart in the Cminor memory state, or $\lfloor b', \delta \rfloor$, meaning that the block b of the Clight memory state corresponds to a sub-block of block b' at offset δ in the Cminor memory state.

A memory injection α defines a relation between Clight values v and Cminor values v', written $\alpha \vdash v \approx v'$ and defined as follows:

$$\alpha \vdash \mathtt{Vint}(n) \approx \mathtt{Vint}(n) \qquad \alpha \vdash \mathtt{Vfloat}(n) \approx \mathtt{Vfloat}(n) \qquad \alpha \vdash \mathtt{Vundef} \approx v$$

$$\frac{\alpha(b) = \lfloor b', \delta \rfloor \quad i' = i + \delta \pmod{2^{32}}}{\alpha \vdash \mathtt{Vptr}(b, i) \approx \mathtt{Vptr}(b', i')}$$

This relation captures the relocation of pointer values implied by α. It also enables Vundef Clight values to become more defined Cminor values during the translation, in keeping with the general idea that compilation can particularize some undefined behaviors.

The memory injection α also defines a relation between Clight and Cminor memory states, written $\alpha \vdash M \approx M'$, consisting of the conjunction of the following conditions:

- Matching of block contents: if $\alpha(b) = \lfloor b', \delta \rfloor$ and $L(M, b) \le i < H(M, b)$, then $L(M', b') \le i + \delta < H(M', b')$ and $\alpha \vdash v \approx v'$ where v is the contents of block b at offset i in M and v' the contents of b' at offset i' in M'.
- No overlap: if $\alpha(b_1) = \lfloor b'_1, \delta_1 \rfloor$ and $\alpha(b_2) = \lfloor b'_2, \delta_2 \rfloor$ and $b_1 \ne b_2$, then either $b'_1 \ne b'_2$, or the intervals $[L(M, b_1) + \delta_1, H(M, b_1) + \delta_1)$ and $[L(M, b_2) + \delta_2, H(M, b_2) + \delta_2)$ are disjoint.
- Fresh blocks: $\alpha(b) = \mathtt{None}$ for all blocks b not yet allocated in M.

The memory injection relations have nice commutation properties with respect to the basic operations of the memory model. For instance:

- Commutation of loads: if $\alpha \vdash M \approx M'$ and $\alpha \vdash \mathtt{Vptr}(b, i) \approx \mathtt{Vptr}(b', i')$ and $\mathtt{load}(\kappa, M, b, i) = \lfloor v \rfloor$, there exists v' such that $\mathtt{load}(\kappa, M', b', i') = \lfloor v' \rfloor$ and $\alpha \vdash v \approx v'$.

- Commutation of stores to mapped blocks: if $\alpha \vdash M \approx M'$ and $\alpha \vdash \mathtt{Vptr}(b, i) \approx \mathtt{Vptr}(b', i')$ and $\alpha \vdash v \approx v'$ and $\mathtt{store}(\kappa, M, b, i, v) = \lfloor M_1 \rfloor$, there exists M_1' such that $\mathtt{store}(\kappa, M', b', i', v') = \lfloor M_1' \rfloor$ and $\alpha \vdash M_1 \approx M_1'$.
- Invariance by stores to unmapped blocks: if $\alpha \vdash M \approx M'$ and $\alpha(b) = \mathtt{None}$ and $\mathtt{store}(\kappa, M, b, i, v) = \lfloor M_1 \rfloor$, then $\alpha \vdash M_1 \approx M'$.

To enable the memory injection α to grow incrementally as new blocks are allocated during execution, we define the relation $\alpha' \geq \alpha$ (read: α' extends α) by $\forall b, \ \alpha'(b) = \alpha(b) \lor \alpha(b) = \mathtt{None}$. The injection relations are preserved by extension of α. For instance, if $\alpha \vdash M \approx M'$, then $\alpha' \vdash M \approx M'$ for all α' such that $\alpha' \geq \alpha$.

4.2 Relating Execution Environments

Execution environments differ in structure between Clight and Cminor: the Clight environment E maps local variables to references of blocks containing the values of the variables, while in Cminor the environment E' for local variables map them directly to values. We define a matching relation $EnvMatch(\gamma, \alpha, E, M, E', sp)$ between a Clight environment E and memory state M and a Cminor environment E' and reference to a stack block sp as follows:

- For all variables x of type τ, if $\gamma(x) = \mathtt{Local}$, then $\alpha(E(x)) = \mathtt{None}$ and there exists v such that $\mathtt{load}(\kappa(\tau), M, E(x), 0) = \lfloor v \rfloor$ and $\alpha \vdash v \approx E'(x)$.
- For all variables x of type τ, if $\gamma(x) = \mathtt{Stack}(\delta)$, then $\alpha \vdash \mathtt{Vptr}(E(x), 0) \approx \mathtt{Vptr}(sp, \delta)$.
- For all $x \neq y$, we have $E(x) \neq E(y)$.
- If $\alpha(b) = \lfloor sp, \delta \rfloor$ for some block b and offset δ, then b is in the range of E.

The first two conditions express the preservation of the values of local variables during compilation. The last two rule out unwanted sharing between environment blocks and their images through α.

At any point during execution, several function calls may be active and we need to ensure matching between the environments of each call. For this, we introduce abstract call stacks, which are lists of 4-tuples (γ, E, E', sp) and record the environments of all active functions. A call stack cs is globally consistent with respect to C memory state M and memory injection α, written $CallInv(\alpha, M, cs)$, if $EnvMatch(\gamma, \alpha, E, M, E', sp)$ holds for all elements (γ, E, E', sp) of cs. Additional conditions, omitted for brevity, enforce separation between Clight environments E and between Cminor stack blocks sp belonging to different function activations in cs.

4.3 Proof by Simulation

The proof of semantic preservation for the translation proceeds by induction over the Clight evaluation derivation and case analysis on the last evaluation rule used. The proof shows that, assuming suitable consistency conditions over the abstract call stack, the generated Cminor expressions and statements evaluate in ways that simulate the evaluation of the corresponding Clight expressions and statements.

We give a slightly simplified version of the simulation properties shown by induction over the Clight evaluation derivation. Let G' be the global Cminor environment obtained by translating all function definitions in the global Clight environment G. Assume $CallInv(\alpha, M, (\gamma, E, E', sp).cs)$ and $\alpha \vdash M \approx M'$. Then there exists a Cminor environment E'_1, a Cminor memory state M'_1 and a memory injection $\alpha_1 \geq \alpha$ such that

- (R-values) If $G, E \vdash a, M \Rightarrow v, M_1$, there exists v' such that $G', sp, L \vdash \mathcal{R}_\gamma(a), E', M' \to v', E'_1, M'_1$ and $\alpha_1 \vdash v \approx v'$.
- (L-values) If $G, E \vdash a, M \overset{l}{\Rightarrow} loc, M_1$, there exists v' such that $G', sp, L \vdash \mathcal{L}_\gamma(a), E', M' \to v', E'_1, M'_1$ and $\alpha_1 \vdash \mathtt{Vptr}(loc) \approx v'$.
- (Statements) If $G, E \vdash s, M \Rightarrow out, M_1$ and τ_r is the return type of the function, there exists out' such that $G', sp \vdash \mathcal{S}_\gamma(s), E', M' \to out', E'_1, M'_1$ and $\alpha_1, \tau_r \vdash out \approx out'$.

Moreover, the final Clight and Cminor states satisfy $\alpha_1 \vdash M_1 \approx M'_1$ and $CallInv(\alpha_1, M_1, (\gamma, E, E'_1, sp).cs)$.

In the case of statements, the relation between Clight and Cminor outcomes is defined as follows:

$$\alpha, \tau_r \vdash \mathtt{Out\_normal} \approx \mathtt{Out\_normal} \qquad \alpha, \tau_r \vdash \mathtt{Out\_continue} \approx \mathtt{Out\_exit}(0)$$
$$\alpha, \tau_r \vdash \mathtt{Out\_break} \approx \mathtt{Out\_exit}(1) \qquad \alpha, \tau_r \vdash \mathtt{Out\_return} \approx \mathtt{Out\_return}$$

$$\frac{\alpha \vdash \mathtt{cast}(v, \tau, \tau_r) \approx v'}{\alpha, \tau_r \vdash \mathtt{Out\_return}(v, \tau) \approx \mathtt{Out\_return}(v')}$$

In addition to the outer induction over the Clight evaluation derivation, the proofs proceed by copious case analysis, over the placement $\gamma(x)$ for accesses to variables x, and over the types of the operands for applications of overloaded operators. As a corollary of the simulation properties, we obtain the correctness theorem for the translation:

Theorem 1. *Assume the Clight program p is well-typed and translates without errors to a Cminor program p'. If $\vdash p \Rightarrow v$, and if v is an integer or float value, then $\vdash p' \to v$.*

This semantic preservation theorem applies only to terminating programs. Our choice of big-step operational semantics prevents us from reasoning over non-terminating executions.

The whole proof represents approximately 6000 lines of Coq statements and proof scripts, including 1000 lines (40 lemmas) for the properties of memory injections, 1400 lines (54 lemmas) for environment matching and the call stack invariant, 1400 lines (50 lemmas) for the translations of type-dependent operators and memory accesses, and 2000 lines (51 lemmas, one per Clight evaluation rule) for the final inductive proof of simulation. By comparison, the source code of the Clight to Cminor translator is 800 lines of Coq function definitions. The proof is therefore 7.5 times bigger than the code it proves. The whole development (design and semantics of Clight; development of the translator; proof of its correctness) took approximately 8 person.months.

5   Related Work

Several formal semantics of C-like languages have been defined. Norrish [10] gives a small-step operational semantics, expressed using the HOL theorem prover, for a subset of C comparable to our Clight. His semantics captures exactly the non-determinism (partially unspecified evaluation order) allowed by the ISO C specification, making it significantly more complex than our deterministic semantics. Papaspyrou [11] addresses non-determinism as well, but using denotational semantics with monads. Abstract state machines have been used to give on-paper semantics for C [4,9] and more recently for C# [3].

Many correctness proofs of program transformations have been published, both on paper and machine-checked using proof assistants; see [2] for a survey. A representative example is [5], where a non-optimizing byte-code compiler from a subset of Java to a subset of the Java Virtual Machine is verified using Isabelle/HOL. Most of these correctness proofs apply to source languages that are either smaller or semantically cleaner than C.

The work that is closest to ours is part of the Verisoft project [6,12]. Using Isabelle/HOL, they formalize the semantics of C0 (a subset of the C language) and a compiler from C0 down to DLX assembly code. C0 is a type-safe subset of C, close to Pascal, and significantly smaller than our Clight: there is no pointer arithmetic, nor side effects, nor premature execution of statements and there exists only a single integer type, thus avoiding operator overloading. They provide both a big step semantics and a small step semantics for C0, the latter enabling reasoning about non-terminating and concurrent executions, unlike our big-step semantics. Their C0 compiler is a single pass compiler that generates unoptimized machine code. It is more complex than our translation from Clight to Cminor, but considerably simpler than our whole certified compiler.

6   Concluding Remarks

The C language is not pretty; this shows up in the relative complexity of our formal semantics and translation scheme. However, this complexity remains manageable with the tools (the Coq proof assistant) and the methodology (big-step semantics; simulation arguments; extraction of an executable compiler from its functional Coq specification) that we used.

Future work includes 1- handling a larger subset of C, especially **struct** types; and 2- evaluating the usability of the semantics for program proof and static analysis purposes. In particular, it would be interesting to develop axiomatic semantics (probably based on separation logic) for Clight and validate them against our operational semantics.

References

1. S. Blazy and X. Leroy. Formal verification of a memory model for C-like imperative languages. In *Proc. of Int. Conf. on Formal Engineering Methods (ICFEM)*, volume 3785 of *LNCS*, pages 280–299, Manchester, UK, Nov. 2005. Springer-Verlag.
2. M. A. Dave. Compiler verification: a bibliography. *SIGSOFT Softw. Eng. Notes*, 28(6):2–2, 2003.
3. E. Börger, N. Fruja, V.Gervasi, and R. Stärk. A high-level modular definition of the semantics of C#. *Theoretical Computer Science*, 336(2-3):235–284, 2005.
4. Y. Gurevich and J. Huggins. The semantics of the C programming language. In *Proc. of CSL'92 (Computer Science Logic)*, volume 702 of *LNCS*, pages 274–308. Springer Verlag, 1993.
5. G. Klein and T. Nipkow. A machine-checked model for a Java-like language, virtual machine and compiler. Technical Report 0400001T.1, National ICT Australia, Mar. 2004. To appear in ACM TOPLAS.
6. D. Leinenbach, W. Paul, and E. Petrova. Towards the formal verification of a C0 compiler. In *Proc. Conf. on Software Engineering and Formal Methods (SEFM)*, pages 2–11, Koblenz, Germany, Sept. 2005. IEEE Computer Society Press.
7. X. Leroy. The Compcert certified compiler back-end – commented Coq development. Available on-line at http://cristal.inria.fr/~xleroy, 2006.
8. X. Leroy. Formal certification of a compiler back-end, or: programming a compiler with a proof assistant. In *Proc. Symp. Principles Of Programming Languages (POPL)*, pages 42–54, Charleston, USA, Jan. 2006. ACM Press.
9. V. Nepomniaschy, I. Anureev, and A. Promsky. Verification-oriented language C-light and its structural operational semantics. In *Ershov Memorial Conference*, pages 103–111, 2003.
10. M. Norrish. *C formalised in HOL*. PhD thesis, University of Cambridge, Dec. 1998.
11. N. Papaspyrou. *A formal semantics for the C programming language*. PhD thesis, National Technical University of Athens, Feb. 1998.
12. M. Strecker. Compiler verification for C0. Technical report, Université Paul Sabatier, Toulouse, Apr. 2005.

A Memory Model Sensitive Checker for C#

Thuan Quang Huynh and Abhik Roychoudhury

Department of Computer Science, National University of Singapore
{huynhqua, abhik}@comp.nus.edu.sg

Abstract. Modern concurrent programming languages like Java and C# have a programming language level memory model; it captures the set of all allowed behaviors of programs on any implementation platform — uni- or multi-processor. Such a memory model is typically weaker than Sequential Consistency and allows reordering of operations within a program thread. Therefore, programs verified correct by assuming Sequential Consistency (that is, each thread proceeds in program order) may not behave correctly on certain platforms! The solution to this problem is to develop program checkers which are memory model sensitive. In this paper, we develop such an invariant checker for the programming language C#. Our checker identifies program states which are reached only because the C# memory model is more relaxed than Sequential Consistency. Furthermore, our checker identifies (a) operation reorderings which cause such undesirable states to be reached, and (b) simple program modifications — by inserting memory barrier operations — which prevent such undesirable reorderings.

1 Introduction

Modern mainstream programming languages like Java and C# support multi-threading as an essential feature of the language. In these languages multiple threads can access shared objects. Moreover, synchronization mechanisms exist for controlling access to shared objects by threads. If every access to a shared object by any thread requires prior acquisition of a common lock, then the program is *guaranteed* to be "properly synchronized". On the other hand, if there are two accesses to a shared object/variable v by two different threads, at least one of them is a write, and they are not ordered by synchronization — the program is then said to contain a data race, that is, the program is *improperly synchronized*. Improperly synchronized programs are common for more than one reason — (a) programmers may want to avoid synchronization overheads for low-level program fragments which are executed frequently, (b) programmers may forget to add certain synchronization operations in the program, or (c) programmers forget to maintain a common lock guarding accesses to some shared variable v since there are often many lock variables in a real-life program.

Problem Statement. The work in this paper deals with formal verification (and subsequent debugging) of multi-threaded C# programs which are improperly synchronized. As a simple example consider the following schematic program

J. Misra, T. Nipkow, and E. Sekerinski (Eds.): FM 2006, LNCS 4085, pp. 476–491, 2006.
© Springer-Verlag Berlin Heidelberg 2006

fragment, and suppose initially x = y = 0. Moreover 11, 12 are thread-local variables while x, y are shared variables.

$$
\begin{array}{c|c}
\texttt{x = 1;} & \texttt{11 = y;} \\
\texttt{y = 1;} & \texttt{12 = x;}
\end{array}
$$

If this program is executed on a uni-processor platform, we cannot have 11 = 1, 12 = 0 at the end of the program. However, on a multiprocessor platform which allows reordering of writes to different memory locations this is possible. On such a platform, the writes to x, y may be completed out-of-order. As a result, the following completion order is possible $\langle y = 1, 11 = y, 12 = x, x = 1 \rangle$.

Since an improperly synchronized program can exhibit different sets of behaviors on different platforms, how do we even specify the semantics of such programs and reason about them? Clearly, we would like to reason about programs in a *platform-independent* fashion, rather than reasoning about a program's behaviors separately for each platform. Languages like Java, C# allow such platform-independent reasoning by defining a *memory model* at the programming language level. Now, what does a memory model for a programming language like C# mean? The C# memory model (also called the .NET memory model [15]) is a set of abstract rules which capture the behaviors of multi-threaded programs on *any* implementation platform — uni-processor or multi-processor. Given a multi-threaded C# program P, the set of execution traces of P permitted under the .NET memory model is a superset of the traces obtained by interleaving the operations of program P's individual threads. The operations in any thread include read/write of shared variables and synchronization operations like lock/unlock. The .NET memory model permits *certain operations* within a thread to be completed out-of-order, that is, the programming language level memory model essentially specifies which reorderings are allowed. So, to consider all program behaviors we need to take into account — (a) arbitrary interleavings of threads, and (b) certain (not all) reorderings within a thread. This makes the formal verification of improperly synchronized multi-threaded programs especially hard.

Basic Approach. In this paper, we develop a memory-model sensitive invariant checker for the programming language C#. Our checker verifies a C# program at the level of bytecodes. The checker proceeds by representing and managing states at the level of C#'s stack-based virtual machine. Moreover, the checker's state space exploration takes the .NET memory model into account. In other words, it allows the reorderings permitted by .NET memory model to explore additional reachable states in a program. Thus, the programming language level memory model is treated as a formal contract between the program and the language implementation; we then take this contract into account during software verification.

Furthermore, we note that programmers usually understand possible behaviors of a multi-threaded program by using a stronger model called *Sequential Consistency* [10]. An execution model for multi-threaded programs is sequentially consistent if for any program P (a) any execution of P is an interleaving of the operations in the constituent threads (b) the operations in each constituent thread execute in program order. Thus, if we are model checking an invariant φ, our checker may uncover counter-example traces which (a) violate φ , and (b) are not allowed under Sequential Consistency. Disallowing such counter-example traces requires disabling reorderings among operations. This is usually done by inserting *memory barriers or fence operations*; a memory barrier is an operation such that instructions before the barrier must complete before the starting of instructions after the barriers. Since memory barriers are expensive operations (in terms of performance) we use a maxflow-mincut algorithm to insert minimal number of barriers/fences for ruling out program states which are unreachable under Sequential Consistency.

Technical Contributions. Our work involves the following steps — which taken together constitute the technical contributions of this paper.

- *Memory Model Specification* We first understand and formally specify the .NET memory model. Previous works [23] have investigated this issue and discussed certain corner cases in the .NET memory model description. Unlike [23], our specification is not operational/executable, making it more accessible to system designers (who may not have formal methods background).
- *The Checker* We use the .NET memory model specification to develop a memory model sensitive invariant checker at the level of bytecodes. It allows all execution traces permitted by .NET memory model. The checker issues operations in program order but allows them to complete out-of-order as long as the reordering is permitted by .NET memory model.
- *Memory Barrier Insertion* Our checker is useful for uncovering all execution traces allowed by the .NET memory model. However, when the programmer finds "unexpected" execution traces using our checker how does (s)he disallow this behavior? We use the well-known maxflow-mincut algorithm [7] to rule out program states unreachable under Sequential Consistency. The mincut yields (a minimal number of) places in the program where the memory barriers are to be inserted.

In Section 3 we show a simple working example to explain our identification and removal of undesirable program behaviors.

2   Related Work

Programming language level memory models are relatively new. In the recent years, substantial research efforts have been invested in developing the Java Memory Model (*e.g.* see [1,11,13]). These works mostly focus on what should be the programming language level memory model for Java.

For the .NET memory model, a formal executable specification based on Abstract State Machines has been discussed in [23]. In this paper, we formally present the .NET memory model in a tabular non-operational format — clearly showing which pairs of operations can be reordered. This makes the formal specification more accessible to system designers as well. Furthermore, even though our memory model specification itself is not executable (unlike [23]) we show how it can be exploited for exploring the state space of a program.

As far as program verification is concerned, typically most works on multi-threaded program verification are oblivious of the programming language memory model. For all such works, the execution model implicitly assumed is Sequential Consistency — operations in a thread proceed in program order and any interleaving among the threads is possible. Integrating programming language level memory models for reasoning about programs has hardly been studied. In particular, our previous work [21] integrated an operational specification of the Java Memory Model for software model checking. Also, the work of [24] integrates an executable memory model specification for detecting data races in multi-threaded Java programs.

Our checker verifies programs at the level of bytecodes; its state space representation has similarities with the Java Path Finder (JPF) model checker [9]. However, JPF is not sensitive to Java memory model, and it implicitly considers sequential consistency as the program execution model. In fact, works on bytecode level formal reasoning (e.g., see [18] and the articles therein) typically have not considered the programming language level memory model.

The work of [12] develops a behavioral simulator to explore program behaviors allowed by the Java memory model. Apart from the differences in programming language (Java and C#) there are at least two conceptual differences between our work and [12]. First of all, their explorer works at the level of abstract operations such as read/write/lock/unlock whereas our checker operates at the lower (and more realistic) bytecode level. Secondly, and more importantly, our tool does not only explore all program executions allowed by the .NET memory model. It can also suggest which barriers are to be inserted for disallowing program executions which are not sequentially consistent but are allowed by the (more relaxed) .NET memory model. This technique is *generic* and is not restricted to C#.

Finally, an alternative to our strategy of inserting memory barriers might be to mark all shared variables in the program as *volatile* [14]. We however note this does not work due to the weak definition and implementation of volatiles in C#. In particular, C# language documents [14] and C# implementations (e.g., .NET 2.0) seem to allow reordering of volatile writes occurring before volatile reads in a program thread. On the other hand, memory barriers have a clear well-understood semantics but they incur performance overheads. For this reason, given an invariant property φ we insert *minimal* memory barriers in the program text which disallow all non-sequentially consistent execution traces violating invariant φ. Note that we are inserting memory barriers to disallow execution traces (in a state transition graph) which violate a *given* invariant property. Thus, we do not seek to avoid all data races, our aim is to avoid violations of a given program invariant.

3 A Working Example

We consider Peterson's mutual exclusion algorithm [20] to illustrate our approach. The algorithm uses two lock variables and one shared turn variable to ensure mutually exclusive access to a critical section; a shared variable `counter` is incremented within the critical section. Initially, we have `lock0 = lock1 = turn = counter = 0`.

Thread 1	Thread 2
1. `lock0 = 1;`	A. `lock1 = 1;`
2. `turn = 1;`	B. `turn = 0;`
3. `while(1){`	C. `while(1) {`
4. `if (lock1!=1)||(turn==0)`	D. `if (lock0!=1)||(turn==1)`
5. `break; }`	E. `break; }`
6. `counter++;`	F. `counter++;`
7. `lock0 = 0;`	G. `lock1 = 0;`

In this program we are interested in the value of the variable `counter` when the program exits. Under sequential consistency, the algorithm is proven to allow only a single thread running in the critical section at the same time and thus when the program exits, we always have *counter == 2*. However when we run the program in a relaxed memory model (such as the .NET memory model) we can observe *counter == 1* at the end. One execution trace that can lead to such an observable value is as follows.

Thread 1	Thread 2
write `lock0 = 1` (line 1)	
write `turn = 1` (line 2)	
read 0 from `lock1`, break (line 4,5)	
read 0 from `counter` (line 6)	
	write `lock1 = 1` (line A)
	write `turn=0` (line B)

At this point, **Thread 1** can write 1 to `counter` (line 6), then write 0 to `lock0` (line 7). However if the writes to `counter` and `lock0` are reordered, `lock0 = 0` is written while `counter` still holds the old value 0. Thread 2 reads `lock0 = 0`, it will break out of its loop and load the value of `counter` which is now still 0. So both threads will write the value 1 to `counter`, leading to *counter == 1* at the end of the program.

Finding out such behaviors is a complex and error-prone task if it is done manually. Moreover even after we find them, how do we disable such behaviors? A quick way to fix the problem is to disable all reorderings within each thread; this clearly ensures Sequential Consistency. Recall that a memory barrier requires all instructions before the barrier to complete before the starting of all operations after the barrier. We can disable all reorderings allowed by a given relaxed memory model by inserting a memory barrier after each operation which can possibly be reordered. This will lead to very high performance overheads.

Note that running the above code with all shared variables being volatile also does not work. In Microsoft .NET Framework 2.0 on Intel Pentium 4, the variable `counter` is still not always observed to be 2 at the end of the program. This seems to be due to the possibility of (volatile-write → volatile-read) reorderings, an issue about which the CLI specification is also ambiguous. We discuss this matter in more details in the next section.

In this paper, we provide a solution to the problem of finding additional behaviors under a relaxed memory model and then disabling those behaviors without compromising program efficiency. Using our checker we can first explore all reachable states under Sequential Consistency and confirm that *counter* == *2* is guaranteed at the end of the program. This amounts to verifying the invariant property $AG((pc == end) \Rightarrow (counter == 2))$ expressed in Computation Tree Logic (CTL). Here *pc* stands for the program counter (capturing the control locations of both the threads) and *end* stands for the last control location (where both threads have terminated). We then check the same invariant property under the .NET memory model; this check amounts to exploring more reachable states from the initial state (as compared to the set of reachable states computed under Sequential Consistency). We find that under the .NET memory model, our property can be violated since *counter* == *1* is possible at the end of the program. The checker does a full reachable state space exploration and returns all the counter-example traces, that is, all possible ways of having *counter* $\neq$ 2 at the end of the program.

However, more importantly, our checker does not stop at *detecting* possible additional (and undesirable) behaviors under the .NET memory model. After finding that the property $AG((pc == end) \Rightarrow (counter == 2))$ is violated under .NET memory model, our checker employs a memory barrier insertion heuristic to suggest an error *correction* strategy; it finds three places in each thread for inserting memory barriers. We only show the modified code for Thread1; Thread2's modification is similar.

```
lock0 = 1; MemoryBarrier; turn = 1;
while(1){
        MemoryBarrier; if((lock1 != 1) || (turn == 0)) break;
}
counter++; MemoryBarrier; lock0 = 0;
```

The inserted memory barriers are sufficient to ensure that the algorithm will work correctly under the relaxed memory model of C# (while still allowing the compiler/hardware to reorder other operations for maximum performance). This claim can again be verified using our checker — that is, by running the checker on the program with barriers under the relaxed .NET memory model we can verify that $AG((pc == end) \Rightarrow (counter == 2))$ holds. Moreover, the number of inserted barriers is also "optimal" — that is, at least so many barriers are needed to disallow all possible violations of $AG((pc == end) \Rightarrow (counter == 2))$ under the .NET memory model.

4   .NET Memory Model and Its Implementation

In this section, we first describe the programming language level memory model for C#, also called the .NET memory model, based on the information in two Microsoft's official ECMA standard document [15] and [14].

We present which reorderings are allowed by .NET memory model as a reordering table. We first describe the bytecode types it considers and then present allowed bytecode reorderings. The bytecode types are:

- Volatile reads/writes: Reads/writes to volatile variables (Variables in a C# program can be marked by the programmer by the keyword "volatile" indicating that any access to such a variable should access its master copy).
- Normal reads/writes: Reads/writes to variables which have not been marked as volatile in the program.
- Lock/unlock: The synchronization operations.

Among these operations, the model allows the reorderings summarized by Table 1. The model leaves a lot of possibility for optimization as long as program dependencies within a thread are not violated (*e.g.*, `store x; load x` is never executed out-of-order due to data dependency on `x`). While data-dependency removal may allow more optimizations, the CLI documents explicitly *prohibit* doing so — see execution order rules in section 10.10 of [14]. Furthermore, here we are presenting the memory model in terms of *allowed bytecode reorderings* and not in terms of reorderings of abstract program actions. Optimizations which remove dependencies are usually performed by the compiler (the hardware platforms respect program dependencies) and hence would already be reflected in the bytecode.

Table 1. Bytecode reordering allowed by the .NET memory model

Reorder	2nd bytecode					
1st bytecode	Read	Write	Volatile Read	Volatile Write	Lock	Unlock
Read	Yes	Yes	Yes	No	Yes	No
Write	Yes	Yes	Yes	No	Yes	No
Volatile-Read	No	No	No	No	No	No
Volatile-Write	Yes	Yes	*Yes*	No	Yes	No
Lock	No	No	No	No	No	No
Unlock	Yes	Yes	Yes	No	No	No

Our reordering table is constructed based on the following considerations.

- Normal Reads and Writes are freely reordered.
- Locks and Unlocks are never reordered.
- Volatile Reads and writes have acquire-release semantics, that is, operations after (before) volatile-read (volatile-write) cannot be moved to before (after) the volatile-read (volatile-write).

An interesting case is when a volatile write is followed by a volatile read (to a different variable). If we adhere to a strict ordering of all volatile operations, this reordering is disallowed.[1] But it seems that Microsoft's .NET 2.0 allows this

---

[1] Note that even if we allow (volatile-write → volatile-read) reorderings, we can still ensure that all writes to volatile variables are seen in the same order from all threads of execution.

reordering on Peterson's mutual exclusion example shown in Section 3 e.g., the reads in Line 4 (or Line D) can get reordered w.r.t. writes in Lines 1,2 (Lines A, B) thereby leading to violation of mutual exclusion. The ECMA documents [15] and [14] are also silent on this issue; they only mention that operations cannot be moved before (after) a volatile read (volatile write), thus leaving out the case when a volatile write is followed by a volatile read.

Our checker implements the .NET Common Language Infrastructure (CLI) instruction set specified in [15]. We allow reordering of operations by (a) requiring all bytecodes to issue in program order and (b) allow certain bytecodes (whose reordering is allowed by the memory model) to complete out-of-order. Allowing reorderings according to the .NET memory model involves additional data structures in the state representation of our checker. In particular, for each thread we now need to maintain a list of "incomplete" bytecodes — bytecodes which have been issued but have not completed. The execution model allows a program thread to either execute its next bytecode or complete one of the incomplete bytecodes. We now proceed to elaborate on the state space representation and the reachability analysis.

5   Invariant Checker

The core of our checker is a virtual machine that executes .NET Common Language Infrastructure (CLI) bytecode using explicit state representation. It supports many threads of execution by interleaving issuing and completing of bytecodes from all threads. We implemented only a subset of the CLI features. Features such as networking, I/O, class polymorphism and exception handling are not included in the implementation.

5.1   State Representation

We first consider the global state representation without considering the effects of the reorderings allowed by .NET memory model. To describe a global state we use the notion of *data units* of the CLI virtual machine. The virtual machine uses *data units* to hold the value of variables and stack items in the program. Each data unit has an identifier (for it to be referred to), and a modifiable value. The type of the modifiable value can be (a) one of the primitive data types, (b) reference types (pointers to objects), or (c) objects. New data units are created when a variable or a new object instance is allocated, or when a load instruction is executed. A global state of a program now consists of the following data units, corresponding to the different memory areas of the CLI virtual machine [15].

Program counter for each thread. Each thread has a program counter to keep track of the next bytecode to be issued.

Stack for each thread. Each thread has a stack which is used by most bytecodes to load/store data, pass parameters and return values from functions (or certain arithmetic / branch operations).

Heap. The virtual machine has a single heap shared among all threads. Object instances and arrays are allocated from the heap. A data unit is created for each object as well each of its fields.

Static variables. A data unit is allocated for each static variable on its first use and this data unit is maintained for subsequent accesses.

Frame. Frames store local variables, arguments and return address of a method. Each time a method is called, a new frame is created and pushed into frame stack; this frame is popped when the method returns. Each local variable/ argument is assigned one data unit.

All of the above data areas of the virtual machine are included in the global state space representation of a program. Now, in order to support the memory model, a new data structure is added to each thread: a list of incomplete bytecodes (given in program order). Each element of this list is one of the following type of operations — read, write, volatile read, volatile write, lock, unlock (the operation types mentioned in the .NET memory model, see Table 1). This completes the state space representation of our checker. We now describe the state space traversal.

5.2   Search Algorithm

Our checker performs reachability analysis by an explicit state depth-first search (starting from the initial state) over the state space representation discussed in the preceding. Given any state, how do we find the possible next states? This is done by picking any of the program threads, and letting it execute a single step. So, what counts as a single step for a program thread? In the usual model checkers (which implicitly assume Sequential Consistency), once a thread is chosen to take one step, the next operation from that thread forms the next step. In our checker the choices of next-step for a thread includes (a) issuing the next operation and (b) completing one of the pending operations (*i.e.*, operations which have started but not completed). The ability to complete pending operations out of order allows the checker to find all possible behaviors reachable under a given memory model (in this case the .NET memory model).

Thus, the search algorithm in our checker starts from the initial state, performs depth-first search and continues until there are no new states to be traversed. In order to ensure termination of this search, our checker of course needs to decide whether a given state has been already encountered. In existing explicit state software model checkers, this program state equivalence test is often done by comparing the so-called *memory image* in the two states, which includes the heap, stacks, frames and local variables. Our checker employs a similar test; however it also considers the list of incomplete operations in the two states. Formally, two states s and s' with two sets of data units $D = \{d_1, d_2, ..., d_n\}$ and $D' = \{d'_1, d'_2, ..., d'_n\}$ are equivalent if and only if the program counters in all threads are equal and there exists a bijective function $f : D \rightarrow D'$ satisfying:

 - For all $1 \leq i \leq n$, the value stored in d_i and $f(d_i)$ are equal.
 - A static variable x in s is allocated data unit d_i if and only if it is allocated data unit $f(d_i)$ in s'.

- Data unit d_i is the kth item on the stack (or frame, local variable, argument list, list of incomplete bytecodes) of the jth thread in s iff $f(d_i)$ is the kth item on the stack (or frame, local variable, argument list, list of incomplete bytecodes) of the jth thread in s'.
- The reference type data unit d_i points to data unit d_j in s if and only if $f(d_i)$ points to $f(d_j)$ in s'.

In our implementation, the global state representation is saved into a single sequence so that if two state's sequences are identical, the two states are equivalent. Like the Java Path Finder model checker [9], we also use a hash function to make the state comparison efficient.

Search Optimizations. By allowing program operations to complete out-of-order, our checker explores more behaviors than the normal model checkers based on Sequential Consistency. We employ the following search optimization to speed up our checker. For each thread, we classify its bytecodes into two categories — thread-local and non thread-local. In particular, the following are considered thread-local bytecodes — load/store of local variables, method invocation, memory allocation, computation and control transfer operations; all others are considered non thread-local bytecodes. Now, our checker exploits this categorization by trying to atomically execute sequences of thread-local bytecodes in a thread. Furthermore, our checker *does not allow two thread-local operations to execute out-of-order even if such reordering is allowed by the .NET memory model.* The justification of this optimization is simple — even if thread-local operations execute out-of-order, the effects of such additional behavior are not observable by other threads.

6   Disabling Undesirable Program Behaviors

Given a multi-threaded C# program, we are interested in computing the set of reachable states from the initial state. The set of reachable states under the .NET memory model is guaranteed to be a superset of the reachable state set under Sequential Consistency. In this section, we discuss tactics for disallowing the additional states reached under the .NET memory model. Since these additional states are reached due to certain reordering of operations within program threads, we can avoid those states if such reorderings are disabled by inserting barriers/fences in the program text.

While doing reachability analysis we build (on-the-fly) the state transition graph. Each vertex represents one state, each directed edge represents a transition from one state to another. Consider the state transition system constructed for the .NET memory model. Because this memory model is more relaxed than Sequential Consistency, we can divide the graph edges into two types: solid edges correspond to transitions which can be performed under the Sequential Consistency (complete the bytecodes in order within a thread) and dashed edges correspond to transitions which can *only* be performed under .NET memory model (requires completing bytecodes out-of-order). From initial state, if we traverse only solid edges we can visit all states reachable under Sequential Consistency. We color the corresponding vertices as white and the remaining vertices as black. The black vertices denotes the additional states which are reached due to the reorderings allowed by the relaxed memory model (see Figure 1 for illustration). Note that if (a) we are seeking to verify an invariant property φ under Sequential Consistency as well as the .NET model, (b) φ is true under Sequential Consistency and (c) φ is false under the .NET memory model — the states violating φ must be black states. However, not all the black states may denote violation of φ as shown in the schematic state transition graph of Figure 1.

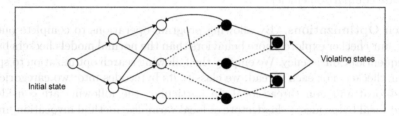

Fig. 1. State transition graph under a relaxed memory model; only white states can be reached under Sequential Consistency. A cut is shown separating the initial state from "violating" states.

Basic Mincut Formulation. To prevent the execution from reaching the violating black states, we need to remove some of the edges from the graph. The solid edges cannot be removed because their corresponding transitions are allowed under Sequential Consistency. The dashed edges can be removed selectively by putting barriers. However note that the barriers will appear in the program text, so inserting *one barrier* in the program can disable *many dashed edges* in the state transition graph. We find out the minimal number of dashed edges to be removed so that the violating black states become unreachable; we then find out the memory barriers to be inserted in the program text for removing these dashed edges. Now we describe our strategy for computing the minimal number of dashed edges to be removed. We compute the minimum cut $C = \{e_1, e_2, ..., e_n\}$ where $e_1, \ldots, e_n$ are dashed edges in the state transition graph such that there is no directed path from the initial state to any violating black state (denoting violation of the invariant φ being verified) without passing through an edge in C. We find the minimal set of dashed edges by employing the well-known Ford-Fulkerson maxflow-mincut algorithm [7]. To find the minimal number of dashed edges in the state transition graph as the mincut, we can set the capacity of each dashed edge to 1 and each solid edge to infinity.

How can we locate the barrier insertion point in the program such that a given dashed edge in the state transition graph is removed? Recall that a dashed edge in the state transition graph denotes a state transition which is caused by out-of-order completion of a bytecode. In Figure 2 state s has m incomplete bytecodes $\langle b_1, b_2, \ldots, b_k, \ldots, b_m \rangle$ (given in program order). The transition that completes bytecode b_1 does not require an out-of-order completion of bytecodes while the

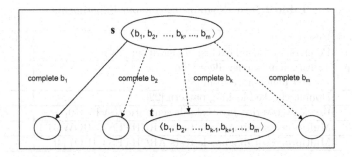

Fig. 2. Transitions from a state, a dashed edge indicates the transition requires an out-of-order completion of bytecodes

transitions that complete b_k with $2 \leq k \leq m$ do. The removal of edge from state s to state t (corresponding to the completion of bytecode b_k, see Figure 2) is identified with inserting a barrier before bytecode b_k.

Modified Mincut Formulation. Note that the minimal set of dashed edges in the state transition graph may not always produce the minimal number of barriers in the program text. At the same time, inserting minimal number of barriers in the program text may not be desirable in the first place since they do not indicate the actual number of barriers encountered during program execution.[2] However if we want to minimize the number of barriers inserted into the program, we can do so by simply modifying the capacities of the dashed edges in the state transition graph. We partition the dashed edges in the state transition graph into disjoint partitions s.t. edges e, e' belong to the same partition iff disabling of both e and e' can be achieved by inserting a single barrier in the program. We can then assign capacities to the edges in such a way that the sum of capacities of the edges in each partition is equal — thereby giving equal importance to each possible program point where a barrier could be inserted. The maxflow-mincut algorithm is now run with these modified capacities (of the dashed edges); the solid edges still carry a weight of infinity to prevent them from appearing in the min cut.

Complexity. The Maxflow-mincut algorithm has time complexity of $O(m * f)$ where m is the number of edges in the state transition graph and f is the value of the maximum flow. The quantity f depends on how the capacities of the state transition graph edges are assigned. In all our experiments, f was less than 150 for all our test programs (using basic or modified mincut formulation).

7   Experiments

In this section, we report the experiments used to evaluate our checker. The multi-threaded programs used in our experiments are listed in Table 2. Out of these,

---

[2] A single barrier inside a loop which is iterated many times can introduce higher performance overheads than several barriers outside the loop.

Table 2. Test Programs used in our Experiments

Benchmark	Description	# bytecodes
peterson	Peterson's Mutual exclusion algorithm [20]	120
tbarrier	Tournament barrier algorithm — *Barrier* benchmark from [8]	153
dc	Double-checked locking pattern [22]	77
rw-vol	Read-after-Write Java volatile semantic test by [19]	92
rowo	Multiprocessor diagnostic tests ARCHTEST (ROWO)[4]	87
po	Multiprocessor diagnostic tests ARCHTEST (PO) [4]	132

peterson, and tbarrier are standard algorithms that work correctly under Sequential Consistency, but require more synchronizations to do so in the C# memory model. The tournament barrier algorithm (taken from Java Grande benchmarks) provides an application program level implementation of the concurrency primitive "barrier" (*different from our memory barriers which prevent reordering of operations*) which allows two or more threads to handshake at a certain program point.

The programs rw-vol and dc have been discussed recently in the context of developing the new Java memory model [1]. In particular, dc has been used in recent literature as a test program to discuss the possible semantics of volatile variables in the new Java memory model [6]; this program involves the lazy initialization of a shared object by several threads.

The other programs rowo and po are test programs taken from the ARCHTEST benchmark suite [4,17]. ARCHTEST is a suite of test programs where the programs have been systematically constructed to check for violations of memory models (by generating violation of memory ordering rules imposed by the memory models). In particular, the program rowo checks for violation of ordering between multiple reads as well as multiple writes within a program thread; the program po checks for violation of program order among all operations in a program thread. These programs are effective for evaluating whether our checker can insert memory barriers to avoid behaviors not observable under Sequential Consistency.

For all of the above benchmarks we employ our checker to find all reachable states under (a) Sequential Consistency and (b) .NET memory model. For the latter, recall that we allow each program thread to maintain a list of incomplete bytecodes so that bytecodes can be completed out of order. For our experiments we do not impose a bound on the size of this list of incomplete bytecodes. So in practice it is bounded only by the (finite) number of bytecodes in a program thread. This exposes *all* possible behaviors of a given program under the .NET memory model.

Our checker for C# programs is itself implemented in C#. It takes the binaries of the benchmarks, disassembles them and checks the bytecode against a given invariant property via state space exploration. For each of our benchmarks in Table 2 we provide a program invariant for the reachability analysis to proceed and report violations. For the Peterson's algorithm (peterson) this invariant is the mutually exclusive access of shared resource. The invariant for tbarrier follows from the definition of the concurrency primitive "barrier". For the Double checked Locking

Table 3. Summary of Experimental Results. Column 4 shows the time to perform full reachability analysis under Sequential Consistency. Under the heading .NET, the CE column shows time to find the first counter-example, while FR shows time for full reachability analysis under .NET memory model. The column Mflow indicates the time to run the Maxflow algorithm for inserting barriers. The *Total* column denotes time for full reachability and barrier insertion, that is, *Total = FR + Mflow*.

Benchmark	# states	# transitions	S.C. (secs)	.NET				
				Time (secs)				# barriers
				CE	FR	Mflow	Total	
peterson	903	2794	0.09	0.05	1.06	0.04	1.10	3
tbarrier	1579	5812	0.21	1.57	3.99	0.05	4.04	3
dc	228	479	0.10	0.11	0.27	0.03	0.30	1
rw-vol	1646	5616	0.20	0.29	2.75	0.23	2.98	4
rowo	1831	4413	0.16	0.23	1.87	0.05	1.92	2
po	6143	22875	0.29	0.60	13.07	1.48	14.55	6

pattern (dc) this invariant states that whenever the shared object's data is read, it has been initialized. The invariant for rw-vol benchmark is obtained from [19]. For the ARCHTEST programs rowo and po, this invariant is obtained from the rules of read/write order and program order respectively (see [4,17]).

Our checker performs reachability analysis to explore the reachable states under Sequential Consistency and the .NET memory model. Clearly, the reachability analysis under the .NET memory model takes more time since it involves exploring a superset of the states reachable under Sequential Consistency. In Table 3 we report the running time of our checker for obtaining the first counter-example (column *CE*) and for performing full reachability analysis (column *FR*). The time taken to find the first counter-example is not high; so if the user is only interested in detecting a violation our checker can produce one in a short time. The time to perform full reachability analysis (thereby finding all counter-example traces) is tolerable, but much larger than the time to find one counter-example. All experiments were conducted on a 2.2 Ghz machine with 2.5 GB of main memory.

After exploring all reachable states under the .NET memory model, our checker can insert barriers via a maxflow-mincut algorithm (we used the "Modified Mincut Formulation" presented in Section 6). The time to run the maxflow algorithm is small as shown in column *Mflow* of Table 3. The results of the barrier insertion step are shown in the *# barriers* column of Table 3. This column shows the total number of barriers inserted by our tool into the program so that any program execution trace which (a) violates the invariant being verified and (b) is disallowed by Sequential Consistency, — is not observed even when the program is run under the relaxed .NET memory model.

Interestingly, the reader may notice that our checker inserts only one barrier for the Double Checked Locking pattern (same as the solution in [16], [3] and [2]) while the solution using "explicit memory barriers" given in [6] suggests putting two barriers. Both solutions are correct, because they work for different memory models. Our checker only inserts those barriers that enforce the program's correctness under *a .NET memory model compliant implementation*. It will not insert barriers to disable behaviors which are not even allowed by the .NET memory model (the additional barrier in [6] is needed if the memory model allows reorderings which do not respect program dependencies).

More details about our checker (including its source code) and the test programs are available from http://www.comp.nus.edu.sg/~release/mmchecker.

8   Discussion

In this paper, we have presented an invariant checker which works on the byte-code representation of multi-threaded C# programs. The main novelties of our work are (a) we can expose non sequentially consistent execution traces of a program which are allowed by the .NET memory model, and (b) after inspecting the counter-example traces violating a given invariant, we can automatically insert barriers to disallow such executions.

We are now in the process of integrating partial order reduction with dynamic escape analysis [5] into our checker. This will allow us to safely reduce the set of explored program states during invariant checking.

Acknowledgments. This work was supported partly by a grant from Microsoft under the Shared Source CLI (SSCLI aka Rotor) programme, partly by a Public Sector grant from A*STAR (Singapore) and partly by an internal grant from NUS (Singapore). Tulika Mitra and Weng-Fai Wong gave us useful feedback during the project.

References

1. Java Specification Request (JSR) 133. Java Memory Model and Thread Specification revision, 2004.
2. B. Abrams. http://blogs.msdn.com/brada/archive/2004/05/12/130935.aspx
3. C. Brumme. Weblog: Memory model. http://blogs.msdn.com/cbrumme/archive/2003/05/17/51445.aspx.
4. W. W. Collier. *Reasoning about Parallel Architectures*. Prentice Hall, 1992.
5. M. B. Dwyer et al. Using static and dynamic escape analysis to enable model reductions in model-checking concurrent object-oriented programs. Technical report, Kansas State Univ., 2003.
6. D. Bacon et al. The "Double-checked Locking is Broken" declaration. http://www.cs.umd.edu/pugh/java/memoryModel/DoubleCheckedLocking.html.
7. L.R. Ford and D.R. Fulkerson. Maximum flow through a network. In *Canad. J. Math*, volume 8, pages 399–404, 1956.
8. JGF. The Java Grande Forum Multi-threaded Benchmarks, 2001. http://www.epcc.ed.ac.uk/computing/research_activities/java_grande/threads.html.
9. JPF. The Java Path Finder model checking tool, 2005. http://javapathfinder.sourceforge.net/.
10. L. Lamport. How to make a multiprocessor computer that correctly executes multiprocess programs. *IEEE Transactions on Computers*, 28(9), 1979.

11. D. Lea. The JSR-133 cookbook for compiler writers. http://gee.cs.oswego.edu/dl/jmm/cookbook.html.
12. J. Manson and W. Pugh. The Java Memory Model Simulator. In *Workshop on Formal Techniques for Java-like Programs, in association with ECOOP*, 2002.
13. J. Manson, W. Pugh, and S. Adve. The Java Memory Model. In *ACM Symposium on Principles of Programming Languages (POPL)*, 2005.
14. Microsoft. Standard ECMA-335 C# Specification, 2005. http://www.ecma-international.org/publications/files/ECMA-ST/Ecma-334.pdf.
15. Microsoft. Standard ECMA-335 Common Language Infrastructure (CLI), 2005. http://www.ecma-international.org/publications/standards/Ecma-335.htm.
16. V. Morrison. Dotnet discussion: The DOTNET Memory Model. http://discuss.develop.com/archives/wa.exe?A2=ind0203B&L=DOTNET&P=R375..
17. R. Nalumusu et al. The "test model checking" approach to the verification of memory models of multiprocessors. In *Computer Aided Verification (CAV)*, 1998.
18. T. Nipkow et al. Special issue on Java bytecode verification. *Journal of Automated Reasoning (JAR)*, 30(3–4), 2003.
19. W. Pugh. Test for sequential consistency of volatiles. http://www.cs.umd.edu/pugh/java/memoryModel/ReadAfterWrite.java.
20. M. Raynal. *Algorithms for mutual exclusion*. MIT Press, 1986.
21. A. Roychoudhury and T. Mitra. Specifying multithreaded Java semantics for program verification. In *ACM Intl. Conf. on Software Engineering (ICSE)*, 2002.
22. D. Schmidt and T. Harrison. Double-checked locking: An optimization pattern for efficiently initializing and accessing thread-safe objects. In *3rd annual Pattern Languages of Program Design conference*, 1996.
23. R.F. Stark and E. Borger. An ASM specification of C# threads and the .NET memory model. In *ASM Workshop, LNCS 3065*, 2004.
24. Y. Yang, G. Gopalakrishnan, and G. Lindstrom. Memory model sensitive data race analysis. In *Intl. Conf. on Formal Engg. Methods (ICFEM)*, 2004.

Changing Programs Correctly: Refactoring with Specifications

Fabian Bannwart and Peter Müller

ETH Zürich
peter.mueller@inf.ethz.ch

Abstract. Refactorings change the internal structure of code without changing its external behavior. For non-trivial refactorings, the preservation of external behavior depends on semantic properties of the program that are difficult to check automatically before the refactoring is applied. Therefore, existing refactoring tools either do not support non-trivial refactorings at all or force programmers to rely on (typically incomplete) test suites to check their refactorings.

The technique presented in the paper allows one to show the preservation of external behavior even for complex refactorings. For a given refactoring, we prove once and for all that the refactoring is an equivalence transformation, provided that the refactored program satisfies certain semantic correctness conditions. These conditions can be added automatically as assertions to the refactored program and checked at runtime or verified statically. Our technique allows tools to apply even complex refactorings safely, and refactorings automatically improve program documentation by generating assertions.

1 Introduction

Refactorings are equivalence transformations on source code that change the internal structure of code without changing its external behavior [10]. They are applied to improve the understandability of code and to reduce its resistance to change.

The application of a refactoring is *correct* if it preserves the external behavior of the program. Whether an application of a refactoring is correct depends on certain correctness conditions. For instance, replacing the (side effect free) condition of a loop by a different condition generally preserves the external program behavior only if the old and the new condition yield the same value in all program executions.

Refactoring by hand is tedious and error-prone. Refactoring tools simplify the application of refactorings, but they guarantee the preservation of the program's external behavior only for refactorings with very simple correctness conditions such as "Rename Method" [10]. More complex refactorings such as "Move Field" are either not supported at all or not guaranteed to be applied correctly. That is, their application potentially alters the external behavior of the program.

Consequently, programmers rely on unit testing to determine whether a refactoring was applied correctly. This approach works well if the program has a

J. Misra, T. Nipkow, and E. Sekerinski (Eds.): FM 2006, LNCS 4085, pp. 492–507, 2006.
© Springer-Verlag Berlin Heidelberg 2006

complete set of unit tests that execute rapidly. However, in most practical applications, the set of unit tests is highly incomplete, for instance, because programmers have to make a trade-off between the completeness of the test suite and the time it takes to run all tests.

In this paper, we present a technique that guarantees that refactorings are applied correctly. For each refactoring, we perform the following three steps.

First, we determine the refactoring's *essential applicability conditions*. These syntactic conditions ensure that applying the refactoring results in a syntactically-correct program. In the "Move Field" example, a field f can be moved from a class S to a class T only if the field and both classes exist and if the target class does not already contain a field called f. Essential applicability conditions can easily be checked syntactically and are therefore not discussed in this paper.

Second, we determine the refactoring's *correctness conditions*. These semantic conditions ensure that each application of the refactoring preserves the external behavior of the program. For instance, an application of "Replace Expression" is correct only if the old and the new expression evaluate to the same value in all program executions. One of the novelties of our approach is that correctness conditions can be expressed in terms of the refactored program and added to the program as assertions such as JML [15] or Spec# [3] specifications. They can then be checked at runtime to make sure that the execution of a test actually covers the correctness condition. Alternatively, they can be checked statically by a program verifier such as Boogie [3] or ESC/Java2 [13]. Some correctness conditions can also be approximated and checked syntactically.

Third, we provide a formal proof that each application of the refactoring preserves the external behavior of the program, provided that the program satisfies the refactoring's essential applicability conditions and correctness conditions. We consider the original and the refactored program to have equivalent external behavior if they perform the same sequence of I/O operations. This notion of equivalence allows us to handle even complex changes of the program's internal structure. It is important to note that this correctness proof is done once and for all for each refactoring, whereas correctness conditions must be checked for each particular application of a refactoring.

Our technique improves the state of the art in three significant ways: (a) It handles refactorings with complex correctness conditions. Expressing these conditions as assertions improves test coverage and enables static verification. (b) It works on the source code level as opposed to more abstract models such as UML class diagrams. Working on the code level is important because refactorings are mainly applied during implementation rather than during design. Moreover, many correctness conditions depend on the intricacies of concrete code. For instance, the correctness conditions for "Move Field" fall on the field accesses, which are not present in an abstract model. (c) The specifications added to the transformed program convey the programmer's tacit knowledge why a particular refactoring is applicable. Therefore, they improve the documentation and facilitate the application of program verifiers.

In this paper, we present our technique and apply it to "Move Field", a prototypical example for a complex refactoring. Our technical report [2] describes several other successful applications of our technique as well as an implementation of "Move Field" in Eclipse and Visual Studio.

Overview. The rest of this paper is structured as follows. In the next section, we discuss correctness conditions. Section 3 formalizes the notion of external equivalence for a language with objects, references, and I/O operations. We apply our approach to "Move Field" in Sect. 4. Section 5 discusses related work.

2   Correctness Conditions

The correctness conditions for a refactoring can be split into *a-priori conditions* that are checked statically in the original program before the refactoring is applied and *a-posteriori conditions* that are checked in the refactored program. A-priori conditions are semantic conditions that can be easily checked or aptly approximated syntactically. For instance, splitting a loop is possible if there is no data dependency between the statements in the loop, which can be checked a-priori by data dependency analyses.

However, for many interesting refactorings, correctness conditions cannot be checked a-priori. Consider for instance the following code fragment, which calculates and prints the hypotenuse of a right triangle with legs a and b.

```
print(a/cos(atan(b/a)));
```

A possible refactoring is to replace the expression `a/cos(atan(b/a))` by the simpler expression `sqrt( a*a + b*b )`.

The correctness conditions for this refactoring are that both expressions (a) are side effect free and (b) evaluate to the same result (we ignore differences due to rounding here). While property (a) can be checked a-priori by a static analysis, property (b) must be checked at runtime or verified statically. Runtime assertion checking is not useful for a-priori conditions because it would be cumbersome to force programmers to run their test suite before applying a refactoring. Therefore, property (b) is better formulated as an a-posteriori condition and turned into a specification of the refactored program:

```
assert sqrt( a*a + b*b ) == a/cos(atan(b/a));
print(sqrt( a*a + b*b ));
```

The assertion can be checked at runtime when testing the refactored program or proved by a program verifier.

Assertions for a-posteriori conditions of refactorings document knowledge about the design of the code. Therefore, it is important that they stay in the program, even after a successful test or static verification. They are an important guideline for future modifications of the code.

To avoid cluttering up programs with assert statements, it is vital that assertions themselves can be refactored. In the above example, the assert statement could, for instance, be replaced by the stronger assertion `assert a > 0`. If a is a field, this assertion could then be further refactored into an object invariant.

We believe that the process of automatically generating assertions during refactoring and later refactoring the assertions into interface specifications greatly contributes to the documentation of the code by making design decisions explicit. This is an important side effect of our technique.

3   External Equivalence

Depending on the application domain, different aspects of external behavior are of interest such as functional behavior, timing, or resource consumption. In this paper, we focus on functional behavior. That is, we consider two programs to be externally-equivalent if they perform the same sequence of I/O operations.

In this section, we present the programming language that is used in the rest of the paper, formalize our notion of external equivalence, and explain how to prove the correctness of refactorings.

3.1   Programming Language

We present our results in terms of a small sequential class-based programming language. The language has the following statements: local variable update $l:=e$, field read $l:=o.f$, field update $o.f:=e$, object allocation $o:=\texttt{new } C$, I/O operation $l:=\texttt{io}(p)$, sequential composition $t_1; t_2$, and loop $\texttt{while}(e)\{t\}$, where l and o are local variables, e is an expression, p is a vector of expressions, f is a field name, and t is a statement. For simplicity, we ignore the declaration of local variables, but we assume that they are correctly typed and that the language is type-safe. We do not discuss methods, inheritance, and subtyping in this paper, but our technical report does [2].

Assertions are not part of the program representation and do therefore not have any operational meaning. For runtime assertion checking however, these assertions have to be compiled into executable code.

The program representation is denoted by Γ. $code_\Gamma$ is the executable program code of Γ. $fields_\Gamma(C)$ is the set of field names for a given class C in program Γ. After object creation, each field is initialized to the zero-equivalent value of its type T, denoted by $zero(T)$. $ctt(name)$ returns the compile-time type of variable or field $name$.

States. A state s of a program execution consists of variables $vars$, object heap $heap$ and I/O interactions ext: $s = (vars, heap, ext)$. We refer to the components of a state s by using $s.vars$, $s.heap$, and $s.ext$, respectively. The variables map names to values: $vars(l) = v$. The heap maps references to objects, which in turn map field names to values: $heap(o)(f) = v$. The I/O interactions accumulate the executed I/O operations: $ext = [\ldots, v:=\texttt{io}(v_1, \ldots, v_n), \ldots]$. The result of an I/O operation is given by the exogenous input decision function inp. Program executions start in the initial state ini, where all local variables hold default values, and the heap as well as the I/O sequence is empty.

Operational Semantics. Expression evaluation $[\![e]\!]s$ is defined compositionally by mapping the operator symbols to the respective operations:

$[\![f(e_1,\ldots,e_n)]\!]s = [\![f]\!]([\![e_1]\!]s,\ldots,[\![e_n]\!]s)$. Variable accesses are simply lookups in the state: $[\![l]\!]s = s.vars(l)$. Field accesses are not allowed in expressions. The big-step operational semantics is defined in Table 1. Updating the image of a value x in a map m with a value v is denoted by $m[x \leftarrow v]$. The state obtained from a state s by updating a local variable l with a value v is denoted by $s[l \leftarrow v]$. We use an analogous notation for updates of $s.heap$ and $s.ext$. The function $\mathrm{rtt}(v)$ yields the (runtime) type of a value. The transition relation for a statement t from a state s to a state r in a program Γ is written as $\Gamma| - s\xrightarrow{t}r$.

Table 1. Operational semantics. Statement t of Γ (first column) performs a transition from state s to the terminal state (second column), provided that the antecedents (third column) hold.

Statement t	Terminal state	Condition
$l := e$	$s[l \leftarrow [\![e]\!]s]$	–
$o.f := e$	$s[heap(s.vars(o))(f) \leftarrow [\![e]\!]s]$	$s.vars(o) \neq \mathbf{null}$
$l := o.f$	$s[l \leftarrow s.heap(s.vars(o))(f)]$	$s.vars(o) \neq \mathbf{null}$
$o := \mathbf{new}\ C$	$s[o \leftarrow p, heap(p) \leftarrow m]$	$p \notin \mathrm{dom}\ heap \wedge \mathrm{rtt}(p) = C \wedge m = \{f \leftarrow zero(\mathrm{ctt}(f)) | f \in \mathit{fields}_\Gamma(C)\}$
$l := \mathbf{io}(p)$	$s[ext \leftarrow ext', l \leftarrow i]$	$i = inp([\![p]\!]s, ext) \wedge ext' = ext \cdot [i := \mathbf{io}([\![p]\!]s)]$
$t_1; t_2$	r	$\Gamma| - s\xrightarrow{t_1}q \wedge \Gamma| - q\xrightarrow{t_2}r$
$\mathbf{while}(e)\{t_1\}$	r	$[\![e]\!]s \wedge \Gamma| - s\xrightarrow{t_1}q \wedge \Gamma| - q\xrightarrow{t}r$
$\mathbf{while}(e)\{t_1\}$	s	$\neg[\![e]\!]s$

3.2 Correspondence Between Original and Transformed Program

A refactoring R is defined by a transformation function μ_R, which maps a program Γ to the refactored program $\Gamma' \equiv \mu_R(\Gamma)$ and occurrences t of statements in Γ to their respective counterparts: $t' \equiv \mu_R(t)$. For simplicity, we assume that μ_R is applied only to programs that satisfy the essential applicability conditions of R. Consequently, μ_R can be assumed to yield syntactically-correct programs.

Γ and Γ' are equivalent if they perform the same I/O operations, that is, if $r.ext = r'.ext$ for their respective terminal states r and r':

$$(\Gamma| - ini\xrightarrow{code_\Gamma}r) => \exists r' : (\Gamma'| - ini\xrightarrow{code_{\Gamma'}}r') \wedge r.ext = r'.ext \qquad (1)$$

For simplicity, we consider only terminating executions here. Non-terminating programs can be handled by considering prefixes of executions of Γ.

Simulation Method. Although Implication (1) expresses external equivalence of Γ and Γ', it is not useful for an equivalence proof because it is inaccessible to any inductive argument. This problem is avoided by using the simulation method for proving correspondence of two transition systems $\Gamma| - \_\xrightarrow{}\_$ and $\Gamma'| - \_\xrightarrow{\mu_R(\_)}\_$.

To apply the simulation method, one defines a correspondence relation β_R on the states of the transition systems and proves that if both systems are in corresponding states and make a transition, they again reach corresponding states:

$$(\Gamma| - s \xrightarrow{t} r) \wedge \beta_R(s, s') => \exists r' : (\Gamma'| - s' \xrightarrow{\mu_R(t)} r') \wedge \beta_R(r, r') \qquad (2)$$

For Implication (2) to imply the general condition (1), two sanity conditions must hold. First, β_R must imply identity of the *ext* parts of the states so that *external equivalence* is guaranteed: $\forall s, s' : \beta_R(s, s') \Rightarrow s.ext = s'.ext$. Second, the initial states of the program executions must correspond (*initial correspondence*): $\beta_R(ini, ini)$.

To prove that a refactoring R is correct, it suffices to devise a correspondence relation β_R and prove that it satisfies Implication (2) and the two sanity conditions. This method works for many refactorings, but cannot handle several interesting refactorings as we discuss next.

General Correspondence Requirement for Refactorings. Implication (2) is too strong for several important refactorings for the following reasons.

(a) Some refactorings do not define a statement $\mu(t)$ for each statement t of the original program[1]. Consider for instance the inlining of a local variable: $\mu(l{:=}f(p_1); \ l{:=}g(p_2)) \equiv l{:=}g(p_2[f(p_1)/l])$. In this case, $l{:=}f(p_1)$ and $l{:=}f(p_2)$ alone do not have corresponding statements in the refactored program. Therefore, $\mu(l{:=}f(p_1))$ and $\mu(l{:=}f(p_2))$ are undefined, and Implication (2) cannot be applied to these statements individually.

(b) Conversely, some refactorings transform a statement t of the original program into several non-consecutive statements in the transformed program. For instance, when unrolling a loop, the loop body t is duplicated and placed at different locations in the program, namely before and inside the loop. Again, $\mu(t)$ is not well-defined.

(c) Different statements in the original program may require different correspondence relations. Consider for instance the split of a variable l_0 into two fresh variables l_1 and l_2 in $t_0 \equiv t_1; t_2$:

$$\mu(t_1) \equiv l_1{:=}l_0; \ \underbrace{t_1[l_1/l_0]}_{t_b} \qquad\qquad \mu(t_2) \equiv l_2{:=}l_1; \ \underbrace{t_2[l_2/l_0]}_{t_d}; \ l_0{:=}l_2$$

This refactoring requires a different correspondence relation for each active scope of the new variables. During the execution of statement t_b, l_0 and l_1 correspond, whereas l_0 and l_2 in general do not correspond since l_2 is not yet initialized. However, during the execution of statement t_d, l_0 and l_2 correspond, whereas l_1 is not used any more. Implication (2) does not permit such variations of the correspondence relation.

To address these problems, we allow the correspondence relation to be different at each program point: $\beta_{[t,t']}^{\text{before}}(s, s')$ is the correspondence between a state s before the execution of a statement t in the original program Γ and a state s' before the execution of a statement t' in the transformed program Γ'. $\beta_{[t,t']}^{\text{after}}(s, s')$

---

[1] We omit the subscript R when the refactoring is clear from the context.

is the analogous correspondence after the execution of t and t'. External equivalence can then be proved using the following implication:

$$(\Gamma| - s \xrightarrow{t} r) \wedge \beta^{\text{before}}_{[t,t']}(s, s') => \exists r' : (\Gamma'| - s' \xrightarrow{t'} r') \wedge \beta^{\text{after}}_{[t,t']}(r, r') \qquad (3)$$

Implication (3) implies the general condition (1) if the two sanity conditions hold, namely initial correspondence, $\beta^{\text{before}}_{[code_\Gamma, code_{\Gamma'}]}(ini, ini)$, and external equivalence, $\forall r, r' : \beta^{\text{after}}_{[code_\Gamma, code_{\Gamma'}]}(r, r') => r.ext = r'.ext$.

Besides these sanity conditions, the correspondence relation is not constrained. Therefore, Implication (3) provides enough flexibility to handle even complex program transformations. In particular, one is free to choose the statements t and t' to be related. For all statements t' in the refactored program Γ' that are not related to a statement t in the original program Γ, $\beta^{\text{before}}_{[t,t']}$ is simply defined to be empty.

For "Split Variable", we say that (a sub-statement of) t_1 in the original is comparable to (the corresponding sub-statement of) t_b in the transformed program and the same for t_2 and t_d. Moreover, a statement t outside t_0 that is not affected by the refactoring is comparable to its transformation $\mu(t)$. For statements t and t' that are not comparable, $\beta^P_{[t,t']}$ is empty. For comparable statements, corresponding states have an identical heap and identical I/O sequences. The requirement for local variables depends on whether t is (a sub-statement of) t_1, (a sub-statement of) t_2, or outside t_0.

In summary, we prove correctness of a refactoring R by devising a correspondence relation β_R that satisfies Implication (3) as well as initial correspondence and external equivalence. If β_R is simple enough, Implications (3) and (2) coincide. This will be the case for "Move Field", which we discuss in the next section. Examples that require the general correspondence, Implication (3), are presented in our technical report [2].

4   Example: "Move Field"

In this section, we apply our technique to "Move Field" [10]. This refactoring is interesting because it requires non-trivial correctness conditions and is therefore not supported by existing approaches. We describe "Move Field", present an appropriate correspondence relation as well as the required correctness conditions, and prove correctness of the refactoring.

4.1   The Refactoring

"Move Field" removes the declaration of a field f from a class *Source*, inserts it into a different class *Target*, and adjusts all accesses to f. To be able to access f after the refactoring, there must be a *Target* object for each *Source* object. For simplicity, we assume that there is a field *target* in *Source* that points to the corresponding *Target* of each *Source* object. A generalization to arbitrary associations between *Source* and *Target* objects is possible by using ghost fields to express the association.

Transformation Function. We assume that the classes *Source* and *Target* exist and that *Source* declares the distinct fields f and *target*. We assume further that *Target* does not declare a field f.

An original program Γ and the transformed program $\mu(\Gamma)$ are identical except for the following aspects: (a) The field f is moved from *Source* to *Target*:

$$fields_{\mu(\Gamma)}(Source) = fields_\Gamma(Source) - \{f\}$$
$$fields_{\mu(\Gamma)}(Target) = fields_\Gamma(Target) \cup \{f\}$$

(b) Accesses to f are redirected via the *target* field:

$$\mu(l{:=}o.f) \equiv tmp{:=}o.target; l{:=}tmp.f$$
$$\mu(o.f{:=}e) \equiv tmp{:=}o.target; tmp.f{:=}e$$

where $ctt(o) = $ *Source* and *tmp* is a fresh variable.

Since "Move Field" either leaves statements of the original program unchanged or replaces them by simple sequential compositions, this refactoring does not require the general correspondence requirement, Implication (3). We can prove correctness using the simpler Implication (2). We present an appropriate correspondence relation in the next subsection.

4.2 Correspondence Relation

Intuitively, the correspondence relation for "Move Field" requires that $o.f$ in the original program and $o.target.f$ in the transformed program hold the same values. However, this correspondence requires $o.target$ to be different from $\mathtt{null}$, which is not the case for a newly allocated object o before $o.target$ has been initialized. To handle object initialization, we use a more relaxed correspondence. If $target = \mathtt{null}$, f in the original program must hold its zero-equivalent default value, that is, be also uninitialized.

For two states s and s', the correspondence relation $\beta(s, s')$ yields true if and only if:

1. All local variables, except for temporary variables introduced by the refactoring, hold the same value in s and s': $s.vars = s'.vars|_{(\mathrm{dom}\,s.vars)}$, where the domain restriction operator $F|_D$ restricts the domain of function F to D.
2. All references x that are not of type *Source* or *Target* are mapped to the same objects: $\mathrm{dom}\,s.heap = \mathrm{dom}\,s'.heap$ and $s.heap(x) = s'.heap(x)$. For a *Source* reference x, $s.heap(x)(f)$ corresponds to $s'.heap(s'.heap(x)(target))(f)$ or $zero(ctt(f))$, depending on whether $s'.heap(x)(target) \neq \mathtt{null}$ or not. All other field values are identical. We also have to encode that *Target* objects do not have an f field in the original program. That is, for all references $x \in \mathrm{dom}\,s.heap$ and object values $m \equiv s.heap(x)$ and $m' \equiv s'.heap(x)$, we require:

$$m = \begin{cases} m'[f \leftarrow s'.heap(m'(target))(f)] & \text{if } rtt(x) = Source \wedge m'(target) \neq \mathtt{null} \\ m'[f \leftarrow zero(ctt(f))] & \text{if } rtt(x) = Source \wedge m'(target) = \mathtt{null} \\ m'[f \leftarrow undef] & \text{if } rtt(x) = Target \\ m' & \text{otherwise} \end{cases} \quad (4)$$

3. The I/O part of both states is identical: $s.ext = s'.ext$.

This correspondence relation satisfies initial correspondence because there are no references in the initial heap *ini.heap*. External equivalence is trivially satisfies by the third requirement.

4.3   Correctness Conditions

The correctness conditions for "Move Field" have to guarantee that the refactoring preserves the external program behavior. In the following, we suggest sufficient correctness conditions and explain how they can be checked a-posteriori.

A-posteriori Conditions for "Move Field". Any conditions that allow one to prove Implication (2) for any statement t in the original program are possible correctness conditions. A pragmatic approach is to start with the proof of Implication (2) and to determine the weakest conditions that are necessary for the induction to go through. However, these weakest conditions are often difficult to express as assertions or difficult to check. Therefore, one typically has to devise stronger correctness conditions that are easier to express and to check.

In the "Move Field" example, Implication (2) holds trivially for most statements of the original program since $t \equiv \mu(t)$. The interesting cases are if t is (a) a read access to the moved field f, (b) an update of f, or (c) an update of *target*. For these cases, we present sufficient (but not weakest) a-posteriori conditions in the following (o is a variable of type *Source*):

(a) $t \equiv l{:}{=}o.f$: The statement t reads $o.f$ in the original program. It terminates normally if o is different from `null`. The correctness conditions must guarantee that the transformed statement $\mu(t) \equiv tmp{:}{=}o.target;\ l{:}{=}tmp.f$ behaves correspondingly. This is the case if $o.target$ is different from `null`. Therefore, we introduce the following assertion before $\mu(t)$:

$$\textsf{assert}\ o.target \neq \textsf{null}; \tag{5}$$

(b) $t \equiv o.f{:}{=}e$: An update of $o.f$ in the original program changes the value of the f field of exactly one *Source* object, namely o. To achieve the corresponding behavior for the transformed statement $\mu(t) \equiv tmp{:}{=}o.target;\ tmp.f{:}{=}e$, we require that the updated *Target* object is not shared by several *Source* objects. Moreover, we have to make sure the association exists, that is, $o.target$ is different from `null`. Therefore, we introduce the following assertion before $\mu(t)$:

$$\textsf{assert}\ o.target \neq \textsf{null} \wedge \forall Source\ p : p.target = o.target => p = o; \tag{6}$$

Quantifiers over objects range over non-null allocated objects. Both t and $\mu(t)$ terminate normally if and only if o is different from `null`.

(c) $t \equiv o.target{:}{=}e$: An update of $o.target$ in the original program associates the *Source* object o with another *Target* object. For the transformed program, this means that o will potentially access a different f field. Updates of *target* are not transformed, that is, $t \equiv \mu(t)$. They lead to corresponding terminal states in the following cases:

- *o.target* is set to `null` ($e = $ `null`), and the old *o.target* either is already
  `null` (that is, the value remains unchanged), or *o.target.f* holds the
  default value for f's type.
- *o.target* is set from `null` to a proper *Target* object ($e \neq $ `null`) whose f
  field holds the default value.
- *o.target* is set to a proper *Target* object whose f field holds the same
  value as the old *o.target.f*.

These conditions are expressed by the following assertion, which is inserted
before $\mu(t)$:

$$\text{assert } (e = \text{null} \wedge (o.target = \text{null} \vee o.target.f = zero(\text{ctt}(f)))) \vee$$
$$(e \neq \text{null} \wedge ((o.target = \text{null} \wedge zero(\text{ctt}(f)) = e.f) \vee \qquad (7)$$
$$(o.target \neq \text{null} \wedge o.target.f = e.f)));$$

Both t and $\mu(t)$ terminate normally if and only if o is different from `null`.

Checking the Conditions. Assertion (5) is amenable to both runtime assertion checking and static verification. Alternatively, non-null types [9] can be used
to check the condition syntactically.

The second conjunct of Assertion (6) is difficult to check at runtime. It requires code instrumentation to keep track of the number of *Source* objects that
point to a *Target* object. Static verification is possible for this assertion, for
instance, using the ownership discipline of the Boogie methodology [16]. A syntactic alternative is to use pointer confinement type systems such as ownership
types and their descendants [5,7], or linear types [8].

Assertion (7) is straightforward to check at runtime or by static verification.
Nevertheless, it seems reasonable to impose additional restrictions to enforce
this correctness condition. For instance in Java, the field *target* can be declared
`final`, which ensures that *target* cannot be changed after its first initialization. With this restriction, the condition of Assertion (7) can be simplified to
$e = \text{null} \vee zero(\text{ctt}(f)) = e.f$.

4.4 Correctness Proof

In this subsection, we prove that "Move Field" is correct. That is, the transformed program $\mu(\Gamma)$ performs the same sequence of I/O operations as the
original program Γ if the correctness conditions hold.

For the proof, we use the following *auxiliary lemma*: If the states s and s'
correspond then the evaluation of an expression e yields the same value in both
states: $\beta(s, s') \Rightarrow [\![e]\!]s = [\![e]\!]s'$. This lemma is a direct consequence of the
definition of β ($\beta(s, s') \Rightarrow s.vars = s'.vars$) and the fact that expressions do
not contain field accesses.

With this auxiliary lemma, the cases for local variable update, object allocation, I/O operation, sequential composition, and loop are straightforward and
therefore omitted. In the following, we sketch the proof for the interesting cases:
field read and field update. The other cases and further details of the proof are
presented in our technical report [2].

We prove correctness by showing Implication (2) for any statement t in the original program Γ and any states s, s', and r. The proof runs by induction on the shape of the derivation tree for $\Gamma| - s \xrightarrow{t} r$. For each case, we present a terminal state r' and then show (a) that $\mu(\Gamma)| - s' \xrightarrow{\mu(t)} r'$ is a valid transition and (b) that r and r' correspond.

Field Read. Consider $t \equiv l:=o.fld$. If $fld \neq f$, the statement is not transformed and we have $\beta(s, s') => s.heap(x)(fld) = s'.heap(x)(fld)$ for all x. Therefore, the field accesses yield the same value. Consequently $r' = r$ satisfies Implication (2).

For $fld = f$, the original and transformed statements are:

$$t \equiv l:=o.f \qquad \text{and} \qquad t' \equiv tmp:=o.target; \; l:=tmp.f$$

They lead to the following terminal states r and r' from s and s' respectively.

$$r = s[l \leftarrow s.heap(s.vars(o))(f)]$$
$$r' = s'[l \leftarrow s'.heap(s'.heap(s'.vars(o))(target))(f),$$
$$tmp \leftarrow s'.heap(s'.vars(o))(target)]$$

The antecedents that have to hold for the transition in the transformed program, $\Gamma'| - s' \xrightarrow{tmp:=o.target; \; l:=tmp.f} r'$, are:

$$s'.vars(o) \neq \texttt{null} \qquad \text{and} \qquad s'.heap(s'.vars(o))(target) \neq \texttt{null}$$

The first antecedent is implied by the antecedent $s.vars(o) \neq \texttt{null}$ of the corresponding transition in the original program because $\beta(s, s')$ implies $s.vars = s'.vars$. The second antecedent is directly guaranteed by the correctness condition preceding t', Assertion (5).

Next, we prove $\beta(r, r')$. r and r' have the same *heap* and *ext* components as s and s', respectively. Besides the temporary variable tmp, which is irrelevant according to the definition of β, their *vars* components differ from the variables of the initial states only for variable l. Therefore, it suffices to show $r.vars(l) = r'.vars(l)$, that is, we prove the following equation:

$$s.heap(s.vars(o))(f) = s'.heap(s'.heap(s'.vars(o))(target))(f)$$

This equation is directly implied by line 1 in Equation (4), which applies because type safety guarantees that $rtt(o) = Source$ holds and Assertion (5) ensures $s'.heap(s'.vars(o))(target) \neq \texttt{null}$.

Field Update. Consider $t \equiv o.fld:=e$. We present the proof for updates of f and of $target$ in the following. For all other fields, the proof is trivial.

Updates of f. For $fld = f$, the original and transformed statements are:

$$t \equiv o.f:=e \qquad \text{and} \qquad t' \equiv tmp:=o.target; \; tmp.f:=e$$

They lead to the following terminal states r and r' from s and s', respectively.

$$r = s[heap(vars(o))(f) \leftarrow [\![e]\!]s]$$
$$r' = s'[heap(s'.heap(s'.vars(o))(target))(f) \leftarrow [\![e]\!]s,$$
$$tmp \leftarrow s'.heap(s'.vars(o))(target)]$$

where we used the auxiliary lemma to show that the evaluation of e is not affected by the transformation.

The antecedents that have to hold for the transition in the transformed program, $\Gamma' | - s' \xrightarrow{tmp:=o.target;\ tmp.f:=e} r'$, are:

$$s'.vars(o) \neq \texttt{null} \qquad \text{and} \qquad s'.heap(s'.vars(o))(target) \neq \texttt{null}$$

The first antecedent is implied by the antecedent $s.vars(o) \neq \texttt{null}$ of the corresponding transition in the original program and $\beta(s, s')$. The second antecedent is directly guaranteed by the correctness condition preceding t', Assertion (6).

Next, we prove $\beta(r, r')$. Besides the temporary variable tmp, which is irrelevant according to the definition of β, r and r' have the same $vars$ and ext components as s and s', respectively. We get $\operatorname{dom} r.heap = \operatorname{dom} r'.heap$ and $r.heap(x) = r'.heap(x)$ for all references x from $\beta(s, s')$ and the definitions of r and r'. Therefore, it suffices to show that Equation (4) holds for all references $x \in \operatorname{dom} r.heap$. We show this by a case distinction on the value of x.

Case (i): $x = s'.vars(o)$. We have $rtt(x) = Source$ (by type safety) and $s'.heap(x)(target) \neq \texttt{null}$ by Assertion (6). Therefore, line 1 in Equation (4) applies. Since only the f field is updated, it suffices to prove:

$$r.heap(x)(f) = r'.heap(x)[f \leftarrow r'.heap(s'.heap(x)(target))(f)](f)$$

(We used $s'.heap(x)(target) = r'.heap(x)(target)$, which holds because $target$ is not updated.) The right-hand side of the above equation can be trivially simplified to $r'.heap(s'.heap(x)(target))(f)$. Using the definitions of r and r' above reveals that both sides of the equation evaluate to $[\![e]\!]s$, which concludes Case (i).

Case (ii): $x \neq s.vars(o)$. Since t updates a field of a $Source$ object, this case is trivial if $rtt(x) \neq Source$. For $rtt(x) = Source$, we continue as follows. If $s'.heap(x)(target) = \texttt{null}$, line 2 of Equation (4) follows directly from $\beta(s, s')$. Otherwise, line 1 in Equation (4) applies, that is, we have to prove:

$$r.heap(x) = r'.heap(x)[f \leftarrow r'.heap(r'.heap(x)(target))(f)]$$

By the definition of r and the assumption of Case (ii), we get $r.heap(x) = s.heap(x)$. By the definition of r' and type safety, we get $r'.heap(x) = s'.heap(x)$ because x is a $Source$ object and t' updates a field of a $Target$ object. By using these two equalities, we can reduce our proof goal to:

$$s.heap(x) = s'.heap(x)[f \leftarrow r'.heap(s'.heap(x)(target))(f)]$$

Assertion (6) implies $s'.heap(x)(target) \neq s'.heap(s'.vars(o))(target)$. Therefore, we get $r'.heap(s'.heap(x)(target)) = s'.heap(s'.heap(x)(target))$ by the definition of r'. This condition together with $\beta(s, s')$ implies the above equation. This concludes Case (ii) and, thereby, the case for updates of f.

Updates of target. For *fld* = *target*, the original and transformed statements are identical. They lead to the following terminal states r and r' from s and s', respectively.

$$r = s[heap(s.vars(o))(target) \leftarrow \llbracket e \rrbracket s]$$
$$r' = s'[heap(s'.vars(o))(target) \leftarrow \llbracket e \rrbracket s]$$

The proof of the antecedent for the transition $\Gamma'| - s' \overset{t}{\rightarrow} r'$ is analogous to the case for *fld* = f.

Next, we prove $\beta(r, r')$. This part is mostly analogous to the case for *fld* = f. The only new property we have to show is that $r.heap(x)$ and $r'.heap(x)$ satisfy Equation (4), where $x = s.vars(o) = s'.vars(o)$. From type safety, we know $rtt(x) = Source$ because *target* is a field of class *Source*. Therefore, line 1 or line 2 of Equation (4) might apply. We continue by case distinction.

Case (i): $r'.heap(x)(target) = \texttt{null}$. From the definition of r' and the assumption of Case (i), we get $\llbracket e \rrbracket s = \texttt{null}$. Therefore, line 2 in Equation (4) applies and we have to prove:

$$r.heap(x) = r'.heap(x)[f \leftarrow zero(\text{ctt}(f))]$$

Using the definitions of r and r' as well as $\beta(s, s')$ reveals that this is exactly the case if $r.heap(x)(f) = zero(\text{ctt}(f))$ or, equivalently:

$$s.heap(x)(f) = zero(\text{ctt}(f))$$

Due to the assumption of this case, Assertion (7) is known to guarantee:

$$s'.heap(x)(target) = \texttt{null} \lor s'.heap(s'.heap(x)(target))(f) = zero(\text{ctt}(f))$$

If the first disjunct holds, $\beta(s, s')$ implies $s.heap(x)(f) = zero(\text{ctt}(f))$ by line 2 in Equation (4). Otherwise, we get this property by line 1 in Equation (4). This concludes Case (i).

Case (ii): $r'.heap(x)(target) \neq \texttt{null}$. Analogously to Case (i), we derive $\llbracket e \rrbracket s \neq \texttt{null}$. Therefore, line 1 in Equation (4) applies and we have to prove:

$$r.heap(x) = r'.heap(x)[f \leftarrow r'.heap(r'.heap(x)(target))(f)]$$

Again, using the definitions of r and r' as well as $\beta(s, s')$ reveals that this is exactly the case if the following equation holds.

$$s.heap(x)(f) = s'.heap(\llbracket e \rrbracket s)(f)$$

Due to the assumption of this case, Assertion (7) is known to guarantee:

$$(s'.heap(x)(target) = \texttt{null} \land zero(\text{ctt}(f)) = s'.heap(\llbracket e \rrbracket s)(f)) \lor$$
$$(s'.heap(x)(target) \neq \texttt{null} \land s'.heap(s'.heap(x)(target))(f) = s'.heap(\llbracket e \rrbracket s)(f))$$

If the first disjunct of this condition holds then line 2 in Equation (4) implies $s.heap(x)(f) = zero(\text{ctt}(f))$, rendering it equal to $s'.heap(\llbracket e \rrbracket s)(f)$.

If the second disjunct holds, line 1 in Equation (4) yields $s.heap(x)(f) = s'.heap(s'.heap(x)(target))(f)$. This concludes Case (ii) and, thereby, the case for updates of *target*. $\qquad\square$

5   Related Work

There is a vast literature on refactoring, but little on its formalization. Most of the related work discusses the design rationale [12] of individual refactorings or treats refactorings on a syntactic level [14]. In this section, we discuss work that is geared towards reasoning about refactorings.

Opdyke [20] mentions explicitly that refactorings have correctness conditions and argued informally for the correctness of refactorings. He defined the notion of equivalence for refactorings that is also used in this paper, namely identical sequences of I/O operations.

The Smalltalk Refactoring Browser [21] samples the program at runtime to estimate properties that are difficult or impossible to infer statically. Samples are taken before the refactoring because their results are sometimes needed for the transformation itself. For instance, because Smalltalk is untyped, the classes that are receivers of a certain method call have to be determined by sampling before "Rename Method" can be applied. Representative program executions must be available for this approach, which is a serious restriction as explained in Sect. 1. While typed languages remove the need to sample programs in order to carry out the refactoring, sampling the program before refactoring could still be used to check correctness conditions a-priori. However, our approach of adding a-posteriori conditions as assertions to the refactored program has several advantages. It reduces the dependence on a complete unit test suite, enables static verification, and improves program documentation.

Streckenbach and Snelting [22] use the results of static or dynamic analyses to determine possible refactorings of class hierarchies automatically. The analyses guarantee that the refactorings are correct. Two class hierarchies are considered equivalent if the behavior observable by clients is identical. This notion of equivalence is too restrictive for many non-local refactorings such as renaming a public field or method. In a similar approach, Logozzo and Cortesi [18] solve this problem by defining explicitly what aspects of the program behavior are observable. They use abstract interpretation to determine possible refactorings of class hierarchies. We do not aim at finding possible refactorings automatically, but require the user to apply the desired refactorings. Our approach supports complex refactorings whose correctness conditions cannot be checked efficiently by static analyses.

Cornélio [6] uses a refinement relation as the equivalence criterion for refactorings. He shows correctness by decomposing a refactoring into various refinement steps. The refinement relation of the calculus [19] per se does not guarantee external equivalence however. In particular, visible intermediary states may be different. We solve this problem by introducing an explicit I/O model. Cornélio's work does not support important language features such as references and therefore avoids some of the most challenging problems. Our formalism is based on an operational semantics, which allows us to handle realistic languages.

Refactorings have also been applied to models of the program such as a UML diagrams rather than to the source code. There are various efforts to formalize such refactorings [4,11,17,23]. Our work focuses on source code because the main application of refactoring is changing code quickly and correctly with all its intricacies For instance, method calls cannot be adjusted in class diagrams.

Like our work, investigations on representation independence [1] aim at proving that certain changes in the code preserve its external behavior. Representation independence relies on encapsulation to guarantee that modifications of the internal representation of a module cannot be observed by client code. In contrast, refactorings are typically not local to a module and, therefore, require very different correctness conditions.

6   Conclusion

We have presented a technique that guarantees that the application of a refactoring preserves the external behavior of the program if the transformed program satisfies the refactoring's correctness conditions. These conditions are added to the transformed program and can be used for runtime assertion checking, to generate unit tests, and for static verification. We applied our approach successfully to 15 representative refactorings [2].

An important virtue of our approach is that it automatically improves program documentation by adding assertions. Thereby, it prepares the program for the application of specification-based test tools and program verifiers.

We have implemented a prototype for "Move Field" for Spec# in Visual Studio and for JML in Eclipse. As future work, we plan to develop a more comprehensive refactoring tool based on the technique presented here. Moreover, we plan to investigate how the generated assertions can be refactored into invariants and method contracts.

References

1. A. Banerjee and D. A. Naumann. Ownership confinement ensures representation independence for object-oriented programs. *J. ACM*, 52(6):894–960, 2005.
2. F. Bannwart. Changing software correctly. Technical Report 509, Department of Computer Science, ETH Zürich, 2006.
3. M. Barnett, K. R. M. Leino, and W. Schulte. The Spec# Programming System: An Overview. In G. Barthe, L. Burdy, M. Huisman, J.-L. Lanet, and T. Muntean, editors, *CASSIS*, volume 3362 of *LNCS*, pages 49–69. Springer-Verlag, 2005.
4. P. L. Bergstein. Object-preserving class transformations. In *OOPSLA*, pages 299–313. ACM Press, 1991.
5. D. G. Clarke, J. M. Potter, and J. Noble. Ownership types for flexible alias protection. In *OOPSLA*, pages 48–64. ACM Press, 1998.
6. M. Cornélio. *Refactorings as Formal Refinements*. PhD thesis, Universidade de Pernambuco, 2004.
7. W. Dietl and P. Müller. Universes: Lightweight ownership for JML. *Journal of Object Technology (JOT)*, 4(8):5–32, 2005.
8. M. Fähndrich and R. DeLine. Adoption and focus: practical linear types for imperative programming. In *PLDI*, pages 13–24. ACM Press, 2002.
9. M. Fähndrich and K. R. M. Leino. Declaring and checking non-null types in an object-oriented language. In *OOPSLA*, pages 302–312. ACM Press, 2003.

10. M. Fowler. *Refactoring: improving the design of existing code.* Addison-Wesley, 1999.
11. R. Gheyi, T. Massoni, and P. Borba. An abstract equivalence notion for object models. *Electr. Notes Theor. Comput. Sci.*, 130:3–21, 2005.
12. J. Kerievsky. *Refactoring to Patterns.* Addison-Wesley Professional, August 2004.
13. J. R. Kiniry and D. R. Cok. ESC/Java2: Uniting ESC/Java and JML. In G. Barthe, L. Burdy, M. Huisman, J.-L. Lanet, and T. Muntean, editors, *CASSIS*, volume 3362 of *LNCS*, pages 108–128. Springer-Verlag, 2005.
14. R. Lämmel. Towards Generic Refactoring. In *Workshop on Rule-Based Programming (RULE)*. ACM Press, 2002.
15. G. T. Leavens, A. L. Baker, and C. Ruby. Preliminary design of JML: A behavioral interface specification language for Java. Technical Report 98-06-rev28, Iowa State University, 2005.
16. K. R. M. Leino and P. Müller. Object invariants in dynamic contexts. In M. Odersky, editor, *ECOOP*, volume 3086 of *LNCS*, pages 491–516. Springer-Verlag, 2004.
17. K. J. Lieberherr, W. L. Hürsch, and C. Xiao. Object-extending class transformations. *Formal Aspects of Computing*, (6):391–416, 1994.
18. F. Logozzo and A. Cortesi. Semantic hierarchy refactoring by abstract interpretation. In E. A. Emerson and K. S. Namjoshi, editors, *VMCAI*, volume 3855 of *LNCS*, pages 313–331. Springer-Verlag, 2006.
19. C. Morgan. *Programming from specifications.* Prentice-Hall, 1990.
20. W. F. Opdyke. *Refactoring object-oriented frameworks.* PhD thesis, University of Illinois at Urbana-Champaign, 1992.
21. D. B. Roberts. *Practical analysis for refactoring.* PhD thesis, University of Illinois at Urbana-Champaign, 1999.
22. M. Streckenbach and G. Snelting. Refactoring class hierarchies with KABA. In *OOPSLA*, pages 315–330. ACM Press, 2004.
23. L. Tokuda and D. Batory. Evolving object-oriented designs with refactorings. In *Automated Software Engineering*, pages 174–182. IEEE Computer Society, 1999.

Mechanical Verification of Recursive Procedures Manipulating Pointers Using Separation Logic

Viorel Preoteasa

Department of Computer Science
Åbo Akademi University and
Turku Centre for Computer Science
DataCity, Lemminkäisenkatu 14A
Turku 20520, Finland

Abstract. Using a predicate transformer semantics of programs, we introduce statements for heap operations and separation logic operators for specifying programs that manipulate pointers. We prove consistent Hoare total correctness rules for pointer manipulating statements according to the predicate transformer semantics. We prove the frame rule in the context of a programming language with recursive procedures with value and result parameters and local variables, where program variables and addresses can store values of any type of the theorem prover. The theory, including the proofs, is implemented in the theorem prover PVS.

Keywords: Mechanical Verification of Programs. Pointer Programs. Separation Logic. Recursive Procedures. Predicate Transformers Semantics.

1 Introduction

Separation logic [10,11,7,14] is a powerful tool for proving correctness of imperative programs that manipulate pointers. However, without theorem prover support, such tasks are unfeasible. By employing Isabelle/HOL [6] theorem prover and separation logic, Weber [13] implements relatively complete Hoare [4] logics for a simple while programming language extended with heap operations. Nevertheless, his implementation does not treat (recursive) procedures and local variables.

In this paper, we introduce a predicate transformer semantics for imperative programs with pointers and define separation logic constructs. Based on this semantics, we prove Hoare total correctness rules for heap operations (new, dispose, lookup, and update). Our work is implemented in the theorem prover PVS [8] and it is based on a previous formalization [1] of Refinement Calculus [2] with recursive procedures.

The main contribution of this work is the formal proof of the frame rule [5,14] in the context of a programming language with recursive procedures with value and result parameters and local variables, where program variables and addresses can store values of any type of at most a well chosen infinite cardinal γ. Although the cardinal of all procedures is greater than γ, only an infinite countable number of them are of interest in programming, and we can have higher order procedures.

J. Misra, T. Nipkow, and E. Sekerinski (Eds.): FM 2006, LNCS 4085, pp. 508–523, 2006.
© Springer-Verlag Berlin Heidelberg 2006

The overview of the paper is as follows. In Section 2 we present related work. Section 3 introduces the predicate transformer semantics of our programming language. We do not explicitly introduce a programming language syntax, but we rather define programming constructs as semantic entities (predicate transformers). We introduce program variables, addresses, and expressions in Section 4. Section 5 introduces the heap, heap statements, and separation logic. In Section 6 we introduce recursive procedures and a Hoare total correctness and frame rule for recursive procedures. Section 7 introduces the frame rule for programs that can be constructed using program statements defined in the paper. In Section 8 we prove the correctness of a recursive procedure for disposing a binary tree from memory. Finally, Section 9 presents concluding remarks and future work.

2   Related Work

Following [14], Weber [13] implements in theorem prover Isabelle/HOL relatively complete Hoare logics for total and partial correctness of a simple while language with pointers where variables and addresses store only natural numbers.

In [14,13] memory faults are modeled by transitions to a special state *fault*. When giving semantics to partial correctness Hoare triples, the programs are required to avoid the state *fault*. In our approach memory faults are modeled by non-termination and our semantics is equivalent to the total correctness semantics from [14,13].

Reynolds, Yang, O'Hearn and Weber [11,14,13] require an infinite supply of addresses and the assumption that only a finite number of them are allocated during the program execution. This assumption is needed for address allocation statement which should always succeed. We do not need these restrictions. By using the demonic update statement [2] to define address allocation we obtain a simpler semantics which yields the same proof rules as in [11,14,13]. In our approach, if new addresses are not available, then the program terminates successfully. This treatment is equivalent to the one where we require that addresses are always available for allocation. Both of these treatments are unfeasible in practice, but most approaches to pointer semantics use one of them.

The proof of the frame rule in [14] is a consequence of the *frame* and *safety (termination) monotonicity* properties and these are proved by induction on the program structure. Although we could state the termination monotonicity property in our semantics, it does not seem obvious how to represent the frame property. Our proof of the frame rule is done directly by induction on programs.

Like in [14,13], non-deterministically choosing a new available address in the allocation statement is essential in proving the frame rule.

In [11,14,13] addresses are natural numbers and variables and addresses can store only natural numbers. The fields of pointer structures are recorded at successive addresses. Although it is possible to reason in this manner about high level programming languages, the semantics is at the level of an assembly language and we cannot take advantage of any type checking mechanism that would simplify the verification work. In our approach, a given address can store only values of a specified type and this fact is ensured by the theorem prover. We can have record types, and addresses can store these records. We could easily implement address arithmetic, but we would use it for representing dynamically allocated arrays of arbitrary types rather than record fields.

3 Preliminaries

In this section, we introduce a predicate transformer semantics of imperative programs. We do not introduce programs as syntactic entities, but rather we work directly with their semantic interpretations (monotonic predicate transformers). Valid Hoare triples are abbreviations of semantic correctness statements, rather than syntactic constructs whose validity is given by a semantic map. We can however easily implement the classical treatment of Hoare logic by introducing syntactic programs, syntactic Hoare proof rules, and by mapping these constructs into our semantics.

We use higher-order logic [3] as the underlying logic. In this section we recall some facts about refinement calculus [2] and about fixed points in complete lattices.

Let Σ be the state space. Predicates, denoted Pred, are the functions from $\Sigma \to$ bool. We denote by $\subseteq$, $\cup$, and $\cap$ the predicate inclusion, union, and intersection respectively. The type Pred together with inclusion forms a complete boolean algebra.

MTran is the type of all monotonic functions from Pred to Pred. Programs are modeled as elements of MTran. If $S \in$ MTran and $p \in$ Pred, then $S.p \in$ Pred are all states from which the execution of S terminates in a state satisfying the postcondition p. The program *sequential composition* denoted $S \ ; \ T$ is modeled by the functional composition of monotonic predicate transformers, i.e. $(S \ ; \ T).p = S.(T.p)$. We denote by $\sqsubseteq$, $\sqcup$, and $\sqcap$ the pointwise extension of $\subseteq$, $\cup$, and $\cap$, respectively. The type MTran, together with the pointwise extension of the operations on predicates, forms a complete lattice. The partial order $\sqsubseteq$ on MTran is the *refinement relation* [2]. The predicate transformer $S \sqcap T$ models *nondeterministic* choice – the choice between executing S or T is arbitrary.

We often work with predicate transformers based on functions or relations. A deterministic program can be modeled by a function $f : \Sigma \to \Sigma$ where the interpretation of $f.\sigma$ is the state computed by the program represented by f that starts from the initial state σ. We can model a nondeterministic program by a relation on Σ, i.e. a function $R : \Sigma \to \Sigma \to$ bool. The state σ' belongs to $R.\sigma$ if there exists an execution of the program starting in σ and ending in σ'.

If $p, q \in$ Pred, $R : \Sigma \to \Sigma \to$ bool, $f : \Sigma \to \Sigma$, then we define

$[f] :$ MTran $\hat{=} (\lambda q \bullet \lambda \sigma \bullet q.(f.\sigma))$ – the monotonic predicate transformer corresponding to the function f.

$[R] :$ MTran $\hat{=} (\lambda q \bullet \lambda \sigma \bullet \forall \sigma' \bullet R.\sigma.\sigma' \Rightarrow q.\sigma')$ – the monotonic predicate transformer corresponding to the nondeterministic choice given by R.

$\{p\} :$ MTran $\hat{=} (\lambda q \bullet p \cap q)$ – the assert statement.

if p then S else T endif : MTran $\hat{=}$ $(\{p\} ; S) \sqcup (\{\neg p\} ; T)$ – the conditional statement.

If L is a complete lattice and $f : L \to L$ is monotonic, then the least fix-point of f, denoted μf, exists [12]. If $b \in$ Pred and $S \in$ MTran, then the iterative programming construct is define by:

$$\text{while } b \text{ do } S \text{ od} \hat{=} (\mu X \bullet \text{if } b \text{ then } S ; X \text{ else skip fi})$$

Lemma 1. **(Fusion lemma [2])** *If f and g are monotonic functions on complete lattices L and L' and $h : L \to L'$ is continuous then*

1. if $h \circ f \le g \circ h$ then $h.(\mu f) \le \mu g$
2. if $h \circ f = g \circ h$ then $h.(\mu f) = \mu g$

Lemma 2. while b do S od$.q = (\mu X \bullet (b \cap S.X) \cup (\neg b \cap q))$.

Proof. Using Lemma 1.

4 Program Variables, Addresses, Constants, and Expressions

We assume that we have a type value that contains all program variables, program addresses, and constants. The type value is the global type of all values that could be assigned to program variables. We can have program variables of type address, or type integer, and, although not used here, we could have program variables that store other program variables (references). We assume that we have the disjoint subtypes location and constant of value, and the element nil $\in$ constant. Moreover, we assume that variable, and address are disjoint subtypes of location. The elements of variable, address, and constant represents the program variables, program addresses, and program constants, respectively. The element nil represents the null address. For example, the type of integer numbers, int, is a subtype of constant.

For all $x \in$ location, we introduce the type of x, denoted T.x, as an arbitrary subtype of value. T.x represents all values that can be assigned to x. For a type $X \subseteq$ value we define the subtypes Vars.$X \subseteq$ variable, Addrs.$X \subseteq$ address, and AddrsWithNil.$X \subseteq$ address $\cup \{$nil$\}$ by

$$\text{Vars}.X \hat{=} \{x \in \text{variable} \mid \text{T}.x = X\}$$

$$\text{Addrs}.X \hat{=} \{x \in \text{address} \mid \text{T}.x = X\}$$

$$\text{AddrsWithNil}.X \hat{=} \text{Addrs}.X \cup \{\text{nil}\}$$

The type Vars.X represents the program variables of type X. The elements of Addrs.X are the addresses that can store elements of type X. An element of AddrsWithNil.X is either nil or is an address that can store an element of type X. For example, the program variables of type addresses to natural numbers are Vars.(AddrsWithNil.nat). Based on these addresses we define the heap and the heap operations in Section 5.

In the C++ programming language, and in most imperative programming languages, a binary tree structure will be defined by something like:

$$\text{struct btree\{int label; btree *left; btree *right; \}} \qquad (1)$$

In our formalism, binary trees, labeled with elements from an arbitrary type A, are modeled by a type ptree.A. Elements of ptree.A are records with three components: $a : A$, and p, q : AddrsWithNil.ptree.A. Formally, the record structure on ptree.A is given by a bijective function ptree : $A \times$ AddrsWithNil.(ptree.A) $\times$ AddrsWithNil.(ptree.A) $\rightarrow$ ptree.A. If $a \in A$, and $p, q \in$ AddrsWithNil.ptree, then ptree.(a, p, q) is the record containing the elements a, p, q. The inverse of ptree has three components (label, left, right), label : ptree.$A \rightarrow A$ and left, right : ptree.$A \rightarrow$ AddrsWithNil.(ptree.A). The type ptree.int corresponds to btree from definition (1) and the type AddrsWithNil.(ptree.int) corresponds to (btree $*$) from (1).

We access and update program locations using two functions.

$$\text{val}.x : \Sigma \rightarrow \mathsf{T}.x$$

$$\text{set}.x : \mathsf{T}.x \rightarrow \Sigma \rightarrow \Sigma$$

For $x \in$ location, $\sigma \in \Sigma$, and $a \in \mathsf{T}.x$, val.$x.\sigma$ is the value of x in state σ, and set.$x.a.\sigma$ is the state obtained from σ by setting the value of location x to a.

Local variables are modeled using two statements (add and del), which intuitively correspond to stack operations – adding a location to the stack and deleting it from the stack. Of the two statements, only del is a primitive in our calculus, whereas add is defined as the relation inverse of del

$$\text{del}.x : \Sigma \rightarrow \Sigma$$

The behavior of the primitives val, set and del is described using a set of axioms [1].

Program expressions of type A are functions from Σ to A. We denote by Exp.A the type of all program expressions of type A. We lift all operations on basic types to operations on program expressions. For example, if $\oplus : A \times B \rightarrow C$ is an arbitrary binary operation, then $\oplus :$ Exp.$A \times$ Exp.$B \rightarrow$ Exp.C is defined by $e \oplus e' \hat{=} (\lambda \sigma \bullet e.\sigma \oplus e'.\sigma)$. To avoid confusion, we denote by $(e \doteq e')$ the expression $(\lambda \sigma \bullet e.\sigma = e'.\sigma)$.

For a parametric boolean expression (predicate) $\alpha : A \rightarrow \Sigma \rightarrow$ bool, we define the boolean expressions

$$\exists .\alpha \hat{=} \lambda \sigma \bullet \exists a : A \bullet \alpha.a.\sigma$$

$$\forall .\alpha \hat{=} \lambda \sigma \bullet \forall a : A \bullet e.a.\sigma$$

and we denote by $\exists \, a \bullet \alpha.a$ and $\forall a \bullet \alpha.a$ the expressions $\exists .\alpha$ and $\forall .\alpha$, respectively.

If $e \in$ Exp.A, $x \in$ variable, and $e' \in$ Exp.$(\mathsf{T}.x)$, then we define $e[x := e']$, the substitution of e' for x in e by $e[x := e'].\sigma = e.(\text{set}.x.(e'.\sigma).\sigma)$.

We also introduce the notion of x–independence for an expression $e \in$ Exp.A, as the semantic correspondent to the syntactic condition that x does not occur free in e. Given $f \in \Sigma \rightarrow \Sigma$ and $e \in$ Exp.A, then we say that e is f–independent if $f \, ; \, e = e$. We say that e is set.x–independent if e is set.$x.a$–independent for all $a \in \mathsf{T}.x$.

The program expressions defined so far may depend not only on the current values of the program variables, but also on the values from the stack. For example, del.x ; val.x

does not depend on any program variable value (changing any variable, including x, does not change the value of this expression), but it depends on the top value stored in the stack. We define the subclass of program expression which depends only on the current values of the program variables. Two states σ and σ' are val–equivalent if for all program variables x, $\text{val}.x.\sigma = \text{val}.x.\sigma'$. A program expression $e \in \text{Exp}.A$ is called val–determined if for all σ and σ' val–equivalent we have $e.\sigma = e.\sigma'$.

4.1   Program Statements and Hoare Total Correctness Triples

In this subsection we introduce the program statements for assignment and handling local variables and we will also give the Hoare total correctness rules to work with these statements.

Let $x, y \in$ variable such that $\text{T}.x = \text{T}.y$ and $e \in \text{Exp}.(\text{T}.x)$. We recall the definition of the assignment statement from [2] and the definition of local variables manipulation statements from [1].

- $x := e \mathrel{\hat{=}} [\lambda\sigma \bullet \text{set}.x.(e.\sigma).\sigma]$ – assignment
- $\text{add}.x \mathrel{\hat{=}} (\lambda\sigma, \sigma' \bullet \sigma = \text{del}.x.\sigma')$ – add local variable
- $\text{Add}.x \mathrel{\hat{=}} [\text{add}.x]$ – add local variable statement
- $\text{add}.x.e \mathrel{\hat{=}} (\lambda\sigma, \sigma' \bullet \exists\sigma_0 \bullet \sigma = \text{del}.x.\sigma_0 \wedge \text{set}.x.(e.\sigma).\sigma_0 = \sigma')$ – add and initialize local variable
- $\text{Add}.x.e \mathrel{\hat{=}} [\text{add}.x.e]$ – add and initialize local variable statement
- $\text{Del}.x \mathrel{\hat{=}} [\text{del}.x]$ – delete local variable statement
- $\text{del}.x.y \mathrel{\hat{=}} (\lambda\sigma \bullet \text{set}.y.(\text{val}.x.\sigma).(\text{del}.x.\sigma))$ – save and delete local variable
- $\text{Del}.x.y \mathrel{\hat{=}} [\text{del}.x.y]$ – save and delete local variable statement

As mentioned earlier, the program statements $\text{Add}.x$, $\text{Del}.x$ and their variants correspond intuitively to stack operations (adding the value of x to the stack and deleting the top value from the stack and assigning it to x). The behavior of these statements are not defined by an explicit stack, but rather by a set of axioms [1].

If α and β are predicates and S is a program, then a *Hoare total correctness triple*, denoted $\alpha \{\!| S |\!\} \beta$ is true if and only if $\alpha \subseteq S.\beta$.

Theorem 1. *If x, y are lists of program variables, α and β are predicates, and e is a program expression then*

(i) $(\exists a \bullet \alpha.a) \{\!| S |\!\} \beta \Leftrightarrow (\forall a \bullet (\alpha.a \{\!| S |\!\} \beta))$

(ii) $(\text{del}.x \; ; \; \alpha) \{\!| \text{Del}.x |\!\} \alpha$

(iii) $\alpha \{\!| \text{Add}.x |\!\} (\text{del}.x \; ; \; \alpha)$

(iv) $\alpha \{\!| \text{Add}.x.e |\!\} (\text{del}.x \; ; \; \alpha)$

(v) α *is* val–*determined* $\Rightarrow \alpha[x := e] \{\!| \text{Add}.x.e |\!\} \alpha$

(vi) α *is* set.y–*independent* $\Rightarrow (\text{del}.x \; ; \; \alpha) \{\!| \text{Del}.x.y |\!\} \alpha$

(vii) α *is* val–*determined and* set.$(x - y)$–*independent* $\Rightarrow$
       $\alpha[y := x] \{\!| \text{Del}.x.y |\!\} \alpha$

5   Heap Operations and Separation Logic

So far, we have introduced the mechanism of accessing and updating addresses, but we need also a mechanism for allocating and deallocating them. We introduce the type allocaddr $\hat{=}$ address $\rightarrow$ bool, the powerset of address; and a special program variable alloc $\in$ variable of type allocaddr (T.alloc = allocaddr). The set val.alloc.σ contains only those addresses allocated in state σ. The heap in a state σ is made of the allocated addresses in σ and their values.

For $A, B \in$ allocaddr we denote by $A - B$ the set difference of A and B. We introduce two more functions: to add addresses to a state and to delete addresses from a state.

$$\text{addaddr}.A.\sigma \hat{=} \text{set.alloc.}(\text{val.alloc.}\sigma \cup A).\sigma$$

$$\text{dispose.}A.\sigma \hat{=} \text{set.alloc.}(\text{val.alloc.}\sigma - A).\sigma$$

Based on these elements we build all heap operations and separation logic operators.

5.1   Separation Logic Operators

Next, we introduce the separation logic predicates. The predicate emp holds for a state where the set of allocated addresses is empty. If e, f are predicates, then the *separation conjunction* $e * f$ holds in a state where the heap can be divided in two disjoint parts, such that e and f holds for the two parts, respectively. The predicate *singleton heap*, $r \mapsto g$, holds in a state where the only allocated address is r and the value stored in r is g. Formally, we have:

Definition 1. *If e, f : Pred, $r : \Sigma \rightarrow$ AddrsWithNil.X, and $g : \Sigma \rightarrow X$, then we define*

$$\text{emp.}\sigma : \text{bool} \quad \hat{=} \ (\text{val.alloc.}\sigma = \emptyset)$$

$$(e * f).\sigma : \text{bool} \quad \hat{=} \ \exists A \subseteq \text{val.alloc.}\sigma \bullet e.(\text{set.alloc.}A.\sigma) \wedge f.(\text{dispose.}A.\sigma)$$

$$(r \mapsto g).\sigma : \text{bool} \hat{=} \ \text{val.}(r.\sigma).\sigma = g.\sigma \wedge \text{val.alloc.}\sigma = \{r.\sigma\}$$

$$(r \mapsto \_) : \text{Pred} \quad \hat{=} \ \exists g : X \bullet r \mapsto g$$

Lemma 3. *The following relations hold*

1. $\alpha * \text{emp} = \alpha$
2. $\alpha * \beta = \beta * \alpha$
3. $\alpha * (\beta * \gamma) = (\alpha * \beta) * \gamma$
4. $(\exists a \bullet \alpha * \beta.a) = \alpha * (\exists \beta)$
5. If γ is set.alloc–*independent then* $\alpha * (\beta \wedge \gamma) = (\alpha * \beta) \wedge \gamma$
6. $(\bigcup_{i \in I} p_i) * q = \bigcup_{i \in I} (p_i * q)$
7. $(\bigcap_{i \in I} p_i) * q \subseteq \bigcap_{i \in I} (p_i * q)$
8. del.x ; emp = emp
9. del.x ; $(\alpha * \beta) = (\text{del.}x \ ; \ \alpha) * (\text{del.}x \ ; \ \beta)$

10. If e is set.alloc–*independent then* $(\alpha * \beta)[x := e] = \alpha[x := e] * \beta[x := e]$
11. If e is set.alloc–*independent then* $(r \mapsto g)[x := e] = r[x := e] \mapsto g[x := e]$

In [11] a subset of program expressions called pure are defined. These are expressions that do not depend on the heap and are the usual program expressions built from program variables, constants and normal (non separation logic) operators. In our framework we use two different concepts corresponding to pure expressions. If an expression is set.alloc–independent, then its value does not depend on what are the allocated addresses. An expression e is called *set address independent* if e does not depend on the value of any (allocated or not) address, formally

$$(\forall u : \text{address}, \ a : \text{T}.u \bullet e \text{ is set}.u.a\text{–independent}).$$

The pure expressions from [11] correspond to set.alloc–independent and set address independent expressions in our framework.

We also need another subclass of program expressions. An expression e is called *non-alloc independent* if e does not depend on the values of non allocated addresses:

$$(\forall \sigma \bullet \forall u \notin \text{val.alloc}.\sigma \bullet \forall a \in \text{T}.u \bullet e.(\text{set}.u.a.\sigma) = e.\sigma).$$

These expressions include all expressions obtained from program variables and constants using all operators (including separation logic operators).

5.2   Specifying Binary Trees Properties with Separation Logic

Let atreecons be the type of nonempty abstract binary trees with labels from a type A. We assume that nil denotes the empty tree and we take atree $=$ atreecons $\cup$ {nil}. The abstract tree structure on atree is given by an injective function

$$\text{atree} : A \rightarrow \text{atree} \rightarrow \text{atree} \rightarrow \text{atreecons}$$

which satisfies the following induction axiom:

$$\forall P : \text{atree} \rightarrow \text{bool} \bullet P.\text{nil} \wedge (\forall a, s, t \bullet P.s \wedge P.t \Rightarrow P.(\text{atree}.a.s.t)) \Rightarrow \forall t \bullet P.t$$

Using this axiom we can prove that the function atree is also surjective and we denote by label : atreecons $\rightarrow A$ and left, right : atreecons $\rightarrow$ atree the components of atree inverse.

Abstract binary trees are very convenient to specify and prove properties involving binary trees. However, imperative programming languages represent binary trees using pointers. We introduce a predicate tree : atree $\rightarrow$ AddrsWithNil.ptree $\rightarrow$ Pred. The predicate tree.t.p will be true in those states σ in which address p stores the tree t. The predicate tree.t.p is defined by structural induction on t.

tree.nil.$p.\sigma$ $\qquad \hat{=} p = \text{nil} \wedge \text{emp}$

tree.$(\text{atree}(a, t_1, t_2)).p \hat{=} (\exists p_1, p_2 \bullet p \mapsto \text{ptree}(a, p_1, p_2) * \text{tree}.t_1.p_1 * \text{tree}.t_2.p_2)$

We extend the predicate tree to programs expressions, tree : $(\Sigma \rightarrow \text{atree}) \rightarrow (\Sigma \rightarrow$ AddrsWithNil.ptree$) \rightarrow$ Pred, by tree.e.$f.\sigma \hat{=} \text{tree}.(e.\sigma).(f.\sigma).\sigma$.

Lemma 4. *If* $a : \Sigma \to$ atree *and* $p : \Sigma \to$ AddrsWithNil.ptree *then*

tree.$a.p \wedge p \not\equiv$ nil $\subseteq (\exists a_1, a_2, c, t_1, t_2 \bullet (p \mapsto$ ptree.$(c, t_1, t_2)) *$ tree.$a_1.t_1 *$ tree.$a_2.t_2)$

Lemma 5. *If* e *and* f *are two expressions of appropriate types then*

1. del.x ; tree.$a.p =$ tree.$($del.x ; $a).($del.x ; $p)$
2. *If* e *is* set.alloc–*independent then*

$$(\text{tree}.a.p)[x := e] = \text{tree}.(a[x := e]).(p[x := e])$$

5.3   Pointer Manipulation Statements

In this subsection, we introduce the statements for pointer manipulation and their Hoare total correctness rules. There is a significant difference between our semantics for heap statements and the semantics form [14]. In [14] memory faults are modeled by a special state. We model memory faults by nontermination, and we use total correctness to reason about programs. However, our notion of total correctness is equivalent with the total correctness notion from [14].

Definition 2. *If* $X \subseteq$ value, $x \in$ Vars.(AddrsWithNil.X), $e : \Sigma \to X$, $r : \Sigma \to$ AddrsWithNil.X, $y \in$ Vars.X, *and* $f : X \to$ T.y *then we define*

New.$X.(x, e) :$ MTran $\;\hat{=}\; [\lambda\sigma, \sigma' \bullet \exists a \in$ Addrs.$X \bullet \neg$alloc.$\sigma.a \wedge$
$$\sigma' = \text{set}.a.(e.\sigma).(\text{set}.x.a.(\text{addaddr}.a.\sigma))]$$

Dispose.$r :$ MTran $\quad\hat{=}\; \{\lambda\sigma \bullet$ alloc.$\sigma.(r.\sigma)\}$; $[\lambda\sigma \bullet$ dispose.$(r.\sigma).\sigma]$

$y := r \to f :$ MTran $\quad\hat{=}\; \{\lambda\sigma \bullet$ alloc.$\sigma.(r.\sigma)\}$; $[\lambda\sigma \bullet$ set.$y.(f.(\text{val}.(r.\sigma).\sigma)).\sigma]$

$[r] := e :$ MTran $\quad\hat{=}\; \{\lambda\sigma \bullet$ alloc.$\sigma.(r.\sigma)\}$; $[\lambda\sigma \bullet$ set.$(r.\sigma).(e.\sigma).\sigma]$

The statement New.$X.(x, e)$ allocates a new address a of type X, sets the value of x to a, and sets the value of a to e. The new address to be allocated is chosen arbitrary form all available addresses and this fact, similarly to [14,13], is essential in proving the frame rule for the New statement. Unlike [11], we do not need the assumption that we have an infinite supply of free addresses. In the case, when there are no addresses available, our programs satisfies any postcondition and we obtain the same proof rules for New statement as the ones from [11]. The statement Dispose.r deletes the address r from allocated addresses. The lookup statement, $y := r \to f$, assigns to y the value of the field f of the record stored at address r. The update statement, $[r] := e$, sets the value of address r to e. If in dispose, lookup, or update statements r is not an allocated address, then these statements abort (do not terminate).

Next, we introduce Hoare correctness rules for these statements

Lemma 6. *If* $X \subseteq$ value, $x \in$ Vars.(AddrsWithNil.X), $a \in$ AddrsWithNil.X, $e : \Sigma \to X$ *is* set.alloc–*independent and non-alloc independent then*

1. $val.x \doteq a \wedge emp\ \{\!|\ New.X.(x, e)\ |\!\}\ val.x \mapsto e[x := a]$
2. $e\ is\ set.x\text{–}independent \Rightarrow (emp\ \{\!|\ New.X.(x, e)\ |\!\}\ val.x \mapsto e)$
3. $emp\ \{\!|\ New.X.(x, e)\ |\!\}\ (\exists a \bullet val.x \mapsto e[x := a])$

Lemma 7. *Let* $r\ :\ \Sigma\ \rightarrow\ address \cup \{nil\}$ *and* $\alpha\ :\ \Sigma\ \rightarrow\ Pred,$ *if* r *is* set.alloc–*independent then*

$$r \mapsto \_\ \{\!|\ Dispose.r\ |\!\}\ emp$$

Lemma 8. *If* $a\ :\ T.x,\ r\ :\ \Sigma\ \rightarrow\ AddrsWithNil.X$ *is* set.alloc–*independent,* $f\ :\ X\ \rightarrow$ $T.x,$ *and* $e\ :\ \Sigma\ \rightarrow\ X$ *is* set.alloc–*independent then*

1. $val.x \doteq a \wedge (r \mapsto e)\ \{\!|\ x := r \rightarrow f\ |\!\}\ val.x \doteq f \circ e[x := a] \wedge (r \mapsto e)[x := a]$
2. $r\ and\ e\ are\ set.x\text{–}independent \Rightarrow r \mapsto e\ \{\!|\ x := r \rightarrow f\ |\!\}\ val.x \doteq f \circ e \wedge r \mapsto e$

Lemma 9. *If* $r\ :\ \Sigma\ \rightarrow\ AddrsWithNil.X$ *and* $e\ :\ \Sigma\ \rightarrow\ X$ *are set address independent then*

$$r \mapsto \_\ \{\!|\ [r] := e\ |\!\}\ r \mapsto e$$

6   Recursive Procedures

In this subsection we recall some facts about recursive procedures from [1] and we introduce a modified version of the recursive procedure correctness theorem.

A procedure with parameters from A or simply a procedure over A, is an element from $A \rightarrow MTran$. We define the type $Proc.A = A \rightarrow MTran$, the type of all procedures over A. The type A is the range of the procedure's actual parameters. A call to a procedure $P \in Proc.A$ with the actual parameter $a\ :\ A$ is the program $P.a$.

Every monotonic function F from $Proc.A$ to $Proc.A$ defines a recursive procedure $P \in Proc.A,\ P = \mu F$, where μF is the least fixpoint of F. For example, the recursive procedures that disposes a tree from memory is defined by

> procedure DisposeTree(value-result t : AddrsWithNil.ptree)
>   local x : AddrsWithNil.ptree
>   if val.$t \neq$ nil then
> $x := val.t \rightarrow$ left ;
>   DisposeTree.x ;
> $x := val.t \rightarrow$ right ;   (2)
>   DisposeTree.x ;
>   Dispose(val.t) ;
> $t := $ nil
>   endif

The procedure DisposeTree can be called by passing a program variable u of type AddrsWithNil.ptree. The procedure call DisposeTree.u disposes the tree stored in u and sets u to nil. The type of the parameters of the procedure DisposeTree is $A = Vars.(AddrsWithNil.ptree)$. We use the notation (2) as an abbreviation for the following formal definition of the procedure DisposeTree.

$$DisposeTree = \mu\ body\text{–}dt$$

where body–dt : Proc.$A \rightarrow$ Proc.A is given by

$$
\begin{aligned}
&\text{body–dt.}P = (\lambda u : A \bullet \\
&\quad \text{Add.}t.(\text{val.}u) \ ; \ \text{Add.}x \ ; \\
&\quad \text{if val.}t \neq \text{nil then} \\
&\qquad x := \text{val.}t \rightarrow \text{left} \ ; \\
&\qquad P.x \ ; \\
&\qquad x := \text{val.}t \rightarrow \text{right} \ ; \\
&\qquad P.x \ ; \\
&\qquad \text{Dispose.}(\text{val.}t) \ ; \\
&\qquad t := \text{nil} \\
&\quad \text{endif} \\
&\quad \text{Del.}x \ ; \ \text{Del.}t.u)
\end{aligned}
$$

6.1 Frame Rule and Recursive Procedures

In order to to be able to state the correctness and frame rule for recursive procedures we need to extend all operations on predicates, and programs to parametric predicates and procedures. For example, if B is a type of specification parameters, $p, q : B \rightarrow A \rightarrow$ Pred, and $P, Q \in$ Proc.A, then we define the *procedure Hoare total correctness triple* by:

$$ p \ \{\!| \ P \ |\!\} \ q \Leftrightarrow (\forall b, a \bullet p.b.a \ \{\!| \ P.a \ |\!\} \ q.b.a) $$

We assume that all operations on predicates and programs are lifted similarly. Sometimes we use in examples the notation $(p.b.a \ \{\!| \ P.a \ |\!\} \ q.b.a)$ for $(p \ \{\!| \ P \ |\!\} \ q)$.

The specification of the procedure DisposeTree is:

$$ \text{tree.}u.a \ \{\!| \ \text{DisposeTree.}u \ |\!\} \ \text{emp} \wedge u = \text{nil} \tag{3} $$

This Hoare total correctness triple asserts that if the heap contains only a tree with the root in u, after calling DisposeTree.u the heap is empty and the value of u is nil. However, we cannot use this property in contexts where the heap contains other addresses in addition to the ones specified by tree.$u.a$. For example, in the recursive definition of DisposeTree, the right subtree is still in the heap while we dispose the left subtree. We would like to derive a property like:

$$ \alpha * \text{tree.}u.a \ \{\!| \ \text{DisposeTree.}u \ |\!\} \ \alpha \wedge u = \text{nil} \tag{4} $$

for all predicates α that do not contain u free. This can be achieved using the frame rule.

We introduce a new theorem that can be used when proving the correctness of recursive procedures manipulating pointers. We assume that we have a non-empty type A of procedure parameters and a nonempty type $X \subseteq A \rightarrow$ Pred. The type X denotes those formulas we could add to a Hoare triple when using the frame rule, and they are in general formulas which does not contain free variables modified by the procedure. For procedure DisposeTree the set X is $\{\alpha : \text{Vars.}(\text{AddrsWithNil.ptree}) \rightarrow \text{Pred} \mid (\forall u \bullet \alpha.u$ is set.u–independent)$\}$. We denote by

$$ \text{Proc}_X.A = \{P \in \text{Proc}.A \mid \forall \alpha \in X, \ \forall q : A \rightarrow \text{Pred} \bullet \alpha * P.q \subseteq P.(\alpha * q)\} $$

If we are able to prove that procedure DisposeTree belongs to $\mathsf{Proc}_X.A$ and satisfies (3), then we can use (4), when proving correctness of programs calling DisposeTree. In [14] the concept "local predicate transformers that modify a set V" of program variables is introduced to define the class of predicate transformers that modify only variables from V and satisfy the frame property. $\mathsf{Proc}_X.A$ is a generalization of local predicate transformers to procedures with parameters. The elements of $\mathsf{Proc}_X.A$ are the local predicate transformers when $A = \{\bullet\}$ and $X =$ the set of predicates that do not contain free variables from V.

Next, we introduce the correctness and frame rule for recursive procedures. Let W be a non-empty type and $p_w : B \to A \to$ Pred. If $<$ is a binary relation on W then we define

- $p_{<w} = \bigcup \{p_v \mid v < w\}$
- $p = \bigvee \{p_w \mid w \in W\}$

Theorem 2. *If for all* $w \in W$, $p_w : B \to A \to$ Pred, $q : B \to A \to$ Pred *and* $body : \mathsf{Proc}.A \to \mathsf{Proc}.A$ *is monotonic, then the following Hoare rule is true*

$$(\forall w : W, \ P : \mathsf{Proc}_X.A \bullet p_{<w} \ \{\!| \ P \ |\!\} \ q \Rightarrow p_w \ \{\!| \ body.P \ |\!\} \ q)$$
$$\wedge \ (\forall P : \mathsf{Proc}_X.A \bullet \mathsf{Proc}_X.A.(body.P))$$
$$\overline{\qquad (p \ \{\!| \ \mu \, body \ |\!\} \ q) \ \wedge \ \mathsf{Proc}_X.A.(\mu \, body) \qquad}$$

Proof. See [9].

When proving a recursive procedure, this theorem lets us assume a stronger property (like (4)), and prove a weaker property (like (3)). When using the procedure correctness statement in proving other programs, we can also use a stronger property (like (4)).

7   Frame Rule

In this section, we prove the frame rule for the program statements we have introduced so far. Our proof of the frame rule is different from the proof done in [14] mainly because we use a predicate transformer semantics instead of an operational semantics. In [14] a frame property of the reflexive and transitive closure of the operational semantics relation is proved by induction on programs. The frame rule is a consequence of this frame property. Expressing the frame property does not seem possible in our framework, and we prove the frame rule directly by induction on programs.

Definition 3. *If* $f : \Sigma \to \Sigma$ *then we call a relation* $R \in \Sigma \to \Sigma \to$ bool $f-$ *independent if for all* $\sigma, \sigma' \in \Sigma$, $R.\sigma.\sigma' \Rightarrow R.(f.\sigma).(f.\sigma')$. *The relation* R *is* set.alloc– *independent if it is* set.alloc.A–*independent for all* $A \subseteq$ address.

The relation R *is called* address preserving *if for all* $\sigma, \sigma' \in \Sigma$, $R.\sigma.\sigma' \Rightarrow$ val.alloc.$\sigma =$ val.alloc.σ'.

A function $f : \Sigma \to \Sigma$ *is called* set.alloc–independent *(address preserving) if the relation* $(\lambda\sigma, \sigma' \bullet f.\sigma = \sigma')$ *is.*

Lemma 10. *The relations* add.x *and* add.$x.e$ *and the functions* del.x *and* del.$x.y$ *are* set.alloc–*independent and address preserving.*

Definition 4. *A predicate transformer S is called* $*$–super-junctive *if for all predicates* $\alpha, \beta \in$ Pred, $S.\alpha * S.\beta \subseteq S.(\alpha * \beta)$.

Lemma 11. *If $R : \Sigma \to \Sigma \to$ bool $(f : \Sigma \to \Sigma)$ is set.alloc–independent and address preserving then $[R]$ $([f])$ is $*$–super-junctive.*

Corollary 1. Add.x, Add.$x.e$, Del.x, *and* Del.$x.y$ *are* $*$–super-junctive.

Theorem 3. (Frame rule for parameters and local variables)

1. *if α is* set.y–indep *and* $(\forall q \bullet (\text{del}.x \; ; \; \alpha) * S.q \subseteq S.((\text{del}.x \; ; \; \alpha) * q))$ *then*

$$(\forall q \bullet \alpha * (\text{Add}.x.e \; ; \; S \; ; \; \text{Del}.x.y).q \subseteq (\text{Add}.x.e \; ; \; S \; ; \; \text{Del}.x.y).(\alpha * q))$$

2. *if* $(\forall q \bullet (\text{del}.x \; ; \; \alpha) * S.q \subseteq S.((\text{del}.x \; ; \; \alpha) * q))$ *then*

$$(\forall q \bullet \alpha * (\text{Add}.x \; ; \; S \; ; \; \text{Del}.x).q \subseteq (\text{Add}.x \; ; \; S \; ; \; \text{Del}.x).(\alpha * q))$$

Proof. Using Lemma 11 and Lemma 1.

Lemma 12. *If $x \in V(B(X))$, $e \in \Sigma \to X$, such that α is* set.x–independent *and is non alloc independent, and e is* set.alloc–independent, *then*

$$\alpha * \text{New}(X)(x, e).q \subseteq \text{New}(X)(x, e).(\alpha * q)$$

Lemma 13. *If r is* set.alloc–independent *then*

$$\alpha * \text{Dispose}(r).q \subseteq \text{Dispose}(r).(\alpha * q)$$

Lemma 14. *If $r \in \Sigma \to$ AddrsWithNil.B and $f : X \to$ T.y, such that r is* set.alloc– independent *and α is* set.y–independent, *then*

$$\alpha * (y := r \to f).q \subseteq (y := [r] \to f).(\alpha * q)$$

Lemma 15. *If $r \in \Sigma \to$ AddrsWithNil.X and $e : \Sigma \to X$, such that r is* set.alloc– independent, *e is* set.alloc–independent, *and α is non alloc independent, then*

$$\alpha * ([r] := e).q \subseteq ([r] := e).(\alpha * q)$$

Lemma 16. *If b is* set.alloc–independent *and* $(\forall q \bullet \alpha * S.q \subseteq S.(\alpha * q))$, *then*

$$\forall q \bullet \alpha * (\text{while } b \text{ do } S \text{ od}.q) \subseteq \text{while } b \text{ do } S \text{ od}.(\alpha * q)$$

Proof. $\qquad \alpha * (\text{while } b \text{ do } S \text{ od}.q) \subseteq \text{while } b \text{ do } S \text{ od}.(\alpha * q)$

$\Leftrightarrow$ {Lemma 2}

$\qquad \alpha * (\mu X \bullet b \wedge S.X \vee \neg b \wedge q) \subseteq (\mu X \bullet b \wedge S.X \vee \neg b \wedge (\alpha * q))$

$\Leftarrow$ {Lemma 1 using $h.X = \alpha * X$}

$\qquad \alpha * (b \wedge S.X \vee \neg b \wedge q) \subseteq b \wedge S.(\alpha * X) \vee \neg b \wedge (\alpha * q)$

- Subderivation

$$\alpha * (b \wedge S.X \vee \neg b \wedge q)$$

$= \{\text{Lemma 3}\}$

$$\alpha * (b \wedge S.X) \vee \alpha * (\neg b \wedge q)$$

$= \{b \text{ is set.alloc–independent and Lemma 3}\}$

$$b \wedge (\alpha * S.X) \vee \neg b \wedge (\alpha * q)$$

$= \{\text{Assumption}\}$

$$b \wedge S.(\alpha * X) \vee \neg b \wedge (\alpha * q)$$

$= \{\text{Subderivation}\}$

true

Although we work at the semantic level, we can define the subclass of programs, denoted Prog, built using the program constructs presented in this paper, where Add and Del statements are used in pairs, like in the definition of the procedure DisposeTree. For a program $S \in$ Prog, we define by induction on the program structure the set of variables modified by S, in a usual manner.

Theorem 4. (Frame rule) *If $S \in$ Prog, V is the set of variables modified by P, $\alpha, q \in$ Pred, and $(\forall x \in V \bullet \alpha$ is set.x–independent), then*

$$\alpha * S.q \subseteq S.(\alpha * q)$$

Proof. By using Lemmas 3, 12, 13, 14, 15, 16, and similar results that are true for assignment statement and sequential composition of programs.

8 Disposing a Binary Tree from Memory

In this section, we outline the correctness proof of the procedure DisposeTree (2). Let $X = \{\alpha : A \to \text{Pred} \mid \alpha.u \text{ is set.}u\text{–indep}\}$

Lemma 17. *The procedure DisposeTree is an element of $\text{Proc}_X.A$ and*

$$(\forall a, u \bullet \text{tree.}(\text{val.}u, a) \ \{\!| \ \text{DisposeTree}(u) \ |\!\} \ \text{emp} \wedge \text{val.}u \doteq \text{nil}) \quad (5)$$

Proof. We apply Theorem 2 for body–dt with

- $W = $ atree
- $<$ on W given by $a < b$ iff a is a subtree of b.
- $p_w = (\lambda a \bullet \lambda u \bullet \text{tree.}(\text{val.}u, a) \wedge a < w)$.
- $q = (\lambda a \bullet \lambda u \bullet \text{emp} \wedge \text{val.}u \doteq \text{nil})$

If $\text{Proc}_X.A.P$ then $\text{Proc}_X.A.(\text{body–dt.}P)$ follows from Theorem 4. For $w \in$ nat, and $P : \text{Proc}_X.A.P$ we assume

$$(\forall u, a, \alpha : \text{set.}u\text{–indep} \bullet \alpha * \text{tree.}(\text{val.}u, a) \wedge a < w \ \{\!| \ P.u \ |\!\} \ \alpha \wedge \text{val.}u \doteq \text{nil}) \quad (6)$$

and we prove

$$(\forall u, a \bullet \text{tree.}(\text{val.}u, a) \wedge a \doteq w \ \{\!| \ \text{body-dt.}P.u \ |\!\} \ \text{emp} \wedge \text{val.}u \doteq \text{nil}) \quad (7)$$

By expanding the definition of body-dt, (7) becomes:

$$\text{tree.}(\text{val.}u, a) \wedge a \doteq w$$

$$\{\!\!|$$

Add.t.(val.u) ; Add.x ;
if val.$t \not\doteq$ nil then
$\quad x := \text{val.}t \rightarrow \text{left}$;
$\quad P.x$;
$\quad x := \text{val.}t \rightarrow \text{right}$;
$\quad P.x$;
$\quad \text{Dispose.}(\text{val.}t)$;
$\quad t := \text{nil}$
endif ;
Del.x ; Del.$t.u$

$$|\!\!\}$$

$$\text{emp} \wedge \text{val.}u \doteq \text{nil}$$

$$(8)$$

We have proved (8) in PVS using (6) and the Hoare rules presented in this paper, without unfolding the definition of Hoare triples or the definitions of the separation logic operators.

9   Conclusions and Future Work

Based on earlier work on local variables and recursive procedures [1], we have mechanically verified separation logic properties and Hoare total correctness rules for heap operations. We have proved a frame rule that can be applied to recursive procedures with value and value–result parameters and local variables. All results were carried out in the theorem prover PVS.

We have also mechanically verified a more complex example [9] of a collection of mutually recursive procedures which build the abstract syntax trees of expressions generated by a context free grammar. In this example, we have used the procedure presented in this paper for disposing a binary tree. This shows the flexibility of our approach: we can use general procedures like DisposeTree in specific situations when the type of the tree labels are strings. We can also use in programs different datatypes: strings, integers, abstract trees, pointer represented trees.

The program constructs introduced in this paper cover an important subclass of programs that can be written in an imperative programming language. We can easily add more features that are present in real programming languages. Pointer arithmetic can be added easily by taking the set of all addresses to be nat and by extending the allocation statement with the possibility of allocating an arbitrary number of addresses. We deal already in [1] with lists of values in multiple assignments, and we can use these lists here as well. As we have mentioned in the introduction, for a given infinite cardinal γ, we can have program variables types of cardinals up to γ. The cardinal of all programs (and of procedures of a given type) is strictly greater than γ which would prevent us from having higher order procedures. However, in practice we are interested only in procedures that can be defined using the program constructs introduced in the paper, and these are only an infinite countable number, therefore we can introduce program variables of type procedures, and then pass them as parameters to other procedures.

Acknowledgments

The author wishes to thank anonymous referee whose comments lead to a substantial improvement of the paper.

References

1. R.J. Back and V. Preoteasa. An algebraic treatment of procedure refinement to support mechanical verification. *Formal Aspects of Computing*, 17:69 – 90, May 2005.
2. R.J. Back and J. von Wright. *Refinement Calculus. A systematic Introduction.* Springer, 1998.
3. A. Church. A formulation of the simple theory of types. *J. Symbolic logic*, 5:56–68, 1940.
4. C.A.R. Hoare. An axiomatic basis for computer programming. *Communications of the ACM*, 12(10):576–580, 1969.
5. S.S. Ishtiaq and P.W. O'Hearn. Bi as an assertion language for mutable data structures. In *POPL '01: Proceedings of the 28th ACM SIGPLAN-SIGACT symposium on Principles of programming languages*, pages 14–26, New York, NY, USA, 2001. ACM Press.
6. T. Nipkow, L.C. Paulson, and M. Wenzel. *Isabelle/HOL — A Proof Assistant for Higher-Order Logic*, volume 2283 of *LNCS*. Springer, 2002.
7. P.W. O'Hearn, J.C. Reynolds, and H. Yang. Local reasoning about programs that alter data structures. In *CSL '01: Proceedings of the 15th International Workshop on Computer Science Logic.*, volume 2142 of *Lecture Notes In Computer Science*, pages 1–19, London, UK, 2001. Springer-Verlag.
8. S. Owre, N. Shankar, J.M. Rushby, and D.W.J. Stringer-Clavert. PVS language reference. Technical report, Computer Science Laboratory, SRI International, dec 2001.
9. V. Preoteasa. Mechanical verification of mutually recursive procedures for parsing expressions using separation logic. Technical Report 771, TUCS - Turku Centre for Computer Science, May 2006.
10. J. Reynolds. Intuitionistic reasoning about shared mutable data structure. In *Millenial Perspectives in Computer Science*, 2000.
11. J. Reynolds. Separation logic: A logic for shared mutable data structures. In *17th Annual IEEE Symposium on Logic in Computer Science*. IEEE, July 2002.
12. A. Tarski. A lattice-theoretical fixpoint theorem and its applications. *Pacific J. Math.*, 5:285–309, 1955.
13. Tjark Weber. Towards mechanized program verification with separation logic. In Jerzy Marcinkowski and Andrzej Tarlecki, editors, *Computer Science Logic – 18th International Workshop, CSL 2004, 13th Annual Conference of the EACSL, Karpacz, Poland, September 2004, Proceedings*, volume 3210 of *Lecture Notes in Computer Science*, pages 250–264. Springer, September 2004.
14. H. Yang and P.W. O'Hearn. A semantic basis for local reasoning. In *FoSSaCS '02: Proceedings of the 5th International Conference on Foundations of Software Science and Computation Structures*, volume 2303 of *Lecture Notes In Computer Science*, pages 402–416, London, UK, 2002. Springer-Verlag.

Model-Based Variable and Transition Orderings for Efficient Symbolic Model Checking

Wendy Johnston, Kirsten Winter, Lionel van den Berg,
Paul Strooper, and Peter Robinson

University of Queensland
School of ITEE
4072 Brisbane (St.Lucia), Australia
{wendy, kirsten}@itee.uq.edu.au
http://www.itee.uq.edu.au/~sigtools

Abstract. The symbolic model checker NuSMV has been used to check safety properties for railway interlockings. When the size of the models increased, the model checking efficiency decreased dramatically to a point at which the verification failed due to lack of memory. At that point the models we could check were still small in the real world of railway interlockings. Various standard options to the NuSMV model checker were tried, mostly without significant improvement. However, the analysis of our model provided information on how to optimise the variable orderings and also the ordering and clustering of the partitioned transition relation. The NuSMV code was adapted to enable user control for ordering and clustering of transitions. This replacement of the tool's generic algorithm improved efficiency enormously, enabling the checking of safety properties for very large models. This paper discusses how the characteristics of our model are used to find the optimised parameters.

Keywords: Symbolic model checking, Binary Decision Diagrams, image computation, partitioned transition relations, clustering, railway interlockings.

1 Introduction

The SigTools toolset [1] automatically generates models from railway interlocking data in the design phase and checks the models for safety properties using the NuSMV model checker [2]. The aim is to detect errors early in the design process by applying an automated tool for verification [3].

NuSMV is a symbolic model checker which uses Reduced Ordered Binary Decision Diagrams (ROBDDs) as internal representation of states and state transitions [4]. When exploring the state space of the model, the checker iteratively applies the transition relation to the current state resulting in the next state. This is called *image computation*.

The size of an ROBDD is determined by the *variable ordering* that is used when building the diagram. In order to minimise runtime and memory usage of

J. Misra, T. Nipkow, and E. Sekerinski (Eds.): FM 2006, LNCS 4085, pp. 524–540, 2006.
© Springer-Verlag Berlin Heidelberg 2006

the checking process it is essential to provide the tool with a good variable ordering [5]. For the image computation it is found that it is beneficial to partition the transition relation into *clusters* [6]. Each cluster is in turn applied to the state, building ROBDDs as intermediate products. The size of the intermediate product is often responsible for the successful termination of the checking process. Large ROBDDs quickly exhaust the available memory. How to partition the transition relation and build the clusters critically determines the shape of the intermediate product graphs. It has to be decided which transitions are grouped into a cluster and in which order the resulting clusters should be applied to the state and intermediate product, respectively. The model checker forms clusters by processing a list of transitions. The specified maximal cluster size, the *threshold*, determines the cut-off point, i.e., the number of transition ROBDDs in each cluster. Thus, the *order of transitions* within the list determines which transitions form a cluster.

Related research has mainly focused on defining heuristics for finding good partitions that can be generated independently of domain knowledge. While the initial suggestion for partitioning the transition relation in [6] "requires intimate knowledge" [7] of the model (usually a complex digital hardware circuit), [7], [8], and [9] follow an approach that deduces information automatically from the model and does not require user intervention.

In our project the chosen variable ordering that leads to the best result is based on expert knowledge of the application domain. The order of transitions and also the definition of cluster cut-off points cannot be customised by the given NuSMV tool. We found, however, that a good model-based variable ordering could also be used to define a good order for transition partitions and is helpful when forming the clusters. We modified the NuSMV code to allow for user control over both parameters. The results show a major increase in efficiency of the checking process and extend the scope of model checking in our domain significantly. Therefore, we argue for user-controlled orderings where possible. This paper analyses our model and provides characteristics that lead to an improved heuristic. Similar characteristics, we believe, can be found in other domains too.

The paper is organised as follows. Section 2 provides some technical background to symbolic model checking. Section 3 describes the application domain and the important characteristics. Section 4 details the customising of the orderings. Results on runtime and memory usage for various models is discussed in Section 5 and Section 6 documents related work. We conclude and give an outlook on future work in Section 7.

2   Background

We use the symbolic model checker NuSMV [4,2]. The tool checks if a state transition system, the *model*, satisfies a temporal logic formula or an invariant. The model is described by means of state variables Var, whose evaluation determines a state, and a transition relation between state and next state.

In symbolic model checking, states or sets of states and transition relations are represented as Binary Decision Diagrams (BDDs) which are reduced and ordered (ROBDDs). ROBDDs are a succinct representation of boolean formulas. NuSMV is implemented using the CUDD package [10] which provides very efficient algorithms for the operations on ROBDDs.

State variables Var are encoded by a set of boolean variables V. A state of the model is represented by $S(V)$ and the transition relation by $N(V, V')$. Both are stored as ROBDDs.

Variable Ordering. ROBDDs are very sensitive to the variable ordering (see [11,5,12]). The efficient reduction of BDDs into ROBDDs is based on the combination of isomorphic subtrees and the elimination of redundant decision nodes in the tree. Thus, the size of the final ROBDD will be closely related to the variable ordering used. Identifying good variable orderings for ROBDDs is the focus of many research papers [13][14][15][16]. The following *heuristics* are suggested in the literature.

1. Declare closely related variables together. In the variable ordering, each variable should be close to the variables that support its transition [5,12].
2. For each transition, having the support variables closer to the top of the order than the variable being transformed, gives the smallest ROBDD [5].
3. Declare global variables firstly [12].
4. Initially order variables manually and run the model checker iteratively to produce an ideal ordering. This is called *dynamic reordering* [2].

Partitioning the Transition Relation. The state space is explored by iteratively applying the transition relation to the states. This is done in a forward fashion starting with the initial state and is called *image computation*. The operation on ROBDDs used for image computation is called *relational product* and is for synchronous system (as in our case) defined as follows (we follow the notation from [6]).

$$S'(V') = \exists_{v \in V}[S(V) \wedge N(V, V')] \qquad (1)$$

V' is the set of primed state variables and $S'(V')$ describes the set of next states reachable from $S(V)$ via one transition step.

The transition $N(V, V')$ can be conjoined and applied to the state as one big transition or it can be envisaged as a conjunct of several smaller transition relations $N_i(V, V')$. The aim is to compute the image without building the whole of $N(V, V')$:

$$S'(V') = \exists_{v \in V}[S(V) \wedge N_0(V, V') \wedge \ldots \wedge N_{n-1}(V, V')] \qquad (2)$$

Each $N_i(V, V')$ usually depends on a smaller set of variables $D_i \subset V$. A good ordering for the $N_i(V, V')$ allows variables to be moved out of the scope of existential quantification if later transitions do not depend on those. Let $E_i = D_{\rho(i)} - \bigcup_{k=i+1}^{n-1} D_{\rho(k)}$ be the set of variables that are not used in transitions later in a given order ρ. Then $S'(V')$ can be computed in a number of steps each eliminating the corresponding variables E_i and building an *intermediate product* $S_{i+1}(V, V')$:

$$S_1(V, V') = \exists_{v \in E_0}[S(V) \wedge N_{\rho(0)}(V, V')]$$
$$S_2(V, V') = \exists_{v \in E_1}[S_1(V, V') \wedge N_{\rho(1)}(V, V')]$$
$$\vdots \tag{3}$$
$$S'(V') = \exists_{v \in E_{n-1}}[S_{n-1}(V, V') \wedge N_{\rho(n-1)}(V, V')]$$

The aim is to choose the order ρ such that variables can be eliminated as early as possible, thus reducing the size of the intermediate product [6].

For many applications the transition relation is given as a set of small transitions, each describing the behaviour of one state variable that is dependent on some other state variables, called *support variables*. The aim is to group those transitions together into one cluster that have the same support variables. Selective grouping of transitions into clusters, and the order ρ of application of the clusters leads to smaller and fewer intermediate products that are manipulated faster [7]. If transitions do not naturally fall into clear-cut divisions, the grouping of transitions within clusters and the order of application of the clusters should be such that early elimination of support variables is maximised.

NuSMV implements algorithms that approximate the *affinity* of transitions. The *affinity* between two transitions is defined as the quotient of the number of variables supporting both transitions at the same time and the total number of variables used in either of the transitions (i.e., the intersection of the support variables over their union)[1]. The transitions are then grouped according to maximal affinities and a cluster is formed when the group size reaches a certain threshold [9,8]. The user may decide the threshold or use the default threshold size. The clusters are progressively *prepended* into a cluster list. The clusters are applied to the state in turn from the beginning of the list.

If applications have very large and very small transitions and the threshold used is not considerably larger than the large transitions, this method will predictably select the large transitions first, thus putting the large transition clusters at the end of the cluster list. This is not necessarily desirable as the transition may be large because it is using many support variables that therefore cannot be eliminated before the end of the cluster application.

3   The Application

A railway interlocking prescribes the behaviour of signal equipment for a specific area, called *verification area*. Different railway interlockings have different input data, some much more complex than others, but the profile of the data is the same for each verification area. We have conducted research into the use of model checking in this context for a number of years. The complexity of the data is a problem for a medium-sized model causing the model checker to run out of

---

[1] In the code this is approximated by the ratio of the size of the conjoined ROBDDs to the sum of the sizes of the individual ROBDDs.

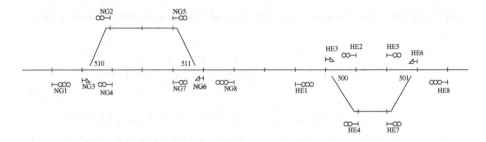

Fig. 1. Track Layout of a small verification area

memory quickly. Thus, in order to be applicable in practice, it is necessary to improve the efficiency of the model-checking process. Particularly, memory usage has to be minimised.

The data in the signalling plan for a railway interlocking includes information about track circuits, signals, points, distances, time, speed, etc. Signals use colour indications as aspects (e.g., green for go), to give authorities for trains to travel a particular route through the layout. Points are movable components in the track that permit a train to move from one track to another. The lie of the points is referred to as *normal* or *reverse*. Points move and signal aspects change depending on calls from the control centre, the lie of other points, aspects of other signals, and the route used and tracks occupied by trains. Our model prescribes the points and signals and the rules for altering the lie of points and the aspects of signals. The abstracted data set required for verification is a small subset of the original data.

Figure 1 depicts the *track layout* of a small verification area. Generally, a track layout shows where signals (e.g., NG1, NG2, NG3, etc.), points (e.g., 500, 501, 510, and 511), and tracks are located in relation to each other. Tracks are not named in Figure 1 but they are indicated on the horizontal line representing the railway by small vertical bars. A route is defined as a path traversing the tracks between two consecutive signals.

Our model includes information on train movement that is possible in a given verification area. This allows us to model the safety requirements simply by means of train collision and train derailment. It is sufficient to maximally consider two trains moving along the tracks (see also [17]). Trains move according to the condition of the points and signals. Although in real railways, trains have many different attributes (such as speed or braking capacity), in order to check the safety of train movement with respect to collision and derailment on the main routes, the train data is limited to the identity of the train, which route it is on, and which track it is occupying. Trains stop at stations. In our model we stop trains non-deterministically. Model checking will include the case in which trains stop at stations and other places too, but we do not need any extra data to determine where stations are. Commands from the control centre are modelled as input variables that change non-deterministically. That is, in any situation, there can be a command to change the status of a particular point or signal [17].

3.1   Characteristics of the Data

The data in our models can be divided into three groups. One group of data applies to the whole system and is called *global data*. The second group applies to local areas within the system and is called *local data*. The third group is non-deterministic *input data* and at each iteration of the model checking all values for those variables are considered.

Our global data represents train attributes like the current position (given in terms of a track) and the currently used route. This is modelled by four variables of enumerated type. Typically 30 -130 different values, depending on the number of tracks and routes in the interlocking, are required. The larger and more complex the verification area, the larger becomes the global data. Typically this data requires five to seven booleans for each attribute in the implementation (see [5] for details on implementing enumerated types efficiently).

The local data, representing the lie of the individual points and current aspect of the signals, is represented by simple booleans (points are set normal or reverse, and signals are set proceed or stop).

Input data, representing signalling and train control commands, includes a number of simple booleans and one variable of enumerated type. The number of enumerated values again depends on the size of the verification area, i.e., the number of points, signals and routes. The implementation of the enumerated input variable typically requires five to seven booleans.

An increase in the complexity of models (more signals, points and tracks), introduces more local variables, and maintains the same number of global and input variables but adds more values to the enumerated types. Adding more values to the enumerated types does not impact significantly on the number of booleans used to implement them but does impact on the size of the ROBDD used to distinguish particular values of the variables.

3.2   Characteristics of the Transition Relations

In our model the transition relation is described using the next operator of the SMV input language [4,18]. For each variable the evaluation in the next state is modelled depending on the previous values of a number of support variables. The size of the ROBDD representing the transition for each variable is dependent on the variable ordering.

Transitions for global variables, called *global transitions*, for which the transition is specified by a case for each possible previous state of the variables, are supported by all the variables. For example, each variable in the system is used in some case when specifying the next train position. Transitions for local variables, *local transitions*, depend on a limited number of variables. Specifically they are supported by the global variables, the input variables and some of the other local variables. For example, only the occupation of particular nearby or local tracks and the input command variable are relevant to the movement of a particular point.

An analysis of the dependencies between all the variables using a dependency matrix (see [9]) resulted in a very dense matrix.

4   Customising the Orderings

Applying the model checker to larger models quickly leads to either a memory overflow or an unacceptable runtime – the checking process might not terminate at all. We have to improve on the efficiency of the process in order to be useful for industrial application, in our case the checking of railway interlockings.

We target this aim by customising the variable ordering and the order of transition partitions and their clustering. The following sections describe how this is successfully done in our project.

Let $Var = \{v_1, \ldots, v_{m+n+p}\}$ be the set of state variables in our model with $\{g_1, \ldots, g_m\} \subset Var$ the set of global variables, $\{l_1, \ldots, l_n\} \subset Var$ the set of local variables and $\{req_1, \ldots, req_p\} \subset Var$ the set of input variables. V denotes the set of boolean variables representing the variables in Var, such that the intersection of V and Var is not necessarily empty. Let $N_{v_i}(V, v_i')$, $1 \leq i \leq (m+n)$, be the transitions, local or global, that changes (local or global) variable v_i dependent on the support variables in V.

4.1   The Variable Ordering

In our project the transitions are such that if $\{v_i, v_k, v_l\}$ is the set of support variables for transition $N_{v_i}(V, v_i')$ then the set of support variables for transition $N_{v_k}(V, v_k')$ is likely to include v_i. That is, there is a cross-dependence between transitions and it is not obvious which variable should come first.

As shown in Figure 1 our data including signals, tracks and points can be drawn as symbols on a graph, i.e. the track layout. The global transitions represent a progression of a train/trains from some starting point along the tracks (or routes) shown in the layout. Each train moves according to the lie of the points and stops at red signals along its way. The local data in our model are attributes of some symbols on that graph. For example, local data for each point is the status of the point, whether it is lying normal or reverse. The local transitions represent the rules for altering these attributes depending on attributes of other symbols in the vicinity on the track-layout graph.

The dependencies between the state variables are therefore related to the *geographical* arrangement that can be read from the track layout. Taking the local data $\{l_1, .., l_n\} \subset Var$ in an order of the associated symbols, left to right across the track layout or vice-versa, i.e., in *geographic order* γ, gives a permutation of local variables $l_{\gamma(1)}, .., l_{\gamma(n)}$. For each local variable $l_{\gamma(j)}$, $1 \leq j \leq n$, the corresponding transition $N_{l_{\gamma(j)}}(V, l_{\gamma(j)}')$ then depends on local variables in reasonably close proximity to $l_{\gamma(j)}$ in the order, e.g. $l_{\gamma(j)-1}$, $l_{\gamma(j)+1}$, etc.

The local data also depend on the global variables. Experimentation shows that putting the global variables higher in the variable order than all the local variables gives the smallest local transitions (supporting heuristics 3 in Section 2). The transitions for the four global variables of enumerated type depend on all the variables and are large.

Placement of the input variables in the variable order is problematic. Input variables are in the support variables for all transitions. When they are placed

Varible Order

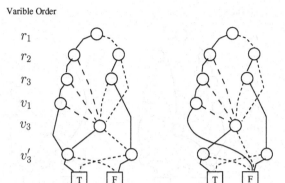

Fig. 2. Left: Transition ROBDD $N_{v_3}(V, v_3')$ with variable ordering $r_1 < r_2 < r_3 < v_1 < v_3 < v_3'$, Right: transition applied to state $v_1 = 0, v_3 = 1$

at the beginning of the order, small transitions $N_{v_i}(V, v_i')$, $1 \le i \le (m+n)$, are produced for the state variables v_i. However, this does not necessarily lead to small intermediate products as the following reasoning shows.

When a transition ROBDD $N_{v_i}(V, v_i')$ is applied to a state ROBDD $S(V)$ we build the relation product

$$S'(V') = \exists_{v \in V}[S(V) \wedge N_{v_i}(V, v_i')]$$

Only those variable evaluations in $N_{v_i}(V, v_i)$ that satisfy the values of the variables in $S(V)$ are included in the product. In the following, we refer to a particular variable evaluation in an ROBDD as a *path* through the diagram.

Figure 2 gives an example for two ROBDDs[2]. It shows on the left the ROBDD for the transition

$$N_{v_3}(V, v_3') = ((r_1 \wedge r_2 \wedge r_3) \wedge v_1 \wedge \neg v_3 \wedge v_3')$$
$$\vee ((\neg r_1 \wedge r_2 \wedge r_3) \wedge \neg v_3')$$
$$\vee (v_3 \Leftrightarrow v_3').$$

N_{v_3} depends on variables v_1 and v_3 and an input variable represented by binaries r_1, r_2, and r_3. The variable ordering is $r_1 < r_2 < r_3 < v_1 < v_3 < v_3'$, i.e., the input variable comes before the other support variables. The formula for N_{v_3} shows that the transition has three cases to consider. In two of the cases a value for the input variable is specified, namely (r_1, r_2, r_3) equals $(1, 1, 1)$ and $(0, 1, 1)$ respectively.

The right-hand side of Figure 2 shows the result of applying N_{v_3} to state $S = \neg v_1 \wedge v_3$ by building the relational product S'. There are eleven nodes in the ROBDD of N_{v_3}, and there are eleven nodes in the ROBDD of S'. The input

---

[2] Each nodes in the graph is labelled by the variable that is at the same level in the variable order. The solid line from a node represents its evaluation to true and the dashed line its evaluation to false. The leaf nodes represent the values true or false for the overall function.

Varible Order

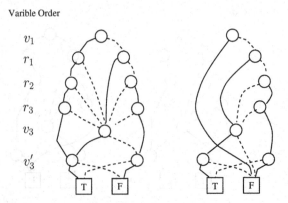

Fig. 3. Left: Transition ROBDD $N_{v_3}(V, v_3')$ with variable ordering $v_1 < r_1 < r_2 < r_3 < v_3 < v_3'$, Right: transition applied to state $v_1 = 0, v_3 = 1$

variables are not restricted to pre-state values but the variables v_1 and v_3 are restricted, so changing the shape of the product S' from the level of v_1 down. In this simple case there is no change in the number of nodes in the product.

Figure 3 shows the same transition as in Figure 2 but with a different ordering. Variable v_1 now precedes the input variable in the variable ordering. N_{v_3} now has twelve nodes, the input variable being required twice. However, when applied to state $S = \neg v_1 \land v_3$, the fixed value for v_1 eliminates a part of the ROBDD for S'. Only one path through the input variable remains which reduces the number of nodes in the product to nine.

The number of nodes in the relational product may be smaller than the number of nodes in the transition ROBDD since the pre-state values of the state variables can restrict the paths (like in Figures 2 and 3). Input variables, however, are not restricted to pre-state values and there is no reduction in the number of nodes in the relational product when applying the transition ROBDD.

A path through the diagram depends on a number of state variables and these are evaluated according to the variable ordering. If the value of a state variable does not satisfy the requirement of the transition, the path is not explored further and subsequent nodes on the path are ignored. Since the value of the input variable selection depends on many nodes (in our project 1-259 nodes) and does not restrict the path, this reasoning suggests that the number of nodes in the relational product is minimised by evaluating the input variable last. That is, state variables higher in the variable ordering than the input variables can eliminate the need to check the input variable on certain paths in the ROBDD.

Each of our local transitions depend on the values of a large input variable representing the control centre commands. Experimentation has shown that placing the large input variable lower in the order increases the size of the local transitions and the size of the clusters. However, as expected from the previous reasoning, this gives smaller intermediate products and uses less memory overall. There are time and memory efficiency penalties for manipulating large transitions, large clusters, and large intermediate products and for our data, experimentation has shown that the best results are obtained by placing the large input variable about 2/3 down the order.

Our model has other state variables of similar size and complexity to the input variable for control centre commands but their values start at a specific value and are changed only by transition rules, ensuring the complexity of their BDD is kept to a minimum.

NuSMV can be used without the user supplying a variable order or any other options. For a medium-sized model using NuSMV this way took 9620 seconds and used 1098 Megabytes (Mb) of memory (see also Table 1 in Section 5). We were unable to produce a good ordering by running the dynamic reordering algorithm implemented in NuSMV as suggested in the heuristic 4 in Section 2. Ordering the variables as they appeared in the assignments, heuristic 3, was not possible as the cross-dependence was too strong.

Using the option to provide a customised variable ordering in the order global and simple boolean input variables followed by local variables in geographic order with the large input variable about 2/3 down the order, NuSMV checked the above medium model in 734 seconds, using 114 Mb of memory. Running the same model but moving the large input variable towards the top of the variable order, took 3739 seconds and used 334 Mb.

4.2 Partitioning the Transition Relation

NuSMV does not have provision for the user to supply a transition order. It has its own generic algorithm for estimating the affinity of transitions [9] and progressively builds clusters based on this affinity. A cluster is closed off when its size reaches a threshold that the user supplies or the default threshold. This results in evenly sized clusters.

For our application the dependency matrix on which the affinity is based is very dense. The behaviour of all variables is heavily interrelated. Therefore, computing the affinity between variables by itself did not provide the necessary improvements in efficiency.

Examining the railway interlocking model and its semantics has enabled us to define an order in which transitions can be conjoined and the points in the order at which to cut the conjunctions to form clusters. When these clusters are applied in turn in the image computation, the variables are quantified efficiently from the intermediate product.

Transition Ordering. It is reasoned that transitions that are supported by the maximal number of variables should be grouped together in a cluster and applied first. Subsequent transitions that are supported by fewer variables should be grouped into clusters so that as many of their support variables as possible do not support transitions in clusters yet to be applied. This enables some of the support variables to be quantified out progressively from the intermediate products giving smaller intermediate products (see equation 3 in Section 2).

In our application, the global transitions, $N_{g_1}, \ldots, N_{g_m}$, are supported by all the other variables including the input variables. The above argument suggests that global transitions should be applied first. The local transitions, $N_{l_1}, \ldots, N_{l_n}$, depend on global variables and other local variables associated with nearby symbols in the track layout, an argument that was used to define the geographic variable ordering (see Section 4.1). A transition order that reflects the geographic order of variables γ for the local transitions results in a permutation $N_{l_{\gamma(1)}}, \ldots, N_{l_{\gamma(n)}}$ of local transition which then can be progressively grouped into clusters with some overlap of support variables. That is, the same argument of vicinity of symbols on the track layout that is used for finding a good variable ordering can be reused for ordering the partitioned transition.

Removing variables at the leaf end of an ROBDD (lowest in the variable order) favours BDD reduction and results in smaller diagrams than removing variables from the middle or root end of the diagram (higher in the variable order). If the local variables indexed progressively by $\gamma(1), \ldots, \gamma(n)$ within the geographic order, the transition for the $\gamma(n)$th variable is applied before the transition for the $(\gamma(n) - 1)$th variable to facilitate early elimination of the $\gamma(n)$th variable. While the $\gamma(n)$th variable may not be eliminated immediately after application of its transition, it should be soon after since all transitions using it will be within close range. This ordering is similar to the variable ordering but the transitions are applied in reverse order for the local variables.

The order of application of transitions is the global transitions followed by the local transitions in the order $\gamma(n)$ to $\gamma(1)$. That is, assuming the NuSMV principle of prepending the cluster list, the transition order for this application is the local transitions in the order $\gamma(1)$ to $\gamma(n)$, followed by the global variable transitions:

$$N_{l_{\gamma(1)}}, \ldots, N_{l_{\gamma(n)}}, N_{g_1}, \ldots, N_{g_m}$$

The NuSMV code was augmented so that the user could manipulate the transition order by entering an ordered list of the corresponding variables, $l_{\gamma(1)}, \ldots, l_{\gamma(n)}, g_1, \ldots, g_m$. The default threshold method was then applied to form the clusters. The medium model used in Section 4.1 was checked in 321 seconds and used 78 Mb of memory which is a significant improvement over former results (c.f. Table 1).

Forming the Clusters. Transitions are conjoined in order according to the transition order. Having defined a good transition order that supports the elimination of variables as early as possible, the question becomes where to cut the transition conjunction and form a cluster. If all transitions are in one cluster, no elimination of variables can occur and the ROBDD representing the cluster becomes very large.

Clusters should not be so large that significant time is lost building the clusters. On the other hand, many small clusters give many intermediate products that are computationally inefficient to process. There should be enough clusters so that significant elimination of variables can occur.

The global transitions are applied first and it is logical to put all of these into the first cluster. The size of this cluster varied from 98401 nodes for a small model, 196301 nodes for a medium model, and 554235 nodes for a large model. After application of the global cluster only the *next* values for the global variables can be quantified out. However, there should be local variables to be eliminated after the second cluster application of local transitions and each subsequent application as this is the criteria on which the transition order was based. Using a transition order and the default threshold to form the clusters resulted in between ten and fourteen clusters for our models.

Assuming the transition order reflects the geographic order, it is possible by referencing the track layout to nominate where in the transition order the dependencies change. For example, Figure 1 shows us that variables related to symbols to the right of signal *HE1* will be supported mostly by variables lower in the transition order than the variable for signal *HE1* since we ordered the variables inspecting the track layout from left to right. Similarly, variables related to symbols to the left of signal *HE1* will be mostly supported by variables higher in the variable ordering than the variable for signal *HE1*. Thus, the local transitions fall naturally into two clusters at this point. Including the global cluster gives three clusters for this track layout.

The code for NuSMV was augmented to allow the user to define clusters. Choosing three clusters by reference to the track layout for the same model as used previously, the altered NuSMV took 152 seconds and used 49 Mb to check the model. That is, runtime is halved and memory usage reduced by a third compared to previous results. The cluster sizes generated are: global cluster 196301 nodes, first local cluster 39018 nodes, second local cluster 18636 nodes. In general we found the models fell naturally into three or four clusters and using this improved the efficiency of our model checking.

However, while one large model fell naturally into three clusters, one of these clusters was very large and the model checker spent significant time building it. While specifying this very large cluster as two clusters fixed the problem, it was not a satisfactory solution.

From our experimentation it is clear that with a good transition order, few clusters are required. Another way to achieve few clusters is to specify a large threshold. The clusters will not be cut as precisely as before but because the order is good, progressive elimination of variables will occur. Running NuSMV on the same model as used previously, with a transition order, and a threshold of 100000 took 222 seconds and used 63 Mb. The cluster sizes for this model check are more even: 1st cluster 196301 nodes, 2nd cluster 303042 nodes, 3rd cluster 153550 nodes. This result is not as good as the customised formation of clusters described above, but is a worthwhile improvement on the default threshold used by standard NuSMV. The result is suggested that this approach is a reasonable alternative as it requires no specialist knowledge of the model or the application domain.

5   Experimental Results

Table 1 compares our results for each of 3 different sized models - small, medium, and large, using the options indicated. The numbers show that a large improvement over runtime and memory usage was achieved by choosing a good variable ordering that was based on geographical information from the track layout, i.e., domain knowledge over the dependencies. This result is not surprising as this correlation is often stated in the literature.

Table 1. Comparison of various sized models using the discussed options

	User Options	Time(secs)	Memory Used
Small model	1	4081	655Mb
	2	651	98Mb
	3	124	42Mb
	4	61	29Mb
	5	88	36Mb
Medium model	1	9620	1098Mb
	2	734	114Mb
	3	321	78Mb
	4	152	49Mb
	5	222	63Mb
Large model	1	N/A	ran out of memory
	2	N/A	ran out of memory
	3	68872	3.6Gb
	4	33641	980Mb
	5	29357	1160Mb

where
option 1: using NuSMV defaults for variable and transition orders and clustering
option 2: using user-defined variable order with default transition order and clustering
option 3: using user-defined variable ordering and user-defined transition orders with default clustering
option 4: using user-defined variable ordering, user-defined transition order and clusters selected by user
option 5: using user-defined variable order, user-defined transition order and clusters selected by threshold

Improvements of similar scale could also be achieved by customising the order of transition partitions and by forming the clusters. Both parameters were chosen using the same reasoning as was used for choosing the variable ordering – in our case geographic order of dependencies. NuSMV does not allow the user to set these parameters. The tool could be improved by given the user an input option.

6   Related Work

Model checking has been applied before to the analysis of interlocking systems. Closest to our approach are the contributions by Eisner [19] and Huber et. al [20].

Both use a symbolic model checker to analyse the interlocking logic of a given track layout and discuss strategies for optimisation. In both works, however, the model is significantly different from our model and different strategies apply. In [20], for instance, the interlocking model is given on the program level of geographical data. The variable ordering is optimised using the dynamic re-ordering of the NuSMV tool. In our case, however, we were able to significantly improve on this option by using an application specific ordering. Huber also suggests splitting the transition relation but does not elaborate on the ordering.

Early work on generally gaining improvements by partitioning the transition relations is published in [6]. While this paper suggests that the order for the transitions partitions should be provided by the user, later publications, e.g. [8,7,9], argue that for large models this task is too complex. Thus, Geist and Beer [7] suggest an algorithmic approach that chooses the transition order based on computable heuristics independently of user knowledge. Ranjan et al. [8] later improved on these heuristics using a cost function. Moon et al. [9] introduce a dependency matrix showing the dependencies between variables. Based on this matrix the *affinity* of transitions is computed, a value that measures the overlap in support variables. Transitions with high affinity should thus form a cluster.

The algorithm in [8] is implemented in NuSMV, referred to as IWLS ordering. However, the function is overwritten by the implementation of the algorithm in [9], referred to as MHS_affinity. Changing the NuSMV code enabled us to experiment with both algorithms but neither of them provided good enough results for our application. In our experiments, we worked with matrices similar to the dependency matrix suggested in [9]. When our matrix contained all variables it was very dense. Any permutation of the rows in the matrix would not lead to improved results. Since in our model global variables are supported by all other variables, we found it to be beneficial to determine the *geographical closeness* (which is similar to the notion of affinity) only for local variables and prepend the global variables.

Wang et al. [21] extended the work of [9] by firstly reducing the transition size by over-approximating the image that is computed, and computing later the exact image by applying a *clipping function*. This approach constrains the next-state values of the variables, i.e., the v_i', instead of the previous state values as in the earlier approaches. This work, similar to the other approaches, does not consider the use of model or domain knowledge. Since an implementation of this approach is not available we cannot compare our results with those gained from using this new algorithm.

7 Conclusion

For checking railway interlockings, this work has shown great improvement of efficiency by allowing the user to define not only the variable order (as is currently available as an option in NuSMV) but also a transition order and cut-off points for forming clusters of transitions. Both the variable order and the transition order come from an analysis of the domain data.

Moon et al. [9] use affinity amongst all variables to derive the transition order, which indicates the overlap of support variables amongst two transitions. In contrast, we recognise global transitions that are supported by all variables and ensure these are applied first to the state. Only local transitions are ordered by *geographical closeness*, which is similar to affinity but based on graphical information. We also place the large input variable low in the variable order since small transition sizes are not necessarily a good indicator of overall model checking efficiency. For our application, our ordering heuristics shows significant improvements over the heuristics suggested in [9]. Since the designer of the model knows both, the global and the input variables, setting the parameters does not require specific domain knowledge. We suggest the following heuristics when defining the *variable ordering*:

1. Declare closely related variables together.
2. Declare global variables first.
3. Consider the size of input variables and experiment by placing any large input variables low in the order.
4. Consider the order of application of transitions so that the variables last in the variable order are the first to be eliminated from the intermediate clusters.

Furthermore, we suggest the following heuristics when defining a *transition order* and the *formation of clusters*:

1. Declare the global variables so that their transitions are applied first.
2. Declare closely related variables together in a sequence depending on support variables.
3. Declare the sequence of local variables so that their transitions are applied in reverse order to the variable order.
4. Put the global variables into 1 cluster.
5. Apply at least 3 clusters.

This project relies on a geographical track layout to get efficient orderings. For even very large verification areas our heuristics rendered the model checking process applicable. In future work, we will apply our approach to those few railway interlockings, such as those found in very large interchanges, in which complex point systems and crossovers make the selection of related groups of signals and points based on graphical information difficult or impossible.

Acknowledgements. This work has been supported by the ARC Linkage Grant LP0455155. We would like to thank George Nikandros, David Barney and David Tombs from Queensland Rail for fruitful discussions.

References

1. Robinson, N., Barney, D., Kearney, P., Nikandros, G., Tombs, D.: Automatic generation and verification of design specification. In: Proc. of Int. Symp. of the International Council On Systems Engineering (INCOSE). (2001)

2. Cimatti, A., Clarke, E., Giunchiglia, E., Giunchiglia, F., Pistore, M., Roveri, M., Sebastiani, R., Tacchella, A.: NuSMV 2: an OpenSource tool for symbolic model checking. In Brinksma, E., Larsen, K.G., eds.: Proc. of Int. Conference on Computer Aided Verification (CAV 2002). Volume 2404 of LNCS., Springer Verlag (2002) 359–364

3. Winter, K., Robinson, N.J.: Modelling large interlocking systems and model checking small ones. In Oudshoorn, M., ed.: Proc. of Australasian Computer Science Conference (ACSC 2003). Volume 16 of Australian Computer Science Communications. (2003)

4. McMillan, K.: Symbolic Model Checking. Kluwer Academic Publishers (1993)

5. Clarke, E., Grumberg, O., Peled, D.: Model Checking. MIT Press (2000)

6. J.R. Burch, E.M. Clarke, D.E. Long: Symbolic model checking with partitioned transition relations. In A. Halaas, P.B. Denyer, eds.: Proc. of Int. Conference on Very Large Scale Integration, North-Holland (1991) 49–58

7. D. Geist, I. Beer: Efficient model checking by automated ordering of transition relation. In David L. Dill, ed.: Proc. of Int. Conference on Computer-Aided Verification (CAV'94). Volume 818 of LNCS., Springer-Verlag (1994) 299–310

8. Ranjan, R., Aziz, A., Brayton, R., Plessier, B., Pixley, C.: Efficient BDD algorithms for FSM synthesis and verification. In: Proc. of IEEE/ACM Int. Workshop on Logic Synthesis. (1995)

9. I.Moon, G.D.Hachtel, F.Somenzi: Border-block triangular form and conjunction schedule in image computation. In: Proc. of Formal Methods in Computer-Aided Design (FMCAD 2000). Volume 1954 of LNCS. (2000) 73–90

10. Somenzi, F.: CUDD: CU Decision Diagram package — release 2.3.0. In: Department of Electrical and Computer Engineering — University of Colorado at Boulder. (September 1998)

11. Bryant, R.E.: Graph-based algorithms for boolean function manipulation. IEEE Transactions On Computers **C-35**(8) (1986)

12. G.Lewis, S.Comella-Dorda, D.Gluch, J.Hudak, C.Weinstock: Model-based verification: Analysis guidelines. Technical Report CMU/SEI-2001-TN-028, Carnegie Mellon Software Engineering Institute (2001)

13. Chan, W., Anderson, R.J., Beame, P., Burns, S., Modugno, F., Notkin, D., Reese, J.D.: Model checking large software specifications. IEEE Transactions on Software Engineering **24**(7) (1998) 498–520

14. Kamhi, G., Fix, L.: Adaptive variable reordering for symbolic model checking. In: Proc. of IEEE/ACM Int. Conference on Computer-aided design (ICCAD'98), ACM Press (1998) 359–365

15. Lu, Y., Jain, J., Clarke, E., Fujita, M.: Efficient variable ordering using a BDD based sampling. In: Proc. of Int. Conference on Design automation (DAC'00), ACM Press (2000) 687–692

16. Rudell, R.: Dynamic variable ordering for ordered binary decision diagrams. In: Proc. of IEEE/ACM Int. Conference on Computer-aided design (ICCAD'93), IEEE Computer Society Press (1993) 42–47

17. Winter, K., Johnston, W., Robinson, P., Strooper, P., van den Berg, L.: Tool support for checking railway interlocking designs. In Cant, T., ed.: 10th Australian Workshop on Safety Related Programmable Systems (SCS'05). Volume Vol. 55., Australian Computer Society, Inc. (2005) to appear.

18. Cavda, R., Cimatti, A., Olivetti, E., Pistore, M., Roveri, M.: NuSMV 2.0 User Manual, http://nusmv.irst.itc.it. (2001)

19. Eisner, C.: Using symbolic model checking to verify the railway stations of hoorn-kersenboogerd and heerhugowaard. In: Proc. of the 10th IFIP Working Conference on Correct Hardware Design and Verification Methods (CHARME'99). Volume 1703 of LNCS., Springer-Verlag (1999) 97–109
20. Huber, M., King, S.: Towards an integrated model checker for railway signalling data. In Eriksson, L.H., Lindsay, P., eds.: Proc. on Formal Methods Europe (FME'2002). Volume 2391., Springer-Verlag (2002) 204–223
21. Wang, C., Hachtel, G.D., Somenzi, F.: The compositional far side of image computation. In: Proc. of IEEE/ACM Int. Conference on Computer-Aided Design (ICCAD'03), IEEE Computer Society (2003) 334–340

Exact and Approximate Strategies for Symmetry Reduction in Model Checking

Alastair F. Donaldson* and Alice Miller

Department of Computing Science
University of Glasgow
Glasgow, Scotland
{ally, alice}@dcs.gla.ac.uk

Abstract. Symmetry reduction techniques can help to combat the state space explosion problem for model checking, but are restricted by the hard problem of determining equivalence of states during search. Consequently, existing symmetry reduction packages can only exploit *full* symmetry between system components, as checking the equivalence of states is straightforward in this special case. We present a framework for symmetry reduction with an *arbitrary* group of structural symmetries. By generalising existing techniques for efficiently exploiting symmetry, and introducing an approximate strategy for use with groups for which fast, exact strategies are not available, our approach allows for significant state-space reduction with minimal time overhead. We show how computational group theoretic techniques can be used to analyse the structure of a symmetry group so that an appropriate symmetry reduction strategy can be chosen, and we describe a symmetry reduction package for the SPIN model checker which interfaces with the computational algebra system GAP. Experimental results on a variety of Promela models illustrate the effectiveness of our methods.

Keywords: Promela/SPIN, model checking, symmetry, computational group theory, GAP.

1 Introduction

Symmetry reduction techniques can help to combat the state space explosion problem when model checking systems with replicated structure. Replication of components in a concurrent system frequently induces replication, or *symmetry*, in a Kripke structure modelling the system, which allows the set of states of the model to be partitioned into equivalence classes. To model check temporal logic properties it is often sufficient to search one state per equivalence class, potentially resulting in more efficient verification. Given a symmetry group G, a common approach to ensure that equivalent states are recognised during search is to convert each newly encountered state s into $min[s]_G$ the *smallest* state in its equivalence class (under a suitable total ordering) before it is stored. However,

---

* Supported by the Carnegie Trust for the Universities of Scotland.

J. Misra, T. Nipkow, and E. Sekerinski (Eds.): FM 2006, LNCS 4085, pp. 541–556, 2006.
© Springer-Verlag Berlin Heidelberg 2006

the problem of computing $min[s]_G$ for an arbitrary group, called the *constructive orbit problem* (COP), is NP-hard [5].

Existing symmetry reduction packages, such as SymmSpin [1] and SMC [18], are limited as they can only exploit *full* symmetry between identical components of a system. Such symmetry arises in systems where all components of the same type are interchangeable, and has been of primary interest since the COP can be efficiently solved in this special case. However, many other kinds of symmetry commonly occur in models of concurrent systems with a regular structure. For example, cyclic/dihedral groups are typically associated with systems which have uni-/bi-directional ring structures, and wreath product groups occur when dealing with tree topologies.

In this paper we generalise existing techniques for efficiently exploiting symmetry under a simple model of computation, and give an approximate strategy for use with symmetry groups for which fast, exact strategies cannot be found. We use computational group theory to automatically determine the structure of a group before search so that an appropriate symmetry reduction strategy can be chosen, and give encouraging experimental results to support our techniques using TopSPIN, a new symmetry reduction package for the SPIN model checker [14] which interfaces with the GAP computational algebra system [12]. We then illustrate the problems associated with extending our model of computation to apply to Promela specifications, where full symmetry reduction may no longer be guaranteed.

2   Symmetry in Model Checking

2.1   Model of Computation

We use a simple model to represent the computation of a system comprised of n communicating components, interleaving concurrently [10,11]. Let $I = \{1, 2, \ldots, n\}$ be the set of component identifiers, and for some $k > 0$, let $L = \{1, 2, \ldots, k\}$ denote the possible local states of the components. A Kripke structure is a pair $\mathcal{M} = (S, R)$, where $S \subseteq L^n$, is a non-empty set of states, and $R \subseteq S \times S$ is a total transition relation. The lexicographical ordering of vectors in L^n provides a total ordering on S. If $s = (l_1, l_2, \ldots, l_n) \in S$ then we use $s(i)$ to denote l_i, the local state of component i.

This model of computation allows us to reason about concurrent systems consisting of processes and channels, since a positive integer can be assigned to each valuation of the local variables of a process or the contents of a channel. We assume that the local variables of components do not refer to component identifiers. We discuss the implications of lifting this assumption in Section 5.1.

2.2   Group Theoretic Notation

We assume some knowledge of basic group theory, but recap some notation here. Let G be a group, and let $\alpha_1, \alpha_2, \ldots, \alpha_n \in G$. The smallest subgroup of G containing the elements $\alpha_1, \ldots, \alpha_n$ is denoted $\langle \alpha_1, \alpha_2, \ldots, \alpha_n \rangle$, and is called the subgroup *generated* by $\alpha_1, \alpha_2, \ldots, \alpha_n$. The elements α_i $(1 \leq i \leq n)$ are called *generators* for this subgroup. Let $X = \{\alpha_1, \ldots, \alpha_n\}$ be a finite subset of G. Then we use $\langle X \rangle$ to denote $\langle \alpha_1, \ldots, \alpha_n \rangle$, the subgroup generated by X. Let H be a subgroup of G, denoted $H \leq G$, and let $\alpha \in G$. The set $H\alpha = \{\beta\alpha : \beta \in H\}$ is called a (right) *coset* of H in G. The set of all cosets of H in G provides a partition of G into disjoint equivalence classes.

The set of all permutations of I forms a group under composition of mappings, denoted S_n (the symmetric group on n points). If $J \subseteq I$ and $\alpha \in S_n$, then $\alpha(J) = \{\alpha(i) : i \in J\}$. For $\alpha \in S_n$ and $H \leq S_n$, define $moved(\alpha) = \{i \in I : \alpha(i) \neq i\}$, and $moved(H) = \{i \in I : i \in moved(\alpha)$ for some $\alpha \in H\}$. For $i \in I$, the *stabiliser* of i under H is the subgroup $stab_H(i) = \{\alpha \in H : \alpha(i) = i\}$, and the *orbit* of i under H is the set $orb_H(i) = \{\alpha(i) : \alpha \in H\}$. The orbit $orb_H(i)$ is *non-trivial* if $|orb_H(i)| > 1$, and H is said to act *transitively* on I if it induces a single orbit.

2.3 Symmetry Reduction

Let $\mathcal{M} = (S, R)$ be a Kripke structure, and let $\alpha \in S_n$. Then α acts on a state $s = (l_1, l_2, \ldots, l_n) \in S$ in the following way: $\alpha(s) = (l_{\alpha^{-1}(1)}, l_{\alpha^{-1}(2)}, \ldots, l_{\alpha^{-1}(n)})$. If $(\alpha(s), \alpha(t)) \in R \; \forall \; (s,t) \in R$, α is an *automorphism* of $\mathcal{M}$. The set of all automorphisms of $\mathcal{M}$ forms a group $Aut(\mathcal{M}) \leq S_n$ under composition of mappings.

A subgroup $G \leq Aut(\mathcal{M})$ induces an equivalence relation $\equiv_G$ on the states of $\mathcal{M}$ thus: $s \equiv_G t \Leftrightarrow s = \alpha(t)$ for some $\alpha \in G$. The equivalence class under $\equiv_G$ of a state $s \in S$, denoted $[s]_G$, is called the *orbit* of s under the action of G (so G induces orbits on both the set I of component identifiers and the set S of states), and $min[s]_G$ denotes the *smallest* element of $[s]_G$ under the total ordering discussed in Section 2.1. The quotient Kripke structure for $\mathcal{M}$ with respect to G is a pair $\mathcal{M}_G = (S_G, R_G)$ where $S_G = \{min[s]_G : s \in S\}$, and $R_G = \{(min[s]_G, min[t]_G) : (s,t) \in R\}$. In general $\mathcal{M}_G$ is a smaller structure than $\mathcal{M}$, but $\mathcal{M}_G$ and $\mathcal{M}$ are equivalent in the sense that they satisfy the same set of logic properties which are *invariant* under the group G (that is, properties which are "symmetric" with respect to G). For a proof of the following theorem, together with details of the temporal logic CTL^*, see [6].

Theorem 1. *Let $\mathcal{M}$ be a Kripke structure, G a subgroup of $Aut(\mathcal{M})$ and ϕ a CTL^* formula. If ϕ is invariant under G then*

$$\mathcal{M}, s \models \phi \Leftrightarrow \mathcal{M}_G, min[s]_G \models \phi$$

Thus by choosing a suitable symmetry group G, model checking can be performed over $\mathcal{M}_G$ instead of $\mathcal{M}$, often resulting in considerable savings in memory and verification time [2,11]. Algorithm 1, adapted from [15], explores a quotient Kripke structure given an initial state s_0. An extension of this algorithm for on-the-fly model checking of LTL properties using a nested depth first search is presented in [1].

In practice, for an arbitrary group G, it may be infeasible to implement the function *min* exactly. In such cases the requirements of *min* can be relaxed so

Algorithm 1. Algorithm to explore a quotient Kripke structure

$reached := \{min[s_0]_G\};$
$unexplored := \{min[s_0]_G\};$
while $unexplored \neq \emptyset$ **do**
   remove a state s from $unexplored$;
   for all successor states t of s **do**
     if $min[t]_G$ is not in $reached$ **then**
       add $min[t]_G$ to $reached$;
       add $min[t]_G$ to $unexplored$;
     end if
   end for
end while

that $min[s]_G$ yields *some* state $t \in [s]_G$ with $t \leq s$. This does not compromise the safety of symmetry reduced model checking since at least one state per orbit is searched, but does not result in memory-optimal verification. However, an efficient implementation of min which maps any element s to one of a small number of orbit representatives can result in fast verification, maintaining a significant reduction in model states (this use of *multiple representatives* is employed in e.g. [2,5]). We refer to such an implementation of min as an *approximate* symmetry reduction strategy, whereas a true implementation of min is an *exact* strategy. Note that exact verification results are still obtained using an approximate symmetry reduction strategy, if enough memory is available.

Throughout the rest of the paper, let G be a subgroup of $Aut(\mathcal{M})$, where M models a concurrent system comprised of n components.

2.4 Symmetry Detection

In this paper, we are concerned with techniques for *exploiting* component symmetries during model checking, rather than *detecting* symmetry before search. Structural symmetries of a model $\mathcal{M}$ are typically inferred by extracting a *communication graph* from the initial specification. The vertex set of this graph is the set I, representing the components of the system. Provided that the specification obeys certain restrictions ensuring that components of the same type are not explicitly distinguished, automorphisms of the communication graph induce automorphisms of $\mathcal{M}$. Since the communication graph is typically small, these automorphisms can be computed automatically using a package such as *saucy* [7]. Practical examples of communication graphs include the *static channel diagram* of a Promela specification [8], and the *coloured hypergraph* [5] of a shared variable concurrent program.

For illustration, throughout the paper we consider a system with a three-tiered architecture consisting of a *database*, a layer of *server* components, and a layer of *client* components, each of which communicates with exactly one server. Figure 1 shows a possible communication graph for this system, which we assume has been extracted from a specification of the system by some symmetry detection tool. Let $\mathcal{M}_{3T}$ be a model of the system. Using the *saucy* program, we compute generators for G_{3T}, the automorphism group of the communication graph:

$$G_{3T} = \langle (1\ 2), (2\ 3), (4\ 5), (5\ 6), (7\ 8), (8\ 9), (10\ 11),$$
$$(12\ 13)(1\ 4)(2\ 5)(3\ 6), (13\ 14)(4\ 7)(5\ 8)(6\ 9) \rangle.$$

Note that the last two elements of the generating set of G_{3T} are products of transpositions. We assume that $G_{3T} \leq Aut(\mathcal{M}_{3T})$, and will use this group and its subgroups as examples to illustrate some of our techniques.

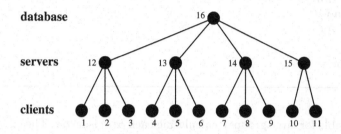

Fig. 1. Communication structure for a three-tiered architecture

3 Exploiting Basic Symmetry Groups

3.1 Enumerating Small Groups

The most obvious strategy for computing $min[s]_G$ is to consider each state in $[s]_G$, and return the smallest. This can be achieved by *enumerating* the elements $\alpha(s)$, $\alpha \in G$. If G is small then this strategy is feasible in practice, and provides an exact symmetry reduction strategy. The SymmSpin package provides an enumeration strategy for fully symmetric groups, which is optimised by generating permutations incrementally by composing successive transpositions. This is more efficient than applying permutations to s directly.

We generalise this optimisation for arbitrary groups using *stabiliser chains*. A stabiliser chain for G is a series of subgroups of the form $G = G^{(1)} \geq G^{(2)} \geq \cdots \geq G^{(k)} = \{id\}$, for some $k > 1$, where $G^{(i)} = stab_{G^{(i-1)}}(x)$ for some $x \in moved(G^{(i-1)})$ $(2 \leq i \leq k)$. If $U^{(i)}$ is a set of representatives for the cosets of $G^{(i)}$ in $G^{(i-1)}$ $(2 \leq i \leq k)$, then each element of G can be uniquely expressed as a product $u_{k-1}u_{k-2}\ldots u_1$, where $u_i \in U^{(i)}$ $(1 \leq i < k)$ [3]. Permutations can be generated incrementally using elements from the coset representatives, and the set of images of a state s under G computed using a sequence of partial images (see Algorithm 2). To ensure efficient application of permutations, the coset representatives are stored as a list of transpositions, applied in succession. GAP provides functionality to efficiently compute a stabiliser chain and associated coset representatives for an arbitrary permutation group. Although this approach still involves enumerating the elements $\alpha(s)$ for every $\alpha \in G$ (and is

Algorithm 2. Computing $min[s]_G$ using a stabiliser chain

$min[s]_G := s$
  for all $u_1 \in U_1$ **do**
    $s_1 := u_1(s)$
    for all $u_2 \in U_2$ **do**
      $s_2 := u_2(s_1)$
      $\vdots$

      for all $u_k \in U_k$ **do**
        $s_k := u_k(s_{k-1})$
        if $s_k < min[s]_G$ **then**
          $min[s]_G := s_k$
      end if
      end for
      $\vdots$

    end for
  end for

---

thus infeasible for large groups), calculating each $\alpha(s)$ is faster. The experimental results of Section 5.3 show an improvement over basic enumeration. Additionally, it is only necessary to store coset representatives, rather than all elements of G.

3.2   Minimising Sets for G if $G \cong S_m$ $(m \leq n)$

For systems where there is full symmetry between components, the smallest state in the orbit of $s = (l_1, l_2, \ldots, l_n)$ can be computed by *sorting* the tuple s lexicographically. [2,5]. For example, for a system with four components, sorting equivalent states $(3, 2, 1, 3)$ and $(3, 3, 2, 1)$ yields the state $(1, 2, 3, 3)$, which is clearly the smallest state in the orbit. Since sorting can be performed in polynomial time, this provides an efficient solution for the COP for this group.

Recall the group G_{3T} of automorphisms of the communication graph of Figure 1. Consider the subgroup

$$H = \langle (12\ 13)(1\ 4)(2\ 5)(3\ 6), (13\ 14)(4\ 7)(5\ 8)(6\ 9) \rangle.$$

This group permutes *server* components 12, 13 and 14, with their associated blocks of *client* components. It is clear that H is isomorphic to S_3, the symmetric group on 3 objects. However, we cannot compute $min[s]_H$ by sorting s in the obvious way, since this is equivalent to applying an element $\alpha \in S_{16}$ to s, which may not belong to H.

In some cases we can deal with groups of this form using a *minimising set* for G. Using terminology from [11], G is said to be *nice* if there is a small set $X \subseteq G$ such that, for any $s \in S$, $s = min[s] \Leftrightarrow s \leq \alpha(s) \; \forall \, \alpha \in X$. In this case we call X a *minimising set* for G. If a small minimising set X can be found for a large group G, then computing the representative of a state involves iterating over the small set X, minimising the state until a fix-point is reached. At this point, no element of the minimising set maps the state to a smaller image, thus the minimal element has been found.

We show that, for a large class of groups which are isomorphic to S_m for some $m \leq n$, a minimising set with size polynomial in m can be efficiently found. This minimising set is derived from the swap permutations used in a selection sort algorithm.

Theorem 2. *Suppose that, for each $i \in I$ such that $orb_G(i)$ is non-trivial, $stab_G(i)$ fixes exactly one element from each non-trivial orbit of G acting on I, and that $G \cong S_m$, where $m = |orb_G(i)| > 1$ for some $i \in I$. Then there is an isomorphism $\theta : S_m \to G$ such that $\{(i\ j)^\theta : 1 \leq i < j \leq m\}$ is a minimising set for G.*

Proof. Since for each $i \in I$ such that $|orb_G(i)| > 1$ the set of elements fixed by $stab_G(i)$ contains exactly one element from each orbit, there is a set of *columns* $C_1, C_2, \ldots, C_m$ such that each column contains one element from each orbit of G, and G permutes the columns. There is an isomorphism θ from G' (the action of G on the columns) to G acting on I. Since $G \cong S_m$, G' contains all column transpositions $(i\ j)$ where $i < j$, so $(i\ j)^\theta \in G$. The element $(i\ j)^\theta$ maps all elements of column i to elements of column j.

Now consider states s and s', where $s' = \alpha(s)$ for some $\alpha \in G$. Let i be the smallest index for which $s(i) \neq s'(i)$. Let j be the index such that $j = \alpha^{-1}(i)$. All of the elements in the column containing j (column j' say) are mapped via α to the column containing i (column i' say). Then $s' < s$ iff $(i'\ j')^\theta s < s$. Hence s is minimal in its orbit iff $(i\ j)^\theta(s) \geq s$ for all $i < j$. So the set $\{(i\ j)^\theta : 1 \leq i < j \leq m\}$ is a minimising set for G.

Note that the minimising set is much smaller than G, and the conditions of Theorem 2 can be easily checked using GAP. It may seem that these conditions are unnecessary, and that, given any isomorphism $\theta : S_m \to G$, the set $\{(i\ j)^\theta : 1 \leq i < j \leq m\}$ is a minimising set for G. However, consider the group G below, which is a subgroup of the symmetry group of a hypercube (see Section 5.3).

$$G = \langle (1\ 2)(5\ 6)(9\ 10)(13\ 14), (1\ 2\ 4\ 8)(3\ 6\ 12\ 9)(5\ 10)(7\ 14\ 13\ 11) \rangle \leq S_{14}$$

G is isomorphic to S_4, with an isomorphism $\theta : S_4 \to G$ is defined on generators by $(1\ 2\ 3\ 4)^\theta = (1\ 2\ 4\ 8)(3\ 6\ 12\ 9)(5\ 10)(7\ 14\ 13\ 11)$, $(1\ 2)^\theta = (4\ 8)(5\ 9)(6\ 10)(7\ 11)$. The state $s = (6, 10, 3, 6, 3, 5, 7, 10, 4, 8, 2, 1, 9, 3) \in \{1, 2, \ldots, 10\}^{14}$ *cannot* be minimised using the set $\{(i\ j)^\theta : 1 \leq i < j \leq 4\}$.

3.3 Local Search for Unclassifiable Groups

If G is large group then computing $min[s]_G$ by enumeration of the elements of G may be infeasible, even with the group-theoretic optimisations discussed in Section 3.1. If no minimising set is available for G, and G cannot be classified as a composite symmetry group (see Section 4) then we must exploit G via an approximate symmetry reduction strategy.

We propose an approximate strategy based on *hillclimbing local search*, which has proved successful for a variety of search problems in artificial intelligence [17, Chapter 4]. In this case the function *min* works by performing a local search of $[s]_G$ starting at s, using the generators of G as operations from which to compute a successor state. The search starts by setting $t = s$, and proceeds iteratively. On each iteration, $\alpha(t)$ is computed for each generator α of G. If $t \leq \alpha(t)$ for all α then a local minimum has been reached, and t is returned as a representative for $[s]_G$. Otherwise, t is set to the smallest image $\alpha(t)$, and the search continues. In Section 5.3 we show that this local search algorithm is effective when exploring the state spaces of various configurations of message routing in a hypercube network.

There are various local search techniques which could be employed to attempt to improve the accuracy of this strategy. *Random-restart* hill-climbing [17] involves the selection of several random elements of $[s]_G$ in addition to s, and performing local search from each of them, returning the smallest result. In our case we could apply such a technique by finding the image of a state s under distinct, random elements of G (GAP provides functionality for generating random group elements). Another potential improvement would be to use *simulated annealing* [16] to escape local minima.

4   Exploiting Composite Symmetry Groups

Certain kinds of symmetry groups can be decomposed as a product of subgroups. In this case solving the COP separately for each subgroup provides a solution to the COP for the whole group. In particular, if a symmetry group permutes disjoint sets of components independently then the group can be described as the *disjoint product* of the groups acting on these disjoint sets. On the other hand, if the symmetry group partitions the components into subsets such that there is analogous symmetry within each subset, and symmetry between the subsets, then the group can be described as the *wreath product* of the group which acts on one of the subsets, and the group which permutes the subsets. It has been shown that, if G is known to be a disjoint or wreath product of subgroups, then the COP can be solved for G by restricting attention to these subgroups [5]. We now present solutions to the problem of detecting, before search, whether or not G can be decomposed.

4.1   Disjoint Products

Definition 1. *Let $H \leq S_n$. Suppose that $H_1, H_2, \ldots, H_k$ are subgroups of H ($1 \leq i \leq k$, $k > 1$). If $H = H_1 H_2 \ldots H_k = \{\alpha_1 \alpha_2 \ldots \alpha_k : \alpha \in H_i \ (1 \leq i \leq k)\}$ then H is called the product of the H_i. If $moved(H_i) \cap moved(H_j) = \emptyset$ for all $1 \leq i \neq j \leq k$ then H is written $H_1 \bullet H_2 \bullet \cdots \bullet H_k$, and called the disjoint product of the H_i. The disjoint product is said to be non-trivial if $H \neq H_i \neq \{id\}$ for all $1 \leq i \leq k$.*

Disjoint products occur frequently in model checking problems. For example, the symmetry group associated with a model of the *readers writers* problem [10] may be a disjoint product of two groups, which independently permute *reader* and *writer* components respectively. In our three-tiered architecture example (see Section 2.4), the group G_{3T} can be shown to decompose as a disjoint product $G_{3T} = H_1 \bullet H_2$ where:

$$H_1 = \langle (1\ 2), (2\ 3), (4\ 5), (5\ 6), (7\ 8), (8\ 9),$$
$$(12\ 13)(1\ 4)(2\ 5)(3\ 6), (13\ 14)(4\ 7)(5\ 8)(6\ 9) \rangle$$
$$H_2 = \langle (10, 11) \rangle.$$

If G is a disjoint product of subgroups $H_1, H_2, \ldots, H_k$ then $min[s]_G = min[\ldots min[min[s]_{H_1}]_{H_2} \cdots]_{H_k}$ [5], so the COP for G can be solved by considering each subgroup H_i in turn. This result is only useful when designing a fully automatic symmetry reduction package if it is possible to efficiently determine, before search, whether or not G decomposes as a disjoint product of subgroups. We present two solutions to this problem.

Efficient, Sound, Incomplete Approach

Let $G = \langle X \rangle$ for some $X \subseteq G$ with $id \notin X$. Define a binary relation $B \subseteq X^2$ as follows: for all $\alpha, \beta \in X$, $(\alpha, \beta) \in B \Leftrightarrow moved(\alpha) \cap moved(\beta) \neq \emptyset$. Clearly B is symmetric, and since for any $\alpha \in G$ with $\alpha \neq id$, $moved(\alpha) \neq \emptyset$, B is reflexive. It follows that the transitive closure of B, denoted B^*, is an equivalence relation on X. We now show that if B^* has multiple equivalence classes then each class generates a subgroup of G which is a non-trivial factor for a disjoint product decomposition of G.

Lemma 1. *Suppose that $\alpha, \beta \in X$, and that $(\alpha, \beta) \notin B^*$. Then $moved(\alpha) \cap moved(\beta) = \emptyset$ and α and β commute.*

Theorem 3. *Suppose $C_1, C_2, \ldots, C_k$ are the equivalence classes of X under B^* where $k \geq 2$. For $1 \leq i \leq k$ let $H_i = \langle C_i \rangle$. Then $G = H_1 \bullet H_2 \bullet \cdots \bullet H_k$, and $H_i \neq \{id\}$ $(1 \leq i \leq k)$.*

Proof. Clearly $H_1 H_2 \ldots H_k \subseteq G$. If $\alpha \in G$ then $\alpha = \alpha_1 \alpha_2 \ldots \alpha_d$ for some $\alpha_1, \alpha_2, \ldots, \alpha_d \in X$, $d > 0$. By Lemma 1 we can arrange the α_l so that elements of C_i appear before those of C_j whenever $i < j$. It follows that $G = H_1 H_2 \ldots H_k$. By Lemma 1, $moved(H_i) \cap moved(H_j) = \emptyset$ for $1 \leq i \neq j \leq k$ and so $G = H_1 \bullet H_2 \bullet \cdots \bullet H_k$, where (since $id \notin X$) the H_i are non-trivial.

The approach is incomplete as it does not guarantee the finest decomposition of G as a disjoint product. However, in practice we have not found a case in which the finest decomposition is not detected when generators have been computed by a graph automorphism program. The approach is very efficient as it works purely with the generators of G, of which there are typically few.

Sound and Complete Approach

It is straightforward to show that if $G = H \bullet K$, then H and K are *normal* subgroups of G. Thus a complete method for determining whether or not G is a non-trivial disjoint product of subgroups H and K involves the computation of all normal subgroups of G and searching for a pair such that $G = H \bullet K$. This method could be applied recursively to the factors of the disjoint product to compute the finest disjoint product decomposition of G. Although for certain groups (e.g. abelian groups), all subgroups are normal, in many cases the number of normal subgroups of a group is significantly smaller than the number of arbitrary subgroups.

4.2   Wreath Products

Definition 2. *For $r > 1$ let $B_1, B_2, \ldots, B_r$ be disjoint subsets of I, where $B_i = \{b_{i,1}, b_{i,2}, \ldots, b_{i,m}\}$ for some $m > 1$. Let $H \leq S_n$ with $moved(H) \subseteq B_1$. For any $\alpha \in H$ and $1 \leq i \leq r$, define $\alpha^{(i)}$ by: $\alpha^{(i)}(x) = x$ if $x \notin B_i$; $\alpha^{(i)}(b_{i,j}) = b_{i,l}$ where $\alpha(b_{1,j}) = b_{1,l}$. For $\beta' \in S_r$, define $\beta \in S_n$ by: $\beta(x) = x$ if $x \notin \bigcup_{1 \leq i \leq r} B_i$ and $\beta(b_{i,j}) = b_{\beta'(i),j}$. Let $K = \langle \beta_1, \beta_2, \ldots, \beta_d \rangle$ where $d > 0$ and each β_i is derived from some $\beta'_i \in S_r$). If every element of G can be expressed in the form $\beta \alpha_r^{(r)} \ldots \alpha_2^{(2)} \alpha_1^{(1)}$, where $\beta \in K$ and $\alpha_1, \alpha_2, \ldots, \alpha_r \in H$, then G is the* wreath product *of H and K, denoted $H \wr K$.*

Intuitively, an element of G applies a permutation to each set B_i, then applies a permutation which permutes the sets. This definition of wreath products is specific to those that occur in model checking problems, typically when a system has a tree structure. For a more general definition, see [4]. In Section 4.1, we showed that the group G_{3T} decomposes as a disjoint product. Consider the factor H_1 of this product. This group itself decomposes as a wreath product $H_1 = H \wr K$ where:

$$H = \langle (1\ 2), (2\ 3) \rangle$$
$$K = \langle (12\ 13)(1\ 4)(2\ 5)(3\ 6), (13\ 14)(4\ 7)(5\ 8)(6\ 9)(10, 11) \rangle.$$

Here, the sets are $B_1 = \{1, 2, 3, 12\}$, $B_2 = \{4, 5, 6, 13\}$ and $B_3 = \{7, 8, 9, 14\}$. If $G = H \wr K$ then, for $1 \leq i \leq k$ define H_i by $\{\alpha^{(i)} : \alpha \in K$. Then $min[s]_G = min[min[\ldots min[min[s]_{H_1}]_{H_2} \ldots]_{H_r}]_K$ [5].

We sketch an approach for detecting whether an arbitrary group is a wreath product of subgroups. If G acts transitively on I, a subset B of I is a *block* if, for any $\alpha \in G$, $\alpha(B) = B$ or $B \cap \alpha(B) = \emptyset$. The set $\mathcal{B} = \{\alpha(B) : \alpha \in G\}$ is a *block system* for G. Given block systems $\mathcal{B}, \mathcal{C}$ for G, $\mathcal{C}$ is *strictly coarser* than $\mathcal{B}$ if $\forall B \in \mathcal{B} \; \exists C \in \mathcal{C}$ such that $B \subset C$, and $\mathcal{B}$ is *maximal* for G if each $B \in \mathcal{B}$ is a proper subset of I, and the only block system strictly coarser than $\mathcal{B}$ is the trivial system $\{I\}$.

If $\{B_1, B_2, \ldots, B_r\}$ is a block system for a transitive group G, where $B_i = \{b_{i,1}, b_{i,2}, \ldots, b_{i,m}\}$ then $G \leq H \wr K$, where $H = \bigcap_{i \notin B_1} stab_G(i)$, and $K = \bigcap_{1 \leq i \leq m} stab_G(\{b_{1,i}, b_{2,i}, \ldots, b_{r,i}\})$ [4]. To check whether or not $G = H \wr K$ it is sufficient to compare orders, and it can be shown that $|H \wr K| = |H|^r |K|$. However, in general G does not act transitively on I. We solve the general problem of determining whether or not G is a wreath product of subgroups by considering the action of G separately on each non-trivial orbit of I.

Lemma 2. *If $G = H \wr K$ then each non-trivial orbit O of I under G has a single maximal block system: $\{O \cap moved(H_i) : 1 \leq i \leq r)\}$.*

If G can be shown to have exactly one maximal block system per orbit, then candidate groups H and K can be constructed. Suppose the non-trivial orbits are $O_1, O_2, \ldots, O_d$. For $1 \leq i \leq d$, the group K_i is computed as follows: let $\{B_1, B_2, \ldots, B_u\}$ be the maximal block system for O_i, where each B_j has the form $\{b_{j,1}, b_{j,2}, \ldots, b_{j,v}\}$ (for some $u, v > 0$). Then $K_i = \bigcap_{1 \leq l \leq v} stab_G(\{b_{1,l}, b_{2,l}, \ldots, b_{u,l}\})$. The candidate group K is the intersection of the K_i. Candidate group H is initially set to G. For each orbit O_i a maximal block B is chosen such that $B \subseteq moved(H)$. Then H is recomputed as $\bigcap_{j \in O_i \setminus B} stab_H(j)$. We now have groups H and K with $G \leq H \wr K$, and we can check whether $G = H \wr K$ by comparing orders, as before.

4.3 Choosing a Strategy for G

The strategies which we have presented for minimising a state with respect to basic and composite groups can be combined to yield a symmetry reduction strategy for the arbitrary group G by classifying the group using a top-down recursive algorithm.

The algorithm starts by searching for a minimising set for G of the form prescribed in Theorem 2, so that $min[s]_G$ can be computed as described in Section 3.2. If no such minimising set can be found, a decomposition of G as a disjoint/wreath product is sought. In this case the algorithm is applied recursively to obtain a minimisation strategy for each factor of the product so that $min[s]_G$ can be computed using these strategies as described in Sections 4.1 and 4.2 respectively. If G remains unclassified and $|G|$ is sufficiently small, enumeration is used, otherwise local search is selected.

5   Symmetry Reductions in Practice

5.1   Extending the Model of Computation

When components do not hold references to other components, the simple model of computation and the action of a permutation on a state (described in Sections 2.1 and 2.3 respectively) are sufficient to reason about concurrent systems, since it is always possible to represent the local state of a component using an integer. However, if components *can* hold references to one another then any permutation that moves component i will also affect the local state of any components which refer to component i.

Sophisticated specification languages, such as Promela, include special datatypes to represent process and channel identifiers. An extended model of computation for Promela is presented in [8]. Both the results presented in [5] on solving the COP for groups which decompose as disjoint/wreath products, and our results on minimising sets for fully symmetric groups (see Section 3.2) do not hold in general for this extended model of computation.

Thus for Promela specifications where local variables refer to process and channel identifiers, the efficient symmetry reduction strategies presented above are not always exact—in some cases they may yield an *approximate* implementation of the function *min*, as discussed in Section 2.3. This does not compromise the safety of symmetry reduced model checking, and in any case, for a large model, there will be many states for which the strategies *will* give exact representatives in an extended model of computation as the experimental results in Section 5.3 show.

For the simple case of full symmetry between identical components, the Symm-Spin package deals with local variables which are references to component identifiers by dividing the local state of each component into two portions, one which does not refer to other components (the *insensitive* portion say), and another which consists entirely of such references (the *sensitive* portion). A state is minimised by first sorting it with respect to the insensitive portion. Then, for each subset of components with identical insensitive portions, every permutation of the subset is considered, and the permutation which leads to the smallest image is applied. This is known as the *segmented* strategy. Our approach using minimising sets is similar to the *sorted* strategy which SymmSpin also provides. Here a state is minimised only with respect to the insensitive portions of the local states. This strategy is much faster than the segmented strategy, but is approximate. It may be possible to extend our approach to be exact by generalising the segmented strategy.

5.2   A Symmetry Reduction Package for SPIN

We have implemented the strategies discussed in Sections 3 and 4 as TopSPIN, a fully automatic symmetry reduction package for SPIN [9]. In order to check properties of a Promela specification, SPIN first converts the specification into a C source file, pan.c, which is then compiled into an executable verifier. The state space thus generated is then searched. If the property being checked is proved to be false, a counterexample is given. TopSPIN follows the approach used by the SymmSpin symmetry reduction package, where pan.c is generated as usual by SPIN, and then converted to a new file, sympan.c, which includes algorithms for symmetry reduction. With TopSPIN, because we allow for arbitrary system topologies, symmetry must be detected before sympan.c can be generated. This is illustrated in Figure 2.

First, the *static channel diagram* (SCD) of the Promela specification is extracted by the SymmExtractor tool, which is described in detail in [8]. The SCD is a graphical representation of potential communication between components of the specification. The group of symmetries of the SCD, $Aut(SCD)$, is computed using the *saucy* tool [7], which we have extended to handle directed graphs. The generators of $Aut(SCD)$ are checked against the Promela specification for validity (an assurance that they induce symmetries of the underlying state space).

TopSPIN uses GAP to compute, from the set of valid generators, the largest group $G \leq Aut(SCD)$ which can be safely used for symmetry-reduced model checking. GAP is then used to classify the structure of G in order to choose an efficient symmetry reduction strategy. The chosen strategy is merged with `pan.c` to form `sympan.c`, which can be compiled and executed as usual. In order to compare strategies it is possible to manually select the strategy used (rather than let TopSPIN choose the most efficient). For experimental purposes, TopSPIN also allows generators of an arbitrary group of component symmetries to be specified manually, as long as the group elements do not permute components with different types.

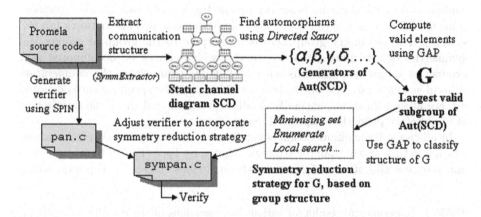

Fig. 2. The symmetry reduction process

5.3 Experimental Results

In Table 1 we present experimental results applying TopSPIN to four families of Promela specifications. For each specification, we give the number of model states without symmetry reduction (**orig**), with full symmetry reduction (**red**), and using the strategy chosen by TopSPIN (**best**). If the latter two are equal, '=' appears for the TopSPIN strategy. The use of state compression, provided by SPIN, is indicated by the number of states in italics. For each strategy (**basic** for enumeration without the optimisations described in Section 3.1, **enum** for optimised enumeration, and **best** for the strategy chosen by TopSPIN), and when symmetry reduction is not applied (**orig**), we give the time taken for verification (in seconds). Verification attempts which exceed available resources, or do not terminate within 5 hours, are indicated by '-'. All experiments are performed on a PC with a 2.4GHz Intel Xeon processor, 3Gb of available main memory, running SPIN version 4.2.3.

The first family of specifications model flow of control for a system similar to the three-tiered architecture example of Section 2.4, but with a layer of p servers with q clients connected to each server (a D-S-C system). Here models exhibit wreath product symmetry: there is full symmetry between the q clients in each block, and the blocks of clients, with their associated servers, are interchangeable. A configuration with p servers and q clients per server is denoted p/q. The second family of specifications model a resource allocator process which controls access to a resource by a competing set of prioritised clients (an R-C system). Models of these specifications exhibit disjoint product symmetry: there is full symmetry between each set of clients with the same priority level. A configuration with p_i clients of priority level i is denoted $p_1, \ldots, p_k$, where k is the number of priority levels. The next family of specifications which model an email system where *client* processes exchange messages via a *mailer* process. The symmetries of models of these specifications permute the client processes, simultaneously permuting their input channels, and can be handled using a minimising set. A configuration with p clients is simply denoted p. Finally, we consider specifications modelling message routing in an n dimensional hypercube network (an HC system). The symmetry group here is isomorphic to the group of geometrical symmetries of a n dimensional hypercube, which cannot be decomposed as a product of subgroups, and thus must be handled using either the *enumeration* or *local search* strategies. An n-dimensional hypercube specification is denoted nd. For all specifications, we verify deadlock freedom, and check the satisfaction of basic safety properties expressed using assertions.

In all cases, basic enumeration is significantly slower optimised enumeration, which is in turn slower than the strategies chosen by TopSpin. For the three-tiered and resource allocator configurations the strategies chosen by TopSpin, which

Table 1. Experimental results for various configurations of the three-tiered (D-S-C), resource allocator (R-C), email (email) and hypercube (HC) specifications

system	config.	states orig	time orig	$|G|$	states red	time basic	time enum	states best	time best
D-S-C	2/3	103105	5	72	2656	7	4	=	2
D-S-C	2/4	1.1×10^6	37	1152	5012	276	108	=	2
D-S-C	3/3	2.54×10^7	4156	1296	50396	4228	1689	=	19
D-S-C	3/4	-	-	82944	-	-	-	130348	104
R-C	3,3	16768	0.2	36	1501	0.9	0.3	=	0.1
R-C	4,4	199018	2	576	3826	57	19	=	0.4
R-C	5,5	2.2×10^6	42	14400	8212	4358	1234	=	2
R-C	4,4,4	2.39×10^7	1587	13824	84377	-	12029	=	17
R-C	5,5,5	-	-	1728000	-	-	-	254091	115
email	3	23256	0.1	6	3902	0.9	0.8	3908	0.2
email	4	852641	9	24	36255	13	6	38560	2
email	5	3.04×10^7	3576	120	265315	679	253	315323	40
email	6	-	-	720	1.7×10^6	-	13523	2.3×10^6	576
email	7	-	-	5040	-	-	-	1.53×10^7	6573
HC	3d	13181	0.3	48	308	0.6	0.3	468	0.2
HC	4d	380537	18	384	1240	58	34	6986	13
HC	5d	9.6×10^6	2965	3840	3907	7442	5241	90442	946

decompose the symmetry group as a wreath/disjoint product of groups which are then handled by minimising sets, provide exact symmetry reduction, despite the potential problems discussed in Section 5.1. This is not the case for email configurations, for which TopSPIN uses minimising sets. Nevertheless, a large factor of reduction is still obtained, and verification is fast. For hypercube configurations, TopSPIN chooses local search, requiring more states than enumeration, but still resulting in a greatly reduced state space.

6 Related Work

The simple model of computation which we have used throughout the paper is common to numerous works on symmetry reductions for model checking [5,10,11], and is adequate for reasoning about input languages where components do not individually hold references to other components, e.g. the input languages of SMC [18] and SYMM [5], or where components are specified using *synchronisation skeletons* [10]. The problem of extending symmetry reduction techniques to a model of computation where such references are allowed is tackled, for the simple case of full symmetry between identical components, by the *segmented* strategy of the SymmSpin package.

Methods for exploiting the disjoint/wreath product structure of symmetry groups were proposed in [5], but this work did not investigate the problem of classifying the structure of an arbitrary group, as we have done. Stabiliser chains (see Section 3.1) are used extensively in computational group theory [3,12], and have been utilised in symmetry breaking approaches for constraint programming [13]. This paper is, to our knowledge, the first to apply these techniques to model checking. The construction of minimising sets for fully symmetric groups which we presented in Section 3.2 builds on the concept of a *nice* group [11], and generalises the idea of computing orbit representatives by sorting [2,5,11].

7 Conclusions and Future Work

In this paper, we have proposed exact and approximate strategies for tackling the NP-hard problem of computing orbit representatives in order to exploit symmetry when model checking concurrent systems, and we have generalised existing results in this area. We have applied techniques from computational group theory to speed up representative computation, and to classify the structure of a symmetry group as a disjoint/wreath product of subgroups before search. We have described TopSPIN, a fully automatic symmetry reduction package for SPIN, and presented encouraging experimental results for a variety of Promela examples.

We are currently investigating further the use of local search techniques as an approximate symmetry reduction strategy. We are also developing an approach to generalise the *segmented* strategy used by the SymmSpin package to overcome potential inefficiencies associated with extending our simple model of computation to the Promela language. TopSPIN is currently limited to verifying the absence of deadlock and the satisfaction of safety properties of Promela specifications. Future work includes extending TopSPIN to allow symmetry-reduced verification of temporal properties with weak fairness, as described in [1].

References

1. D. Bosnacki. A light-weight algorithm for model checking with symmetry reduction and weak fairness. In *SPIN'03*, LNCS 2648, pages 89–103. Springer, 2003.
2. D. Bosnacki, D. Dams, and L. Holenderski. Symmetric spin. *International Journal on Software Tools for Technology Transfer*, 4(1):65–80, 2002.
3. G. Butler. *Fundamental Algorithms for Permutation Groups*, volume 559 of *LNCS*. Springer-Verlag, 1991.
4. P.J. Cameron. *Permutation Groups*. Cambridge University Press, 1999.
5. E.M. Clarke, E.A. Emerson, S. Jha, and A.P. Sistla. Symmetry reductions in model checking. In *CAV'98*, LNCS 1427, pages 147–158. Springer, 1998.
6. E.M. Clarke, O. Grumberg, and D. Peled. *Model Checking*. The MIT Press, 1999.
7. P.T. Darga, M.H. Liffiton, K.A. Sakallah, and I.L. Markov. Exploiting structure in symmetry detection for CNF. In *DAC'04*, pages 530–534. ACM Press, 2004.
8. A.F. Donaldson and A. Miller. Automatic symmetry detection for model checking using computational group theory. In *FM'05*, LNCS 3582, pages 418–496. Springer, 2005.
9. A.F. Donaldson and A. Miller. A computational group theoretic symmetry reduction package for the SPIN model checker. In *AMAST'06*, LNCS 4019, pages 374–380. Springer, 2006.
10. E.A. Emerson and R.J. Trefler. From asymmetry to full symmetry: new techniques for symmetry reduction in model checking. In *CHARME'99*, LNCS 1703, pages 142–156. Springer, 1999.
11. E.A. Emerson and T. Wahl. Dynamic symmetry reduction. In *TACAS'05*, LNCS 3440, pages 382–396. Springer, 2005.
12. The Gap Group. *GAP–Groups Algorithms and Programming, Version 4.2*. Aachen, St. Andrews, 1999. http://www-gap.dcs.st-and.ac.uk/~gap.
13. I.P. Gent, W. Harvey, and T. Kelsey. Groups and constraints: symmetry breaking during search. In *CP'02*, LNCS 2470, pages 415–430. Springer, 2002.
14. G. J. Holzmann. *The SPIN model checker: primer and reference manual*. Addison Wesley, 2003.
15. C.N. Ip and D.L. Dill. Better verification through symmetry. *Formal Methods in System Design*, 9(1/2): 41–75, 1996.
16. K.S. Kirkpatrick, C.D. Gelatt, and M.P. Vecchi. Optimization by simulated annealing. *Science*, 220: 671–680, 1983.
17. S. Russel and P. Norvig. *Artificial Intelligence, a Modern Approach*. Prentice Hall, 1995.
18. A.P. Sistla, V. Gyuris, and E.A. Emerson. SMC: a symmetry-based model checker for verification of safety and liveness properties. *ACM Transactions on Software Engineering and Methodology*, 9(2):113–166, 2000.

Monitoring Distributed Controllers: When an Efficient LTL Algorithm on Sequences Is Needed to Model-Check Traces

Alexandre Genon, Thierry Massart, and Cédric Meuter

Université Libre de Bruxelles
Boulevard du Triomphe - CP-212, 1050 Bruxelles, Begium
Tel.: +32 2 650.5603; Fax:+32 2 650.5609
{tmassart, cmeuter}@ulb.ac.be

Abstract. It is well known that through code instrumentation, a distributed system's finite execution can generate a finite trace as a partially ordered set of events. We motivate the need to use LTL model-checking on sequences and not on traces as defined by Diekert and Gastin, to validate distributed control systems executions, abstracted by such traces, and present an efficient symbolic algorithm to do the job. It uses the standard method proposed by Vardi and Wolper, which from the LTL formula, builds a monitor that accepts all the bad sequences. We show that, given a monitor and a trace, the problem to check that both the monitor and the trace have a common sequence is NP-complete in the number of concurrent processes. Our method explores the possible configurations symbolically, since it handles sets of configurations. Moreover, it uses techniques similar to the partial order reduction, to avoid exploring as many execution interleavings as possible. It works very well in practice, compared to the standard exploration method, with or without partial order reduction (which, in practice, does not work well here).

Keywords: testing of asynchronous distributed systems, monitor, global properties, model checking of traces.

1 Introduction

A distributed control system is a set of distributed hardware equipments such as small computers or Programmable Logic Controllers (PLCs), which run concurrent processes, communicating asynchronously through some network. The design and implementation of such a distributed reactive system is a non-trivial task. Validation and debugging techniques can be used during the design and the implementation to help the developer in his work [DMM04, DGMM05]. *Verification* tools (e.g. [Hol97, McM92b, CCG+02]) can be used to validate a model. Unfortunately in practice, the system's implementation code contains thousands of lines and dozens of variables. The *state-explosion problem* generally prevents the designer from its exhaustive verification even with efficient exploration techniques such as partial order reduction [God96, Val93] or symbolic model checking [CGP99, McM92a, Bry92].

J. Misra, T. Nipkow, and E. Sekerinski (Eds.): FM 2006, LNCS 4085, pp. 557–572, 2006.
© Springer-Verlag Berlin Heidelberg 2006

The designer generally falls back to *testing*, which cannot guarantee that a system is completely bug-free, but if achieved on a large number of test-cases (e.g. covering all the system's functionalities), can give a *reasonable* confidence that the system is correct. For that purpose, the implementation is generally instrumented to record relevant events. A special process, called *monitor*, records the system's events and must then check that the observed execution satisfies the desired properties. This monitoring can either be done offline, i.e. after the complete trace is recorded, or online, at runtime. Notice that this monitoring technique can also be used to validate runs of a system's *model*, if too complex to be exhaustively verified. Hence, both at the design and implementation level, it is an important activity where efficient methods must be provided.

For distributed asynchronous systems [Lyn96], a run is generally not seen as a totally ordered sequence of events, but as a partially ordered set where unordered events may have occurred in any order. In a simple approach, the monitor just assumes that the events happened in the order they are received, and check that the property is satisfied. In a predictive approach [SRA04], the monitor must check that every compatible total order of events satisfies the property. The causal *partial order* between the fired events can be obtained through correct code instrumentation using, e.g. vector clocks [Lam78, Mat89]. The collected information of an execution is therefore abstracted as a *trace*, i.e. a partially ordered set of events where two consecutive events of the same site are temporally ordered and where communications (e.g. message transfers or shared variable manipulations) impose an order between some distributed events.

An important point to note is that even if the control is distributed and provides a partially ordered trace, the *exact sequence the control actions are taken is generally crucial*. One can for instance think to a controlled system where a valve A must be closed before another valve B can be opened and where each valve is controlled by another PLC; the *controlled environment* is therefore seen as centralized. *Testing* that an execution satisfies a *global property* ϕ reduces therefore to verifying that every sequential execution *compatible* with the partial order satisfies ϕ or, in other terms, model checking ϕ on the corresponding *trace*. Therefore, we will see that our traces can not be seen as Mazurkiewicz traces [Maz86] where the order of independent events is meaningless.

Unfortunately, even if the monitor is already built, this problem is hard and in practice, the number of compatible sequential executions may be exponential in the number of concurrent processes. Therefore, in the same spirit as what is done with partial order reduction techniques, which try to minimize the exploration of execution interleavings as much as possible, we investigate here an efficient method to practically reduce the verification time. Moreover our proposed method is symbolic since it handles sets of configurations. We show in practice that our method is very efficient in execution time, compared to the standard exploration method with or without partial order reduction.

This paper is organized as follows. In section 2, we detail related proposals and explain why the problem needs model-checking on sequences and not on traces. In section 3, we introduce our model for traces and monitors, formalize the trace monitoring problem and show that this problem is hard even with an already built monitor. In section 4, we present our symbolic method and show its correctness, and in section 5, we show how this method can be refined into a symbolic exploration algorithm. Next, in section 6, we present our experimental results of various examples. Finally, further works are given in section 7.

2 Related Works and Motivation

In the literature, papers on *global predicate detection* and *trace model-checking* have generally a common starting point since the *system* to verify is composed of various concurrent processes synchronized by some mean. This system is modeled, possibly after some code instrumentation (using e.g. [Lam78, Mat89]), as a *trace*, i.e. a set of temporally partially ordered events.

Global Predicate Detection. initially aims at answering reachability questions, i.e. does there exist a possible global configuration of the system, that satisfies a given global predicate ϕ. Numerous works have been done on the detection of global predicates. Garg and Chase showed in [CG98] that this problem is NP-complete for an arbitrary predicate, even when there is no inter-process communication. Chandy and Lamport [CL85], present a technique for stable predicates, i.e. predicates that never turn false once they become true. In [CDF95], Charron-Bost *et al* present an algorithm for observer independent predicates. In [GW94, GW96], Garg and Waldecker give polynomial procedures for *conjunctive* predicates, i.e. predicates that are conjunctions of local predicates. In [CG98], Chase and Garg introduce the classes of *linear* and *semi-linear* predicates and give an efficient procedure to solve the predicate detection problem for these classes of systems. In [GM01], Garg and Mittal introduce the notion of *regular* predicates, a subset of the linear predicates, for which they present a procedure that solves the predicate detection problem in polynomial time. This procedure makes use of *computation slicing*, that is, computing all cuts compatible with a given execution satisfying a given predicate. They present an efficient procedure for computing such slices. Computation slicing on regular predicates is examined in details in [MG01]. In [SG03], A. Sen and Garg present the temporal logic RCTL (for *regular*-CTL), which is a subset of the temporal logic CTL (and an extension, RCTL+). Every RCTL formula is a regular predicate; thus with RCTL formulae, we can use computation slicing to solve the predicate detection problem. In [SRA04] K. Sen et al. use an automaton to specify the system's monitor. The authors provide an explicit exploration of the state space and to limit this exploration a *window* is used. The choice of a linear temporal logic as LTL rather than a branching temporal logic as CTL seems natural since the aim is to verify that for all total orderings of the occurred events, the corresponding runs satisfy the property. In [SVAR04] K. Sen et al. define the logic PT-DTL which is a variant of past time linear temporal logic, suitable for efficient distributed model-checking on execution traces. However, if it allows efficient check, neither PT-DTL of K. Sen et al nor RCTL of A. Sen and Garg can verify properties as LTL (or equivalent CTL formula) $\Box(a \rightarrow \Diamond(b \wedge c))$, i.e. every a is eventually followed by a state (or a transition) where b and c are true; formula that may be very useful during validation. Our work uses a similar framework to what is used in [SRA04]. We investigate here on the possibility to define a method, efficient in practice to be able to model-check any LTL formula. Therefore, we do not limit the exploration as in [SRA04], but prefer to increase its efficiency with a symbolic method.

Trace Model Checking. has been studied through the definition of several linear temporal logics for Mazurkiewicz traces. A Mazurkiewicz trace [Maz86], over an alphabet Σ with a independence relation I, can be defined as a Σ-labelled partial order set of events with special properties not explained here. For Mazurkiewicz traces, *local* and *global* trace logics have been defined. Local trace logics have been proposed in the work of Thiagaranjan on TrPTL [Thi94] and Alur, Peled and Penczek on TLC [APP95]. Global trace logics include, among others, LTrL [TW02] proposed by Thiagarajan and Walukiewicz, and LTL on traces [DG02] defined by Diekert and Gastin.

However, in our problem, the *trace* is an input which models a run that must be checked to see if the possible ordering of events is correct. For instance if it is required that an event a must occur before b, and if, in the trace, actions a and b are independent and can be executed in any order, the system is seen as incorrect. But, *trace temporal logics* are not "designed" to express constraints on the particular order independent actions are executed. For instance if actions a and b are independent, the trace $\mathcal{T} = ab$ expresses that a and b are concurrent. Therefore, the LTL formula $a \rightarrow \Diamond b$ which expresses on semantics on sequences, that a is eventually followed by b is not so easily expressible in *trace-LTL*. Therefore, since we do not have a priori the independence relation, these trace logics are not adapted to model-check our runs.

3   Trace Monitoring Problem

In this section, we first introduce our framework with the notions of *finite trace* which models a run of a concurrent system, and *monitor* which is an automata representation of the formula to check. Then, we formalize the trace monitoring problem and prove its NP-completeness in the number of concurrent processes.

Trace. Our runs are obtained by concurrent processes, each executing a finite sequence of variables assignments. Moreover, due to inter-process communications, other causal relations are added. A run is modeled as a finite trace, i.e. a finite partially ordered set of events, where each event is labeled by the assignment which took place during this event. Formally:

Definition 1 (Trace). *For a set of variables Var, a (finite) trace $\mathcal{T}$ is a finite labeled partially ordered set $(E, \lambda, \preceq)$ where:*

- *E is a finite set of events,*
- *$\lambda : E \mapsto Var \times \mathbb{N}$ is a labeling function, mapping each event e to an assignment of the form $x := v$. For the event e, $\mathsf{var}(e)$ and $\mathsf{val}(e)$ denote respectively the simple variable x and value v of the corresponding assignment.*
- *$\preceq\, \subseteq E \times E$ is a partial order relation on E*

In the following, we will use the following notations: $\downarrow e$ denotes $\{e' \mid e' \preceq e\}$ and $\uparrow e$ denotes $\{e' \mid e \preceq e'\}$ (the reflexo-transitive closure of resp. causal predecessors and successors). Moreover, for any set S of events, $\uparrow S = \cup_{e \in S} \uparrow e$ and $\downarrow S = \cup_{e \in S} \downarrow e$. We also define a *cut* C of a trace $\mathcal{T}$, which models an "execution point" of the corresponding distributed execution, as a consistent set of already executed events $C \subseteq E$ such that $\downarrow C = C$. We note $\mathcal{C}_\mathcal{T}$ the set of all cuts of $\mathcal{T}$. The *set of enabled events of a cut* is defined by: $\mathsf{enabled}(C) = \{e \in E \setminus C \mid \downarrow e \setminus \{e\} \subseteq C\}$. Note that for a cut C and any event $e \in \mathsf{enabled}(C)$, the set $C \cup \{e\}$ is also a cut.

As mentioned earlier, even if our systems are finite traces, their particular nature, i.e., the fact that they come from a distributed controller of a global environment which can be seen as centralized, induces that their semantics is defined classically by the sets of (finite) sequences of events they can do.

Definition 2 (Semantics of a trace). *For a set of variables Var, and a trace $\mathcal{T} = (E, \lambda, \preceq)$ defined with these variables, the semantics $[\![\mathcal{T}]\!]$ is defined as the set of sequences of execution $\mathcal{T}$ can have. Formally:*

$$[\![\mathcal{T}]\!] = \left\{\sigma = e_1, e_2, ..., e_{|E|} \mid \forall 1 \leq i, j \leq |E| : \begin{matrix} (e_i \in E) \wedge (e_i \preceq e_j) \Rightarrow (i \leq j) \wedge \\ (i \neq j) \Rightarrow (e_i \neq e_j) \end{matrix} \right\}$$

Remark: if needed we can easily define the value of the variables at some point in the execution. At the beginning of the execution, we can assume all variables to be equal to 0. However, with our model, we cannot in general, talk about the value of a variable x in some cut C; this value can depend on the particular path σ taken to reach C.

Monitor. Now that we have defined the model $\mathcal{T}$ of a distributed system, we need to define how a property can be expressed on $\mathcal{T}$.

Since events in a trace are single assignment, we naturally first define basic formulae as boolean expressions on variables of the trace. We restrict ourselves to expressions using arithmetic operators $(+,-,*,/)$, comparison operators $(<,>,=)$ and boolean connectors $(\wedge, \vee, \neg)$. Moreover, since each trace's event is a simple assignment, each *basic formula* uses only one variable of the trace. Example of such basic formulae are $(x = 3)$ or $((0 < 2 * x) \wedge (2 * x < 5))$. We denote by $\mathcal{F}$ the set of such basic formulae and by $\mathsf{var}(\phi)$, the variable appearing in a basic formula ϕ. For a given basic formula ϕ, and an event e which executes the assignment $x := v$, we naturally define :

Definition 3 (Formula triggering). *An event e triggers a formula ϕ, if e assigns the variable appearing in ϕ and if ϕ evaluates to true after the assignment.*

Formally, if $\phi[x \leftarrow v]$ denotes the formula ϕ where the variable x is substituted by v, then we have:

$$(\phi \models e) \Leftrightarrow ((\mathsf{var}(e) = \mathsf{var}(\phi)) \wedge (\phi[\mathsf{var}(e) \leftarrow \mathsf{val}(e)] = \top))$$

Those basic formulae can be used as propositions to build more complex temporal constraints, using LTL.

A particular care must be taken to the fact that it will be checked on finite sequences. This can be done, as explained e.g. in [LMC01] by an obvious translation of any LTL formula into an "LTL with Δ actions" (where Δ is not in the initial alphabet). Semantically the finite sequences are extended by an infinite sequence of Δ actions, to mark the deadlock. For example, intuitively a system S should satisfy $\neg a$ iff S can not perform a a as next action. Hence S may either perform only actions b different from a or it may deadlock. Similarly, if $\bigcirc$ denotes the *next* operator in LTL, a system which satisfies $\neg \bigcirc a$ can either deadlock immediately or perform some visible action and then satisfy $\neg a$. To capture the intuition, any formula $\bigcirc\phi$ is first translated into $(\neg\Delta \wedge \bigcirc\phi)$ and $\neg \bigcirc \phi$ into $(\Delta \vee \bigcirc\neg\phi)$.

Then, the classical procedure defined by Vardi and Wolper [VW86] to build from a LTL formula a corresponding *(Büchi) automaton* $\mathcal{B}$ able to do all the sequences of $|\neg\phi|$ can be used to build our monitor (seen as a standard non deterministic finite automaton). The construction is restricted to our systems where only one variable is modified at each event. As explained in [LMC01], the Δ-transitions can be removed from the *monitor* obtained and a finite automaton is provided where transitions are labeled by basic formulae and with a standard and not the Büchi acceptance condition. Note that the size of the obtained monitor may be exponential in the size of the corresponding LTL formula [VW86]; but generally, since in practice the size of the formula is small, it is not a problem.

We will show that our main contribution in this paper, is an algorithm which outperforms classical methods to compose $\mathcal{B}$ and $\mathcal{T}$ and verify that $|\mathcal{T}| \cap |\neg\phi| = \emptyset$, i.e. check that no sequence of the system has the property ϕ.

In the following, we simply define our monitors as any non deterministic finite automata with basic formulae on transitions. The formal definition of a monitor follows.

Definition 4 (Monitor). *A monitor $\mathcal{M}$ is a tuple $(M, m^0, B, \rightarrow_m)$ where:*

- *M is a finite set of states,*
- *$m^0 \in M$ is the initial state,*
- *$B \subseteq M$ is a set of final "bad" states,*
- *$\rightarrow \subseteq M \times \mathcal{F} \times M$ is a transition relation.*

The Monitoring Problem. We have seen that the monitoring problem reduces to determine if a given trace $\mathcal{T} = (E, \lambda, \preceq)$ and monitor $\mathcal{M} = (M, m^0, B, \rightarrow_m)$ have a common accepted sequence of events; or in other words does there exist a total order on E, compatible with $\preceq$ such that, if the events of E are executed in that order, $\mathcal{M}$ can reach to a "bad" state. A priori, we need to examine how the monitor reacts to every interleaving of the events in E compatible with the partial order $\preceq$. A monitor reacts to an event e if, in its current state, there exists an outgoing transition labeled with a guard ϕ such that e triggers ϕ. $\mathsf{next}(e, m)$ denotes the set of monitor states reached by triggering an event e, from a monitor state m. Formally, next is defined as follows:

$$\mathsf{next}(m, e) = \begin{cases} \{m\} & \text{if } \forall m \xrightarrow{\phi}_m m' : e \not\models \phi \\ \{m' \mid \exists m \xrightarrow{\phi}_m m' : e \models \phi\} & \text{otherwise} \end{cases}$$

This leads us to the following definition of composition of a trace with a monitor.

Definition 5 (Composition). *The composition of a trace $\mathcal{T}$ and a monitor $\mathcal{M}$, noted $\mathcal{T} \otimes \mathcal{M}$ is a transition system $(Q, q^0, \rightarrow)$ where:*

- *$Q \subseteq 2^E \times M$ is the set of configurations*
- *$q^0 = (\emptyset, m^0)$ is the initial configuration*
- *$\rightarrow \subseteq Q \times E \times Q$ is the transition relation defined as follows: $\forall (s, m) \in Q, \forall e \in$ $\mathsf{enabled}(s), \forall m' \in \mathsf{next}(m, e)$*

$$(s, m) \xrightarrow{e} (s \cup \{e\}, m')$$

We note $(s, m) \xrightarrow{\rho} (s', m')$ iff $\exists (s_0, m_0), (s_1, m_1), ..., (s_n, m_n)$, such that $(s, m) = (s_0, m_0), (s', m') = (s_n, m_n)$ and the path $\rho = e_1 e_2 \cdots e_n$ with $\forall \ 0 \le i < n \ :$ $(s_i, m_i) \xrightarrow{e_i} (s_{i+1}, m_{i+1})$. We also note $(s, m) \rightsquigarrow (s', m')$ if $\exists \rho : (s, m) \xrightarrow{\rho} (s', m')$, and $\mathsf{reachable}(s, m) = \{m' \in M \mid (s, m) \rightsquigarrow (E, m')\}$. An simple example of composition is presented in figure 1 where e.g. the vactor $[2, 1]$ represents the cut reached after execution of 2 events in $P1$ (x:=0; y:=3) and 1 event in $P2$ (w:=4).

Using these notations, we can reformulate the monitoring problem.

Definition 6 (Trace monitoring problem (TMP)). *Given a trace $\mathcal{T} = (E, \lambda, \preceq)$ and a monitor $\mathcal{M} = (M, m^0, B, \rightarrow_m)$ the trace monitoring problem (TMP) is to check whether $\mathsf{reachable}(\emptyset, m_0) \cap B = \emptyset$*

Remember that, by the definition of $\mathsf{reachable}$, we ask here to execute the complete trace before checking that the reached state is in B.

NP-Completeness. We now show that the monitoring problem is NP-complete in the number of concurrent processes in the trace even if the formula only uses boolean variables and where every formula on transitions is of the form $x = v$. This result is *a priori* not completely obvious since we consider restricted monitors that use single variables predicates on each transition and it is known ([GW96, GW94]) that checking conjunction of local predicates is polynomial in the size of the conjunction. We present a polynomial time reduction from 3-SAT to our problem.

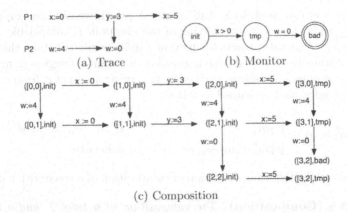

Fig. 1. Example of composition

Theorem 1 (NP-completeness of TMP). *[GMM06] The trace monitoring problem is* NP-*complete.*

Proof sketch. It is easy to see that the TMP is in NP. Indeed, one could use a non deterministic algorithm to guess an execution (of size $|E|$) and check, in polynomial time, if the corresponding total order is compatible with T_ϕ and if this execution leads to a state in B. For NP-hardness, we reduce from 3-SAT. The main idea is to use a monitor to model a 3-SAT formula and the trace to model all possible valuations of its propositions. The only technicality resides in the fact that the valuations must not contain any pair of complementary literals. This is accomplished by properly choosing the partial order.

Note on Partial Order Reduction. Using partial order reduction [God96] to improve the explicit exploration will not work to solve the TMP. This is because in the trace monitoring problem, the monitor expresses constraints on all, or most of the events of the trace. Therefore, no events is seen as "invisible"; and the partial order reduction brings no improvement. This was another motivation to find an effective method for the TMP. Our method is presented in the following section.

4   Symbolic Composition

The main idea behind the symbolic exploration is to exploit the fact that the monitor is not always sensitive to all events. Indeed, in the classical exploration, if an event e does not assign any variable appearing in a guard of an outgoing transition, we consider two cases: one where e is fired, and one where e is not. But both executions correspond to the same evolution of the monitor. Hence, it would be more efficient to consider only one execution, where e has been *optionally* fired. However, we must remember these events, because they might become relevant in the future, i.e. they could become *mandatory* in the future.

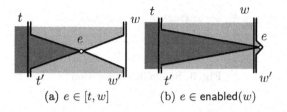

(a) $e \in [t, w]$ (b) $e \in \mathsf{enabled}(w)$

Fig. 2. Symbolic transition $(t, w, m) \xrightarrow{e}_s (t', w', m')$ with $e \in \mathsf{sensitive}(m)$

Therefore, in our approach, each symbolic configuration will separate both kinds of events: *optional* events, i.e. events that did not produce a monitor move and do not change its state if they are not taken, and *mandatory* events, i.e. events that did produce, directly or indirectly, a monitor move. In practice, a symbolic configuration is a tuple (t, w, m), where t and w are cuts. *Mandatory* events are contained in t, and *optional* events are contained in $w \backslash t$ (denoted $[t, w]$ in the following). Such a symbolic configuration represents an entire set of explicit configurations $\{(s, m) \mid s \in \mathcal{C}_{\mathcal{T}} \wedge t \subseteq s \subseteq w\}$.

In order to define the symbolic composition based on this idea, we first need to introduce some notations. We define $\mathsf{sensitive}(m) = \{e \in E \mid \exists m \xrightarrow{\phi}_m m' : e \models \phi\}$, the set of all events that will trigger a monitor move when it is in state m.

Definition 7 (Symbolic Composition). *The symbolic composition of a trace $\mathcal{T}$ and a monitor $\mathcal{M}$, noted $\mathcal{T} \otimes_s \mathcal{M}$ is a transition system $(Q_s, q_s^0, \rightarrow_s)$ where:*

- *$Q_s \subseteq 2^E \times 2^E \times M$ is the set of symbolic configurations*
- *$q_s^0 = (\emptyset, \emptyset, m^0)$ is the initial symbolic configuration*
- *$\rightarrow_s \subseteq Q_s \times E \times Q_s$ is the transition relation defined $\forall (t, w, m) \in Q_s$, as follows:*
  (i) if $e \notin \mathsf{sensitive}(m) \wedge e \in \mathsf{enabled}(w)$, then

$$(t, w, m) \xrightarrow{e}_s (t, w \cup \{e\}, m)$$

  (ii) if $e \in \mathsf{sensitive}(m) \wedge e \in \mathsf{enabled}(w) \cup [t, w]$, then $\forall m' \in \mathsf{next}(m, e)$

$$(t, w, m) \xrightarrow{e}_s (t \cup \downarrow e, (w \backslash \uparrow e) \cup \{e\}, m')$$

We note $(t, w, m) \xrightarrow{\rho}_s (t', w', m')$ iff $\exists (t_0, w_0, m_0), ..., (t_n, w_n, m_n)$, such that $(t, w, m) = (t_0, w_0, m_0), (t', w', m') = (t_n, w_n, m_n)$ and such that the path $\rho = e_1 e_2 \cdots e_n$ with $\forall 0 \leq i < n : (t_i, w_i, m_i) \xrightarrow{e_i}_s (t_{i+1}, w_{i+1}, m_{i+1})$. We also note $(t, w, m) \rightsquigarrow_s (t', w', m')$ if $\exists \rho : (t, w, m) \xrightarrow{\rho}_s (t', w', m')$, and $\mathsf{reachable}_s(t, w, m) = \{m' \in M \mid (t, w, m) \rightsquigarrow (t', E, m')\}$, the set of monitor states, reachable at the end of a trace's run.

From a symbolic configuration (t, w, m), we can fire events that were not previously examined before (events in $\mathsf{enabled}(w)$), or events that were examined before as *optional* and that allows now to change the current minitor state (event

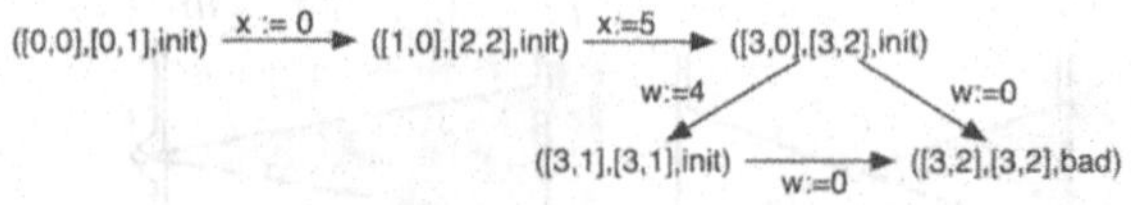

Fig. 3. Symbolic exploration

in $[t, w] \cap$ sensitive(m). When firing an event e, we consider two cases. The first case is when e is not sensitive in m. In this case, since e becomes *optional*, it is simply added to w. On the other hand, if e is sensitive in m, it becomes *mandatory* and must be added to t *together with all its causal predecessors* ($\downarrow e$). Moreover, we add e to w in order to keep t included in w, and all events added to w in the strict future of e must be removed from w since e changed from *optional* to *mandatory*.

We now need to prove that this symbolic composition is correct w.r.t the classical explicit exploration.

Theorem 2 (Correctness of symbolic composition). *[GMM06] The symbolic composition is correct w.r.t the classical explicit composition*

$$\text{reachable}_s(\emptyset, \emptyset, m^0) = \text{reachable}(\emptyset, m^0)$$

Proof sketch. First prove that the symbolic composition is consistent, i.e. that $((\emptyset, \emptyset, m^0) \rightsquigarrow_s (t, w, m)) \Rightarrow ((\downarrow t = t) \wedge (\downarrow w = w) \wedge (t \subseteq w))$. Then, we prove that it is sound, i.e. that $((\emptyset, \emptyset, m^0) \rightsquigarrow_s (t, w, m)) \Rightarrow (\forall s : (t \subseteq s \subseteq w) \wedge (\downarrow s = s) \Rightarrow (\emptyset, m^0) \rightsquigarrow (s, m))$. Finally, we prove that the symbolic composition is complete, i.e. $((\emptyset, m^0) \rightsquigarrow (s, m)) \Rightarrow (\exists t, w : (t \subseteq s \subseteq w) \wedge (\emptyset, \emptyset, m^0) \rightsquigarrow_s (t, w, m))$.

5   Symbolic Exploration

Taking advantage of the symbolic composition presented in the previous section, we propose our method, given in algorithm 1, which can efficiently solve the TMP, i.e. compute if $\text{reachable}_s(\emptyset, \emptyset, m^0) \cap B = \emptyset$. The idea behind this algorithm is simple. Given a symbolic configuration (t, w, m), we first explore all non-sensitive events. Since these events do not influence the monitor when fired, the order in which they are fired is not important. Therefore, we can just consider them in any order. In practice, we add to w all non-sensitive event of enabled(w), and this repeatedly until a stabilization (lines 7–10). Afterwards, from there, we fire all sensitive events yielding several new symbolic configurations (lines 1–14). The sets W and T contain the symbolic configuration resp. remaining to handle and already handled. The resulting state space for the monitor and trace presented in figure 1 is presented in figure 3.

In order to prove the correctness of this algorithm, we need to prove that firing non-sensitive events first is sufficient to detect if $\text{reachable}_s(\emptyset, \emptyset, m^0)_s \cap B = \emptyset$ is not empty. For this, we introduce a covering operator.

Algorithm 1. Symbolic exploration

```
    input  : T = (E, λ, ⪯), M = (M, m⁰, B, →ₘ)
    output: reachableₛ(∅, ∅, m⁰) ∩ B ≠ ∅
 1  begin
 2  │    T ← ∅, W ← {(∅, ∅, m⁰)}
 3  │    while W ≠ ∅ do
 4  │    │    let (t, w, m) ∈ W
 5  │    │    W ← W \ {(t, w, m)}
 6  │    │    T ← T ∪ (t, w, m)
 7  │    │    repeat
 8  │    │    │    x ← w
 9  │    │    │    w ← w ∪ {e ∈ enabled(w) | e ∉ sensitive(m)}
10  │    │    until (w = x)
11  │    │    if (w = E) ∧ (m ∈ B) then
12  │    │    └    return false
    │    │
13  │    │    forall (t', w', m') : (t, w, m) →ₛᵉ (t', w', m') ∧ (t', w', m') ∉ T do
14  │    │    └    W ← W ∪ {(t', w', m')}
    │
15  │    return true
16  end
```

Definition 8 (Covering operator ⊑). *A symbolic configuration* (t, w, m) *is covered by a symbolic configuration* (t', w', m'), *noted* $(t, w, m) \sqsubseteq (t', w', m')$, *iff*

$$(t' \subseteq t) \wedge (w \subseteq w') \wedge (m = m')$$

Intuitively, (t', w', m') covers (t, w, m) if (t', w', m') represents more explicit configurations than (t, w, m).

Lemma 1 (Monotonicity of ⊑). *[GMM06] The covering operator is monotonic w.r.t the symbolic composition.*

$$\left((t_1, w_1, m_1) \xrightarrow{e}_s (t'_1, w'_1, m'_1) \wedge (t_1, w_1, m_1) \sqsubseteq (t_2, w_2, m_2) \right)$$
$$\Rightarrow$$
$$\left(\exists (t'_2, w'_2, m'_2) : (t_2, w_2, m_2) \xrightarrow{e}_s (t'_2, w'_2, m'_2) \wedge (t'_1, w'_1, m'_1) \sqsubseteq (t'_2, w'_2, m'_2) \right)$$

Theorem 3 (Correctness of algorithm 1). *Given a trace* $T = (E, \lambda, \preceq)$ *and a monitor* $M = (M, m^0, B, \rightarrow_m)$, *algorithm 1 terminates and returns true iff* reachableₛ$(\emptyset, \emptyset, m^0) \cap B \neq \emptyset$.

Proof. First, we can see that E and M are finite, so is the set of possible symbolic configurations. Therefore, termination is guaranteed since we do not explore a symbolic configuration more than once. Moreover, theorem 2 ensures soundness, since only valid symbolic transition are taken. However, completeness is not that trivial, because the algorithm explore only a subset of all symbolic configurations. This comes from the fact that non-sensitive events are always fired first. However, if c denotes the configuration after the loop at lines 7–10, then any configuration c' computed during the loop is covered by c. Therefore, lemma 1 guarantees that any configuration reachable from c' is covered by a configuration reachable from c. Thus, only exploring c is sufficient.

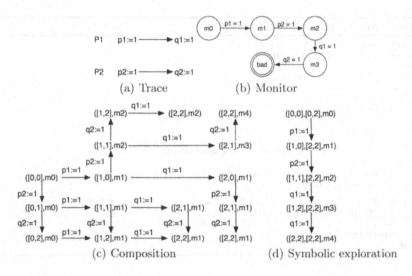

Fig. 4. Example of where algorithm 1 leads to an exponential gain

Note that using lemma 1, we could improve algorithm 1 by replacing the test $(t', w', m') \in T$, in line 1, by $(t', w', m') \sqsubseteq T$, i.e does there exist a configuration in T that covers (t', w', m'). An efficient data structure which handles set of tuples-intervals (see [DRV04] and its variant [Gan02]) can be used to perform efficiently these tests. The same efficient data structure can be used to represent W; then the union in line 1 adds a new configuration only if it is not already covered by W.

Possible Exponential Improvement. In practice, as shown in the next section, our symbolic method, given in algorithm 1, allows generally to reduce significantly the explored state space and the verification time. We show here the simple example given in figure 4 which provides a state space which is linear with our symbolic method while exponential in the explicit method. Note that this example can be extended to k processes. Hence, by using algorithm 1, we benefit from an exponential improvement (w.r.t. k) for the state space size. For instance for 8 processes, 17 states are explored by the symbolic algorithm against 8020 for the explicit one.

6   Experimental Results

In this section, we experimentally validate our method. We compared on randomly generated traces, both in time and in number configurations, our symbolic algorithm with a straightforward explicit trace exploration. Moreover, we compared our testing method with a complete model-checking using the tool *spin* [Hol97], with partial order reduction.

We conducted experiments on several examples (seen as distributed controllers). For each example, we examined a correct model and a faulty model,

Table 1. Experimental results ("-" means that the execution ran out of memory)

Experiment				Explicit			Symbolic			*Spin*
Model	Processes	Events	Property	Error	Time	Conf.	Error	Time	Conf.	Error
Peterson	2	10000	Mutex	NO	1.39s	21551	NO	0.35s	4001	0.06s
	2	100000	Mutex	NO	16.88s	215544	NO	3.45s	40001	0.06s
	2	1000000	Mutex	-	-	-	NO	34.75s	400002	0.06s
Peterson	2	10000	Mutex	YES	1.11s	21384	YES	0.01s	4	0.05s
Faulty	2	100000	Mutex	YES	15.95s	214727	YES	0.05s	4	0.05s
	2	1000000	Mutex	-	-	-	YES	0.53s	4	0.05s
ABProtocol	2	10000	Received	NO	2.17s	31185	NO	0.42s	4654	0.15s
	2	100000	Received	NO	31.08s	316414	NO	4.25s	46684	0.15s
	2	1000000	Received	-	-	-	NO	43.09s	466887	0.15s
ABProtocol	2	10000	Received	YES	2.06s	31495	YES	0.01s	5	0.13s
Faulty	2	100000	Received	YES	29.70s	315808	YES	0.06s	5	0.13s
	2	1000000	Received	-	-	-	YES	0.53s	5	0.13s
Philosopher	3	100	Fork	NO	1.03s	6190	NO	0.05s	299	0.40s
	5	100	Fork	NO	87.02s	60727	NO	0.21s	2875	12.01s
	10	100	Fork	-	-	-	NO	1.52s	26791	-
Philosopher	3	100	Fork	YES	0.09s	1187	YES	0.01s	63	0.38s
Faulty	5	100	Fork	YES	78.72s	55982	YES	0.01s	78	11.01s
	10	100	Fork	-	-	-	YES	0.01s	55	-

where a bug was intentionally introduced. Traces were generated by instrumenting the code to emit relevant events (i.e. assignments). The partial order relations were obtained using vector clocks.

Table 1 presents the results of these experiments. For each experiment, the first four columns respectively present the model, the number of processes, the number of events in the trace and the property. Next, for both the explicit, and symbolic method, columns 5 to 10 show if an error was found or not, the time needed for exploration and the number of configurations used. The last column present the times needed for the complete model-checking with partial order reduction. A "-" in the table indicates that no result could be obtained because the process ran out of memory.[1]

The first example we considered was the *Peterson* mutual exclusion protocol with two processes, where communication is done through shared variables. We used a monitor to check mutual exclusion (a safety property).

The second model we considered was the *Alternating-bit protocol* between two process, i.e. a sender and a receiver. This time the communication is achieved using asynchronous channel. We used a monitor to check that every message sent was correctly received.

On those two examples, we can see that the symbolic exploration works well in practice, compared to the explicit exploration method, both with safety and liveness property. It is worth noting that, in the faulty version of both models, the error was detected rapidly. However, on those two examples, the complete *spin* model checking can be done very efficiently. This should be expected since the model is relatively small.

The last example we considered was the *Dining Philosopher* problem. The monitor was used to check that when the first philosopher takes his left fork, then

---

[1] Explorations and model-checking were limited to 1GB of memory.

his left neighbor cannot eat until he has finished to eat. Note that this property cannot be expressed in RCTL+ of [SG03] because it involves an *until* operator. We considered 3, 5 and 10 philosophers. On this example, we can see that using the symbolic method allows to handle a larger number of processes. Indeed, when dealing with 10 philosophers, the explicit exploration fails to terminate, whereas the symbolic method still works. Moreover, in the faulty model, with 10 philosophers, the complete *spin* model checking fails to terminate, whereas the symbolic exploration still detects the error that was introduced.

7   Future Works

Our symbolic method will be integrated into our distributed controllers design environment $_d$SL [DMM04, DGMM05] to allow efficient testing of real industrial distributed controllers. For this purpose, our method should be extended to online monitoring, and further developed to handle more complex formulae. A comparison between our tool and other existing tools could then be done both at the expressivity and performance levels.

We also intend to investigate the use of our method in different frameworks. A first candidate is the validation of Message Sequence Charts (MSC). We must study how our method can improve the efficiency of existing MSC validation methods. Moreover, we would like to explore the possibility of integrating other techniques such as computation slicing [MG05], in order to gain in time an space during the validation.

Finally, we are also interested in the extension of our method to the model-checking of complete systems. The combined use of our method with unfolding technique developed by McMillan [McM95] and further refined by Esparza [ERV96] seems a priori a promising approach.

Acknowledgments. We would like thank the anonymous reviewers, whose comments allowed us to significantly improve the quality of this paper.

References

[APP95]   Rajeev Alur, Doron Peled, and Wojciech Penczek. Model checking of causality properties. In *Proceedings of the 10th Annual IEEE Symposium on Logic in Computer Science (LICS'95)*, pages 90–100, San Diego, California, 1995.

[Bry92]   Randal E. Bryant. Symbolic boolean manipulation with ordered binary-decision diagrams. *ACM Comput. Surv.*, 24(3):293–318, 1992.

[CCG$^+$02]   Alessandro Cimatti, Edmund M. Clarke, Enrico Giunchiglia, Fausto Giunchiglia, Marco Pistore, Marco Roveri, Roberto Sebastiani, and Armando Tacchella. Nusmv 2: An opensource tool for symbolic model checking. In *CAV*, pages 359–364, 2002.

[CDF95]   Bernadette Charron-Bost, Carole Delporte-Gallet, and Hugues Fauconnier. Local and temporal predicates in distributed systems. *ACM Trans. Program. Lang. Syst.*, 17(1), 1995.

[CG98]   Craig M. Chase and Vijay K. Garg. Detection of global predicates: Techniques and their limitations. *Distributed Computing*, 11(4):191–201, 1998.

[CGP99]   E.M. Clarke, O. Grumberg, and D. Peled. *Model Checking*. The MIT Press, 1999.

[CL85]   K. Mani Chandy and Leslie Lamport. Distributed snapshots: Determining global states of distributed systems. *ACM Trans. Comput. Syst.*, 3(1):63–75, 1985.

[DG02]   Volker Diekert and Paul Gastin. LTL is expressively complete for Mazurkiewicz traces. *Journal of Computer and System Sciences*, 64(2):396–418, March 2002.

[DGMM05]   Bram De Wachter, Alexandre Genon, Thierry Massart, and Cédric Meuter. The formal design of distributed controllers with dsl and spin. *Formal Aspects of Computing*, 17(2):177–200, 2005. (24 pages).

[DMM04]   Bram De Wachter, Thierry Massart, and Cédric Meuter. dsl : An environment with automatic code distribution for industrial control systems. In *Lecture Notes in Computer Sciences*, volume 3144, pages 132–145. Springer, 2004. (14 pages).

[DRV04]   Giorgio Delzanno, Jean-François Raskin, and Laurent Van Begin. Covering sharing trees: a compact data structure for parameterized verification. *STTT*, 5(2-3):268–297, 2004.

[ERV96]   Javier Esparza, Stefan Römer, and Walter Vogler. An improvement of mcmillan's unfolding algorithm. In *TACAS*, pages 87–106, 1996.

[Gan02]   Pierre Ganty. Algorithmes et structures de données efficaces pour la manipulation de contraintes sur les intervalles. Master's thesis, Université Libre de Bruxelles, 2002.

[GM01]   Vijay K. Garg and Neeraj Mittal. On slicing a distributed computation. In *ICDCS*, pages 322–329, 2001.

[GMM06]   Alexandre Genon, Thierry Massart, and Cédric Meuter. Monitoring distributed controllers : When an efficient ltl algorithm on sequences is needed to model-check traces. Technical Report 2006-59, CFV - Université Libre de Bruxelles, 2006.

[God96]   P. Godefroid. *Partial-Order Methods for the Verification of Concurrent Systems - An Approach to the State-Explosion Problem*, volume 1032 of *Lecture Notes in Computer Science*. Springer, 1996.

[GW94]   Vijay K. Garg and Brian Waldecker. Detection of weak unstable predicates in distributed programs. *IEEE Trans. Parallel Distrib. Syst.*, 5(3):299–307, 1994.

[GW96]   Vijay K. Garg and Brian Waldecker. Detection of strong unstable predicates in distributed programs. *IEEE Trans. Parallel Distrib. Syst.*, 7(12):1323–1333, 1996.

[Hol97]   Gerard J. Holzmann. The model checker spin. *IEEE Trans. Software Eng.*, 23(5):279–295, 1997.

[Lam78]   Leslie Lamport. Time, clocks, and the ordering of events in a distributed system. *Commun. ACM*, 21(7):558–565, 1978.

[LMC01]   M. Leuschel, T. Massart, and A. Currie. How to make fdr spin : Ltl model checking of csp by refinement. In *Lecture Notes in Computer Sciences*, volume 2021, pages 99–118. Springer, 2001. (20 pages).

[Lyn96]   Nancy A. Lynch. *Distributed Algorithms*. Morgan Kaufmann Publishers Inc., San Francisco, CA, USA, 1996.

[Mat89]   Friedemann Mattern. Virtual time and global states of distributed sys-
            tems. In Cosnard M. et al., editor, *Proc. Workshop on Parallel and
            Distributed Algorithms*, pages 215–226, North-Holland / Elsevier, 1989.
[Maz86]   Antoni W. Mazurkiewicz. Trace theory. In *Advances in Petri Nets*, pages
            279–324, 1986.
[McM92a]   K. L. McMillan. *Symbolic model checking: an approach to the state ex-
            plosion problem*. Carnegie Mellon University, 1992.
[McM92b]   K.L. McMillan. The smv system. Technical Report CMU-CS-92-131,
            Carnegie Mellon University, 1992.
[McM95]   Kenneth L. McMillan. A technique of state space search based on un-
            folding. *Formal Methods in System Design*, 6(1):45–65, 1995.
[MG01]   Neeraj Mittal and Vijay K. Garg. Computation slicing: Techniques and
            theory. In *DISC*, pages 78–92, 2001.
[MG05]   Neeraj Mittal and Vijay K. Garg. Techniques and applications of com-
            putation slicing. *Distributed Computing*, 17(3):251–277, 2005.
[SG03]   Alper Sen and Vijay K. Garg. Detecting temporal logic predicates in
            distributed programs using computation slicing. In *OPODIS*, pages 171–
            183, 2003.
[SRA04]   Koushik Sen, Grigore Rosu, and Gul Agha. Online efficient predictive
            safety analysis of multithreaded programs. In *TACAS*, pages 123–138,
            2004.
[SVAR04]   K. Sen, A. Vardhan, G. Agha, and G. Rosu. Efficient decentralized
            monitoring of safety in distributed systems. In *Proceedings of 26th In-
            ternational Conference on Software Engineering (ICSE'04), Edinburgh,
            UK*, pages 418–427. IEEE, May 2004.
[Thi94]   P. S. Thiagarajan. A trace based extension of linear time temporal
            logic. In Samson Abramsky, editor, *Proceedings of the Ninth Annual
            IEEE Symp. on Logic in Computer Science, LICS 1994*, pages 438–447.
            IEEE Computer Society Press, July 1994.
[TW02]   P. S. Thiagarajan and I. Walukiewicz. An expressively complete linear
            time temporal logic for mazurkiewicz traces. *Inf. Comput.*, 179(2):230–
            249, 2002.
[Val93]   Antti Valmari. On-the-fly verification with stubborn sets. In *CAV*, pages
            397–408, 1993.
[VW86]   M. Y. Vardi and P. Wolper. An automata-theoretic approach to auto-
            matic program verification. In *Proc. 1st Symp. on Logic in Computer
            Science*, pages 332–344, Cambridge, June 1986.

PSL Model Checking and
Run-Time Verification Via Testers

A. Pnueli and A. Zaks

New York University, New York
{amir, zaks}@cs.nyu.edu

Abstract. The paper introduces the construct of *temporal testers* as a compositional basis for the construction of automata corresponding to temporal formulas in the PSL logic. Temporal testers can be viewed as (non-deterministic) transducers that, at any point, output a boolean value which is 1 iff the corresponding temporal formula holds starting at the current position.

The main advantage of testers, compared to acceptors (such as Büchi automata) is that they are compositional. Namely, a tester for a compound formula can be constructed out of the testers for its sub-formulas. In this paper, we extend the application of the testers method from LTL to the logic PSL.

Besides providing the construction of testers for PSL, we indicate how the symbolic representation of the testers can be directly utilized for efficient model checking and run-time monitoring.

1 Introduction

The standard way of model checking an LTL property φ over a finite-state system S, represented by the automaton M_s, is based on the construction of an ω-automaton $\mathcal{A}_{\neg\varphi}$ that accepts all sequences that violate the property φ. Having both the system and its specification represented by automata, we may form the product automaton $M_s \times \mathcal{A}_{\neg\varphi}$ and check that it accepts the empty language, implying that there exists no computation of S which refutes φ [14].

Usually, the automaton $\mathcal{A}_{\neg\varphi}$ is a non-deterministic Büchi automaton, which is constructed using an explicit-state representation. In order to employ it in a symbolic (BDD-based) model checker, it is necessary to encode the automaton by the introduction of auxiliary variables. Another drawback of the normal (tableau-based) construction is that it is not compositional. That is, having constructed automata $\mathcal{A}_\varphi$ and $\mathcal{A}_\psi$ for LTL formulas φ and ψ, there is no simple recipe for constructing the automaton for a compound formula which combines φ and ψ, such as $\varphi \, U \, \psi$.

The article [9] introduces a compositional approach to the construction of automata corresponding to LTL formulas. This construction is based on the notion of a *temporal tester* that has been introduced first in [8]. A tester for an LTL formula φ can be viewed as a *transducer* that keeps observing a state sequence σ and, at every position $j \geq 0$, outputs a boolean value which equals 1 iff $(\sigma, j) \models \varphi$. While acceptors, such as the Büchi automaton $\mathcal{A}_\varphi$, do not compose, transducers do. In Fig. 1, we show how transducers for the formulas φ, ψ, and $p \, U \, q$ can be composed into a transducer for the formula $\varphi \, U \, \psi$.

J. Misra, T. Nipkow, and E. Sekerinski (Eds.): FM 2006, LNCS 4085, pp. 573–586, 2006.
© Springer-Verlag Berlin Heidelberg 2006

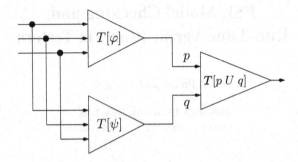

Fig. 1. Composition of transducers to form $T[\varphi\ U\ \psi]$

There are several important advantages to the use of temporal testers as the basis for the construction of automata for temporal formulas:

- The construction is compositional. Therefore, it is sufficient to specify testers for the basic temporal formulas: $X!p$ and $p\ U\ q$, where p and q are assertions (state formulas). Testers for more complex formulas can be derived by composition as in Fig. 1 .
- The testers for the basic formulas are naturally symbolic. Thus, a general tester, which is a synchronous parallel composition (automata product) of symbolic modules can also be easily represented symbolically.
- As shown below, the basic processes of model checking and run-time monitoring can be performed directly on the symbolic representation of the testers. There is no need for determinization or reduction to explicit state representation.

In the work presented in this paper, we generalize the temporal tester approach to the more expressive logic PSL, recently introduced as a new standard logic for specifying hardware properties [1]. Due to compositionality, it is only necessary to provide the construction of testers for the basic operators introduced by PSL.

In addition, we show how to construct an optimal symbolic run-time monitor. By optimality, we mean that the monitor extracts as much information as possible from the observed trace. In particular, an optimal monitor stops as soon it can be deduced that the specification is violated or satisfied, regardless of the possible continuations of the observed trace.

2   Accellera PSL

In this paper, we only consider a subset of PSL. For brevity, we omit the discussions of OBE (Optional Branching Extension) formulas that are based on CTL. Note that using testers we can obtain a model checking algorithm even for CTL* branching formulas by combining PSL testers with the work in [9]. Regarding run-time monitoring, which together with model checking is the primary motivation for our work, branching formulas are not applicable at all. In addition, we do not consider clocked formulas and formulas with *abort* operator. This is not a severe limitation since none of the above add any expressive power to PSL. One can find a rewriting scheme for the @ operator (clock operator) in [6] and for the *abort* operator in [12]. The rewriting rules produce a semantically equivalent formula not containing the operators, which is linear in the size of the original.

Due to lack of space, we do not formally define logic PSL but follow very closely the definitions from [6]. The only exceptions are the one mentioned above, and, for convenience, we define one additional operator $\langle r \rangle \varphi$ as

$$ v \vDash \langle r \rangle \varphi \iff \exists j < |v| \text{ s.t. } \bar{v}^{0..j} \Vdash r, \; v^{j..} \vDash \varphi. $$

3 Computational Model

3.1 Fair Discrete Systems with Finite Computations

We take a *just discrete system*(JDS), which is a variant of *fair transition system* [10], as our computational model. Under this model, a system $\mathcal{D} : \langle V, \Theta, R, \mathcal{J}, F \rangle$ consists of the following components:

- V: A finite set of *system variables*. A *state* of the system $\mathcal{D}$ provides a type-consistent interpretation of the system variables V. For a state s and a system variable $v \in V$, we denote the value assigned to v by the state s by $s[v]$.
- Θ: The *initial condition*. This is an assertion (state formula) characterizing the initial states. A state is defined to be *initial* if it satisfies Θ.
- $R(V, V')$: The *transition relation*, which is an assertion that relates the values of the variables in V interpreted by a state s to the values of the variables V' in an *R-successor* state s'.
- $\mathcal{J}$: A set of *justice* (*weak fairness*) requirements. Each justice requirement is an assertion. An infinite computation must include infinitely many states satisfying the assertion.
- F: The *termination condition*, which is an assertion specifying the set of *final* states. Each finite computation must end in a final state.

A *computation* of an JDS $\mathcal{D}$ is a non-empty sequence of states $\sigma : s_0, s_1, s_2, ...,$ satisfying the requirements:

- *Initiality*: s_0 is initial.
- *Consecution*: For each $i \in [0, |\sigma|)$, the state s_{i+1} is a R-successor of state s_i. That is, $\langle s_i, s_{i+1} \rangle \in R(V, V')$ where, for each $v \in V$, we interpret v as $s_i[v]$ and v' as $s_{i+1}[v]$.
- *Justice*: If σ is infinite, then for every $J \in \mathcal{J}$, σ contains infinitely many occurrences of J-states.
- *Termination*: If $\sigma = s_0, s_1, s_2, ..., s_k$ is finite, then s_k must satisfy F.

A sequence of states $\sigma : s_0, s_1, s_2, ...$ that only satisfies all conditions for being a computation except initiality is called an *uninitialized computation*.

Given two JDS's, $\mathcal{D}_1$ and $\mathcal{D}_2$, their *synchronous parallel composition*, $\mathcal{D}_1 \; ||| \; \mathcal{D}_2$, is the JDS whose sets of variables and justice requirements are the unions of the corresponding sets in the two systems, whose initial and termination conditions are the conjunctions of the corresponding assertions, and whose transition relation is a conjunction of the two transition relations. Thus, a step in an execution of the composed system is a joint step of the systems $\mathcal{D}_1$ and $\mathcal{D}_2$.

3.2 Interpretation of PSL Formulas over JDS

We assume that the set of atomic propositions P is a subset of the variables V, so we can easily evaluate all the propositions at a given state of a JDS. We say that a letter $l \in 2^P$ *corresponds* to a state s if $p \in l$ iff $s[p] = 1$. Similarly, we define a correspondence between words and computations. We say, that a computation σ models (or satisfies) PSL formula φ, denoted $\sigma \models \varphi$, if the corresponding word v satisfies PSL formula φ.

4   Temporal Testers

One of the main problems in constructing a Büchi automaton for a PSL formula (or for that matter any ω-regular language) is that the conventional construction is not compositional. In particular, given Büchi automata $\mathcal{A}_\varphi$ and $\mathcal{A}_\psi$ for formulas φ and ψ, it is not trivial to build an automaton for $\varphi\ U\ \psi$. Compositionality is an important consideration, especially in the context of PSL. It is expected that specifications are written in a modular way, and PSL has several language constructs to facilitate that. For example, any property can be given a name, and a more complex property can be built by simply using a named sub-property instead of an atomic proposition.

One way to achieve compositionality with Büchi automata is to use alternation [3]. Nothing special is required from the Büchi automata to be composed in such manner, but the presence of universal branching in the resulting automaton is undesirable. Though most model checkers can deal with existential non-determinism directly and efficiently, universal branching is usually preprocessed at exponential cost.

Our approach is based on the observation that while the main property of Büchi automata (as well as any other automata) is to correctly identify a language membership of a given sequence of letters, starting from the very first letter; it turns out that for composition it is also very useful to know whether a word is in the language starting from an arbitrary position i. We refer to this new class of objects as *testers*. Essentially, testers are transducers that at each step output whether the suffix of the input sequence is in the language. Of course, the suffix is not known by the time the decision has to be made, so the testers are inherently non-deterministic.

Formally, a *tester* for a PSL formula φ is a JDS T_φ, which has a distinguished boolean variable x_φ, such that:

- **Soundness:** For every computation $\sigma : s_0, s_1, s_2, \ldots$ of T_φ, $s_i[x_\varphi] = 1$ iff $\sigma^{i\cdots} \models \varphi$
- **Completeness:** For every sequence of states $\sigma' : s'_0, s'_1, s'_2, \ldots$, there is a matching computation $\sigma : s_0, s_1, s_2, \ldots$ such that for each i, s_i and s'_i agree on the interpretation of φ-variables.

Intuitively, the second condition requires that a tester must be able to correctly interpret x_φ for an arbitrary input sequence. Otherwise, the first condition can be trivially satisfied by a JDS that has no computations.

5   LTL **Testers**

We are going to continue the presentation of testers by considering two very important PSL operators, namely $X!$(next) and U(until). First, we show how to build testers for two *basic formulas* $X!b$ and $b_1 \ U \ b_2$, where b, b_1, and b_2 are boolean expressions. Then, we demonstrate high compositionality of the testers by easily extending the result to cover full LTL. Note that our construction for LTL operators is very similar to the one presented in [8].

5.1   A Tester for $\varphi = X!b$

Let $T_\varphi = \langle V_\varphi, \Theta_\varphi, R_\varphi, \mathcal{J}_\varphi, F_\varphi \rangle$ be the tester we wish to construct. The components of T_φ are defined as follows:

$$T(X!b) : \begin{cases} V_\varphi : P \cup x_\varphi, \text{ where } P \text{ is a set of atomic propositions} \\ \Theta_\varphi : 1 \\ R_\varphi(V, V') : x_\varphi = b' \\ \mathcal{J}_\varphi : \emptyset \\ F_\varphi : \neg x_\varphi \end{cases}$$

It almost immediately follows from the construction that $T(X!b)$ is indeed a good tester for $X!b$. The soundness of the $T(X!b)$ is guaranteed by the transition relation with the exception that we still have a freedom to incorrectly interpret x_φ at the very last state. This case is handled separately by insisting that every final state must interpret x_φ as *false*. The completeness follows from the fact that we do not restrict P variables by the transition relation, and we can always interpret x_φ properly, by either matching b' or setting it to *false* in the last state.

5.2   A Tester for $\varphi = b_1 \ U \ b_2$

The components of T_φ are defined as follows:

$$T(b_1 \ U \ b_2) : \begin{cases} V_\varphi : P \cup x_\varphi \\ \Theta_\varphi : 1 \\ R_\varphi(V, V') : x_\varphi = b_2 \vee (b_1 \wedge x'_\varphi) \\ \mathcal{J}_\varphi : b_2 \vee \neg x_\varphi \\ F_\varphi : b_2 \vee \neg x_\varphi \end{cases}$$

Unlike the previous tester, $T(b_1 \ U \ b_2)$ has a non-empty justice set. A technical reason is that the transition relation allows x_φ to be continuously set to true without having a single state that actually satisfies b_2. The situation is ruled out by the justice requirement. Another way to look at the problem is that R_φ represents an expansion formula for the U(strong until) operator, namely $b_1 \ U \ b_2 \iff b_2 \vee (b_1 \wedge X![b_1 \ U \ b_2])$. In general, starting with an expansion formula is a good first step when building a tester. However, the expansion formula alone is usually not sufficient for a proper tester. Indeed, consider the operator $\mathcal{W}$(weak until), defined as $b_1 \ \mathcal{W} \ b_2 \equiv \neg(true \ U \ \neg b_1) \vee b_1 \ U \ b_2$, which has exactly the same expansion formula, namely $b_1 \ \mathcal{W} \ b_2 \iff b_2 \vee (b_1 \wedge X![b_1 \ \mathcal{W} \ b_2])$. We use justice to differentiate between the two operators.

6   Tester Composition

In Fig. 2, we present a recursive algorithm that builds a tester for an arbitrary LTL formula φ. In Example 1, we illustrate the algorithm by applying the tester construction for the formula $\varphi = true\ U\ \big(X![b_1\ U\ b_2] \vee (b_3\ U\ [b_1\ U\ b_2])\big)$.

- **Base Case**: If φ is a basic formula (i.e., $\varphi = X!b$ or $\varphi = b_1\ U\ b_2$), use construction from Section 5. For a trivial case, when the formula φ does not contain any temporal operators, we can use a tester for $false\ U\ \varphi$.

- **Induction Step**: Let ψ be an innermost basic sub-formula of φ, then $T_\varphi = T_{\varphi[\psi/x_\psi]}\ |||\ T_\psi$, where $\varphi[\psi/x_\psi]$ denotes the formula φ in which each occurrence of the sub-formula ψ is replaced with x_ψ.

Fig. 2. Tester construction for an arbitrary LTL formula φ

Example 1. *Tester Construction for* $\varphi = true\ U\ \big(X![b_1\ U\ b_2] \vee [b_1\ U\ b_2]\big)$

We start by identifying $b_1\ U\ b_2$ to be the innermost basic sub-formula and building the corresponding tester, $T_{b_1 U b_2}$ with the output variable y. Let $\alpha = \varphi[b_1\ U\ b_2/y]$; after the substitution $\alpha = true\ U\ \big(X!z \vee y\big)$. Note that we performed the substitution twice, but there is no need for two testers, which can result in significant savings. We proceed in similar fashion and build one more tester $T_{X!y}$ with the output variable x. After the substitutions, we obtain $\beta = true\ U\ [x \vee y]$, which satisfies the conditions of the base case. The final result can be expressed as:

$$T_\varphi = T_\beta\ |||\ T_{X!y}\ |||\ T_{b_1 U b_2}.$$

Though we have assumed φ is an LTL formula, the algorithm can be extended to PSL by considering additional basic formulas.

7   Associating a Regular Grammar with a SERE

Following [7], a grammar $\mathcal{G} = \langle \mathcal{V}, \mathcal{T}, \mathcal{P}, \mathcal{S} \rangle$ consists of the following:

- $\mathcal{V}$: A finite set of *variables*.
- $\mathcal{T}$: A finite set of *terminals*. We assume that $\mathcal{V}$ and $\mathcal{T}$ are disjoint. In our framework, $\mathcal{T}$ consists of boolean expressions and a special terminal ϵ.
- $\mathcal{P}$: A finite set of *productions*. We only consider right-linear grammars, so all productions are of the form $V \to aW$ or $V \to a$, where a is a terminal, and V and W are variables.
- $\mathcal{S}$: A special variable called a *start symbol*.

We say a grammar $\mathcal{G}$ is *associated* with a SERE r if, intuitively, they both define the same language. While this definition is not accurate, we show a precise construction of an associated grammar for a given SERE in [12]. For example, we associate the following grammar $\mathcal{G}$ with SERE $r = (a_1 b_1)[*] \&\& (a_2 b_2)[*]$

$$V_1 \rightarrow \epsilon \mid (a_1 \wedge a_2)V_2$$
$$V_2 \rightarrow \quad (b_1 \wedge b_2)V_1$$

Theorem 1. *For every SERE r of length n, there exists an associated grammar $\mathcal{G}$ with the number of productions $O(2^n)$. If we restrict SERE's to the three traditional operators: concatenation (;), union (|), and Kleene closure ([*]), the number of productions becomes linear in the size of r.*

8   PSL Testers

There are only two additional basic formulas that we need to consider to handle full PSL, namely $\varphi = \langle r \rangle b$ and $\varphi = r$, where r is a SERE and b is a boolean expression. All other PSL temporal operators can be expressed using those two and the LTL operators, $X!$ and U. For example, $r! \equiv \langle r \rangle \mathit{true}$, and $r \mapsto b \equiv \neg(\langle r \rangle \neg \varphi)$.

8.1   A Tester for $\varphi = \langle r \rangle b$

Let $T_\varphi = \langle V_\varphi, \Theta_\varphi, R_\varphi, \mathcal{J}_\varphi, F_\varphi \rangle$ be the tester we wish to construct. Assume that x_φ is the output variable. Let $\mathcal{G} = \langle V, T, \mathcal{P}, \mathcal{S} \rangle$ be a grammar associated with r. Without the loss of generality, we assume $\mathcal{G}$ has variables $V_1, \ldots, V_n$ with V_1 being the start symbol. In addition, each variable V_i, has derivations of the form:

$$V_i \rightarrow \alpha_1 \mid \cdots \mid \alpha_m \mid \beta_1 V_1 \mid \cdots \mid \beta_n V_n$$

where $\alpha_1, \ldots, \alpha_m, \beta_1, \ldots, \beta_n$ are boolean expressions. The case that variable V_i does not have a particular derivation $V_i \rightarrow \beta_j V_j$ or $V_i \rightarrow \alpha_k$, is covered by having $\beta_j = \mathit{false}$, and similarly, $\alpha_k = \mathit{false}$. Note that by insisting on this specific form, which does not allow ϵ productions, we can not express whether an empty string is in the language. However, since, by definition of $\langle \rangle$ operator, a prefix that satisfies r must be non-empty, we do not need to consider this. The tester T_φ is given by:

$$T_\varphi : \begin{cases} V_\varphi : P \cup x_\varphi \cup \{X_1, \ldots, X_n, Y_1, \ldots, Y_n\} \\ \Theta_\varphi : 1 \\ R_\varphi : \text{Each derivation } V_i \rightarrow \alpha_1 \mid \cdots \mid \alpha_m \mid \beta_1 V_1 \mid \cdots \mid \beta_n V_n \\ \quad \text{contributes to } \rho \text{ the conjunct} \\ \quad X_i = (\alpha_1 \wedge b) \vee \cdots \vee (\alpha_m \wedge b) \vee (\beta_1 \wedge X_1') \vee \cdots \vee (\beta_n \wedge X_n') \\ \quad \text{and the conjunct} \\ \quad Y_i \rightarrow (\alpha_1 \wedge b) \vee \cdots \vee (\alpha_m \wedge b) \vee (\beta_1 \wedge Y_1') \vee \cdots \vee (\beta_n \wedge Y_n') \\ \quad \text{the output variable is constrained by the conjunct} \\ \quad x_\varphi = X_1 \\ \mathcal{J}_\varphi : \{\neg Y_1 \wedge \cdots \wedge \neg Y_n, \quad X_1 = Y_1 \wedge \cdots \wedge X_n = Y_n\} \\ F_\varphi : \text{Each derivation } V_i \rightarrow \alpha_1 \mid \cdots \mid \alpha_m \mid \beta_1 V_1 \mid \cdots \mid \beta_n V_n \\ \quad \text{contributes to } F \text{ the conjunct} \\ \quad X_i = (\alpha_1 \wedge b) \vee \cdots \vee (\alpha_m \wedge b) \end{cases}$$

Example 2. *A Tester for* $\varphi = \langle\{pq\}[*]\rangle b$.

To illustrate the construction, consider formula $\langle\{pq\}[*]\rangle b$. Following the algorithm from [12] and removing ϵ productions, the associated right-linear grammar for the SERE $\{pq\}[*]$ is given by

$$V_1 \rightarrow pV_2$$
$$V_2 \rightarrow q \mid qV_1$$

Consequently, a tester for $\langle\{pq\}[*]\rangle b$ is given by

$$T(\langle\{pq\}[*]\rangle b) : \begin{cases} V_\varphi : P \cup x_\varphi \cup \{X_1, X_2, Y_1, Y_2\} \\ \Theta_\varphi : 1 \\ R_\varphi(V, V') : \begin{pmatrix} (X_1 = (p \wedge X_2')) & \wedge \\ (X_2 = (q \wedge b) \vee (q \wedge X_1')) \wedge \\ (Y_1 \rightarrow (p \wedge Y_2')) & \wedge \\ (Y_2 \rightarrow (q \wedge b) \vee (q \wedge Y_1')) \wedge \\ x_\varphi = X_1 \end{pmatrix} \\ J_\varphi : \{\neg Y_1 \wedge \neg Y_2, \quad X_1 = Y_1 \wedge X_2 = Y_2\} \\ F_\varphi : (X_1 = \textit{false}) \wedge (X_2 = q \wedge b) \end{cases}$$

The variables $\{X_1, \ldots, X_n, Y_1, \ldots, Y_n\}$ are expected to check that the rest of the sequence from now on has a prefix satisfying the SERE r. Thus, the subsequence $s_j, \ldots, s_k, \ldots \models \langle r \rangle b$ iff there exists a generation sequence $V^j = V_1, V^{j+1}, \ldots, V^k$, such that for each $i, j \leq i < k$, there exists a grammar rule $V^i \rightarrow \beta V^{i+1}$, where $s_i \models \beta, V^k \rightarrow \alpha$, and $s_k \models (\alpha \wedge b)$.

The generation sequence is represented in a run of the tester by a sequence of true valuations for the variables $Z^j = Z_1, Z^{j+1}, \ldots, Z^k$ where $Z^i \in \{X^i, Y^i\}$ for each $i \in [j..k]$. An important element in this checking is to make sure that any such generation sequence is finite. This is accomplished through the double representation of each V_i by X_i and Y_i. The justice requirement $(X_1 = Y_1) \wedge \cdots \wedge (X_n = Y_n)$ guarantees that that any true X_i is eventually copied into Y_i. The justice requirement $\neg Y_1 \wedge \cdots \wedge \neg Y_n$ guarantees that all true Y_i's are eventually falsified. Together, they guarantee that there exists no infinite generation sequence. The double representation approach was introduced in [11].

8.2   A Tester for $\varphi = r$

We start the construction exactly the same way as we did for $\varphi = \langle r \rangle b$, in Section 8.1. Let $T_\varphi = \langle V_\varphi, \Theta_\varphi, R_\varphi, J_\varphi, F_\varphi \rangle$ be the tester we wish to construct. Assume that x_φ is the output variable. Let $\mathcal{G} = \langle \mathcal{V}, \mathcal{T}, \mathcal{P}, \mathcal{S} \rangle$ be a grammar associated with r.

The tester T_φ is given by:

$$T_\varphi : \begin{cases} \quad V_\varphi : P \cup x_\varphi \cup \{X_1, \ldots, X_n, Y_1, \ldots, Y_n\} \\ \quad \Theta_\varphi : 1 \\ \quad R_\varphi(V, V') : \text{Each derivation } V_i \to \alpha_1 \mid \cdots \mid \alpha_m \mid \beta_1 V_1 \mid \cdots \mid \beta_n V_n \\ \qquad\qquad \text{contributes to } \rho \text{ the conjunct} \\ \qquad\qquad X_i = \alpha_1 \vee \cdots \vee \alpha_m \vee (\beta_1 \wedge X_1') \vee \cdots \vee (\beta_n \wedge X_n') \\ \qquad\qquad \text{and the conjunct} \\ \qquad\qquad \alpha_1 \vee \cdots \vee \alpha_m \vee (\beta_1 \wedge Y_1') \vee \cdots \vee (\beta_n \wedge Y_n') \to Y_i \\ \qquad\qquad \text{the output variable is constrained by the conjunct} \\ \qquad\qquad x_\varphi = X_1 \\ \quad \mathcal{J}_\varphi : \{Y_1 \wedge \cdots \wedge Y_n, \quad X_1 = Y_1 \wedge \cdots \wedge X_n = Y_n\} \\ \quad F_\varphi : \text{Each derivation } V_i \to \alpha_1 \mid \cdots \mid \alpha_m \mid \beta_1 V_1 \mid \cdots \mid \beta_n V_n \\ \qquad\qquad \text{contributes to } F \text{ the conjunct} \\ \qquad\qquad X_i = \alpha_1 \vee \cdots \vee \alpha_m \vee \beta_1 \vee \cdots \vee \beta_n \end{cases}$$

The variables $\{X_1, \ldots, X_n, Y_1, \ldots, Y_n\}$ are expected to check that the rest of the sequence from now on has a prefix that does not violate SERE r. We follow a similar approach as for the tester $\varphi = \langle r \rangle b$. However, now we are more concerned with false values of the variables $X_1 \ldots X_n$. The duality comes from the fact that, now, we are trying to prevent postponing the violation of the formula r forever.

8.3 Complexity of the Construction

Theorem 2. *For every* PSL *formula φ of length n, there exists a tester with $O(2^n)$ variables. If we restrict SERE's to three traditional operators: concatenation (;), union (|), and Kleene closure ([∗]), the number of variables is linear in the size of φ.*

To justify the result, we can just count the fresh variables introduced at each step of the tester construction. There is only linear number of sub-formulas, so there is a linear number of output variables. The only other variables introduced are the ones that are used to handle SERE's. According to Theorem 1, the associated grammars contain at most $O(2^n)$ non-terminals ($O(n)$ - for the restricted case). We conclude by observing that testers for the formulas $\varphi = \langle r \rangle b$ and $\varphi = r$ introduce exactly two variables, X_i and Y_i, for each non-terminal V_i.

9 Using Testers for Model Checking

One of the main advantages of our construction is that all the steps, as well as the final result – the tester itself, can be represented symbolically. That is particularly handy if one is to use symbolic model checking [2]. Assume that the formula under consideration is φ, and $T_\varphi = \langle V_\varphi, \Theta_\varphi, R_\varphi, \mathcal{J}_\varphi, F_\varphi \rangle$ is the corresponding tester. Let JDS $\mathcal{D}$ represent the system we wish to model check.

We are going to use traditional automata theoretic approach based on synchronous composition, as in [2]. We perform the following steps:

- Compose $\mathcal{D}$ with T_φ to obtain $\mathcal{D} \,|||\, T_\varphi$.
- Check if $\mathcal{D} \,|||\, T_\varphi$ has a (fair) computation, such that $s_0[x_\varphi] = 0$. $\mathcal{D} \,|||\, T_\varphi$ has such a computation iff $\mathcal{D}$ does not satisfy φ.

As you can see, a tester can be used anywhere instead of an automaton. Indeed, we can always obtain an automaton from a tester by restricting the initial state to interpret x_φ as *true*.

10   Run-Time Monitoring with Testers

The problem of *run-time monitoring* can be described as follows. Assume a reactive system $\mathcal{D}$ and a PSL formula φ, which formalizes a property that $\mathcal{D}$ should satisfy. In order to test the conjecture that $\mathcal{D}$ satisfies φ, we construct a program M, to which we refer as a *monitor*, that observes individual behaviors of $\mathcal{D}$. Behaviors of $\mathcal{D}$ are fed to the monitor state by state. After observing the finite sequence $\sigma : s_0, \ldots, s_k$ for some $k \geq 0$, we expect the monitor to be able to answer a subset of the following questions:

1. Does σ satisfy the formula φ?
2. Is φ *negatively determined* by σ? That is, is it the case that $\sigma \cdot \eta \not\models \varphi$ for all finite or infinite completions η.
3. Is φ *positively determined* by σ? That is, is it the case that $\sigma \cdot \eta \models \varphi$ for all finite or infinite completions η?
4. Is φ $\sigma-$*monitorable*? That is, is it the case that there exists a finite η such that φ is positively or negatively determined by $\sigma \cdot \eta$. If $\mathcal{D}$ is expected to run forever then it is useless to continue monitoring after observing σ such that φ is not $\sigma-$*monitorable*.

Solving the above questions leads to a creation of an *optimal* monitor - a monitor that extracts as much information as possible from the observation σ. In particular, an optimal monitor detects a violation of the property as early as possible. Of course, a monitor can do better if we supply it with some implementation details of the system $\mathcal{D}$, which may allow to deduce a violation even earlier [13]. In the extreme case, when a monitor knows everything about $\mathcal{D}$ the monitoring problem is reduced to model checking.

10.1   Monitoring with Testers

Let $\mathcal{D} : \langle P, \Theta, R, \mathcal{J}, F \rangle$ be a reactive system with observable variables P, and let φ be a PSL formula over P, which validity with respect to $\mathcal{D}$ we wish to test. Assume that $T_\varphi = \langle V_\varphi, \Theta_\varphi, R_\varphi, \mathcal{J}_\varphi, F_\varphi \rangle$ is the tester for φ, where the variables $V_\varphi = P \cup A$ are partitioned into the variables of $\mathcal{D}$ and additional auxiliary variables A. Let x_φ be the distinguished output variable of the tester T.

For an assertion (state formula) α, we define the R_φ-*predecessor* and R_φ-*successor* of α by

- $R_\varphi \diamond \alpha = \exists V'_\varphi : R_\varphi(V_\varphi, V'_\varphi) \wedge \alpha'$
- $\alpha \diamond R_\varphi = unprime(\exists V_\varphi : R_\varphi(V_\varphi, V'_\varphi) \wedge \alpha)$

where *unprime* simply replaces all next state variables with current state variable. Remember that the transition relation R_φ has two copies of each variable, one representing a current state and the other copy (a primed one) the next state.

Let $\sigma \ : \ s_0, s_1, \ldots, s_k$ be a finite observation produced by system $\mathcal{D}$. That is, a sequence of evaluations of the variables P. We define the *symbolic monitoring trace* $\mathcal{M} = \alpha_0, \alpha_1, \ldots, \alpha_k$ as the sequence of assertions given by

$$\alpha_0 = \Theta_\varphi \wedge x_\varphi \wedge (P{=}s_0), \text{ and } \alpha_{i+1} = (\alpha_i \diamond R_\varphi) \wedge (P{=}s_{i+1}), i \in [0, k),$$

where $P = s$ stands for $\bigwedge_{v \in P} v = s[v]$.

Essentially, α_i represents a "current" state of the monitor, which is more precisely just a set of states of the tester T_φ. Whenever the system makes a step from s_i to s_{i+1}, a monitor takes the corresponding step from α_i to α_{i+1} according to the transition relation R_φ and the interpretation of the propositions by the state s_{i+1}. The whole process can be described as, on the fly, synchronous, composition of the system and the tester, in which the later is determinized using classical subset construction. Note that we only need to worry about the existential non-determinism, A similar approach, but for alternating automata was also used for a so called breadth-first traversal in [**?**]. The monitoring sequence can be used to answer the first of the monitoring questions as stated by the following claim:

Claim 1 (Finitary satisfaction). *For a PSL formula* φ*, the finite sequence* $\sigma \ : \ s_0, s_1,$ $\ldots, s_k$ *satisfies* φ*, i.e.,* $\sigma \models \varphi$*, iff the formula* $\alpha_k \ \wedge \ F_\varphi$ *is satisfiable.*

The correctness of the claim results from the following observations. The tester T_φ can be interpreted as a non-deterministic automaton for acceptance of sequences satisfying φ if we insist that x_φ is *true* in the initial state. Furthermore, the assertion α_k represents all the automaton (tester) states which can be reached after reading the input σ. If any such evaluation is consistent with the assertion F_φ, which represents the set of final states, then this points to an accepting run of the automaton.

10.2 Deciding Negative Determinacy

Claim 1 has settled the first monitoring task. Next we consider one of the remaining tasks. Namely, we show how to decide whether, for a given σ, $\sigma \cdot \eta \not\models \varphi$ for all infinite or finite completions η.

In order to do this, we have to perform some offline calculations as a preparation. We generalize the notion of a single-step predecessor to an *eventual* predecessor by defining

$$R_\varphi^* \diamond \alpha = \alpha \vee R_\varphi \diamond \alpha \vee R_\varphi \diamond (R_\varphi \diamond \alpha) \vee \cdots$$

Consider the fix-point expression presented in Equation (1).

$$feas = [\mu X : (R_\varphi \diamond X) \vee F_\varphi] \ \bigvee \ [\nu Y : R_\varphi \diamond Y \ \wedge \ \bigwedge_{J \in \mathcal{J}} R_\varphi^* \diamond (Y \wedge J_\varphi)] \quad (1)$$

The first expression captures all the states that have a path to a final state. The second expression captures a maximal set of tester states Y such that every non-final state $s \in Y$ has an Y-successor and, for every justice requirement J, s has a Y-path leading to some Y-state which also satisfies J. The following can be proven:

Claim 2 (Feasible states). *The set feas characterizes the set of all states which origi-nate an uninitialized computation.*

Assuming that we have precomputed the assertion *feas*, the following claim tells us how to decide whether a finite observation σ is sufficient in order to negatively determine φ:

Claim 3 (Negative Determinacy). *The PSL formula φ is negatively determined by the finite observation $\sigma = s_0, s_1, \ldots, s_k$ iff $\alpha_k \wedge feas$ is unsatisfiable.*

The claim is justified by the observation that $\alpha_k \wedge feas$ being unsatisfiable means that there is no way to complete the finite observation σ into a finite or infinite observation which will satisfy φ.

10.3 Deciding Positive Determinacy

In order to decide positive determinacy, we need to monitor the incoming observations not only by assertion sequences which attempt to validate φ but also by an assertion sequence which attempts to refute φ. Consequently, we define the *negative symbolic monitoring trace* $\mathcal{M}^- = \beta_0, \beta_1, \ldots, \beta_k$ by

$$\beta_0 = \Theta_\varphi \wedge \neg x_\varphi \wedge (P = s_0), \text{ and } \beta_{i+1} = (\beta_i \diamond R_\varphi) \wedge (P = s_{i+1}), i \in [0, k)$$

Claim 4 (Positive Determinacy). *The PSL formula φ is positively determined by the finite observation $\sigma = s_0, s_1, \ldots, s_k$ iff $\beta_k \wedge feas$ is unsatisfiable.*

10.4 Detecting Non-monitorable Prefixes

Unfortunately, not all properties can be effectively monitored. Consider a property $\square \diamond p$, which is not σ-monitorable for any σ prefix. No useful information can be gained after observing a finite prefix if the property only depends on the things that must happen infinitely often. A good monitor should be able to detect such situations and alert the user. Next, we show how to decide whether φ is σ-monitorable, for a given σ.

Let $\mathcal{M} = \alpha_0, \alpha_1, \ldots, \alpha_k$ and $\mathcal{M}^- = \beta_0, \beta_1, \ldots, \beta_k$ be the positive and negative symbolic monitoring traces that correspond to σ. Let Γ represent a set of assertions. We define the R_φ-*successor* and *eventual* R_φ-*successor* of Γ by

- $\Gamma \diamond R_\varphi = \{(\gamma \diamond R_\varphi) \wedge (P = s) \mid \gamma \in \Gamma, s \text{ is some state of the system } \mathcal{D}\}$
- $\Gamma \diamond R_\varphi^* = \Gamma \vee R_\varphi \diamond \Gamma \vee R_\varphi \diamond (R_\varphi \diamond \Gamma) \vee \cdots$

Claim 5 (Monitorability). *A PSL formula φ is σ-monitorable, where $\sigma = s_0, s_1, \ldots, s_k$, iff there exists an assertion γ such that either $\gamma \in (\alpha_k \diamond R_\varphi^*)$ or $\gamma \in (\beta_k \diamond R_\varphi^*)$, and $(\gamma \wedge feas)$ is unsatisfiable.*

The claim almost immediately follows from the definition of σ-monitorable proper-ties, Claim 3, and Claim 4. Note that the algorithm can be very inefficient due to the double-exponential complexity. One way to cope with the problem is to consider each state in α_k and β_k individually. The idea is very similar to never-violate states intro-duced in [5]. A state of a Büchi automaton is called *never violate* if, on any input letter, there is a transition to another *never-violate* state. Similarly, we can define *never-satisfy* states and obtain a reasonable approximation to the problem of monitorability. Note that the complexity of this solution is exponential, which hopefully can be managed using BDD's. In addition, the never-violate and never-satisfy states can be pre-computed before the monitoring starts. However, it remains to be seen whether the approximation works well in practice.

11 Related Work

It is very interesting to compare our approach to the one suggested in [4], which uses alternating automata. We have already mentioned some high-level distinctions between testers and alternating automata in Section 4. However, the question remains about which construction is better. It turns out that both approaches yield very similar results, assuming universal non-determinism is removed from the alternating automata. Although that is a somewhat unexpected conclusion, it is not hard to justify it.

Without going into the details of algorithm described in [4], it is enough to mention that each state in the alternating automaton is essentially labeled with a sub-formula. To remove universal non-determinism, we follow classical subset construction. In particular, we assign a boolean variable x for each sub-formula φ to represent whether the corresponding state is in the subset. One can easily verify that x is nothing more but the output variable of the tester T_φ and follows the same transition relation.

To finish the partial determinization and define the final states in the new automata, the authors of [4] use the same trick with double representation as we do. At this step, the automata obtained after the subset construction is composed with itself via a cartesian product. This step is conceptually the same as introducing Y variables in the tester construction. However, we only introduce the extra variables when dealing with SERE's. For the LTL portion of the formula, the tester construction avoids the quadratic blow out associated with the cartesian product by essentially building a generalized Büchi with multiple acceptance sets (i.e., multiple justice requirements). If one to insist on a single acceptance set, our approach would yield an automaton identical to the one obtained in [4]. Note that, for symbolic model checking, using a generalized Büchi automaton might be more efficient then the corresponding Büchi automaton.

While our approach may not necessarily yield a better automaton, it never performs worse, and there are several significant benefits. Since model checking is very expensive, we expect that, in practice, automata for commonly occurring sub-properties will be hand-tuned. In such a case, it is more beneficial to work with testers since an alternating automaton requires an exponential blow-up due to universal non-determinism that cannot be locally optimized.

Another important advantage is that PSL testers can be used anywhere instead of LTL testers. For example, if one were to extend CTL* with PSL operators, our approach combined with [9] immediately gives a model checking algorithm for the new logic.

12 Conclusion

In this paper, we have shown a new approach towards model checking logic PSL, recently introduced as a new standard for specifying hardware properties. Our approach is based on testers that, unlike automata, are highly compositional, which is very advantageous in the context of PSL.

In addition, we have described a framework for symbolic run-time monitoring. In particular, we have identified some of the major questions that a good monitor should be able to answer and shown how to answer those questions using symbolic algorithms.

Acknowledgement

The authors wish to thank the anonymous reviewers as well as Cindy Eisner for their helpful comments.

References

1. Accellera Organization, Inc. *Property Specification Language Reference Manual, Version 1.01*, 2003. http://www.accellera.org/.
2. E.M. Clarke andO. Grumberg and D.A. Peled. *Model checking*. MIT Press, 2000.
3. A.K. Chandra, D.C. Kozen, and L.J. Stockmeyer. Alternation. *Journal of ACM*, 28(1):114–133, 1981.
4. Bustan D., Fisman D., and Havlicek J.   Automata Construction for PSL.   2005. http://www.wisdom.weizmann.ac.il/dana/publicat/automta_constructionTR.pdf.
5. Marcelo d'Amorim and Grigore Rosu. Efficient monitoring of omega-languages. In *CAV*, pages 364–378, 2005.
6. Cindy Eisner, Dana Fisman, John Havlicek, Michael Gordon, Anthony McIsaac, and David Van Campenhout.   Formal Syntax and Semantics of PSL.   2003. http://www.wisdom.weizmann.ac.il/dana/publicat/formal_semantics_standalone.pdf.
7. John E. Hopcroft and Jeffrey D. Ullman. *Introduction to Automata Theory, Languages, and Computation*. Addison Wesley, Reading, Massachussetts, 1979.
8. Y. Kesten, A. Pnueli, and L. Raviv. Algorithmic verification of linear temporal logic specifications. In *Proc. 25th Int. Colloq. Aut. Lang. Prog.*, volume 1443 of *Lect. Notes in Comp. Sci.*, pages 1–16, 1998.
9. Yonit Kesten and Amir Pnueli. A compositional approach to CTL* verification. *Theoretical Computer Science*, 331:397–428, 2005.
10. Z. Manna and A. Pnueli. *Temporal Verification of Reactive Systems: Safety*. Springer-Verlag, New York, 1995.
11. Satoru Miyano and Takeshi Hayashi. Alternating finite automata on ω-words. *Theoretical Computer Science*, 32:321–330, 1984.
12. Amir Pnueli and Aleksandr Zaks. PSL model checking and run-time verification via testers. Technical Report, Dept. of Computer Science, New York University, 2006.
13. Amir Pnueli, Aleksandr Zaks, and Lenore Zuck. Monitoring interfaces for faults. In H. Barringer, B. Finkbeiner, Y. Gurevich, and H. Sipma, editors, *Fifth International Workshop on Run-time Verification (RV)*, July 2005. Edinburgh, Scotland, UK.
14. M.Y. Vardi and P. Wolper. An automata-theoretic approach to automatic program verification. In *Proc. First IEEE Symp. Logic in Comp. Sci.*, pages 332–344, 1986.

Formal Methods for Security: Lightweight Plug-In or New Engineering Discipline

Werner Stephan

German Research Center for Artificial Intelligence (DFKI GmbH)
Stuhlsatzenhausweg 3, 66123 Saarbrücken, Germany
Werner.Stephan@dfki.de

Abstract. This contribution discusses two main lines of developments concerning the use of formal methods in security engineering. Fully automated and highly specialized methods that hide most of the formal theory from its users are compared to formal security models centered around explicit formal system models. It is argued that only the latter offer the perspective to comprehensively control the development process with its various security aspects and phases. In putting more emphasis on the combination of theories, fragmentation could be overcome by an integration of the specialized methods that are presently still applied in isolation.

1 Introduction

For most of the questions concerning the industrial perspective of formal techniques including the topics addressed at this I-Day there will be no simple answers. The current situation in formal methods is characterized by a vast amount of approaches most often pursued in isolation and difficult to overlook even by experts. To assess obstacles, potential benefits, and costs for an industrial use, first of all it is therefore necessary to roughly classify the main lines of development.

In the author's view, approaches like the AbsInt tool for execution time analysis [2] and the ongoing Boogie development [6], are very likely to be adopted on a broad basis by industrial users. There is no reason not to believe that in security engineering program analysis to detect covert channels, following approaches developed in [1] and specialized tools for analyzing security protocols, like the AVISPA tool [3] are on the right track toward commercial applications.

Such approaches *hide* a deep and complex theory and highly sophisticated implementation[1] behind a front end that seamlessly fits to existing, well established programming environments and notations. They are easy to use since the formal analysis is carried out *automatically* with results that can be interpreted directly in the given context. Hiding the internal structure of the underlying model also provides protection against *inadequate usage*. Finally, the *extra costs* for the acquisition and application of these tools make no real difference, neglecting the expenses for research that was necessary to develop them.

---

[1] From this point of view to call them "lightweight plugins'" is much too disrespectful.

J. Misra, T. Nipkow, and E. Sekerinski (Eds.): FM 2006, LNCS 4085, pp. 587–591, 2006.
© Springer-Verlag Berlin Heidelberg 2006

However, even if support for error prone and tedious activities is offered at a high level of expertise beyond that of typical human experts, and even if the approaches scale up to the size of real world applications, their isolated use will limit the impact of formal methods on the overall development process. Fragmentation seems to be a consequence of the advantages mentioned above.

The strength in automatic problem solving comes along with restrictions to certain aspects, like protocol correctness, and development phases, like coding. Hiding the underlying formal models and theory makes it difficult to adapt these methods to new scenarios and, above all, *combine* them into an integrated approach necessary for a comprehensive treatment of complex developments. A multi-applicative smart card, for example, might use access control to protect the applications (against each other), protocols to communicate with the outside world, in particular to download new applications, and non-generic but security critical mechanisms inside the applications.

What seems to be missing is an explicit, sufficiently rich system model at various levels of abstraction that is shared by highly specialized analysis methods for generic mechanisms like access control and cryptographic protocols.

The author is not completely confident that we will see formal methods used to *control*, *record*, and *assess* comprehensive developments on a scientifically objectified basis in the near future. Nevertheless, after arguing that the program indicated above seems to suit the spirit of the Common Criteria framework, some encouraging own experiences will be mentioned as a basis for a brief discussion of steps necessary to keep this vision on the agenda.

2   Formal Methods in the Common Criteria

To a large extent the engineering practice for critical systems will (and in the opinion of the author has to be) shaped by mandatory guidelines like the Common Criteria (CC) for IT security. Formal methods will never leave the state of an unsystematic, accidental, and largely incompatible use without such frameworks. Most of the (commercial) formal activities of the DFKI group related to IT security were part of developments intended to meet the CC requirements.

Although not stipulating a particular development method or life cycle model, the CC insists on laying down requirements and tracking them through appropriately documented design stages connected by well defined relationships.

In our work we adopt the view that the *formal* Security Model (as required by the CC) should consist of an (abstract) specification of the relevant parts of the system together with certain security mechanisms (or measures). Although this is not explicitly requested we then proved that the intended security properties (or principles) are actually satisfied. This is the place where the specific techniques for modeling and proving security properties, like protocol analysis [3,7] and information flow analysis at the specification level [5], come into play. In this context specialized automated techniques, if integrated into the overall formal model, will lower the burden of proof work. However, in this setting one has to be prepared to establish a formal relationship to the system model and to possibly integrate several security issues.

To allow for such an integration an explicit formal system model is needed. This has to be given by the developer using a specification language which is expressive and general enough to cover all necessary aspects. In most cases this means that in the general case we have to carry out interactive proofs.

Whether or not one day automatic techniques used *in this setting* will reduce the interactive proof work to some residue that can be neglected remains an open question.

The formal model also serves as a starting point for a subsequent refinement to technical solutions, for example on platforms like smart cards. This includes the relationship to non-formal technical documents. In cases where the specification technique did not guarantee (logical) consistency, refinements were used for model construction by prototypic implementations.

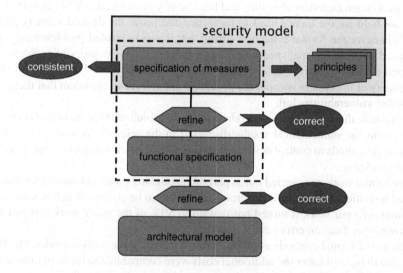

Fig. 1. CC-Components for Formal Development

During the design stage formal debugging techniques are useful since interactive proofs still are very sensible to changes despite reasonable progress in (proof) reuse.

Yet it should be stated that the use of formal methods advocated here can be "trivialized" (intendedly or unintendedly). This is due to the open nature of formal modeling which is difficult to restrict by guidelines or official CC interpretations. For example, a pure restatement of, say, some access control rules without relation to a system model and its refinement or the proof of information flow properties realized by them will not offer much benefit except that the formal[2] requirements of the CC are (possibly) met. Such a use of formal techniques will sooner or later discredit the whole community.

---

[2] In the legal sense.

3 Experience

The group at DFKI developed several security models as part of industrial consortia following the scheme above. Specifications and proofs were carried out in the Verification Support Environment (VSE) [4].

In all cases the formal model covered the critical part of the system under consideration. Moreover, the models contained all details and cases mentioned in the non-formal design documents.

In particular, when discussing the possible benefits of formal methods, this working use of formal methods should well be distinguished from the idealized and simplified models often appearing in case studies performed to *demonstrate* the principal theory behind some method.

The formal specifications were readable and understandable by most of the other (technical) team members after they had been briefly introduced to VSE. However, this does not hold for the theory used to formulate and prove the desired security properties. Whenever the formal reflection (using that theory) revealed problems they were discussed using the formal specification as a reference. The majority of problems was detected (by our experts) while writing down the specification. However, due to the complexity of the system without the proofs no one felt really confident that there were no *further* vulnerabilities left.

Again note that it is not enough to show that some solution is secure *in principle*. This is sufficient for mathematical results discussed in the scientific community. Here we use formal methods to control developments in all their detail using tools that guarantee sound reasoning.

The formal work was carried out as part of the ongoing project including revisions. It caused no critical delays. Redoing proofs turned out to be critical. When in some cases we monitored our work it turned out that up to 50% of the proof work resulted from (our own) specification errors and revisions.

The use of formal methods as outlined above increased the costs considerably. However, due to our estimates the additional costs were comparable to those of other expert teams.

Taking all this as an indication that formal modeling and analysis along the lines briefly described above is not just a mere vision, what are the necessary steps on the road to a comprehensive use of formal methods in security engineering?

- All of our developments were basically built from scratch. Except for the basic modeling techniques (abstract data types, state based systems, concurrency, information flow, protocol traces) we could not build on any formal (security) engineering experiences manifested in guidelines or even generic models (or parts thereof). To develop such patterns for formal modeling on top of the existing theories and to extend these where necessary from an application oriented point of view seems to be the most important task.
- In particular, notions of refinement for security mechanisms (analyzed in a formal way) have to be developed.
- Combination of theories is another critical issue.
- In the academic community there seems not to be enough appreciation for the kind of work indicated above.

- On the other hand collaboration with industrial partners (for example in application oriented research projects) is absolutely necessary to obtain the appropriate domain knowledge.
- The academic community should take part in and (try to) influence the further development of criteria like the CC.

References

1. Andrei Sabelfeld and David Sands. A Per Model of Secure Information Flow in Sequential Programs. In *European Symposium on Programming*, pages 40–58, 1999
2. AbsInt: Advanced Compiler Technology for Embedded Systems. http://www.absint.com
3. The AVISPA project. http://www.avispa-project.org/
4. Dieter Hutter, Bruno Langenstein, Claus Sengler, Jörg H. Siekmann, Werner Stephan, and Andreas Wolpers. Verification support environment (vse). *High Integrity Systems*, 1(6): 523–530, 1996.
5. Heiko Mantel. Information Flow Control and Applications – Bridging a Gap. In Jose Nuno Olivera and Pamela Zave, editors, *FME 2001: Formal Methods for Increasing Software Productivity, International Symposium of Formal Methods Europe*, pages 153–172, LNCS 2021, Springer, Berlin, Germany, 2001
6. Leino, K. R. M. and Müller, P. Modular verification of static class invariants. In Fitzgerald, J. and Hayes, I. and Tarlecki, A., editors, *Formal Methods (FM)*, pages 26 – 42, LNCS 3582, Springer-Verlag, 2005
7. L. C. Paulson. The inductive approach to verifying cryptographic protocols. *Journal of Computer Security*, 6:85–128, 1998.

Formal Methods in the Security Business: Exotic Flowers Thriving in an Expanding Niche

David von Oheimb

Siemens Corporate Technology, Munich, Germany
David.von.Oheimb@siemens.com

Abstract. Formal methods in the industrial wild, outside the academic greenhouse, are still considered rather exotic, or even esoteric. Sometimes they are admired, more often smiled at, and most times simply ignored. There are some niches, though, where they display their abstract beauty. One of those places offering suitable environmental conditions is security. Which are the specific fertilizers there? Which particular sub-species have proven versatile and sturdy enough to survive in harsh industrial climate? Who recognizes the strong blessings of their hardly accessible blossoms? We share our grower's experience with them in the security field.

Keywords: Formal methods, security, software engineering, evaluation, models.

1 Security as a Software Engineering Problem

In the development of large IT systems, design errors and implementation bugs inevitably occur. Similarly to safety-critical systems, systems involving security-sensitive data face high risks because their failure can cause great damage. The risk involved with them is even higher than with safety-critical systems, because their deficiencies will not only cause problems accidentally, but will be searched for actively and exploited systematically.

One cannot expect to cope with the problem by legal or educational means, and organizational and physical measures have limited strength and scope. So the only really effective way to prevent attacks is by removing any potential loopholes and vulnerabilities. This is hard to achieve though: since security is a non-functional and holistic property that pervades the whole system and thus intricate to specify, and since systems are usually fairly complex, security flaws are notoriously hard to avoid, find, and correct. It's even harder to convince oneself, or one's contractors/customers, of the absence of such flaws.

2 The Solution Offered by Formal Methods

System security can only be approximated, by careful requirements analysis, systematic design and development, and extensive reviews and checks during all development phases. Formal methods provide the most rigorous tools for this.

J. Misra, T. Nipkow, and E. Sekerinski (Eds.): FM 2006, LNCS 4085, pp. 592–597, 2006.
© Springer-Verlag Berlin Heidelberg 2006

During requirements analysis, abstract models help keeping the overview (by concentration on the essentials) and understanding the security issues and by a systematic approach, e.g. generic patterns simplifying the analysis.

During design and documentation, formalizations enhance the quality of specifications and other descriptions by preventing ambiguities, incompleteness, and inconsistencies.

During implementation, formal analysis can be used for systematically testing — or even verifying with mathematical precision — the correctness of the actual product wrt. its specification.

Although formal methods usually require high sophistication and large effort, in the security area the risks are often so high that it still pays to use them since they offer a higher level of assurance than any other known method. This explains why IT developers like Siemens are willing to apply them for their most security-critical products and solutions, and why standardized and widely used security evaluation criteria like the Common Criteria require their use for higher levels of assurance.

The use of security evaluation and certification is motivated in two ways:

intrinsically: developers can use it for internal quality control

extrinsically: developers are forced into it by market pressure or, more often, by legal requirements. According to our observations, in most cases this form of motivation is the decisive factor.

3   Formal Security Modeling

Every formal method naturally requires a formal model of the system to be analyzed. A *formal security model* is an abstract description (in an appropriate formal notation) of the real system and its desired properties, focusing on the relevant security issues.

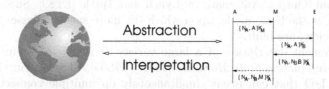

The description includes the *security policy*, defining what actions, data flow, etc. is allowed, typically by a relationship between subjects and objects. The model usually describes also the mechanisms that are meant to enforce the given policy, typically in terms of system state or sequences of states. Security verification can then check (at the abstraction level of the model) whether the mechanisms actually enforce the policy. Even if the model is not used for subsequent testing or verification, the very act of producing a formal model is already of enormous value, since many errors already show up during this process.

Several factors influence the shape of a formal model.

The formality level should be adequate:
- the more formal, the more precision
- the less formal, the less special skills are required

The choice of formalism depends on:
- the application domain, modeler's experience, tool availability, ...
- its quality: it should be simple, expressive, flexible, and mature

The abstraction level should be:
- high enough to maintain overview and to minimize efforts
- low enough not to loose important detail

The use of refinement promises to offer the best of both high-level and low-level descriptions, yet at the cost of some extra effort

When formalizing a system, information on the following is required.

System architecture: which components exist and how they are connected

Security-related concepts: e.g., actors, objects, states, messages, ...

Threats, security goals, and objectives: describing which attacks shall be countered, e.g. for integrity: which data contents are only allowed to be modified by whom during which times, or on transit from where to where

Security mechanisms: their relation to the goals and how they are applied, e.g. who signs which contents for what purpose and where signatures are checked. They should be described precisely but at high level, e.g., abstract message format/contents but not concrete syntax.

There are four classes of practically relevant formal security models, about which we briefly share our experience.

3.1 Automata Models

The most general way of describing systems at an abstraction level suitable for security analysis is by state transition automata. Many such formalisms exist, e.g. the Input/Output Automata by Lynch and Tuttle [LT89]. Such automata can be seen as the basic model upon which the more specific classes of models, described below, are built.

For convenient description of a large variety of reactive systems, we have introduced *Interacting State Machines (ISMs)* [OL04], whose distinctive feature is buffered I/O that can occur simultaneously on multiple connections. ISM models

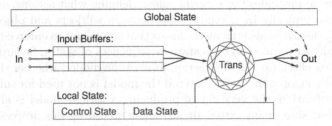

can be verified with the interactive theorem prover Isabelle [NPW02]. We have
applied ISMs when updating the Lotz-Kessler-Walter model [LKW99] employed
as the formal security model of the Infineon SLE 66 smart card processor, which
— with the help of the LKW model — was the first of its kind to receive an
EAL5 certification. An ISM model [OLW05] was employed also for the EAL5
certification of the memory management of the successor chip, the SLE 88.

3.2 Access Control Models

Classical access control models, like the well-known Bell-LaPadula model [BL73],
have proven too restricted for practical use. Currently much more important are
role-based access control (RBAC) models [SCFY96]. Subjects are related with
roles, which may be hierarchically structured, and finally roles are related with
access rights to objects.

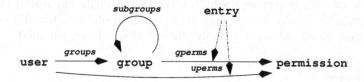

We have used an RBAC model to describe the complex access control policies
of a medical information system. It involves two independent hierarchies, one of
roles and sub-roles determining privileges to perform certain actions, and one
of groups and subgroups determining the permissions to access certain data elements. When we modeled the system according to the specifications provided
by our customers, we asked them many "nagging questions", which lead to clar-
ifications that boosted the quality of the specifications.

3.3 Information Flow Models

Classical information flow models include the noninterference model by Goguen
and Meseguer [GM82] and many others, and prominent recent examples include
[Man03]. They describe which information may flow between which domains in
a very abstract way such that they can capture also indirect and partial flow of
information.

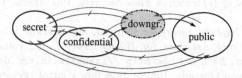

Although we have contributed to this research field ourselves [Ohe04], we
consider such models on the one hand too powerful and on the other hand too
difficult to be of much practical use these days.

3.4 Crypto Protocol Models

Probably the most successful class of security models so far are crypto protocol models describing the message traffic of security protocols. Mostly secrecy and authentication goals can be specified and then verified automatically using model-checkers tailored for this application.

We have participated in a recent EU-funded project called *Automated Validation of Internet Security Protocols and Applications (AVISPA)* [AH-03], which dealt with the subject very successfully. One of its highlight applications was the H.530 authentication for mobile roaming in a multimedia scenario. Two vulnerabilities were found and corrected, and the solution is being patented.

References

[AH-03]   The AVISPA project homepage, 2003. http://www.avispa-project.org/.

[BL73]   D.E. Bell and L. LaPadula. Secure Computer Systems: Mathematical Foundations (NTIS AD-770 768), A Mathematical Model (NTIS AD-771 543), A Refinement of the Mathematical Model (NTIS AD-780 528). Technical Report MTR 2547, Mitre Corporation, Bedford MA, 1973.

[GM82]   J. A. Goguen and J. Meseguer. Security policies and security models. In *Symposium on Security and Privacy*. IEEE Computer Society Press, 1982.

[LKW99]   Volkmar Lotz, Volker Kessler, and Georg Walter. A Formal Security Model for Microprocessor Hardware. In *Proc. of FM'99 World Congress on Formal Methods*, volume 1708 of *LNCS*, pages 718–737. Springer-Verlag, 1999.

[LT89]   Nancy Lynch and Mark Tuttle. An Introduction to Input/Output Automata. *CWI Quarterly*, 2(3):219–246, 1989. http://theory.lcs.mit.edu/tds/papers/Lynch/CWI89.html.

[Man03]   H. Mantel. *A Uniform Framework for the Formal Specification and Verification of Information Flow Security*. PhD thesis, Univ. d. Saarlandes, 2003.

[NPW02]   Tobias Nipkow, Lawrence Paulson, and Markus Wenzel. *Isabelle/HOL — A Proof Assistant for Higher-Order Logic*, volume 2283 of *LNCS*. Springer, 2002. See also http://isabelle.in.tum.de/docs.html.

[Ohe04]   David von Oheimb. Information flow control revisited: Noninfluence = Noninterference + Nonleakage. In P. Samarati, P. Ryan, D. Gollmann, and R. Molva, editors, *Computer Security – ESORICS 2004*, volume 3193 of *LNCS*, pages 225–243. Springer, 2004. http://ddvo.net/papers/Noninfluence.html.

[OL04]   David von Oheimb and Volkmar Lotz. Formal Security Analysis with In-
            teracting State Machines. In Gerwin Klein, editor, *Proc. NICTA Formal
            Methods Workshop on Operating Systems Verification*, pages 37–72, Syd-
            ney, Australia, 2004. National ICT Australia, Technical Report 0401005T-
            1. http://ddvo.net/papers/FSA_ISM.html.

[OLW05]   David von Oheimb, Volkmar Lotz, and Georg Walter.   Analyzing
            SLE 88 memory management security using Interacting State Ma-
            chines. *International Journal of Information Security*, 4(3):155–171, 2005.
            http://ddvo.net/papers/SLE88_MM.html.

[SCFY96]   Ravi S. Sandhu, Edward J. Coyne, Hal L. Feinstein, and Charles E.
            Youman. Role-based access control models. *IEEE Computer*, 29(2):38–47,
            1996.

Connector-Based Software Development: Deriving Secure Protocols

(Abstract)

Dusko Pavlovic

Kestrel Institute, Palo Alto,
California, USA
dusko@kestrel.edu

While most branches of engineering consist of methodologies for building complex systems from simple components, formulating incremental and compositional methods for Security Engineering has been a daunting task: in general, security properties are not preserved under refinement or composition. The reason is that the nondestructive composition operations require that their static assumptions about the environment are maintained; but Security Engineering is concerned with dynamic, adversarial environments, and what happens when the assumptions fail.

The problem is compounded by the fact that establishing security of a system often involves not only logical and computational structures, but also a wide range of mathematical methods of cryptography. The notions of security thus span across a multi-dimensional space of methods and approaches, which have not yet been systematized on a solid semantical foundation. But practice is faster than theory, and complex secure protocols are being designed and deployed in many systems, often complex and critical.

The goal of our research effort towards the Protocol Derivation System (PDS), and of our development towards the Protocol Derivation Assistant (PDA) is to capture, formalize and advance the sound rules and methods of incremental protocol development, that have evolved in practice of Security Engineering. In this talk, I shall summarize the results of this effort so far, and present a case study of GDoI, the standard protocol for group communication and multicast over IPSec [3]. Although carefully designed and thoroughly analyzed, through seven internet drafts prior to standardization, this protocol turned out to have vulnerabilities invalidating the basic stated requirements: an attempt to derive it incrementally, together with the desired security properties, led to a derivation of an attack, which in turn allowed evaluation of the repair options [4]. The derivations were built and will be presented using the Protocol Derivation Assistant, a development environment with support for collaboration and integration [1,2].

GDoI was analyzed in joint work with Catherine Meadows. PDA can be freely downloaded from [1].

J. Misra, T. Nipkow, and E. Sekerinski (Eds.): FM 2006, LNCS 4085, pp. 598–599, 2006.
© Springer-Verlag Berlin Heidelberg 2006

References

1. Matthias Anlauff and Dusko Pavlovic. The protocol derivation assistant, 2005. URL http://www.kestrel.edu/software/pda.
2. Matthias Anlauff, Dusko Pavlovic, Richard Waldinger, and Stephen Westfold. Proving authentication properties in the protocol derivation assistant, May 2006. submitted.
3. M. Baugher, B. Weis, T. Hardjono, and H. Harney. The group domain of interpretation. Network Working Group, Internet Engineering Task Force. RFC 3547, July 2003.
4. Catherine Meadows and Dusko Pavlovic. Deriving, attacking and defending the gdoi protocol. In Peter Ryan, Pierangela Samarati, Dieter Gollmann, and Refik Molva, editors, *Proceedings of ESORICS 2004*, volume 3193 of *Lecture Notes in Computer Science*, pages 53–72. Springer Verlag, 2004.

Model-Based Security Engineering for Real

Jan Jürjens

Software & Systems Engineering,
Dep. of Informatics, TU Munich, Germany
http://www4.in.tum.de/~juerjens

Abstract. We give an overview over a soundly based secure software engineering methodology and associated tool-support developed over the last few years under the name of Model-based Security Engineering (MBSE). We focus in particular on applications in industry.

The difficulty of designing security mechanisms correctly has motivated very successful research using mathematical concepts and tools to ensure correct design of security-critical components of bounded size such as security protocols, including [BAN89, KMM94, Low96, Pau98]. Unfortunately, due to a perceived high cost in personnel training and use, formal methods have not yet been employed very widely in industrial development [Hoa96, Hei99, KK04]. To increase industry acceptance in the context of security-critical systems, it would be beneficial to integrate security requirements analysis with a standard development method, which should be easy to learn and to use [CW96]. Also, security concerns must be considered in every phase of software development, from requirements engineering to design, implementation, testing, and deployment [DS00].

Some other challenges for using sound engineering methods for secure systems development exist. Currently a large part of effort both in analyzing and implementing specifications is wasted since these are often formulated imprecisely and unintelligibly, if they exist at all. If increased precision by use of a particular notation brings an additional advantage, such as automated tool support for security analysis, this may however be sufficient incentive for providing it. Since software developers often hesitate to learn a particular formal method to do this, because of limited resources in time and training, one needs to instead use the artifacts that are at any rate constructed in industrial software development. Examples include specification models in the Unified Modeling Language (UML), source code, and configuration data. Also, the boundaries of the specified components with the rest of the system need to be carefully examined, for example with respect to implicit assumptions on the system context. Lastly, a more technical issue is that formalized security properties are not always preserved by refinement, which is the so-called *refinement problem*. Since an implementation is necessarily a refinement of its specification, an implementation of a secure specification may, in such a situation, not be secure, which is clearly undesirable, and also hinders the use of stepwise development. In this paper, we give an overview over an approach that aims to address these problems.

J. Misra, T. Nipkow, and E. Sekerinski (Eds.): FM 2006, LNCS 4085, pp. 600–606, 2006.
© Springer-Verlag Berlin Heidelberg 2006

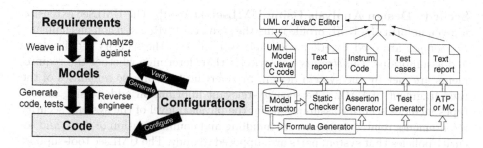

Fig. 1. a) Model-based Security Engineering; b) Model-based Security Tool Suite

Model-based Security Engineering. In MBSE [Jür02, Jür04, Jür05a, Jür05b, Jür06, Jür07], recurring security requirements (such as secrecy, integrity, authenticity and others) and security assumptions on the system environment, can be specified either within a UML specification, or within the source code (Java or C) as annotations. The associated tools [UML04] (Fig. 1b) generate logical formulas formalizing the execution semantics and the annotated security requirements. Automated theorem provers and model checkers automatically establish whether the security requirements hold. If not, a Prolog-based tool automatically generates an attack sequence violating the security requirement, which can be examined to determine and remove the weakness. This way we encapsulate knowledge on prudent security engineering as annotations in models or code and make it available to developers who may not be security experts. Since the analysis that is performed is too sophisticated to be done manually, it is also valuable to security experts.

One can use MBSE within model-based development (Fig. 1a). Here one first constructs a model of the system. Then, the implementation is derived from the model: either automatically using code generation, or manually, in which case one can generate test sequences from the model to establish conformance of the code regarding the model. The goal is to increase the quality of the software while keeping the implementation cost and the time-to-market bounded. For security-critical systems, this approach allows one to consider security requirements from early on in the development process, within the development context, and in a seamless way through the development cycle: One can first check that the system fulfills the relevant security requirements on the design level by analyzing the model and secondly that the code is in fact secure by generating test sequences from the model. However, one can also use our analysis techniques and tools within a traditional software engineering context, or where one has to incorporate legacy systems that were not developed in a model-based way. Here, one starts out with the source code. Our tools extract models from the source code, which can then again be analyzed against the security requirements. Using MBSE, one can incorporate the configuration data (such as user permissions) in the analysis, which is very important for security but often neglected.

Security Design Analysis Using UMLsec [Jür04]. The UMLsec extension is given in form of a UML profile using the standard UML extension mechanisms. *Stereotypes* are used together with *tags* to formulate the security requirements and assumptions. *Constraints* give criteria that determine whether the requirements are met by the system design, by referring to a precise semantics of the used fragment of UML. The security-relevant information added using stereotypes includes security assumptions on the physical level of the system, security requirements related to the secure handling and communication of data, and security policies that system parts are supposed to obey. The UMLsec tool-support in Fig. 1b) can be used to check the constraints associated with UMLsec stereotypes mechanically, based on XMI output of the diagrams from the UML drawing tool in use [UML04, Jür05b]. There is also a framework for implementing verification routines for the constraints associated with the UMLsec stereotypes. Thus advanced users of the UMLsec approach can use this framework to implement verification routines for the constraints of self-defined stereotypes. The semantics for the fragment of UML used for UMLsec is defined in [Jür04] using so-called *UML Machines*, which is a kind of state machine with input/output interfaces similar to Broy's Focus model, whose behavior can be specified in a notation similar to that of Abstract State Machines (ASMs), and which is equipped with UML-type communication mechanisms. On this basis, important security requirements such as secrecy, integrity, authenticity, and secure information flow are defined. To support stepwise development, we show secrecy, integrity, authenticity, and secure information flow to be *preserved* under refinement and the composition of system components. We have also developed an approach that supports the secure development of layered security services (such as layered security protocols). UMLsec can be used to specify and implement security patterns, and is supported by dedicated secure systems development processes, in particular an Aspect-Oriented Modeling approach which separates complex security mechanisms (which implement the security aspect model) from the core functionality of the system (the primary model) in order to allow a security verification of the particularly security-critical parts, and also of the composed model.

Code Security Assurance [Jür05a, Jür06]. Even if specifications exist for the implemented system, and even if these are formally analyzed, there is usually no guarantee that the implementation actually conforms to the specification. To deal with this problem, we use the following approach: After specifying the system in UMLsec and verifying the model against the given security goals as explained above, we make sure that the implementation correctly implements the specification with techniques explained below. In particular, this approach is applicable to legacy systems. In ongoing work, we are automating this approach to free one of the need to manually construct the UMLsec model.

Run-Time Security Monitoring Using Assertions. A simple and effective alternative is to insert security checks generated from the UMLsec specification that remain in the code while in use, for example using the assertion statement that is part of the Java language. These assertions then throw security exceptions when violated at run-time. In a similar way, this can also be done for C code.

Model-Based Test Generation. For performance-intensive applications, it may be preferable not to leave the assertions active in the code. This can be done by making sure by extensive testing that the assertions are always satisfied. We can generate the test sequences automatically from the UMLsec specifications. More generally, this way we can ensure that the code actually conforms to the UMLsec specification. Since complete test coverage is often infeasible, our approach automatically selects those test cases that are particularly sensitive to the specified security requirements.

Automated Code Verification Against Interface Specifications. For highly non-deterministic systems such as those using cryptography, testing can only provide assurance up to a certain degree. For higher levels of trustworthiness, it may therefore be desirable to establish that the code does enforce the annotations by a formal verification of the source code against the UMLsec interface specifications. We have developed an approach that does this automatically and efficiently by proving locally that the security checks in the specification are actually enforced in the source code.

Automated Code Security Analysis. We developed an approach to use automated theorem provers for first-order logic to directly formally verify crypto-based Java implementations based on control flow graphs that are automatically generated (and without first manually constructing an interface specification). It supports an abstract and modular security analysis by using assertions in the source code. Thus large software systems can be divided into small parts for which a formal security analysis can be performed more easily and the results composed. Currently, this approach works especially well with nicely structured code (such as created using the MBSE development process).

Secure Software-Hardware Interfaces. We have tailored the code security analysis approach to software close to the hardware level. More concretely, we considered the industrial Cryptographic Token Interface Standard PKCS 11 which defines how software on untrustworthy hardware can make use of tamper-proof hardware such as smart-cards to perform cryptographic operations on sensitive data. We developed an approach for automated security analysis with first-order logic theorem provers of crypto protocol implementations making use of this standard.

Analyzing Security Configurations. We have also performed research on linking the UMLsec approach with the automated analysis of security-critical configuration data. For example, our tools automatically checks SAP R/3 user permissions for security policy rules formulated as UML specifications [Jür04]. Because of its modular architecture and its standardized interfaces, the tool can be adapted to check security constraints in other kinds of application software, such as firewalls or other access control configurations.

Industrial Applications of MBSE include:

Biometric Authentication. For a project with an industrial partner, MBSE was chosen to support the development of a biometric authentication system at the specification level, where three significant security flaws were found [Jür05b]. We also applied it to the source-code level for a prototypical implementation constructed from the specification [Jür05a].

Common Electronic Purse Specifications. MBSE was applied to a security analysis of the Common Electronic Purse Specifications (CEPS), a candidate for a globally interoperable electronic purse standard supported by organizations representing 90 % of the world's electronic purse cards (including Visa International). We found three significant security weaknesses in the purchase and load transaction protocols [Jür04], proposed improvements to the specifications and showed that these are secure [Jür04]. We also performed a security analysis of a prototypical Java Card implementation of CEPS.

Web-Based Banking Application. In a project with a German bank, MBSE was applied to a web-based banking application to be used by customers to fill out and sign digital order forms [Jür04]. The personal data in the forms must be kept confidential, and orders securely authenticated. The system uses a proprietary client authentication protocol layered over an SSL connection supposed to provide confidentiality and server authentication. Using the MBSE approach, the system architecture and the protocol were specified and verified with regard to the relevant security requirements.

In other applications [Jür04], MBSE was used . . .

- to uncover a flaw in a variant of the Internet protocol TLS proposed at IEEE Infocom 1999, and suggest and verify a correction of the protocol.
- to perform a security verification of the Java implementation Jessie of SSL.
- to correctly employ advanced Java 2 or CORBA security concepts in a way that allows an automated security analysis of the resulting systems.
- for an analysis of the security policies of a German mobile phone operator.
- for a security analysis of the specifications for the German Electronic Health Card in development by the German Ministry of Health.
- for the security analysis of an electronic purse system developed for the Oktoberfest in Munich.
- for a security analysis of an electronic signature pad based contract signing architecture under consideration by a German insurance company.
- in a project with a German car manufacturer for the security analysis of an intranet-based web information system.
- with a German chip manufacturer and a German reinsurance company for security risk assessment, also regarding Return on Security Investment.
- in applications specifically targeted to service-based, health telematics, and automotive systems.

Outlook. Given the current insatisfactory state of computer security in practice, MBSE seems a promising approach, since it enables developers who are not experts in security to make use of security engineering knowledge encapsulated in a widely used design notation. Since there are many highly subtle security requirements which can hardly be verified with the "naked eye", even security experts may profit from this approach. Thus one can avoid mistakes that are difficult to find by testing alone, such as breaches of subtle security requirements, as well as the disadvantages of the "penetrate-and-patch" approach. Since preventing security flaws early in the system life-cycle can significantly reduce costs, this gives a potential for developing securer systems in a cost-efficient way. MBSE has been successfully applied in industrial projects involving German government agencies and major banks, insurance companies, smart card and car manufacturers, and other companies. The approach has been generalized to other application domains such as real-time and dependability. Experiences show that the approach is adequate for use in practice, after relatively little training. On the basis of the book [Jür04] and the associated tutorial material and tools [UML04], usage of UMLsec can in fact be rather easily taught to industrial developers.

References

[BAN89]   M. Burrows, M. Abadi, and R. Needham. A logic of authentication. *Proceedings of the Royal Society, Series A*, 426(1871):233–271, December 1989.

[CW96]   E. Clarke and J. Wing. Formal methods: State of the art and future directions. *ACM Computing Surveys*, 28(4):626–643, 1996.

[DS00]   P. Devanbu and S. Stubblebine. Software engineering for security: a roadmap. In *The Future of Software Engineering (ICSE 2000)*, pages 227–239, 2000.

[Hei99]   C. Heitmeyer. Formal methods for developing software specifications: Paths to wider usage. In H. R. Arabnia, editor, *PDPTA'99*, 1999.

[Hoa96]   C. A. R. Hoare. How did software get so reliable without proof? In *Formal Methods Europe (FME'96)*, volume 1051 of *LNCS*, pages 1–17. Springer, 1996.

[Jür02]   J. Jürjens. UMLsec: Extending UML for secure systems development. In *5th Int. Conf. on the Unified Modeling Language (UML)*, LNCS. Springer, 2002.

[Jür04]   J. Jürjens. *Secure Systems Development with UML*. Springer, 2004.

[Jür05a]   J. Jürjens. Code security analysis of a biometric authentication system using automated theorem provers. In *ACSAC'05*. IEEE, 2005.

[Jür05b]   J. Jürjens. Sound methods and effective tools for model-based security engineering with UML. In *27th Int. Conf. on Softw. Engineering*. IEEE, 2005.

[Jür06]   J. Jürjens. Security analysis of crypto-based Java programs using automated theorem provers. In *21st IEEE/ACM Int. Conf. Autom. Softw. Eng.*, 2006.

[Jür07]   J. Jürjens. *IT-Security*. Springer, 2007. In preparation.

[KK04]   R. Kilian-Kehr. Can formal verification become mainstream in software engineering ? In J. Jürjens, editor, *2nd Works. of the GI-WG FoMSESS*, 2004.

[KMM94]   R. Kemmerer, C. Meadows, and J. Millen. Three systems for cryptographic protocol analysis. *Journal of Cryptology*, 7(2):79–130, Spring 1994.

[Low96]   G. Lowe. Breaking and fixing the Needham-Schroeder public-key protocol using FDR. *Software Concepts and Tools*, 17(3):93–102, 1996.

[Pau98]   L. C. Paulson. The inductive approach to verifying cryptographic protocols. *Journal of Computer Security*, 6(1–2):85–128, 1998.

[UML04]   UMLsec group. Security analysis tool, 2004. http://www.umlsec.org.

Cost Effective Software Engineering for Security

D. Randolph Johnson

National Security Agency, STE 6511, 9800 Savage Road,
Fort Meade, MD, 20755-6511, USA
drjohns@orion.ncsc.mil

Abstract. In this talk I will discuss our experience with one particular development methodology for security related software. I will describe the general principles it follows, the tools used, and the resources needed. Then I will offer some opinions on why this approach is effective and practical for achieving even moderate levels of security. When the goal is a very high level security, I will explain why I believe that at least the general principles, if not the specific details, are probably essential.

1   Introduction

I will begin by describing the development of a security related software system, the Tokeneer ID Station (TIS). I will discuss the nature of the system and the approach taken by the experienced software devlopment professionals at Praxis Critical Systems, now Praxis High Integrity Systems. This work was carried out as an evaluation exercise organized by a research team in my organization. Then I will describe a further exercise in which we had a small group of student interns try to use the same methodology and support tools on the same basic problem. Finally, I will take a step back and make some general comments on the use of formal techniques in the development of security related software.

2   Praxis Professionals Tackle the Problem

2.1   The Problem

Tokeneer is an access control system for a secure enclave such as a secure computer room or laboratory[2]. It is used as a technology demonstration vehicle for token technologies and biometric technologies. By its nature, it is a realistic, but not quite real, security system. The basic usage scenario is that a person approaches a locked door and follows the instructions on a display panel to insert a token, such as a smart card, then places his finger on a fingerprint reader. If the user is known, the token is authentic, and the fingerprint matches the owner of the token, the door is unlocked for a set period of time. Once inside the enclave, he has the privileges authorized for his identity. There are facilities for an alarm, a guard station with emergency override capability, an audit log, etc.

In our exercise, Praxis was hired to develop the control software to the standards called for at Common Criteria EAL5 or better. The Common Criteria is an

J. Misra, T. Nipkow, and E. Sekerinski (Eds.): FM 2006, LNCS 4085, pp. 607–611, 2006.
© Springer-Verlag Berlin Heidelberg 2006

open internation standard for security related software development and evaluation. It has seven Evaluation Assurance Levels, EAL1-EAL7. EAL4 is, roughly,
best commercial practice. By implication, then, EAL5-EAL7 are beyond current
commercial development practices. In particular, they require increasing use of
formal techniques.

2.2   Methodology and Artifacts

The basic development process is really quite conventional in outline. The
added power comes from the use of notations solidly grounded in appropriate
mathematics.

The process began with a review of all available documentation and discussions with the stakeholders. The goal in this stage was an accurate understanding of the customer's requirements and the scope of the desired system. This
included identifying what was contained in the system to be developed, what
was in the environment and interacted with the system, and what was external
and did not interact directly with the system. The artifact produced was a fairly
conventional but quite carefully done requirements document.

The next stage was writing a formal functional specification in the formal
specification notation Z and English. This covered all the things the system was
supposed to do but not how it did those things.

Because we were developing a security related system within the general
framework described in the Common Criteria, we provided the contractor with
a somewhat generic Protection Profile describing the desired security properties. From this, Praxis produced a Security Target describing exactly what they
would deliver for the agreed cost and schedule. In our role as customers, we
worked with Praxis to make sure that the items we cared about were included
and unnecessary items were excluded. From the Security Target, in English,
Praxis wrote a shorter document, in English and Z, with precise statements of
the critical system security properties.

From the formal functional specification, Praxis wrote a design document, also
in Z and English. This document described how the specified functionality would
be implemented. They also produced a more architectural document describing
the components and subsystems and the data repositories and flows.

In their final stage, Praxis wrote the inputs, outputs, preconditions, postconditions, invariants, and other annotations for each of the code modules using ths
SPARK annotation language and the executable SPARK code itself.

Our contract with Praxis did not require them to deliver any specific test
plan or results. In fact, they did deliver some assurance evidence in the form of
sample proofs of the identified security properties.

The delivered code and other artifacts were sent to an independent company,
SPRE, Inc. in Albuqueque New Mexico, for independent testing. The results were
outstanding[2]. A few key statistics: a team of three people working part time
wrote 9,939 lines of Spark executable code plus 16,564 lines of annotations over
a nine month period. The all-inclusive rate was 38 LOC/day, significantly better
than the industry average. The stated reliability goal was 99.99% reliability with

a 90% confidence level. When the independent testers had enough test results to justify this confidence level, they had found *zero* failures.

2.3   Principles

All steps in the development methodology are guided by some basic principles of good engineering:

- Write right - write clearly, simply, unambiguously using the most suitable language for the purpose
- Step, don't leap - the step from one stage of the development to the next should be semantically small
- Say something once - each stage should add some information or decisions not stated earlier
- Check here before going there - each step should be reviewed and verified as soon as possible, usually against the previous step(s)
- Argue your corner - document the reasons for each design decision
- Use the right tools for the job - at each step, use the most effective verification technique or tool
- Use you brains - there is no substitute for rigorous, careful thought

3   Amateurs Get Involved

When the contract with Praxis and SPRE ended, we felt that we had good evidence that the methodology worked very well when followed by experienced professionals. An important unanswered question was whether anyone else could do it. Fortunately, we had an ideal group of test subjects available. We had three summer student interns almost completely uncorrupted by knowledge of any aspect of the methodology. There were two undergraduate students of mathematics and computing and one computer science graduate student. One had seen Spark in a course and none had encountered Z previously.

3.1   Support Provided

We gave them a short 4 day course in reading and writing Z, using the Z Reference Manual[3] and the Z/EVES tool. We spent about 5 days on Spark and gave them each a copy of the Spark textbook[1]. Praxis provided a version of their tool set under an academic license. We also explained the whole development methodology.

3.2   The Challenge and Results

We spent a few days explaining the Tokeneer system and then told the students that there were some new requirements. Specifically, security policy now required three factors for identification and authentication. In addition to a token (something you have) and a biometric reading (an aspect of who you are), the user had to enter a password (something you know).

The students were told to exercise the entire methodology. That is, they were given all the artifacts produced by Praxis and had to update the requirements document, the functional specification, the formal design documents, the security properties, the Spark annotations, and the executable code. A few of us were available to play the role of customers and state what we wanted delivered, and to answer any questions they might have on Z or Spark. Praxis provided the same kind of support they provide to their corporate customers; they answered Spark questions by email.

Once again, the results were everything we hoped for. In the 10 - 12 weeks they were with us, the students did everythig we asked them to do. There was neither time nor budget for independent testing, but the work was subjected to human review and checking by Z/EVES and the Spark tools.

4 Conclusions

4.1 Bottom Line

The experiences with Tokeneer described here, as well as my experience on other projects, have convinced me that it is feasible to produce software reaching the high assurance levels in the Common Criteria. There is a body of objective evidence that the use of formal techniques can produce results more quickly and reliably and at lower cost than traditional methods. To me, it is an indication of the maturity of formal techniques that a philosophy of correctness by construction, guided by sound engineering practices and supported by appropriate mathematics, is proven and practical. Can we explain why these techniques are so effective?

4.2 Why?

This is more speculative and less objective, I believe that there are some attributes of formal techniques which might account for their good results.

- Clarity (no ambiguity). Z, like a number of other specification notations, has a mathmatically defined semantics. The meaning of a Z specification is unambiguous. Spark allows no implementation dependent constructs, unlike the majority of programming languages.
- Abstraction (chosen level of detail). Z and other specification languages allow the user to express information he considers important and omit minor details. Good judgement is needed to establish the right level of abstraction, but this is very helpful in reaching a proper understanding of the system.
- Precision (as much as is useful). Specification languages such as Z have the mathematical power to make very precise statements when necessary.
- Organization (logical structure). When writing in a language based on mathematical logic, organization is often easier to get than to avoid.

4.3 What Choice Do We Have?

We certainly have a choice of formal techniques. Z and Spark were suitable technologies for the Tokeneer work and, indeed, for a wide range of security critical systems. However, other formal techniques have the basic attributes listed above and could also be used. And, for specifying some systems, Z would not be suitable at all.

That said, my opinion is that formal techniques are the only way to achieve high assurance of security for the complex systems we are developing today. The attributes listed above are helpful in achieving functional goals, but are essential in reaching security goals. Security is basically a negative property, establishing that certain potential bad things won't happen. The only way I know to establish such a property relies on a thorough understanding of the system involved, reached with the help of the attributes listed above. And formal techniques are the only way I know to bring those attributes to bear on the problem.

References

1. Barnes, J., High Integrity Software: The SPARK Approach to Safety and Security, Addison Wesley, ISBN 0-321-13616-0.
2. Barnes, J., Chapman, R., Cooper, D., Everett, B., Johnson, R., Widmaier, J.: Engineering the Tokeneer Enclave Protection Software. In: Redwine, S., Hall, A., Wing, J. (eds.): IEEE International Symposium on Secure Software Engineering, 13-15 March 2006, IEEE Computer Society, 2006.
3. Spivey, J. M., The Z Notation: a reference manual, 2nd edn., http://spivey.oriel.ox.ac.uk/mike/zrm/index.html

Formal Methods and Cryptography

Michael Backes[1], Birgit Pfitzmann[2], and Michael Waidner[3]

[1] Saarland University, Saarbrücken, Germany
backes@cs.uni-sb.de
[2] IBM Research, Rueschlikon, Switzerland
bpf@zurich.ibm.com
[3] IBM Software Group, Somers, NY, USA
wmi@zurich.ibm.com

Abstract. Security-critical systems are an important application area for formal methods. However, such systems often contain cryptographic subsystems. The natural definitions of these subsystems are probabilistic and in most cases computational. Hence it is not obvious how one can treat cryptographic subsystems in a sound way within formal methods, in particular if one does not want to encumber the proof of an overall system by probabilities and computational restrictions due only to its cryptographic subsystems.

We survey our progress on integrating cryptography into formal models, in particular our work on reactive simulatability (RSIM), a refinement notion suitable for cryptography. We also present the underlying system model which unifies a computational and a more abstract presentation and allows generic distributed scheduling. We show the relation of RSIM and other types of specifications, and clarify what role the classical Dolev-Yao (term algebra) abstractions from cryptography can play in the future.

1 Secure Channels as an Example of Cryptography Within Larger Systems

Imagine you are using formal methods to prove the correctness of a distributed system with respect to an overall specification. This system uses SSL/TLS for secure communication between its components; this is a widely used standard for cryptographically protecting messages on otherwise insecure channels [10]. What does the use of SSL mean for the overall proof?

Clearly, the nicest solution would be if you would not need to bother that SSL is a cryptographic subsystem, but could simply abstract from it by a secure channel, as if that channel were realized by a dedicated and protected wire. Most formal methods for distributed systems have a notion of secure channels as a basic communication mechanism, or can easily specify one. Essentially, a unidirectional secure channel correctly delivers messages from one specific sender to one specific recipient and to no other party. Hence simply using such a secure-channel abstraction for SSL would be perfect for the overall system proof. However, is this abstraction sound? SSL is realized with cryptographic primitives,

J. Misra, T. Nipkow, and E. Sekerinski (Eds.): FM 2006, LNCS 4085, pp. 612–616, 2006.
© Springer-Verlag Berlin Heidelberg 2006

such as Diffie-Hellman key exchange and symmetric encryption and authentication. These systems are not perfectly unbreakable; e.g., an adversary with sufficient computing time can deterministically insert forged messages or learn the messages sent by honest participants. Hence the simple secure-channel abstraction that we discussed is certainly not sound in the standard absolute sense. Nevertheless, it seems "essentially" correct in the sense that for adversaries with reasonably bounded computational power, and if one ignores very small probabilities, the differences seem to disappear. Hence the two main questions are:

- Can we rigorously define a soundness notion in which a cryptographic realization like SSL can be a refinement of a non-cryptographic specification like simple secure channels?
- Does SSL have features that differ so much from the secure-channel abstraction that they are not abstracted away by this potential soundness notion, and if yes, can the secure-channel abstraction be slightly modified to accomodate these features?

As an answer to the first question, we introduced in [15] the notion of *reactive simulatability (RSIM)*, which we survey below. It is not only applicable to the example of secure channels, but very broadly for abstractions of cryptographic systems. As to the second question, SSL indeed has such features (imperfections). For instance, an adversary who observes the underlying communication lines can easily see who communicates when with whom, and even the length of the communicated messages, because typical encryption leaves this length more or less unchanged. The adversary can also suppress messages.

Similar to this example, the overall approach when proving a system with cryptographic subsystems is usually as follows: First, find a good "natural" abstraction of the cryptographic subsystem. Secondly, investigate whether the natural abstraction has to be extended by certain imperfections such as leaking traffic patterns and message lengths. Thirdly, prove the real cryptographic system sound with respect to this modified abstraction in the RSIM sense. During the third step, one often also changes the cryptographic implementation a little because typical classical realizations concentrated on specific security properties and did not aim at realizing an overall abstraction.

2   Reactive Simulatability

Reactive simulatability (RSIM) is a notion for comparing two systems, typically called real and ideal system [15,16]. In terms of the formal-methods community one might call RSIM an implementation or refinement relation, specifically geared towards the preservation of what one might call secrecy properties compared with functional properties. In Figure 1, the ideal system is called TH (trusted host), and the protocol machines of the real system are called M_1, $\dots M_n$. The ideal or real system interacts with arbitrary so-called honest users, collectively denoted by a machine H, and an adversary A, who is often given

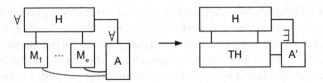

Fig. 1. Overview of reactive simulatability (RSIM)

more power than the honest users. In real systems A typically controls the network and can manipulate messages on the bitstring level. The option for A and H to communicate directly corresponds to known- and chosen-message attacks.

Reactive simulatability between the real and ideal system essentially means that for every adversary A on the real system there exists an equivalent adversary A′ on the ideal system, such that arbitrary honest users H cannot distinguish whether they interact with the real system and A, or with the ideal system and A′. Indistinguishability of families of random variables, here the two families of views of the honest users, is a well-known cryptographic notion from [18]. There exist stronger universal and blackbox version of this definition [15], depending mainly on the quantifier order.

The RSIM notion is based on simulatability definitions for secure (one-step) function evaluation [11,12,5,14,8]. It is also highly related to the observational equivalence notions for a probabilistic π-calculus from [13]. A notion very similar to RSIM was later also called UC [9].

3   System Model

In principle, RSIM can be defined over many system models by regarding the boxes in Figure 1 as (possibly probabilistic) I/O automata, Turing machines, CSP or π-calculus processes, etc.. Even large parts of most theorems and proofs about RSIM are on this box-level and could be instantiated in many ways. For the rigorous definitions, we have used a system model with probabilistic I/O automata, and with a well-defined computational realization by Turing machines for computational aspects. Two important aspects are:

- It is usually not sufficient that individual transitions of the automata are polynomial-time ("transaction poly"), and not even that the runtime of each automaton is polynomial in the entire inputs so far ("weakly poly"), because these notions do not compose. One usually needs overall polynomial-time restrictions in the initial inputs.
- We allow generic distributed scheduling for the asynchronous case. This means that for each part of the distributed computation that may be scheduled separately, we can designate an arbitrary other machine as the scheduler. This allows us to define adversarial scheduling with realistic information as well as, e.g., adversary-scheduled secure channels, local distributed algorithms not under control of the adversary, and specific fair schedulers.

4   Individual Security Properties

Reactive simulatability is great once it has been proved for a pair of an abstraction and a cryptographic realization, because then arbitrary larger systems can be proved with the abstraction and the results are also true with the realization. However, it is a strong property, and sometimes the consequences for the realization are not desired. Hence it is important to also have notions of individual security properties, such as the integrity of certain messages or the absence of information flow between certain parties. These properties can be given similar links between abstract formulations usual in formal methods and cryptographic realizations; see, e.g., [15,2,3].

5   Dolev-Yao Models

In the past, formal methods have usually abstracted from cryptographic operations by term algebras called Dolev-Yao models or symbolic cryptography. Justifying these abstractions is non-trivial because the term algebras are used as initial models; in particular it is assumed that terms for which no explicit equations and derivation rules for an adversary exist in the algebra are perfectly secret from the adversary. We have shown that a Dolev-Yao model of several important core cryptographic primitives, with small extensions similar to those we mentioned for SSL above, can indeed be implemented soundly in the sense of RSIM under standard cryptographic assumptions, see in particular [4,17]. However, we have also shown recently that extending these results to other primitives like hashing or XOR is not possible, at least not in the same very strong sense and with similar generality as our positive results.

In the context of larger systems, we see Dolev-Yao models as a tool on a middle level, useful for proving protocols that use standard cryptography in a blackbox way, but still rather explicitly. Within proofs of overall systems, we believe that even more abstract specifications of cryptographic subsystems, such as entire secure channels or entire secure payments, are more suitable.

6   Conclusion

An overview of all our own results on relating cryptography and formal methods, including concrete abstractions from cryptography that are sound in the RSIM sense, can be found at http://www.zurich.ibm.com/security/models/. The papers listed there also contain more references to related literature by others.

A particular area of where we can see formal methods for cryptography gaining more industrial relevance is web services security, at least if the current trend continues to make web services security specification, like all web services specifications, highly extensible and configurable, so that one may not be able to prove all standards-compatible realizations in advance. A first analysis of how formal-methods considerations and cryptographic considerations play together in this context can be found in [1]. For purely formal considerations based on Dolev-Yao models we also refer to [7,6].

Acknowledgments. This work is partially supported by the European Commission through the IST Programme under Contract IST-4-026764-NOE ReSIST.

References

1. M. Backes, S. Mödersheim, B. Pfitzmann, and L. Viganò. Symbolic and cryptographic analysis of the Secure WS-ReliableMessaging Scenario. In *Proc. 9th FOSSACS*, volume 3921 of *LNCS*, pages 428–445. Springer, 2006.
2. M. Backes and B. Pfitzmann. Intransitive non-interference for cryptographic purposes. In *Proc. 24th IEEE Symp. on Security & Privacy*, pages 140–152, 2003.
3. M. Backes and B. Pfitzmann. Relating symbolic and cryptographic secrecy. *IEEE Transactions on on Dependable and Secure Computing*, 2(2):109–123, 2005.
4. M. Backes, B. Pfitzmann, and M. Waidner. A composable cryptographic library with nested operations. In *Proc. 10th ACM CCS*, pages 220–230, 2003.
5. D. Beaver. Secure multiparty protocols and zero knowledge proof systems tolerating a faulty minority. *Journal of Cryptology*, 4(2):75–122, 1991.
6. K. Bhargavan, R. Corin, C. Fournet, and A. Gordon. Secure sessions for web services. In *ACM Workshop on Secure Web Services (SWS)*. ACM Press, to appear, 2004.
7. K. Bhargavan, C. Fournet, A. Gordon, and R. Pucella. TulaFale: A security tool for web servics. In *Proc. 2nd Intern. Symp. on Formal Methods for Components and Objects (FMCO03)*, volume 3188 of *LNCS*, pages 197–222. Springer, 2004.
8. R. Canetti. Security and composition of multiparty cryptographic protocols. *Journal of Cryptology*, 3(1):143–202, 2000.
9. R. Canetti. Universally composable security: A new paradigm for cryptographic protocols. In *Proc. 42nd IEEE FOCS*, pages 136–145, 2001.
10. T. Dierks and C. Allen. The TLS Protocol Version 1.0, 1999. Internet RFC 2246.
11. O. Goldreich, S. Micali, and A. Wigderson. How to play any mental game – or – a completeness theorem for protocols with honest majority. In *Proc. 19th ACM STOC*, pages 218–229, 1987.
12. S. Goldwasser and L. Levin. Fair computation of general functions in presence of immoral majority. In *Proc. CRYPTO '90*, volume 537 of *LNCS*, pages 77–93. Springer, 1990.
13. P. Lincoln, J. Mitchell, M. Mitchell, and A. Scedrov. A probabilistic poly-time framework for protocol analysis. In *Proc. 5th ACM CCS*, pages 112–121, 1998.
14. S. Micali and P. Rogaway. Secure computation. In *Proc. CRYPTO '91*, volume 576 of *LNCS*, pages 392–404. Springer, 1991.
15. B. Pfitzmann and M. Waidner. Composition and integrity preservation of secure reactive systems. In *Proc. 7th ACM CCS*, pages 245–254, 2000.
16. B. Pfitzmann and M. Waidner. A model for asynchronous reactive systems and its application to secure message transmission. In *Proc. 22nd IEEE Symp. on Security & Privacy*, pages 184–200, 2001.
17. C. Sprenger, M. Backes, D. Basin, B. Pfitzmann, and M. Waidner. Cryptographically sound theorem proving. In *Proc. 19th IEEE CSFW*, 2006. To appear.
18. A. C. Yao. Theory and applications of trapdoor functions. In *Proc. 23rd IEEE FOCS*, pages 80–91, 1982.

Verified Software Grand Challenge

Jim Woodcock

Abstract. Some practitioners in industry and researchers from universities believe its now practical to use formal methods to produce software, even non-critical software, and that this will turn out to be the cheapest way to do it. Given the right computer-based tools, the use of formal methods could become widespread and transform the practice of software engineering. The computer science community recently committed itself to making this a reality within the next fifteen to twenty years. Collectively, we have a lot of experience in the successful use of formal methods in industry, and this is being strengthened by a new wave of tools shielding users from deep technical issues. The time is now right for a concerted push at software verification, and considerable activity is already under way in the Verified Software Grand Challenge and its pilot projects.

J. Misra, T. Nipkow, and E. Sekerinski (Eds.): FM 2006, LNCS 4085, p. 617, 2006.
© Springer-Verlag Berlin Heidelberg 2006

Author Index

Aiguier, Marc   364
Amálio, Nuno   252
Artho, Cyrille Valentin   412

Bacherini, Stefano   179
Backes, Michael   612
Balser, Michael   32
Bannwart, Fabian   492
Berkani, Karim   364
Biere, Armin   412
Blazy, Sandrine   460
Botaschanjan, Jewgenij   163
Bouquet, Fabrice   428
Boute, Raymond   316
Brunet, Greg   98
Butler, Michael   221

Cavalcanti, Ana Lucia Caneca   115
Chechik, Marsha   98
Cohen, Ernie   81
Cunha, Alcino   284

Dadeau, Frédéric   428
Dargaye, Zaynah   460
Delahaye, David   48
Donaldson, Alastair F.   541
Donzeau-Gouge, Véronique Viguié   48

Étienne, Jean-Frédéric   48
Evans, Neil   221

Fantechi, Alessandro   179
Freitas, Angela   115

Genon, Alexandre   557
Grandy, Holger   16
Gruler, Alexander   163

Haneberg, Dominik   16
Harhurin, Alexander   163
Henzinger, Thomas A.   1
Hoffmann, Alwin   32
Höfner, Peter   300
Honiden, Shinichi   412
Hooman, Jozef   147

Hoover, H. James   396
Huynh, Thuan Quang   476

Johnson, D. Randolph   607
Johnston, Wendy   524
Jürjens, Jan   600

Kassios, Ioannis T.   268
Khedri, Ridha   300
Kof, Leonid   163

Langari, Zarrin   348
Larsen, Kim G.   82
Larsen, Peter Gorm   147
Le Gall, Pascale   364
Legeard, Bruno   428
Leroy, Xavier   460
Li, Xin   396
Lund, Mass Soldal   380
Lynch, Nancy   64

Marcos, Mar   32
Massart, Thierry   557
McComb, Tim   205
McIver, Annabelle K.   131
Meuter, Cédric   557
Miller, Alice   541
Möller, Bernhard   300
Mostowski, Wojciech   444
Müller, Peter   492

Nyman, Ulrik   82

Oheimb, David von   592
Oliveira, José Nuno   236, 284

Pavlovic, Dusko   598
Pfitzmann, Birgit   612
Pnueli, Amir   573
Polack, Fiona   252
Preoteasa, Viorel   508

Reif, Wolfgang   16, 32
Robinson, Peter   524
Rodrigues, César Jesus   236
Roychoudhury, Abhik   476
Rudnicki, Piotr   396

Schellhorn, Gerhard   16
Schmitt, Jonathan   32
Sifakis, Joseph   1
Smith, Graeme   205
Spichkova, Maria   163
Stephan, Werner   587
Stepney, Susan   252
Stølen, Ketil   380
Strooper, Paul   524

Tempestini, Matteo   179
Trachtenherz, David   163
Trefler, Richard   348

Uchitel, Sebastian   98
Umeno, Shinya   64

van den Berg, Lionel   524
Verhoef, Marcel   147
Visser, Joost   284

Waidner, Michael   612
Wang, Jinquan   190
Wang, Kan   190
Wąsowski, Andrzej   82
Winter, Kirsten   524
Woodcock, Jim   617

Xue, Jinyun   190

Zaks, Aleksandr   573
Zave, Pamela   332
Zheng, Yujun   190
Zingoni, Niccolò   179

Lecture Notes in Computer Science

For information about Vols. 1–4017

please contact your bookseller or Springer

Vol. 4144: T. Ball, R.B. Jones (Eds.), Computer Aided Verification. XV, 564 pages. 2006.

Vol. 4127: E. Damiani, P. Liu (Eds.), Data and Applications Security XX. X, 319 pages. 2006.

Vol. 4121: A. Biere, C.P. Gomes (Eds.), Theory and Applications of Satisfiability Testing - SAT 2006. XII, 438 pages. 2006.

Vol. 4115: D.-S. Huang, K. Li, G.W. Irwin (Eds.), Computational Intelligence and Bioinformatics, Part III. XXI, 803 pages. 2006. (Sublibrary LNBI).

Vol. 4114: D.-S. Huang, K. Li, G.W. Irwin (Eds.), Computational Intelligence, Part II. XXVII, 1337 pages. 2006. (Sublibrary LNAI).

Vol. 4113: D.-S. Huang, K. Li, G.W. Irwin (Eds.), Intelligent Computing, Part I. XXVII, 1331 pages. 2006.

Vol. 4112: D.Z. Chen, D. T. Lee (Eds.), Computing and Combinatorics. XIV, 528 pages. 2006.

Vol. 4111: F.S. de Boer, M.M. Bonsangue, S. Graf, W.-P. de Roever (Eds.), Formal Methods for Components and Objects. VIII, 447 pages. 2006.

Vol. 4109: D.-Y. Yeung, J.T. Kwok, A. Fred, F. Roli, D. de Ridder (Eds.), Structural, Syntactic, and Statistical Pattern Recognition. XXI, 939 pages. 2006.

Vol. 4108: J.M. Borwein, W.M. Farmer (Eds.), Mathematical Knowledge Management. VIII, 295 pages. 2006. (Sublibrary LNAI).

Vol. 4106: T.R. Roth-Berghofer, M.H. Göker, H. A. Güvenir (Eds.), Advances in Case-Based Reasoning. XIV, 566 pages. 2006. (Sublibrary LNAI).

Vol. 4104: T. Kunz, S.S. Ravi (Eds.), Ad-Hoc, Mobile, and Wireless Networks. XII, 474 pages. 2006.

Vol. 4099: Q. Yang, G. Webb (Eds.), PRICAI 2006: Trends in Artificial Intelligence. XXVIII, 1263 pages. 2006. (Sublibrary LNAI).

Vol. 4098: F. Pfenning (Ed.), Term Rewriting and Applications. XIII, 415 pages. 2006.

Vol. 4097: X. Zhou, O. Sokolsky, L. Yan, E.-S. Jung, Z. Shao, Y. Mu, D.C. Lee, D. Kim, Y.-S. Jeong, C.-Z. Xu (Eds.), Emerging Directions in Embedded and Ubiquitous Computing. XXVII, 1034 pages. 2006.

Vol. 4096: E. Sha, S.-K. Han, C.-Z. Xu, M.H. Kim, L.T. Yang, B. Xiao (Eds.), Embedded and Ubiquitous Computing. XXIV, 1170 pages. 2006.

Vol. 4094: O. H. Ibarra, H.-C. Yen (Eds.), Implementation and Application of Automata. XIII, 291 pages. 2006.

Vol. 4093: X. Li, O.R. Zaiane, Z. Li (Eds.), Advanced Data Mining and Applications. XXI, 1110 pages. 2006. (Sublibrary LNAI).

Vol. 4092: J. Lang, F. Lin, J. Wang (Eds.), Knowledge Science, Engineering and Management. XV, 664 pages. 2006. (Sublibrary LNAI).

Vol. 4090: S. Spaccapietra, K. Aberer, P. Cudré-Mauroux (Eds.), Journal on Data Semantics VI. XI, 211 pages. 2006.

Vol. 4088: Z.-Z. Shi, R. Sadananda (Eds.), Agent Computing and Multi-Agent Systems. XVII, 827 pages. 2006. (Sublibrary LNAI).

Vol. 4085: J. Misra, T. Nipkow, E. Sekerinski (Eds.), FM 2006: Formal Methods. XV, 620 pages. 2006.

Vol. 4079: S. Etalle, M. Truszczyński (Eds.), Logic Programming. XIV, 474 pages. 2006.

Vol. 4077: M.-S. Kim, K. Shimada (Eds.), Advances in Geometric Modeling and Processing. XVI, 696 pages. 2006.

Vol. 4076: F. Hess, S. Pauli, M. Pohst (Eds.), Algorithmic Number Theory. X, 599 pages. 2006.

Vol. 4075: U. Leser, F. Naumann, B. Eckman (Eds.), Data Integration in the Life Sciences. XI, 298 pages. 2006. (Sublibrary LNBI).

Vol. 4074: M. Burmester, A. Yasinsac (Eds.), Secure Mobile Ad-hoc Networks and Sensors. X, 193 pages. 2006.

Vol. 4073: A. Butz, B. Fisher, A. Krüger, P. Olivier (Eds.), Smart Graphics. XI, 263 pages. 2006.

Vol. 4072: M. Harders, G. Székely (Eds.), Biomedical Simulation. XI, 216 pages. 2006.

Vol. 4071: H. Sundaram, M. Naphade, J.R. Smith, Y. Rui (Eds.), Image and Video Retrieval. XII, 547 pages. 2006.

Vol. 4070: C. Priami, X. Hu, Y. Pan, T.Y. Lin (Eds.), Transactions on Computational Systems Biology V. IX, 129 pages. 2006. (Sublibrary LNBI).

Vol. 4069: F.J. Perales, R.B. Fisher (Eds.), Articulated Motion and Deformable Objects. XV, 526 pages. 2006.

Vol. 4068: H. Schärfe, P. Hitzler, P. Øhrstrøm (Eds.), Conceptual Structures: Inspiration and Application. XI, 455 pages. 2006. (Sublibrary LNAI).

Vol. 4067: D. Thomas (Ed.), ECOOP 2006 – Object-Oriented Programming. XIV, 527 pages. 2006.

Vol. 4066: A. Rensink, J. Warmer (Eds.), Model Driven Architecture – Foundations and Applications. XII, 392 pages. 2006.

Vol. 4065: P. Perner (Ed.), Advances in Data Mining. XI, 592 pages. 2006. (Sublibrary LNAI).

Vol. 4064: R. Büschkes, P. Laskov (Eds.), Detection of Intrusions and Malware & Vulnerability Assessment. X, 195 pages. 2006.

Vol. 4063: I. Gorton, G.T. Heineman, I. Crnkovic, H.W. Schmidt, J.A. Stafford, C.A. Szyperski, K. Wallnau (Eds.), Component-Based Software Engineering. XI, 394 pages. 2006.

Vol. 4062: G. Wang, J.F. Peters, A. Skowron, Y. Yao (Eds.), Rough Sets and Knowledge Technology. XX, 810 pages. 2006. (Sublibrary LNAI).

Vol. 4061: K. Miesenberger, J. Klaus, W. Zagler, A. Karshmer (Eds.), Computers Helping People with Special Needs. XXIX, 1356 pages. 2006.

Vol. 4060: K. Futatsugi, J.-P. Jouannaud, J. Meseguer (Eds.), Algebra, Meaning, and Computation. XXXVIII, 643 pages. 2006.

Vol. 4059: L. Arge, R. Freivalds (Eds.), Algorithm Theory – SWAT 2006. XII, 436 pages. 2006.

Vol. 4058: L.M. Batten, R. Safavi-Naini (Eds.), Information Security and Privacy. XII, 446 pages. 2006.

Vol. 4057: J.P.W. Pluim, B. Likar, F.A. Gerritsen (Eds.), Biomedical Image Registration. XII, 324 pages. 2006.

Vol. 4056: P. Flocchini, L. Gąsieniec (Eds.), Structural Information and Communication Complexity. X, 357 pages. 2006.

Vol. 4055: J. Lee, J. Shim, S.-g. Lee, C. Bussler, S. Shim (Eds.), Data Engineering Issues in E-Commerce and Services. IX, 290 pages. 2006.

Vol. 4054: A. Horváth, M. Telek (Eds.), Formal Methods and Stochastic Models for Performance Evaluation. VIII, 239 pages. 2006.

Vol. 4053: M. Ikeda, K.D. Ashley, T.-W. Chan (Eds.), Intelligent Tutoring Systems. XXVI, 821 pages. 2006.

Vol. 4052: M. Bugliesi, B. Preneel, V. Sassone, I. Wegener (Eds.), Automata, Languages and Programming, Part II. XXIV, 603 pages. 2006.

Vol. 4051: M. Bugliesi, B. Preneel, V. Sassone, I. Wegener (Eds.), Automata, Languages and Programming, Part I. XXIII, 729 pages. 2006.

Vol. 4049: S. Parsons, N. Maudet, P. Moraitis, I. Rahwan (Eds.), Argumentation in Multi-Agent Systems. XIV, 313 pages. 2006. (Sublibrary LNAI).

Vol. 4048: L. Goble, J.-J.C.. Meyer (Eds.), Deontic Logic and Artificial Normative Systems. X, 273 pages. 2006. (Sublibrary LNAI).

Vol. 4047: M. Robshaw (Ed.), Fast Software Encryption. XI, 434 pages. 2006.

Vol. 4046: S.M. Astley, M. Brady, C. Rose, R. Zwiggelaar (Eds.), Digital Mammography. XVI, 654 pages. 2006.

Vol. 4045: D. Barker-Plummer, R. Cox, N. Swoboda (Eds.), Diagrammatic Representation and Inference. XII, 301 pages. 2006. (Sublibrary LNAI).

Vol. 4044: P. Abrahamsson, M. Marchesi, G. Succi (Eds.), Extreme Programming and Agile Processes in Software Engineering. XII, 230 pages. 2006.

Vol. 4043: A.S. Atzeni, A. Lioy (Eds.), Public Key Infrastructure. XI, 261 pages. 2006.

Vol. 4042: D. Bell, J. Hong (Eds.), Flexible and Efficient Information Handling. XVI, 296 pages. 2006.

Vol. 4041: S.-W. Cheng, C.K. Poon (Eds.), Algorithmic Aspects in Information and Management. XI, 395 pages. 2006.

Vol. 4040: R. Reulke, U. Eckardt, B. Flach, U. Knauer, K. Polthier (Eds.), Combinatorial Image Analysis. XII, 482 pages. 2006.

Vol. 4039: M. Morisio (Ed.), Reuse of Off-the-Shelf Components. XIII, 444 pages. 2006.

Vol. 4038: P. Ciancarini, H. Wiklicky (Eds.), Coordination Models and Languages. VIII, 299 pages. 2006.

Vol. 4037: R. Gorrieri, H. Wehrheim (Eds.), Formal Methods for Open Object-Based Distributed Systems. XVII, 474 pages. 2006.

Vol. 4036: O. H. Ibarra, Z. Dang (Eds.), Developments in Language Theory. XII, 456 pages. 2006.

Vol. 4035: T. Nishita, Q. Peng, H.-P. Seidel (Eds.), Advances in Computer Graphics. XX, 771 pages. 2006.

Vol. 4034: J. Münch, M. Vierimaa (Eds.), Product-Focused Software Process Improvement. XVII, 474 pages. 2006.

Vol. 4033: B. Stiller, P. Reichl, B. Tuffin (Eds.), Performability Has its Price. X, 103 pages. 2006.

Vol. 4032: O. Etzion, T. Kuflik, A. Motro (Eds.), Next Generation Information Technologies and Systems. XIII, 365 pages. 2006.

Vol. 4031: M. Ali, R. Dapoigny (Eds.), Advances in Applied Artificial Intelligence. XXIII, 1353 pages. 2006. (Sublibrary LNAI).

Vol. 4029: L. Rutkowski, R. Tadeusiewicz, L.A. Zadeh, J.M. Zurada (Eds.), Artificial Intelligence and Soft Computing – ICAISC 2006. XXI, 1235 pages. 2006. (Sublibrary LNAI).

Vol. 4028: J. Kohlas, B. Meyer, A. Schiper (Eds.), Dependable Systems: Software, Computing, Networks. XII, 295 pages. 2006.

Vol. 4027: H.L. Larsen, G. Pasi, D. Ortiz-Arroyo, T. Andreasen, H. Christiansen (Eds.), Flexible Query Answering Systems. XVIII, 714 pages. 2006. (Sublibrary LNAI).

Vol. 4026: P.B. Gibbons, T. Abdelzaher, J. Aspnes, R. Rao (Eds.), Distributed Computing in Sensor Systems. XIV, 566 pages. 2006.

Vol. 4025: F. Eliassen, A. Montresor (Eds.), Distributed Applications and Interoperable Systems. XI, 355 pages. 2006.

Vol. 4024: S. Donatelli, P.S. Thiagarajan (Eds.), Petri Nets and Other Models of Concurrency - ICATPN 2006. XI, 441 pages. 2006.

Vol. 4021: E. André, L. Dybkjær, W. Minker, H. Neumann, M. Weber (Eds.), Perception and Interactive Technologies. XI, 217 pages. 2006. (Sublibrary LNAI).

Vol. 4020: A. Bredenfeld, A. Jacoff, I. Noda, Y. Takahashi (Eds.), RoboCup 2005: Robot Soccer World Cup IX. XVII, 727 pages. 2006. (Sublibrary LNAI).

Vol. 4019: M. Johnson, V. Vene (Eds.), Algebraic Methodology and Software Technology. XI, 389 pages. 2006.

Vol. 4018: V. Wade, H. Ashman, B. Smyth (Eds.), Adaptive Hypermedia and Adaptive Web-Based Systems. XVI, 474 pages. 2006.